The Power of Critical Thinking

The Power of Critical Thinking

Fourth Canadian Edition

Chris MacDonald
Lewis Vaughn

OXFORD
UNIVERSITY PRESS

OXFORD
UNIVERSITY PRESS

Oxford University Press is a department of the University of Oxford.
It furthers the University's objective of excellence in research, scholarship,
and education by publishing worldwide. Oxford is a registered trade mark of
Oxford University Press in the UK and in certain other countries.

Published in Canada by
Oxford University Press
8 Sampson Mews, Suite 204,
Don Mills, Ontario M3C 0H5 Canada

www.oupcanada.com

First Canadian Edition published in 2008
Second Canadian Edition published in 2010
Third Canadian Edition published in 2013

The Power of Critical Thinking, Fourth Edition was originally published in English in 2012 by Oxford University Press Inc., 198 Madison Avenue, New York, New York, 10016 with the ISBN 9780199856671. This adapted edition is published by arrangement. Oxford University Press Canada is solely responsible for this adaptation from the original work.

Library and Archives Canada Cataloguing in Publication

Vaughn, Lewis, author
The power of critical thinking / Chris MacDonald, Lewis Vaughn. -- Fourth Canadian edition.

Revision of: The power of critical thinking / Lewis Vaughn, Chris MacDonald. -- Third Canadian edition. -- Don Mills, Ontario, Canada : Oxford University Press, [2013]
Includes bibliographical references and index.
ISBN 978-0-19-901868-0 (paperback)

1. Critical thinking--Textbooks. I. MacDonald, Chris, 1969–, author II. Title.

BC177.V38 2016 160 C2016-900287-X

Cover image: Mark Matysia/Getty Images

Oxford University Press is committed to our environment.
Wherever possible, our books are printed on paper which comes from responsible sources.

Printed and bound in the United States of America

1 2 3 4 — 19 18 17 16

CONTENTS

From the Publisher xii
Preface xx

PART ONE BASICS 1

1 THE POWER OF CRITICAL THINKING 2

Why It Matters 4
How It Works 9
- Claims and Reasons 9
- Reasons and Arguments 11
- Arguments in the Rough 16

Summary 18
Field Problems 26
Self-Assessment Quiz 26
Critical Thinking and Writing Exercise 29
Writing Assignments 32

2 THE "ENVIRONMENT" OF CRITICAL THINKING 33

Category 1: How We Think 34
- Am I Really Special? 35
- The Power of the Group 41

Category 2: What We Think 45
- Subjective Relativism 46
- Social Relativism 48
- Skepticism 48

Summary 49
Field Problems 56
Self-Assessment Quiz 57
Integrative Exercises 58
Critical Thinking and Writing Exercise 61
Writing Assignments 63

3 MAKING SENSE OF ARGUMENTS 64

Argument Basics 66
Judging Arguments 71
Finding Missing Parts 78
Argument Patterns 83
Diagramming Arguments 92
Assessing Long Arguments 106
Summary 111
Field Problems 111
Self-Assessment Quiz 112
Integrative Exercises 113
Critical Thinking and Writing Exercise 117
Writing Assignments 120

PART TWO REASONS 121

4 REASONS FOR BELIEF AND DOUBT 122

When Claims Conflict 124
Experts and Evidence 127
Personal Experience 135
- Impairment 135
- Expectation 137
- Innumeracy 139

Fooling Ourselves 140
- Resisting Contrary Evidence 140
- Looking for Confirming Evidence 142
- Preferring Available Evidence 144

Claims in the News 146
- Inside the News 146
- Sorting Out the News 150

Advertising and Persuasion 151
- Identification 153
- Slogans 153
- Misleading Comparisons 154
- Weasel Words 155

Summary 155
Field Problems 160
Self-Assessment Quiz 161
Integrative Exercises 163
Critical Thinking and Writing Exercise 165
Writing Assignments 170

5 FAULTY REASONING 171

Irrelevant Premises 172
- Genetic Fallacy 172
- Appeal to the Person 173
- Composition 175
- Division 176
- Equivocation 177
- Appeal to Popularity 178
- Appeal to Tradition 179
- Appeal to Ignorance 180
- Appeal to Emotion 182
- Red Herring 183
- Straw Man 184

Unacceptable Premises 186
- Begging the Question 186
- False Dilemma 187
- Slippery Slope 190
- Hasty Generalization 191
- Faulty Analogy 192

Summary 193
Field Problems 198
Self-Assessment Quiz 199
Integrative Exercises 200
Critical Thinking and Writing Exercise 203
Writing Assignments 208

PART THREE ARGUMENTS 209

6 DEDUCTIVE REASONING: CATEGORICAL LOGIC 210

Statements and Classes 212
Translations and Standard Form 215
  Terms 216
  Quantifiers 219
Diagramming Categorical Statements 223
Sizing Up Categorical Syllogisms 228
Summary 238
Field Problems 240
Self-Assessment Quiz 241
Integrative Exercises 242
Writing Assignments 243

7 DEDUCTIVE REASONING: PROPOSITIONAL LOGIC 244

Connectives and Truth Values 246
  Conjunction 248
  Disjunction 250
  Negation 253
  Conditional 253
Checking for Validity 259
  Simple Arguments 259
  Tricky Arguments 263
  Streamlined Evaluation 266
Summary 271
Field Problems 275
Self-Assessment Quiz 275
Integrative Exercises 277
Writing Assignments 280

8 INDUCTIVE REASONING 281

Enumerative Induction 283
  Sample Size 286
  Representativeness 287
  Opinion Polls 288

Statistical Syllogisms 298
- Evaluating Statistical Syllogisms 300

Analogical Induction 302
- Relevant Similarities 306
- Relevant Dissimilarities 307
- The Number of Instances Compared 307
- Diversity among Cases 307

Causal Arguments 312
- Testing for Causes 314
- Causal Confusions 319
- Confusing Cause with Temporal Order 323
- Necessary and Sufficient Conditions 326

Mixed Arguments 333
Summary 336
Field Problems 337
Self-Assessment Quiz 337
Integrative Exercises 340
Writing Assignments 343

PART FOUR EXPLANATIONS 345

9 INFERENCE TO THE BEST EXPLANATION 346

Explanations and Inference 348
- Abductive Reasoning 359

Theories and Consistency 360
Theories and Criteria 361
- Testability 364
- Fruitfulness 365
- Scope 367
- Simplicity 368
- Conservatism 370

Telling Good Theories from Bad 376
- A Doomed Flight 379

Summary 386
Field Problems 387
Self-Assessment Quiz 387

Integrative Exercises 389
Writing Assignments 391

10 JUDGING SCIENTIFIC THEORIES 393

Science and Not Science 394
The Scientific Method 396
Testing Scientific Theories 400
Judging Scientific Theories 403
- Copernicus versus Ptolemy 403
- Evolution versus Creationism 406

Science and Weird Theories 416
Making Weird Mistakes 417
- Leaping to the Weirdest Theory 418
- Mixing What Seems with What Is 419
- Misunderstanding the Possibilities 419

Judging Weird Theories 421
- Talking with the Dead 421

Summary 427
Field Problems 430
Self-Assessment Quiz 431
Integrative Exercises 433
Writing Assignments 435

11 CONTEXTS OF APPLICATION: THINKING CRITICALLY ABOUT HEALTH, LAW, AND ETHICS 436

Thinking Critically about Health and Health Care 437
- Key Skills 437
- Evaluating Health Claims in the News 439
- Finding and Evaluating Expert Advice 440
- Stumbling Blocks 442

Thinking Critically about the Law 444
- Key Skills 446
- Stumbling Blocks 448

Thinking Critically about Ethics 450
- Key Skills 450
- Stumbling Blocks 456

Summary 458
Field Problems 461
Self-Assessment Quiz 461
Writing Assignments 462

APPENDIX A ESSAYS FOR EVALUATION 463

APPENDIX B ANSWERS TO SELECT EXERCISES 490

Glossary 521
Notes 527
Index 529
Credits 535

FROM THE PUBLISHER

The fourth Canadian edition of *The Power of Critical Thinking* builds on the successful approach used in the previous Canadian editions that have served instructors and students so well. It gives first-time students a comprehensive, engaging, and clear introduction to critical thinking and its application in the real world.

This latest edition retains the best features of previous editions while adding new features to help students use their critical thinking skills in their everyday life. Highlights include the following:

Student-friendly tone. Without compromising rigor or oversimplifying material, this introductory text is written in an engaging tone that students will enjoy. The authors tackle tough topics with a casual approach, mixed with humour where appropriate, to enhance students' understanding and enjoyment.

10 PART ONE | Basics

- You are a liar.
- You are not a liar.
- I see blue spots before my eyes.
- 7 + 5 = 12
- 7 + 5 = 11
- You should never make fun of someone's disability.
- The best explanation for his behaviour is that he was drunk.
- The capital of Canada is Winnipeg.
- Rap music is better than Celtic fiddle music.
- An electron is a sub-atomic particle.

So statements, or claims, are the kind of things that are either true or false. (Notice that at least three of the claims above are definitely false, but that doesn't stop them from counting as statements!) They assert that some state of affairs is or is not actual. You may know that a specific statement is true, or you may know that it is false, or you may not know either way. There may be no way to find out at the time if the statement is true or false. There may be no one who believes the statement. But it would be a statement nonetheless.

Some of the thoughts we express, though, do *not* express statements:

- Does a triangle have three sides?
- Is that cheese?
- Turn that music off!
- Hey, dude.
- ROFL!

Fly Logic

The first two sentences are questions, the third is a command, the fourth sentence is a greeting, and the fifth is an exclamation that is common in email and text messaging. None of them asserts that something is or is not the case. They are meaningful things to say, but they're not *statements*.

When you're engaged in critical thinking, you're mostly either evaluating statements or formulating them. In both cases your primary task is to figure out how strongly to believe them. The strength of your belief should depend on the quality of the reasons in favour of the statements. Statements backed by good reasons are

Increased practical content. New "Everyday Problems and Decisions" boxes and an increased number of "Field Problem" questions help students apply critical thinking to familiar everyday issues in their lives.

Emphasis on evaluation of evidence, authority, and credibility. Students are encouraged to critically assess evidence and claims put forward by experts, news media, business leaders, and friends. In each case, the main principles and procedures are explained and illustrated.

Extensive treatment of scientific reasoning. The book offers a chapter each on inductive reasoning and causal arguments (Chapter 8), scientific theories and inference (Chapter 9), and scientific method and theory evaluation (Chapter 10). Many helpful examples show how scientific reasoning can be applied to a wide range of questions in many scientific fields, everyday life, and even the realm of the extraordinary, the paranormal, and the supernatural.

Rigorous attention to detail. All exercises, philosophical facts, figures, and diagrams have been checked and validated by a selection of leading experts in the field.

6 | Deductive Reasoning: Categorical Logic 235

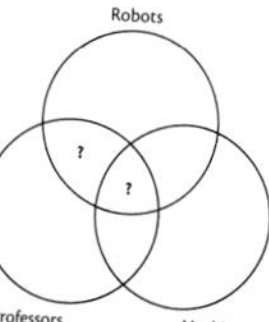

So then the question arises in which subsection we should place the X. (That's why there are question marks in the diagram above—to point out, just for now, the uncertainty). Should we put the X in the area overlapping with the machines circle—or in the part not overlapping with the machines circle? Our choice *does* affect what the diagram says about the validity of the argument. But if we diagram the universal premise first, the decision of where to insert the X is made for us because there would be only one relevant subsection left (and we can't place an X in a shaded area, because shaded means *empty*):

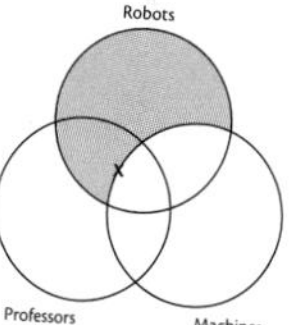

The resulting diagram represents the statement that some professors are machines, which is what the conclusion asserts. The syllogism, then, is valid.

But sometimes, diagramming the universal premise first still leaves us with a question about where the X should go. Consider this syllogism:

All barbers are singers.
Some Italians are singers.
Therefore, some Italians are barbers.

CHAPTER OBJECTIVES

Science and Not Science
You will be able to
- understand why science is not the same thing as technology, ideology, or scientism.

The Scientific Method
You will be able to
- list the five steps of the scientific method.
- understand the logic of scientific testing.
- understand why no scientific hypothesis can be conclusively confirmed or conclusively confuted.

Testing Scientific Theories
You will be able to
- use the steps of the scientific method, and be able to explain how a scientist would go about testing a simple hypothesis in medical science.
- understand why scientists use control groups, make studies double-blind, include placebos in testing, and seek replication of their work.

Judging Scientific Theories
You will be able to
- list the five criteria of adequacy and explain what they mean.
- understand how to apply the criteria of adequacy to the theories of evolution and creationism and why the text says that evolution is the better theory.

Enhanced Pedagogy

This edition of *The Power of Critical Thinking* builds on the pedagogical approach that has successfully helped students practise and refine their critical thinking skills.

EVERYDAY PROBLEMS AND DECISIONS

Self-Image and Consumerism

It is always important to watch out when things get personal. One of the situations in which that is particularly important is when someone is trying to sell you something. Of course, there is a sense in which buying consumer goods *should* be personal—after all, more often than not you are buying things for *yourself*, and your own desires and values have a proper role to play. However, advertisers and salespeople may try to make purchases personal in another sense: they may try to convince you that having their product really is important to your self-conception, your own vision of who you are. In such situations, it is worth taking a step back, and asking:

- Is my sense of worth really tied to how expensive my jeans are?
- Does having a car with more horsepower make *me* more powerful?
- Is this shampoo really going to go beyond cleaning my hair to make me happy?

Consumer purchases can be important decisions: if they are going to be *personal*, that should be your decision, not someone else's!

"EVERYDAY PROBLEMS AND DECISIONS" BOXES allow students to apply their critical thinking skills to real-world problems.

326 PART THREE | Arguments

As you can see, it's not always a simple matter to discern what the nature of a causal link is. Again, we must rely on our rule of thumb: *don't assume that a causal connection exists unless you have good reason for doing so*. This tenet applies not only to our ordinary experience, but also to all states of affairs involving cause and effect, including scientific investigations.

In everyday life, sorting cause from effect is often easy because the situations we confront are frequently simple and familiar—as when we're trying to discover what caused the kettle to boil over. Here, we naturally rely on Mill's methods or other types of causal reasoning. But as we've seen, in many other common circumstances, things aren't so simple. We often cannot be sure that we've identified all the relevant factors or ruled out the influence of coincidence or correctly distinguished cause and effect. Our rule of thumb, then, should be our guide in all the doubtful cases.

Science faces all the same kinds of challenges in its pursuit of causal explanations. And despite its sophisticated methods and investigative tools, it must expend a great deal of effort to pin down causal connections. Identifying the cause of a disease, for example, usually requires not one study or experiment, but many. The main reason is that it's always tough to uncover relevant factors and exclude irrelevant or misleading factors. That's why we should apply our rule of thumb even to scientific research that purports to identify a causal link. In Chapters 9 and 10, we'll explore procedures for evaluating scientific research and for applying our rule of thumb with more precision.

sufficient condition A condition for the occurrence of an event that guarantees that the event occurs.

necessary condition A condition for the occurrence of an event without which the event cannot occur.

Necessary and Sufficient Conditions

To fully appreciate the dynamics of cause and effect and to be able to skilfully assess causal arguments, you must understand two other important concepts: **necessary condition** and **sufficient condition**. Causal processes always occur under specific conditions. So we often speak of cause and effect in terms of *the conditions for the occurrence of an event*. Scientists, philosophers, and others go

REVIEW NOTES

Causal Confusions

- Misidentifying relevant factors
- Overlooking relevant factors
- Confusing coincidence with cause
- Confusing cause with temporal order (post hoc fallacy)
- Confusing cause and effect

A NEW MARGINAL GLOSSARY highlights key terms and concepts close to where they are discussed in the text.

REVIEW NOTES

Conflicting Claims

- If a claim conflicts with other claims that we have good reason to accept, we have good grounds for doubting it.
- If a claim conflicts with our background information, we have good reason to doubt it.
- We should proportion our belief to the evidence.
- It's not reasonable to believe a claim when there is no good reason for doing so.
- If a claim conflicts with expert opinion, we have good reason to doubt it.
- When the experts disagree about a claim, we have good reason to suspend judgment.

"REVIEW NOTES" BOXES appear throughout each chapter to reiterate the main points of chapter sections, improving comprehension and making later review more efficient.

FOOD FOR THOUGHT

Standard Form versus Fuzziness

We take the trouble to translate categorical statements into standard form for several reasons—one of them being that language is fuzzy, fuzzy, fuzzy. The famed logician Bertrand Russell agreed: "Because language is misleading, as well as because it is diffuse and inexact when applied to logic (for which it was never intended), logical symbolism is absolutely necessary to any exact or thorough treatment of our subject" (*Introduction to Mathematical Philosophy*).

We can see a good example of language fuzziness in this type of categorical statement: "All *S* are not *P*." Take the statement "All Bigfoot monsters are not apes." Does this mean that (1) no Bigfoot monsters are apes or (2) that some Bigfoot monsters are not apes? Statement 1 is an E-statement; statement 2 is an O-statement. To defeat fuzziness, we have to apply some categorical logic and translate the original sentence into either an E- or O-statement.

CREDIT: Mark Heath/Cartoon Stock.

"FOOD FOR THOUGHT" BOXES provide additional, sometimes humorous, material on a topic and challenge students to apply the critical thinking skills they are learning. The material is purposely diverse in both subject matter and format.

70 PART ONE | Basics

REVIEW NOTES

Deductive and Inductive Arguments

A deductive argument

- is intended to provide conclusive support for its conclusion;
- is said to be *valid* if it succeeds in providing conclusive support for its premise. (A valid argument is such that if its premises are true, its conclusion must be true.); and
- is said to be *sound* if it is valid and has true premises.

An inductive argument

- is intended to provide probable support for its conclusion;
- is said to be *strong* if it succeeds in providing probable support for its conclusion. (A strong argument is such that if its premises are true, its conclusion is probably true.); and
- is said to be *cogent* if it is strong argument and has true premises.

Both deductive and inductive arguments can be manipulated in various ways to yield new insights. For example, let's say that you have formulated a valid deductive argument and you know that the conclusion is false. From these facts you can infer (based on the definition of a valid deductive argument) that at least one of the premises must be false. Using this approach, you can demonstrate that a premise is false because in a valid argument it leads to a false conclusion. Or let's say that you've constructed a valid argument and you know that your premises are true. Then you can infer that the conclusion must be true—even if it's contrary to your expectations. Or maybe you put forth a strong inductive argument and you know that the premises are questionable. Then you know that the conclusion also can't be trusted.

EXERCISE 3.1

Answers to exercises marked with an asterisk (*) may be found in Appendix B, Answers to Exercises.

1. What is a deductive argument?
2. What is an inductive argument?
3. Are inductive arguments truth-preserving? Why or why not?
*4. What type of arguments do the terms *valid* and *invalid* apply to?
5. What kind of support does a deductive argument provide when it is valid?

3 | Making Sense of Arguments 71

6. Can an inductive argument guarantee the truth of the conclusion if the premises are true? Why or why not?
7. What is the difference between an inductively strong argument and an inductively weak one?
*8. What is the term for valid arguments that have true premises?
9. What is the term for strong arguments that have true premises?
10. Can a valid argument have false premises and a false conclusion? Can it have false premises and a true conclusion?
11. What logical conclusion can you draw about an argument that is valid but has a false conclusion?
*12. Is it possible for a valid argument to have true premises and a false conclusion?
13. In what way are conclusions of deductive arguments absolute?

JUDGING ARGUMENTS

When it comes to deductive and inductive arguments, the most important skills you can acquire are being able to identify both kinds of arguments and determining whether they are good or bad. Much of the rest of this text is devoted to helping you become proficient in these skills. This chapter will serve as your first lesson and give you a chance to practise what you learn.

So the obvious questions here are the following: When you come face to face with an argument to evaluate, (1) how can you tell whether it's deductive or inductive, and (2) how can you determine whether it gives you good reasons for accepting the conclusion (whether it's sound or cogent)? The following is a suggested four-step procedure for answering these questions, one that will be elaborated on here and in later chapters.

Step 1. Find the conclusion of the argument and then its premises. Use the techniques you learned in Chapter 1. You'll have plenty of chances to hone this skill in later chapters.

Step 2. Ask, "Is it the case that if the premises are true the conclusion *must* be true?" If the answer is yes, treat the argument as *deductive*, for it is very likely meant to offer conclusive support for its conclusion. The argument, then, is deductively valid, and you should check to see if it's sound. If the answer is no, proceed to the next step.

Step 3. Ask, "Is it th...

ABUNDANT EXERCISES cover a wide range of topics, with selected answers given at the back of the book (Appendix B). There are hundreds of exercises, found throughout each chapter, presented progressively, from simple to complex, elementary to more advanced, and familiar to unusual.

Contemporary Design

The design of the fourth Canadian edition reflects the vibrancy and excitement of learning how to think critically without sacrificing content or authoritativeness.

Aids to Student Learning

CHAPTER OBJECTIVES

Statements and Classes

You will be able to

- define subject term, predicate term, copula, quantifier, quantity, and quality.
- memorize the four standard-form categorical statements.

Translations and Standard Form

You will be able to

- translate ordinary statements into standard categorical form.
- translate singular statements into standard form.

Diagramming Categorical Statements

You will be able to

- construct a Venn diagram for any categorical statement.
- memorize the Venn diagrams for the four standard-form categorica
- use Venn diagrams to tell if two statements are, or are not, equivale

Sizing Up Categorical Syllogisms

You will be able to

- understand the structure of categorical syllogisms.
- check the validity of a categorical argument by drawing Venn diagr

CHAPTER OPENERS preview the contents of each chapter with chapter objectives that provide a concise overview of the key concepts to be covered.

CHAPTER SUMMARIES provide additional support and the end of each chapter to ensure students have identified and understood key concepts.

2 | The "Environment" of Critical Thinking 61

Critical Thinking and Writing Exercise

From Issue to Thesis

For many students, the biggest challenge in writing an argumentative essay is deciding on an appropriate thesis—the claim, or conclusion, that the essay is designed to support or prove. Very often, when an essay runs off track and crashes, the derailment can be traced to a thesis that was bad from the beginning.

Picking a thesis out of the air and beginning to write is usually a mistake. Any thesis statement that you craft without knowing anything about the subject is likely to be ill-formed or indefensible. It's better to begin by selecting an issue—a question that's controversial or in dispute—then researching it to determine what arguments or viewpoints are involved. To research it, you can survey the views of people or organizations involved in the controversy. Read articles and books, talk to people, and do some research online. This process should not only inform you about various viewpoints but also tell you what arguments are used to support them. It should also help you narrow the issue down to one that you can easily address in the space you have.

Suppose you begin with the issue of whether Canada has serious industrial pollution problems. After investigating this issue, you would probably see that it is much too broad to be addressed in a short paper. You should then restrict the issue to something more manageable—for example, whether recent legislation to allow coal-burning power plants to emit more sulphur dioxide will harm people's health. With the scope of the issue narrowed, you can explore arguments on both sides. You cannot examine every single argument, but you should assess the strongest ones, including those that you devise yourself. You can then use what you've already learned about arguments to select one that you think provides good support for its conclusion. The premises and conclusion of this argument can then serve as the bare-bones outline of your essay. Your argument might look like this:

> [Premise 1] High amounts of sulphur dioxide in the air have been linked to increases in the incidence of asthma and other respiratory illnesses.
> [Premise 2] Many areas of the country already have high amounts of sulphur dioxide in the air.
> [Premise 3] Most sulphur dioxide in the air comes from coal-burning power plants.
> [Conclusion] Therefore, allowing coal-burning power plants to emit more sulphur dioxide will most likely increase the incidence of respiratory illnesses.

WRITING MODULES, embedded within the end-of-chapter student activities in five chapters, introduce the rudiments of argumentative essay writing.

STUDENT ACTIVITIES, included at the end of each chapter, reinforce concepts and ideas through a variety of formats, including the following:

- "Field Problems" that invite students to apply newly acquired and refined critical thinking skills to "real world" problems.
- "Self-Assessment Quizzes" that allow students to test their understanding of the material.
- "Integrative Exercises" that help students bring information and techniques from multiple chapters together, ensuring that their understanding of critical thinking is comprehensive.
- "Writing Assignments" that allow students to apply their knowledge and practise working in longer formats, such as essays.

240 PART THREE | Arguments

Field Problems

1. Go online and check the opinion or editorial section of your local newspaper or one of the national newspapers (the *Globe and Mail* or *National Post*). Within one of the editorials or letters to the editor, find a categorical syllogism that you suspect is invalid. Assess its validity using the Venn diagram method. If it is indeed invalid, write a 150–200 word explanation of how you would explain, to someone who doesn't know about categorical logic, what's wrong with the argument.
2. Check recent news reports to find one categorical statement made by the prime minister of Canada, a federal cabinet minister, the mayor of your city, or one of the premiers. Translate the statement into standard form. (1) Construct a *valid* categorical syllogism using the statement as the conclusion and supplying whatever premises you deem appropriate. Assume that your premises are true. (2) Then construct an *invalid* syllogism using the same statement as the conclusion and supplying premises, also assumed to be true. In both arguments, try to keep the statements as realistic as possible (e.g., close to what you may actually read in a newsmagazine).
3. Think of a piece of *advice* you have been given that was presented in syllogistic form. (Hint: this often happens when a speaker's first premise is a general rule of thumb, and his or her second premise relates that rule to your current situation. The conclusion will be advice aimed specifically at you.) Is the argument a good one? Did you take the advice?

Self-Assessment Quiz

1. What is a quantifier? What are the two quantities that can be used in categorical statements?
2. What are the two qualities that can be expressed in categorical statements?
3. What are the four standard-form categorical statements? (Specify them by quality and quantity and by letter designation.)

For each of the following statements, identify the subject and predicate terms, the quality, the quantity, and the name of the form (universal affirmative, universal negative, particular affirmative, or particular negative).

4 | Reasons for Belief and Doubt 163

Integrative Exercises

These exercises pertain to material in Chapters 1–4.

1. What is a deductive argument? An inductive one?
2. How can background information help us determine the soundness of a deductive argument or the cogency of an inductive one?
3. Is expertise more important for determining the validity of a deductive argument or the strength of an inductive one?
4. What is the appeal to authority? Is appealing to authority always fallacious?

For each of the following arguments, specify the conclusion and premises and say whether it is deductive or inductive. If it's inductive, say whether it is strong or weak; if deductive, say whether it is valid or invalid. If necessary, add implicit premises and conclusions.

5. "In Canada, the new Canadian Strategy on HIV/AIDS contains, for the first time, a component on legal, ethical, and human-rights issues. This represents a huge step forward and a recognition that these issues must be an integral part of any strategy to fight HIV, for three reasons: because work aimed at ensuring that laws and policies facilitate rather than hinder efforts to prevent HIV/AIDS must be supported; because work aimed at ensuring that laws and policies facilitate rather than hinder efforts to provide care, treatment, and support to people with HIV/AIDS must be supported; and because work aimed at ensuring that laws and policies respect and protect the rights of people with HIV/AIDS and those affected by the disease must be supported." (Editorial, *Canadian HIV/AIDS Policy & Law Newsletter*, 4, no. 2/3, Spring 1999)
6. "The people of PEI have a voice and it deserves to be heard in return for a vote. Too many times people have voted for the Liberals and PCs and too many times those people have been let down by the party they voted for because the party has their own hidden agendas." (Online comment, 4 February 2011, *The Guardian*, Charlottetown, PEI)
7. If Quebec separates from Canada, Quebec will suffer economically. Fortunately, Quebec won't separate from Canada. So, Quebec will not suffer economically.
8. No one is going to support the prime minister if he follows the United States in refusing to lower greenhouse gas emissions. But it looks as if he's going to follow the United States. Thus, no one will support him.

120 PART ONE | Basics

Writing Assignments

1. Create an outline for Essay 3 ("Marine Parks") in Appendix A. Specify the thesis statement, each premise, arguments supporting premises, any objections considered, and the conclusion.
2. Study the argument presented in Essay 7 ("Yes, Human Cloning Should Be Permitted") in Appendix A. Identify the conclusion and the premises and objections considered. Then write a two-page critique of the essay's argument.
3. Select an issue from the following list and write a three-page paper defending a claim pertaining to the issue. Follow the procedure discussed in the text for outlining the essay and choosing a thesis and an appropriate argument to defend it. Where necessary, clarify terms.
   - Should Canada seek diplomatic ties with North Korea—a dictatorship with a terrible history of human-rights violations?
   - In the fight against terrorism, should law-enforcement agencies be allowed to spy on Canadian citizens by monitoring their email, wire-tapping their phones, and checking records from public libraries—all without warrants?
   - Should a city government celebrate its citizens' cultural diversity or instead focus on its citizens' fundamental similarities?
   - Should children as young as 10 years of age be encouraged to carry cellphones?

Supplements

The Power of Critical Thinking also includes a comprehensive online ancillary package, available at **www.oupcanada.com/MacDonaldVaughn4Ce**. An instructor's manual, a test generator, and a robust set of PowerPoint slides—animated for maximum pedagogical effectiveness—are available to those teaching the course. (Please contact your OUP sales representative for login and password information). A student study guide is also available online (no password required); this effective resource allows students to take advantage of a number of study notes, quizzes, and additional exercises.

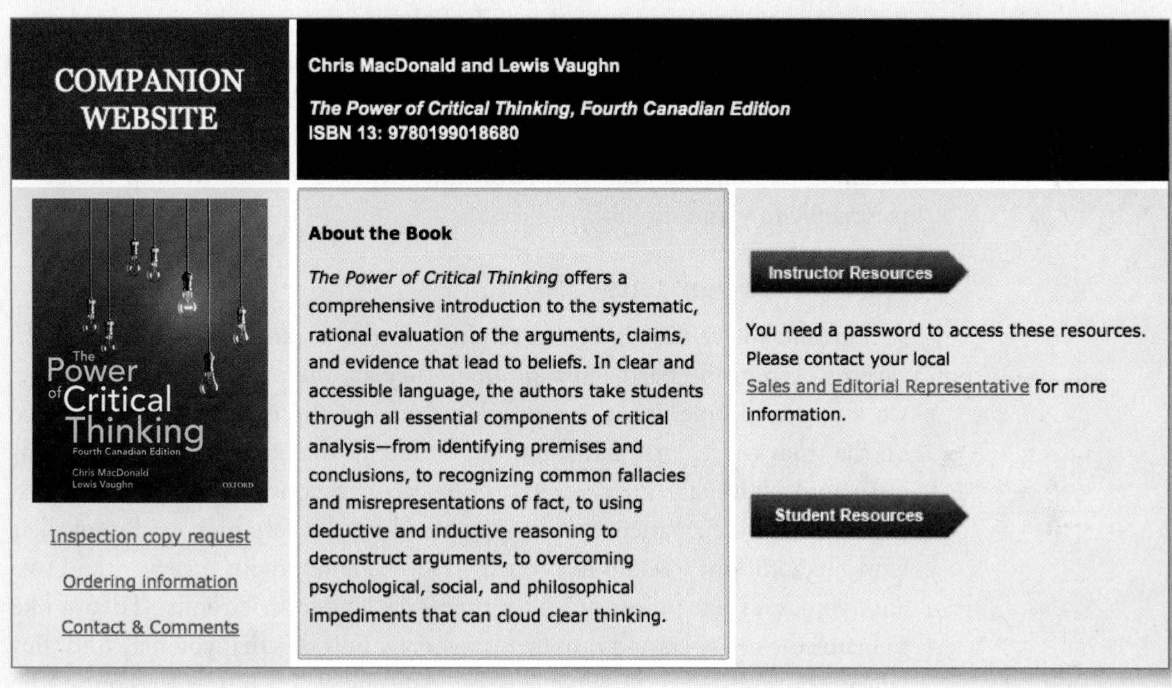

PREFACE

As we enter our fourth edition, the Canadian version of *The Power of Critical Thinking* continues to evolve. The original American version, with its US spelling and cultural references, is an increasingly distant cousin. The current edition features many new end-of-chapter questions, and five new Essays for Evaluation at the back of the book—all on topics of current interest, and all by Canadian authors. Every chapter also now includes one or more Everyday Problems and Decisions boxes, illustrating the application of that chapter's material to the reader's everyday life. Among many other changes, we've also updated many of the end-of-chapter Field Problems, added new material on the dangers of fooling ourselves, and included a useful new textbox on the use of propositional logic in essay-writing in Chapter 7. Overall, we've worked hard to keep the book practical and informal, while at the same time retaining its philosophical rigour and integrity. We've tried to keep the book reasonably fun, and useful.

Acknowledgements

As I'm sure you've heard, critical thinking textbooks are produced by elves in caverns deep in the Earth. Just kidding. They are the product of a lot of hard work by real people, including people other than those whose names you see on the front cover. First and foremost, I'd like to thank, as always, my friends at Oxford University Press, including especially Stephen Kotowych and Meg Patterson, for their patience and support and for the very high quality of their work. In addition, I would like to thank several anonymous reviewers and two anonymous, expert proofreaders for their excellent contributions. (I'd also like to blame the reviewers and proofreaders for any mistakes that you may find. But you're a critical thinker, so you'll see right through me.) In fact, of course, the mistakes that remain are my own fault. If you spot one, let me know. Finally, as always, I would like to thank Professor Nancy Walton, who on a daily basis teaches me the value, and the proper place, of critical thinking, and does so more often than not with a smile.

Reviewers

We gratefully acknowledge the contributions of the following reviewers, whose thoughtful comments and suggestions have helped to shape this new edition:

Kelvin Booth, Thompson Rivers University

Laura Byrne, University of Ottawa

Antoine Goulem, Seneca College

Sam Hillier, University of Alberta
Gregory Lavers, Concordia University
Jeff Vancha, University of Regina
Patrick Walsh, University of Manitoba

Chris MacDonald
Ryerson University

The Power of Critical Thinking

PART ONE

BASICS

1 THE POWER OF CRITICAL THINKING

CHAPTER OBJECTIVES

- To understand the meaning of *critical thinking* and the importance and meaning of the terms *systematic*, *evaluation*, *formulation*, and *rational standards*.
- To understand how critical thinking is related to logic, the truth or falsity of statements, knowledge, and personal empowerment.

Why It Matters

You will be able to

- appreciate why critical thinking is better than the passive acceptance of beliefs.
- appreciate the relevance of the claim "The unexamined life is not worth living" to critical thinking.
- understand why the following claims are dubious: "Critical thinking makes people too critical or cynical," "Critical thinking makes people cold and unemotional," and "Critical thinking is the enemy of creativity."
- appreciate the usefulness of critical thinking in all human endeavours.

How It Works

You will be able to

- distinguish between statements and non-statements.
- understand the basic concepts of reasons, argument, inference, premise, and conclusion.
- use indicator words to help pinpoint premises and conclusions.
- distinguish between passages that do and do not contain an argument.
- identify arguments in various contexts and distinguish between arguments and superfluous material, arguments and explanations, and premises and conclusions.

When you were born, you were completely without opinions or judgments or values or viewpoints—and now your head is overflowing with them. Opinions help you make your way through the world. They guide you to failure and success, ignorance and understanding, good and bad, paralysis and empowerment. Some of your beliefs truly enable you, and some blind you. Some are true; some are not. But the question is, *which ones are which?* This kind of question—a question about the *quality* of your beliefs—is the fundamental concern of **critical thinking**.

critical thinking The systematic evaluation or formulation of beliefs or statements by rational standards.

Determining the quality or value of your beliefs is a function of thinking, and the kind of thinking that does this job best is critical thinking—a skill that a university or college education seeks to foster. This means that critical thinking is not directly about *what* you think, but rather *how* you think.

The quality of beliefs is not about what factors *caused* you to have the beliefs that you do. A sociologist might tell you how society has influenced some of your moral views. A psychologist might describe how your emotions cause you to cling to certain opinions. Your best friend might claim that you have unconsciously absorbed most of your beliefs directly from your parents. But none of these speculations have much to do with the central task of critical thinking.

"The recipe for perpetual ignorance is: be satisfied with your opinions and content with your knowledge."

—Elbert Hubbard

Critical thinking focuses not on what *causes* a belief, but on *whether it is worth believing*. A belief is worth believing, or accepting, if we have *good reasons* to accept it. The better the reasons, the more likely the belief is to be true. Critical thinking offers us a set of standards embodied in techniques, attitudes, and principles that we can use to assess beliefs and determine if they are supported by good reasons. After all, we want our beliefs to be true, to be good guides for dealing with the world—and critical thinking is the best tool we have for achieving this goal.

Here's one way to wrap up these points in a concise definition:

CRITICAL THINKING: The systematic evaluation or formulation of beliefs or statements by rational standards.

Critical thinking is *systematic* because it involves distinct procedures and methods. It entails *evaluation* and *formulation* because it's used both to assess existing beliefs (yours or someone else's) and to devise new ones. And it operates according to *rational standards* in that beliefs are judged by how well they are supported by reasons.

The effort involved in thinking critically is well worth it, because it is one of the few tools we have to counteract the natural limitations of the human brain. Some of those limitations are pretty easy to spot, of course. All of us make mistakes of reasoning from time to time: we fail to give enough attention to key facts, we forget things, we jump to conclusions, and so on. But some errors of reasoning are more common than others. Some are so common that psychologists have studied them and given them names. These are called "cognitive biases," and evidence suggests that some of them are nearly universal. For example, we tend to judge facts differently depending on just how they are stated, or "framed." We might react quite positively to an announcement that a struggling company had been able to "save" 300 jobs (out of 1000) but quite negatively to an announcement that the company was "laying off" 700 people (out of 1000)—even though the result is exactly the same. Framing the issue in terms of jobs saved—which sounds like a good thing—makes us think more positively about the whole scenario. Another example: if you ask people to estimate how likely it is that 200 people will die in Canada this month in a plane crash versus how likely it is that 200 people will die in Canada this month in car accidents, they're likely to overestimate the relative likelihood of a plane crash, just because they've seen scary images on TV of planes crashing and can readily call those images to mind. In general, we tend to overestimate how common dramatic events are and underestimate how common more boring events are. (Some more of these cognitive biases are touched upon again in Chapter 4.) We know that mistakes of reasoning like these are common, and it's easy to see how they can lead to bad conclusions and bad decisions. Our best defence is to look at the facts carefully and think critically.

logic The study of good reasoning, or inference, and the rules that govern it.

Critical thinking, of course, involves **logic**. Logic is the study of good reasoning, or inference, and the rules that govern it. Critical thinking is broader than logic because it involves not only logic but also the examination of the truth or falsity of individual statements, the evaluation of arguments and evidence, the use of analysis and investigation, and the application of many other skills that help us decide what to believe or do.

Ultimately, what critical thinking leads you to is knowledge, understanding, and—if you put these to work—empowerment. In Chapters 2 and 3 you'll get a more thorough grounding in critical thinking and logical argument as well as plenty of opportunities to practise your new skills. Consider this chapter an introduction to those important lessons. Focus on soaking up the big ideas. They will help you prepare for the skills you'll learn in later chapters.

WHY IT MATTERS

In large part, our lives are defined by our actions and choices, and our actions and choices are guided by our thinking—so our thinking had better be good. Almost every day we are hit by a blizzard of assertions, opinions, arguments, and pronouncements from all directions. They all try to get us to believe, to agree, to accept, to follow, to submit. If we care whether our choices are right and our beliefs true, if we want to rise above blind acceptance and random choices, we need to use the tools provided by critical thinking.

FOOD FOR THOUGHT

Dumb and Dumber

Often when we don't know something, that's bad. But when we *don't know* that we don't know something, that's worse. At least, that's the view of researchers who studied the effects of this kind of double-edged ignorance (*Journal of Personality and Social Psychology,* December 1999). In several studies, the researchers assessed the ability of study participants in areas that demanded "knowledge, wisdom, or savvy"—logical reasoning, English grammar, and humour.

The results: people whose abilities were very weak tended to greatly overestimate them (see Figure 1.1). Those who got the lowest test scores thought they had achieved much higher scores. The data suggested that the overestimations arose because the subjects couldn't distinguish accuracy from error. They didn't know what they didn't know. Ironically, when the researchers helped the participants improve their abilities and increase their knowledge, the participants could recognize their limitations.

Hmm. Increase your knowledge and recognize your limitations—isn't that what critical thinking helps you do?

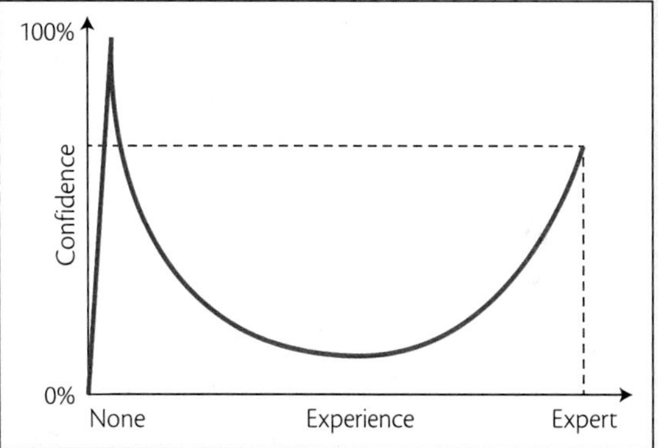

FIGURE 1.1 Dunning-Kruger Effect
Unskilled and unaware of it: how difficulties in recognizing one's own incompetence lead to inflated self-assessments. Kruger, J., Dunning, D. (1999). Available at http://bobbins.info/2014/12/dunning-kruger-effect/

Of course we always have the option of taking the easy way out. We can simply grab on to whatever beliefs or statements come blowing by in the wind, adopting viewpoints either because others hold them or because they make us feel good. But then we give up control over our lives and let the wind take us wherever it will, as if we had no more say in the outcome than a leaf in a storm.

A consequence of going with the wind is a loss of personal freedom. If you passively accept beliefs that have been handed to you by your parents, your culture, or your teachers, then those beliefs are *not really yours.* You just happened to be in a certain place and time when they were handed out. If they are not really yours and if you still let them guide your choices and actions, then they—not you—are in charge of your life. Your beliefs are yours only if you critically examine them for yourself and decide that they are supported by good reasons.

Our choice to apply critical thinking skills is not an all-or-nothing decision. Each of us already uses critical thinking to some degree in our lives. We often evaluate reasons for (and against) believing that someone famous has committed

"Are you not ashamed of caring so much for the making of money and for fame and prestige, when you neither think nor care about wisdom and truth and the improvement of your soul?"

—*Socrates*

CREDIT: xkcd.com.

a crime, that one candidate in an election is better than another, that regulation of genetically modified foods should be strengthened or weakened, that we should buy a particular kind of car, that a new friend is trustworthy, that one university is better than another, that the bill being considered in Parliament would be bad for the environment, or that buying stock in Apple is a good investment. But the more urgent consideration is not just whether we sometimes use critical thinking, but *how well* we use it.

Many people, however, will reject all of this—and perhaps you are one of them. They believe that critical thinking—or what they assume to be critical thinking—makes a person excessively critical or cynical, emotionally cold, and creatively constrained. For example, there are some who think that anything that sounds like logic and rationality must be negative—designed to attack someone else's thinking and score points by putting people in their place. A few of these take the word "critical" here to mean "faultfinding" or "whiny" or "picky."

Now, no doubt some people try to use critical thinking primarily for offensive purposes, but this approach goes against critical thinking principles. The *critical* in critical thinking is used in the sense of "exercising or involving careful judgment or judicious evaluation." Critical thinking is about determining what

EVERYDAY PROBLEMS AND DECISIONS

What Should I Believe?

Decisions about what to believe are some of the most important decisions we ever make. What we believe shapes who we are, and our beliefs guide us in what we decide to do. Decisions about what to believe, in other words, are the foundations for all of our *other* decisions. Consider the importance of each of the following decisions about what to believe:

Whether I believe . . .	**influences whether I . . .**
the flu is a serious public health risk	get a flu shot.
that a particular politician is honest	vote for her.
I can afford mortgage payments	buy a house.
the oncoming car is going to stop	step off the sidewalk and into the street.

FOOD FOR THOUGHT

Passion and Reason

"Reason is, and ought only to be the slave of the passions." That's what Scottish philosopher David Hume wrote in his *Treatise on Human Nature* (1738). What did he mean by this? He meant roughly that reason, far from being at odds with emotion, is best thought of as serving it. Our emotions tell us what we want; our reason tells us what to do about it, based in part on what we can reasonably believe will be effective in achieving our goals.

we are justified in believing, and that involves an openness to other points of view, a tolerance for opposing perspectives, a focus on the issue at hand, and fair assessments of arguments and evidence.

Some people fear that if they apply critical thinking to their lives, they will become cold and unemotional—just like a computer that works strictly according to logic and mathematical functions. But this fear is misplaced. Critical thinking and feelings actually work best together. Certainly part of thinking critically is ensuring that we don't let our emotions distort our judgments, but critical thinking can also help us clarify our feelings and deal with them more effectively. Our emotions often need the guidance of reason. Likewise, our reasoning needs our emotions. It is our feelings that motivate us to action, and without motivation our reasoning would never get off the ground.

Then there's the dubious assumption that critical thinking is the enemy of creativity. To some people, critical thinking is a sterile and rigid mode of thought that limits the imagination, hinders artistic vision, and prevents "thinking outside the box." But critical thinking and creative thinking are not opposed to one another. Good critical thinkers can let their imaginations run free, just like anyone else. They can create and enjoy poetry, music, art, literature, and plain old fun in the same way and to the same degree as the rest of the world. Critical thinking can complement creative thinking because it is needed to assess and enhance the creation. Scientists, for example, often dream up some very far-fetched theories (an important part of doing science). These theories pop into their heads in the same way that the idea for a great work of art appears in the mind of a painter. But then scientists use all of their critical thinking skills to evaluate what they have produced (as artists sometimes do)—and this critical examination enables them to select the most promising theories and to weed out those that are unworkable.

In a very important sense, critical thinking *is* thinking outside the box. When we passively absorb the ideas we encounter, when we refuse to consider any alternative explanations or theories, when we conform our ideas to the wishes of

FOOD FOR THOUGHT

Architecture: Creativity through Critical Thinking

CREDIT: Eric Fruhauf

"Creativity and critical thinking are inseparable in the field of architecture. Facing regulatory constraints (building codes, municipal bylaws), physical constraints (structural requirements, material limitations), and project-specific constraints (client desires and budget), an architect adds his or her personal experience, knowledge of precedent, and abstract problem-solving to develop a clear physical design solution. The most creative architectural designs result from a complex web of information, skillfully interpreted.

In architecture school, it is the design critique session or 'crit' that prepares architects for this design process. Each student's design is presented to a group of fellow students, professors, and practitioners; its merits are tested, difficult questions are asked, and alternatives suggested. This process of critical thinking, over time, hones the architect's creative skills."

—Eric Fruhauf, OAA. Professor of architecture, civil, and building science at Algonquin College, Ottawa.

the group, and when we let our thinking be controlled by bias, stereotypes, superstition, and wishful thinking, that's when we are deep, deep in the box. But we rise above all that when we have the courage to think critically. When we are willing to put our beliefs on trial in the court of critical reason, we open ourselves up to new possibilities, the dormant seeds of creativity.

"Sometimes you get a brainstorm, sometimes you only get the clouds."

Critical thinking covers a lot of territory. It's used across the board in all disciplines, all areas of public life, all the sciences, all sectors of business, and all occupations. It has played a major role in all the great endeavours of humankind— scientific discoveries, technological innovations, philosophical insights, social and political movements, literary creation and criticism, judicial and legal reasoning, democratic nation building, and more. The *lack* of critical thinking has also left its mark. The great tragedies of history—the wars, massacres, holocausts, tyrannies, bigotries, epidemics, and witch hunts—grew out of famines of the mind where clear, careful thinking was much too scarce.

HOW IT WORKS

As you can see, critical thinking has extremely broad applications. Principles and procedures used to evaluate beliefs in one discipline or issue can be used to assess beliefs in many other arenas (and we will examine several of those in detail in Chapter 11). But the basics of good critical thinking are the same everywhere. Here are the common threads that make them universal.

Claims and Reasons

Critical thinking is a rational, systematic process that we apply to beliefs of all kinds. Of course, we can really only evaluate beliefs that are made explicit; for obvious reasons, it's hard to evaluate beliefs that are kept hidden from us. We can only evaluate our *own* beliefs once we say (or maybe admit!) to ourselves, "This is what I believe." And we can only evaluate other people's beliefs by looking at the things those people actually say or write. So although we are interested in evaluating the quality of beliefs in general, we are mostly limited to evaluating beliefs that someone makes explicit by making some statement or claim. (We'll say something about the role unstated beliefs can play in arguments, and about how to bring them to light and assess them, in Chapter 3.)

A **statement** is an assertion that something is or is not the case. The following are all statements:

statement (claim) An assertion that something is or is not the case.

- A triangle has three sides.
- I am cold.

REVIEW NOTES

Why Critical Thinking Matters

- Our thinking guides our actions, so it should be of high quality.
- If you have never critically examined your beliefs, they are not truly yours.
- Critical thinking is one way of defending against the cognitive biases that tend to lead us to false conclusions and bad decisions.
- To examine your beliefs is to examine your life. Socrates said: "The unexamined life is not worth living."
- Critical thinking involves determining what we're justified in believing, being open to new perspectives, and fairly assessing the views of others and ourselves.
- Critical thinking complements both our emotions and our creativity.
- Critical thinking is thinking outside the box.

- You are a liar.
- You are not a liar.
- I see blue spots before my eyes.
- 7 + 5 = 12
- 7 + 5 = 11
- You should never make fun of someone's disability.
- The best explanation for his behaviour is that he was drunk.
- The capital of Canada is Winnipeg.
- Rap music is better than Celtic fiddle music.
- An electron is a sub-atomic particle.

So statements, or claims, are the kind of things that are either true or false. (Notice that at least three of the claims above are definitely false, but that doesn't stop them from counting as statements!) They assert that some state of affairs is or is not actual. You may know that a specific statement is true, or you may know that it is false, or you may not know either way. There may be no way to find out at the time if the statement is true or false. There may be no one who believes the statement. But it would be a statement nonetheless.

Some of the thoughts we express, though, do *not* express statements:

- Does a triangle have three sides?
- Is that cheese?
- Turn that music off!
- Hey, dude.
- ROFL!

The first two sentences are questions, the third is a command, the fourth sentence is a greeting, and the fifth is an exclamation that is common in email and text messaging. None of them asserts that something is or is not the case. They are meaningful things to say, but they're not *statements.*

When you're engaged in critical thinking, you're mostly either evaluating statements or formulating them. In both cases your primary task is to figure out how strongly to believe them. The strength of your belief should depend on the quality of the reasons in favour of the statements. Statements backed by good reasons are

CREDIT: Nate Fakes/Cartoon Stock

Fly Logic

worthy of strong acceptance. Statements that fall short of this standard deserve weaker acceptance.

Sometimes you may not be able to assign any substantial weight at all to the reasons for or against a statement—there simply may not be enough evidence to decide rationally. Generally when that happens, good critical thinkers do not arbitrarily choose to accept or reject a statement. They suspend judgment until there is enough evidence to make an intelligent decision.

Reasons and Arguments

Reasons provide support for a statement. That is, they provide us with grounds for believing that a statement is true. Reasons are themselves expressed as statements. So a statement expressing a reason or reasons is used to show that another statement is true or likely to be true. This combination of statements—a statement (or statements) supposedly providing reasons for accepting another statement—is known as an **argument**. Arguments are the main focus of critical thinking; they are the most important tool we have for evaluating the truth of statements (our own and those of others) and for formulating statements that are truly worthy of acceptance. Arguments are, therefore, essential for the advancement of knowledge in all fields. Often people use the word *argument* to indicate a debate or an angry exchange. In critical thinking, however, *argument* refers to the assertion of reasons in support of a statement.

argument A group of statements in which some of them (the premises) are intended to support another of them (the conclusion).

The statements (reasons) given in support of another statement are called the **premises**. The statement that the premises are intended to support is called the **conclusion**. We can define an argument, then, like this:

premise In an argument, a statement, or reason, given in support of the conclusion.

conclusion In an argument, the statement that the premises are intended to support.

> **ARGUMENT:** A group of statements in which some of them (the premises) are intended to support another of them (the conclusion).

The following are some simple arguments:

1. Because you want a job that will allow you to make a difference in the world, you should consider working for a charitable organization.
2. The *Globe and Mail's Report on Business* says that people should invest heavily in gold. Therefore, investing in gold is a smart move.
3. When Joseph takes the bus, he's always late. And he's taking the bus today, so I'm sure he's going to be late.
4. Wow! This movie is on Netflix, but it was never even shown in theatres. It's not a good sign when a movie goes straight to video without ever being shown in theatres. This one must be pretty bad.
5. No one should drink a beer brewed by a giant corporation. Labatt's Blue is brewed by a giant corporation, so no one should drink it.

Here are the same arguments where the parts are easily identified:

1. [Premise] Because you want a job that will allow you to make a difference in the world, [Conclusion] you should consider working for a charitable organization.
2. [Premise] *The Globe and Mail's Report on Business* says that people should invest heavily in gold. [Conclusion] Therefore, investing in gold is a smart move.
3. [Premise] When Joseph takes the bus, he's always late. [Premise] And he's taking the bus today, [Conclusion] so I'm sure he's going to be late.
4. Wow! [Premise] This movie is on Netflix, [Premise] but it was never even shown in theatres. [Premise] It's not a good sign when a movie goes straight to video without being shown in theatres. [Conclusion] This one must be pretty bad.
5. [Premise] No one should drink a beer brewed by a giant corporation. [Premise] Labatt's Blue is brewed by a giant corporation. [Conclusion] So no one should drink it.

"What danger can ever come from ingenious reasoning and inquiry? The worst speculative skeptic ever I knew was a much better man than the best superstitious devotee and bigot."

—David Hume

What all of these arguments have in common is that reasons (the premises) are offered to support or prove a claim (the conclusion). This logical link between premises and conclusion is what distinguishes arguments from all other kinds of discourse. This mental process of reasoning from a premise or premises to a conclusion based on those premises is called **inference**. We infer the conclusion of an argument from its premise or premises. Being able to identify arguments, to pick them out of a larger chunk of non-argumentative writing if need be, is an important skill on which many other critical thinking skills are based.

inference The process of reasoning from a premise or premises to a conclusion based on those premises.

Next, consider this passage:

> The cost of the new XJ fighter jet is $650 million. The cost of three AR21 bombers is $1.2 billion. The Canadian government intends to fund such projects.

Is there an argument here? No. This passage consists of several claims, but no reasons are presented to support any particular claim (conclusion). This passage can be turned into an argument, though, with some minor editing:

> Canada's auditor general says that any weapon that costs more than $50 million apiece will actually impair our military readiness. The cost of the new XJ fighter jet is $650 million dollars. The cost of three AR21 bombers is $1.2 billion. We should never impair our readiness. Therefore, the Canadian government should cancel both these expensive projects.

Now we have an argument because *reasons* are given for accepting a conclusion. Here's another passage:

> Allisha used the online banking app on her iPhone to check the balance of her chequing account. It said that the balance was $125. Allisha was stunned that it was so low. She called her brother to see if he had been playing one of his stupid pranks. He said he hadn't. She wondered: was she the victim of bank fraud?

Where is the conclusion? Where are the reasons? There are none. This is a little story built out of descriptive claims, but it's not an argument. It's not trying to convince you, the reader, of anything. It could be turned into an argument if, say, some of the claims were restated as reasons for the conclusion that bank fraud had been committed.

Being able to distinguish between passages that do and do not contain arguments is a very basic skill—and an extremely important one. Many people think that if they have clearly stated their beliefs on a subject, they have presented an argument. But a mere declaration of beliefs never counts as an argument. Often such assertions of opinion are just a jumble of unsupported claims without an argument of any kind. A writer or speaker of these claims gives the readers or listeners no grounds for believing the claims. In writing courses, this kind of absence of supporting premises is sometimes called a "lack of development."

Here are two more examples of discussion without argument:

> There's a pattern developing that suggests [Prime Minister Stephen] Harper's pledge of a sharply limited, six-month engagement may be so much dust in the desert wind. Before this goes any further, the government should urge our allies to cool their jets. We should complete our six-month mission, and Parliament should weigh the results, before we bow to pressure to do more. (Editorial, *Toronto Star*, 6 November 2014)

> Bank of Canada governor Stephen Poloz says young adults looking for work in this country should be willing to work for free to gain a foothold in the job market. Young Canadians should cross Poloz off their list of career counsellors. He may be very good at setting interest rates and sending signals to financial markets but he sent a very bad message recently to both those trying to break into the workforce and their potential employers. (Editorial, *Vancouver Sun*, 6 November, 2014)

The passage about Stephen Harper is an expression of doubt (which may or may not be justified), but no reasons supporting a conclusion are offered. Note the contentious tone in the second passage. This passage smells like an argument—it certainly expresses an opinion. But, unfortunately, there is no argument. It's just a point of view presented without any support at all.

explanation A statement or statements intended to tell why or how something is the case.

Sometimes people also confuse **explanations** with arguments. An argument gives us reasons for believing *that something is the case*—that a claim is true or at least probably true. An explanation, though, tells us *why or how something is the case.* Arguments have something to prove; explanations do not. Look carefully at this pair of statements:

1. Adam obviously stole the money—he was the only one with access to it.
2. Yes, Adam stole the money, but he did it because he needed it to buy food.

Statement 1 is an argument. Statement 2 is an explanation. Statement 1 tries to show that something is the case—that Adam stole the money—and the reason offered in support of this statement is that he alone had access to it. That's why we should believe it. Statement 2 does not try to prove that something is the case (that Adam stole the money). Instead, it attempts to explain why something is the case (why Adam stole the money). Statement 2 takes for granted that Adam stole the money and then tries to explain *why* he did it. In a different context, of course, the fact that Adam had a motive—hunger—that might be liable to make people steal could be offered as a reason to believe that he did, in fact, steal on this occasion. But in the absence of such a context, this sentence is most naturally read as an explanation, rather than an argument. (Note that explanations can be used as integral *parts* of arguments. When they play that role, they are powerful intellectual and scientific tools that help us understand the world; that is why this text has several chapters in Part 4 devoted to explanations used in this way.)

indicator words Words that frequently accompany arguments and signal that a premise or conclusion is present.

It's not always easy to recognize an argument and to locate both premises and a conclusion, but there are a few tricks that can make the job more manageable. For one, there are **indicator words** that frequently accompany arguments and signal that a premise or conclusion is present. For example, in argument 1, presented earlier in this chapter, the indicator word *because* tips us off to the presence of the premise "Because you want a job that will allow you to make a difference in the world." In argument 2, *therefore* points to the conclusion "Therefore, investing in stocks is a smart move."

Here are some common premise indicators:

because	due to the fact that	inasmuch as
in view of the fact	being that	as indicated by
given that	since	for
seeing that	assuming that	the reason being
as	for the reason that	

These words almost always introduce a premise – something given as a reason to believe some conclusion.

And here are some common conclusion indicators:

therefore	it follows that	it must be that
thus	we can conclude that	as a result
which implies that	so	which means that
consequently	hence	ergo

Using indicator words to spot premises and conclusions, however, is not foolproof. They're just good clues. You will find that some of the words just listed are used when no argument is present. For example,

- I am here *because* you asked me to come.
- I haven't seen you *since* Canada Day.
- He was *so* sleepy he fell off his chair.

Note also that arguments can be put forth without the use of *any* indicator words:

> We must each take steps to protect our environment. We can't rely on the government—federal and provincial regulators already have their hands full. Government can't be everywhere at once, and they usually get involved only after some environmental catastrophe has already happened.

As you may have noticed from these examples, the basic structure of arguments can have several simple variations. For one thing, arguments can have any number of premises. Arguments 1 and 2 on page 12 have one premise; arguments 3 and 5 each have two premises, and argument 4 has three premises. In extended arguments that often appear in essays, editorials, reports, and other works, there can be many more premises. Also, the conclusion of an argument may not always appear after the premises. As in the above argument about the environment, the conclusion may be presented first.

Occasionally the conclusion of an argument can be disguised as a question—even though a question is usually not a claim at all. (For purposes of examining such arguments, we may need to rewrite the conclusion as a statement; in some arguments, we may also need to do the same for the premises.) Most of the time readers have no difficulty discerning what the implied conclusion is, even when it is stated as a question. See for yourself:

> Do you think for one minute that backbench Conservatives in Parliament will be happy about the prime minister's refusal to re-open the

REVIEW NOTES

Claims, Reasons, and Arguments

- *Statement* (claim): An assertion that something is or is not the case.
- *Premise:* A statement given in support of another statement.
- *Conclusion:* A statement that premises are used to support.
- *Argument:* A group of statements in which some of them (the premises) are intended to support another of them (the conclusion).
- *Explanation:* A statement or statements asserting why or how something is the case.
- *Indicator words:* Words that frequently accompany arguments and signal that a premise or conclusion is present.

abortion debate? A lot of Conservative Members of Parliament were elected by constituents who have very strong anti-abortion views.

The opening sentence of this passage is a question, but the answer is one that the writer assumes will be clear and obvious to the reader—namely, "no."

Probably the best advice for anyone trying to uncover or dissect arguments is this: *Find the conclusion first.* Once you know what claim someone is trying to prove, it becomes much easier to isolate the premises being offered in support of it. Ask yourself, "What claim is this writer or speaker trying to persuade me to believe?" If the writer or speaker is not trying to convince you of anything, there is no argument to examine.

Arguments in the Rough

As you've probably guessed by now, in the real world arguments almost never appear neatly labelled as they are here. As suggested earlier, they usually come embedded in a tangle of other sentences that serve many other functions besides articulating an argument. They may be long and hard to follow. And sometimes a passage that sounds like an argument isn't one. Your main challenge is to identify the conclusion and premises without getting lost in all the "background noise."

Consider this passage:

[1] A.L. Jones used flawed reasoning in his letter yesterday praising this newspaper's decision to publish announcements of same-sex unions. [2] Mr Jones asserts that same-sex unions are a fact of life and therefore should be acknowledged by the news media as a legitimate variation on social partnerships. [3] But the news media are not in the business of endorsing or validating lifestyles. [4] They're supposed to report on

> lifestyles, not bless them. [5] In addition, by validating same-sex unions or any other lifestyle, the media abandon their objectivity and become political partisans—which would destroy whatever respect people have for news outlets. [6] All of this shows that the news media—including this newspaper—should never endorse lifestyles by announcing those lifestyles to the world.

There's an argument here, but it's surrounded by extraneous material. The conclusion is sentence 6—"All of this shows that the news media—including this newspaper—should never (explicitly or implicitly) endorse lifestyles by announcing those lifestyles to the world." Since we know what the conclusion is, we can identify the premises and separate them from other information. Sentences 1 and 2 are not premises; they're background information about the nature of the dispute. Sentence 3 presents the first premise, and sentence 4 is essentially a restatement of that premise. Sentence 5 is the second premise.

Stripped clean of non-argumentative material, the argument looks like this:

> [Premise] The news media are not in the business of endorsing or validating lifestyles. [Premise] In addition, by validating same-sex unions or any other lifestyle, the media abandon their objectivity and become political partisans—which would destroy whatever respect people have for news outlets. [Conclusion] All of this shows that the news media—including this newspaper—should never endorse lifestyles by announcing those lifestyles to the world.

Now see if you can spot the conclusion and premises in this one:

> [1] You have already said that you love me and that you can't imagine spending the rest of your life without me. [2] Once, you even tried to propose to me. [3] And now you claim that you need time to think about whether we should be married. [4] Well, everything that you've told me regarding our relationship has been a lie. [5] In some of your letters to a friend you admitted that you were misleading me. [6] You've been telling everyone that we are just friends, not lovers. [7] And worst of all, you've been secretly dating someone else. [8] Why are you doing this? [9] It's all been a farce!

And you thought that romance had nothing to do with critical thinking! In this passionate paragraph, an argument is alive and well. The conclusion is in sentence 4: "Everything that you've told me . . . has been a lie." Sentence 9, the concluding remark, is essentially a repetition of the conclusion with a little extra information abut what the speaker is going to do next. Sentences 1, 2, and 3 are background information on the current conflict. Sentences 5, 6,

> "I respect faith, but doubt is what gets you an education."
>
> —*Wilson Mizner*

and 7 are the premises, the reasons that support the conclusion. And sentence 8 is an exasperated query that's not part of the argument.

You will discover that in most extended argumentative passages, premises and conclusions make up only a small portion of the total number of words. A good part of the text is background information and restatements of the premises or conclusion. Most of the rest consists of explanations, digressions, examples or illustrations, and descriptive passages.

As you can see, learning the principles of critical thinking or logic requires at least some prior knowledge and ability. But, you may wonder (especially if this is your first course in critical or logical reasoning), "Where does this prior knowledge and ability come from?"—and do you have these prerequisites? Fortunately, the answer is yes. Since you are, as the ancient Greek philosopher Aristotle says, a rational animal, you already have the necessary equipment—namely, a logical sense that helps you reason in everyday life and enables you to begin honing your critical reasoning.

SUMMARY

Critical thinking is the systematic evaluation or formulation of beliefs, or statements, by rational standards. Critical thinking is *systematic* because it involves distinct procedures and methods. It entails *evaluation* and *formulation* because it's used both to assess existing beliefs (yours or someone else's) and to devise new ones. And it operates according to *reasonable standards* in that beliefs are judged according to the reasons and reasoning that support them.

Critical thinking matters because our lives are defined by our actions and choices, and our actions and choices are guided by our thinking. Critical thinking helps guide us toward beliefs that are worthy of acceptance and that can help us be successful in life, however we define success.

A consequence of not thinking critically is a loss of personal freedom. If you passively accept beliefs that have been handed to you by your family and your culture, then those beliefs are not really yours. If they are not really yours and you let them guide your choices and actions, then they—not you—are in charge of your life. Your beliefs are yours only if you examine them critically for yourself to see if they are supported by good reasons.

Some people believe that critical thinking will make them cynical, emotionally cold, and creatively constrained. But there is no good reason to believe that this is the case. Critical thinking does not necessarily lead to cynicism. It can complement our feelings by helping us sort them out. And it doesn't limit creativity—it helps perfect it.

Critical thinking is a rational, systematic process that we apply to beliefs of all kinds. As we use the term here, *belief* is just another word for statement or claim. A *statement* is an assertion that something is or is not the case. When you're engaged in critical thinking, you are mostly either evaluating a statement or trying to formulate one. In both cases your primary task is to figure out how strongly to believe the statement (on the basis of how likely it is to be true). The strength of your belief will depend on the strength of the reasons in favour of the statement.

In critical thinking an argument is not a fight but a set of statements—statements supposedly providing reasons for accepting another statement. The statements given in support of another statement are called the *premises.* The statement that the premises are used to support is called the *conclusion.* An argument then is a group of statements in which some of them (the premises) are intended to support another of them (the conclusion).

Being able to recognize an argument is an important skill on which many other critical thinking skills are based. The task is made easier by indicator words that often accompany arguments and signal that a premise or conclusion is present. Premise indicators include *for*, *since*, and *because.* Conclusion indicators include *so*, *therefore*, and *thus.*

Arguments almost never appear neatly labelled for identification. They usually come embedded in a lot of statements that are not part of the arguments. Arguments can be complex and long. Your main task is to identify the conclusion and premises without getting lost in the maze of words.

EXERCISE 1.1

Answers to exercises marked with an asterisk (*) may be found in Appendix B, Answers to Exercises.

Review Questions

*1. What is critical thinking?

2. Is critical thinking primarily concerned with *what* you think or with *how* you think?

3. How do the terms *systematic*, *evaluation*, and *formulation* relate to critical thinking?

*4. According to the text, what does it mean to say that critical thinking is done according to rational standards?

5. According to the text, how does a lack of critical thinking cause a loss of personal freedom?

*6. What does the term *critical* refer to in critical thinking?

7. What is logic, and what vital role does it play in critical thinking?

*8. What is a statement?

9. Give an example of a statement. Then give an example of a sentence, on the same topic, that is not a statement.
10. According to the text, how should we go about proportioning our acceptance of a statement?
*11. What is an argument?
12. Give an example of an argument with two premises.
13. What is a premise?
*14. What is a conclusion?
15. Why can't a mere assertion or statement of beliefs constitute an argument?
16. True or false: All disagreements contain an argument.
*17. Does the following passage contain an argument? *Sample passage:* Jail sentences for criminals should be longer. No, I won't provide evidence that longer sentences lead to reduced crime rates. I know I'm right!
18. Does the following passage contain an argument? *Sample passage:* I know you want to take the 8:00 bus to the concert. But that's crazy—if we leave at 8:00, we'll never get to the concert on time!
*19. What role do indicator words play in arguments?
20. List three conclusion indicator words.
21. List three premise indicator words.
22. Give an example of a sentence that uses the word *since* as something *other than* an indicator word.
*23. What is probably the best strategy for trying to find an argument in a complex passage?
24. True or false: You can almost always find an argument in narrative writing.

EXERCISE 1.2

Which of the following are *statements?* Which are not?

*1. Should I go to class today?
2. Do not allow your emotions to distort your thinking.
3. Being able to speak your mind in public places is a fundamental right.
*4. Given that you believe in free speech, do you agree that we have the right to hold a protest march on campus?
5. Should our religious beliefs be guided by reason, emotion, or faith?
6. Puppies!
*7. Eating at Denny's was a terrible mistake.
8. The burgers at Burger King made me sick.
9. Maybe you should drink some tea.
*10. What have you done to serve your country?

EXERCISE 1.3

Which of the following passages are *arguments*? For each argument you find, specify what the conclusion is.

*1. Coffee is delicious, and it helps me stay awake while I'm studying. So you should give it a try.
2. Coffee is full of caffeine, which is why it helps me stay awake while I'm studying.
3. This weather is perfect for going to the beach! There's also a discount on surfing lessons that's good today only!
4. Where is Alexei planning on taking us for the annual ski trip this year?
5. Freeze! You're under arrest!
6. If you light that cigarette in here, I will leave the room.
*7. *The Heat* was a terrible movie, and not even Sandra Bullock could save it.
8. I know that humans evolved from monkeys, because my biology professor taught us that in class.
9. *Iron Man* was a better superhero movie than *Thor* because technology is just way cooler than mythology.
10. "Whether our argument concerns public affairs or some other subject, we must know some, if not all, of the facts about the subject on which we are to speak and argue. Otherwise, we can have no materials out of which to construct arguments." (Aristotle, *Rhetoric*)
*11. If guns are outlawed, then only outlaws will have guns. Don't outlaw guns.
12. Many believe that consciousness is a purely physical phenomenon. There is no soul, they say, and the mind is simply a result of electrical and chemical signals interacting in the brain. I reject this notion!
13. "Citizens who so value their 'independence' that they will not enroll in a political party are really forfeiting independence, because they abandon a share in decision-making at the primary level: the choice of the candidate." (Bruce L. Felknor, *Dirty Politics*)
14. If someone says something that offends me, I cannot and should not try to stop them from speaking. After all, in free countries like Canada, speech—even offensive speech—is protected.
*15. "Piercing car alarms have disturbed my walks, cafe meals, or my sleep at least once during every day I have lived in the city; roughly 3,650 car alarms. Once, only once, was the wail a response to theft. . . . Silent car alarms connect immediately to a security company, while the noisy ones are a problem, not a solution. They should be banned, finally." (Letter to the editor, *New York Times*, 4 October 2002)

16. Are NHL teams really good for local business? A recent article says that's not necessarily the case. According to the article, "Ivey School of business economist Mike Moffat says that while it could very likely aid in that respect, studies show that the overall economic impact of sports teams is typically low." (*Canadian Business*, 31 May 2011)

EXERCISE 1.4

Which of the following passages are *arguments?* For each argument specify both the conclusion and the premise or premises.

*1. It's a law of economics that if prices go up, demand will fall. Raising the price of our shoes is sure to dampen sales.

2. You have neglected your duty on several occasions, and you have been absent from work too many times. Therefore, you are not fit to serve in your current position.

3. Racial profiling is not an issue for white people, but it is a serious issue for visible minorities.

*4. The flu epidemic on the east coast is real. Government health officials say so. And I personally have read at least a dozen news stories that characterize the situation as a "flu epidemic."

5. People who place their trust in financial analysts are crazy. If analysts were any good they'd all be rich and wouldn't need to spend their time writing advice for other people.

6. Those protesters think the city should close down our local animal shelter because the animals are making too much noise. I bet they like to kick kittens in their spare time too. People who don't love animals make me sick.

*7. "I am writing about the cost of concert tickets. I am outraged at how much ticket prices are increasing every year. A few years ago, one could attend a popular concert for a decent price. Now some musicians are asking as much as $200 to $300." (Letter to the editor, *Buffalo News*, 10 October 2002)

8. "Comparing the culling of animals for economic reasons to the difficult decision that has to be made by thousands of women each year—whether to end a pregnancy through abortion—is reprehensible. If those who oppose abortion used their resources more wisely and became advocates of better sex education in the classroom, condom machines in all washrooms including high schools, and getting the Catholic Church to change its archaic, dangerous stance on all forms of contraceptives, I believe the rates

of abortion around the world would drop significantly." (Tony Matthews, letter to the editor, *Halifax Chronicle-Herald,* 12 May 2006)

9. Buying Microsoft stock is a sure thing! Several financial analysts have already predicted that the price will rise 50 per cent by the end of the month. Also, my friend thinks Bill Gates is cute.
*10. Stretched upon the dark silk night, bracelets of city lights glisten brightly.
11. Dianne's blog is always interesting. Her commentaries are tough, but they're always fair. Her blog should definitely be on your reading list!

EXERCISE 1.5

For each of the following conclusions, write at least two premises that could reasonably be offered in support of it. Your proposed premises can be entirely imaginary. To come up with premises, think of what kind of statement (if true) would persuade a reasonable person to believe the conclusion.

Example

Conclusion: Pet psychics can diagnose a dog's heartburn 100 per cent of the time.
Premise 1: In the past 50 years, in dozens of scientific tests, pet psychics were able to correctly diagnose heartburn in dogs 100 per cent of the time.
Premise 2: Scientists have confirmed the existence of energy waves that can carry information about the health of animals.

1. Canada is the best place to live in the world.
2. Wearing sunglasses indoors doesn't make you cool.
*3. Aboriginal Canadians have the right to hunt and fish on their traditional lands.
4. Nickelback is a terrible band.
5. The smartphone is the most important invention since the steam engine.
*6. When it comes to animals, MacDonald doesn't know what he's talking about.
7. The mayor doesn't seem to understand the rules related to the ethics of "conflict of interest."
8. If Steve Jobs came back to life he'd hate the new, bigger iPhone too.
*9. The Internet is the best tool that law enforcement officials have against terrorists.
10. Pornography is good for society because it educates people about sexuality.
11. Pornography is bad for society because it misleads people about sexuality.
*12. *The Walking Dead* is the greatest series in the history of television.
13. Students are right to be protesting against rising tuition.
14. Cheese is awesome.

EXERCISE 1.6

For each of the following sets of premises, write a conclusion that would be supported by the premises (your conclusion should depend at least in part on all of the premises). Neither the conclusion nor the premises need to be statements that are actually true.

Example

Premise 1: The price of your shares in the stock market will continue to decline for at least a year.

Premise 2: Anyone with shares whose price will continue to decline for at least a year should sell now.

Conclusion: You should sell now.

1. Premise 1: You don't know how to type.
   Premise 2: You don't like sitting at a desk all day.

*2. Premise 1: Several Canadian cities have banned smoking in bars and restaurants.
   Premise 2: Bans on smoking in bars and restaurants typically result in lower rates of smoking overall.

3. Premise 1: The new CEO is unhappy with our department's performance.
   Premise 2: CEO is known for firing managers of departments that aren't performing well.

*4. Premise 1: All married people are happier than unmarried people.
   Premise 2: You are married.

5. Premise 1: Yoni will be happy if the government introduces tough new gas mileage standards for all car manufacturers.
   Premise 2: It looks like the government is indeed about to introduce tough new gas mileage standards for all car manufacturers.

6. Premise 1: If there is no God, then there is no morality.
   Premise 2: There is no God.

7. Premise 1: Adding long-term bonds to an investment portfolio will lower its return.
   Premise 2: Luke just added long-term bonds to his investment portfolio.

*8. Premise 1: There is a great deal of pornography of all kinds on the Internet.
   Premise 2: Laws in Canada essentially allow everyone access to the Internet.
   Premise 3: A society that allows access to pornography doesn't care about its children.

9. Premise 1: People who don't recycle their cans and bottles aren't serious about sustainability.

Premise 2: People who aren't serious about sustainability don't care about the environment.
Premise 3: China doesn't recycle at all.

EXERCISE 1.7

For each of the following passages, determine if there is an argument present. If so, identify the premises and the conclusion.

*1. Advertising is not manipulative, as some people seem to think. The main thing advertising does is to provide us with information about products. And ads that don't provide much information are really just trying to entertain us, not manipulate us.

2. Ted Rogers (founder of Rogers Communications) was a great leader. He turned the tiny media company he inherited from his father into a multi-billion dollar corporation. He was renowned for his passion and energy. And he donated millions of dollars to worthy charities.

*3. "Is there archaeological evidence for the [Biblical] Flood? If a universal Flood occurred between five and six thousand years ago, killing all humans except the eight on board the Ark, it would be abundantly clear in the archaeological record. Human history would be marked by an absolute break. We would see the devastation wrought by the catastrophe in terms of the destroyed physical remains of pre-Flood human settlements. . . . Unfortunately for the Flood enthusiasts, the destruction of all but eight of the world's people left no mark on the archaeology of human cultural evolution." (Kenneth L. Feder, *Frauds, Myths, and Mysteries*)

4. It's wrong to treat corporations as if they're people. People—people like you and me—have the right to free speech, and corporations don't. Corporations also don't have a conscience. Corporate lawyers may try to convince you that corporations have rights, just like you and I do. But all rights are *human* rights, and one thing is for sure . . . there's nothing human about a corporation.

5. Although Canadians like to think that we tax the wealthy more than the poor, this is a boldfaced lie. Low-income families actually lose a much greater proportion of their earnings to sales tax when buying basic necessities than do higher-income families. There are also many tax loopholes that can be exploited by the wealthy to lower their effective tax rate. People can talk about our progressive tax brackets all they want, but there is no doubt that Canada's tax system is actually a regressive one.

Field Problems

1. Find a blog topic that interests you. Select an entry that contains at least one argument. Locate the conclusion and each premise.
2. From the same blog, find an entry that presents a point of view but that contains no argument at all. Rewrite the letter so that it contains at least one argument. Try to preserve as much of the original letter as possible, and stay on the same topic.
3. Go to the website of a major newspaper (or your own town's main newspaper). Find a story that has reader comments posted below it. Find a comment that presents an argument—not just an opinion!—and identify the premise and conclusion.

Self-Assessment Quiz

1. What is an argument?
2. Name at least three premise indicators and three conclusion indicators.
3. From the following sentences, indicate which ones are *not* statements:
   a. Are you sure this is the right room for the Critical Thinking class?
   b. Find an example of an argument and analyze it.
   c. The Canadian Charter of Rights and Freedoms guarantees the rights and freedoms set out in it, subject only to such reasonable limits prescribed by law as can be demonstrably justified in a free and democratic society.
   d. The best pizza in town is at Pizzeria Libretto.
4. From the list below, select the conclusion that is supported by the premises in the following argument:

   I spoke to a number of students on campus who see nothing wrong with downloading music from the Internet without paying for it. I tried to explain the issue to them, but they just didn't get it. They didn't understand that taking songs without paying for them is just like shoplifting. And they didn't seem to think downloading hurts anyone, even though it means hard-working musicians aren't getting paid for their work. If some bands want to give away music for free, that's fine, but that doesn't mean that all music is then free for the taking.

   a. University students are not intelligent.
   b. Downloading music is illegal.

c. Some university students should learn more about ethical arguments related to downloading music.
d. University students generally don't respect the law.

5. Does the following passage contain an argument? If it does, specify the conclusion.

   While it initially seems preposterous that Prince Charles has his shoelaces ironed every day—I mean, who thinks of such things?—its plausibility increases given earlier reports that he has someone to put toothpaste on his toothbrush (Social Studies – Nov. 2). Where will this end? Does he have a "Chief hint-giver" for the daily crossword, perhaps? (Letter to the editor, theglobeandmail.com, 3 November 2011)

6. Does the following passage contain an argument? If it does, specify the conclusion.

   "The news" is an invaluable part of how we understand and relate to the world. But news is only one kind of storytelling, only one way to make sense of the world. There are other powerful and meaningful forms of storytelling practiced by artists—by singers, poets, dancers and more—that can help us to make a different kind of sense out of our shared experiences. In moments of crisis, the power of artists to heal, to unite, to challenge inequalities, and to reaffirm our faith in each other and in our community's values, is tangible. It is, in fact, essential. Without culture, as I wrote in my book, there is no future. (Simon Brault, *Ottawa Citizen*, 22 October 2014)

7. Does the following passage contain an argument? If it does, specify the conclusion.

   Some people seem to think that the provincial government can't do anything right. If the government raises taxes, they get upset over that. But if the government lowers taxes, those same people complain that it's going to result in the government providing fewer services. If the province introduces new programs, these folks complain that they're not as good as the old programs. But if the government doesn't do something new every year, then the complaint is that the government isn't doing enough.

Which of the following sentences and sentence fragments are likely to be conclusions, and which are likely to be premises?

8. Therefore, Nova Scotia's lobster fishery will need to be managed carefully if it is to be sustainable.

9. Given that you didn't even pass first-year Calculus!
10. This suggests that you're likely to vote Conservative in the next election.
11. Given all the excitement surrounding the football team.
12. It follows that sexual harassment should be a crime.

For questions 13–15, write at least two premises for each of the conclusions. You can make up the premises, but you must ensure that they support the conclusion.

13. Eyewitness evidence is the best kind of evidence there is.
14. Computers will never be able to play *Jeopardy* well enough to be indistinguishable from humans.
15. Dean Brown, who for years was "the voice of the Ottawa Senators," is the best hockey announcer alive!

Read the following argument. Then in questions 16–20, supply the information requested.

> [1] Is global warming a real threat? [2] Or is it hype propagated by tree-hugging, nutty environmentalists? [3] The prime minister apparently thinks that the idea of global climate change is nonsense. [4] But a recent American study showed him to be wrong. [5] The US government issued a report on global warming called the *US Climate Action Report 2002.* [6] It gave no support to the idea that global warming isn't happening and we should all go back to sleep. [7] Instead, it asserted that global warming was definitely real and that it could have catastrophic consequences if ignored. [8] For example, global climate change could cause heat waves, extreme weather, and water shortages in many parts of North America. [9] The report is also backed by many other reports, including a very influential one from the United Nations. [10] Yes, prime minister, global warming is real. [11] It is as real as hurricanes and ice storms.

Identify by number all the sentences in the argument that fulfill each of the following roles:

16. Conclusion
17. Premise or premises
18. Background information
19. Example or illustration
20. Repetition of conclusion or premise

Critical Thinking and Writing Exercise

This is the first of five end-of-chapter lessons, or modules, designed to help you think about, plan, and write good argumentative essays. The modules are progressive, starting here with a few fundamentals of the writing process and then later covering basic guidelines and concepts that can help you think critically and write intelligently about arguments and issues. Though each module is linked in some fashion to material in the corresponding chapters, they are meant to serve as a stand-alone (though cumulative) tutorial to be used as your instructor sees fit.

Arguments and Argumentative Essays

As we note in this chapter, an argument is a group of statements in which some of them (the premises) are intended to support another of them (the conclusion). This configuration of statements-supporting-another-statement is not only the basic structure of an argument—it's the general design of an argumentative essay. An argumentative essay tries to support a particular conclusion or position on an issue by offering reasons to support that conclusion. Arguments (in the critical thinking sense) are not passionate exchanges of unsupported views or pointless contests of the is-too-is-not variety, and neither are argumentative essays. A mere sequence of statements expressing your views is not an argument, just as several pages of such statements do not constitute an argumentative essay.

In an argumentative essay, your main task is to provide rational support for a claim. If you are successful, you will have shown that there are good reasons to accept your view of things. Readers who think critically may well be persuaded by your arguments. If you write well, you may be able to make your essay even more persuasive through rhetorical or stylistic devices that add emphasis, depth, and vividness to your writing. No one wants to read a boring essay. What you should not do, however, is rely entirely on non-argumentative elements to persuade your audience. Strong emotional appeals, for example, can indeed persuade some people some of the time, but they prove nothing. In truly effective argumentative essays, the primary persuasive device is critical reasoning.

Basic Essay Structure

Good argumentative essays generally contain the following elements, though not necessarily in the order shown here:

- Introduction (or opening)
- Statement of thesis (the claim to be supported)
- Argument supporting the thesis
- Assessment of objections
- Conclusion

In the *introduction,* you want to do at least two things: (1) grab the reader's attention and (2) provide background information for the thesis. Effective attention grabbers include startling statistics, compelling quotations, interesting anecdotes, opinions of experts, shocking or unexpected claims, and vivid imagery. Whatever attention grabbers you use, *they must be related to the topic of the essay.* There's no use telling a good story if it has nothing to do with your thesis. Providing background for your thesis often means explaining why your topic is important, telling how you became concerned, or showing that there is a problem to be solved or a question to be answered. Very often the introduction, sometimes consisting of no more than a sentence or two, is laid out in the first paragraph of the essay. In general, the shorter the introduction, the better.

The *thesis statement* also usually appears in the first paragraph. This is the statement that you hope to support or prove in your essay; it is the conclusion of the argument that you intend to present. You want to state the thesis in a single sentence and do so as early as possible in the essay. Your thesis statement is like a compass to your readers, guiding them through your essay from premise to premise, showing them a clear path. It also helps *you* stay on course by reminding you to keep every part of the essay related to your single unifying idea. Your thesis statement should be restricted to a claim that can be defended in the space allowed (often only 750 to 1000 words). Not restricted enough: "Tuition is too high." Better: "Tuition increases at Degrassi College are unacceptable." Better still: "The recent tuition increase at Degrassi College is unnecessary for financial reasons." (More on how to devise a properly restricted thesis statement in a moment.)

The main body of the essay is the fully developed *argument supporting the thesis.* This means that the basic essay structure consists of the thesis statement followed by each premise or reason that supports the thesis. Each premise in turn is stated clearly, explained and illustrated sufficiently, and supported by examples, statistics, expert opinion, and other evidence. Sometimes you can develop the essay very simply by devoting a single paragraph to each premise. At other times, each premise may demand several paragraphs. In any case, you should develop just one point per paragraph, and every paragraph should be clearly related to the thesis statement.

A sketch of the argument for the Degrassi College essay, then, might look like this:

- Premise: If the college has a budget surplus, then a tuition increase is unnecessary.
- Premise: The college has had a budget surplus for the last five years.
- Premise: If the college president says that the school is in good shape financially and therefore doesn't need a tuition increase, then it's probably true that the school doesn't need a tuition increase.

- Premise: In an unguarded moment, the president admitted that the school is in good shape financially and therefore doesn't need a tuition increase.
- Thesis statement: Therefore, the recent tuition increase at Degrassi College is probably unnecessary for financial reasons.

Good argumentative essays also include an *assessment of objections*—an honest effort to take into account any objections that readers are likely to raise about the thesis statement or its premises. When you deal with such objections in your essay, you lend credibility to it because you're making an attempt to be fair and thorough. In addition, when you carefully examine objections, you can often see ways to make your argument or thesis statement stronger. It isn't necessary to consider every possible objection, just the strongest or the most common ones. Sometimes it's best to deal with objections when you discuss premises that are related to them. At other times it may be better to handle objections near the end of the essay after defending the premises.

Finally, your essay—unless it's very short—must have a *conclusion.* The conclusion usually appears in the last paragraph of the essay. Usually it reiterates the thesis statement (though usually not in exactly the same words). If the argument is complex or the essay is long, the conclusion may contain a summary of the argument. Good conclusions may reassert the importance of the thesis statement, challenge readers to do something about a problem, tell a story that emphasizes the relevance of the main argument, or bring out a disturbing or unexpected implication of a claim defended in the body of the essay.

Guidelines for Writing the Essay

1. *Determine your thesis statement.* Do *not* write on the first thesis idea that pops into your head. Select a topic you're interested in and narrow its scope until you have a properly restricted thesis statement. Research the topic to find out what issues are being debated. When you think you have an idea for a thesis statement, stop. Dig deeper into the idea by examining the arguments associated with that claim. Choose a thesis statement that you think you can defend. If you come to a dead end, start the process over.
2. *Create an outline.* Establish the basic framework of your outline by writing out your thesis statement and all the premises that support it. Then fill in the framework by jotting down what points you will need to make in defence of each premise. Decide what objections to your argument you will consider and how you will respond to them.
3. *Write a first draft.* As you write, don't be afraid to revise your outline or even your thesis statement. Writing will force you to think carefully about the strengths and weaknesses of your argument. If need be, write

a second draft and a third. Good writers aren't afraid of revisions; they depend on them.

4. *Stay on track.* Make sure that each sentence of your essay is related somehow to your thesis statement and argument.
5. *Zero in on your audience.* Decide what audience your essay is intended for and *write to them.* Is it readers of the local paper? Fellow students? People who are likely to disagree with you?
6. *Support your premises.* Back up the premises of your argument with examples, expert opinion, statistics, analogies, and other kinds of evidence.
7. *Let your final draft sit.* If possible, when you've finished writing your paper, set it aside and read it the next day. You may be surprised how many mistakes this fresh look can reveal. If you can't set the essay aside, ask a friend to read it and give you some constructive criticism.
8. *Revise.* Your first effort will almost never be your very best work. Every good writer knows that editing and revising is the key to putting their best work forward.

Writing Assignments

1. Read Essay 7 ("Yes, Human Cloning Should Be Permitted") in Appendix A and outline the argument presented. Specify the thesis statement or main conclusion and each supporting premise.
2. Write a 500-word paper in which you defend a claim that *contradicts* the thesis statement in Essay 2 ("Hurray! No One's Watching") in Appendix A. Pretend that all the evidence cited in Essay 2 actually supports your thesis statement. You may alter the details of the evidence accordingly.
3. Study the argument presented in Essay 3 ("Marine Parks") in Appendix A. Identify the conclusion and the premises and objections considered, then write a two-page rebuttal to the essay. That is, defend the claim that marine mammals should continue to be kept in marine parks.
4. Select an issue from the following list and write a 750-word paper defending a claim pertaining to the issue:
   - Should professors ban laptops from their classrooms?
   - When Canadian companies are operating overseas, should they follow Canadian ethical standards or the standards of their "host" country?
   - Should flu shots be mandatory for health care workers?
   - Should Canadian law make a distinction between the ownership of a rifle and the ownership of a handgun?

2 THE "ENVIRONMENT" OF CRITICAL THINKING

CHAPTER OBJECTIVES

- To appreciate that there are ways to (1) detect errors in our thinking, (2) restrain the attitudes and feelings that can distort our reasoning, and (3) achieve a level of objectivity that makes critical thinking possible.
- To understand that the most common impediments to critical thinking can be sorted into two categories: (1) those hindrances that arise because of *how* we think and (2) those that occur because of *what* we think.

Category 1: How We Think

You will be able to

- detect and overcome self-interested thinking by (1) watching out for instances when your deliberations get personal, (2) being alert to ways that critical thinking can be undermined, and (3) ensuring that no relevant evidence or ideas have been left out.
- appreciate how group thinking can distort critical thinking.
- understand the meaning of *peer pressure, appeal to popularity,* and *stereotyping* and be able to cite examples of each.

Category 2: What We Think

You will be able to

- understand what a world view is and how certain crucial ideas in a world view can undermine critical thinking.
- critique the notion of subjective relativism.
- critique the notion of social relativism.
- define *philosophical skepticism* and explain how it relates to critical thinking.

Critical thinking does not happen in a vacuum but in an "environment" that is often hostile to it. It takes place in the real world in the minds of real people who almost always have thoughts and feelings and experiences that, given half a chance, would sabotage critical reasoning at every turn.

Recall our definition of critical thinking: *The systematic evaluation or formulation of beliefs or statements by rational standards.* This means, of course, that several factors must be present for the process of critical thinking to be fully realized. If the process fails to be systematic, or falls short of being a true evaluation or formulation, or ignores rational standards, critical thinking can't happen. Because we are fallible (capable of making errors) there are thousands of ways that this failure of reason could occur. And there is no cure for our fallibility.

We should expect then that thinking critically will often be difficult and even unpleasant, and indeed it is. But there are ways to (1) detect errors in our thinking, (2) restrain the attitudes and feelings that can distort our reasoning, and (3) achieve a level of objectivity that makes critical thinking possible.

Doing all this—and doing it consistently—requires *awareness*, *motivation*, and *practice*. If we are to think critically, we must be aware, not only of what is involved in good critical thinking, but also of what can result from sloppy thinking. Then we must *practise* avoiding the pitfalls and using the skills and techniques that critical thinking requires. And we must be *motivated* to do all of this because it is unlikely that we will use critical thinking very much if we can't appreciate its value—if we can't appreciate its value, we would have little motivation to make the extra effort.

We can sort the most common barriers to critical thinking into two main categories: (1) those hindrances that arise because of *how* we think and (2) those that occur because of *what* we think. There is some overlap in these categories since how people think is often a result of what they think and vice versa. But in general, category 1 barriers are those that come into play because of psychological factors (our fears, attitudes, motivations, and desires), and category 2 barriers are those that arise because of certain philosophical ideas we have (our beliefs about beliefs). For example, a category 1 hindrance is the tendency to shape our opinions to match those of our peers. A common category 2 problem is the belief that objectivity in thinking is impossible or that we really don't know anything or that we don't truly know what we think we know.

In this chapter we review the most common category 1 and 2 barriers to critical thinking and practise uncovering and neutralizing them. The motivation to learn these lessons well and to watch for these barriers is up to you.

CATEGORY 1: HOW WE THINK

No one is immune to category 1 barriers. We all have psychological tendencies and habits that affect our behaviour and channel our thinking. They tend to persist or recur, haunting our minds until we have the awareness and the will to break free of them.

CREDIT: Jack Ziegler/The New Yorker Collection/The Cartoon Bank

Am I Really Special?

As humans we spend a great deal of time protecting, maintaining, and comforting our own mental life, our own *selves*—a perfectly natural urge that does no harm until we push our self-serving efforts too far. How far is too far? From the standpoint of critical thinking, we have taken things too far when we accept claims for no good reason—when our thinking is no longer systematic and rational. In effort to protect ourselves, we distort our judgment and raise our risk of error, which is ironically a risk to ourselves.

Self-interested thinking takes several forms. We may decide to accept a claim *solely on the grounds that it advances, or coincides with, our interests.* You may think, "I believe the province should lower the sales tax on anything bought at a convenience store because I own a convenience store," or "I am against all forms of gun control because I am a hunter," or "This university should not raise tuition fees because I am a student, and I don't want to pay more tuition." There is nothing inherently wrong with accepting a claim that furthers your own interests. The problem arises when you accept a claim *solely because* it furthers your interests. Self-interest alone simply cannot establish the truth of a claim. If you base your beliefs on self-interest alone, you are abandoning critical thinking.

Here's a classic example of self-interested thinking inspired by the film *Twelve Angry Men:*

> Twelve jurors sit in a room deliberating over whether to find the defendant guilty of murder. The accused is a Puerto Rican teenager who has grown up in the rough and impoverished streets of the inner city. At first, all but one juror (the jury foreman) vote guilty. The foreman persuades the other jurors to examine the evidence once again. Their deliberations go on for hours, and as they do, the prosecution's case slowly falls apart. Apparently damning evidence that had seemed so strong earlier was now shown to be full of holes. They take another vote, but this time 11 jurors, including the foreman, vote not guilty, while one man (juror number 10) insists that the other jurors are deluded and that the boy is undoubtedly guilty. The jurors ask him to explain his

> reasons. He angrily insists again that the boy is guilty, but he can't provide any evidence or reasons that suggest the boy's guilt. He just rants at the other jurors, muttering something about his dead son and Puerto Ricans being "no good" and "against everything I believe in." Finally the other jurors think they understand what's behind the seemingly irrational stance of juror number 10: He wants to convict the boy for personal reasons—perhaps because he wants to avenge his son's death, because he feels threatened by ethnic minorities, because he had been wronged by another Puerto Rican boy, or because of some other bias that has nothing to do with the guilt or innocence of the defendant.

In this example, the other members of the jury eventually realize that the judgments of juror number 10 are self-serving and linked to his own emotional needs. What gave him away? An obvious clue is his emotional protestations. But an even more telling clue is his rejection of all relevant evidence. The reasons for acquitting are perfectly clear to the other jurors, but he won't (or can't) consider them. In everyday life, these two clues often signal the presence of powerful self-interest at work.

The influence of self on your thinking can take another form. You may be tempted to accept claims *for no other reason than that they help you save face.* We all like to think of ourselves as excelling in various ways. We may believe

CREDIT: Showtime/The Kobal Collection/Art Resource

In *Twelve Angry Men,* one juror, for personal reasons, holds out for a guilty verdict despite overwhelming evidence that the accused is innocent. How often do you think this kind of self-interested thinking occurs in real-life juries?

that we are above average in intelligence, integrity, talent, compassion, physical beauty, athletic ability, and much more. But we not only like to think such things about ourselves; we want others to think the same about us. The challenge comes, however, when we accept or defend claims just to cover up the cracks in our image. You make a mistake, and so you blame it on someone or something else. You behave badly, and you try to justify your behaviour. You make a judgment or observation that turns out to be wrong, and you're too embarrassed or proud to admit it. (In Chapter 4 we'll learn that sometimes self-interested thinking can even alter our perceptions.)

The consequences of self-centred thinking can be self-destructive. In the realm of critical thinking, this devotion to yourself can prevent careful evaluation of claims, limit critical inquiry, blind you to the facts, provoke self-deception, encourage rationalizations, lead you to suppress or ignore evidence, and promote wishful thinking. And these mistakes can decrease your chances of success (however you define success) and hamper your personal growth, maturity, and self-awareness. This tendency toward being self-centred can also leave you wide open to propaganda and manipulation by people who appeal to your personal desires and prejudices. How easy would it be for people to control your choices and thoughts if they told you exactly what you wanted to hear? (There are in-depth discussions of these lapses in critical thinking in Chapters 4 and 5.)

When examining a claim or making a choice, how can you overcome the excessive influence of your own needs? Sometimes you can do it only with great effort, and sometimes the task is much easier, especially if you remember these three guidelines:

> "To be conscious that you are ignorant is a great step to knowledge."
>
> —*Benjamin Disraeli*

- Watch out when things get personal.
- Be alert to ways that critical thinking can be undermined.
- Ensure that nothing has been left out.

Watch Out When Things Get Personal

You are most likely to let your self-interest get in the way of clear thinking when you have a big personal stake in the conclusions you reach. You may be deeply committed to a particular view or belief, or you may desperately want a particular claim to be false or unjustified, or you may be devoted not to particular claims but to *any* claims that contradict those of someone you dislike. Such excessive enthusiasm can wreck any attempt at a careful, fair evaluation of a claim.

The twentieth-century philosopher Bertrand Russell asserts that the passionate holding of an opinion is a sure sign of a lack of reasons to support the opinion:

> When there are rational grounds for an opinion, people are content to set them forth and wait for them to operate. In such cases, people do

FOOD FOR THOUGHT

When We Construct the Facts Ourselves

Psychologists have long known that a great deal of what we experience is subconsciously fabricated by our own brains. That is, our own desires and expectations help form an impressive proportion of our perceptions, memories, and beliefs. Here are a few examples documented by scientific research:

CREDIT: REUTERS/Keith Bedford

Pareidolia or not: The Virgin Mary in the bark of a tree? In 2012, people in West New York, New Jersey, spotted what seemed to be a Christian icon in the bark of this Gingko biloba tree.

- Often what we think we see in vague stimuli turns out to be something that our minds have made up. We see bunnies, bearded men, and Elvis in formless clouds and smoke. We hear words and animal noises in garbled audio (like records played backward). This phenomenon is known as *pareidolia.* To this day tabloid newspapers run stories on the Great Stone Face of Mars, a supposed one-mile wide stone monument built by aliens. That's what some people say they see in a very fuzzy 1976 NASA photograph of the Martian surface. Scientists say it's a natural formation like a thousand others in the area. A later NASA photo was much clearer and showed that the "face" was just an illusion of shadows and wishful thinking.
- There are probably hundreds of stories about ghosts and aliens showing up in people's bedrooms. Whatever is going on here, it certainly doesn't need to be supernatural. Researchers have shown that when people are in that drowsy state just before sleep, they often have weird hallucinations known as *hypnagogic imagery.* These images come on suddenly, are not under the sleeper's control, and can seem as real as physical objects in the room. Images range from faces in the dark to ghostly shapes and coloured geometric shapes.
- Research has shown that our memories are not exact copies of past events. The recall of eyewitnesses, for instance, is notoriously unreliable. In the act of recall, they try to reconstruct a memory—but the reconstruction is frequently inexact, resulting in distortions and missing details. Stress can exaggerate these problems. Our memories can be drastically changed if we later come across new information—even if the new information is brief and flimsy. Most amazing of all, our expectations about the way things should be can insert or delete elements of a memory. If we expect to see a gun in the hand of a bank robber, we may remember exactly that even though no gun was involved.

Part of the job of critical thinking, of course, is to counteract all these tendencies—or help you recognize them when they happen.

> not hold their opinions with passion; they hold them calmly, and set forth their reasons quietly. The opinions that are held with passion are always those for which no good ground exists; indeed the passion is the measure of the holder's lack of rational conviction.[1]

The dead giveaway that you are skewing your thinking is a surge of strong emotions (like the one that gripped juror number 10). If your evaluation or defence of a position evokes anger, passion, or fear, your thinking could be prejudiced or clouded. It is possible, of course, to be emotionally engaged in an issue and still think critically and carefully. But most of the time, getting worked up over a claim or conclusion is reason enough to suspect that your thinking is not as clear as it should be.

The rule of thumb is this: If you sense a rush of emotions when you deal with a particular issue, pause for a moment. Think about what's happening and why. Then continue at a slower pace and with greater attention to the basics of critical reasoning, double-checking to ensure that you are not ignoring or suppressing evidence or getting sloppy in your evaluations.

Be Alert to Ways That Critical Thinking Can Be Undermined

If you understand the techniques and principles of critical thinking, and you have practised applying them in a variety of situations, you are more likely than not to detect your own one-sided, self-centred thinking when it occurs. An alarm should go off in your head: "Warning—faulty reasoning!"

EVERYDAY PROBLEMS AND DECISIONS

Self-Image and Consumerism

It is always important to watch out when things get personal. One of the situations in which that is particularly important is when someone is trying to sell you something. Of course, there is a sense in which buying consumer goods *should* be personal—after all, more often than not you are buying things for *yourself*, and your own desires and values have a proper role to play. However, advertisers and salespeople may try to make purchases personal in another sense. They may try to convince you that having their product really is important to your self-conception, your own vision of who you are. In such situations, it is worth taking a step back, and asking:

- Is my sense of worth really tied to how expensive my jeans are?
- Does having a car with more horsepower make *me* more powerful?
- Is this shampoo really going to go beyond cleaning my hair to make me happy?

Consumer purchases can be important decisions: if they are going to be *personal*, that should be your decision, not someone else's!

When your alarm sounds, double-check your thinking, look for lapses in arguments and claims, and weed them out.

Ensure That Nothing Has Been Left Out

A common flaw in reasoning is the failure to consider evidence or arguments that *do not support* your preferred claims or positions. For example, you may secretly want a particular claim to be true, so you knowingly or unknowingly look for evidence in its favour but ignore evidence against it. The chances of making this mistake increase markedly when you are reasoning for the sake of self.

This kind of preferential treatment for some statements and not others is part of a common phenomenon called *selective attention* (see Chapters 4 and 5). In selective attention, we notice certain things and ignore others—usually without even being aware that we're doing it. We may ignore facts that contradict our beliefs and search out facts that support them. Scientific research has repeatedly confirmed this behaviour. In a typical study, researchers showed subjects both *evidence for* and *evidence against* the reality of extrasensory perception (ESP). Subjects who already doubted the existence of ESP recalled both kinds of evidence accurately. But subjects who already believed in ESP remembered both kinds of evidence as *proving* ESP. They somehow recalled even the disconfirming evidence as supporting their belief in ESP!

The remedy for this problem is to *make a conscious effort to look for opposing evidence.* Don't consider your evaluation of a statement or argument finished until you've carefully considered *all the relevant reasons.* Ask yourself, "What

FOOD FOR THOUGHT

Is It Unethical to Believe without Good Reasons?

Some philosophers have asserted that it is morally wrong to believe a proposition without justification or evidence. One of these is the famous biologist Thomas Henry Huxley. Another is the mathematician W.K. Clifford (1845–79). This is how Clifford states his view:

> It is wrong always, everywhere, and for anyone, to believe anything upon insufficient evidence. If a man, holding a belief which he was taught in childhood or persuaded of afterwards, keeps down and pushes away any doubts which arise about it in his mind . . . and regards as impious those questions which cannot easily be asked without disturbing it—the life of that man is one long sin against mankind.[2]

Clifford thinks that belief without evidence is immoral because our actions are guided by our beliefs, and if our beliefs are unfounded, our actions (including morally relevant actions) are likely to be imprudent.

REVIEW NOTES

Avoiding Self-Interested Thinking

- Watch out when things get personal and you become emotionally invested in an issue.
- Beware of the urge to distort your thinking to save face.
- Be alert to ways that critical thinking can be undermined.
- Ensure that nothing has been left out of consideration.
- Avoid selective attention.
- Make a conscious effort to look for opposing evidence.

is the evidence or reasons against this statement?" Doing so is often psychologically difficult. Our natural tendency is to look for evidence that supports our views. But a willingness to look for opposing evidence is a key element of intellectual honesty.

This approach is at the heart of science. A basic principle of scientific work is not to accept a favoured theory until competing (alternative) theories are thoroughly examined (more on this in Chapter 10).

The Power of the Group

In the television series *Star Trek: The Next Generation,* the crew of the starship *Enterprise* encounters an unusual threat: the Borg. The Borg is a collective of individual minds that have been stripped of individuality and merged into a single group-mind with evil intentions. Much of the Borg storyline (which spans several episodes) is about the dignity and importance of individualism as opposed to the conformism of the Borg hive. The thought of losing one's self in the monolithic Borg is presented as a profound tragedy—a theme that strikes a chord with humans. Individualism, independence, and freedom of thought are what we want and what we must have.

Or so we say. Although we frequently proclaim the importance of individualism, we humans spend a great deal of our time trying to conform to groups or be part of them. We want to belong, we want the safety and comfort of numbers, and we want the approval of our beloved tribe. All of that is perfectly normal. We are, after all, social creatures. Conformist tendencies are a fact of life, and are in some cases useful. But trouble appears when our conformism hampers—or obliterates—critical thinking.

We all belong to multiple groups—family, work groups, gender, church, clubs, professional societies, political parties, advocacy groups, you name it—and we can be susceptible to pressure from all of them. Much of the time there is intense pressure to fit into groups and to adopt the ideas, attitudes, and goals

CREDIT: © n8n photo/Alamy

Critical thinking helps you avoid becoming one of the Borg.

endorsed by them. Sometimes the influence of the group is subtle but strong, and it can occur in the most casual, unofficial gatherings. The claims and positions adopted by the group can be implicit, never spoken, but well understood. The Facebook group, the cluster of Christians or Muslims or Jews who happen to meet on the bus, the collection of peers who support the same political cause—all of these groups can exert a surprising influence on our beliefs.

Group pressure to accept a statement or to act in a certain way has several different faces (some of which we cover in more detail in later chapters). When we're talking about the pressure to conform that comes from your peers, it's called—not surprisingly—**peer pressure**. When we're talking about an argument that tries to support a conclusion on the basis of the mere popularity of a belief, that's known, appropriately enough, as an **appeal to popularity** (also known as an appeal to the masses). In all cases, the lapse in critical thinking comes from the fact that the views or behaviour of the group *alone* is taken as reason to support a claim (see Chapter 5).

peer pressure Group pressure to accept or reject a claim solely on the basis of what one's peers think or do.

appeal to popularity (or to the masses) The fallacy of arguing that a claim must be true merely because a substantial number of people believe it.

Group pressure can happen quickly. For example, if you're listening to a speech by a member of your own political party, you may immediately find yourself positively disposed toward the speaker—not because you agree with him or her, but because he or she is a member of your group.

"Believe nothing, no matter where you read it, or who said it, no matter if I said it, unless it agrees with your own reason and your own common sense."

—*The Buddha*

Group pressure can also take a while to have an effect. Consider this example:

> Aimee has just become a new member of the Eco-Awareness Club on campus. She's been considering joining ever since Frosh Week. She's away from home for the first time and hasn't made very many new friends. She likes to feel that she belongs to something, and she shares most of the group's beliefs. And the club includes some of the smartest and most active students on campus, so being part of the club makes her feel like part of the "in" crowd. She soon finds out that she agrees with members of the club on every social and political issue—except one. Everyone else in the group is strongly in favour of decriminalizing possession of marijuana. Aimee is against it because she's read a lot about it

and the arguments against decriminalization seem to be stronger than the arguments in favour. But she doesn't want to jeopardize her membership in the club—or her new friendships—over this one issue. So, when the topic comes up, she stays quiet. The arguments she hears from her new friends seem faulty. But, as time goes on, she stops thinking about the arguments and tries not to think about the topic at all. Over time, her views on the subject start to change, until finally she finds herself being wholeheartedly in favour of decriminalizing marijuana.

"If all your friends were looting and pillaging, would you do it, too?"

CREDIT: Marty Bucella

Here, the need to belong slowly overcomes critical reasoning in a specific subject area (decriminalization of marijuana). On other topics, Aimee may be an astute critical thinker.

There's another kind of group influence that we have all fallen prey to: the pressure that comes from assuming that our own group is the best, the right one, the chosen one, and all other groups are, well, not as good. You can see this kind of ethnocentrism in religions, political parties, generations, social classes, and many other groups. The assumption that your group is better than others is at the heart of prejudice. If we are honest with ourselves, most of us recognize that we are susceptible to this force.

"A great many people think they are thinking when they are really rearranging their prejudices."

—*William James*

This we-are-better pressure is probably the most powerful of all. We all have certain beliefs, not because we have thought critically about them, but because our parents raised us to believe them or because the conceptual push and pull of our social group has instilled them in us. That is, we may believe what we believe—and assume that our beliefs are better than anyone else's—because we were born into a family or society that maintains such views. We may be a Catholic or a Conservative or a racist primarily because we were born into a Catholic or Conservative or racist family or society. Like the influence of the self, this external pressure can lead to wishful thinking, rationalization, and self-deception. Group thinking can also easily generate narrow-mindedness, resistance to change, and **stereotyping** (drawing conclusions about people without sufficient reasons). (Again, more on these problems in Chapters 4 and 5.)

stereotyping Drawing conclusions about people without sufficient reasons.

FOOD FOR THOUGHT

Prejudice, Bias, and Racism

Group pressure often leads to prejudice, bias, and racism. (To a lesser extent, so does self-interest.) But what do these terms mean?

Prejudice in its broadest sense is a judgment or opinion—whether positive or negative—based on insufficient reasons. To be prejudiced literally means to pre-judge—to judge before we have the relevant information. But usually the term is used in a more narrow sense to mean a negative or adverse belief (most often about people) without sufficient reasons. At the heart of prejudice, then, is a failure of critical thinking. And the use of critical thinking is an important part of eradicating prejudiced views.

Bias is another word for prejudice, both in the general and the narrow sense. Sometimes the word is also used to mean a simple inclination of temperament or outlook—as in "My bias is in favour of tougher laws."

Racism is a lack of respect for the value and rights of people of different races or geographical origins. Usually this attitude is based on prejudice—specifically an unjustified belief that one group of people is somehow superior to another.

CREDIT: Canada, Department of National Defence/Library and Archives Canada/PA-112539

During World War II, Canadians of Japanese heritage were removed from their homes and sent to internment camps by the Canadian government. They were not charged with crimes, but were subject to harsh treatment simply because of their heritage. In this image, a Canadian navy officer interrogates a Japanese-Canadian fisherman while confiscating his boat.

As comfortable as our inherited beliefs are, when we accept them without good reason we risk error, failure, and delusion. And as we discussed in Chapter 1, if we have certain beliefs solely because they were given to us, they are not really our beliefs. The sign of a maturing intellect is having the will and the courage to gradually eliminate those beliefs that we come to realize are groundless.

For critical thinkers, the best way to deal with the power of the group is to make a conscious effort to proportion your belief to the strength of reasons. We should only hold strongly to those beliefs for which there are strong reasons.

After thinking critically about claims favoured by groups, you may find that the claims are actually on solid ground and you really do have good reason to accept them. Or you may find that there is no good reason for believing them, and so you don't accept them. Either way, critical thinking will give you a clearer view of the group and yourself.

Critical thinking then is independent thinking. That's why, to many people, those who have most dramatically achieved independent thinking—the Aristotles, the Einsteins, the Shakespeares, the Michelangelos—are heroes.

CATEGORY 2: WHAT WE THINK

A **world view** is a philosophy of life, a set of fundamental ideas that helps us make sense of a wide range of important issues in life. The ideas are fundamental because they help guide us in the evaluation or acceptance of many other less basic ideas. They are answers to the "big questions" of life, such as "What do I know?" "Is knowledge possible?" "What is real and what is not?" "How do I know which actions are morally right?" "Are people basically good or bad?"

world view A philosophy of life; a set of fundamental ideas that helps us make sense of a wide range of important issues in life. A world view defines for us what exists, what should be, and what we can know.

The interesting thing about world views is that we all have one; all of us have adopted (or inherited) certain fundamental ideas about the world. You may have unknowingly absorbed the ideas from your family or society, and you

REVIEW NOTES

Avoiding Group Pressure on Your Thinking

- Group pressure can come in the form of peer pressure, appeals to popularity, and appeals to common practice.
- Group-centred thinking can degenerate into narrow-mindedness, resistance to change, and stereotyping.
- The best way to defend yourself against group thinking is to always proportion your acceptance of a claim according to the strength of reasons.

may not have thought much about them, but you have a world view nonetheless. Even the rejection of all world views is a world view.

Elements of some world views—certain fundamental but problematic ideas—may undermine critical thinking. These notions can give rise to category 2 barriers to critical reason, for they may affect our thinking through the content of our beliefs.

Subjective Relativism

Like science, critical thinking is based on a number of propositions that few people would think to question. Science, for example, is based on the proposition that the world is publicly understandable—that the world has a certain structure (independent of what anyone thinks), that we can know the structure, and that this knowledge can, in principle, be acquired by anyone. Critical thinking is based on similar ideas. Among the most basic is the notion that the truth of a claim does not depend on what a person thinks. That is, your believing that something is true *does not make it true.*

The alternative idea that truth depends on what someone believes is called **subjective relativism**, and if you accept this notion or use it to try to support a claim, you are said to be committing an error of reasoning known as the **subjectivist fallacy**. This view says that truth depends, not on the way things are, but solely on what someone believes. Truth, in other words, is relative to individuals. Truth is a matter of what a person believes—not a matter of how the world is. This means that a proposition can be true for one person but not for another. If you believe that dogs can fly, then it is true (for you) that dogs can fly. If someone else believes that dogs cannot fly, then it is true (for him) that dogs cannot fly.

subjective relativism The idea that truth depends on what someone believes.

subjectivist fallacy Accepting the notion of subjective relativism or using it to try to support a claim.

You've probably encountered subjective relativism more often than you realize. You may have heard someone (maybe even yourself!) say, "This is *my* truth, and that's *your* truth," or, "This statement is true *for me*."

Subjective relativism can undermine critical thinking in a fundamental way. In large part, critical thinking is about determining whether statements are true or false. But if we can make a statement true just by believing it to be true, then critical thinking would seem to be unnecessary. The subjectivist fallacy, they say, may be an excuse to forgo the tough job of critical inquiry.

Most philosophers see the situation this way: We use critical thinking to find out whether a statement is most likely to be true or false. Objective truth is about the world, about the way the world is regardless of what we may believe about it. To put it differently, there is a way the world is, and our beliefs do not make it. The world is the way it is, regardless of how we feel about it.

These same philosophers would probably be quick to admit that some objective truths *are* about our subjective states or inner processes. It might be true, for example, that you're feeling pain right now. But if so, the claim that you are feeling pain right now is an *objective* truth about your *subjective* state. I could be wrong about whether you are in pain, even if you could not be wrong about that yourself.

Also, they would readily admit that there are some things about ourselves that obviously *are* relative because they are one way for us and another way for someone else. You may prefer chocolate ice cream, and someone else may prefer vanilla. Your preference for chocolate ice cream is then relative to you. But the truth about these states of affairs is not relative.

Subjective relativism (as well as other forms of relativism) is controversial, and we needn't spend much time on it here. But you should know at least that philosophers have (through the use of critical thinking!) uncovered some odd implications of subjective relativism, ones that seem to render it implausible. First, they point out that if we could make a statement true just by believing it to be true, we would each be infallible. We could not possibly be in error about anything that we sincerely believed. We could never be mistaken about where we parked the car or what the capital of Nigeria is or which planet is the largest or the smallest. Personal infallibility is, of course, absurd, and this is a pretty compelling argument against subjective relativism.

Many critics think the biggest problem with subjective relativism is that it's self-defeating. It defeats itself because its truth implies its falsity. The relativist says, "All truth is relative." If this statement is objectively true, then it refutes itself because if it is objectively true that "All truth is relative," then the statement itself is an example of an objective truth, which is precisely the kind of truth that it denies exists! So if "All truth is relative" is objectively true, it is objectively false.

FOOD FOR THOUGHT

Having Everything Your Own Way Is . . . Impossible?

If you like relativism, you'll love a notion similar to relativism that has been advocated by, among others, the actress and New Age guru Shirley MacLaine. In a nutshell, the idea is that we each create our own reality—that is, each of us creates physical reality, everything from stars and galaxies to chocolate pudding. As MacLaine says, "Life doesn't happen to us. We make it happen. Reality isn't separate from us. We are creating our reality every moment of the day."[3] Believe it, and it will come true.

But a little critical thinking shows this theory to be flawed because it involves a logical contradiction. If we each create our own reality, what happens when people have opposing beliefs? If you believe that the Earth is round, and someone else believes that the Earth is not round, we would have a state of affairs that was both existing and not existing at the same time—which is a logical impossibility. We would have a situation like a square circle or a married bachelor, which simply can't be. Since the theory leads to such absurdities, we must conclude that we really can't create our own reality.

Social Relativism

social relativism The view that truth is relative to societies.

To escape the difficulties of subjective relativism, some people posit **social relativism**, the view that truth is relative to societies. The idea here is that truth depends not on an individual's beliefs, but on your society's beliefs. So a claim can be true for the Chinese but false for Americans, true for college students but false for public officials, true for Protestants or Muslims but false for atheists. To many, this kind of relativism, like the subjective kind, also seems to render critical thinking superfluous. After all, why bother to think critically when your own society's traditional beliefs are, by definition, always true?

Social relativism is attractive to many because it seems to imply an admirable egalitarianism—the notion that the beliefs of different societies are all in some important sense equal. And in general, respect for other cultures is a good thing. But we shouldn't confuse the idea that all societies are worthy of equal respect with the idea that all claims are worthy of equal respect. The former is an important moral principle; the latter is a recipe for disaster.

In fact, a lot of philosophers maintain that social relativism has most of the same defects that subjective relativism has. For example, according to social relativism, individuals may not be infallible, but societies are. In other words, it implies that the beliefs of whole societies cannot possibly be mistaken. But this notion of societal infallibility is no more plausible than the idea of individual infallibility. Is it plausible that no society has ever been wrong about anything—never been wrong about the causes of disease, the best form of government, the number of planets in our solar system, the burning of witches, or the beliefs behind the Nazi policies that resulted in the killing of six millionJews?

"What we need is not the will to believe, but the will to find out."

—*Bertrand Russell*

Critics like to point out that just as subjective relativism is self-defeating, so is social relativism. The claim that "all truth is relative to societies" is self-defeating because if it is objectively true, it is an example of an objective truth—true for all people everywhere. And that means that the claim (that all truth is relative) must be objectively false.

If you accept relativism, you may be tempted to care very little about critical thinking, and that would be your loss. Fortunately, there is no good reason why you should neglect critical thinking in the name of relativism.[4]

Skepticism

If knowledge were impossible, critical thinking—as a way of coming to know the truth or falsity of claims—would seem to be out of a job. Most of us, though, believe that we *can* acquire knowledge. We feel confident that we know a great many things—that we are alive, that our shoes are a certain colour, that there is a tree on the lawn, that the Earth is not flat, that rabbits cannot fly, that

2 + 2 = 4. But not everyone would agree. There are some who believe that we know much less than we think we do, or perhaps even nothing at all. This view is known as **philosophical skepticism**, and thinkers who raise doubts about how much we know are known as **philosophical skeptics**.

philosophical skepticism The view that we know much less than we think we do or that we know nothing at all.

philosophical skeptics Those who embrace philosophical skepticism.

This is no place to dive into a debate on skepticism, but we can take a quick look at the most important type of philosophical skepticism and see what, if anything, it has to do with critical thinking. This form of skepticism says that knowledge requires certainty—if we are to know anything, we must be certain of it. This means that our knowledge isn't really knowledge unless it is beyond any *possibility* of doubt. If knowledge requires certainty, however, there is very little that we know because there are always considerations that can undermine our certainty. There is always, it seems, room for at least some doubt.

But a more reasonable approach is to say that our knowledge *does not* require absolute certainty. All of us can cite many situations in which it does seem reasonable to say we have knowledge—even though we do not have absolutely conclusive reasons. We usually would claim to know, for example, that it is raining, that our dog has spots, that we were born, and that the moon is not made of green cheese—even though we are perhaps not absolutely certain of any of these. These examples suggest that we do know many things. We know them not because they are beyond all *possible* doubt, but because they are beyond all *reasonable* doubt. For practical purposes, that is enough. Doubt is always possible, but it is not always reasonable or useful. Rejecting a reasonable claim to knowledge just because of the bare possibility that you may be wrong is neither reasonable nor necessary.

Critical thinking does have a job to do in our efforts to acquire knowledge. Its task, however, is not to help us find claims that we cannot possibly doubt but to help us evaluate claims that vary in degrees of reasonable doubt—that is, from weak reasons (or no reasons) to very strong reasons.

SUMMARY

Critical thinking takes place in a mental environment consisting of our experiences, thoughts, and feelings. Some elements in this inner environment can sabotage our efforts to think critically or can at least make critical thinking more difficult. Fortunately, we can exert some control over these elements. With practice, we can detect errors in our thinking, restrain attitudes and feelings that can disrupt our reasoning, and achieve enough objectivity to make critical thinking possible.

The most common of these hindrances to critical thinking fall into two main categories: (1) those barriers that crop up because of *how* we think and (2) those that occur because of *what* we think. The first category is composed of psychological factors such as our fears, attitudes, motivations, and desires. The second category is made up of certain philosophical beliefs.

None of us is immune to the psychological obstacles. Among them are the products of egocentric thinking. We may accept a claim solely because it advances our interests or just because it helps us save face. To overcome these pressures, we must (1) be aware of strong emotions that can warp our thinking, (2) be alert to ways that critical thinking can be undermined, and (3) ensure that we take into account *all* relevant factors when we evaluate a claim.

The first category of hindrances also includes those that arise because of group pressure. These obstacles include conformist pressures from groups that we belong to and ethnocentric urges to think that our group is superior to others. The best defence against group pressure is to proportion our beliefs according to the strength of reasons.

We may also have certain core beliefs that can undermine critical thinking (the second category of hindrances). Subjective relativism is the view that truth depends solely on what someone believes—a notion that may make critical thinking look pointless. But subjective relativism leads to some strange consequences. For example, if the doctrine were true, each of us would be infallible. Also, subjective relativism has a logical problem—it's self-defeating. Its truth implies its falsity. There are no good reasons to accept this form of relativism.

Social relativism is the view that truth is relative to societies—a claim that would also seem to make critical thinking unnecessary. But this notion is undermined by the same kinds of problems that plague subjective relativism.

Philosophical skepticism is the doctrine that we know much less than we think we do. One form of philosophical skepticism says we cannot know anything unless the belief is beyond all possible doubt. But this is not a plausible criterion for knowledge. To count as knowledge, claims need not be beyond all possible doubt but beyond all *reasonable* doubt.

EXERCISE 2.1

Answers to exercises marked with an asterisk (*) may be found in Appendix B, Answers to Exercises.

Review Questions

*1. According to the text's definition of critical thinking, what factors must be present for us to think critically?
2. What are the two main categories of common barriers to critical thinking?
3. What did W.K. Clifford say about the morality of believing claims?
4. What is stereotyping?

*5. From the standpoint of critical thinking, what suggests that we have allowed our bias in favour of ourselves go too far?
6. According to the text, what effect can our urge to save face have on our thinking?
*7. When are you most likely to let your self-interest get in the way of clear thinking?
8. According to the text, what should you do if you sense a rush of emotion when you think about a particular issue?
9. What is selective attention? What is a remedy for this problem?
10. According to the text, how might selective attention affect your thinking when you are examining evidence for or against a claim?
*11. How might the influence of a group that you belong to affect your attempts to think critically?
12. What are some of the possible consequences of self-centered thinking?
13. What is the appeal to popularity?
*14. What is a world view?
15. How is subjective relativism different from social relativism?
16. According to the text, how could subjective relativism make critical thinking unnecessary?
*17. Is critical thinking concerned with the *objective* or the *subjective* truth of claims?
18. What is social relativism?
19. What is philosophical skepticism?
20. Why is it incorrect to say that knowledge requires certainty?
*21. What kind of doubt is involved in the acquisition of knowledge?

EXERCISE 2.2

Indicate whether each of the following passages most likely contains examples of self-interested thinking, face-saving, or group pressure.

*1. Christopher: Corporations have the same rights as humans.
Andrew: What makes you think that?
Christopher: I've got money invested in several corporations, and if corporate rights aren't protected, my investment would be in danger. I could be ruined financially!
2. Jonathan: My essay is better than Julio's.
Betty: Why do you think yours is better than all the others? Do you agree that the content and writing of all the essays are similar?
Jonathan: Well, yes.

Betty: Do you agree that all the other indicators of quality are nearly identical?
Jonathan: Yes, but mine is still better.

3. Don't waste your inheritance by donating to feed the homeless. They're mostly just drug addicts anyway. But I'm involved with a great charity that would put that money to good use.
*4. Yeah, I did badly on the essay. But it's not my fault because the prof hates me.
5. I oppose women becoming members of this club. If I endorsed their claims, every friend I've got in the club would turn their backs on me.
6. Amanda: This song isn't very good.
Ben: But it's on all the top charts. I also happen to really like this song.
Amanda: Oh wow you're right! I just listened to it again and it does sound pretty good.
*7. Hinduism is superior to all other religions. I was raised Hindu, and all my relatives are Hindus. This is the only religion I've known, and everyone I know and trust tells me it's the one true religion.
8. Don't tell me how to run my company! I've already *forgotten* more about how to run a business than you'll ever learn!
9. Molson Canadian is the best beer in the world. I've never tried any of those weird foreign beers, and I don't intend to.
*10. If Joan is appointed to the committee, I am guaranteed to have a job for the rest of my life. I think Joan would be a great addition to the committee.
11. Free speech should not extend to pornographers. Right now they are allowed to espouse their smut on the Internet and many other places. That's just not how I was raised.

EXERCISE 2.3

Read each of the following claims. Then select from the list any statements that, if true, would constitute good reasons for accepting the claim. Be careful: In some questions, none of the choices are correct.

*1. John: The newspaper account of the charges of pedophilia lodged against Father J. Miller, a Catholic priest in our town, should never have been printed.
   a. The charges come from a single source who is a known liar.
   b. John is a Catholic.

   c. Important evidence that would exonerate Father Miller was not mentioned in the newspaper account.
   d. The town is predominately Catholic.

2. Alice: You should always buy vegetables that have been grown locally.
   a. Alice owns a local vegetable farm.
   b. Studies show that locally grown vegetables are more environmentally friendly.
   c. You've noticed that the food seems to be better at restaurants that feature locally grown food.
   d. Alice has a degree in nutrition.

*3. Janette: Women are less violent and less emotional than men.
   a. A study from McGill University shows that women are less violent and less emotional than men.
   b. Janette is a woman.
   c. Janette is a member of a group of women who are fighting for the rights of women.
   d. Janette and all her friends are women.

4. Nanako: You should visit Japan for your next holiday.
   a. Nanako was born in Japan and knows how beautiful it is there.
   b. Nanako knows you well enough to know what kind of vacation you would enjoy.
   c. Nanako's brother owns a travel agency that specializes in trips to Japan.
   d. You've told Nanako before that you've always wanted to visit Asia.

5. A recent report submitted to our finance department indicates that ACME Inc. can supply us with the best materials at the lowest price.
   a. ACME has a good reputation in the industry.
   b. The person in charge of preparing the report is a board member of ACME.
   c. ACME has a history of being accused of using shady business practices to drive down their costs.
   d. A separate report submitted by an independent 3rd party has produced the same result, although not to the same extent.

*6. Zaid: "This product is sure to be a failure."
   a. Zaid wasn't included in the product design process.
   b. The product faces stiff competition from many excellent similar products.
   c. Zaid's boss, Jen, has doubts about this product.
   d. Everyone in the lunch room is making jokes about the product.

7. Angelo: Marijuana should be legalized.
   a. All of Angelo's friends smoke marijuana.

b. Legalizing marijuana would reduce the consumption of marijuana and save lives, money, and resources.
c. Angelo has already said on television that marijuana should be legalized.
d. Angelo likes to smoke marijuana.

EXERCISE 2.4

Read the following passages. Determine whether each one contains examples of the kind of group pressure that encourages people to conform (peer pressure or appeal to popularity) or the type that urges people to think that one's own group is better than others. For each example of group pressure, specify the possible negative consequences of such pressure. A couple of these are very difficult to classify.

*1. Marie-Eve is deeply religious, attending church regularly and trying to abide by church law and the Scriptures. She has never considered any other path. She believes that laws should be passed that forbid Sunday shopping and that designate Easter as a national statutory holiday.

2. Prathamesh is trying out for his university's varsity lacrosse team. Nearly everyone on the team has a girlfriend. Prathamesh hasn't ever had a girlfriend, and he's not even sure that he likes girls. He notices that he hasn't been invited to many of the team events, particularly not the ones where guys bring girlfriends or dates.

*3. An Atlantic Canadian university has invited a famous writer to be a guest speaker in the campus-wide distinguished-speaker series. She is an accomplished poet and essayist. She is also a Marxist and favours more socialism in Canada. During her speech she is shouted down by a small group of conservative students and faculty.

4. Yang Lei is a conservative columnist for one of the best conservative journals in the country. But she yearns for bigger and better things—most especially, a regular column for a weekly newsmagazine. She gets her dream job, though the magazine does have liberal leanings. The first few columns she writes for the magazine are a shock to her friends. Politically, her new columns are middle-of-the-road or even suspiciously left-leaning.

5. Adam is afraid of water and can't swim. His friends are having a party on a boat and really want him to go, but he has so far resisted their efforts to persuade him. Running out of ideas, his friends decide to have a cute girl in their statistics class ask him to go with her. They are delighted

on the day of the party when they see Adam clinging onto the railing of the boat.

6. A prominent politician in Ottawa presents a carefully reasoned argument against the use of quotas to make sure that women have equal access to government jobs. He points to studies that show that women are relatively successful at getting such jobs, and he argues that there are strong moral reasons in favour of always hiring the most well-qualified candidate. That evening, his office receives dozens of angry emails from women and men who say his statement was sexist and who threaten not to vote for him in the next election. The next day, he issues a press release apologizing for his comments. He states that he is a strong supporter of woman's rights and that his comments on hiring quotas were "taken out of context."

*7. Advertisement: When you make the best car in the world, everyone wants it. Audi TT. A car in demand.

EXERCISE 2.5

Read the following scenarios. Indicate whether each one contains examples of self-interested thinking or face-saving and, for each instance, specify the possible negative consequences.

*1. Last year, Neera Co. operated at a loss for the first time since being founded 60 years ago. The new CEO blamed poor market conditions for the loss. So far this year, Neera Co. has been losing even more money than last year and its shareholders have started voicing their concerns. The CEO is planning to release a statement that blames the workers' union's unfair demands for driving up costs and hurting the company.

*2. City councillor Jackson is in a position to cast the deciding vote on two proposals for the development of a new city park. Proposal 1 offers a parcel of land near Jackson's house, which affords him a beautiful view. Its drawbacks are that it costs twice as much as proposal 2 and is not easily accessible to most of the public. Proposal 2 suggests a parcel of land near the centre of town. It is convenient to the public, has a more beautiful setting, and will raise property values in the area. Councillor Jackson says that the obvious best choice is proposal 1.

3. Antonio is running in the municipal election for a position on his City Council. On election night, he has two speeches prepared. If he wins, he plans on stating in his speech that he is glad that the people have spoken so clearly and given him this honourable task. If he loses, he plans to

express his disappointment in the crooked campaign tactics used by his key opponent.

4. Sheila is a bright medical scientist. For years she has been working on a series of clinical studies that could establish her favourite medical hypothesis—that high doses of vitamin E can cure skin cancer. Each study in the series has added more evidence suggesting that the hypothesis is probably true. The last study in the series is crucial. It is a much larger study than the others, and it will confirm or invalidate the usefulness of vitamin E for skin cancer. When the study is completed, she examines the data. Instead of confirming her hypothesis, the study suggests not only that her pet idea is unfounded, but also that the doses of vitamin E used are toxic, causing terrible side effects in patients. She concludes, though, that the study results do not disconfirm her hypothesis but are merely inconclusive.
5. David and Max are in a heated debate about the theory of biological evolution. David rejects the theory in favour of creationism, which says that life on Earth was created or facilitated by a supreme intelligence. Max rejects creationism in favour of evolution. David marshals an abundance of facts that seem to prove his case. In addition, he alleges that evolution is false because there are huge gaps in the fossil record, suggesting that there has never been a smooth, tidy progression of species from earlier forms to later forms. Max has no answer for this fossil-record gap argument and looks exasperated. David is about to declare victory when Max suddenly begins to quote the research findings of reputable biologists showing that there really are no gaps. After the debate, some of Max's friends quietly congratulate him for being clever enough to quote research findings that are fictitious.

Field Problems

1. Recall a situation in your past in which your beliefs were skewed by self-interest, face-saving, or group pressure. Think about (1) how one or more of these three factors affected your beliefs, (2) what the consequences (negative or positive) of the event were, and (3) what beliefs you might have acquired if you had used critical thinking. Take notes to help you remember the facts and be prepared to present your story in class.
2. Recall a situation in which the beliefs of someone you know were skewed by self-interest, face-saving, or group pressure to conform. Identify the three factors mentioned in the preceding question.

3. Assess a speech by a Canadian politician—federal, provincial, or municipal. Examine the speech for evidence of *peer pressure, appeal to popularity,* or *stereotyping*. Explain briefly what you found.

Self-Assessment Quiz

1. According to the definition of critical thinking given in the text, what factors must be present for critical thinking to take place?
2. From the standpoint of critical thinking, what suggests that we have allowed our bias in favour of ourselves to go too far?
3. According to the text, what single word is used to describe a philosophy of life, a set of fundamental ideas that helps us make sense of a wide range of important issues in life?
4. What is subjective relativism?
5. According to the text, what is a world view?
6. What kind of doubt is involved in the acquisition of knowledge?
7. According to the text, why is it important to look for opposing evidence when evaluating claims?

Read the following scenarios. State whether each one contains examples of self-interested thinking, face-saving, or both.

8. Trevor predicts that Farley Windblower will win the 2016 mayoral election in his city. In fact, he bets money on it and brags that he always predicts the winners. Windblower then loses by the widest margin in the city's history. At first, Trevor refuses to pay the bet but finally gives in. He claims that the election was rigged from the very beginning.
9. Lois believes strongly that an economic crash is imminent. She says this truth is unavoidable: she has had several friends lose jobs in the last three months. However, economists state that this is very unlikely. Key economic statistics are strong, including overall employment numbers. Lois doesn't say anything else about her "evidence," but she asserts, "You'll all be sorry when it happens and you see that I'm right!"
10. One day Julie and Jill hear their instructor read a list of arguments for and against abortion. Half the arguments are pro, and half are con. Julie is on the pro side, and Jill is on the con side. Later, when they discuss the abortion arguments, they recall the facts differently. Julie remembers that most of the arguments heard in class were in favour of abortion rights. Jill

remembers only the arguments against abortion and recalls very few pro arguments.

Specify whether the following passages are examples of face-saving, self-serving, or group pressure thinking, or a combination of these.

11. They made a huge mistake by not offering me the job. They'll see!
12. Everyone believes in affirmative action. That fact alone ought to persuade you to do the same.
13. Look, every student I know cheats on exams once in a while. So why not you? Why do you have to be such a Boy Scout?
14. People should do whatever makes them happy.
15. Member of Parliament Aneesah Syed: "Anyone who doesn't believe in God shouldn't have a say in how this nation is run. I don't think that atheists should even be citizens."
16. Why won't you get an iPhone already? We all have one, and group messaging you would be so much easier if you had iMessage.
17. In Canada about 90 per cent of the population has some kind of religious belief or affiliation with some religious organization. In light of this, how can you say you're an unbeliever? If you're an unbeliever, you're un-Canadian.

Read each of the following passages and state whether it is an example of the subjectivist fallacy or social relativism.

18. This may not be your truth, but it's my truth.
19. It's true for me that killing innocent civilians is morally wrong. It may not be true for you.
20. Russian diplomat: "My country cannot be judged by some universal standard. It must be judged by its own unique values and norms."

Integrative Exercises

These exercises pertain to material in Chapters 1 and 2.

1. What is an argument?
2. What is a statement or claim? (Give an example of a statement and an example of a sentence that is not a statement.)

3. Name one way in which a "haunted world view" can influence your evaluation of a claim.
4. According to the text, what critical thinking principle should you keep in mind when you're trying to think clearly under group pressure?

For each of the following passages indicate whether it contains an argument. For each argument, specify what the conclusion is and whether the passage contains an appeal to popularity or peer pressure.

5. Unlike beliefs, desires cannot be false because they aren't intended to reflect the external world.
6. Cloning any biological entity (including humans) is not worth the risks involved. Scientists have already reported some unexpected, dangerous side effects in the cloning of plants, and Dolly, the famous cloned sheep, has exhibited some cellular abnormalities.
7. You bought a Prius? You'll be the laughingstock of the whole town if anyone sees you in that thing.
8. Some day, perhaps, the government will be willing to listen to people who elect them, instead of just listening to wealthy corporations.
9. A woman's place is in the kitchen. That's just the way I was raised.
10. You can't deny that the mayor is terrific. Most folks in town believe that she is doing a great job, and you can't argue with the people.
11. Your family loves you and we all think you're wrong about Frank. That should be enough to convince you not to marry him.

Read each of the following claims. Then select from the list any statements that, if true, would constitute good reasons for accepting the claim. Some statements may have no good reasons listed.

12. There should be harsher punishments for doctors who behave negligently.
    a. Countries with the harshest punishments against negligent doctors have the lowest number of deaths from medical procedures.
    b. Polls show that Canadians think that overall, doctors are much more irresponsible than they should be.
    c. The president of the United States has voiced his support for this course of action in the US and your friends agree with him as well.
    d. Punishing doctors for negligence is the only way to ensure the integrity of our health care system and so is the only morally correct course of action.
13. It's getting harder and harder for young Canadians to find a job.
    a. I haven't found a job, despite graduating over three months ago.

b. Surveys show that joblessness among Canadians aged 18–25 is higher than last year.
c. Many Canadian companies are opening up branches in foreign countries.
d. My cousin has a university degree, but she has been working at McDonald's for over a year now.

14. There is an afterlife. After you die, your essence lives on.
    a. I have to believe in an afterlife. The alternative is too terrible to contemplate.
    b. Over 80 per cent of Canadians believe in an afterlife.
    c. This society believes that there is an afterlife.
    d. On the radio I told two million people that there is an afterlife. So I have to believe in it. Otherwise, I'll look like a fool.

For each of the following passages, determine whether an argument is present and whether peer pressure or an appeal to popularity is being used. Some passages may not contain arguments, and some may not contain examples of group pressure.

15. "Barbara Ehrenreich wrote tongue-in-cheek in her June column, 'First, challenge anyone to find in the Bible . . . a single phrase or sentence forbidding the fondling or sodomizing of altar boys.' . . . In fact, the Bible does have at least a single phrase or sentence forbidding just such a thing. In 1 Corinthians 6:9 (New International Version), Paul has a list of those who will not inherit the Kingdom. Although far from settled, one of the words in the list suggests that men in a mentoring relationship with young boys are 'wicked' if they engage in sexual acts with the boys." (Letter to the editor, *The Progressive*, 1 July 2002)
16. "Remote voting by way of the Internet would privatize one of our few remaining civic rituals. Balloting technology is not politically neutral. The history of elections administration in this country shows that different ways of voting allocate political values differently." (Letter to the editor, *New York Times*, 31 October 2002)
17. You must reject the proposition that rising levels of gun violence in Canada's major cities proves the need for the federal government's Firearm Registry. First, there's no documented connection between violence and the availability of guns. Second, if you accept the need for a Registry, you'll be the laughingstock of all your fellow Westerners!
18. To teens, getting fake IDs to sneak into bars and pubs may seem like a good idea, but it's not. I think every teenager who tries it should be arrested.
19. You cannot seriously believe that Seattle is more beautiful than Vancouver!

Critical Thinking and Writing Exercise

From Issue to Thesis

For many students, the biggest challenge in writing an argumentative essay is deciding on an appropriate thesis—the claim, or conclusion, that the essay is designed to support or prove. Very often, when an essay runs off track and crashes, the derailment can be traced to a thesis that was bad from the beginning.

Picking a thesis out of the air and beginning to write is usually a mistake. Any thesis statement that you craft without knowing anything about the subject is likely to be ill-formed or indefensible. It's better to begin by selecting an issue—a question that's controversial or in dispute—then researching it to determine what arguments or viewpoints are involved. To research it, you can survey the views of people or organizations involved in the controversy. Read articles and books, talk to people, and do some research online. This process should not only inform you about various viewpoints but also tell you what arguments are used to support them. It should also help you narrow the issue down to one that you can easily address in the space you have.

Suppose you begin with the issue of whether Canada has serious industrial pollution problems. After investigating this issue, you would probably see that it is much too broad to be addressed in a short paper. You should then restrict the issue to something more manageable—for example, whether recent legislation to allow coal-burning power plants to emit more sulphur dioxide will harm people's health. With the scope of the issue narrowed, you can explore arguments on both sides. You cannot examine every single argument, but you should assess the strongest ones, including those that you devise yourself. You can then use what you've already learned about arguments to select one that you think provides good support for its conclusion. The premises and conclusion of this argument can then serve as the bare-bones outline of your essay. Your argument might look like this:

> [Premise 1] High amounts of sulphur dioxide in the air have been linked to increases in the incidence of asthma and other respiratory illnesses.
>
> [Premise 2] Many areas of the country already have high amounts of sulphur dioxide in the air.
>
> [Premise 3] Most sulphur dioxide in the air comes from coal-burning power plants.
>
> [Conclusion] Therefore, allowing coal-burning power plants to emit more sulphur dioxide will most likely increase the incidence of respiratory illnesses.

For the sake of the example, the premises of this argument are made up. But the argument of your essay must be real, with each premise that could be called into question supported by an additional argument. After all, your readers are not likely to accept the conclusion of your argument if they doubt your premises.

In some cases, your paper may contain more than one argument supporting a single conclusion, or it may offer a critique of someone else's argument. In either case, investigating an issue and the arguments involved will follow the pattern just suggested. In a critique of an argument (or arguments), you offer reasons why the argument fails and you thereby support the thesis that the conclusion is false or at least unsupported.

This process of devising a thesis statement and crafting an argument to back it up is not linear. You will probably have to experiment with several arguments before you find one that's suitable. Even after you decide on an argument, you may later discover that its premises are dubious or that they cannot be adequately supported. Then you will have to backtrack to investigate a better argument. Backtracking in this preliminary stage is relatively easy. But if you postpone this rethinking process until you are almost finished with your first draft, it will be harder—and more painful.

Argument and Emotion

As we saw earlier, the point of an argument is to provide rational support for a claim by supplying good reasons for accepting a conclusion. And argument, of course, is the main focus of a good argumentative essay. Nonetheless, experienced writers often enhance the persuasive power of their argumentative essays through the use of various emotional appeals. Inexperienced writers, though, sometimes get the argumentative and emotional elements confused or out of balance. To avoid such problems, try to stick to these rules of thumb:

- Be fair to the opposing view. Summarize or restate the opposing arguments accurately. Avoid sarcasm, ridicule, or loaded (emotive) words in describing other viewpoints. Don't say, for example, "this so-called argument," "that ridiculous view," or "this idiotic proposal."
- Be fair to your opponent. Avoid personal attacks, insults, stereotyping, and innuendo. Keep the main focus on the quality of your opponent's arguments, not on his or her character.
- Avoid appeals to your own self-interest or the wishes of your preferred group.
- If you have strong feelings about an issue, try to channel those feelings into creating the best arguments possible—not into emotional displays on paper.

Writing Assignments

1. Read Essay 2 ("Hurray! No One's Watching") in Appendix A and write a summary of the essay in 75–100 words. Mention the thesis statement and each supporting premise.
2. Study the argument presented in Essay 10 ("Unrepentant Homeopaths") in Appendix A. Identify the conclusion and the premises and objections considered. Then write a 500-word rebuttal to the essay. That is, defend the claim that it is morally right to promote homeopathy.
3. Select an issue from the following list and write a 600-word paper defending a statement pertaining to the issue. Follow the procedure discussed in the text for identifying a thesis and an appropriate argument to defend it.
   - Are the media biased?
   - Should a single corporation be allowed to buy up as many media outlets (newspapers, radio and TV stations, book publishers, etc.) as it wants?
   - Should the Canadian government be allowed to arrest and indefinitely imprison, without trial, any Canadian citizen who is suspected of terrorism?
   - Should corporate taxes be raised or lowered?

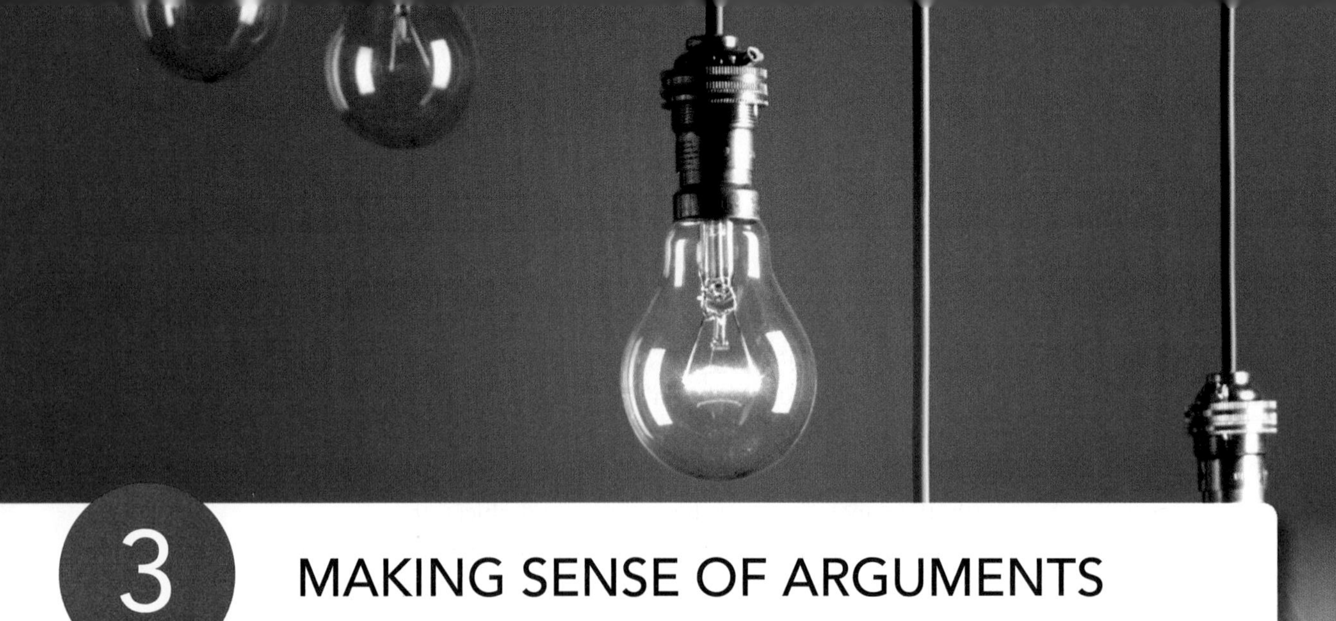

3 MAKING SENSE OF ARGUMENTS

CHAPTER OBJECTIVES

Argument Basics

You will be able to

- distinguish between deductive and inductive arguments.
- understand the terms *valid, invalid,* and *sound.*
- understand the terms *strong, weak,* and *cogent.*

Judging Arguments

You will be able to

- follow the four-step procedure for determining whether an argument is deductive or inductive, good or bad.
- obtain a familiarity with indicator words that suggest that an argument is deductive or inductive.

Finding Missing Parts

You will be able to

- use the three-step procedure for uncovering implicit premises.

Argument Patterns

You will be able to

- memorize and be able to recognize the argument patterns known as *modus ponens, modus tollens, hypothetical syllogism, denying the antecedent, affirming the consequent,* and *disjunctive syllogism.*
- use the counterexample method for determining if a deductive argument is valid or invalid.

Diagramming Arguments

You will be able to

- understand the definition of *dependent* and *independent premises.*
- follow the three-step procedure to diagram arguments, both simple and complex ones, including those embedded in extraneous material.

Assessing Long Arguments

You will be able to

- understand the challenges involved in assessing long arguments.
- follow the procedure for diagramming long arguments.

In this chapter we resume our discussion of arguments begun in Chapter 1, dig deeper into the dynamics and structure of different types of argument, and get a lot more practice identifying and critiquing simple (and not so simple) arguments in their "natural habitat."

Remember, in Chapter 1 we defined an argument as a group of statements in which some of them (the premises) are intended to support another of them (the conclusion). An essential skill is the ability to identify arguments in real-life contexts and to distinguish them from non-arguments. To recognize an argument you must be able to identify the premises and the conclusion. Indicator words such as *because* and *since* often signal the presence of premises, and words such as *therefore* and *thus* can point to a conclusion.

ARGUMENT BASICS

The point of *devising* an argument is to try to show that a statement or claim is worthy of acceptance. The point of *evaluating* an argument is to see whether this task has been successful—whether the argument shows that the statement (the conclusion) really is worthy of acceptance. When the argument shows that the statement is worthy of acceptance, we say that the argument is *good.* When the argument fails to show that the statement is worthy of acceptance, we say that the argument is *bad.* There are different ways, however, that an argument can be good or bad. This is because there are different types of arguments.

Arguments come in two forms—**deductive** and **inductive**. A deductive argument is intended to provide, and potentially capable of providing, logically *conclusive* support for its conclusion. An inductive argument is intended to provide, and only capable of providing, *probable*—not conclusive—support for its conclusion.

deductive argument An argument intended to provide logically conclusive support for its conclusion.

inductive argument An argument in which the premises are intended to provide probable, not conclusive, support for its conclusion.

FOOD FOR THOUGHT

Persuading or Reasoning?

There is a fundamental distinction in critical thinking between persuading and reasoning. Persuading someone to agree with you is not the same thing as presenting them with a good argument, though a good argument might end up being persuasive. You can influence people's opinions by using words to appeal to their ego, gullibility, bigotry, greed, anger, prejudice, and more. You just have to use emotional language, psychological ploys, tricky wording, and outright lies. But having done so, you would not have demonstrated that any belief is true or warranted. You would not have shown that a claim is worthy of acceptance. This latter task is a matter of logic and argument. The techniques of raw persuasion are not.

Certainly the presentation of a good argument (in the critical thinking sense) can often be psychologically compelling. And there are times when persuasion through psychological or emotional appeals is appropriate, even necessary. You just have to keep these two functions straight in your mind.

CREDIT: The Art Archive/Art Resource

Great persuaders aren't necessarily great critical thinkers.

invalid argument A deductive argument that fails to provide conclusive support for its conclusion.

valid argument A deductive argument that succeeds in providing conclusive support for its conclusion.

truth-preserving A characteristic of a valid deductive argument in which the logical structure guarantees the truth of the conclusion if the premises are true.

A deductive argument that succeeds in providing such decisive logical support is said to be **valid**; a deductive argument that fails to provide such support is said to be **invalid**. A deductively valid argument is such that if its premises are true, its conclusion *must* be true. That is, if the premises are true, there is no way that the conclusion can be false. In logic, *valid* is not a synonym for true. A deductively valid argument simply has the kind of logical structure that *guarantees* the truth of the conclusion *if* the premises are true. "Logical structure" refers not to the content of an argument, but to its construction, that is, the way the premises and conclusion fit together. Because of the guarantee of truth in the conclusion, deductively valid arguments are said to be **truth-preserving**.

Here's a simple deductively valid argument:

Dorothy is an engineer.
All engineers are good at math.
So Dorothy is good at math.

And here's a golden oldie:

All men are mortal.
Socrates is a man.
Therefore, Socrates is mortal.

And one in regular paragraph form:

[Premise] All motorcycle gang members ride motorcycles. [Premise] Jax is a member of a motorcycle gang. [Conclusion] Therefore Jax rides a motorcycle.

CREDIT: © skynesher/iStockphoto

An argument containing a false premise such as "Dolphins are plotting to take over the planet" may be logically valid, but it is definitely flawed (and a little strange).

In each of these arguments, if the premises are true, the conclusion must be absolutely, positively true. You may or may not agree with the premises, but it is impossible for the premises to be true and the conclusions false. The conclusion *follows logically* from the premises. And the order of the premises makes no difference.

A deductively *invalid* version of these arguments might look like this:

Dorothy is an engineer.
Dorothy is a mother.
So all engineers are mothers.

If Socrates has horns, he is mortal.
Socrates is mortal.
Therefore, Socrates has horns.

In each of these, the conclusion does *not* follow logically from the premises. Each is an attempt at a deductively valid argument, but the attempt fails—even if the premises were true, they would not guarantee that their conclusions are true. And again, this would be the case regardless of the order of the premises. Note that even an argument with a conclusion that is obviously true can be invalid if that conclusion is not supported by the premises offered. Look at this argument, for example:

> "The most perfidious way of harming a cause consists of defending it deliberately with faulty arguments."
>
> *—Friedrich Nietzsche*

All whales have tails.
All whales have eyes.
Therefore, all whales are mammals.

The conclusion here is obviously true, but the argument is invalid: the conclusion doesn't *follow from* the premises offered.

An inductive argument that succeeds in providing probable—but not conclusive—logical support for its conclusion is said to be **strong**. An inductive argument that fails to provide such support is said to be **weak**. An inductively strong argument is such that if its premises are true, its conclusion is *probably* or

strong argument An inductive argument that succeeds in providing probable—but not conclusive—support for its conclusion.

weak argument An inductive argument that fails to provide strong support for its conclusion.

likely to be true. The structure of an inductively strong argument cannot guarantee that the conclusion is true if the premises are true—but the conclusion can be rendered probable and worthy of acceptance. (Here again, the structure and content of an argument are separate issues.) Because the truth of the conclusion cannot be guaranteed by the truth of the premises, inductive arguments are not truth-preserving.

Let's turn our first two deductively valid arguments into inductively strong arguments:

> Most engineers are good at math.
> Therefore, Larry Page (co-founder of Google, and an engineer), is probably good at math.

> Most humans cannot play the banjo.
> June is a human.
> Therefore, June cannot play the banjo.

Notice that in the first argument, it's entirely possible for the premise to be true and the conclusion false. After all, if only *most* engineers are good at math, there is no guarantee that Larry Page is good at math. Yet the premise, if true, makes the conclusion probably true. Likewise, in the second argument it is possible that even if 99.9 per cent of humans cannot play the banjo and June is human, the conclusion that June cannot play the banjo could be false. But the premises, if true, make it likely that the conclusion is true.

CREDIT: Nick Kim/Cartoon Stock

Logical validity or logical strength is an essential characteristic of good arguments. But there is more to good arguments than having the proper structure. Good arguments also have *true premises.* A good argument is one that has the proper structure *and* true premises. Take a look at this argument:

> All pigs can fly.
> Michael is a pig.
> Therefore, Michael can fly.

The premises of this argument are false, but the conclusion follows logically from those premises. It's a deductively valid argument with all the parts in the right place—even though the premises and conclusion are false. But it is not a good argument, because a good argument must also have true premises, and this argument doesn't. A deductively valid argument that also has true premises is said to be

sound. A sound argument is a good argument that gives you good reasons for accepting its conclusion.

sound argument A deductively valid argument that has true premises.

Note, however, that deductively valid arguments can have true or false premises and true or false conclusions. Specifically, deductively valid arguments can have false premises and a false conclusion, false premises and a true conclusion, and true premises and a true conclusion. See for yourself:

False Premises, False Conclusion
All restaurants are bars.
All bars are places that serve pancakes.
Therefore, all restaurants are places that serve pancakes.

False Premises, True Conclusion
My friend Mike is a cat.
All cats like broccoli.
Therefore, my friend Mike is a mammal.

True Premises, True Conclusion
Mike is a human.
All humans are mammals.
Therefore, Mike is a mammal.

A valid argument, though, cannot have true premises and a false conclusion—that's impossible.

A good inductive argument must also have true premises. This example illustrates why:

> It's a proven fact that 99 per cent of men love money more than they love their children.
> So it's likely that the next person I meet will love money more than he loves his children.

This is an inductively strong argument (because its premise, if true, would provide plenty of support for its conclusion) but it's not a good argument because its premise is false. When inductively strong arguments have true premises, they are said to be **cogent**. Good inductive arguments are cogent; bad inductive arguments are not cogent.

cogent argument A strong inductive argument with all true premises.

You may have noticed another important difference between deductive and inductive arguments. The kind of support that a deductive argument can give a conclusion is *absolute*. Either the conclusion is shown to be true, or it is not. There is no sliding scale of truth or falsity for deductive arguments. The support that an inductive argument can provide a conclusion, however, can range from very weak to extremely strong. An inductive argument, that is, might provide a little support, a moderate amount of support, or a lot of support for its conclusion.

REVIEW NOTES

Deductive and Inductive Arguments

A deductive argument

- is intended to provide conclusive support for its conclusion;
- is said to be *valid* if it succeeds in providing conclusive support for its premise. (A valid argument is such that if its premises are true, its conclusion must be true.); and
- is said to be *sound* if it is valid and has true premises.

An inductive argument

- is intended to provide probable support for its conclusion;
- is said to be *strong* if it succeeds in providing probable support for its conclusion. (A strong argument is such that if its premises are true, its conclusion is probably true.); and
- is said to be *cogent* if it is strong argument and has true premises.

Both deductive and inductive arguments can be manipulated in various ways to yield new insights. For example, let's say that you have formulated a valid deductive argument and you know that the conclusion is false. From these facts you can infer (based on the definition of a valid deductive argument) that at least one of the premises must be false. Using this approach, you can demonstrate that a premise is false because in a valid argument it leads to a false conclusion. Or let's say that you've constructed a valid argument and you know that your premises are true. Then you can infer that the conclusion must be true—even if it's contrary to your expectations. Or maybe you put forth a strong inductive argument and you know that the premises are questionable. Then you know that the conclusion also can't be trusted.

EXERCISE 3.1

Answers to exercises marked with an asterisk (*) may be found in Appendix B, Answers to Exercises.

1. What is a deductive argument?
2. What is an inductive argument?
3. Are inductive arguments truth-preserving? Why or why not?
*4. What type of arguments do the terms *valid* and *invalid* apply to?
5. What kind of support does a deductive argument provide when it is valid?

6. Can an inductive argument guarantee the truth of the conclusion if the premises are true? Why or why not?
7. What is the difference between an inductively strong argument and an inductively weak one?
*8. What is the term for valid arguments that have true premises?
9. What is the term for strong arguments that have true premises?
10. Can a valid argument have false premises and a false conclusion? Can it have false premises and a true conclusion?
11. What logical conclusion can you draw about an argument that is valid but has a false conclusion?
*12. Is it possible for a valid argument to have true premises and a false conclusion?
13. In what way are conclusions of deductive arguments absolute?

JUDGING ARGUMENTS

When it comes to deductive and inductive arguments, the most important skills you can acquire are being able to identify both kinds of arguments and determining whether they are good or bad. Much of the rest of this text is devoted to helping you become proficient in these skills. This chapter will serve as your first lesson and give you a chance to practise what you learn.

So the obvious questions here are the following: When you come face to face with an argument to evaluate, (1) how can you tell whether it's deductive or inductive, and (2) how can you determine whether it gives you good reasons for accepting the conclusion (whether it's sound or cogent)? The following is a suggested four-step procedure for answering these questions, one that will be elaborated on here and in later chapters.

Step 1. Find the conclusion of the argument and then its premises. Use the techniques you learned in Chapter 1. You'll have plenty of chances to hone this skill in later chapters.

Step 2. Ask, "Is it the case that if the premises are true the conclusion *must* be true?" If the answer is yes, treat the argument as *deductive,* for it is very likely meant to offer conclusive support for its conclusion. The argument, then, is deductively valid, and you should check to see if it's sound. If the answer is no, proceed to the next step.

Step 3. Ask, "Is it the case that if the premises are true its conclusion is *probably* true?" If the answer is yes, treat the argument as *inductive,* for it is very likely meant to offer probable support for its conclusion. The argument, then, is inductively strong, and you should check to see if it's cogent. If the answer is no, proceed to the next step.

Step 4. Ask, "Is the argument intended to offer conclusive or probable support for its conclusion but *fails* to do so?" If you reach this step, you will have already eliminated two possibilities: a valid argument and a strong one. The remaining options are an invalid argument or a weak one. So here you must discover what type of (failed) argument is intended. There are two guidelines that can help you do that.

GUIDELINE 1: Generally, if an argument looks deductive or inductive because of its form, assume that it is intended to be so.

Bad arguments may sometimes look like good arguments because the arrangement of their premises and conclusion—their form—is similar to that found in reliable arguments. (You saw some of these reliable argument forms in the argument examples presented earlier in this chapter.) Such argument forms are an indication of what kind of argument is intended, and that fact gives you some guidance on determining argument type.

GUIDELINE 2: Generally, if an argument looks deductive or inductive because of the types of indicator words used (and its form yields no other clues), assume that it is intended to be so.

Arguments are often accompanied by words or phrases that identify them as deductive or inductive. Terms that tend to signal a deductive argument include "It necessarily follows that," "it logically follows that," "absolutely," "necessarily," and "certainly." Words signalling an inductive argument include "likely," "probably," "chances are," "odds are," and "it is plausible that." Such indicator words, though, are not foolproof clues to the type of argument because they are sometimes used in misleading ways. For example, someone might end an inductively strong argument with a conclusion prefaced with "it necessarily follows that," suggesting (incorrectly) that the argument is deductively valid.

But argument-type indicators may still be useful, especially when the argument form provides no clues (i.e., when Guideline 1 doesn't apply).

In step 4, once you discover which kind of argument is intended, you will know that it is either invalid or weak (because in steps 2 and 3 we eliminated the possibility of a valid or strong argument). The only remaining task is to determine whether the premises are true (whether the argument is sound or cogent).[1]

"He who strikes the first blow admits he's lost the argument."

—*Chinese proverb*

Let's try out the four-step procedure on a few arguments. Consider this one:

> [Premise] Unless we do something about the massive Ebola epidemic in Africa, the whole continent will be decimated within six months. [Premise] Unfortunately, we won't do anything about the Ebola epidemic in Africa. [Conclusion] It necessarily follows that the population of Africa will be decimated within six months.

Step 1 is already done for us; the premises and conclusion are clearly labelled. In step 2 we must ask, "Is it the case that if the premises are true, the conclusion must be true?" The answer is yes, if it's true that the Ebola epidemic in Africa will decimate the population in six months unless "we do something," and it's true that "we won't do anything," then the conclusion that the population of Africa will be decimated in six months *must* be true. So this argument is deductively valid. To determine if it's sound, we would need to check to see if the premises are true. In this case, the first premise is false because, under current conditions, it would take longer than six months for the epidemic to decimate the population of the whole continent. The other premise ("we won't do anything") is at least dubious since we can't predict the future. So what we have here is a deductively valid argument that's unsound—a bad argument.

Now let's analyze this one:

> [Premise] The Quebec-based French-language group "l'impératif français" works diligently to make sure businesses in Quebec use French in their daily operations. [Premise] The Quebec government has affirmed its commitment to preserving the French language. [Premise] And most Canadians are in favour of official bilingualism. [Conclusion] Let's face it, the French language is guaranteed to survive in Quebec!

Again, step 1 is already done for us. At step 2 we can see that even if the three premises of this argument are all true, the conclusion can still be false. After all, even if everything described in the premises is true, the French language could still die out in Quebec (perhaps because new immigrants speak English or other languages, or because of the influence of American TV, movies, and magazines). So the argument can't be deductively valid. But if we go through step 3, we can see that if all the premises are true, the conclusion is

FOOD FOR THOUGHT

When Reasoning Crashes . . . Leave the Scene of the Accident

Sometimes an argument goes off into a ditch and you don't know why. Here's an example of a wrecked argument from the great American satirical writer Ambrose Bierce (1842–1914?). What's wrong here?

> Sixty men can do a piece of work sixty times as quickly as one man.
> One man can dig a posthole in sixty seconds.
> Therefore, sixty men can dig a posthole in one second.

likely to be true, making the argument inductively strong. If the premises *are* true, the argument would be cogent.

See what you think of this one:

> [Premise] If you act like Bart Simpson, you will be respected by all your classmates. [Premise] But you don't act like Bart Simpson. [Conclusion] It follows that you will not be respected by all of your classmates.

This argument flunks the tests in steps 2 and 3: it is not deductively valid, and it is not inductively strong. But it does have features that suggest it is a deductive argument. First, it displays a pattern of reasoning that can, at first glance, seem deductive. Actually, it uses an argument pattern that is always deductively *invalid* (called denying the antecedent, an argument form we will look at shortly). This alone should be evidence enough that the argument is indeed deductive but invalid. But it also contains a phrase ("it follows that") that suggests an attempt at a deductive form.

You'll get a lot more exposure to argument forms and indicator words in the rest of this chapter (and the rest of this text). Ultimately, practice in distinguishing different types of arguments and their relative worth is the only way to gain proficiency (and confidence!) in making these judgments.

So far we've spent most of our time assessing the logical structure of arguments—that is, whether they are valid or invalid, or strong or weak. We haven't focused as much attention on evaluating the truth of premises because that's a big issue that's best considered separately—which is what we do in Part 2 of this book.

EXERCISE 3.2

Answers to exercises marked with an asterisk (*) may be found in Appendix B, Answers to Exercises.

For each of the following arguments, follow the four-step procedure to determine whether it is deductive or inductive, valid or invalid, and strong or weak. State the results of applying each step.

Example 1

Colonel Mustard did not commit the murder. After all, someone who had committed the murder would have dirt on his shoes and blood on his hands. Colonel Mustard's shoes and hands are clean.

Step 1: Conclusion: Colonel Mustard did not commit the murder. Premises: Someone who had committed the murder would have dirt on his shoes and blood on his hands. Colonel Mustard's shoes and hands are clean.
Step 2: Deductively valid.
Step 3: Does not apply.
Step 4: Does not apply.

Example 2

Most people who smoke pot are irresponsible and forgetful. Looks like you smoke pot all the time! Therefore, you're irresponsible and forgetful. Can you remember that?

Step 1: Conclusion: Therefore, you're irresponsible and forgetful. Premises: Most people who smoke pot are irresponsible and forgetful. Looks like you smoke pot all the time.
Step 2: Not deductively valid.
Step 3: Inductively strong.
Step 4: Does not apply.

*1. Ethel graduated from Queen's University. If she graduated from Queen's, she probably has a superior intellect. She has a superior intellect.
2. You're a university student, and all university students drink coffee, so you must drink coffee!
3. You would have to be crazy to be dating Barry. And you've been dating Barry for months now. So I think you're clearly crazy.
4. "Good sense is of all things in the world the most equally distributed, for everybody thinks himself so abundantly provided with it, that even those most difficult to please in all other matters do not commonly desire more of it than they already possess." (René Descartes, *A Discourse on Method*)
5. All cats are playful. All cats are natural hunters. It necessarily follows that all playful animals are natural hunters.
*6. Every musician has had special training, and everyone with special training has a university degree. Thus, every musician has a university degree.

7. People with high IQs also have psychic abilities. People with high grades—which are comparable to high IQ scores—also probably have psychic abilities.
8. If Greenpeace is against the Keystone XL pipeline, then the pipeline must be a terrible risk to the environment. Greenpeace is against the pipeline. Therefore, it must be a terrible risk to the environment.
*9. Some actors sing, and some play a musical instrument. So some actors who sing also play a musical instrument.
10. Anyone who is not a bigot will agree that Chris is a good fellow. Some people in this neighbourhood think that he's anything but a good fellow. Some people in this neighbourhood are bigots.
11. We shouldn't waste our time participating in the protest march, because public protest has never accomplished anything.
12. A vase was found broken on the floor, some money had been taken out of the safe, and there were strange scratches on the wall. It follows that someone must have burglarized the place.
13. All the evidence in this trial suggests that Paul Bernardo is guilty of murder. Let's face it: he's probably guilty.
14. If everything were all right, there would be no blood on the floor. Of course, there is plenty of blood on the floor. Therefore, everything is not all right.
*15. If minds are identical to brains—that is, if one's mind is nothing but a brain—androids could never have minds because they wouldn't have brains. Clearly, a mind is nothing but a brain, so it's impossible for androids to have minds.
16. "From infancy, almost, the average girl is told that marriage is her ultimate goal; therefore her training and education must be directed towards that end." (Emma Goldman, "Marriage and Love")
17. If you have scratches on your body that you can't account for, and you feel that you have been visited by space aliens, then you really have been visited by space aliens. You have such scratches, and you have experienced such feelings. Doubtless, space aliens have visited you.
18. If store windows are being broken all over town, the hockey riot has started. Dozens of windows have already been broken. The riot has begun.

EXERCISE 3.3

For each of the following arguments, indicate whether it is valid or invalid, strong or weak.

1. Brandon says this new iPad app is totally awesome. So it must be great.
2. Welfare is by definition a handout to people who have not worked for it. But giving people money they have not earned through labour is not helping anyone. It follows then that social welfare does not help anyone.
*3. If the *Globe and Mail* reports that the war in Afghanistan is over, then the war in Afghanistan is over. The *Globe and Mail* has reported exactly that. The war must be over.
4. If $r = 12$, then $s = 8$; $r = 12$; therefore, $s = 8$.
5. Any sitcom that tries to imitate *Seinfeld* probably sucks. All of this season's sitcoms try to imitate *Seinfeld.* They've all gotta suck.
6. "Poetry is finer and more philosophical than history; for poetry expresses the universal and history only the particular." (Aristotle, *Poetics*)
7. Either you're lying or you're not telling the whole story. You're obviously not lying, so you're just telling part of the story.
*8. Either your thinking is logical or it is emotional. It's obviously not logical. It's emotional.
9. It is unwise to skip your baby's scheduled vaccinations. Those vaccinations could save her life.
10. A recent Gallup poll says that 69 per cent of Canadians believe in the existence of heaven, but only 43 per cent say they believe in hell. People are just too willing to engage in wishful thinking.
11. Tequila makes people violent. Anything that makes people violent should be banned. We ought to ban the sale of tequila in campus pubs.
12. "We say that a person behaves in a given way because he possesses a philosophy, but we infer the philosophy from the behavior and therefore cannot use it in any satisfactory way as an explanation, at least until it is in turn explained." (B.F. Skinner, *Beyond Freedom and Dignity*)
13. You failed your driver's test twice. You've had three traffic tickets in the last two years. And your own brother won't let you drive him to hockey practice. It's pretty clear you're not a very good driver.
*14. Bachelors are unmarried. George is a bachelor. He has never taken a wife.
15. Bachelors are unmarried, and George acts as if he's not married. He's a bachelor for sure.
16. If there is a tax cut this year, the deficit will rise. There has already been a tax cut. The deficit is sure to rise.
17. If the universe had a beginning, then it was caused to begin. We know that the universe did have a beginning in the form of the big bang. So it was caused to come into existence. If it was caused to come into existence, that cause must have been God. God caused the universe to come into existence.

*18. If the United States is willing to wage war in the Middle East, it can only be because it wants the oil supplies in the region. Obviously, the United States is willing to go to war there. The United States wants that oil.

19. "Someone must have been telling lies about Joseph K., for without having done anything wrong he was arrested one fine morning." (Franz Kafka, *The Trial*)

20. Anyone willing to take the lives of innocent people for a cause is a terrorist. Many Christians, Jews, and Muslims have taken innocent lives in the name of their religious cause. Many Christians, Jews, and Muslims have been terrorists.

21. If the landlady is at the door, it's probably because she's looking for this month's rent. There she is. She must want the rent.

22. If you're a woman, then you understand sexism. But you're a man. You're just never going to understand what I'm going through.

*23. I like geometry. My geometry teacher likes me. Therefore I will pass my geometry course with flying colours.

FINDING MISSING PARTS

Sometimes arguments, especially informal ones, may seem to have a few pieces missing. Premises (and sometimes even conclusions)—material needed to make the argument work—are often left unstated. These implicit premises, or assumptions, are essential to the argument. Of course, certain assumptions are frequently left unsaid for good reason: they are obvious and understood by all parties to the argument, and boredom would set in fast if you actually tried to mention them all. If you wish to prove that "Socrates is mortal," you normally wouldn't need to explain what *mortal* means and that the name "Socrates" refers to an ancient philosopher, and not to a type of garden tool. But many arguments do have unstated premises that are necessary to the chain of reasoning and so must be made explicit to fully evaluate the arguments.

For instance:

> Handguns are rare in Canada, but the availability of shotguns and rifles poses a risk of death and injury. Shotguns and rifles should be banned, too!

Notice that there is a kind of disconnect between the premise and the conclusion. The conclusion is about banning something, but the premises—the reasons given—don't say anything about banning anything. The conclusion follows from the premise *only* if we assume an additional premise, perhaps something like this: "Anything that poses any risk of death or injury should be banned." With this additional premise, the argument becomes:

> Handguns are rare in Canada, but the availability of shotguns and rifles poses a risk to public safety. Anything that poses any risk of death or injury should be banned. Therefore, shotguns and rifles should be banned, too!

Now that all the premises are spelled out, you can evaluate the *full* argument just as you would any other. Not only that, but you can see that the unstated premise is questionable, which is the case with many implicit premises. Not everyone would agree that absolutely anything raising the risk of death or injury should be banned, for if that were the case we would have to outlaw cars, airplanes, most prescription drugs, most occupations, and who knows how many kitchen appliances! Many unstated premises are like this one—they're controversial and hence unstated. But they're also important to evaluate, and therefore should not be left unexamined.

Here's another argument with an unstated premise:

> Anyone who craves political power cannot be trusted to serve the public interest. So I say Premier Blowhard can't be trusted to serve the public interest.

As stated, this argument seems like a rush to judgment because the first premise concerns *anyone* who craves power, and suddenly Premier Blowhard is denounced as untrustworthy. Something's missing. What we need is another premise connecting the first premise to the conclusion: "Premier Blowhard craves political power." Now let's plug the implicit premise into the argument:

> Anyone who craves political power cannot be trusted to serve the public interest. Premier Blowhard craves political power. He can't be trusted to serve the public interest.

So exactly when should we try to ferret out an unstated premise? The obvious answer is that we should do so when there appears to be something essential missing—an implied, logical link between premises and conclusion that is not a commonsense, generally accepted assumption. Such implicit premises should never be taken for granted because, among other things, they are often deliberately hidden or downplayed to make the argument seem stronger.

"The difficult part in an argument is not to defend one's opinion, but rather to know it."

—*André Maurois*

Be aware, though, that many times the problem with an argument is not unstated premises, but invalid or weak structure. Consider this:

> If that potion contains arsenic, he will die. But it does not contain arsenic, so he will not die.

This argument is invalid; the conclusion does not follow from the premises. (After all, arsenic isn't the only poison that could be in that potion! So even if the premises are true, the conclusion need not be.) Like most invalid arguments, it can't be salvaged without altering it beyond what is clearly implied. It's just a bad argument. The same goes for weak arguments. They usually can't be fixed without adding or changing premises gratuitously. Remember, the point of articulating unstated premises is to make explicit what is already implicit. Your job as a critical thinker is not to make bad arguments good; that task belongs to the one who puts forward the argument in the first place.

To make sure that your investigation of implicit premises is thorough and reasonable, work through the following three-step process:[2]

Step 1. Search for a credible premise that would make the argument *valid,* one that would furnish the needed link between premise (or premises) and conclusion. Choose the supplied premise that

a. is most plausible

and

b. fits best with the author's intent.

The first stipulation (a) means that you should look for premises that are either true or, at least, not obviously false. The second stipulation (b) means that premises should fit—that is, at least not conflict—with what seems to be the author's point or purpose (which, of course, is often difficult to figure out).

straw man The fallacy of distorting, weakening, or oversimplifying someone's position so it can be more easily attacked or refuted.

These two requirements embody what is sometimes known as "the Principle of Charity in Interpretation" or just "the Principle of Charity." The Principle of Charity says that, whenever we find someone's meaning unclear, we should attempt to interpret it in a way that makes sense. That's the *fair* thing to do, and it's the thing that's most likely to aid in clear communication. And when it comes to *criticizing* someone else's argument, you want to be especially fair in stating what you think their argument is. Criticizing a version of their argument into which you've inserted a silly or irrelevant premise isn't very productive, and it isn't very fair. In fact, that amounts to a well-known fallacy known as the **straw man** fallacy, which we'll discuss in more detail in Chapter 5.

CREDIT: Betsy Streeter/Cartoon Stock

If the premise you supply is plausible and fitting (with the author's intent), use it to fill out the argument. If the premise you supplied is either not plausible or not fitting, go to step 2.

Step 2. Search for a credible premise that would make the argument as *strong* as possible. Choose the supplied premise that fulfills stipulations (a) and (b). If the premise you supply is plausible and fitting, use it to fill out the argument. If it is either not plausible or not fitting, consider the argument beyond repair and reject it.

Step 3. Evaluate the reconstituted argument. If you're able to identify a credible, implicit premise that makes the argument either valid or strong, assess this revised version of the argument, paying particular attention to the plausibility of the other premise or premises.

Now let's apply the procedure above to a few arguments:

> If the Bank of Canada lowers interest rates one more time, there will be a deep recession. So, I'm telling you there's going to be a deep recession.

The first step is to see if there's a credible premise that would make the argument valid. We can see right away that one premise will do the trick: "The Bank of Canada is about to lower interest rates again." Adding it to the argument will supply the link needed between the existing premise and the conclusion. We also can see that our new premise is plausible (the Bank of Canada has in fact lowered interest rates many times in the past) and seems to fit with the point of the argument (to prove that there will be a recession). Our resulting argument, though, is probably not a good one because the premise about the effect of the Bank of Canada's lowering interest rates is questionable.

Now examine this one:

> Security officer Blart lied on her employment application about whether she had a criminal record. Security officer Blart will do a bad job of screening passengers for weapons.

The sentence "Security officer Blart will do a bad job of screening passengers for weapons" is the conclusion here. To try to make this argument valid, we would need a premise like "Any security officer at Pearson International Airport who has lied on his or her employment application about having a criminal record will do a bad job of screening passengers for weapons." This premise fits the point of the argument, but it isn't plausible. Surely it cannot be the case that *any* security officer who has lied will do a bad job of screening. A more plausible premise is "Most security officers at Pearson International Airport who have lied on their employment applications about having a criminal record will do a bad job of screening passengers for weapons." This premise will do, and this is now a good argument—assuming that the other premise is true.

What about this one?:

> The use of marijuana should be legal because it's an act that brings pleasure to people's lives.

To make this argument valid, we need a premise that connects the idea of something being legal with the idea of bringing pleasure. We would need to add this premise (or one like it): "Any act that brings pleasure to people's lives should be legal." But this premise is hard to accept since many heinous acts—such as murder and theft—may bring pleasure to some people, yet few of us would think those acts should be legal. To try to make the argument strong, we might add this premise instead: "Some acts should be legal simply because they bring pleasure to people's lives." This premise is actually controversial, but it at least is not obviously false. It also fits with the point of the argument. If we decide that the premise is neither plausible nor fitting, we would declare the argument beyond repair.

EXERCISE 3.4

For exercises marked with an asterisk (*), there are answers in Appendix B, Answers to Exercises.

I. For each of the following arguments, state the implicit premises that will make the argument valid.

Example

The engine is sputtering. It must be out of gas.
Implicit premise: Whenever the engine sputters, it's out of gas.

*1. Any member of Parliament who is caught misusing campaign funds should resign his or her seat. The honourable member from Algoma-Manitoulin-Kapuskasing should resign.
2. Kelly is a very strong student, so she is almost certain to get an A in critical thinking.
3. Orange juice has lots of vitamin C. So it must be healthy for you.
4. The RCMP doesn't have a very serious focus on stopping terrorism. A major terrorist attack *will* happen in this country.
*5. The author of this new book on interventionist wars is either biased or incompetent as a journalist. So she's biased.
6. Mavis goes to church every Sunday. So you can definitely trust her.
7. The government of Saudi Arabia is bound to fall! After all, the Taliban regime in Afghanistan fell because it persecuted women.
8. The Canadian government should limit its military activities to the western hemisphere because it doesn't have the resources to cover the whole world.

9. If the engine starts right away, it's because of the tune-up I gave it. Must be because of the tune-up I gave it.

*10. Taslima did not criticize US military action in the Gulf War or in the war in Afghanistan. She must be pro-American.

II. For each of the following arguments, change or add a premise that will make the argument strong.

1. Professor Fullbrook graduated from a second-rate university. He's probably not a very good professor.
2. Morgan has a habit of keeping junk that she really should throw out, so she is likely going to end up on one of those reality shows about "hoarders."

*3. Six out of 10 of my teenage friends love rap music. So 60 per cent of all teens love rap music.

4. Seventy-one per cent of the faculty and staff at Spadina College are New Democrats. So most of the students are probably New Democrats.
5. Miriam was in the library when the books were stolen from the librarian's desk. She was also seen hanging around the desk. So she's probably the one who stole them.

*6. If Assad's fingerprints are on the vase, then he's probably the one who broke it. He's probably the one who broke it.

7. If the prime minister needs more money to balance the federal budget, he will get it by cutting defence spending. Well, he's almost certainly going to get it by cutting defence spending.
8. Ninety per cent of students at the University of Northern Saskatchewan graduate with a BA degree. Li Fong will probably graduate from the University of Northern Saskatchewan with a BA degree.

*9. The murder rates in the Atlantic provinces are very low. The murder rates in most large cities in the western provinces are very low. So the murder rate in Toronto must be very low.

10. Paul is a typical Canadian. He probably eats way too many doughnuts.

ARGUMENT PATTERNS

Earlier we discussed the importance of being familiar with patterns, or forms, of argument—that is, the structures on which the content of an argument is laid. The point was that knowing some common argument forms makes it easier to determine whether an argument is deductive or inductive. But being

FOOD FOR THOUGHT

Arguments on the Net

The Internet is fertile ground for all manner of arguments—good, bad, benign, and benighted. Here's one that has gone around the world a few times in cyberspace:

> Adolf Hitler was evil.
> Adolf Hitler was a vegetarian.
> Therefore, vegetarianism is evil.

What's wrong with this argument? If you don't know, the following section on argument patterns will help you. An important clue that something is fishy here is that any argument of this form can be used to try to "frame" anybody. Consider:

> Dominic lives in Montreal.
> Dominic is tall.
> Therefore, everyone who lives in Montreal is tall.

familiar with argument forms is also helpful in many other aspects of argument evaluation. Let's take a closer look at some of these forms.

Since argument forms are structures distinct from the content of an argument, we can easily signify different forms by using letters to represent statements in the arguments. Each letter represents a different statement in much the same way that letters are used to represent values in a mathematical equation. Consider this argument:

> If the job is worth doing, then it's worth doing well.
> The job is worth doing.
> Therefore, it's worth doing well.

We can represent this argument like this:

> If *p*, then *q*.
> *p*.
> Therefore, *q*.

Notice that the first line in the argument is a compound statement. That means it's composed of at least two constituent statements—"the job is worth doing" and "it's worth doing well"— which are represented in this case by *p* and *q*. So we have two statements in this argument that are arranged into an argument form, one that is both very common and always valid. We can plug any statements we want into this form, and we will still get a valid argument. The premises may be true or false, but the form will be valid.

Some of the more common argument patterns that you encounter are like this pattern—they're deductive and **conditional**. They are conditional in that they contain at least one conditional, or "if–then," premise. We describe such premises as conditional because they state the *conditions under which* a certain state of affairs will obtain. The first statement in a conditional premise (the *if* part) is known as the **antecedent**. The second statement (the *then* part) is known as the **consequent**.

conditional statement An "if–then" statement; it consists of the antecedent (the part introduced by the word *if*) and the consequent (the part introduced by the word *then*).

antecedent The first part of a conditional statement (If *p*, then *q*), the component that begins with the word *if.*

consequent The part of a conditional statement (If *p*, then *q*) introduced by the word *then.*

The conditional pattern shown here is called **affirming the antecedent** or, to use the Latin term, ***modus ponens***. Any argument in the *modus ponens* form is valid—if the premises are true, the conclusion absolutely must be true. In the argument form shown here, this means that if "If *p*, then *q*" and "*p*" are both true, the conclusion has to be true also. (Try your own example, filling in any true statements you want for "If *p*, then *q*" and "*p*." If your premises are true, then your conclusion will also be true.) These facts, then, provide a way to quickly size up any conditional argument. If an argument is in the form of *modus ponens*, it's valid, regardless of the content of the statements. That's a very handy thing to know.

affirming the antecedent/ *modus ponens* A valid argument form:

If *p*, then *q*.
p.
Therefore, *q*.

Another common conditional argument form is called **denying the consequent**, or ***modus tollens***:

If Austin is happy, then Barb is happy.
Barb is not happy.
Therefore, Austin is not happy.

denying the consequent/ *modus tollens* A valid argument form:

If *p*, then *q*.
Not *q*.
Therefore, not *p*.

The form of *modus tollens* is:

If *p*, then *q*.
Not *q*.
Therefore, not *p*.

Like *modus ponens, modus tollens* is always valid. If the premises are true, the conclusion must be true. Make up your own example to see for yourself! So any argument that's in the *modus tollens* pattern is valid.

A third common conditional argument form is called **hypothetical syllogism**. *Hypothetical* is just another term for conditional. A **syllogism** is an argument (usually deductive) made up of three statements—two premises and a conclusion. *(Modus ponens* and *modus tollens* are particular kinds of syllogisms. We'll discuss "categorical" syllogisms—deductive syllogisms that show the logical relationships between three categories of things—in Chapter 6, and we'll discuss inductive "statistical" syllogisms in Chapter 8.) In a hypothetical syllogism, all three statements are conditional, and the argument is always valid:

hypothetical syllogism A valid argument made up of three hypothetical, or conditional, statements:

If *p*, then *q*.
If *q*, then *r*.
Therefore, if *p*, then *r*.

syllogism A deductive argument made up of three statements—two premises and a conclusion. See **affirming the antecedent** and **denying the consequent**.

If you leave the door open, the cat will get out.
If the cat gets out, it will get hit by a car.
Therefore, if you leave the door open, the cat will get hit by a car.

Here's the symbolized version:

If *p*, then *q*.
If *q*, then *r*.
Therefore, if *p*, then *r*.

People often use hypothetical syllogisms to reason about causal chains of events. They try to show that one event will lead unavoidably to a sequence of events that will finally conclude in a single event that seems far removed from the first. This linkage has prompted some to label hypothetical syllogisms "chain arguments."

Here's another example of a hypothetical syllogism:

If the Habs lose this game, they're out of the playoffs.
If they're out of the playoffs, there will be riots in Montreal.
Therefore, if the Habs lose this game, there will be riots in Montreal.

Because the *structure* of this argument is the same as the structure of the previous argument (that is, they're both hypothetical syllogisms), the symbolized version is exactly the same:

If *p*, then *q*.
If *q*, then *r*.
Therefore, if *p*, then *r*.

denying the antecedent An invalid argument form:

If *p*, then *q*.
Not *p*.
Therefore, not *q*.

There are also two common conditional argument forms that are *not* valid, though they superficially resemble valid forms. One is called **denying the antecedent**. For example:

If Einstein invented the steam engine, then he's a great scientist.
Einstein did not invent the steam engine.
Therefore, he is not a great scientist.

Denying the antecedent is represented like this:

If *p*, then *q*.
Not *p*.
Therefore, not *q*.

"Mistakes are made on two counts: an argument is either based on error or incorrectly developed."

—*Thomas Aquinas*

You can see the problem with this form in the preceding argument. Even if the antecedent, *p*, is false (if Einstein did not invent the steam engine), that doesn't show that he's not a great scientist, because he could be a great scientist on account of some other great achievement. Thus, denying the antecedent is clearly an invalid pattern because it's possible for the premises to be true and the conclusion false.

REVIEW NOTES

Valid Conditional Argument Forms

AFFIRMING THE ANTECEDENT (*Modus Ponens*)	**Example**
If *p*, then *q*.	If Spot barks, a burglar is in the house.
p.	Spot is barking.
Therefore, *q*.	Therefore, a burglar is in the house

DENYING THE CONSEQUENT (*Modus Tollens*)	**Example**
If *p*, then *q*.	If it's raining, the park is closed.
Not *q*.	The park is not closed.
Therefore, not *p*.	Therefore, it's not raining.

HYPOTHETICAL SYLLOGISM	**Example**
If *p*, then *q*.	If Tanvir steals the money, he will go to jail.
If *q*, then *r*.	If Tanvir goes to jail, his family will suffer.
Therefore, if *p*, then *r*.	Therefore, if Tanvir steals the money, his family will suffer.

Here's another example of this form:

If Alexander the Great jumped off the CN Tower without a parachute, then Alexander the Great is dead.
Alexander the Great did not jump off the CN Tower without a parachute.
Therefore, Alexander the Great is not dead.

Even if Alexander the Great did not jump off the CN Tower without a parachute, that in itself does not show that he is not dead. After all, there are lots of ways to die. And in fact, we know that he died (of illness) over 2300 years ago. In other words, it's possible for both premises in this argument to be true while the conclusion is false.

There's another common invalid form you should know about: **affirming the consequent**.

Here's an instance of this form:

If Brandon is the capital of Manitoba, then Brandon is in Manitoba.
Brandon is in Manitoba.
Therefore, Brandon is the capital of Manitoba.

affirming the consequent
An invalid argument form:
If *p*, then *q*.
q.
Therefore, *p*.

We represent this form like this:

If *p*, then *q*.
q.
Therefore, *p*.

Obviously, in this form it's possible for the premises to be true while the conclusion is false, as this example shows. This pattern, therefore, is invalid.

The final pattern we will look at is a common non-conditional argument form called **disjunctive syllogism**. It's valid and extremely simple:

disjunctive syllogism A valid argument form:

Either *p* or *q*.
Not *p*.
Therefore, *q*.

In the second premise of the syllogism, either disjunct can be denied.

Either Ralph walked the dog, or he stayed home.
He didn't walk the dog.
Therefore, he stayed home.

It's called a disjunctive syllogism because it starts with a disjunction—a statement that says that one or another of two things is true. Each of those things (in this case "Ralph walked the dog" and "he stayed home" is called a **disjunct**. The symbolized form of the argument above is thus:

Either *p* or *q*.
Not *p*.
Therefore, *q*.

REVIEW NOTES

Invalid Conditional Argument Forms

AFFIRMING THE CONSEQUENT	EXAMPLE
If *p*, then *q*.	If the cat is on the mat, she is asleep.
q.	She is asleep.
Therefore, *p*.	Therefore, she is on the mat.

DENYING THE ANTECEDENT	EXAMPLE
If p, then *q*.	If the cat is on the mat, she is asleep.
Not *p*.	She is not on the mat.
Therefore, not *q*.	Therefore, she is not asleep.

Disjunctive Syllogism (Valid)

SYMBOLIZED VERSION	EXAMPLE
Either *p* or *q*.	Either we light the fire or we will freeze.
Not *p*.	We cannot light the fire.
Therefore, *q*.	Therefore, we will freeze.

Keep in mind that in a disjunctive syllogism, either disjunct can be denied, not just the first one. Here's an example in which the second of the two disjuncts is denied:

> Either Rick Mercer was joking, or he is out of touch with current events.
> But I *know* he's not out of touch with current events!
> So, he must have been joking.

These six deductive argument forms (four valid ones and two invalid ones) can help you streamline the process of argument evaluation. If you want to find out quickly if a deductive argument is valid, you can compare it to these patterns to do that. (But remember, a good deductive argument has both a valid form and true premises.) You need only to see if the argument fits one of the forms. If it fits a valid form, it's valid. If it fits an invalid form, it's invalid. If it doesn't fit any of the forms, then you need to find another way to evaluate the argument. The easiest way to use this form-comparison technique is to memorize all six forms so that you can recognize them whenever they arise.

Sometimes you can see right away that an argument has a valid or invalid form. At other times, you may need a little help figuring this out, or you may want to use a more explicit test of validity. In either case, the *counterexample method* can help. With this technique you check for validity by simply devising a parallel argument that has the same form as the argument you're evaluating (the test argument) but has obviously *true premises and a false conclusion.* Recall that any argument having true premises and a false conclusion cannot be valid. So if you can invent such an argument that also has the same pattern as the test argument, you've proved that the test argument is invalid.

For example, let's say that you are confronted with this argument:

> If old-fashioned values are lost, then young people will abandon marriage.
> Young people have abandoned marriage.
> Therefore, old-fashioned values have been lost!

And to check this test argument, you come up with this parallel argument, which has exactly the same form:

> If George is a dog, then he is warm-blooded.
> George is warm-blooded.
> Therefore, he is a dog.

This argument has the same pattern as the previous one—but the premises can easily be true and the conclusion false (assuming, for example, that George is your brother!). So the test argument too has to be invalid. You may have already guessed that it is an instance of affirming the consequent. The counterexample method, though, works not just for the deductive forms we've discussed but for all deductive forms. (We will discuss other deductive forms in upcoming chapters.)

EXERCISE 3.5

Answers to exercises marked with an asterisk (*) may be found in Appendix B, Answers to Exercises.

For each of the following arguments, determine whether it is valid or invalid and indicate the argument pattern.

*1. If the Vikings built that wall, there would be archeological evidence of that.
But there is no such evidence.
So the Vikings did not build that wall.

2. If it doesn't have the Fairtrade Foundation's mark on it, then it's not fair-trade coffee.
This coffee doesn't have the Fairtrade Foundation's mark on it.
So it's not fair-trade coffee.

3. Either Tarvinder is pregnant or she has been eating too much.
She isn't pregnant.
Therefore, she has been eating too much.

4. If my iPod hasn't been plugged in, the battery must be dead.
The battery isn't dead.
Therefore, my iPod must have been plugged in.

5. If my iPod has been plugged in, the battery must be OK.
My iPod has not been plugged in.
Therefore, the battery must be dead.

*6. If CBC News omits important news stories, then it is irresponsible.
It is not irresponsible.
So CBC News does not omit important news stories.

7. If ESP (extrasensory perception) were real, psychic predictions would be completely reliable.
Psychic predictions are completely reliable.
Therefore, ESP is real.

8. If I take the toll route, I'll get to the meeting a half-hour before everybody else.

I didn't take the toll route.
I won't get to the meeting a half-hour before everybody else.

*9. If ESP (extrasensory perception) were real, psychic predictions would be completely reliable.
ESP is real.
Therefore, psychic predictions are completely reliable.

10. If Tammy has a PhD, she will be hired.
Tammy was not hired.
Therefore, Tammy does not have a PhD.

11. If interest rates go up, bond prices must go down.
Bond prices went down.
Therefore, interest rates went up.

12. If it rains, Alex will get wet.
If Alex gets wet, he will be upset.
Therefore, if it rains, Alex will be upset.

EXERCISE 3.6

For each of the following premises, add another premise and a conclusion to make it valid in two different ways—*modus ponens* and *modus tollens.*

1. If McDonald's manages to buy Burger King, they will become the largest foods company that the world has ever seen.
*2. If Lino is telling the truth, he will admit to all charges.
3. If China adopts North American patterns of consumption, then the environment is doomed.
4. If the new vaccine prevents the spread of Ebola, the researchers who developed the vaccine should get the Nobel Prize.
*5. If religious conflict in Nigeria continues, thousands more will die.
6. If *p*, then *q*.
7. If it's cold on my birthday, in January, we should spend my birthday in Mexico.
8. If our politicians realize that they serve the people, and not the other way around, our laws would be much more reflective of our society's values and beliefs
*9. If solar power can supply six megawatts of power in Vancouver (which is certainly not the sunniest place in the world), then solar power can transform the energy systems in sunnier places like Edmonton and Calgary.
10. If Toni and Tracy don't return our calls, then we should go to the baseball game without them.

EXERCISE 3.7

Use the counterexample method to create a parallel argument for each of the invalid arguments in Exercise 3.5. Write out each parallel argument and represent its form with letters as discussed earlier. Answers are provided for 4, 5, 7, 8, and 11.

Example

Test Argument.

If the government mismanages the economy, there will be a long-term recession.
We are in a long-term recession.
Therefore, the government has mismanaged the economy.

Parallel Argument.

If Beyoncé could fly, she sure would be famous.
She is famous.
Therefore, Beyoncé can fly.

If *a*, then *b*.
b.
Therefore, *a*.

DIAGRAMMING ARGUMENTS

Most of the arguments we've looked at so far have been relatively simple. When arguments are more complex (and in real life they usually are!), you may find it increasingly difficult to sort out premises from conclusions and parts of an argument from non-argumentative background noise. If you can visualize the structure of an argument, though, the job gets much easier. That's where argument diagramming comes in.

Let's begin by diagramming the following very simple argument, before moving on to more complicated ones.

Justin Trudeau has great ideas for preserving the natural environment. That's for sure! Therefore, Trudeau being elected is good for Canada.

The first thing we do is underline any premise- or conclusion-indicator words (e.g., "therefore," "since," and "because"):

Justin Trudeau has great ideas for preserving the natural environment. That's for sure! <u>Therefore</u>, Trudeau being elected is good for Canada.

Next we number all the statements (and *only* the statements, not questions, etc.) in the passage in sequential order.

> (1) Justin Trudeau has great ideas for preserving the natural environment. (2) That's for sure! (3) Therefore, Trudeau being elected is good for Canada.

And then we cross out all extraneous statements—those that are neither premises nor conclusions, those that are redundant, and those that are nothing more than background information or other logically irrelevant material.

> (1) Justin Trudeau has great ideas for preserving the natural environment. (2) ~~That's for sure!~~ (3) Therefore, Trudeau being elected is good for Canada.

We've crossed out claim (2) because it is redundant—it just adds emphasis to what is said in claim (1).

Finally, we draw the diagram. Put the numbers associated with the premises inside squares and place those squares above the number for the conclusion, which is itself put inside a circle. (In our diagramming method, squares will always represent premises, and circles will always represent conclusions.) Then draw arrows from the premises to the conclusion they support. Each arrow represents a logical relationship between premise and conclusion, a relationship that we might normally indicate with the word "therefore" or with the words "is a reason or premise for."

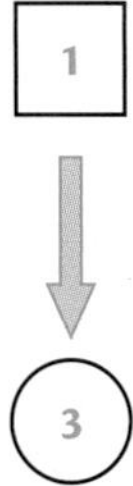

This diagram is very simple, because the argument it represents is very simple. It has just one premise and one conclusion. And it has just one arrow, showing that premise (1) is being used here in support of conclusion (3).

Now we're ready to try a slightly more complicated example.

> What do I think of shopping at H&M? I'll tell you! They've got great prices, and they've got a good selection of men's clothes. So H&M is a great place to shop!

The first thing we do is underline any premise- or conclusion-indicator words (e.g., "therefore," "since," and "because"):

> What do I think of shopping at H&M? I'll tell you! They've got great prices, and they've got a good selection of men's clothes. So H&M is a great place to shop!

Next we number all the statements (and *only* the statements) in the passage in sequential order.

> What do I think of shopping at H&M? (1) I'll tell you! (2) They've got great prices, and (3) they've got a good selection of men's clothes. (4) So H&M is a great place to shop!

We haven't numbered that first sentence, because it's a question, not a statement—it's merely there to introduce the topic.

And then we cross out all extraneous statements—those that are neither premises nor conclusions, those that are redundant, and so on.

> ~~What do I think of shopping at H&M?~~ (1) ~~I'll tell you!~~ (2) They've got great prices, and (3) they've got a good selection of men's clothes. (4) So H&M is a great place to shop!

We've crossed out the first two sentences because they're not essential to the structure of this argument. The first sentence isn't a statement at all. And the second one, though it *is* a statement, doesn't really have any content: it just announces that an argument is on its way.

Finally, we draw the diagram. Place the numbers of the premises inside squares and put the number for the conclusion inside a circle. Put the premises above the conclusion on your page. Then draw arrows from the premises to the conclusion they support.

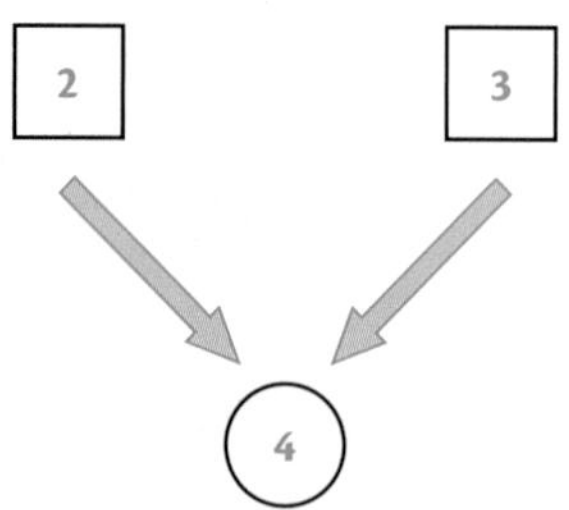

Here we see that our diagram—our argument—is one step more complicated than in our previous example. This one has two premises, each lending some support to the conclusion. The logical "flow" from the two premises to the conclusion is represented by the two arrows.

Next, let's try something more complicated still.

> There is no question in my mind. I therefore maintain that Colonel Mustard is the murderer. Because if he did it, he would probably have

bloodstains on the sleeve of his shirt. The bloodstains are tiny, but they are there. Any observant person could see them. Also the murder weapon was within the colonel's reach for quite a while before the crime was committed. And since of all the people in the house at the time he alone does not have an airtight alibi, he must be the killer.

Again, the first thing we do is underline any premise- or conclusion-indicator words (e.g., "therefore," "since," and "because"):

> There is no question in my mind. I therefore maintain that Colonel Mustard is the murderer. Because if he did it, he would probably have bloodstains on the sleeve of his shirt. The bloodstains are tiny, but they are there. Any observant person could see them. Also the murder weapon was within the colonel's reach for quite a while before the crime was committed. And since of all the people in the house at the time he alone does not have an airtight alibi, he must be the killer.

Next we number all the statements (and *only* the statements) in the passage in sequential order. (For the purposes of diagramming, an if–then statement is considered one statement, and multiple statements in a single compound sentence are to be counted as separate statements. Such statements are usually joined by "and," "or," or "but.")

> (1) There is no question in my mind. (2) I therefore maintain that Colonel Mustard is the murderer. (3) Because if he did it, he would probably have bloodstains on the sleeve of his shirt. (4) The bloodstains are tiny, but they are there. (5) Any observant person could see them. (6) Also the murder weapon was within the colonel's reach for quite a while before the crime was committed. (7) And since of all the people in the house at the time he alone does not have an airtight alibi, (8) he must be the killer.

Allen is far less argumentative since Angie's introduction to falconry.

And then we cross out all extraneous statements, noise, redundancies, and anything else that is neither a premise nor a conclusion.

> (1) ~~There is no question in my mind.~~ (2) I therefore maintain that Colonel Mustard is the murderer. (3) Because if he did it, he would probably have bloodstains on the sleeve of his shirt. (4) The bloodstains are tiny, but they are there. (5) ~~Any observant person could see them.~~ (6) Also the murder weapon was within the colonel's reach for quite a while before the crime was

committed. (7) And since of all the people in the house at the time he alone does not have an airtight alibi, ~~he must be the killer.~~

Finally, we draw the diagram. Again, place the numbers of the premises inside squares and above the number for the conclusion, which is itself placed inside a circle. Squares will represent premises, and circles will represent conclusions. Draw arrows from the premises to the conclusion they support.

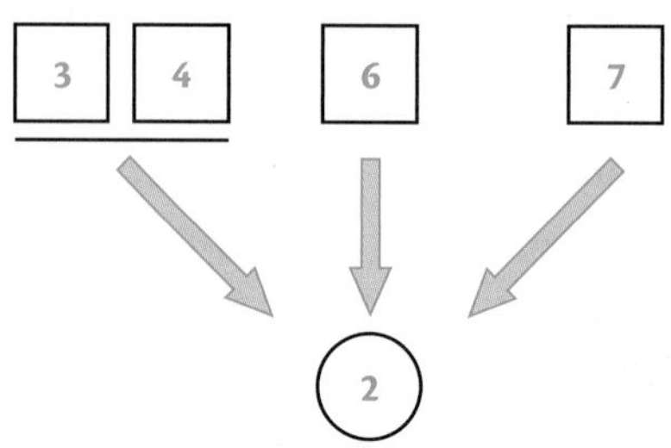

independent premise A premise that does not depend on other premises to provide support to a conclusion. If an independent premise is removed, the support that other premises supply to the conclusion is not affected.

dependent premise A premise that depends on at least one other premise to provide joint support to a conclusion. If a dependent premise is removed, the support that its linked dependent premises supply to the conclusion is undermined or completely cancelled out.

In this diagram you can see that premises 3 and 4 are handled differently from premises 6 and 7. The reason is that some premises are **independent** and some are **dependent**.

An independent premise offers support to a conclusion *without the help of any other premises.* If other premises are omitted or undermined in an argument, the support supplied by an independent premise does not change. We represent this fact in the diagram by drawing separate arrows to the conclusion from premises 6 and 7, both of which give it independent support. If we delete one of these premises, the support that the other one gives does not change.

Premises 3 and 4 are dependent premises. They do depend on each other to jointly provide support to a conclusion. If either premise 3 or 4 is removed, the support that the remaining premise supplies is undermined or completely cancelled out. By itself, premise 3 ("Because if he did it, he would probably have bloodstains on the sleeve of his shirt") offers no support whatsoever to the conclusion ("Colonel Mustard is the murderer"). And by itself, premise 4 ("The bloodstains are tiny, but they are there") doesn't lend any support to the conclusion. But together, premises 3 and 4 offer a good reason to accept the conclusion. We represent dependent premises by underlining them *together,* as in our diagram. Since dependent premises together act as a single premise, or reason, we draw a single arrow from the combined premises (from the line between 3 and 4, each of which is inside its own square) to the conclusion. With the diagram complete, we can see clearly that two independent premises and one set of dependent premises provide support for the conclusion (statement 2).

Now, consider this argument:

(1) The famous trial lawyer Clarence Darrow (1857–1938) made a name for himself by using the "determinism defence" to get his clients

acquitted of serious crimes. (2) The crux of this approach is the idea that humans are not really responsible for anything they do because they cannot choose freely— they are "determined," predestined, if you will, by nature (or God) to be the way they are. (3) So in a sense, Darrow says, humans are like wind-up toys with no control over any action or decision. (4) They have no free will. (5) Remember that Darrow was a renowned agnostic who was skeptical of all religious claims. (6) But Darrow is wrong about human free will for two reasons. (7) First, in our moral life, our own commonsense experience suggests that sometimes people are free to make moral decisions. (8) We should not abandon what our commonsense experience tells us without good reason—and (9) Darrow has given us no good reason. (10) Second, Darrow's determinism is not confirmed by science, as he claims—but actually conflicts with science. Modern science says that there are many things (at the subatomic level of matter) that are not determined at all: (12) they just happen.

Indicator words are scarce in this argument, unless you count the words *first* and *second* as signifying premises, but they're not reliable indicators. After we number the statements consecutively and cross out extraneous statements, the argument looks like this:

~~(1) The famous trial lawyer Clarence Darrow (1857–1938) made a name for himself by using the "determinism defence" to get his clients acquitted of serious crimes. (2) The crux of this approach is the idea that humans are not really responsible for anything they do because they cannot choose freely—they are "determined," predestined, if you will, by nature (or God) to be the way they are. (3) So in a sense, Darrow says, humans are like wind-up toys with no control over any action or decision. (4) They have no free will. (5) Remember that Darrow was a renowned agnostic who was skeptical of all religious claims.~~ (6) But Darrow is wrong about human free will for two reasons. (7) First, in our moral life, our own commonsense experience suggests that sometimes people are free to make moral decisions. (8) We should not abandon what our commonsense experience tells us without good reason—and (9) Darrow has given us no good reason. (10) Second, Darrow's determinism is not confirmed by science, as he claims—but actually conflicts with science. (11) Modern science says that there are many things (at the subatomic level of matter) that are not determined at all: (12) ~~they just happen.~~

Clarence Darrow was skilled at argumentation, which he used to good effect in his most famous case, the so-called Scopes Monkey Trial of 1925, in which he defended a man (John Scopes) charged with teaching evolution in a public school.

CREDIT: © Corbis

To simplify things, we can eliminate several statements right away. Statements 1 through 4 are just background information on Darrow's views. Statement 5 is irrelevant to the argument; his agnosticism has no logical connection to the premises or conclusion. Statement 12 is a rewording of statement 11.

After this elimination process, only the following premises and conclusion (statement 6) remain:

(6) But Darrow is wrong about human free will for two reasons.
(7) First, in our moral life, our commonsense experience suggests that sometimes people are free to make moral decisions.
(8) We should not abandon what our commonsense experience tells us without good reason.
(9) Darrow has given us no good reason.
(10) Second, Darrow's determinism is not confirmed by science, as he claims—but actually conflicts with science.
(11) Modern science says that there are many things (mostly at the subatomic level of matter) that are not determined at all.

The question is, how are these premises related to the conclusion? Well, premises 7, 8, and 9 are dependent premises supporting the conclusion. Taken separately, these premises are weak, but together they constitute a plausible reason for accepting statement 6. Premise 10 directly supports the conclusion, and it in turn is supported by premise 11. These logical relationships can be diagrammed like this:

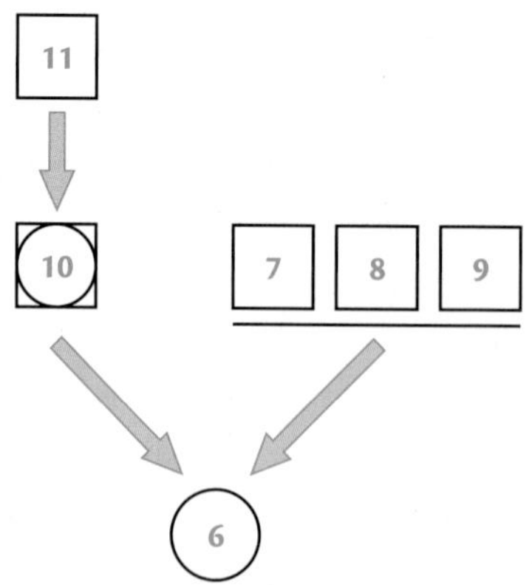

Notice how statement 10 is diagrammed. It is a premise leading to the conclusion (6), so it needs to be inside a square. But it is also a conclusion (supported by premise 11), so it also needs to be inside a circle. The circle–square combination indicates that the statement is a sub-conclusion, a statement that serves as both a premise *and* a conclusion.

REVIEW NOTES

Diagramming Arguments: Step by Step

1. Underline all premise- or conclusion-indicator words such as "since," "therefore," and "because." Then number the statements.
2. Cross out all extraneous material—redundancies, irrelevant sentences, questions, exclamations.
3. Draw the diagram using numbered squares to represent premises and numbered circles to represent conclusions. Connect premises and conclusions with arrows showing logical connections. Include both dependent and independent premises, and draw a line under dependent premises to connect them.

Now read this passage:

As the Islamic clerics cling to power in Iran, students there are agitating for greater freedom and less suppression of views that the clerics dislike. Even though ultimate power in Iran rests with the mullahs, it is not at all certain where the nation is headed. Here's a radical suggestion: the Islamic republic in Iran will fall within the next five years. This is because the majority of Iranians are in favour of democratic reforms, and no regime can stand for very long when citizens are demanding access to the political process. Also, Iran today is a mirror image of the Soviet Union before it broke apart—there's widespread dissatisfaction and dissent at a time when the regime seems to be trying to hold the people's loyalty. Every nation that has taken such a path has imploded within five years. Finally, the old Iranian trick of gaining support for the government by fomenting hatred of America will not work anymore because Iran is now trying to be friends with the United States.

When we number the statements and underline the indicators, we get this:

(1) As the Islamic clerics cling to power in Iran, students there are agitating for greater freedom and less suppression of views that the clerics dislike. (2) Even though ultimate power in Iran rests with the mullahs, it is not at all certain where the nation is headed. Here's a radical suggestion: (3) the Islamic republic in Iran will fall within the next five years. (4) This is <u>because</u> the majority of Iranians are in favour of democratic reforms, (5) and no regime can stand for very long when citizens are demanding access to the political process. (6) Also, Iran today is a mirror image of the Soviet Union before it broke apart—there's widespread dissatisfaction and dissent at a time when the regime

> seems to be trying to hold the people's loyalty. (7) Every nation that has taken such a path has imploded within five years. (8) Finally, the old Iranian trick of gaining support for the government by fomenting hatred of America will not work anymore (9) because Iran is now trying to be friends with the United States.

And here's the passage with the extraneous material crossed out:

> ~~(1) As the Islamic clerics cling to power in Iran, students there are agitating for greater freedom and less suppression of views that the clerics dislike. (2) Even though ultimate power in Iran rests with the mullahs,~~ it is not at all certain where the nation is headed. Here's a radical suggestion: (3) the Islamic republic in Iran will fall within the next five years. (4) This is because the majority of Iranians are in favour of democratic reforms (5) and no regime can stand for very long when citizens are demanding access to the political process. (6) Also, Iran today is a mirror image of the Soviet Union before it broke apart—there's widespread dissatisfaction and dissent at a time when the regime seems to be trying to hold the people's loyalty. (7) Every nation that has taken such a path has imploded within five years. (8) Finally, the old Iranian trick of gaining support for the government by fomenting hatred of America will not work anymore (9) because Iran is now trying to be friends with the United States.

The conclusion is statement 3, and the premises are statements 4 through 9. The first two statements are extraneous. Statements 4 and 5 are dependent premises, and so are statements 6 and 7. Statements 8 and 9 constitute an argument that gives support to the conclusion of the passage. Statement 8 is the conclusion; statement 9, the premise. The diagram of this argument is as follows:

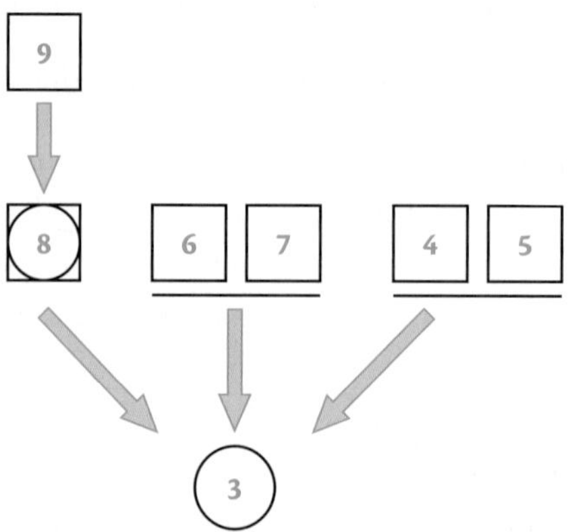

By the time you work through the diagramming exercises in this chapter, you will probably be fairly proficient in diagramming arguments of all kinds.

Just as important, you will have a better appreciation of how arguments are built, how they are dissected, and how you can judge their value in a penetrating, systematic way.

EXERCISE 3.8

Answers to exercises marked with an asterisk (*) may be found in Appendix B, Answers to Exercises.

For each of the following diagrams, devise an argument whose premises and conclusion can be accurately depicted in the diagram. Write out the argument, number each statement, and insert the numbers into the diagram at the right places.

*1.

2.

3.

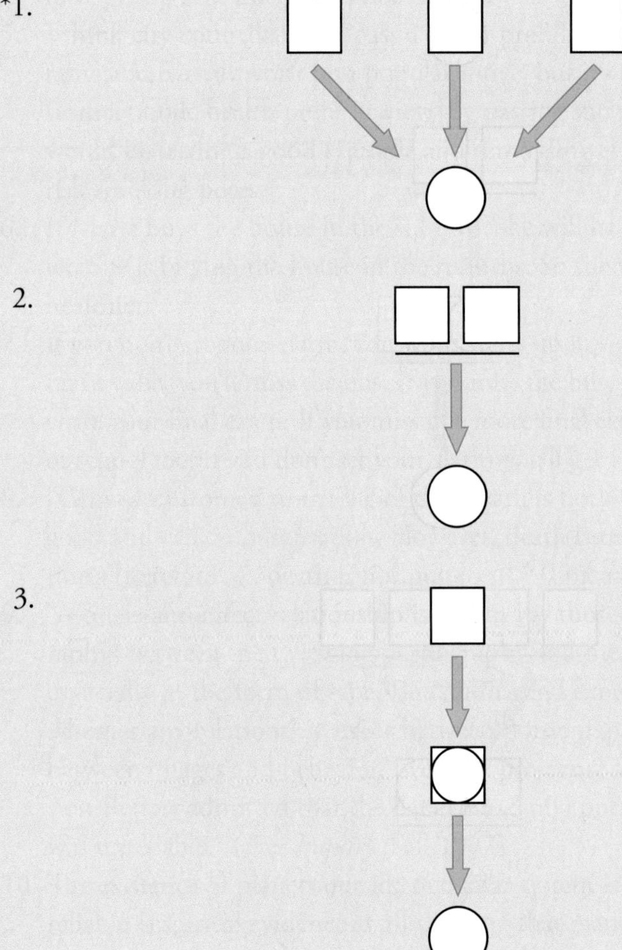

or habitat damage. We also have programs like Oceans Wise that will tell you if the shrimp you want to buy for the barbecue or order in a restaurant won't harm the oceans they come from. Shrimp should be something special we eat in celebration of special events like World Oceans Day! Fortunately the timing coincides with the B.C. spot prawn season. Yes, you will pay more for the shrimp you eat but the oceans will pay less for your choices. Your long-term gain will be appreciating and eating other marine life for much longer." (Sarah Foster, InformedOpinions.org, 5 June 2014)

3. "The fifth way [of proving that God exists] is taken from the governance of the world. We see that things that lack knowledge, such as natural bodies, act for an end, and this is evident from their acting always, or nearly always, in the same way, so as to obtain the best result. Hence it is plain that they achieve their end, not fortuitously, but designedly. Now whatever lacks knowledge cannot move towards an end, unless it be directed by some being endowed with knowledge and intelligence; as the arrow is directed by the archer. Therefore some intelligent being exists by whom all natural things are directed to their end; and this being we call God." (Thomas Aquinas, *Summa Theologica*)
4. "The first thing that must occur to anyone studying moral subjectivism [the view that the rightness or wrongness of an action depends on the beliefs of an individual or group] seriously is that the view allows the possibility that an action can be both right and not right, or wrong and not wrong, etc. This possibility exists because, as we have seen, the subjectivist claims that the moral character of an action is determined by individual subjective states; and these states can vary from person to person, even when directed toward the same action on the same occasion. Hence one and the same action can evidently be determined to have—simultaneously—radically different moral characters. . . . [If] subjectivism . . . does generate such contradictory conclusions, the position is certainly untenable." (Phillip Montague, *Reason and Responsibility*)
5. I just heard about another lawsuit accusing the Vatican of hiding instances of sexual abuse by priests in Canada and the United States. Sexual abuse is never OK, but I think such cases should be dismissed by courts in light of the community stature and function of priests and the benefits that accrue to society in the aftermath of the decision. Let's consider community stature first. The community stature of priests must always be taken into account in these abuse cases. A priest is not just anybody; he performs a special role in society—namely, to provide spiritual guidance and to remind people that there is both a moral order and a divine order in the world. The priest's role is special because it helps to underpin and secure society itself. Anything that could undermine this role must be neutralized as soon as possible. Among those things that can weaken the

priestly role are publicity, public debate, and legal actions. Abuse cases are better handled in private by those who are keenly aware of the importance of a positive public image of priests. And what of the benefits of curtailing the legal proceedings? The benefits to society of dismissing the legal case outweigh all the alleged disadvantages of continuing with public hearings. The primary benefit is the continued nurturing of the community's faith, without which the community would cease to function effectively.

SUMMARY

Arguments come in two forms: deductive and inductive. A deductive argument is intended to provide logically conclusive support for a conclusion; an inductive one is intended to provide probable support for a conclusion. Deductive arguments can be valid or invalid, whereas inductive arguments are strong or weak. A valid argument with true premises is said to be sound. A strong argument with true premises is said to be cogent.

Evaluating an argument is the most important skill of critical thinking. It involves finding the conclusion and premises, checking to see if the argument is deductive or inductive, determining its validity or strength, and discovering if the premises are true or false. Sometimes you also have to ferret out implicit, or unstated, premises.

Arguments can come in certain common patterns, or forms. Two valid forms that you will often run into are *modus ponens* (affirming the antecedent) and *modus tollens* (denying the consequent). Two common invalid forms are denying the antecedent and affirming the consequent.

Analyzing the structure of arguments is easier if you diagram them. Argument diagrams can help you visualize the function of premises and conclusions and the relationships among complex arguments with several sub-arguments.

Assessing very long arguments can be challenging because they may contain lots of verbiage but few or no arguments, and many premises can be implicit. Evaluating long arguments, though, requires the same basic steps as assessing short ones: (1) ensure that you understand the argument, (2) find the conclusion, (3) find the premises, and (4) diagram the argument to clarify logical relationships.

Field Problems

1. Find a short passage online claiming to present an argument for a particular view but that actually contains no real arguments at all. A good way to begin is by doing the following Google search: Google the phrase "I

strongly believe" or something similar (in quotation marks), along with a word representing a favourite topic of your choosing—politics, religion, sports, animal rights, whatever. Such a search will almost certainly lead you to some strong statement of opinion presented without sufficient argumentation. Then rewrite the passage and include an argument for the original view.

2. Visit a website intended to support a particular view on a social or political issue. Using the information on the website, write a 300-word passage containing an argument for a view that the website might endorse.
3. The next time you're watching television with commercials, find the argument in one commercial (why should you buy this car or visit that place or vote for that person). Write out its premises and conclusion. Are any of its premises hidden? Find another that contains no argument at all. If it contains no argument, does it still try to convince you of something? How?

Self-Assessment Quiz

1. What is a deductive argument? An inductive argument?
2. What is a valid argument? An invalid one? What is an inductive argument? What is a *strong* inductive argument?
3. What is the difference between a cogent argument and a sound argument?

Say whether the following arguments are deductive or inductive.

4. If you don't stop talking, then you're going to embarrass yourself. You seem determined to keep talking. So, you're just going to end up embarrassing yourself.
5. There's an 80 per cent chance that the hurricane will veer northward tomorrow and hit Halifax. So Halifax will probably feel the force of the hurricane tomorrow.
6. Professor Goss is an expert. Whatever he says about accounting has got to be true.
7. Whatever Bill Nye the Science Guy says is true. He says that the Earth's climate is getting warmer. So the climate must really be getting warmer.

In each of the following arguments, identify the implicit premise that will make the argument either valid or strong.

8. Spizzirri has ordered his engineers to design a perpetual motion machine. Clearly he has no idea how the laws of physics work.

9. KC Roberts and the Live Revolution is a funk band. So they're not likely to play any Nickelback tunes during their show Saturday night.
10. If 60 per cent of people believe in astrology or tarot cards, the future of the country does not look bright. Grades in university science courses will probably drop dramatically.
11. For each of the following exercises, give an example of the argument pattern indicated.
    a. *Modus ponens*
    b. *Modus tollens*
    c. Denying the antecedent
    d. Affirming the consequent

Diagram the following arguments:

12. Bullock is in a bad mood. He was rude to me this morning, and Martha said he didn't even apologize when he bumped into her this afternoon.
13. The TV is on. The only people who could have turned it on are my girlfriend or me. Since my girlfriend is at work, and I didn't turn it on, no person could have turned it on. Oh my goodness it must have been a ghost!
14. If dolphins have minds comparable to ours, then these creatures are self-conscious, intelligent, and creative. If they are self-conscious, then they should react appropriately when they see their reflections in a mirror. They do react appropriately. If they're intelligent, they should be able to solve complex problems. They can solve such problems. If they're creative, they should be able to create some form of art. In a rudimentary way, they do create art. They are definitely self-conscious, intelligent, and creative.
15. If the rule against lying were really a universal moral rule, then it should come naturally to everyone. But it does not come naturally to everyone, because we all know lying is actually very common. So the rule against lying is not a universal moral rule.
16. It is absolutely unacceptable for anyone to bring cats into my house. Cats shed everywhere, and I have a serious allergy to fur. I also can't stand their constant meowing. The sound drives me crazy!
17. Creationism is an inadequate theory about the origins of life. It conflicts with science, and it is incapable of predicting any new facts.

Integrative Exercises

These exercises pertain to material in Chapters 1–3. For each of the following passages, state whether it contains an argument. If it does, specify the conclusion and premises, any argument-indicator words, whether the argument is deductive or inductive, and whether it contains an example of face-saving or group-pressure thinking. Also identify any implicit premises and diagram the argument.

1. Dr Jeckel, the world's leading expert on schizophrenia, has suggested that the mental disorder is a direct result of psychological trauma suffered during early childhood. He sounds like he knows what he's talking about, so that must be the cause of schizophrenia.
2. If today's more-potent marijuana were more dangerous than the marijuana of days gone by, then you would expect to see more drug-related deaths in Europe, where hashish—a more-potent drug from the same plant as marijuana—is more common. But we do not, in fact, see higher rates of drug-related deaths in Europe. So marijuana that is more potent is not necessarily more dangerous.
3. "In the wake of the attacks of September 11th, 2001, the governments of Canada and the United States have passed sweeping anti-terrorism bills that effectively lay the groundwork for the criminalization of ideas. One consequence has been . . . the policing of freedom of expression. In Canada, a post–September 11th exhibit of contemporary Arab-Canadian art at the National Museum in Ottawa was abruptly cancelled by the organizers to allow the curators to 'reconsider' the political works on display: the exhibition did go ahead as scheduled, but only after a determined public campaign challenging the museum's actions." (*Alternative Press Review*, Spring 2002)
4. "[Is] there scientific evidence that prayer really works? . . . The problem with . . . any so-called controlled experiment regarding prayer is that *there can be no such thing as a controlled experiment concerning prayer.* You can never divide people into groups that received prayer and those that did not. The main reason is that there is no way to know that someone did not receive prayer. How would anyone know that some distant relative was not praying for a member of the group . . . identified as having received no prayer?" (*Free Inquiry,* Summer 1997)
5. "The handling of Occupy Vancouver by the authorities is eroding public faith in the rule of law. It is clear that what started as a protest with significant public sympathy for the core cause has now settled into a squat by people who either believe they are not covered by the laws that govern everyone else or who are spoiling for a confrontation with authorities." (*Vancouver Sun*, 11 November 2011)
6. "[C]urrent-day Christians use violence to spread their right-to-life message. These Christians, often referred to as the religious right, are well

known for violent demonstrations against Planned Parenthood and other abortion clinics. Doctors and other personnel are threatened with death, clinics have been bombed, there have even been cases of doctors being murdered." (Letter to the editor, *Daily Wildcat,* 17 September 2002)

7. Life on Earth today is better than it has ever been. We have technologies that our grandparents could only dream of. Life expectancies keep going up and up. And, despite all the criticisms, I just don't think there's anything wrong with our modern consumer culture.
8. Alfred has decided that the best way for his company to save money is for it to dump its waste into the ocean instead of paying to dispose of it properly. Unfortunately, this practice is highly controversial. Therefore, it is very likely that Alfred's company will be featured in the local magazine's next issue as the worst business in town.
9. We evaluated the accuracy of recent news reports on a wide range of news topics. We focused on reports aired or published by three major media outlets. We found that 40 per cent of their news reports were highly inaccurate. So, though it's hard to believe, 40 per cent of all the news reports that people are exposed to are questionable.
10. Allow me to explain to you why I think that hockey is the greatest sport ever in the history of the entire world. It is incredibly fast paced since skating allows the players to move at great speeds. Also, there is a lot of skill is involved in controlling such a small puck with something like a hockey stick with so much precision. Lastly, the checking and even fighting makes the sport very physical and exciting to watch.
11. People who have more than 10 pairs of shoes are not financially responsible. There's no reason to have that many pairs of shoes since there wouldn't even be time to wear them all. And people who spend money on things they can't use are obviously irresponsible with their money. Also, my mom only has a couple of pairs of shoes and she's the most financially responsible person I know.
12. If sex education in the schools can reduce the teen pregnancy rate or help delay the onset of teen sexual activity, I'm all for it. A recent study of several hundred teens showed that sex education in school lowered the incidence of teen pregnancy. We should have sex ed in all public schools.
13. The worst calamity that will befall the world in the next 20 years will be the use of small nuclear weapons by terrorists or rogue states. The death toll from such a state of affairs is likely to be higher than that of any other kind of human devastation. The United Nations just issued a report that comes to the same conclusion. We should act now to prevent the proliferation of nuclear weapons and nuclear-weapons-grade material from falling into the wrong hands.

14. Many surveys show that most people not only believe in "remote viewing" (the ability to observe distant locations without using the physical senses), but also think that science has already proved its existence. This demonstrates that the majority of people are scientifically illiterate. If they understood the least bit about the methods of science and how it reaches conclusions, they would denounce silly ideas like remote viewing—or at least not accept them blindly.
15. Magazines regularly publish articles on "the sexiest man alive" or "the most beautiful woman in the world." All you have to do to see that these claims of superior attractiveness are crazy is to stroll down any main thoroughfare in any nation's capital. There you will see people—male and female—who make the magazines' favourite personifications of beauty or sexiness look like dogs.
16. The movie *The Godfather* is praised by many as one of the greatest mobster films ever produced. Even Mafia members have remarked on the astounding accuracy with which their lifestyles were recreated on the big screen, and critics consider historical accuracy a vital characteristic of a good mobster film. Marlon Brando and Al Pacino were both credited with delivering outstanding performances.
17. Peanuts are good for you. A million little monkeys can't be wrong.
18. "There is no justice in the world. Amelia Earhart's plane went down, and despite 50 years of looking, no one has ever been able to find her. But Yasser Arafat's plane goes down, and he's rescued in 15 minutes." (Jay Leno, *The Tonight Show*)
19. "So Stephen Harper has officially declared that the time for debating Canada's presence in Afghanistan is over (*Now* magazine, 16–22 March 2006). I have the utmost respect for our soldiers, but don't we owe it to them to have a legitimate debate on the issue to ensure they're there for the right reasons? Years into the mission, the government has completely lost sight of why we went in the first place and has become more concerned with saving face. Now that we're being told Canada might be in Afghanistan upwards of 10 years, there's never been a more important time for debating the issue. This idea of giving the government unquestioned support for war is dangerously close to the backwards mentality of the US." (Letter to the editor, *Now* magazine, 23–29 March 2006)
20. Freedom is a necessary component of the good life. The good life is something that every human being has a right to. Everything that humans have a right to should be acquired by any means necessary. Therefore, any war conducted to secure freedom for any of us is justified.

Critical Thinking and Writing Exercise

From Thesis to Outline

In the Critical Thinking and Writing Exercise in Chapter 1, we saw that the second step in writing an argumentative essay (after determining your thesis statement, or conclusion) is to create an outline. Outlines are useful because, among other things, they help avert disaster in the essay-writing phase. Imagine writing two-thirds of your essay, then discovering that the second premise of your argument cannot be supported and is, in fact, false. You might have to throw out the whole argument and start over.

At the head of your outline, insert your thesis statement, expressing it as clearly and as precisely as possible. At every stage of outlining, you can then refer to the statement for guidance. The premises and conclusion of your argument (or arguments) will constitute the major points of your outline. The following, for example, is the preliminary outline for the essay discussed in Module 2:

> Thesis: Allowing coal-burning power plants to emit more sulphur dioxide will most likely increase the incidence of respiratory illnesses.
>
> I. High amounts of sulphur dioxide in the air have been linked to increases in the incidence of asthma and other respiratory illnesses.
> II. Many areas of the country already have high amounts of sulphur dioxide in the air.
> III. Most sulphur dioxide in the air comes from coal-burning power plants.
> IV. Therefore, allowing coal-burning power plants to emit more sulphur dioxide will most likely increase the incidence of respiratory illnesses.

After you clearly state the premises, you need to ask yourself whether any of them need to be defended. As we discussed in Module 1, any premise likely to be questioned by your readers will need support. That is, the premise itself will need arguments to back it up, and the supporting arguments should be indicated in your outline. (Some premises, though, may not need support because they are obvious or generally accepted.) As discussed in this chapter, you can support a premise (claim) through deductive or inductive arguments with premises made up of examples, analogies, empirical evidence (such as scientific research or trustworthy observations), and authoritative judgments (such as those from reliable experts). Here's how the preceding outline might look with (fictional) supporting arguments clearly shown:

> **THESIS:** Allowing coal-burning power plants to emit more sulphur dioxide will most likely increase the incidence of respiratory illnesses.

I. High amounts of sulphur dioxide in the air have been linked to increases in the incidence of asthma and other respiratory illnesses.
   A. Environment Canada data show an association between high amounts of sulphur dioxide and increased respiratory illnesses.
   B. Cities that monitor air pollution have noted increases in hospital admissions for asthma and other respiratory illnesses when sulphur dioxide emissions are high.
II. Many areas of the country already have high amounts of sulphur dioxide in the air.
   A. Scientists have reported high levels of sulphur dioxide in the air in 15 major cities.
III. Most sulphur dioxide in the air comes from coal-burning power plants.
   A. Many environmental scientists assert that coal-burning power plants are the source of most sulphur dioxide.
   B. A few owners of coal-burning power plants admit that their plants emit most of the sulphur dioxide in their region.
IV. Therefore, allowing coal-burning power plants to emit more sulphur dioxide will most likely increase the incidence of respiratory illnesses.

You should expand your outline until you've indicated how you intend to provide support for each claim that requires it. This level of detail helps ensure that you will not encounter any nasty surprises in the writing phase.

Your essay should somehow address objections or criticisms that your readers are likely to raise, and your outline should show how you intend to do this. Answering objections can make your case stronger and lend credibility to you as the writer. Sometimes it's best to address objections where they are likely to arise—in connection with specific premises or arguments. At other times, your essay may be more effective if you deal with objections at the end of it, near the conclusion.

As you work through your outline, don't be afraid to rework your thesis statement or to make changes in arguments. Satisfy yourself that the outline is complete and that it reflects a logical progression of points.

Argument and Ambiguity

Good writing is clear writing. Writing that lacks clarity is ineffective—not to mention exasperating to its readers and sometimes embarrassing to its writer. An argument with unclear premises or conclusion is likewise ineffective. The lack of clarity undermines the argument, perhaps even rendering it useless.

Ambiguity is one of the many ways that a piece of writing can be unclear. A term or statement is ambiguous if it has more than one meaning and if the context doesn't reveal which meaning is intended. Consider these claims:

1. Morgan ate the ice cream with relish.

2. Kids make nutritious snacks.
3. It is impossible to live on water.
4. John met the girl that he married at a dance.
5. Helen saw the bird with powerful binoculars.
6. Luc hit the boy with the book.
7. The guy was all over the road; I had to swerve a number of times before I hit him.
8. Officers help dog bite victims.
9. Include your children when baking cookies.

All these claims are ambiguous, but they are ambiguous in different ways. Claims 1, 2, and 3 involve *semantic ambiguities.* Semantic ambiguities are due to possible multiple meanings of a word or phrase. In claim 1 the phrase "with relish" could mean "accompanied by a condiment" or "with pleasure or delight." In claim 2 the word "make" could mean either "prepare" or "constitute"—a difference between the kids' making food and *being* food. In claim 3 the phrase "live on water" could mean "subsist by ingesting water" or "reside on water"—a distinction between the culinary and the sociological.

Semantic ambiguities often spark unnecessary and tedious debates. Disputants, for example, may disagree dramatically over whether a photo in a magazine is pornographic—but they disagree only because they have different ideas about what the term *pornographic* means. They may actually be in agreement about which photos they find offensive. But to one person, *pornographic* may describe any representation of nudity. To another person, *pornographic* may refer only to depictions of sexual acts.

Claims 4, 5, and 6 involve *syntactic ambiguities.* Syntactic ambiguities arise because of the sloppy way that words are combined. In claim 4 did John meet his bride-to-be at a dance, or did he marry her at a dance? In claim 5 did Helen use the binoculars, or did the bird use them? In claim 6 did Luc use a book to smack the boy, or did Luc smack a boy who was carrying a book?

Claims 7, 8, and 9 are not plainly either semantically or syntactically ambiguous, but they are unclear (and silly) just the same. In claim 7 was the writer deliberately trying to hit the guy or not? In claim 8 are the officers helping people who had been bitten, or are they using dogs to bite people? In claim 9 are we supposed to bake cookies alongside our children—or bake the children *into the cookies*?

As a critical reader, your job is to be on alert for possible ambiguities, to understand the contexts that can help clear up ambiguities, and to constantly ask, "What does this mean?" If the meaning of a claim is unclear, you are under no obligation to accept it. Likewise, if an argument contains ambiguous claims, you need not accept the argument.

As a critical writer, your job is *not* to suppose that your readers will understand exactly what you mean but to strive to be perfectly clear about what you mean. Inexperienced writers too often assume that because they know what they mean, others will know too. The best corrective for unclear or ambiguous writing is the objective stance—the viewing of your writing from the standpoint of others. Good writers try hard to view their writing as others will, to step back mentally and try to imagine coming to their writing for the first time. In effect, they ask themselves, "Will my audience understand what I mean?" Achieving an objective attitude toward your writing is not easy. One thing that helps is to put your writing aside for a day or two after you complete it and then read it cold. Often after this "cooling down" period, passages that you thought were unambiguous turn out to be murky.

Another good tactic, of course, is to state explicitly what you intend your words to mean by offering a definition. But of course, you can't offer definitions for *every* word you use—not without ruining the "flow" of your essay. So definitions, while useful, must be used sparingly. (For more about definitions, see "Defining Terms" on page 168.)

Writing Assignments

1. Create an outline for Essay 3 ("Marine Parks") in Appendix A. Specify the thesis statement, each premise, arguments supporting premises, any objections considered, and the conclusion.
2. Study the argument presented in Essay 7 ("Yes, Human Cloning Should Be Permitted") in Appendix A. Identify the conclusion and the premises and objections considered. Then write a two-page critique of the essay's argument.
3. Select an issue from the following list and write a three-page paper defending a claim pertaining to the issue. Follow the procedure discussed in the text for outlining the essay and choosing a thesis and an appropriate argument to defend it. Where necessary, clarify terms.
   - Should Canada seek diplomatic ties with North Korea—a dictatorship with a terrible history of human-rights violations?
   - In the fight against terrorism, should law-enforcement agencies be allowed to spy on Canadian citizens by monitoring their email, wire-tapping their phones, and checking records from public libraries—all without warrants?
   - Should a city government celebrate its citizens' cultural diversity or instead focus on its citizens' fundamental similarities?
   - Should children as young as 10 years of age be encouraged to carry cellphones?

PART TWO

REASONS

4 REASONS FOR BELIEF AND DOUBT

CHAPTER OBJECTIVES

When Claims Conflict

You will be able to

- understand that when a claim conflicts with other claims we have good reason to accept, we have good grounds for doubting it.
- recognize that if a claim conflicts with our background information, we have good reason to doubt it.
- appreciate that when we are confronted with a claim that is neither completely dubious nor fully credible, we should proportion our belief to the evidence.
- realize that it is not reasonable to believe a claim when there is no good reason for doing so.

Experts and Evidence

You will be able to

- understand what makes someone an expert and what does not.
- understand that if a claim conflicts with expert opinion, we have good reason to doubt it.
- realize that when the experts disagree about a claim, we have good reason to suspend judgment.
- recognize fallacious appeals to authority.
- distinguish true experts from non-experts by using the four indicators of expertise.

Personal Experience

You will be able to

- understand that it is reasonable to accept the evidence provided by personal experience only if there is no good reason to doubt it.

- appreciate the importance of the common factors that can give us good reason to doubt the reliability of personal experience—impairment, expectation, and innumeracy.

Fooling Ourselves

You will be able to

- appreciate why we need to resist the human tendency to resist contrary evidence.
- become sensitive to the possibility of confirmation bias.
- be alert to the possibility of the availability error.

Claims in the News

You will be able to

- gain a basic understanding of how the news media work and what factors influence the claims they generate.
- understand the skills involved in evaluating claims in the news.

Advertising and Persuasion

You will be able to

- understand and apply the guiding principle for thinking critically about advertising.
- exhibit familiarity with common tactics of persuasion used in advertising.

Let's remind ourselves once again why we've come this way. If we care whether our beliefs are true or reliable, whether we can safely use them to guide our steps and inform our choices, then we must care about the reasons for accepting those beliefs. The better the reasons for acceptance, the more likely are the beliefs, or statements, to be true. Inadequate reasons, no reasons, or fake reasons (discussed in the next chapter) should lead us not to accept a statement, but to doubt it.

As we saw in earlier chapters, the reasons for accepting a statement are often spelled out in the form of an argument, with the statement being the conclusion. The reasons and conclusion together might compose a deductive argument or an inductive argument. In such cases, the reasons are normally there in plain sight. But in our daily lives, statements or claims usually confront us alone without any accompanying stated reasons. An unsupported claim may be the premise of an argument (and its truth value may then determine whether the argument is sound or cogent). Or it may simply be a stand-alone assertion of fact. Either way, if we care whether the claim is acceptable, we must try to evaluate the claim as it stands.

Of course, it helps to be knowledgeable about the subject matter of a claim. But it can be even more useful to understand and apply some critical thinking principles for assessing unsupported claims. Let's take a close look at these principles.

WHEN CLAIMS CONFLICT

> "The whole problem with the world is that fools and fanatics are always so certain of themselves, but wiser people so full of doubts."
>
> —*Bertrand Russell*

Suppose you come across this claim in a reputable local newspaper:

> [Claim 1] The historic CHUM–CityTV building at the corner of Queen and John was demolished yesterday to make way for a parking lot.

But say you also have very good reasons to believe this claim:

> [Claim 2] The historic CHUM–CityTV building at the corner of Queen and John was *not* demolished yesterday to make way for a parking lot.

What do you make of such a conflict between claims? Well, as a good critical thinker, you can know at least that this conflict means that you have good reason to doubt claim 1 and therefore have no good grounds for accepting it. You have good reason to doubt it because it conflicts with another claim you have good reason to believe (claim 2). When two claims conflict, they simply cannot both be true; at least one of them has to be false. So the following principle comes into play:

> *If a claim conflicts with other claims we have good reason to accept, we have good grounds for doubting it.*

With conflicting claims, you are not justified in believing either one of them until you resolve the conflict. Sometimes this job is easy. If, for example, the competing claims are reports of personal observations, you can often decide between them by making further observations. If a friend says your dog is sleeping on top of your car, and you say your dog is not sleeping on top of your car (because you checked a short time ago), you can see who's right by simply looking at the roof of your car. (Remember, though, that even personal observations can sometimes mislead us, as we'll soon see.)

Many times, however, sorting out conflicting claims requires a deeper inquiry. You may need to do some research to see what evidence exists for each of the claims. In the best-case scenario, you may quickly discover that one of the claims is not credible because it comes from an unreliable source (a subject taken up in the next few pages).

background information
The large collection of very well-supported beliefs that we all rely on to inform our actions and choices. It consists of basic facts about everyday things, beliefs based on very good evidence (including our own personal observations and excellent authority), and justified claims that we would regard as "common sense" or "common knowledge."

Now suppose that you're confronted with another type of conflict—this time a conflict between a claim and your **background information**. Background information is that huge collection of very well-supported beliefs that

FOOD FOR THOUGHT

Fact and Opinion

When we evaluate claims, we are often concerned with making a distinction between facts and opinions. But just what is the difference? We normally use the word *fact* in two senses. First, we may use it to refer to a state of affairs—as in "We should examine the evidence and find out the facts." Second, and more commonly, we use *fact* to refer to true statements—as in "John smashed the dinnerware—that's a fact." Thus, we say that some claims, or statements, are facts (or are factual) and some are not. We use the word *opinion*, however, to refer to a belief—as in "It's John's opinion that he did not smash the dinnerware." Some opinions are true, so they are facts. Some opinions are not true, so they are not facts.

Sometimes we may hear somebody say, "That's a matter of opinion." What does this mean? Often it's equivalent to something like "Opinions differ on this issue" or "There are many different opinions on this." But it also frequently means that the issue is not a matter of objective fact but is entirely subjective, a matter of individual taste. Statements expressing matters of opinion in this latter sense are not the kind of things that people can disagree on, just as two people cannot sensibly disagree about whether they like chocolate ice cream.

we all rely on to inform our actions and choices. A great deal of this knowledge consists of basic facts about everyday things, beliefs based on very good evidence (including our own personal observations and excellent authority), and justified claims that we would regard as "common sense" or "common knowledge." Suppose, then, that you're asked to accept this unsupported claim:

> Some babies can bench-press a 500-kilogram weight.

You are not likely to give much credence to this claim for the simple reason that it conflicts with an enormous number of your background beliefs concerning human physiology, gravity, weightlifting, and who knows what else. Given what you already know, the odds of that claim being true are very low.

Or how about this claim:

> The prime minister is entirely under the control of the chief justice of the Supreme Court of Canada.

This claim is not as ridiculous as the previous one, but it too conflicts with our background beliefs, specifically those having to do with the structure and workings of the Canadian government. So we would have good reason to doubt this one also.

The principle we are using here is this:

> *If a claim conflicts with our background information, we have good reason to doubt it.*

Other things being equal, the more background information the claim conflicts with, the more reason we have to doubt it. We would normally—and rightfully—assign a low probability to any claim that conflicts with a great deal of our background information.

You would be entitled, for example, to have a *little* doubt about the claim that Joan is late for work if it conflicts with your background information that Joan has never been late for work in the 10 years you've known her. But you are entitled to have very *strong* doubts about, and to assign very low credibility to, the claim that André can turn a stone into gold just by touching it. You could even reasonably dismiss the claim without further investigation. Such a claim conflicts with too much of what we know about the physical world.

It's always possible, of course, that a conflicting claim is true and some of our background information is unfounded. So in many cases it's reasonable for us to examine a conflicting claim more closely. If we find that it has no good reasons in its favour and that it is not credible, we may reject it. If, on the other hand, we discover that there are strong reasons for accepting the new claim, we may need to revise our background information. For example, we may be forced to accept the claim about André's golden touch (and to rethink some of our background information) if the claim is backed by strong supporting evidence. Our background information would be in need of some serious revision if André could produce this stone-to-gold transformation repeatedly under scientifically controlled conditions that ruled out error, fraud, and trickery.

So it is not reasonable to accept a claim if there is good reason to doubt it. And sometimes, if the claim is dubious enough, we may be justified in dismissing a claim out of hand. But what should we believe about a claim that is not quite dubious enough to discard immediately and yet not worthy of complete acceptance? We should measure out our belief according to the strength of reasons. That is,

We should proportion our belief to the evidence.

"A belief which leaves no place for doubt is not a belief; it is a superstition."

—José Bergamin

The more evidence a claim has in its favour, the stronger our belief in it should be. Weak evidence for a claim warrants weak belief; strong evidence warrants strong belief. And the strength of our beliefs should vary across this spectrum as the evidence dictates.

Implicit in all of the foregoing is a principle that deserves to be made explicit because it's so often ignored:

It's not reasonable to believe a claim when there is no good reason for doing so.

The famous twentieth-century philosopher Bertrand Russell tried hard to drive this idea home. As he put it, "It is undesirable to believe a proposition when there is no ground whatever for supposing it true."[1]

FOOD FOR THOUGHT

Folk Psychology

A big part of our "background information" comes from folk psychology, the skill we all have for correctly attributing to other people (and sometimes animals) moods, beliefs, desires, intentions, memories, and so on. We use the fact that other people have those things as a way to explain and predict their behaviour.

Have you ever seen someone lifting cushions off a couch one at a time, or lifting up pieces of paper on a desk to look under them? If you have, you probably immediately knew what was going on: he or she was *searching for something*. You recognize the behaviour: that's what searching looks like. Or imagine you know that your friend John loves chocolate and hates vanilla. The waiter at lunch tells you that the desert special today is chocolate or vanilla. What will John choose? Yes, you can predict the future here, and quite easily. John will choose chocolate. How do you know? Not just because you know that John loves chocolate, but because you know that *people tend to choose things they love.*

The term *folk psychology* was coined by the philosopher Daniel Dennett in 1981. It consists, according to Dennett, of the stuff *everyone knows* about how other people's minds work. You know that other people have hopes and dreams; that they love some things and hate other things; that they remember things that happen to them; that they can perceive the world around them using their senses of sight, smell, hearing, touch, and so on.

Our capacity for folk psychology is truly essential; it's what allows us to live and work together in groups. Folk psychology is what lets you know that punching someone will make them *mad*, that gossiping about them will hurt their *feelings*, and that flirting with their girlfriend will make them *jealous*. And you can typically predict how they might act *in response*. Folk psychology is also what allows you to motivate them to alter their behaviour: you know that they will have a tendency to do more of something if you reward them for it, and to do less of something if you punish them for it.

For that matter, if it weren't for our command of folk psychology, how could we ever do something like driving on a highway? Think about it: hundreds of vehicles zooming all around us, each one of them a potentially lethal threat. How do we know that this is actually a pretty safe activity? Because we know that humans generally try to avoid getting killed, and so you can generally expect other drivers to behave in ways that will help them avoid an accident that might kill them as well as you.

Our capacity for folk psychology is, however, imperfect. Sometimes people make no sense to us: we see their behaviour, but can't map it onto any particular understanding of what is on their mind. Sometimes it may simply reflect the fact that different people are different – we don't all think identically. So we may find ourselves truly puzzled, and ask ourselves, "What on earth are they *doing*?" But the very fact that we sometimes ask this question just reinforces the fact that we do understand other people as creatures with minds, beings that have beliefs and act upon them. If we didn't see other people that way, if we didn't see them as *doing* things intentionally, we wouldn't bother to wonder *why* they do what they do.

EXPERTS AND EVIDENCE

When an unsupported claim—one for which no premises have been provided—doesn't conflict with what we already know, we are often justified in believing it because it comes from experts. An **expert** is someone who is more knowledgeable in a particular subject area or field than most other people are.

expert Someone who is more knowledgeable in a particular subject area or field than most others are.

Experts provide us with reasons for believing a claim because, in their specialty areas, they are more likely to be right than we are. They are more likely to be right because (1) they have access to *more information* on the subject than we do and (2) they are *better at judging* that information than we are. Experts are familiar with the established facts and existing data in their field and know how to properly evaluate that information. Essentially, this means that they have a handle on the information and know how to assess the evidence and arguments for particular claims involving that information. They are true authorities on a specified subject. Someone who knows the basic information relevant to a particular field but who can't evaluate the reliability of a claim is no expert.

In a complex world where we can never be knowledgeable in every field, we must rely on experts—a perfectly legitimate state of affairs. But good critical thinkers are careful about expert opinion, guiding their use of experts by some commonsense principles. One such principle is this:

If a claim conflicts with expert opinion, we have good reason to doubt it.

This principle follows from our definition of experts. If they really are more likely to be right than non-experts about claims in their field, then any claims that conflict with expert opinion are, at least initially, dubious.

Here's the companion principle to the first:

When there is disagreement about a claim among the relevant experts, we have good reason to doubt it.

If a claim is in dispute among experts, then non-experts can have no good reason for accepting (or rejecting) it. Throwing up your hands and arbitrarily deciding to believe or disbelieve the claim is not a reasonable response. The claim must remain in doubt until the experts resolve the conflict or you resolve the conflict yourself by becoming informed enough to decide competently on the issues and evidence involved—a course that's possible but usually not feasible for non-experts.

Sometimes we may have good reason to be suspicious of unsupported claims, even when they are purportedly derived from expert opinion. Our doubt is justified when a claim comes from someone deemed to be an expert who in fact is not an expert. When we rely on

"Your wife feels that your cat needs to hear an authoritative male voice."

CREDIT: J.B. Handelsman: J.B. Handelsman/The New Yorker Collection/The Cartoon Bank

EVERYDAY PROBLEMS AND DECISIONS

It's at the Drugstore. Should I Buy It?

One of the most important decisions you can make—one of the most important *kinds* of decisions—concerns the question of who you should trust when seeking health advice. Health is an area in which we are almost certain to need to rely on the advice of experts. Health is complex because the human body is complex, as is the way that body interacts with its environment. And good health is what allows us to enjoy many of the other things we enjoy in life, so making good decisions is important. Some health-related decisions necessarily involve the input of licensed health professionals such as physicians and public-health nurses. Other decisions are ones we might make on our own. A trip to the local pharmacy, for example, might leave us asking whether to buy some of the products we see on the shelves there. Should we trust them just because the packages imply that these products will keep us healthy or restore our health when we're sick? What about the fact that these products are being sold at a pharmacy, rather than at a corner store? Is that a guarantee of quality? In fact, there are all sorts of products for sale at your local drugstore that you probably should not trust. Before you buy that "amazing" and "all-natural" cold remedy or that bracelet that is "guaranteed" to improve your "overall well-being," ask yourself:

- Does the product packaging clearly specify what the product will do, or does it use vague weasel words, with claims that it will "support" health or "boost" your immune system?
- Does the packaging include warnings to the effect that "these claims have not been verified by Health Canada" or fine print stating that "this product is not intended to treat or cure any disease"?
- Does the product claim to be "amazing," "revolutionary," or "all-natural"? Reputable makers of health products rarely use such words.

If in doubt, talk directly to the pharmacist, and ask tough questions: is there substantial, reliable evidence that this product will work? It's the pharmacist's job to know such things. So if he or she says no, or doesn't know, don't buy!

such bogus expert opinion, we commit the fallacy known as the **appeal to authority**.

appeal to authority The fallacy of relying on the opinion of someone deemed to be an expert who in fact is not an expert.

The fallacious appeal to authority usually happens in one of two ways. First, we may find ourselves disregarding this important rule of thumb: just because someone is an expert in one field, he or she is not necessarily an expert in another. The opinion of experts generally carries more weight than our own—but only in their own areas of expertise. Any opinions that they put forward outside their fields are no more authoritative than those of non-experts. Outside their fields, they are not experts.

We don't need to look far for real-life examples of such skewed appeals to authority. On any day of the week we may be urged to accept claims in one field that are based on the opinion of an expert from unrelated fields. An electrical engineer or Nobel Prize–winning chemist may assert that certain herbs can cure cancer. A radio talk-show host with a degree in physiology may give relationship advice. A geneticist expresses opinions about how to reform financial institutions. Sometimes the lack of relevant expertise is quite subtle: a scientist with expertise relevant to detecting global warming may not have the relevant expertise to tell us what we can or should *do* about global warming. The point is not that these experts can't be right, but that their expertise in a particular field doesn't give us reason to believe their pronouncements in another. There is no such thing as a general expert, only experts in specific subject areas.

Second, we may fall into a fallacious appeal to authority by regarding a non-expert as an expert. We forget that a non-expert—even one with prestige, status, or sex appeal—is still a non-expert. Movie stars, TV actors, renowned athletes, and famous politicians endorse products of all kinds in TV and print advertising. Such people may be very good at what they do, but they are not experts in the sense in which we are using the word here. And when they speak outside their areas of talent and experience (which is almost always the case), they give us no good reason for believing that the products are as advertised. Advertisers, of course, know this, but they hope that we will buy the products anyway because of the appeal or attractiveness of the celebrity endorsers.

Historically regarding a non-expert as an expert has probably been the most prevalent form of the appeal to authority—with disastrous results. Political, religious, tribal, and cultural leaders have often been considered to be authorities, not because they knew the facts and could judge the evidence correctly, but because culture, tradition, or whim dictated that they be regarded as authorities. When these "authorities" spoke, people listened and believed—then went to war, persecuted unbelievers, or undertook countless other ill-conceived projects. If we are to avoid this trap, we must look beyond mere labels and titles and ask, "Does this person provide us with any good reasons or evidence?"

This question, of course, is just another way of asking if someone is a true expert. How can we tell? To be considered an expert, someone must have shown that he or she can assess relevant evidence and arguments and arrive at well-supported conclusions in a particular field. What are the indicators that someone has this essential kind of expertise? There are several that provide clues to someone's ability, but they do not guarantee the possession of true expertise.

In most fields, the following two indicators are considered minimal prerequisites for being considered an expert:

1. Education and training from reputable institutions or programs in the relevant field (usually evidenced by degrees or certificates).
2. Experience in making reliable judgments in the field (generally the more years of experience the better).

FOOD FOR THOUGHT

Are Doctors Experts?

Yes and no. Physicians are certainly experts in the healing arts, in diagnosing and treating disease and injury. They know and understand the relevant facts and they have the wherewithal to make good judgments regarding those facts. But are physicians experts in determining whether a particular treatment is safe and effective? Contrary to what many believe, the answer is, in general, no. Determining the safety and efficacy of treatments is a job for scientists (who may also be physicians). Medical scientists conduct controlled studies to try to ascertain whether treatment X can safely alleviate disease A—something that usually cannot be determined by a doctor interacting with her patients in a clinical setting. Medical studies are designed to control all kinds of extraneous variables that can skew the study results, the same extraneous variables that are often present in the doctor's office. What we expect from doctors is that they have a good knowledge of what it is that the relevant experts have figured out.

Critical thinkers should keep this distinction in mind, because they will often hear people assert that Treatment Y works just because Dr Wonderful says so.

(For an example of the process used for testing medical treatments, see the section in Chapter 10 on "Testing Scientific Theories," page 400.)

But, unfortunately, people can have the requisite education and experience and still not know what they're talking about in the field in question. Sadly, in the real world there are well-trained, experienced auto mechanics who do terrible work—and tenured professors with PhDs whose professional judgment is iffy. Two additional indicators, though, are more revealing:

3. Reputation among peers (as reflected in the opinions of others in the same field, relevant prestigious awards, and positions of authority).
4. Professional accomplishments.

CREDIT: Allstar Picture Library/Alamy

Appeal to authority: The actress Gwyneth Paltrow has endorsed products such as agave nectar.

These two indicators are more helpful because they are likely to be correlated with the intellectual qualities expected in true experts. People with excellent reputations among their professional peers and with significant accomplishments to their credit are usually true experts.

As we've seen, we are often justified in believing an otherwise unsupported claim because it's based on expert opinion. But if we have reason to doubt the opinion of the experts, we are not justified in believing the claim on the basis of that opinion. And chief among possible reasons for doubt (aside from conflicting expert opinion) is bias. When experts are biased, they are motivated by something other than the search for the truth—perhaps financial gain, loyalty to a cause, professional ambition, emotional needs, political outlook, sectarian dogma, personal ideology, or some other judgment-distorting factor. Therefore, if we have reason to believe that an expert is biased, we are not justified in accepting the expert's opinion without further investigation.

"An expert is a man who has made all the mistakes which can be made in a very narrow field."

—*Niels Bohr*

But how can we tell when experts are biased? There are no hard-and-fast rules here. In the more obvious cases, we often suspect bias when an expert is being paid by special interest groups or companies to render an opinion, or when the expert expresses very strong belief in a claim even though there is no evidence to support it, or when the expert stands to gain financially from the actions or policies that he or she supports.

It's true that many experts can render unbiased opinions and do high-quality research even when they have a conflict of interest. Nevertheless, in such situations we have reasonable grounds to suspect bias—unless we have good reason to believe that the suspicion is unwarranted. These good reasons might include the fact that the expert's previous opinions in similar circumstances have been reliable or that he or she has a solid reputation for always offering unbiased assessments.

FOOD FOR THOUGHT

Evaluating Internet Sources

Can you trust the information you find on the Internet? In most cases, no. But if you understand how to judge the reliability of websites, and you're willing to spend some time doing the judging, you can often uncover material that is trustworthy and useful. Finding credible information online takes some effort because, unlike books and magazines, most of the information on the Internet is not screened by editors, fact checkers, or anyone else before it hits cyberspace. Anyone can say anything on the Internet. Thus, your online research should be guided by reasonable skepticism. If you want to know more about evaluating online sources, a good place to start is a college or university library. Many of them have free websites featuring excellent guides to Internet research. Duke University, for example, has such a site. Among other things, it offers a checklist of questions to ask about online sources to help you assess their credibility. Some of these questions follow, broken down by category:

Authority

- Who wrote the material? Look for the author's name near the top or the bottom of the website. If you can't find a name, look for a copyright credit (©) or link to an organization.
- What are the author's credentials? Look for biographical information or the author's affiliations (university department, organization, corporate title, etc.).
- Could the credentials be made up? Anyone who has visited a chat room knows that people don't always identify themselves accurately online.

- Did the author include contact information? Look for an email link, address, or phone number for the author. A responsible author should give you the means to contact him or her.

Whose Website Is This?

- What organization is sponsoring the website? Look at the domain (.ca, .edu, .org, etc.). Look for an "about this site" link. Also look for a tilde (~) in the URL, which usually identifies a personal directory on a website—be careful of a website that has a tilde in its URL. Internet service provider sites (AOL, Sympatico, MSN, etc.) and online community sites (MySpace, Facebook, Google+, etc.) feature personal pages. Be careful of online material from those sites, too.

Purpose or Intended Audience

- What is the purpose of the site? Why did the author create it? The purpose could be advertising, advocacy, news, entertainment, opinion, fandom, scholarship, satire, and so on. Some pages have more than one purpose. For example, www.dowjones.com provides free business information but also encourages you to subscribe to the *Wall Street Journal* or other Dow Jones products.

Is the Website Current?

- Is there a date at the top or bottom of the website? But note: A recent date doesn't necessarily mean the information is current. The content might be years out of date even if the given date is recent. (The last update of the page might have consisted of someone changing an email address or fixing a typo.)
- Is the information up to date? This takes a little more time to determine. Compare the information on the website to information available through other sources. Broken links are one measure of an out-of-date page. In general, information about science, technology, and business ages quickly, whereas information in the humanities and social sciences ages less quickly. However, depending on your research, old information can still be perfectly valid.

Objectivity versus Bias

- Is the author being objective or biased? Biased information is not necessarily "bad," but you must take the bias into account when interpreting or using the information given. Look at the facts the author provides, and the facts the author doesn't provide. Are the facts cited accurately and completely? Is the author fair, balanced, and moderate in his or her views, or overly emotional or extreme? Taking the author's credentials into account, try to identify any conflict of interest. Determine if the advertising is clearly separated from the objective information on the page.

Support

- Does the author support the information he or she uses? Look for links or citations to sources. Some academic websites include bibliographies.
- Is the support respectable? Does the material cite well-known sources or authorities? Does the website cite a variety of sources? Do other websites on the same topic cite some of the same sources? The website in question should have a mix of internal links (links to websites on the same site or by the same author) and external links (links to other sources or experts). If a website makes it hard for you to check the support, be suspicious.[2]

FOOD FOR THOUGHT

Do Non-Experts Know Best?

Some people have a bias against experts—all experts. Their thoughts on the subject might run something like this: "It's the uneducated ones, the simple seekers of knowledge, who are the truly wise, for their thinking has not yet been corrupted by ivory-tower learning and highbrow theorizing that's out of touch with the real world. Thus the wisdom of the non-expert is to be preferred over the expert whenever possible." This attitude is, oddly enough, sometimes embraced by very highly educated people. There's a strong strain of it, for example, among New Agers and advocates of some alternative, or unconventional, medicine.

This non-expertism is related to the appeal to ignorance discussed in Chapter 5. (The appeal to ignorance says that since there's no evidence refuting a position, it must be true.) The problem is that both tacks, though psychologically compelling, are fallacious. A lack of good reasons—evidence or expert testimony—does not constitute proof of a claim.

The history of science shows that virtually all notable scientific discoveries have been made by true experts—men and women who were fully knowledgeable about their subject matter. There have been many more instances, however, of cocksure non-experts who proposed theories, cures, and solutions to problems that turned out to be worthless.

Finally, keep in mind that there are certain kinds of issues that we probably don't want experts to settle for us. Indeed, in most of these cases the experts cannot settle them for us. These issues usually involve moral, social, or political questions. If we're intellectually conscientious, we want to provide our own final answers to such questions, though we may draw heavily on the analyses and arguments provided by experts. We may study what the experts have to say and the conclusions they draw. But we want ultimately to come to our own conclusions. We prefer this approach in large part because the questions are so important and because the answers we give help define who we are. What's

REVIEW NOTES

Conflicting Claims

- If a claim conflicts with other claims that we have good reason to accept, we have good grounds for doubting it.
- If a claim conflicts with our background information, we have good reason to doubt it.
- We should proportion our belief to the evidence.
- It's not reasonable to believe a claim when there is no good reason for doing so.
- If a claim conflicts with expert opinion, we have good reason to doubt it.
- When the experts disagree about a claim, we have good reason to suspend judgment.

more, the experts usually disagree on these issues. So even if we wanted the experts to settle one of these questions for us, they probably couldn't.

PERSONAL EXPERIENCE

We accept a great many claims because they are based on personal experience—our own or someone else's. Personal experience, broadly defined, arises from our senses, memory, and judgment involved in those faculties. In countless cases, personal experience is our evidence (or part of the evidence) that something is or is not the case. You believe that Jack caused the traffic accident because you, or someone else, witnessed it. You think that the herbal tea cured your headache because the pain went away after you drank it. You believe that your friend can bend spoons with her mind because you saw her do it at a party. You're sure that it was the other guy, not you, who threw the first punch, because that's how you remember the incident. Or, as a member of a jury, you vote to convict the defendant because eyewitness testimony puts him at the scene of the crime with a gun in his hand. But can you trust personal experience to reveal the truth?

The answer is a qualified and cautious "yes." And here's the qualification in the form of an important principle:

> *It's reasonable to accept the evidence provided by personal experience only if there's no good reason to doubt it.*

If we have no good reason to doubt what our personal experience reveals to us, then we're justified in believing it. This means that if our faculties are working properly and our use of them is unimpeded by anything in our environment, we're entitled to accept what our personal experience tells us. If we seem to see a cat on the mat under good viewing conditions—that is, we have no reason to believe that our observations are impaired by, say, poor lighting, cracked glasses, or too many beers—then we're justified in believing that there's a cat on the mat.

The problem is that personal experience, though generally reliable, is not infallible. Under certain circumstances, our senses, memory, and judgment can't be trusted. It's easy enough to identify these circumstances in an abstract way, as you'll see later. The harder job is to (1) determine when they actually occur in real-life situations and (2) avoid them or take them into account.

The rest of this section is a rundown of some of the more common factors that can give us good reason to doubt the reliability of personal experience.

Impairment

This should be obvious: if our perceptual powers are somehow impaired or impeded, we have reason to doubt them. The unambiguous cases are those in which our senses are debilitated because we are ill, injured, tired, stressed out, excited, drugged, drunk, distracted, or disoriented. And just as clear are the situations that interfere with sensory input—when our environment is, say, too dark, too bright, too noisy, or too hazy. If any of these factors are in play, the risk of misperception is high, which gives us reason to doubt the trustworthiness of what we experience.

> "Besides learning to see, there is another art to be learned—not to see what is not."
>
> —*Maria Mitchell*

Memories can be affected by many of the same factors that interfere with accurate perception. They are especially susceptible to distortion if they are formed during times of stress—which helps explain why the memories of people who witness crimes or alleged ghosts are so often unreliable. These situations are understandably stressful.

The impairment of our faculties is complicated by the peculiar way they operate. Contrary to what many believe, they are not like recording devices that make exact mental copies of objects and events in the world. Research suggests that they are more like artists who use bits of sensory data or memory fragments to concoct creative representations of things, not exact replicas. Our perception and memory are constructive, which means that what we perceive and remember is to some degree fabricated by our minds. For example, you see a man standing in the shadows by the road—then discover when you get closer that the man is a tree stump. Or you are anxiously awaiting a phone call from

FOOD FOR THOUGHT

Tinkering with Your Memory

The memories of eyewitnesses are notoriously unreliable. One reason is that your memory of an event can be altered if you later receive new information regarding the event. Research shows that your memory can be changed in this way, but you don't even know it. You will be sincerely convinced that your altered memory is the original memory. Research studies have uncovered this phenomenon again and again. Here's a description of the classic case:

> Once upon a time, a man (whom we'll call Mike) stumbled upon an armed robbery in a hardware store. The robber rummaged around the cluttered store brandishing a silver weapon; finally, he stole all the money. Then, almost as an afterthought, he grabbed a hand calculator and a hammer, putting these in his satchel as he left the store. The police were summoned immediately, but before they arrived Mike talked to another customer about the robbery. We'll call her Maria. Maria told Mike that she saw the robber grab a calculator and a screwdriver, stuffing them in his satchel as he left the store. The police arrived, and when they questioned Mike he recounted the robbery at some length. He described in detail the silver weapon, the money, and the calculator. When the police asked him about a tool that they heard had been taken, "Did you see if it was a hammer or a screwdriver?" he said, "Screwdriver."[3]

your elderly aunt Mary, and when a call comes and you hear the person's voice, you're sure it's her—then realize that it's a much younger woman asking for a charitable donation. Or while you're in the shower you hear the phone ring—but no one is calling, and the ringing is something your mind is making up.

The constructive workings of our minds help us solve problems and deal effectively with our environment. But they can also hinder us by manufacturing too much of our experiences from too little data. Unfortunately, the constructive tendency is most likely to lead us astray precisely when our powers of perception and memory are impaired or impeded. Juries, for example, are expected to be suspicious of the testimony of eyewitnesses who swear they plainly saw the dirty deed committed but were frightened, enraged, or a little tipsy at the time.

Expectation

A tricky thing about perception is that we often perceive exactly what we expect to perceive—regardless of whether there's anything there to detect. Have you

FOOD FOR THOUGHT

Look! Martian Canals

How easy it is for even a trained observer to see what isn't there! This famous example, one of many, is explained by the psychologist Terrence Hines:

> The constructive nature of perception accounts for a famous astronomical illusion—the canals of Mars. These were first reported in 1877 by the Italian astronomer Schiaparelli. They were popularized in the early twentieth century by the American astronomer Percival Lowell. . . . Lowell argued that the canals were constructed by an advanced Martian civilization. It turns out, however, that the canals of Mars don't exist. [Carl Sagan and P. Fox (1975)] have compared the photos taken by Mariner 9, which photographed the entire Martian surface, with maps of the canals. When the actual Martian surface is examined, there are no canals and no other physical features that could account for what Schiaparelli and Lowell reported. So, where did the canals come from? Sagan and Fox state that "the vast majority of the canals appear to be largely self-generated by the visual observers of the canal school, and stand as monuments to the imprecision of the human eye-brain-hand system under difficult observing conditions."[4]

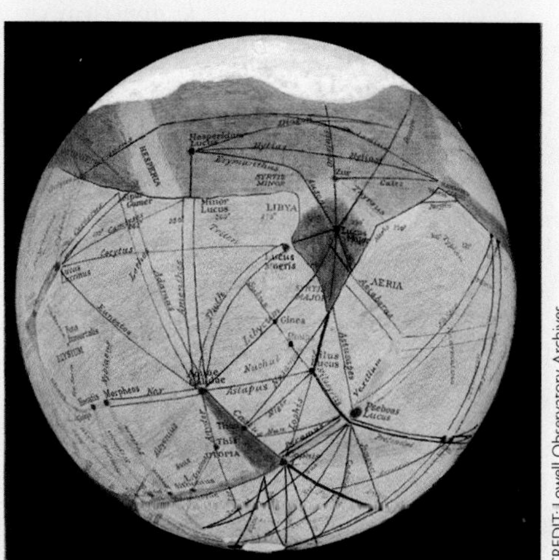

Lowell's drawings of Martian canals.

CREDIT: Lowell Observatory Archives

ever watched the second hand on an electric clock move—then suddenly realize that the clock is not running at all? You "see" it moving because that's what you expect to see; after all, *moving* is what second hands *do*! Ever been walking through a crowd looking for a friend and hear her call your name—then find out later that she was actually 10 blocks away at the time? Such experiences—again the result of the constructive tendencies of mind—are common examples of how expectation can distort your perceptions.

Scientific research shows that expectation can have a more powerful effect on our experiences than most people think. In numerous studies, subjects who expected to see a flash of light, smell a certain odour, or feel an electric shock did indeed experience these things—even though suitable stimuli were never present. The mere suggestion that the stimuli would occur was enough to cause the subjects to report perceiving things that did not in fact exist.

Our tendency to sometimes perceive things that are not really there is especially pronounced when the stimuli are vague or ambiguous. For example, we may perceive completely formless stimuli—clouds, smoke, "white noise," garbled voices, random-patterned wallpaper, blurry photos, lights in the night sky, stains on the ceiling—yet think we observe very distinct images or sounds. In the formlessness we may see ghosts, faces, and words and hear songs, screams, or verbal warnings. We may see or hear exactly what we expect to see or hear. Or the mere suggestion of what we should perceive helps us perceive it. This phenomenon is a kind of illusion known as *pareidolia*. It's the reason some people claim to hear Satanic messages when rock music is played backwards, or to observe a giant stone face in fuzzy pictures of the surface of Mars, or to see the perfect likeness of Jesus in the marks left on a burned tortilla by the pan it was fried in.

Scientists are keenly aware of the possible distorting influence of expectancy, so they try to design experiments that minimize it. We too need to minimize it as much as possible. Our strong expectations are a signal that we should double-check our sensory information and be careful about the conclusions we draw from it.

FOOD FOR THOUGHT

Expecting Racism?

Many studies demonstrate the effect of expectation and belief on our perceptions, but one classic study seems to really hit home. Years ago researchers asked students to look at a picture and describe what they saw. It showed two men standing next to one another in a subway car. One man was white, the other black. The white man was holding an open straight razor. Later the students were asked to recall what they saw. Half of them said that the razor was in the black man's hand.

Innumeracy

When we make an off-the-cuff judgment about the chances of something happening (whether an event in the past or one in the future), we should be extra careful. Why? Because, generally, we humans are terrible at estimating probabilities.

Here's a classic example. Imagine there are 23 students, including you, in your classroom. What are the chances that at least 2 of the students have exactly the same birthday? (Not the same date of birth, but the same birthday out of the 365 possible ones.) Most people are surprised to find out that the answer is neither 1 chance in 365 (1/365), nor 1 in 52 (1/52). It's 1 chance in 2 (1/2, or 50–50)—a completely counterintuitive result. Math can give you the right answer, but guessing or estimating is very unlikely to do so.

Another common error is the misjudging of coincidences. Many of us often believe that an event is simply too improbable to be a mere coincidence and that something else must surely be going on—such as paranormal or supernatural activity. But we mustn't forget that surprising coincidences occur all the time and, in fact, must occur according to elementary laws of statistics. The probability that a particular strange event will occur—say, that an ice cube tossed out of an airplane will hit the roof of a barn—may be extremely low, maybe one in a billion. But given enough opportunities to occur, that same event may be highly probable over the long haul. It may be unlikely in any given instance for you to flip a coin and get tails seven times in a row. But this "streak" is virtually certain to happen if you flip the coin enough times.

Here is another example. What are the odds that someone will be thinking of a person she knew, or had heard of, and then suddenly learn that the person is seriously ill or dead? Believe it or not, such a strange event is likely to occur several times a day somewhere in the world. If we make the reasonable assumption that someone would recognize the names of a few thousand people (both famous and not so famous) and that a person would, each year, learn of the illness or death of several of those people, then the chances of our eerie coincidence happening to someone somewhere are pretty good. We could reasonably expect that each day several people would have this experience.[5]

Another error is to think that previous events can affect the probabilities in the random event at hand. This mistake is known as the **gambler's fallacy**. Let's say you toss an unbiased coin six times in a row. On the first toss, the odds are, of course, one in two, or 50–50, that it will land tails. It lands tails. Astoundingly, on the other five tosses the coin also lands tails. That's six tails in a row. So what are the odds that the coin will land tails on the seventh toss? Answer: 50–50. Each toss has exactly the same probability of landing tails (or heads): 50–50. The coin does not remember previous tosses, and to think otherwise is to commit the gambler's fallacy. You see it a lot in casinos, sporting events, and—alas—everyday decision making.

gambler's fallacy The error of thinking that previous events can affect the probabilities in the random event at hand.

REVIEW NOTES

Personal Experience

- It's reasonable to accept the evidence provided by personal experience only if there's no good reason to doubt it.
- If our perceptual powers are impaired or impeded, we have reason to doubt them.
- Our perception and memory are constructive, which means that our minds are capable of manufacturing what we seem to have experienced.
- We often perceive exactly what we expect to perceive, and this tendency is enhanced when stimuli are vague or ambiguous.
- The gambler's fallacy is the mistake of thinking that previous events can affect the probabilities in the random event at hand.

"The first principle is that you must not fool yourself—and you are the easiest person to fool."

—*Richard P. Feynman*

The lesson here is not that we should mistrust all judgment about probabilities, but that we shouldn't rely solely on our intuitive sense in evaluating them. Relying entirely on intuition, or "gut feeling," in assessing probabilities is usually not a reason to trust the assessment, but to doubt it.

FOOLING OURSELVES

As we've seen, it is not reasonable to believe a claim unless we have good reasons for doing so. If we care whether our beliefs about the world are reliable, we must base them on the relevant evidence. Beliefs backed by good evidence are more likely to be true, and true beliefs are more likely to help us get what we want out of life.

The kink in this straightforward arrangement is that we too often fail to give evidence the respect it deserves. We ignore evidence, deny it, manipulate it, and distort it. Somehow there is very little comfort in knowing that everyone occasionally does this dance. What truly is encouraging is that we can learn to be alert to missteps in using and assessing evidence and that we can usually minimize, though not eliminate, the problems. This section looks at three of the most common and most serious mistakes we make when we deal with evidence.

Resisting Contrary Evidence

An all too human tendency is to try to resist evidence that flies in the face of our cherished beliefs. We may deny evidence, ignore it, or reinterpret it so it fits better with our prejudices. Resisting evidence may be psychologically comforting (for a while, anyway), but it gets in the way of any search for knowledge and stunts our understanding.

The will to resist contrary evidence is especially strong—and tempting—in forays into the paranormal. Remember the study mentioned in Chapter 2 about researchers who showed subjects both evidence for and evidence against the reality of extrasensory perception (ESP)? The subjects who already had doubts about the existence of ESP recalled both kinds of evidence accurately. But the true believers—the subjects who already believed in ESP—remembered both kinds of evidence as proving ESP. They resisted the disconfirming evidence by mentally transforming it into confirming evidence. These results are typical of studies focusing on the paranormal.

Another typical case involves believers in the paranormal who, when confronted with evidence counting against their beliefs, simply refuse to accept it. For example, belief in fairies was given a boost a century ago when two little girls presented the world with photographs they had allegedly taken of fairies playing with them in the garden. (The episode was the basis for the movie *Fairy Tale: A True Story*.) The photos looked fake, the fairies resembling cut-outs from a children's book—which is exactly what they were. But brushing that aside, many people (including the renowned writer Sir Arthur Conan Doyle, creator of the fictional Sherlock Holmes) were convinced that the photos showed real fairies. Many years later, when the girls were grown up, they confessed that the whole thing had been a hoax. But some believers—even those who heard the confession first-hand—refused to accept it.[6]

But we need not look to the fringes of reality to find instances of the denial of evidence. Scientific research and everyday experience show that the practice permeates all walks of life. A political activist may refuse to consider evidence that conflicts with his party's principles. A scientist may be so committed to her theory that she refuses to accept any evidence that undermines it. A sports fan believes deeply that her favourite team is the greatest team there is, despite a string of losing seasons.

Often our resistance to contrary evidence takes a subtle form. If we encounter evidence against our views, we frequently don't reject it outright. We simply apply more critical scrutiny to it than we would to evidence in favour of our

CREDIT: Photo by SSPL/Getty Images

Taken in August 1920, *Fairy Offering Posy of Harebells to Elsie* was initially thought to be a genuine photograph of the Cottingley fairies. In the 1980s, Elsie Wright and Frances Griffiths admitted that the fairies were cardboard cutouts.

views, or we seek out additional confirming information, or we find a way to interpret the data so it doesn't conflict with our expectations.

In one study, proponents and opponents of the death penalty were presented with evidence about whether capital punishment deterred crime. Both those opposed to and in favour of capital punishment were given two types of evidence—(1) some that supported the practice and (2) some that discredited it. Psychologist Thomas Gilovich describes the outcome of the study:

> The results of this experiment were striking. The participants considered the study that provided evidence consistent with their prior beliefs—regardless of what type of study that was—to be a well-conducted piece of research that provided important evidence concerning the effectiveness of capital punishment. In contrast, they uncovered numerous flaws in the research that contradicted their initial beliefs. . . . Rather than ignoring outright the evidence at variance with their expectations, the participants cognitively transformed it into evidence that was considered relatively uninformative and could be assigned little weight.[7]

There is no cure for our tendency to resist opposing evidence. The only available remedy is our commitment to examine our favourite claims critically—which means trying our best to be even-handed in scrutinizing the evidence we like and the evidence we don't like.

Looking for Confirming Evidence

We often not only resist conflicting evidence, but also seek out and use only confirming evidence—a phenomenon known as confirmation bias. When we go out of our way to find only confirming evidence, we can end up accepting a claim that's not true, seeing relationships that aren't there, and finding confirmation that isn't genuine.

In scientific research on confirmation bias, when subjects are asked to assess a claim they often look for confirming evidence only, even though disconfirming evidence may be just as revealing. For example, in one study, a group of subjects was asked to assess whether practising before a tennis match was linked to winning the match; another group, whether practising before a match was linked to losing the match. All the subjects were asked to select the kind of evidence (regarding practice and winning or losing matches) that they thought would be the most helpful in answering the relevant question. Not surprisingly, the subjects deciding whether pre-game practising was linked to winning focused on how many times players practised and then won the match. And subjects assessing whether practising was associated with losing focused on how many times players practised and then lost the match.[8]

Sometimes we look for confirming evidence even when disconfirming evidence is more telling. For example, take this claim: all swans are white. Is it true? How could you find out? You can easily find confirming instances; white swans are plentiful and ubiquitous. But even seeing thousands of white swans will not conclusively confirm that *all* swans are white, because there may be swans in places where you haven't looked. But all you have to do is find one black swan to conclusively show that the claim is false. (People used to believe that the claim was absolutely true—until black swans were discovered in Australia.) In such cases, confirmation bias can lead us way off course.

The moral to this story is that when we evaluate claims, we should look for disconfirming as well as confirming evidence. Doing so requires a conscious effort to consider not only the information that supports what we want to believe, but also the information that conflicts with it. We have to seek out disconfirming evidence just as we keep an eye out for confirming evidence—an approach that goes against our grain. We naturally gravitate to people and policies we agree with, to the books that support our views, to the magazines and newspapers that echo our political outlook. Acquiring a broader, smarter, more critical perspective takes effort—and courage.

FOOD FOR THOUGHT

This Is Lunacy!

When there's a full moon, do people get crazy? Do they behave like lunatics? Folklore says that they do, and many people believe that there's a lunar effect on the way people act. But numerous studies have shown that there is absolutely no causal connection between the moon and human behaviour. So why do so many people believe in lunar power? Part of the reason is the availability error. Since strange behaviour is more noticeable (and so more available) than normal behaviour, we tend to think that weird behaviour is more frequent. And if we look only for confirming instances (and we do), we're likely to believe that the moon is indeed the cause of a lot of peculiar behaviour. On the night of a full moon, we may pay more attention to and watch for examples of strange behaviour; other nights, such behaviour is just as common, but we may be less likely to notice it if we're not watching out for it. Of course, many people behave strangely with or without a full moon.

Do full moons have an effect on our actions?

Preferring Available Evidence

Another common mistake in evaluating evidence is the availability error. We commit this error when we rely on evidence not because it's trustworthy, but because it's memorable or striking—that is, psychologically available. In such cases, we put stock in evidence that's psychologically impressive or persuasive, not necessarily logically acceptable. You fall for the availability error if you vote to convict a murder suspect because he looks menacing, not because the evidence points to his guilt; or if you decide that a Honda Civic is an unsafe vehicle because you saw one get smashed up in a highway accident; or if, just because you watched a TV news report about a mugging in your city, you believe that the risk of being mugged is extremely high.

Being taken in by the availability error can lead to some serious misjudgments about the risks involved in various situations. Some people (are you one of them?) believe that air travel is more dangerous than many other modes of transportation, so they shun travel by airplane in favour of the car. Their conclusion is based on nothing more than a few vivid media reports of tragic plane crashes, such as the terrorist attacks of 9/11. But research shows that per mile travelled, flying is far safer than travelling by car. Researchers have calculated that driving a particular distance (say, from Toronto, Ontario, to Fredericton, New Brunswick) is about 65 times as risky as a non-stop flight of the same distance. The fact is, there are plenty of less vivid and less memorable (that is, psychologically unavailable) things that are much more dangerous than air travel: falling down stairs, drowning, choking, and accidental poisoning.[9] But airplane wreckages make dramatic footage on the TV news, and so deaths due to airplane crashes tend to stick in our heads.

Social psychologist John Ruscio gives another example:

> Aside from a close miss by what was reported to be a falling airplane part early in *The Truman Show*, I cannot personally recall ever having heard of such an accident, fictitious or real. Students over the years have told me that they recall stories of people having found fallen airplane parts, but not of an actual fatality resulting from such falling parts. Shark attacks, on the other hand, are easily imagined and widely reported. Moreover, in the first movie that comes to my mind, the shark in *Jaws* actually did cause several fatalities. It may come as some surprise, then, to learn that in an average year in the United States thirty times more people are killed by falling airplane parts than by shark attacks.[10]

The availability error is likely at work in many controversies regarding environmental hazards. Because the alleged hazard and its effects can be easily and vividly imagined, and the scientific data on the issue are not so concrete or memorable, the imagined danger can provoke a public scare even though the fear is completely unwarranted. Brain cancer from the use of cellphones and autism from childhood vaccines—both of these supposed hazards have provoked fear and public demands for action. But scientific studies have shown these concerns to be groundless.[11] Many environmental hazards are real, of course. But to conclude that they exist solely on the basis of scary thoughts is to fall prey to the availability error.

If we're in the habit of basing our judgments on evidence that's merely psychologically available, we will frequently commit the error known as hasty generalization, a mistake discussed in detail in Chapter 8. We're guilty of hasty generalization when we draw a conclusion about a whole group on the basis of an inadequate sample of the group. We fall into this trap when we assert something like this: "Honda Civics are pieces of junk. I owned one for three months, and it gave me nothing but trouble." Since our experience with a car is immediate and personal, for many of us it can be a short step from this psychologically available evidence to a hasty conclusion. If we give in to the availability

FOOD FOR THOUGHT

The Dangers of Fooling Ourselves

In many regards, we are our own worst enemies when it comes to thinking critically. In part, this reflects the fact that we are the ones who have the most *opportunity* to affect our thinking, for better or for worse. Occasionally *other* people have the opportunity to affect our thinking. But we ourselves are the only ones who play a constant role in our own thinking. Whenever we are trying to figure out what to believe, our own thought patterns—including assumptions and biases —are sure to have an effect.

In this chapter, we outline three specific mechanisms by which we tend to fool ourselves, namely resisting contrary evidence, looking for confirming evidence, and preferring available evidence. In reality, that is just a very small sample of the wide range of ways in which we have the tendency to fool ourselves.

In theory, a rational person wants to try to make sure that the ideas inside her head match reality out in the world. For example, imagine that I currently think that the capital of India is Calcutta, but I find out that it is actually New Delhi. In theory, I should change what I think. I should *change my thinking* so that it matches reality. But in practice, we often behave as if the *world* should change to match what we currently think about it. Our prior beliefs are "sticky" in a way that makes them persist even in the face of evidence to the contrary. Of course, in most cases it is impossible for the world literally to change to match our beliefs. But our behaviour often suggests a kind of denial of that fact: we try our best—mostly subconsciously—to try to bend reality so that it fits our prior understanding of it. And so we ignore evidence that the world is different from the way we believe it to be.

This is a common human tendency, one that is very difficult to escape. But the implication is that to be a critical thinker means to at least attempt to be honest with oneself about the tendency we all have—each and every one of us—to fool ourselves. We must all work hard to develop the habit of questioning ourselves. In particular, we need to work hard to seek evidence about how the world really is, especially when such evidence could challenge our own prior assumptions.

error and stick to our guns about Civics being no good in the face of evidence to the contrary (say, automobile reliability research done by the Consumers Union or similar organizations), we should get an F in critical thinking.

CLAIMS IN THE NEWS

In the Information Age, we are drenched with, well, information. And the news media are a major source of the information that drenches us every day. Through newspapers, magazines, television, radio, and the Internet, information about what's happening in the world hits us like rain almost every waking hour. The claims—supported and unsupported—just keep coming at us. How can we cope with such an onslaught?

Once again, critical thinking must play a big role. Remember that information is just pieces of data, bundles of claims—not necessarily true, not always useful, and not the same thing as knowledge. Knowledge is true belief supported by good reasons; information doesn't have this lofty status. And to transform information into knowledge—our most useful commodity—we need critical thinking. Through critical thinking we can make sense of a great deal of the information coming from the news media. As you will see, most of the rest is not relevant and not worth our time.

Let's begin by looking at how the news media work—how and why they generate the claims that they do. Then we'll see how to critically examine these claims embedded in news reports, broadcasts, and multimedia presentations.

Inside the News

The news media include hundreds of newspapers (among the biggest and the best are the *Globe and Mail*, the *Washington Post*, the *New York Times*, and the *Los Angeles Times*), network news organizations (CTV, CBC, Global), cable news networks (CBC News Network, CTV News Channel, CNN), local and national radio broadcasts, local television news, American public television and radio, newsmagazines (notably *Maclean's*, and *L'actualité*), and numerous news-containing websites. Most news can be found in newspapers, where news stories are generally longer, more comprehensive, and more in-depth than those of any other news source. Newspapers, especially the good ones, devote far more resources to gathering and reporting news than the electronic and Internet media do, usually employing many more reporters and producing many more news stories. A large daily newspaper may contain 100,000 words, while a nightly television news broadcast may contain fewer than 4000. Other kinds of news sources (especially television stations and websites) are far more numerous than newspapers and are the primary news sources for millions of people even though they provide less news.

But not all news is created equal. Some news stories or reports are good, some are bad; some are reliable and informative, some are not. Most probably lie somewhere in between. The quality of news reporting depends on many factors, probably most of which are not under the control of the reporters.

> "Everything is being compressed into tiny tablets. You take a little pill of news every day—23 minutes—and that's supposed to be enough."
>
> —*Walter Cronkite*

Foremost among such factors is money. After all, news outlets—whether print, electronic, or online—are businesses with profit margins to maintain, salaries to pay, and shareholders to please. A news organization makes most of its money not from selling its product (news) through subscriptions or direct sales, but from selling opportunities for other companies to advertise to the news outlet's audience. The organization wants a big audience because big audiences bring in big advertising dollars.

The pressure on news organizations to turn an acceptable profit is immense and has been growing in the past two decades. The old ideal of journalism as primarily a public service and not a cash cow has seldom been able to withstand the corporate push for profits. The effects of this trend on the nature and quality of the news have been profound. Two veteran reporters from the *Washington Post* explain some of the changes this way:

> Most newspapers have shrunk their reporting staffs, along with the space they devote to news, to increase their owners' profits. Most owners and publishers have forced their editors to focus more on the bottom line than on good journalism. Papers have tried to attract readers and advertisers with light features and stories that please advertisers—shopping is a favorite—and by de-emphasizing serious reporting on business, government, the country, and the world.
>
> If most newspapers have done poorly, local television stations have been worse. Typically, local stations provide little real news, no matter how many hours they devote to "news" programs. Their reporting staffs are dramatically smaller than even the staffs of shrunken newspapers in the same cities. The television stations have attracted viewers—and the advertising that rewards their owners with extraordinary profits—with the melodrama, violence, and entertainment of "action news" formulas, the frivolity of "happy talk" among their anchors, and the technological gimmicks of computer graphics and "live" remote broadcasting.

"Is this the movie of the week or the news of the day?"

CREDIT: Mick Stevens/The New Yorker Collection/The Cartoon Bank

> The national television networks have trimmed their reporting staffs and closed foreign reporting bureaus to cut their owners' costs. They have tried to attract viewers by diluting their expensive newscasts with lifestyle, celebrity and entertainment features, and by filling their low-budget, high-profit, prime-time "newsmagazines" with sensational sex, crime, and court stories.
>
> All-news cable television channels and radio stations—to which the networks have ceded much of the routine coverage of serious national and foreign news—fill many of their hours as cheaply as possible with repetitive, bare-bones news summaries and talk shows that present biased opinions and argument as though they were news.[12]

Deliberately or unconsciously, editors and reporters may skew their reporting so as not to offend their advertisers, their audience, or their shareholders. They may also moderate their reporting to keep their sources of information open. Reporters get a great deal of their news from sources such as government officials, corporate public relations people, and advocacy-group spokespersons. A reporter who irritates these sources by writing stories that they don't like could end up being shunned by the sources. There is always the temptation, then, to craft inoffensive or watered-down stories to please the source. Not all news people give in to the temptation, but many do.

Editors and reporters are the ones who decide what's newsworthy and what isn't. And these decisions can help give us a clearer picture of the world or a more distorted one. The distortion can happen in several ways. First, it can arise when reporters do what we might call passive reporting. Most reporters aren't investigative reporters, going off into the world and digging up the hard facts. Often, the news is simply handed to them by spokespersons and public relations experts hired by governments, corporations, and others who want to get their own version of the facts into the news media. In these situations, reporters may report only what they're told at press conferences or in press releases. The result is canned news that's slanted toward the views of the people who supply it.

Second, for a variety of reasons, publishers, editors, producers, and reporters may decide not to cover certain stories or specific aspects of a story. With so much going on in the world, some selectivity is necessary and inevitable. Too often, though, decisions not to cover something can lead the public to conclude that there is nothing happening when in fact something very important is happening. During the run-up to the war in Iraq, some massive anti-war protests occurred in the United States and Europe. But, at least at first, the mainstream American news media didn't cover them, leading some observers to accuse the news media of bias in favour of the war. Likewise, some observers complain that the Canadian news media don't cover many international stories that news organizations in other countries cover in depth, such as famines and human rights violations in developing nations. The result, the complaint goes, is that Canadians may be blithely ignorant of what's really happening in the world. Also, many times the news media forgo covering a story because they deem it too complex or too unexciting for an audience hungry for titillation, scandal, and entertainment. The RCMP chasing a car thief on Highway 102 may get a full hour of TV coverage, but a debate over the role of the monarchy in Canada may get two minutes, or less.

Third, editors, reporters, and producers can dramatically alter our perception of the news by playing certain aspects up or down. Television and radio news broadcasts can make a trivial news item seem momentous just by making it the lead story in the broadcast. Or they can make an important story seem inconsequential by devoting only 15 seconds to it near the end of the broadcast. Newspapers can play the same game by putting a story on the front page with a big headline and compelling photo—or embedding it on page 22 with a tiny headline. Parts of a story can also be arranged for the same effect, with the most telling information mentioned last.

Every piece of news is filtered through a reporter (as well as an editor or producer), most of whom try hard to get the story right. But reporters are subject to many pressures—internal and external—to push the story this way or that, to stray far from the laudable ideal of objective reporting based on professional journalistic standards. Reporters can slant the news by using loaded language and manipulating the tone of the writing, leaving out (or leaving in) certain details, putting facts in conspicuous (or inconspicuous) positions, inserting arguments and personal opinions, dramatizing parts of the story, and appealing to the reader's prejudices.

FOOD FOR THOUGHT

Man Shoots Neighbour with Machete

Man shoots neighbour with machete? Yes—so says a headline that actually appeared in a large-circulation newspaper. Probably every newspaper in North America has been guilty of running such ambiguously goofy headlines. Here are a few more:

- Iraqi Head Seeks Arms
- Study Finds Sex, Pregnancy Link
- Kicking Baby Considered to Be Healthy
- Typhoon Rips through Cemetery; Hundreds Dead
- Lack of Brains Hinders Research
- Panda Mating Fails; Veterinarian Takes Over

Unfortunately, there is a trend these days for reporters to deliberately make themselves part of the story—to editorialize as they report the story, to try to exhibit attitudes common in the community, to offer subtle value judgments that the audience is likely to approve of. Here's an extreme example. On the nightly news, a film clip shows the arrest of activists who have chained themselves to some logging machines in a forest in British Columbia, and the reporter on the scene tells the TV audience, "Once again, the police are jailing those who interfere with the loggers' right to feed their families." Or maybe the reporter takes the opposite tack: "Once again, the police are jailing citizens fighting to protect our shared natural heritage."

All of this suggests that we should not assume without good reason that a news report is giving us an entirely accurate representation of events. And deciding whether in fact we have good reason is a job for critical thinking.

> "News reports stand up as people, and people wither into editorials. Clichés walk around on two legs while men are having theirs shot off."
>
> —*Karl Kraus*

Sorting Out the News

Sometimes you won't be able to tell whether a news report is trustworthy, no matter how carefully you scrutinize it. Your only recourse then is reasonable skepticism. But most times you can at least get a few clues about the reliability of the report by taking the following critical approach.

CREDIT: Chris Madden/Cartoon Stock

Consider Whether the Report Conflicts with What You Have Good Reason to Believe

A report that conflicts with other reports that you believe are reliable or with facts you already know is not trustworthy. Likewise, a report that conflicts with expert opinion should not be accepted.

Look for Reporter Slanting

Look for slanting in news accounts just as you would look for it in any set of claims. Check for loaded or biased language; arguments or unsupported opinion; emotional appeals; appeals to authority, popularity, and tradition; and biased or subjective tone.

Consider the Source

Ask what the source is of the information presented in the story. Did the reporter uncover the facts herself—or does the information come directly from the government, corporations, or interest groups? How does the reporter know that the information is accurate? Does the information seem to be a simple statement of facts—or a pack of assertions designed to put someone in the best possible light?

Check for Missing Information

Be suspicious if essential facts are not presented in the story or if it seems so heavily edited that the context of remarks is mysterious. Sound bites, for example, are easy to take out of context because they usually have no context.

Look for False Emphasis

The size of headlines, the position of stories, the order in which facts are presented—all these things can give unmerited emphasis to a story or some of its claims. To counteract this tactic, ask if the emphasis is really deserved—or, more broadly, if the story or story part is really as significant as the reporter would have you believe.

Check Alternative News Sources

How can you tell if the news you're getting is incomplete—if there's important news you're not seeing? You can't, unless you check alternative news sources for any missing stories. Reading a variety of newspapers, newsmagazines, journals of opinion, and websites is the best way to ensure that you're getting the big picture. To avoid confirmation bias, and to ensure that you're fully informed, you should read not only those sources that agree with you, but also those that don't.

ADVERTISING AND PERSUASION

Advertising is like air. It is everywhere, so pervasive and so natural that we forget it's there, sinking into and changing us every day. Advertising messages hit us rapid-fire and non-stop from television, radio, email, websites, blogs, podcasts, movie theatres, magazines, newsletters, newspapers, book covers, junk mail, telephones, fax machines, product labels, billboards, vehicle signs, T-shirts, wall posters, flyers, and who knows what else. Ads permeate all media—print, film, video, television, radio, and cyberspace. Caught in this whirl of words and sounds and images, we can easily overlook the obvious and disconcerting facts behind them: (1) all advertising is designed to influence, persuade, or manipulate us; (2) to an impressive degree and in many ways, it *does* successfully influence, persuade, or manipulate us; and (3) we are often oblivious to—or in outright denial about—how effectively advertising influences, persuades, or manipulates us.

The purpose of advertising is to sell products and services, promote causes or candidates, or alter attitudes and opinions. How well advertising does these jobs can be measured in money. Advertising in most media costs a great deal. A single full-page magazine ad can cost tens of thousands of dollars; a 30-second TV ad can run into the millions (especially on Super Bowl Sunday). But companies are willing to pay the price because advertising works. The revenues garnered from advertising can outweigh its costs by wide margins; in the case of a magazine ad or a TV spot, the gain could easily be hundreds of thousands or millions of dollars. In addition, advertisers and advertising agencies invest heavily each year in scientific consumer research to determine how to configure ads precisely to elicit the desired response from people. Again, they make these investments because there is a sure payoff. Consumers usually respond just as the research says they will. How do your eyes track across a newspaper ad when you are looking at it? Would you respond better to a TV commercial if the voiceover came from CBC news anchor Peter Mansbridge or from the lead singer of the band Nickelback? Would the magazine ad be more likely to sell you the cottage cheese if the headline used the word *creamy* instead of *smooth*? Would the ad copy on the junk-mail envelope increase sales if it were red instead of blue? You may not care about any of this, but advertisers do because such seemingly trivial bits of information can help them influence you in ways you barely suspect.

However averse we are (or think we are) to advertising or to its aims, we cannot deny its appeal. We like advertising, at least some of it. We can easily point to ads that annoy us or insult our intelligence, but most of us can also recall ones that are entertaining, funny, inspiring, even informative. How, then, should good critical thinkers think about advertising? Our guiding principle should be this:

> *We generally have good reason to doubt advertising claims and to be wary of advertising's persuasive powers.*

This means that usually the most reasonable response to advertising is a degree of suspicion. If we prefer truth over falsehood, if we would rather not be mistaken or bamboozled, if we want to make informed choices involving our time and money, then a general wariness toward advertising ploys is justified. This principle does not assume that all ad claims are false or that advertising cannot be genuinely informative or useful. It simply says that we should not accept uncritically an ad's message or impact on us.

Unethical advertising uses falsehoods to deceive the public. Ethical advertising uses the truth to deceive the public.

CREDIT: Mark Dubowski/Cartoon Stock

There are several reasons for this cautious approach. First, recall the purpose of advertising—to *sell or promote something*, whether a product, service, person, or idea. To put the point bluntly, though advertising can be both truthful and helpful, its primary function is *not* to provide objective and accurate information to consumers. Advertisers will tell you many good things about their products, but are unlikely to mention all the bad. Their main job is *not* to help consumers make fully informed, rational choices about available options. Advertising is advertising—it is not intended to be an impartial search for facts or a program of consumer protection. We are therefore justified in maintaining the same attitude toward advertising that we would toward a complete stranger who wants to sell us something. His motives are obviously financial while his commitment to honesty is unknown.

Second, advertising has a reputation for—and a history of—misleading messages. The world is filled with ads that make dubious or false claims, use fallacious arguments (stated or implied), and employ psychological tricks to manipulate consumer responses.

Some of these methods fit neatly in our rundown of fallacies in this chapter and the next. Ads frequently employ fallacious appeals to authority ("As an Olympic gold medal winner, I can tell you that PowerVitamin 2000 really works!"), appeals to emotion ("Enjoy the goodness and warmth of Big Brand Soup, just like mother used to make"), appeals to popularity ("*The Globe and Mail*: Canada's Most Trusted News Source"), hasty generalizations ("Mothers everywhere will love Softie Diapers—our test mothers sure did!"), and faulty analogies ("As a businessman, I got a major corporation out of debt. As premier, I can get this province out of debt!") But advertisers also use an array of other persuasive techniques, most of which do not involve making explicit claims or providing good reasons for acting or choosing. The following are some of the more common ones.

Identification

Many ads persuade by simply inviting the consumer to identify with attractive individuals (real or imagined) or groups. Most ads featuring celebrity endorsements use this ploy. The idea is to get you to identify so strongly with a celebrity that you feel his or her product choices are *your* preferred choices. Without providing a single good reason or argument, endorsement ads say, in effect, that if Christina Aguilera prefers Pepsi, if Halle Berry likes Revlon, if Michael Jordan loves Nike, maybe you should too.

Slogans

Catchy, memorable phrases are the stock-in-trade of advertising. How could we forget such gems as "Nike. Just do it" (Nike); "Reach out and touch someone"

(AT&T); "Like a rock" (Chevrolet); "Don't leave home without it" (American Express); "Built Ford tough!" (Ford); or "Time for Tims" (Tim Hortons)? Such catchphrases may not say much, but they do get our attention, engender appealing emotions or concepts, and get us to associate them with products or companies—again and again and again. Through repetition that seems to embed them in our brains, slogans surreptitiously get us to feel that one product or brand is better than another.

Misleading Comparisons

In advertising, comparisons can mislead in many ways. Consider these examples:

1. BeClean Paper Towels are 30 per cent more absorbent.
2. Big sale! The SuperX CD Player for less than the suggested retail price!
3. Simply better-tasting tacos. No question.
4. Our mobile phone plan beats the competition. Long-distance calling is just 5 cents per minute, compared with our competitors who charge up to 10 cents a minute.

The problem with example 1 is its vagueness, which is of course deliberate. What does "30 per cent more absorbent" mean? Thirty per cent more absorbent than they used to be? Thirty per cent more absorbent than similar products are? If the latter, what similar products are we talking about? Are BeClean Paper Towels being compared to the *least* absorbent paper towels on the market? The *30 per cent* may seem impressive—until we know what it actually refers to. (Another relevant question is how absorbency was determined. As you might imagine, there are many ways to perform such tests, some of them likely to yield more impressive numbers than others.)

The claim in example 2 may or may not be touting a true bargain. We would probably view the "big sale" in a different light if we knew whether the store's *regular* prices are below the suggested retail prices or if *all* stores sell the CD player below the suggested retail price.

Example 3 contains the same sort of vagueness we find in example 1 plus an additional sort of emptiness. The phrase "better-tasting tacos" is a claim about a subjective state of affairs—a claim that *anyone* could make about his or her own eating experience. You and a thousand other people might try the tacos and think they taste terrible. So the claim tells you nothing about whether you will like the tacos. The claim would be empty even if it were stretched to "The best-tasting tacos on Earth!" In the ad world, such exaggerations are known as *puffery*, which is regarded in advertising law as hype that few people take seriously.

Example 4 is misleading because it tries to compare apples and oranges. Maybe the service offered by one phone company is not like that offered by the others. Maybe the former gives you bare-bones service for 5 cents a minute; the latter gives you the same plus caller ID, call waiting, and free long distance on weekends. So comparing the two according to the per-minute charge alone is deceptive.

Weasel Words

When advertisers want to *appear* to make a strong claim but avoid blatant lying or deception, they use what are known as *weasel words*. Weasel words water down a claim in subtle ways—just enough to ensure that it is technically true but superficially misleading. Consider:

1. You may have already won a new 2017 Ford pickup truck!
2. Some doctors recommend ginseng for sexual dysfunction.
3. Relieves up to 60 per cent of headaches in chronic headache sufferers.

Example 1 is typical junk-mail hype that seems to promise a valuable prize. But the weasel word *may* weakens the claim. Technically, you *may* have actually won since your winning is at least (remotely) possible. But in the typical sweepstakes, the odds of your winning anything are millions to one. Yes, you *may* have already won—and you *may* get hit by an asteroid tomorrow. Example 2 plays on the weasel word *some*. It is probably true that *some* (meaning at least one) doctors recommend ginseng for sexual dysfunction, but a huge majority of them do not. Using *some*, we could craft an infinite number of technically true but misleading (and ridiculous) claims about what doctors do and don't do. In Example 3 the weasel words are *up to*. Notice that many states of affairs would be consistent with this (vague) statement. It would be true even if just 1 per cent of headaches were relieved in almost all headache sufferers.

Other weasels include *as many as*, *reportedly*, *possibly*, *virtually*, *many*, *seems*, and *perhaps*. Such words, of course, can have perfectly respectable uses as necessary qualifiers.

SUMMARY

Many times we need to be able to evaluate an unsupported claim—a claim that isn't backed by an argument. There are several critical thinking principles that can help us do this. An important one is this: if a claim conflicts with other claims we have good reason to accept, we have good grounds for doubting it. Sometimes the conflict is between a claim and your background information.

Background information is the large collection of very well-supported beliefs that we rely on to inform our actions and choices. The relevant principle then is this: if a claim conflicts with our background information, we have good reason to doubt the claim.

It's not reasonable to accept a claim if there is good reason to doubt it. In the case of claims that we can neither accept nor reject outright, we should proportion our belief to the evidence.

An expert is someone who is more knowledgeable than most people in a particular subject area. The important principle here is this: if a claim conflicts with expert opinion, we have good reason to doubt it. We must couple this principle with another one: when the experts disagree about a claim, we have good reason to suspend judgment. When we rely on bogus expert opinion, or on the opinion of an expert not backed up by the consensus of his or her peers, we commit the fallacy known as the appeal to authority.

Many claims are based on nothing more than personal experience, ours or someone else's. We can trust our personal experience—to a point. The guiding principle is that it's reasonable to accept the evidence provided by personal experience only if there's no reason to doubt it. Some common factors that can raise such doubts are impairment (stress, injury, distraction, emotional upset, and the like), expectation, and our limited abilities in judging probabilities.

Some of the common mistakes we make in evaluating claims are resisting contrary evidence, looking for confirming evidence, and preferring available evidence. To counteract these tendencies, we need to take deliberate steps to examine even our most cherished claims critically, to search for disconfirming evidence as well as confirming, and to look beyond evidence that is merely the most striking or memorable.

Many of the unsupported claims we encounter are in news reports. Reporters, editors, and producers are under many pressures that can lead to biased or misleading reporting. The biggest factor is money—the drive for profits in news organizations, especially those owned by large corporations or conglomerates. Reporters themselves may introduce inaccuracies, biases, and personal opinions. And the people who produce the news may decide not to cover certain stories (or aspects of stories), thereby sometimes giving a skewed or erroneous picture of an issue or event.

The best defence against being misled by news reports is a reasonable skepticism and a critical approach that involves, among other things, looking for slanting, examining sources, checking for missing facts, and being on the lookout for false emphasis.

Advertising is another possible source of unsupported or misleading claims. We should realize that we generally have good reason to doubt advertising claims and to be wary of the persuasive powers of advertising.

EXERCISE 4.1

Answers to exercises marked with an asterisk (*) may be found in Appendix B, Answers to Exercises.

Review Questions

1. What is a person's background information?
2. What should we do when faced with a claim that conflicts with other claims you have good reason to believe?
3. What degree of belief should we have in a claim that conflicts with some but not all of our background information?
*4. What is the most reasonable attitude toward a claim that is neither worthy of acceptance nor deserving of outright rejection?
5. State two of the usual criteria for identifying someone as an expert.
6. What should our attitude be toward a claim that conflicts with expert opinion?
7. What should our attitude be toward a claim when experts disagree with each other about it?
8. What are the two versions of the fallacy of appeal to authority?
9. What, in most fields, are the two minimal prerequisites for being considered an expert?
*10. Beyond the minimal prerequisites, what are two more telling indicators that someone is an expert?
11. Under what three circumstances should we suspect that an expert might be biased?
12. Why is it important to guide your online research with reasonable skepticism? What are some questions you can ask to determine whether the information you find is accurate?
13. What are two factors that can give us good reason to doubt the reliability of personal experience?
14. What is the gambler's fallacy?
15. What are some ways that people resist contrary evidence?
16. What is confirmation bias?
*17. How can critical thinkers counteract confirmation bias?
18. What is the availability error?
19. What is the connection between the availability error and hasty generalization?
20. According to the text, what is the guiding principle that we should use to treat advertisements?
21. What are some of the strategies that advertisements use to try and make us buy into their claims regarding their products?

EXERCISE 4.2

On the basis of claims you already have good reason to believe, your background information, and your assessment of the credibility of any cited experts, indicate for each of the following claims whether you would accept it, reject it, or proportion your belief to the evidence. Give reasons for your answers. If you decide to proportion your belief to the evidence, state generally what degree of plausibility you would assign to the claim.

1. Most Canadians have very low levels of credit card debt.
2. India is one of the coldest countries in the world.
3. Every year in Canada over 300 people die of leprosy.
*4. According to Dr Feelgood, the spokesperson for Acme Mattresses, the EasyRest 2000 from Acme is the best mattress in the world for those suffering from back pain.
5. Every year in Canada over 50,000 people die from cancer.
*6. Every person has innate psychic ability that, when properly cultivated, can enable him or her to read another person's mind.
7. All major western government powers are monitoring and collecting private information on their citizens, and then sharing the collected information with each other.
8. No video of Canada's first prime minister, Sir John A. Macdonald, exists today.
9. The New Democratic Party has held a majority of seats in Parliament more than a dozen times in Canada's history.
*10. Fifteen women have died this year after smelling a free sample of perfume that they received in the mail.
11. A chain letter describing the struggles of a nine-year-old girl with incurable cancer is circulating on the Internet. The more people who receive the letter, the better the little girl's chances of survival.
12. A report from the Health Canada says there is no evidence that high doses of the herb ephedra can cure cancer.
13. According to renowned biologist Dr Higgs, the modern-day scorpion was one of the first arthropods to exist, and has more or less stayed the same since before the time of the dinosaurs.
*14. Crop circles—large-scale geometric patterns pressed into fields of grain or hay—are the work of space aliens.
15. Crop circles are the work of human hoaxers.
16. Canada is likely to lead the world in medals at the Summer Olympics in 2020.

*17. Dr Xavier, a world-famous astrologer, says the position of the sun, planets, and stars at your birth influences your choice of careers and your marital status.
18. Eleanor Morgan, a Nobel Prize–winning medical scientist, says that modern democratic systems (including developed nations) are not viable.
19. If the price of apples go up, people are more likely to buy oranges instead.
20. The highway speed limit in Alberta is 120 km/h.

EXERCISE 4.3

For each of the following claims, decide whether you agree or disagree with it. If you agree with a claim, say what evidence would persuade you to reject the statement. If you disagree with a claim, say what evidence would persuade you to accept the statement. In each case, ask yourself if you would really change your mind if presented with the evidence you suggested.

1. Canada's system of universal, free health care results in a significantly lower quality of service and much longer wait times compared to other health care systems such as in the United States.
2. Canada needs to promote higher levels of immigration, since immigrants have always been the most productive elements of Canadian society.
*3. An alien spacecraft crashed in Roswell, New Mexico, in 1947.
4. The Earth is about 10,000 years old.
5. There once was life on Mars.
6. My yoga teacher is able to slow his heart rate down to 20 beats per minute.
7. The Russians are planning to release deadly chemical agents in all major US cities within the week.
*8. Meditation and controlled breathing can shrink cancerous tumours.
9. No subatomic particle can travel faster than the speed of light.
10. Once the baby boomers retire, our heavily socialized economy will result in a catastrophic tax burden on the next generation to maintain the country's current standard of living.

EXERCISE 4.4

Examine the following newspaper story and answer the questions that follow.

Work Farce

26 June 2003—Brazen Department of Education construction employees ripped off the city by clocking in but doing little or no work—instead spending their days at the gym, shopping, or moonlighting, a sting operation by Schools Investigator Richard Condon's office found.

Checks of 13 workers—some chosen randomly, others on the basis of complaints—who were monitored beginning last August found eight of them doing little or no work.

The slackers will soon find themselves in handcuffs and unemployment lines, authorities said. . . . Condon charged that time cheating by phantom workers is "common practice."

"Time abuse is a financial drain on the city's public school system. No doubt it plays a role in the overtime that is paid to skilled trade workers," Condon said. . . .

Condon did not release the names of the slackers because they're about to be arrested, he said. Chancellor Joel Klein said they will be fired "immediately."[13]

1. Is the story slanted toward or against a particular group? How?
2. Are there instances of loaded or biased language or emotional appeals in the story or headline? If so, give examples.
3. What significant person or persons did the reporter who wrote this story apparently fail to talk to? What effect might that have had on the reporting?
4. Assume the story above was found on the Internet. What information would you like for to determine whether the website is credible?

Field Problems

1. Find a controversial newspaper story posted on the Internet and answer the questions in Exercise 4.4 about it.
2. Write down a claim in which you strongly believe. Select one that pertains to an important social, religious, or political issue. Then state what evidence would persuade you to change your mind about the claim.
3. Write down a claim that a close friend of yours strongly believes, but that you do not believe. Then state what evidence you think it would take to persuade your friend to change his or her mind about the claim.

4. Think of the range of *experts* whose advice you rely on, either directly or indirectly, in your own life. They may or may not be people you know by name. Try to think of at least five, and make a list. For each, name the source of his or her expertise. Is it extensive education, extensive experience, or something else, that makes them reliable?

Self-Assessment Quiz

1. How should a critical thinker regard an unsupported claim that conflicts with a great deal of his or her background information?
2. State, in your own words, Bertrand Russell's principle regarding unsupported claims.
3. Name at least three of the four factors to consider in deciding whether someone should be considered an expert.
4. According to the text, what are some telltale signs that an expert may be biased?
5. Name three types of perceptual impairment that can give us good reason to doubt the reliability of our personal experience.

For each of the following situations and the claim associated with it, indicate whether there may be good reasons to doubt the claim and, if so, specify the reasons.

6. Eve is driving through a blizzard when she suddenly sees a shape appear just up the road. She concludes that the object is about 250 metres away, so she should have plenty of time to stop the car before she hits it.
7. While walking through the woods on a windy day, Connor thinks he hears a voice whispering his name. It's almost inaudible, but he thinks it says, "Connnnnnorrrrrr . . . come home!"
8. Constable Jones views the videotape of the robbery at the Tim Hortons that occurred last night. He sees the robber look into the camera. "I know that guy," he says. "I put him away last year on a similar charge."

For each of the following claims, say whether it is (a) probably true, (b) probably false, (c) almost certainly true, (d) almost certainly false, or (e) none of the above.

9. Canada has more trees than the United States does.
10. Health Canada says that about 100 children a year die as a result of their mothers smoking during pregnancy or from exposure to smoke at home.

11. Nobody in the world is truly altruistic. Everyone is out for him or herself alone.
12. The reason the current generation is becoming so lazy and entitled is due to the availability of technology to replace work that traditionally needed to be done by hand.
13. "The world shadow government behind the US government is at it again, destroying US buildings and killing people with staged acts of terrorism [on 11 September 2001], the intent of which being—among other things—to start WW III." (Website devoted to 9/11 theories)
14. "What is Pre-Birth Communication? It's something that many people experience, yet very few talk about—the sense that somehow we are in contact with a being who is not yet born! It may be a vivid dream, the touch of an invisible presence, a telepathic message announcing pregnancy, or many other types of encounter. It is a mystery, one that challenges our ideas about ourselves and our children." (Website on pre-birth communication)
15. The reason that funding for research into renewable energy sources is so scarce is that the big oil companies are trying their best continue being the dominant players in the energy sector. They are constantly lobbying for the government to ignore alternative energy.
16. The "financial collapse" of 2008–9 didn't really happen at all. It was a huge lie made up by the government, with the co-operation of the banks, to scare the population into being obedient.

Read the following news story and then answer questions 17–20.

Soldiers Sweep Up Saddam's Hit Goons

1 July 2003—WASHINGTON—US troops captured 319 suspected Ba'ath Party murderers as part of a tough new crackdown on regime diehards yesterday, as Defense Secretary Donald Rumsfeld forcefully denied that the United States is getting into a "quagmire" in Iraq.

Military officials said US forces carried out 27 raids and also seized more than $9 million in cash as well as hundreds of machine guns and grenade launchers over the past two days as part of Operation Sidewinder.

The military offensive is a get-tough display of American power aimed at defeating Saddam Hussein's loyalists and outside terrorists responsible for hit-and-run attacks on US troops and sabotage of Iraq's power and water services. But the Iraqi goon squads continued their guerrilla-style campaign yesterday, ambushing a US Avenger air-defense vehicle in the ultra-tense town of Fallujah, wounding Jeremy Little, an Australian-born sound man for NBC news.

> The Pentagon says 65 soldiers have been killed and scores more wounded in a series of ambushes and attacks by Saddam loyalists since the war was declared over May 1.
>
> But at a Pentagon briefing, Rumsfeld tried to counter growing criticism in Congress and in the media over the US policy toward Iraq and angrily denied that the US is getting into another Vietnam War quagmire. . . .
>
> Rumsfeld admitted that fighting in Iraq "will go on for some time," but said "more and more Iraqis" are starting to cooperate with coalition forces in their hunt for Saddam's goon squads.[14]

17. Is the story slanted toward or against a particular group mentioned in the story? How?
18. Are there instances of loaded or biased language or emotional appeals in the story or headline? If so, give examples.
19. What main source did the reporter use for the details of this story?
20. Is this story lacking another perspective on the events? Is there more to the story that isn't mentioned? If so, explain.

Integrative Exercises

These exercises pertain to material in Chapters 1–4.

1. What is a deductive argument? An inductive one?
2. How can background information help us determine the soundness of a deductive argument or the cogency of an inductive one?
3. Is expertise more important for determining the validity of a deductive argument or the strength of an inductive one?
4. What is the appeal to authority? Is appealing to authority always fallacious?

For each of the following arguments, specify the conclusion and premises and say whether it is deductive or inductive. If it's inductive, say whether it is strong or weak; if deductive, say whether it is valid or invalid. If necessary, add implicit premises and conclusions.

5. "In Canada, the new Canadian Strategy on HIV/AIDS contains, for the first time, a component on legal, ethical, and human-rights issues. This represents a huge step forward and a recognition that these issues must be an integral part of any strategy to fight HIV, for three reasons: because

work aimed at ensuring that laws and policies facilitate rather than hinder efforts to prevent HIV/AIDS must be supported; because work aimed at ensuring that laws and policies facilitate rather than hinder efforts to provide care, treatment, and support to people with HIV/AIDS must be supported; and because work aimed at ensuring that laws and policies respect and protect the rights of people with HIV/AIDS and those affected by the disease must be supported." (Editorial, *Canadian HIV/AIDS Policy & Law Newsletter*, 4, no. 2/3, Spring 1999)

6. "The people of PEI have a voice and it deserves to be heard in return for a vote. Too many times people have voted for the Liberals and PCs and too many times those people have been let down by the party they voted for because the party has their own hidden agendas." (Online comment, 4 February 2011, *The Guardian*, Charlottetown, PEI)
7. If Quebec separates from Canada, Quebec will suffer economically. Fortunately, Quebec won't separate from Canada. So, Quebec will not suffer economically.
8. No one is going to support the prime minister if he follows the United States in refusing to lower greenhouse gas emissions. But it looks as if he's going to follow the United States. Thus, no one will support him.
9. My high school teacher swears that smoking cigarettes is actually good for you. He says his father smoked two packs of cigarettes a day and lived to the ripe old age of 92 without even a hint of cancer or other serious disease. The rest of his family tree never smoked a day in their lives and all died before they reached their seventies..
10. The fear generated by the terrorist attacks on 11 September 2001 allowed the US government to enact legislation that increased their own power and tighten their control over their citizens. It also provided a good excuse to invade the Middle East for oil under the pretext of "hunting down terrorists." That's why many believe that the US government probably had something to do with attacks.
11. Of course Canadians should retain their link to the British monarchy. Sure, Canada is a democracy now, but our link to the monarchy is an important reminder of our history, and an important part of what makes us different from other North American countries.
12. Yes, the monarchy is part of our heritage. But Canada is a modern democracy, and in a modern democracy there is simply no room for the remnants of an outdated form of authoritarian rule.
13. If you cared about social justice, you would be down there with your friends at the Occupy Toronto protest. If you were down at the protest, you wouldn't be sitting on the couch. But there you are, sitting on the couch eating Doritos. You don't care about social justice at all!

14. "Cold-FX is an undeniable Canadian sales success, but this seems to be due more to marketing, rather than science. The data published to date suggest that it may have some sort of a biological effect—but it's a small one, and for many people that take it, the data suggest it will not be effective in preventing colds or the flu." (*Science-Based Pharmacy*, 27 February 2009)
15. Debra says that the restaurant only serves burritos and tacos. Since I can't stand tacos, I'll have to get a burrito.
16. If Maya didn't answer her phone, she wouldn't get invited to the party. She says she wasn't invited to the party, so I guess she didn't answer her phone.

For each of the following unsupported claims, specify whether it seems worthy of acceptance, rejection, or a degree of belief in between.

17. I could swear I saw my Mom yesterday, even though she's on vacation in Mexico. I was home, really sick with flu, and I woke up and there she was at the foot of my bed.
18. Rogers Wireless, Bell Mobility, and Telus Mobility run the oligopoly that is Canada's telecommunications sector and they work together closely to make sure that mobile phone plans stay as expensive—and profitable—as possible.
19. Wearing an evil grin on his face when he was captured, the goon had to be the guy who committed the recent Stanley Park mugging.
20. The head of Canada's second-largest bank says that there's no need to reform Canada's banking regulations.

Critical Thinking and Writing Exercise

From Outline to First Draft

If you have developed a detailed outline, then you have a path to follow as you write. And while you're writing an argumentative essay, having a path is much better than searching for one. Your outline should make the writing much easier.

No outline is a finished work, however. As you write, you may discover that your arguments are not as strong as you thought, or that other arguments would be better, or that changing a point here and there would make an argument more effective. If so, you should amend your outline and then continue writing. The act of writing is often an act of discovery, and good writers are not afraid of revisions or multiple drafts.

Recall from the exercise in Chapter 1 that good argumentative essays generally comprise these elements:

Introduction (or opening)
Statement of thesis (the claim to be supported)
Argument supporting the thesis
Assessment of objections
Conclusion

Start your draft with a solid opening that draws your readers into your essay and prepares the way for your arguments. Good openings are interesting, informative, and short. Grab the attention of your readers with a bold statement of your thesis, a provocative quotation, a compelling story, or interesting facts. Prepare the way for your arguments by explaining why the question you're addressing is important, why you're concerned about it, or why it involves a pressing problem. Don't assume that your readers will see immediately that the issue you're dealing with is worth their time.

Include a clear statement of your thesis in your opening (in the first paragraph or very close by). In many cases, you will want to tell the reader how you plan to develop your argument or how the rest of the essay will unfold (without going into lengthy detail). In any case, by the time your audience reads through your opening, they should know exactly what you intend to prove and why.

Consider this opening for our imaginary essay on air pollution from Chapter 3:

> Respiratory experts at Health Canada say that sulphur dioxide in the air is a poison that we should avoid. Yet the provincial government wants to loosen environmental rules to allow coal-burning power plants to emit more sulphur dioxide than they already do. That's a bad idea. The latest evidence shows that letting the plants emit more of this poison will most likely increase the incidence of respiratory illnesses in hundreds of communities.

This opening gets the reader's attention by sounding the alarm about a serious health hazard. It provides enough background information to help us understand the seriousness of the problem. And the thesis statement in the last sentence announces what the essay will try to prove.

The body of your essay should fully develop the arguments for your thesis statement, or conclusion. You should devote at least one paragraph to each premise, though several paragraphs may be necessary. You may opt to deal with objections to your argument as you go along, perhaps as you put forth each premise or at the end of the essay just before the conclusion. Each paragraph should develop and explain just one idea, which is usually expressed in a topic sentence. Each sentence in each paragraph should relate to the paragraph's main idea. Any sentence that has no clear connection to the main idea should be deleted or revised. Be sure to link paragraphs together in a logical sequence using transitional words and phrases or direct references to material in preceding paragraphs.

Here are two paragraphs that might follow the air pollution opening:

> Scientists used to wonder whether there is a connection between airborne sulphur dioxide and respiratory illness—but no more. Research has repeatedly shown a strong link between high levels of sulphur dioxide in the air and diseases that affect the lungs. For example, data from studies conducted by Health Canada show that when levels of airborne sulphur dioxide in urban areas reach what the agency calls the "high normal" range, the incidence of respiratory illnesses increases dramatically. According to several Health Canada surveys of air quality, many major cities (not just Toronto) often have high normal levels of sulphur dioxide in the air. In addition, data from health departments in large cities show that when levels of airborne sulphur dioxide are at their highest, hospital admissions for asthma and other respiratory illnesses also increase.
>
> These findings, however, tell only half the story. Many parts of the country have more than just occasional surges in levels of airborne sulphur dioxide. They must endure unsafe levels continuously. New studies from Health Canada demonstrate that in at least 10 major cities, the amount of sulphur dioxide in the air is excessive all the time.

In this passage, a single paragraph is devoted to each premise. Each paragraph develops a single idea, which is stated in a topic sentence. (The topic sentence for the first paragraph is "Research has repeatedly shown a strong link between high levels of sulphur dioxide in the air and diseases that affect the lungs." For the second paragraph, the topic sentence is "[Many parts of the country] must endure unsafe levels continuously.") Each sentence in each paragraph relates to the topic sentence, and the relationships among the sentences are clear. Likewise the connection between the discussion in the first paragraph and that of the second is apparent. The transitional sentence in the second paragraph ("These findings, however, tell only half the story.") helps bridge the gap between the paragraphs. Both of them help support the thesis statement.

How you end your essay is often as important as how you start it. In short or simple essays, there may be no need for a conclusion. The thesis may be clear and emphatic without a conclusion. In many cases, however, an essay is strengthened by a conclusion, and sometimes a conclusion is absolutely essential. Often, without an effective conclusion, an essay may seem to end pointlessly or to be incomplete. The typical conclusion reiterates or reaffirms the thesis statement without being repetitious. Or the conclusion of the essay's argument serves as the conclusion for the whole essay. In long or complex essays, the conclusion often includes a summary of the main points discussed.

Sometimes a conclusion is a call to action, an invitation to the reader to do something about a problem. Sometimes it relates a story that underscores the importance of the essay's argument. Sometimes it highlights a provocative aspect of a claim defended earlier. In all cases it serves to increase the impact of the essay.

The conclusion, however, is not the place to launch into a completely different issue, make entirely unsubstantiated claims, malign those who disagree with you, or pretend that your argument is stronger than it really is. These tactics will not strengthen your essay but weaken it.

Defining Terms

Your essay will do its job only if it is understood, and it will be understood only if the meaning of its terms is clear. As noted in the Chapter 3 exercise, sometimes a dispute can hang on the meaning of a single term. Clarify the meaning, and the disagreement dissolves. In an argumentative essay, clarifying terms often comes down to offering precise definitions of words that are crucial to your argument.

There are several different kinds of definitions. A lexical definition reports the meaning that a term has among those who use the language. For example, among English-speaking people, the word *rain* is used to refer to condensed atmospheric moisture falling in drops, which is the lexical definition. A stipulative definition reports a meaning that a term is deliberately assigned, often for the sake of convenience or economy of expression. If you assign a meaning to a familiar term or to a term that you invent, you give a stipulative definition. A precising definition reports a meaning designed to decrease ambiguity or vagueness. It qualifies an existing term by giving it a more precise definition. Someone, for example, might offer a precising definition for the word *old* (as it applies to the age of humans) by specifying that *old* refers to anyone over 80. A persuasive definition reports a meaning designed to influence attitudes or beliefs. It is usually not meant to be purely informative but is calculated to appeal to someone's emotions. Someone who opposes taxation, for example, might define *taxation* as "a form of state-run extortion." Someone who thinks that taxation is generally a good thing might define *taxation* as "a way for individuals to contribute financially to important social programs."

In general, any definition you offer should decrease vagueness or ambiguity and thereby increase the effectiveness of your writing. Your definitions should also be consistent. If you provide a definition for a term in your essay, then you should stick to that definition throughout. Altering the meaning of a term mid-essay or using more than one term to refer to the same thing can be confusing to the reader—and might even subvert your essay's argument.

Good writers are also very much aware of another kind of meaning—the meaning that comes from a word's connotations. Connotations are the feelings, attitudes, or images associated with a word, beyond the literal meaning of the term. Consider these words: *food*, *sustenance*, *cuisine*, and *grub*. These terms have nearly the same literal meaning, but they differ in the emotions or attitudes they convey. Or what about these terms: *tavern*, *saloon*, *bar*, *watering hole*, and *dive*. They refer to the same kind of establishment, but the images or emotions conveyed are diverse, ranging from the respectable and pleasant (tavern) to the lowly and odious (dive).

Good writers make use of both the literal meaning of words and their connotations. Connotations, however, can sometimes mislead by obscuring or minimizing the facts. In debates about, for example, Quebec independence, those who want greater independence for Quebec may characterize their position as favouring "sovereignty and self-determination." Those opposed to it might label it as "seeking to break up Canada." Both these labels are meant to provoke certain attitudes toward the subject matter—attitudes that may not be supported by any evidence or argument. Words used to convey positive or neutral attitudes or emotions in place of more negative ones are known as euphemisms. Words used to convey negative attitudes or emotions in place of neutral or positive ones are called dysphemisms. Consider the disparate impact on the reader of these pairs of terms, both of which refer to the same thing:

downsized	fired
revenue enhancements	tax increases
full-figured	fat
guerrillas	freedom fighters
resolute	pigheaded
emphatic	pushy
sweat	perspire
crippled	disabled
lied to	misled
passed away	died

Keep in mind that euphemisms often perform a useful social purpose by allowing us to discuss sensitive subjects in an inoffensive way. We may spare people's feelings by saying that their loved ones "have passed on" rather than that they "have died," or that their dog "was put to sleep" rather than "killed." Nevertheless, as critical thinkers, we should be on guard against the deceptive use of connotations. As critical writers, we should rely primarily on argument and evidence to make our case.

Writing Assignments

1. Write an alternative opening for Essay 2 ("Hurray! No One's Watching") in Appendix A. If you want, you may invent quotations or stories.
2. Write an outline for Essay 1 ("Deterrence") in Appendix A. Include a thesis statement, each premise, and points supporting each premise.
3. Study Essay 8 ("RIM Is Dead") in Appendix A. Identify the rhetorical use of any euphemisms or dysphemisms.
4. Select one of the following topics and extract an issue from it that you can write about. Investigate arguments on both sides of the issue, and write a three-page paper defending your chosen thesis.
   - the morning-after pill
   - drug testing in the workplace
   - vegetarianism
   - the Occupy Wall Street movement
   - same-sex marriages
   - government censorship of media coverage of military activities
   - commercial whaling
   - religion as a source of knowledge
   - endangered species
   - animal rights
   - the dangers of heavy metal music
   - Aboriginal land claims
   - date rape
   - tougher jail sentences for child pornography
   - an oil pipeline from northern Alberta to Texas.
5. Write a two-page rebuttal to Essay 7 ("Yes, Human Cloning Should Be Permitted") in Appendix A. Use the testimony of experts to help defend your view

5 FAULTY REASONING

CHAPTER OBJECTIVES

Irrelevant Premises

You will be able to

- recognize fallacies of irrelevant premises (genetic fallacy, composition, division, appeal to the person, equivocation, appeal to popularity, appeal to tradition, appeal to ignorance, appeal to emotion, red herring, and straw man).
- understand the concept of burden of proof and when it applies.

Unacceptable Premises

You will be able to

- recognize fallacies of unacceptable premises (begging the question, false dilemma, slippery slope, hasty generalization, and faulty analogy).

An argument is meant to prove a point—to provide good reasons for accepting a claim. As you know, sometimes an argument succeeds, and sometimes it doesn't. When it doesn't, the problem will be that the premises are false, or the reasoning is faulty, or both. In any case, the argument is defective, bad, or bogus—call it what you will. There are countless ways that an argument can be defective. But there are certain types of defective arguments that occur so frequently that they have names (given to them, in many cases, by ancient philosophers or medieval scholars) and are usually gathered into critical thinking texts so students can become aware of them. Such common, flawed arguments are known as **fallacies**, and they are therefore said to be fallacious.

fallacy An argument form that is both common and defective; a recurring mistake in reasoning.

Fallacies are often convincing; they can *seem* plausible. Time and again they are *psychologically* persuasive though *logically* impotent. The primary reason for studying fallacies, then, is to be able to detect them so you're not taken in by them.

We can divide fallacies into two broad categories: (1) those that have *irrelevant* premises and (2) those that have *unacceptable* premises.[1] Irrelevant premises simply have no bearing on the truth of the conclusion they are supposed to support. An argument may seem to offer reasons for accepting the conclusion, but the "reasons" have nothing to do with the conclusion. Unacceptable premises are relevant to the conclusion but are nonetheless dubious in some way. An argument may have premises that pertain to the conclusion, but they do not adequately support it. Premises can be unacceptable because they are as dubious as the claim they're intended to support, because the evidence they offer is too weak to support the conclusion adequately, or because they're otherwise so defective that they provide no support at all.

"Most people think they just appear out of thin air! But the truth is, there's a great deal of very hard work involved!"

CREDIT: Bradford Veley/Cartoon Stock

So, in good arguments, premises must be both relevant and acceptable. In fallacious arguments, at least one of these requirements is not met.

In this chapter we examine numerous fallacies of both types. We won't be able to discuss all known fallacies—there are just too many—but we will scrutinize the most common ones. By the time you have finished this chapter, you should be able to spot these fallacies a mile away.

IRRELEVANT PREMISES

Genetic Fallacy

The **genetic fallacy** consists of arguing that a claim is true or false solely because of its origin. For example:

> Selena's argument regarding Aboriginal rights can't be right because she's of European descent.
>
> We should reject that proposal for solving the current welfare mess. It comes straight from the New Democratic Party.
>
> Russell's idea about tax hikes came to him in a dream, so it must be a silly idea.

genetic fallacy The fallacy of arguing that a claim is true or false solely because of its origin.

These arguments fail because they reject a claim solely on the basis of where it comes from, not on its merits. In most cases, the source of an idea is irrelevant to its truth. Good ideas can come from questionable sources; bad ideas can come from impeccable sources. Generally, judging a claim only by its source is a recipe for error.

"One must accept the truth from whatever source it comes."

—*Moses Maimonides*

There are times, however, when the origins of a claim can be a relevant factor. In court cases, when an eyewitness account comes from someone known to be a pathological liar, the jury is entitled to doubt the account.

Appeal to the Person

The fallacy of **appeal to the person** (or ad hominem, meaning "to the man") is to reject a claim by criticizing the person who makes it rather than the claim itself. For example:

appeal to the person/ ad hominem The fallacy of rejecting a claim by criticizing the person who makes it rather than the claim itself. *Ad hominem* means "to the man."

> Watanabe has argued for an increase in the tax on cigarettes. But he once ran as the NDP candidate in a provincial election, so he's a raving socialist who thinks all taxes are good. Anything he has to say on this issue is sure to be loony.
>
> We should reject Chen's argument for life on other planets. He relies on fortune tellers for financial advice!
>
> You can't believe anything Beauchemin says about the benefits of federalism. She's a known separatist.
>
> You can't believe anything Morris says about welfare reform. He's a left-leaning softy.

Such arguments are fallacious because they attempt to discredit a claim by appealing to something that's almost always irrelevant to it, such as a person's character, motives, or personal circumstances. Claims must be judged on their own merits—they are not guilty by association. We are never justified in rejecting a claim because of a person's faults unless we can show how a person's faults translate into faults in the claim—and this is almost never the case. Even when a person's character *is* relevant to the truth of claims (as when we must consider the merits of testimonial evidence), we are not justified in believing a claim false just because the person's character is dubious. If the person's character is dubious, we are left with no reason to think the claim is either true *or* false.

The fallacy of appeal to the person is usually regarded as a special case of the genetic fallacy. What distinguishes an appeal to the person is that it not only *mentions* a person as the origin of an argument, but it also *attacks* the person (usually his or her character) and usually ignores the argument altogether.

The fallacy of appeal to the person comes in several varieties. One is the personal attack (just mentioned), which often simply consists of insults. The gist of these arguments is familiar enough. The arguer suggests that X's claims, ideas, or theories should be rejected because X is a radical, reactionary, extremist, right-winger, left-winger, fool, bonehead, moron, nutbar, or scum of the earth. Whatever psychological impact such terms of abuse may have, logically they carry no weight at all.

Another form of this fallacy emphasizes, not a person's character, but his or her circumstances. Here someone making a claim is accused of inconsistency—specifically, of maintaining a view that is inconsistent with his or her previous views or social or political commitments.

> Edgar asserts that global warming is real, but he's a card-carrying member of a political party that is officially skeptical about climate change. So he can't believe in global warming; he's got to deny it.

> Madison *says* she's in favour of higher levels of immigration, but you can't take her seriously. That view goes against everything her whole family believes in.

These arguments are fallacious if they're implying that a claim must be true (or false) just because it's inconsistent with some aspect of the claimant's circumstances. The circumstances are irrelevant to the truth of the claim.

When such arguments are put forth as charges of hypocrisy, we get another ad hominem fallacy known as ***tu quoque*** (or "you're another"). The fallacious reasoning goes like this: Ellen claims that X, but Ellen doesn't practise/live by/condone X herself—so X is false. Look:

***tu quoque* ("you're another")** A type of ad hominem fallacy that argues that a claim must be true (or false) just because the claimant is hypocritical.

> West coast granola crunchers tell us we shouldn't drive SUVs because they use too much gas and are bad for the environment. But they drive SUVs themselves.
>
> What hypocrites! I think we can safely reject their stupid pronouncements.

But whether someone is hypocritical about their claims can have no bearing on the truth of those claims. We may, of course, condemn someone for hypocrisy, but we logically cannot use that hypocrisy as a justification for rejecting his or her views. Their views must stand or fall on their own merits.

FOOD FOR THOUGHT

Fighting Fire with Fire

Political discourse is a massive breeding ground for ad hominem arguments. In this example, the writer uses an ad hominem attack while accusing her opponents of using ad hominem attacks!

> The Liberal Party has no real policy direction—nothing Canadian voters would be interested in, anyway. So, instead of coming up with new ideas, they just accuse the Conservatives and NDP of every flaw or failing that comes to mind. So Canadians should ignore the Liberal Party's whining criticisms of the government's new environmental policy initiatives.

In another variation of circumstantial ad hominem reasoning, someone might deduce that a claim is false because the person making it, given his or her circumstances, would be *expected* to make it. For example:

> Wilson claims that the political system in Cuba is exemplary. But he *has* to say that. He's a card-carrying communist. So forget what he says.

But whether Wilson is a communist, and whether he would be expected or required to have certain views because of his connection to communism, is irrelevant to the truth of his claim.

Finally, we have the ad hominem tactic known as "poisoning the well." In this one, someone argues like this: X has no regard for the truth or has non-rational motives for espousing a claim, so nothing that X says should be believed—including the claim in question. The idea is that just as you can't get safe water out of a poisoned well, you can't get reliable claims out of a discredited claimant. This tack is fallacious because the fact that someone might have dubious reasons for making a claim does not show that the claim is false, nor does it mean that everything that comes out of the "poisoned well" can be automatically dismissed.

Composition

The fallacy of **composition** involves arguing that what is true of the parts must be true of the whole. The error here is to think that the characteristics of the parts are somehow transferred to the whole, something that is not always the case. Likewise, the error is committed whenever we assume that what's true of a member of a group is true of the group as a whole. For example:

composition The fallacy of arguing that what is true of the parts must be true of the whole. The error is thinking that the characteristics of the parts are somehow transferred to the whole, something that is not always the case.

> The atoms that make up the human body are invisible. Therefore, the human body is invisible.

> Each member of the club is productive and effective. So the club will be productive and effective.

Each note in the song sounds great. Therefore, the whole song will sound great.

Every part of this motorcycle is lightweight; therefore, the whole motorcycle is lightweight.

Sometimes, of course, the parts do share the same characteristics as the whole. We may safely conclude that since all the parts of the house are made of wood, the house itself is made of wood. We commit the fallacy of composition, though, when we assume that a particular case must be like this.

The fallacy of composition often shows up in statistical arguments. Consider the following:

The average small investor puts $2000 into the stock market every year. The average large investor puts $100,000 into stocks each year. Therefore, large investors as a whole invest more money in the stock market than the small investor group does.

The fact that the average small investor invests less than the average large investor does not mean that small investors as a group invest less than large investors as a group. After all, there may be many more small investors than large investors.

Division

division The fallacy of arguing that what is true of the whole must be true of the parts. The error is thinking that characteristics of the whole must transfer to the parts or that traits of the group must be the same as traits of individuals in the group.

The flip side of the fallacy of composition is the fallacy of **division**—arguing that what is true of the whole must be true of the parts. This fallacy is also committed when we assume that what is true of a group is true of individuals in the group.

This machine is heavy. Therefore, all the parts of this machine are heavy.

The building Dimitri lives in is huge, so his apartment must be huge.

A university degree is a valuable thing to have! So how can you possibly think that this course in underwater basket weaving isn't valuable?

These arguments are fallacious because they assume that characteristics of the whole are transferred to the parts or that traits of the group must be the same as traits of individuals in the group.

Like the fallacy of composition, the fallacy of division is frequently used in statistical arguments:

Of course Mike can run faster than Colleen! It's well known that men are, on average, faster runners than women.

Just because the average man runs faster than the average woman, this doesn't mean that any specific man must necessarily run faster than any

EVERYDAY PROBLEMS AND DECISIONS

The High Cost of a Fallacy

Did you know that fallacies can sell cars? Take a look at this conversation:

BRUNO: I really like this car. Looks like a babe magnet. Is it very expensive?
SALESPERSON: Oh, the price is very reasonable. You can easily afford it. The payments are only $190 a month.
BRUNO: Wow, I'll take it.
SALESPERSON: (Thinking to himself) Sucker. He just bought a $31,000 car.

Don't let the fallacy of composition lead you into making an expensive bad decision.

specific woman. The speeds of individuals, which make up the average, may vary greatly.

Equivocation

The fallacy of **equivocation** is the use of a word in two different senses in an argument. For example:

equivocation The fallacy of using a word in two different senses in an argument.

The end of everything is its perfection.
The end of life is death.
Therefore, death is the perfection of life.

Only man is rational.
No woman is a man.
Therefore, no woman is rational.

Laws can only be created by law givers.
There are many laws of nature.
Therefore, there must be a law giver, namely, God.

In the first argument, *end* is used in two different senses. In the first premise it means *purpose*, but in the second it means *termination*.

"The exact contrary of what is generally believed is often the truth."
—*Jean de la Bruyère*

Because of this flip-flop in meanings, the conclusion doesn't follow from the premises—but it looks as if it should.

In the second argument, *man* is the equivocal term. In the first premise it means humankind, but in the second, male. So the conclusion doesn't follow, making it appear that a sound argument has banished women's rationality.

In the third argument, *laws* is used in two senses—rules of human behaviour in the first premise, regularities of nature (as in "law of gravity") in the second. Consequently, the conclusion trying to establish the existence of God doesn't follow.

The fallacy of equivocation occurs whenever a word has one meaning in one premise and another meaning in another premise or the conclusion. This switch of meaning always invalidates the argument.

Equivocation often plays a central part in arguments over abortion because so much depends on the meaning of terms referring to the unborn. Consider the following:

> Everyone agrees that a fetus is a human.
> All human beings have a right to life.
> Therefore, a fetus has a right to life.

In the first premise, *human* is used in the sense of something having human physical characteristics such as human DNA. In the second premise, the word is used with *beings* in the sense of a person with moral rights. Because of this shift in meaning, the argument fails.

Appeal to Popularity

appeal to popularity (or to the masses) The fallacy of arguing that a claim must be true merely because a substantial number of people believe it.

The fallacy of the **appeal to popularity** (or to the masses) is to argue that a claim must be true merely because a substantial number of people believe it.

The basic pattern of this fallacy is "Everyone (or almost everyone, most people, many people) believes X, so X must be true." For example:

> Most people approve of the provincial government's decision not to pay for in vitro fertilization treatments. So I guess that decision must be a good one.

> Of course Nova Scotia's rules for new drivers are justified. Everyone believes that they're justified.

> The vast majority of Canadians believe that the monarchy is a good thing.

FOOD FOR THOUGHT

Bamboozling the Taxpayers

Suppose you hear these words in a speech by a national politician: "My tax cut plan will be a windfall for the Canadian taxpayer. Under my plan, the average tax savings will be $1100 per person. Think of what each of you could do with that much extra income."

Sounds like great news—except that this is an example of the fallacy of division. Just because the tax savings for Canadian taxpayers as a group is an average of $1100, it doesn't mean that each individual taxpayer will get $1100. It's possible that only a few taxpayers will get $1100 or more while most won't get any tax break at all.

These arguments are fallacious because they assume that a proposition is true merely because a great number of people believe it. But as far as the truth of a claim is concerned, what many people believe is irrelevant. Many people used to believe that certain women were witches and should be burned, that slavery was perfectly acceptable, that Earth was the centre of the universe, and that bleeding and purging were cures for just about every illness. Large groups of people are no more infallible than an individual is. Their belief in a proposition, by itself, is no indication of truth.

What many other people believe, however, can be an indication of truth if they are experts or have expert knowledge in the issue at hand. If almost all farmers say that the fall harvest will be abundant, ordinarily we should believe them.

When the argument at hand is not about what many people *believe*, but rather about what many people *do*, we may have a case of **appeal to common practice**. For example:

appeal to common practice The fallacy of accepting or rejecting a claim solely on the basis of what groups of people generally do or how they behave (when the action or behaviour is irrelevant to the truth of the claim).

> Of course it's OK to speed! Everybody does it.
>
> But Mom, why can't I get a tattoo? All the other girls in my class already have one!
>
> There's nothing wrong with cheating a bit on your taxes. I read somewhere that nearly half of all taxpayers lie about *something* on their tax returns.

The problem, here, is very similar to the problem with appeal to popularity. The fact that a lot of people *do* something is generally not an indication that it's ethical, polite, or wise for you to do it too.

Appeal to Tradition

The **appeal to tradition** is arguing that a claim must be true just because it's part of a tradition. For example:

appeal to tradition The fallacy of arguing that a claim must be true just because it's part of a tradition.

> Acupuncture has been used for a thousand years in China. It must work.
>
> Of course publishing pornography is wrong. In this community there's a tradition of condemning it that goes back to the early days of photography.

Such appeals are fallacious because tradition, like the masses, can be wrong. Remember that an established tradition barred women from voting, stripped Canada's Aboriginal peoples of their land, promoted the vengeful policy of "an eye for an eye," and sanctioned the sacrifice of innocents to the gods.

"Your proposal is bold and innovative but we are a traditional corporation. I would prefer changes like the ones we've tried before."

CREDIT: Aaron Bacall/Cartoon Stock

Be careful, though. It is also not reasonable to automatically reject a claim because it's traditional. The point is that a tradition should be neither accepted nor rejected without good reason. Knee-jerk acceptance of tradition is as bad as knee-jerk rejection.

Appeal to Ignorance

The **appeal to ignorance** consists of arguing that a lack of evidence proves something. In one type of this fallacy, the problem arises by thinking that a claim must be true because it hasn't been shown to be false. For example:

appeal to ignorance The fallacy of arguing that a lack of evidence proves something. In one type of this fallacy, the problem arises by thinking that a claim must be true because it hasn't been shown to be false. In another type, the breakdown in logic comes when you argue that a claim must be false because it hasn't been proven to be true.

> No one has shown that ghosts aren't real, so they must be real.
>
> It's clear that God exists because science hasn't proved that he doesn't exist.
>
> You can't show me one bit of evidence to disprove my theory that the current "Stanley Cup" is a fake, and that the real one is hidden in Wayne Gretzky's basement. Therefore, my theory is correct.

The problem here is that a lack of evidence is supposed to prove something—but it can't. A lack of evidence alone can neither prove nor disprove a proposition. A lack of evidence simply reveals our ignorance about something.

In another variation of this fallacy, the breakdown in logic comes when you argue that a claim must be false because it hasn't been proved to be true. Look at these examples:

> No one has shown that ghosts are real, so they must not exist.
>
> It's clear that God doesn't exist because science hasn't proved that he does.
>
> You can't provide clear evidence for your theory that the current "Stanley Cup" is a fake and that the real one is hidden in Wayne Gretzky's basement. Therefore, your theory is false.

Again, the moral is: Lack of evidence proves nothing. It does not give us a reason for believing a claim.

But what if our moral were wrong? If we could prove something with a lack of evidence, we could prove almost anything. You can't prove that invisible men *aren't* having a keg party on Mars—does this mean that it's true that invisible men are having a keg party on Mars? You can't prove that Gandhi liked chocolate chip cookies—does this prove that he didn't like them?

There are cases, however, that may seem like appeals to ignorance but actually are not. Sometimes when we carefully search for something, and such a thorough search is likely to uncover it if there is anything to uncover, the failure to find what we're looking for can show that it probably isn't there. A botanist, for example, may search a forest looking for a rare plant that used to grow only there but not find it even though she looks in all the likely places. In this case, her lack of evidence—her not finding the plant after a thorough search—may be good evidence that the plant has gone extinct. This conclusion would not rest on ignorance, but on the knowledge that in these circumstances any thorough search would probably reveal the sought-after object if it was there at all.

This kind of inductive reasoning is widespread in science. Drugs, for example, are tested for toxicity on rodents or other animals before they are given to humans. If after extensive testing no toxic effects are observed in the animals (which are supposed to be relatively similar to humans), the lack of toxicity—the fact that we haven't found negative effects—is considered evidence that the drug will probably not cause toxic effects in humans. Likewise, in the realm of "alternative" health care, most scientists regard the failure to find, after decades of testing, any evidence that homeopathic remedies have any physical effect as strong evidence that such remedies do not in fact work.

In order to understand the significance of appeals to ignorance it is important to understand the notion of **burden of proof**. Burden of proof is the weight of evidence or argument required by one side in a debate or disagreement (in the critical thinking sense). Problems arise when the burden of proof is placed on the wrong side. For example, if Louise declares that "no one has shown that zombies aren't real, so they must be real," she implicitly puts the burden of proof on those who don't agree with her. She's asserting, in effect, "I say that zombies are real, and it's up to you to prove I'm wrong." Or to put it another way, "I'm entitled to believe that zombies are real unless you prove that they're not." But as we saw earlier, this line is just an appeal to ignorance, and the burden of proof for showing that zombies are real rests with *her*—not with those who don't share her belief. If her claim is unsupported, you need not accept it. If you take the bait and try to prove that zombies don't exist, you are accepting a burden of proof that should fall on Louise's shoulders, not yours.

burden of proof The weight of evidence or argument required by one side in a debate or disagreement.

Usually, the burden of proof rests on the side that makes a positive claim—an assertion that something exists or is the case, rather than that something does not exist or is not the case. So in general, if a person (the claimant) makes an unsupported positive claim, he or she must provide evidence for it if the claim is to be accepted. If you doubt the claim, you are under no obligation to prove it wrong. You need not—and should not—accept it without good reasons (which the claimant should provide). Of course, you also should not reject the claim without good reasons. If the claimant does give you reasons for accepting the claim, you can either accept them or reject them. If you reject them, you are obligated to explain the reasons for your rejection.

Appeal to Emotion

appeal to emotion The fallacy of using emotions in place of relevant reasons as premises in an argument.

The fallacy of the **appeal to emotion** is the use of emotions as premises in an argument. That is, it consists of trying to persuade someone of a conclusion solely by arousing his or her feelings rather than presenting relevant reasons. When you use this fallacy, you appeal to people's guilt, anger, pity, fear, compassion, resentment, pride—but not to good reasons that could give logical support to your case. Take a look:

> You should hire me for this network analyst position. I'm the best person for the job. If I don't get a job soon my wife will leave me, and I won't have enough money to pay for my mother's heart medication. Come on, give me a break.

> Political ad: If school music programs are cut as part of the school board's new budget, we will save money—and lose our children to a world without music, a landscape without song. Let the children sing. Write to your member of the school board now and let them know what you think!

As arguments, these passages are fallacious not just because they appeal to strong emotions, but because they appeal to almost *nothing but* strong emotions. They urge us to accept a conclusion but offer no good reasons for doing so. We may feel compassion for the job hunter and his mother, but those feelings have no bearing on whether he is truly the best person for the job. We may recoil from the idea of children in a stark, tuneless world, but that overblown image and the emotions it evokes in us provide no logical support for the conclusion.

CREDIT: Joel Carillet/iStockphoto

Apple is famous for using appeals to emotion to get potential customers to stop thinking of iPods and iPads in terms of technology, and to focus instead on feelings.

This kind of wielding of emotion in discourse is an example of *rhetoric*, the use of non-argumentative, emotive words and phrases to persuade or influence an audience. Arguments try to persuade through logic and reasons. Rhetoric tries to persuade primarily through the artful use of language. There's nothing inherently wrong with using rhetoric, but its use becomes fallacious when there's an attempt to support a conclusion by rhetoric alone.

But in such cases the fallacy is easily avoided. Good writers often combine arguments with appeals to emotion in the same piece of writing, and no fallacy need enter the picture. A strong argument is presented, and it's reinforced by strong feelings. Consider this piece of persuasive prose regarding the legal drinking age in various American states:

> I am a mother though my child is dead. He did not die of an incurable disease, of a virus beyond the ken of medical science. He was not taken from me by a foreign enemy while defending his country. No, he was needlessly slaughtered on the highway. A drunk driver ran broadside into his motorcycle. My son was shot fifty feet through the air by the collision and hit the blacktop at forty-five miles per hour.
>
> My son's assassin is not yet out of high school and yet that boy was able to walk into a liquor store and purchase two six-packs of beer, most of which he drank that evening. This boy does not have the mental capability to graduate from high school in the prescribed time (he was held back in his senior year), and yet the law has given him the right to purchase alcohol and decide for himself what is appropriate behavior with regard to alcoholic consumption. I do not trust most of my adult friends to make such mature judgments. How can anyone trust the eighteen-year-old?
>
> The law must change. Statistics have shown that states that have a minimum drinking age of twenty-one years also have significantly fewer automobile accidents caused by drunken teenagers. I lost my son, but why do any of the rest of us have to suffer as I have? Please, support legislation to increase the drinking age to twenty-one.[2]

There are appeals here to the reader's sympathy and indignation—but also an argument using statistics to support a conclusion about the need for new legislation.

Red Herring

Perhaps the most blatant fallacy of irrelevance is the **red herring**, the deliberate raising of an irrelevant issue during an argument. This fallacy gets its name from the practice of dragging a smelly fish across a trail to throw a hunting dog off the scent. The basic pattern is to put forth a claim and then couple it with additional claims that may seem to support it but in fact are mere distractions. For instance:

red herring The fallacy of deliberately raising an irrelevant issue during an argument. The basic pattern is to put forth a claim and then couple it with additional claims that may seem to support it but, in fact, are mere distractions.

> Canada needs tougher immigration policies. I've got a neighbour who says we should let in *more* immigrants. The sixties . . . boy, what a great time that was for druggies and wackos! You should see the way that hippie dresses. . . . He hasn't figured out that the sixties are over!

> The federal government should bring in mandatory minimum sentences for a greater range of serious crimes. I'm telling you, crime is a terrible thing when it happens to you. It causes death, pain, and fear. And I wouldn't want to wish these things on anyone.

"Discourse on virtue and they pass by in droves; whistle and dance the shimmy, and you've got an audience."

—*Diogenes*

Notice what's happening here. In the first example, the issue is whether Canada should have tougher immigration policies. But the arguer shifts the subject to the intelligence and dress of one particular person who favours more immigration. That person's intelligence and way of dressing, of course, have nothing to do with the main issue. The argument is bogus. In the second example, the issue is whether the federal government should institute more mandatory minimum sentences. But the subject gets changed to the terrible costs of crime, which is only remotely related to the main issue. (There's also an appeal to fear, here.) We can agree that crime can have awful consequences, but this fact has little to do with the merits and demerits of instituting mandatory minimum sentences.

Straw Man

straw man The fallacy of distorting, weakening, or oversimplifying someone's position so it can be more easily attacked or refuted.

Related to red herring is the fallacy of the **straw man**—the distorting, weakening, or oversimplifying of someone's position so it can be more easily attacked or refuted. A straw man argument distracts the listener by focusing on a distorted version of the target argument, rather than focusing on that argument itself. A straw man argument works like this: Reinterpret claim X so that it becomes the weak or absurd claim Y. Attack claim Y. Conclude that X is unfounded. For example:

> David says he's in favour of equal marriage rights for gays. Obviously, he thinks gay relationships deserve special treatment, and that the gay lifestyle should be celebrated and promoted. Do you really want your kids being taught that the gay lifestyle is best? David does, and he's dead wrong.

> The official opposition is opposed to the government's plan to increase spending on Canada's military. Why does the opposition always want to leave Canada defenceless? Why do they want the military's budget cut? They want Canada to be stuck with a military that can't defend our borders, let alone participate in our proud tradition of peacekeeping overseas.

> The premier says that the federal government ought to correct the "fiscal imbalance" by transferring more money to the provinces and territories. I think if he had his way, the federal government would give up all its powers and eventually waste away to nothing at all. Then

> there'd be nothing left to hold this country together. We can't let that happen! Oppose the premier's plan!

In the first passage, David is in favour of equal marriage rights for gays. His opponent, however, distorts his view, claiming that David is actually in favour of teaching children that the gay lifestyle is *best*. David, of course, is not asserting this. This *distorted version* of David's position is easy to ridicule and reject, seemingly allowing his actual view to be summarily dismissed.

In the second passage, the official opposition is against increasing military spending. Their position, though, is twisted into the claim that the military's budget should actually be *reduced* to such an extent that the military becomes useless. But it is unlikely that that is what the opposition really wants. They simply don't want the military's budget *increased*.

The third passage is typical of the kind of fallacious arguments that crop up in debates over federal–provincial relations. Here, the premier wants the federal government to transfer more money to the provinces to help correct what some people see as the "fiscal imbalance" (i.e., the supposed mismatch between the responsibility the provinces have for major expenditures such as health care and education, and their relative lack of money compared to the federal government). But the premier's view gets characterized as implying a wasting away of the federal government. But wanting to make *some* change in the balance of power (and financial ability) between the two levels of government is a far cry from wanting the federal government to have no role at all. Characterizing the premier's point of view as so extreme, however, is a way to generate strong opposition to it. Note that in debates over federal–provincial relations, the straw man tactic is also taken to bolster the other side of the dispute. Those who favour *greater* powers for the federal government are sometimes characterized as wanting to reduce the provinces to mere administrators of federal decisions and policies. But, of course, from the fact that someone wants to increase the powers of the federal government, it does not follow that they want to render the provinces entirely powerless.

CREDIT: Mimi and Eunice

REVIEW NOTES

Fallacies with Irrelevant Premises

- *Genetic fallacy:* Arguing that a claim is true or false solely because of its origin.
- *Appeal to the person:* Rejecting a claim by criticizing the person who makes it rather than the claim itself.
- *Composition:* Arguing that what is true of the parts must be true of the whole.
- *Division:* Arguing that what is true of the whole must be true of the parts or that what is true of a group is true of individuals in the group.
- *Equivocation:* The use of a word in two different senses in an argument.
- *Appeal to popularity:* Arguing that a claim must be true merely because a substantial number of people believe it.
- *Appeal to common practice:* Arguing that a practice is ethical or wise merely because a substantial number of people do it.
- *Appeal to tradition:* Arguing that a claim must be true or good just because it's part of a tradition.
- *Appeal to ignorance:* Arguing that a lack of evidence proves something.
- *Appeal to emotion:* The use of emotions as premises in an argument.
- *Red herring:* An irrelevant issue raised during an argument.
- *Straw man:* A distorted, weakened, or oversimplified representation of someone's position that can be more easily attacked or refuted than their true position.

UNACCEPTABLE PREMISES

Begging the Question

begging the question The fallacy of attempting to establish the conclusion of an argument by using that conclusion as a premise. Also called arguing in a circle.

The fallacy of **begging the question** (or arguing in a circle) is the attempt to establish the conclusion of an argument by using that conclusion as a premise. To beg the question is to argue that a proposition is true because the very same proposition supports it:

> *p*
>
> Therefore, *p*.
>
> The classic question-begging argument goes like this:
>
> God exists. We know that God exists because the Bible says so, and we should believe what the Bible says because God wrote it.
>
> Or, more formally:
>
> The Bible says that God exists.
> The Bible is true because God wrote it.
> Therefore, God exists.

FOOD FOR THOUGHT

Are We Begging the Question Yet?

In everyday usage, the phrase "beg the question" often refers to the famous fallacy. But many times it does not. It is sometimes used (some would say misused) to mean something like "prompts the question" or "raises the question," as in, "The rise in the crime rate begs the question of whether we have enough police officers on the job." As a critical thinker, you need to make sure you don't get these two uses confused.

This argument assumes at the outset the very proposition ("God exists") that it is trying to prove. Any argument that does this is fallacious.

Unfortunately, most question-begging arguments are not as obviously fallacious as "*p* is true because *p* is true." They may be hard to recognize because they are intricate or confusing. Consider this argument:

> It is in every case immoral to lie to someone, even if the lie could save a life. Even in extreme circumstances a lie is still a lie. All lies are immoral because the very act of prevarication in all circumstances is contrary to ethical principles.

At first glance, this argument may seem reasonable, but it's not. It reduces to this circular reasoning: "Lying is always immoral because lying is always immoral."

Among the more subtle examples of question begging is this famous one, a favourite of critical thinking texts:

> To allow every man unbounded freedom of speech must always be, on the whole, advantageous to the state; for it is highly conducive to the interests of the community that each individual should enjoy a liberty, perfectly unlimited, of expressing his sentiments.[3]

This argument, as well as the one preceding it, demonstrates the easiest way to subtly beg the question: just repeat the conclusion as a premise, but use different words.

False Dilemma

The fallacy of **false dilemma** consists of either:

- asserting that there are only two alternatives to consider when there are actually more than two,

or

- asserting that there are two distinct alternatives that may in fact not be mutually exclusive.

false dilemma The fallacy of asserting that there are only two alternatives to consider when there are actually more than two.

> "Truth, like light, is blinding. Lies, on the other hand, are a beautiful dusk, which enhances the value of each object."
>
> —*Albert Camus*

Let's start with the first kind. Here's an example:

> Look, either you're in favour of government support for the arts or you're an uncultured thug. You're not in favour of government support for the arts. So you're an uncultured thug.

This argument contends that there are only two alternatives to choose from: either you're in favour of the government spending money to support the arts (painters, musicians, etc.) or you're an uncultured thug. But this argument works only if there really are just two alternatives. (A "dilemma" is a situation where there are two equally undesirable possibilities.) But here there are actually other plausible possibilities. Maybe you like art, but don't want to see the government spending tax dollars on it. Maybe you spend a lot of money on art, and just don't think it's necessary for the arts to be supported by government. Because these possibilities are excluded, the argument is fallacious.

Here's another example:

> Either I saw you at the party with Mark, or I was too drunk to see straight. But I wasn't drunk. So I saw you at the party with Mark!

This argument says that there are only two possibilities: your friend was at the party with Mark, or you were too drunk to see straight. And so your friend must have been there with Mark, because you weren't drunk. But clearly in a situation like this there are more possible explanations than the ones being offered. You might have seen someone (at a distance) who merely looked like your friend. You might not have been wearing your glasses. You might be misremembering and confusing that night with another night. Since the argument ignores these reasonable possibilities, it's fallacious.

Finally:

> We must legalize drugs. We either legalize them or pay a heavy toll in lives and the taxpayers' money to continue the war on drugs. And we cannot afford to pay such a high price.

At first glance, these two alternatives may seem to exhaust the possibilities. But there is at least one other option—to launch a massive effort to prevent drug use and thereby reduce the demand for illegal drugs. The argument does not work because it fails to consider this possibility.

Note that these three arguments are expressed in disjunctive (either–or) form. But they can just as easily be expressed in a conditional (if–then) form, which says the same thing:

> Look, if you aren't in favour of government support for the arts, then you're an uncultured thug. You're not in favour of government support for the arts. So you're an uncultured thug.

If those lights you saw in the night sky were not alien spacecraft (UFOs), then you were hallucinating. You obviously weren't hallucinating. So they had to be UFOs.

We must legalize drugs. If we don't legalize them, then we will pay a heavy toll in lives and the taxpayers' money to continue the war on drugs. And we cannot afford to pay such a high price.

Sometimes we encounter stand-alone disjunctive phrases rather than full-blown false dilemma arguments. These are false choices often presented as one-liners or headlines in tabloid newspapers, TV news programs, and magazines. For example:

Canada's Oil Sands: Economic Boon or Environmental Disaster?
Apple: Innovator or Evil Giant?
Is the Government Incompetent or Just Evil?

By limiting the possibilities, these headlines can imply that almost any outlandish state of affairs is actual—without even directly asserting anything.

People are often taken in by false dilemmas because they don't think beyond the alternatives laid before them. Out of fear, the need for simple answers, or a failure of imagination, they don't ask, "Is there another possibility?" To

FOOD FOR THOUGHT

False Dilemmas, Evolution, and Creationism

False dilemmas seem to crop up in all kinds of controversies, including debates in science and philosophy. The following is an example of how the fallacy is thought to arise in the ongoing dispute between creationism and evolution.

> Creationists also assume that any data that counts against evolution counts in favor of creationism. But to argue in this way is to commit the fallacy of false dilemma: it presents two alternatives as mutually exclusive when, in fact, they aren't. Gish sets up the dilemma this way: "Either the Universe arose through naturalistic, mechanistic evolutionary processes, or it was created supernaturally." This argument is a false dilemma for a number of reasons. In the first place, there is no need to assume that the universe was created even if evolution is not supported. The universe, as many non-Western peoples believe, may be eternal, that is, without beginning or end. . . . Second, evolution is not the only natural account of creation, and Genesis is not the only supernatural account. Theories of creation are as varied as the cultures that conceived them. The Vikings believed that the universe developed naturally from the void whereas the Gnostics believed that it's the supernatural work of the devil. Thus, even if the creationists could totally discredit evolution, they would not thereby prove their own position, for there are many other alternatives.[4]

ask this is to think outside the box and reduce the likelihood of falling for simplistic answers.

False dilemmas also arise when the arguer asserts that there are two distinct alternatives when in fact the two options offered may not be mutually exclusive. For example:

> She's either a lawyer or a doctor, but I can't figure out which!

This counts as a false dilemma because these two possibilities—being a lawyer and being a doctor—are not in fact mutually exclusive. It is possible to be both, and some people *are* both.

Here's another example:

> Why are you so concerned about the rights of the *accused*? Are you interested in the rights of accused criminals, or the rights of their victims?

Again, this is a false dilemma because the two options being offered are not necessarily in opposition to each other. We can be concerned with protecting the rights of those accused of crimes (e.g., presuming them "innocent until proven guilty") while at the same time wanting to work to assist and protect the victims of crime. In the face of a false dilemma of this kind, we should reply, "Why can't I do both?"

Slippery Slope

slippery slope The fallacy of arguing, without good reasons, that taking a particular step will inevitably lead to further, undesirable steps.

The fallacy of **slippery slope** is to argue, without good reasons, that taking a particular step will inevitably lead to a further, undesirable step (or steps). The idea behind the metaphor, of course, is that if you take the first step on a slippery slope, you will have to take others because, well, the slope is slippery. A familiar slippery slope pattern is "Doing action A will lead to action B, which will lead to action C, which will result in calamitous action D. Therefore, you should not do action A." It's fallacious when there is no good reason to think that doing action A will actually result in undesirable action D. Take a look at this classic example:

> Americans absolutely must not lose the war in Vietnam. If South Vietnam falls to the communists, then Thailand will fall to them. If Thailand falls to them, then South Korea will fall to them. And before you know it, all of Southeast Asia will be under communist control.

This argument was commonplace during the Cold War. It was known as the domino theory because it asserted that if one country in Southeast Asia succumbed to communism, they all would succumb, just as a whole row of dominoes will fall if the first one is pushed over. It was fallacious because there was no good evidence that the dominoes would inevitably fall as predicted. In fact, after South Vietnam was defeated, they did not fall as predicted.

Here are some more examples:

> If supporters of the federal government's Firearms Registry get their way, all recreational and hunting weapons will have to be registered with the federal government. Next thing you know, it'll be illegal to own a gun for target practice, or to go hunting for rabbits, like my Dad and I did when I was a boy. Eventually, the government will want to know if you own *any* weapon, whether it's a pocket knife or a baseball bat. So if you support the Firearms Registry, you're inviting the government to invade your privacy and interfere with your basic freedoms.

> We must ban pornography in all forms. Otherwise, rape and other sex crimes will be as common as jaywalking.

> All Canadians should oppose gay marriage. If gay marriage is allowed, before you know it anything goes—polygamy, incest, marrying animals . . . who knows!

These arguments follow the basic slippery slope pattern. They are fallacies, not because they assert that one event or state of affairs can inevitably lead to others, but because there is no good reason to believe the assertions. Some arguments may look like slippery slope fallacies but are not because there is good reason to think that the steps are connected as described. Observe:

> If you have Lyme disease, you definitely should get medical treatment. Without treatment, you could develop life-threatening complications. Man, you could die. You should see your doctor now.

This is not a fallacious slippery slope argument. There are good reasons to believe that the series of events mentioned would actually happen.

Hasty Generalization

In Chapter 4 we pointed out the connection between the availability error and the fallacy known as **hasty generalization**. In Chapter 8 we will examine hasty generalizations at length. Here we need only recall that we are guilty of hasty generalization when we draw a conclusion about a whole group based on an inadequate sample of the group. This mistake is a genuine fallacy of unacceptable premises because the premises stating the sample size are relevant to the conclusion, but they provide inadequate evidence. There is always an additional premise implied, namely that the sample provided is adequate to justify the conclusion given. And that premise is unacceptable. For example:

hasty generalization The fallacy of drawing a conclusion about a target group on the basis of too small a sample.

> You should buy a Dell computer. They're great. I bought one last year, and it has given me nothing but flawless performance.

> The only male professor I've had this year was a chauvinist pig. All the male professors at this school must be chauvinist pigs.

> Psychology majors are incredibly ignorant about human psychology. Believe me, I know what I'm talking about: My best friend is a psych major. What an ignoramus!

> The French are snobby and rude. Remember those two high-and-mighty guys with really bad manners? They're French. I rest my case.

> The food at Pappie's Restaurant is awful. I had a sandwich there once, and the bread was stale.

Note that in each of these cases, the evidence given may be true and relevant, but the assumption that that evidence is *sufficient* is faulty—it is an unstated and false premise.

"One cool judgment is worth a thousand hasty counsels."

—*Woodrow Wilson*

Faulty Analogy

We will also discuss **arguments by analogy** in Chapter 8. Like hasty generalizations, defective arguments by analogy, or **faulty analogies**, are also fallacies involving unacceptable premises. An analogy is a comparison of two or more things that are alike in specific respects. An argument by analogy reasons this way: Because two or more things are similar in several respects, they must be similar in some further respect. For example:

argument by analogy (analogical induction) An argument making use of analogy, reasoning that because two or more things are similar in several respects, they must be similar in some further respect.

faulty analogy A defective argument by analogy.

> The last time we went on vacation and left you in charge of the house, you said you wanted to have "a few friends" over for a party, and the house was a mess when we got home. Likewise, this time you say you want to have "a few friends" over. So if we let you, I'm sure the house will be a disaster area when we get home!

> A watch is a mechanism of exquisite complexity with numerous parts precisely arranged and accurately adjusted to achieve a purpose—a purpose imposed by the watch's designer. Likewise the universe has exquisite complexity with countless parts—from atoms to asteroids—that fit together precisely and accurately to produce certain effects as though arranged by plan. Therefore, the universe must also have a designer.

In a faulty analogy, the things being compared are not sufficiently similar in relevant ways. Such analogical arguments are said to be weak. For instance, you could argue that:

> Dogs are warm-blooded, nurse their young, and give birth to puppies. Humans are warm-blooded and nurse their young. Therefore, humans give birth to puppies too.

REVIEW NOTES

Fallacies with Unacceptable Premises

- *Begging the question:* The attempt to establish the conclusion of an argument by using that conclusion as a premise.
- *False dilemma:* Asserting that there are only two alternatives to consider when there are actually more than two.
- *Slippery slope:* Arguing, without good reasons, that taking a particular step will inevitably lead to a further, undesirable step (or steps).
- *Hasty generalization:* The drawing of a conclusion about a target group based on an inadequate sample size.
- *Faulty analogy:* An argument in which the things being compared are not sufficiently similar in relevant ways.

This argument by analogy is about as weak as they come—and a little silly. Dogs and humans are not sufficiently similar in relevant ways (in physiology, for one thing) to justify such a strange conclusion.

SUMMARY

Certain types of defective arguments that occur frequently are known as fallacies. Fallacies are often psychologically persuasive but logically flawed. We can divide fallacies into two broad categories: (1) those that have *irrelevant* premises and (2) those that have *unacceptable* premises.

Fallacies with irrelevant premises include the genetic fallacy (arguing that a claim is true or false solely because of its origin), composition (arguing that what is true of the parts must be true of the whole), division (arguing that what is true of the whole must be true of the parts or that what is true of a group is true of individuals in the group), appeal to the person (rejecting a claim by criticizing the person who makes it rather than the claim itself), equivocation (the use of a word in two different senses in an argument), appeal to popularity (arguing that a claim must be true merely because a substantial number of people believe it), appeal to ignorance (arguing that a lack of evidence proves something), appeal to tradition (arguing that a claim must be true or good just because it's part of a tradition), appeal to emotion (the use of emotions as premises in an argument), red herring (the deliberate raising of an irrelevant issue during an argument), and straw man (the distorting, weakening, or oversimplifying of someone's position so it can be more easily attacked or refuted).

Fallacies with unacceptable premises include begging the question (the attempt to establish the conclusion of an argument by using that conclusion as a premise), slippery slope (arguing, without good reasons, that taking a particular step will inevitably lead to a further, undesirable step or steps), hasty generalization (the drawing of a conclusion about a group based on an inadequate sample of the group), and faulty analogy (an argument in which the things being compared are not sufficiently similar in relevant ways).

EXERCISE 5.1

Answers to exercises marked with an asterisk (*) may be found in Appendix B, Answers to Exercises.

Review Questions

1. According to the text, what are the two broad categories of fallacies?
2. What is the genetic fallacy?
3. Can the origin of a claim ever be relevant to deciding its truth or falsity?
*4. What is the fallacy of composition? How is it different from the fallacy of division?
5. What are the two forms of the fallacy of division?
6. Why are appeals to the person fallacious?
7. What type of ad hominem argument is put forth as a charge of hypocrisy?
8. What is the fallacy of poisoning the well?
9. What is the fallacy of equivocation?
*10. Why are appeals to popularity fallacious?
11. What is the appeal to tradition?
12. What are the two forms of the appeal to ignorance?
13. What is the proper response to an appeal to ignorance?
14. What is rhetoric?
*15. According to the text, is it ever legitimate to use rhetoric and argument together?
16. What is a red herring? How is it different from the straw man fallacy?
17. What is the basic pattern of argument of the straw man fallacy?
18. What is the fallacy of hasty generalization?
*19. What are two ways that false dilemmas can be presented? Why are people often taken in by this fallacy?
20. What is the burden of proof?
21. What is the fallacy of slippery slope?

EXERCISE 5.2

In the following passages, identify any fallacies of irrelevance (genetic fallacy, composition, division, appeal to the person, equivocation, appeal to popularity, appeal to ignorance, appeal to tradition, appeal to emotion, red herring, and straw man). Some passages may contain more than one fallacy, and a few may contain no fallacies at all.

*1. "Seeing that the eye and hand and foot and every one of our members [i.e., body parts] has some obvious function, must we not believe that, likewise, a human being has a function over and above these particular functions?" (Aristotle)

2. Buying products made in Canada is the way to go. If you buy products that are made in other countries, you are forcing hard-working Canadians out of a job. Ask any Canadian and they'll tell you that's morally wrong.

3. The Occupy Wall Street protestors say they're against greed and corporate corruption. But they're really just a bunch of whiny, unwashed hipsters who are trying to avoid having to get a real job.

4. It was a bad idea for all the countries of Europe to give up their old currencies and adopt the euro. Just ask any German how he feels about linking his country's economic fate to that of Greece!

*5. The *National Post* says that a proposal to force companies to embrace corporate social responsibility amounts to a denial of the basic principles of the market economy. But you know that's false—after all, it's from the *National Post*!

6. Geraldo says that students who cheat on exams should not automatically be expelled from school. I can't believe he thinks cheating is such a trivial thing!

7. Of course there is a God. Almost every civilization in history has believed in a deity of some kind.

8. Wow, your computer was so expensive! Each of its components must have cost a fortune too.

9. The prime minister has misled the country about whether he was behind that decision. Surveys show that almost everyone in Canada thinks so.

*10. Kelly says that many women who live in predominantly Muslim countries are discriminated against. But how the heck would she know? She knows nothing about the world's religions!

11. A lot of people think that football jocks are stupid and rude. That's a crock. Anyone who has seen the fantastic game that our team played on Saturday, with three touchdowns before halftime, would not believe such rubbish.

12. Does acupuncture work? Can it cure disease? Of course. It has been used in China by folk practitioners for at least 3000 years.
13. The study found that 80 per cent of women who took the drug daily had no recurrence of breast cancer. But that doesn't mean anything. The study was funded in part by the company that makes the drug.
*14. "The only proof capable of being given that an object is visible, is that people actually see it. The only proof that a sound is audible, is that people hear it: and so of the other sources of our experience. In like manner, I apprehend, the sole evidence it is possible to produce that anything is desirable, is that people actually desire it." (John Stuart Mill, *Utilitarianism,* 1863)
15. You'll be sorry if you don't give our new revolutionary weight-loss pill a try. But if you try it, you'll thank us when your friends and family start complimenting you on your slim figure. And that feeling you'll get when you notice people staring at you at the beach? Priceless!
16. How do you know that everything you see around you is real and that we aren't actually in a simulation, similar to the world in *The Matrix*? Famous philosophers have accepted this scenario as a very real possibility. Besides, you can't actually know whether or not it's true because it would be impossible to find any evidence that disproves this idea.
17. "The most blatant occurrence of recent years is all these knuckleheads running around protesting nuclear power—all these stupid people who do not research at all and who go out and march, pretending they care about the human race, and then go off in their automobiles and kill one another." (Ray Bradbury)
18. I can't believe that lady got such a big legal settlement from McDonald's by spilling coffee on herself. I guess our legal system just doesn't care much about taking responsibility for your own mistakes. Now everyone will "accidentally" spill hot coffee on themselves and become millionaires.
19. Is the Bible the true word of God? There can be no doubt that it is, for it has inspired millions of believers for centuries.
*20. The former mayor was convicted of drug possession, and he spent time in jail. So you can safely ignore anything he has to say about legalizing drugs.
21. Of course I believe in miracles. I defy you to show me one bit of proof that miracles aren't possible.
22. Professor, I deserve a better grade than a D on my paper. Look, my parents just got a divorce. If they see that I got a D, they will just blame each other, and the fighting will start all over again. Give me a break.
23. We know that at its most basic level, matter is not alive. Clearly a bunch of non-living things can't just come together and make one living thing, so God must have created life.

24. We've built this orchestra by selecting the very best players from over 20 high school orchestras. This is clearly going to be the best orchestra in the province.

EXERCISE 5.3

In the following passages, identify any fallacies of unacceptable premises (begging the question, false dilemma, slippery slope, hasty generalization, and faulty analogy). Some passages may contain more than one fallacy, and a few may contain no fallacies at all.

1. If we don't allow Olympic athletes to make use of steroids, then how can we justify them taking cold medication when they've got a cold? And if cold medications get counted as "performance enhancing," shouldn't we just go all the way and say "no health care at all for Olympic athletes"?
2. John keeps littering! I can't believe he cares so little for the environment. He might as well be taking a chainsaw to the park and cutting down all the trees! I'm sure the police would arrest him in a heartbeat if he started doing that, so why aren't they taking his littering more seriously? I tell you, there'll be anarchy in the streets soon if people find out you can get away with committing crimes like littering!
3. Three thieves are dividing up the $7000 they just stole from the local bank. Robber number one gives $2000 to robber number two, $2000 to robber number three, and $3000 to himself. Robber number two says, "How come you get $3000?" Robber number one says, "Because I am the leader." "How come you're the leader?" "Because I have more money."

*4. Either you are rich or you are poor. If you're rich, you don't have to worry about money. And if you're poor, you don't have any money to worry about. Either way, you've got no worries!

5. Ivan doesn't talk about his political views. But he's got to be either a Liberal or a Conservative. And he's certainly no Liberal. So he must be a Conservative!

*6. I used to work with this engineering major, and, man, they are totally geeky.

7. I met these two guys on a plane, and they said they were from Edmonton. They were total druggies. Almost everyone in that city must be on drugs.
8. It's no coincidence that Rwanda has a very weak economy and that it also has a very high rate of infant mortality.
9. A recent study conducted by PETA has shown that meat eaters are significantly more likely to engage in violent behaviour than are vegetarians and

vegans. Their study involved handing out questionnaires to 20 meat eaters and 20 non–meat eaters and scoring their answers on a behavioural scale.

*10. Either we fire this guy or we send a message to other employees that it's OK to be late for work. Clearly, we need to fire him.

EXERCISE 5.4

For each of the following claims, devise an argument using the fallacy shown in parentheses. Make the argument as persuasive as possible.

1. All drugs should be legalized. (red herring)
2. *Cowboys and Aliens* is the best western ever made. (appeal to popularity)
*3. Mrs Anan does not deserve the Nobel Prize. (appeal to the person)
4. Vampires—just like in the *Twilight* books and movies—are real. (appeal to ignorance)
5. Wall Street needs to be held accountable for the 2008 financial crisis. (slippery slope)
*6. It's great that Scouts Canada welcomes gay kids as members. (begging the question)
7. Quebec should separate from Canada. (false dilemma)
8. That sociology department is absolutely the worst department in the entire university. (hasty generalization)
9. The Canadian government needs to increase health care spending. (appeal to emotion)
10. The Nigerian court was right to sentence that woman to be stoned to death for adultery. (appeal to popularity)
*11. Newfoundland's fisheries are a mess because the Department of Fisheries and Oceans—a federal department—has too much power over them. (red herring)
12. We should reject the American suggestion that Canada needs to reform its banking regulations. (genetic fallacy)

Field Problems

1. Find a letter to the editor in a magazine or newspaper (an online letter is OK, too), that contains at least one fallacy. Point out the fallacious part,

name the fallacy involved, and then rewrite the passage to eliminate the fallacy and strengthen the argument. (To rework the argument effectively, you may have to make up some facts.)

2. Print out at least two pages of comments from an online news story. Look through them all, circling and labelling any examples of fallacies. Find at least three examples.
3. What is one of the major political topics discussed in your city right now? Find a speech or editorial made on the subject. Can you find any fallacies being used? Do you think the fallacious argument is being used on purpose, because it is psychologically persuasive? Or do you think he or she is using it without realizing it is a bad argument?

Self-Assessment Quiz

Name the fallacy or fallacies in the following passages:

1. The mayor is a racist! At a city council meeting last night, he said that he won't support our proposal to name a street after Nelson Mandela. How can we tolerate elected officials who say that minorities shouldn't have rights?
2. People keep repeating anecdotes about how Wall Street bankers caused the financial crisis. But where's the real proof? Show me the proverbial "smoking gun" or stop complaining about people just because they're more successful than you.
3. Legislation to officially recognize gay marriage was opposed by crazy religious groups across the country—which proves that the legislation is on the right track!
4. You want to know about this car's gas mileage? Well, I'll be happy to tell you all about it and I think you'll be pleasantly surprised. But first, have you noticed the detailing on the dashboard? That's pure, hand-cut cherry wood!
5. "Jews are part of the Soviet people. They are a fine people, intelligent, very valued in the Soviet Union. Therefore, the problem of the Jews in the Soviet Union does not exist." (Mikhail Gorbachev)
6. You can safely ignore Helena's argument for a freeze on tuition because she's active in the Canadian Federation of Students.
7. You advocate a woman's right to abortion because you do not understand how hideous and monstrous an abortion procedure is, how it tears a living

fetus away from the uterine wall, crushes it to bleeding pieces, and sucks it away into oblivion.

8. That must have been a terrible film. I don't know anyone who went to see it.
9. True knowledge is unattainable because it is impossible to know anything with certainty.
10. "If the parts of the Universe are not accidental, how can the whole Universe be considered as the result of chance? Therefore the existence of the Universe is not due to chance." (Moses Maimonides)
11. It would appear that war is inevitable. Either we attack our enemies now or hide in our homes and cower down to their every demand like weaklings. And we are no weaklings!
12. Atheistic philosophers have been trying for thousands of years to prove that there is no God, and they haven't succeeded yet. This shows that there is indeed a God after all.
13. How can you, with a straight face, tell me that I should be a vegetarian? You're wearing a leather jacket!
14. Judges should not hand down anything but maximum sentences for all convicted criminals. If you start making exceptions, prosecutors will start asking for lighter sentences. Next thing you know, every criminal will be getting off with mere warnings.
15. Either you're a good Christian or you're a godless heathen!
16. The food at Big Ben's Burger Palace is unlikely to be much good. I mean, have you seen their ads on TV? Those commercials are just awful.
17. If the professor really appreciated my hard work, he would have given me an A+ on my essay. But he only gave me a B+, so he obviously doesn't care about the effort I put into it.
18. When I was in elementary school, we were supposed to stand and recite "The Lord's Prayer" every day before class. That was dead wrong. No child should have to submit to such brainwashing.
19. My doctor says I should stop smoking. But I saw him in the park yesterday, smoking a cigar. So why should I listen?
20. Dilraj was caught stealing office supplies from the supply cabinet. But why should the boss fire him? After all, lots of people steal stuff from that cabinet.

Integrative Exercises

These exercises pertain to material in Chapters 1–5.

For each of the following passages, say whether it contains an argument. If it does, specify the conclusion and premises, whether the argument is deductive or inductive, whether it is a good argument (sound or cogent), and whether it is a fallacy. Some passages may contain no argument.

1. Fernanda always blushes when Dennis walks into the room, so she *must* have a crush on him!
2. Are you seriously trying to tell me that there is no such thing as dragons, when in actual fact you have no proof at all that they aren't out there, somewhere?
3. "Didn't Tom Cruise make a stock-car movie in which he destroyed thirty-five cars, burned thousands of gallons of gasoline, and wasted dozens of tires? If I were given the opportunity, I'd say to Tom Cruise, 'Tom, most people don't own thirty-five cars in their *life*, and you just trashed thirty-five cars for a movie. Now you're telling other people not to pollute the planet? Shut up, sir.'" (Rush Limbaugh)
4. "The large number of female voters for Arnold Schwarzenegger in California announces one thing: the death of feminism. That so many women would ignore his sexual misconduct and vote for him bespeaks the re-emergence of the reckless phallus." (Letter to the editor, *Newsday*)
5. Alanis Morissette and Shania Twain are vegetarians. And Nazi leader Adolf Hitler was also a vegetarian. We are forced to conclude that Morissette and Twain are Nazis!
6. If you park illegally, you're breaking the law. And if you break one law, you'll break another. Soon, you'll be shoplifting. Next thing you know, you'll be committing major crimes and end up in jail.
7. Since it looks like nobody is willing to speak up, I'll come out and say it. I think your clothing designs are awful, and I know for a fact that every other designer in this room thinks so too.
8. Thinking is like swimming. Just as in swimming it's easy to float on the top but hard to dive deep; it's easy in thinking to float along on the surface of an issue but difficult to use your intellect to delve down into the layers.
9. "If a cell, under appropriate conditions, becomes a person in the space of a few years, there can surely be no difficulty in understanding how, under appropriate conditions, a cell may, in the course of untold millions of years, give origin to the human race." (Herbert Spencer)
10. Either you make a donation to our anti-cancer campaign, or you admit that you just don't care about the suffering of the thousands of Canadians diagnosed with cancer each year.

11. Everything must either happen by random accident or by divine intervention. Nothing happens by pure accident, so everything must happen because of divine intervention.
12. Children should never be spanked. Spanking is harmful. I've talked to three mothers about this issue, and they all agree that spanking harms a child's self-esteem and development.
13. Green is the "in" colour this season. It must be true, because everyone is wearing it.
14. My professor says that telling a lie is never morally permissible. But that's ridiculous. The other day I heard him tell a boldfaced lie to one of his students.
15. "Not all forms of gender discrimination are unethical. There are a number of exclusively male or female fitness clubs around the country utilized by religious individuals who shun the meat market scene. If a woman wants to spare herself the embarrassment of being ogled in her sports bra while doing thigh-thrusts, it is her right to work out with women only. Similarly, if a man wants to spare himself the temptation of working out with lingerie models, he should be allowed membership to strictly male fitness clubs. It would be unreasonable to require non-discrimination of these private clubs, or to make them build separate facilities to accommodate everyone." (Letter to the editor, *Arizona Daily Wildcat*)
16. "Highway checkpoints, drug testing, ubiquitous security cameras and now the government's insistence on the use of sophisticated software tools to spy on the American people all point to a single vision. This vision was shared with us years ago, in George Orwell's book *1984*. Big Brother is indeed watching." (Letter to the editor, *Buffalo News*)
17. There are those on campus who would defend a professor's right to question the teachings of Islam. But there is no such right. Racism is wrong, and will always be wrong.
18. We must protect our historical landmarks because they can give us glimpses into what life was like for our ancestors. This is important because it is unlikely that we will be able to build a successful future without learning from the mistakes of the past
19. Give a man a fish, and he'll eat for a day. Teach a man to fish, and he'll ask you to buy a fishing rod for him, and then bait, and then a cooler to store the fish, and then a car so he can drive to the stream. Clearly it's better to just give the man a fish.
20. It's true! The British explorers of the seventeenth century saved the First Nations people from their backward ways. If it weren't true, it wouldn't be in my history textbook!

Critical Thinking and Writing Exercise

An Annotated Sample Paper

Let's see how the lessons of the four previous modules might be applied in an actual student essay.[5] The essay on the following pages incorporates the main elements of good argumentative papers and, as even the best essays do, exhibits both strengths and weaknesses—many of which are noted in the margins. Read the paper carefully, taking in the annotations as you go and making sure you understand each point before moving on to the next.

Free Speech on Campus

In order to meet the goals and purposes of higher education, free speech must remain intact. Thus, the University of Missouri should not adopt a campus hate speech code. (1.) The First Amendment protects all speech outside the university setting, and what happens outside of the university setting also should be allowed inside. (2.) Without an open forum for thought, though it may include hate speech, the university fails in its mission to provide a realistic experience for its students. By abolishing hate speech on university campuses, that open forum for discovery and knowledge is eliminated. As a result, learning and knowledge are stunted. (3.) Without the exchange of controversial ideas and opinions, there can be no real change in our society. Experiencing and debating is almost always better than suppressing, because censoring speech can never invoke real change.

Thesis statement

Seems to be three arguments to discuss, but this summary does not make that as clear as it should.

Summarizes the arguments to be made.

The First Amendment protects the right for every person to express opinions about the government and about each other. It actually "protects speech no matter how offensive the content" (Hate Speech on Campus, 1996). Just because something is offensive to one person does not mean it is offensive to another. Justice John M. Harlan wrote in Cohen v. California (1971), "One man's vulgarity is another's lyric" (Free Speech, 1996). In other words, just because something is offensive to one person does not mean that it is offensive by definition.

Provides background for first argument.

Needs a more explicit transition to first argument.

Sources cited

Speech that is protected outside of the university setting also should be protected inside. Some would argue that hate speech hinders the abilities of minority students to learn, but part of the goal of higher education is to put students out of their comfort zone and to challenge their ways of thinking. In response to a sexual-harassment policy being implemented at the University of Massachusetts, lawyer Harvey A. Silvergate (1995) wrote a memo to university administrators opposing the proposal.

Responds to an objection to thesis.

First argument for thesis

> One of the primary purposes of a college education and experience is to challenge students, to make them question their comfortable lives and assumptions in short, to discomfort them in one way or another (Silvergate, 1995).

Not clear how these quotations—which refer to sexual harassment—relate to hate speech.

In the same memo, Silvergate also wrote:

> If I am allowed to say something on the street corner, in a letter to the editor of a newspaper, or on a radio talk show, surely I should be allowed to say it on the campus of the University of Massachusetts.

First argument for thesis

This is equally true for the University of Missouri. What can possibly be gained by excluding an element of real life such as offensive speech from the campus experience? The university would only serve to deceive its students by shielding them from realistic situations while they are in school. This, in turn, only serves to place them into the real world with false expectations.

Introduces quotation

Alternatively, exploring and debating is almost always better than suppressing. The organization Justice on Campus (1995) contends that:

> When we hear speech or see images that offend us, nothing is more human than our urge to suppress or to destroy them. But as deeply human is our need to think and to share our thoughts with others. Censorship is the greatest evil because the censor's goal is to imprison the human spirit.

Second argument for thesis

In addition to providing a realistic picture of nonacademic life, allowing all types of speech on campus encourages an open forum for the discussion of all types of ideas. Discussion of controversial issues and different points of view are the fuel for a useful education. That is why higher education has a responsibility to ensure that all forms of speech are protected, analyzed, and addressed. "The right of free speech is indivisible. When one of us is denied this right, all of us are denied" (Hate Speech on Campus, 1996). By denying one point of view, we eliminate the open forum. A speech code on any university campus only hinders the ability of students and faculty to fully explore the market of ideas available to them. The University of Missouri is no exception to the idea that academic freedom is the bedrock of a free society.

Third argument for thesis

If we do not allow open expression, however hateful it is, then there can be no change, no growth. Racism, sexism, ageism, etc. are not going to diminish without being addressed in higher education. As noted by the ACLU (Hate Speech on Campus, 1995), "Verbal purity is not social change." Barring certain types of speech would be a seeming quick fix for issues such as racism, sexism, ageism, and homophobia, which often comprise hate speech. But racist statements are not the real problem between the races; racism is. If we bar all racially biased comments on campus, all we have done is fuel the racism. We have then given hatred the power to lurk and grow within us instead of communicating and debating about it in the open.

If hate speech is not allowed to occur openly, the problem of racism is never addressed. Like racism, hate speech itself is not the problem; hate is. As members of a society, we must communicate in order to solve problems and grow as individuals. This includes addressing hateful ideas and opinions. We can make no progress if we do not allow offensive kinds of speech to exist on campus. By barring them, we run the risk of being silenced ourselves.

Conclusion summarizes main arguments

Restatement of thesis

A hate speech code at the University of Missouri would be detrimental to everyone, from students to faculty. The First Amendment protects all kinds of speech, including the offensive. It does this in order to ensure that all voices are heard and that all issues can be addressed. To go through college with the idea that offensive speech does not happen is detrimental to students and to the society in which they live. The educational system is based on the idea that communication leads to learning and that learning leads to personal growth. Without the open forum for thought and the freedom to express controversial ideas, a higher education is worthless. Moreover, no one ever solved a controversial gender issue or a racial conflict in silence. There must be communication so that debate can transpire.

In order for any change in our society to transpire, offensive speech must be allowed to continue. It can only be addressed and learned from if it is equally protected by the Constitution. Mike Godwin, of the Electronic Frontier Foundation, says, "when it comes to the Bill of Rights, what you don't use, you lose. The First Amendment is a terrible thing to waste" (Comments and quotes, 1995). If anyone has a responsibility to use the freedom granted by the First Amendment, higher education is at the top of the list.

References

American Civil Liberties Union. (1996). Hate speech on campus. [Online]. Available: **www.aclu.org/library/pbp16.html**

American Civil Liberties Union. (1996). Free speech. [Online]. Available: **www.aclu.org/issues/freespeech/isfs.html**

Justice on Campus. (1996). Comments and quotes on sexual harassment and free speech. [Online]. Available: **http://joc.mit.edu/comments.html**

Justice on Campus. (1995). Speech codes and disciplinary charges. [Online]. Available: **http://joc.mit.edu/roundup.html**

Silvergate, H.A. (1995, November 23). Memo from Harvey Silvergate. [Online]. Available: **http://joc.mit.edu/amherst/silvergate.112495.txt**

Writing Assignments

1. In a 300-word essay, argue that women are no more nurturing and caring than men are. Avoid fallacies. Then exchange essays with a classmate and write a one-page critique of each other's paper, paying special attention to any fallacies you uncover. Be polite, but honest!
2. Write a 500-word response to Essay 3 ("Marine Parks") in Appendix A, pointing out as many fallacies as possible.
3. Write a 300-word paper arguing that the legal age for obtaining a regular driver's licence should be raised to 21. Include at least three fallacies in the paper, but try to make them as convincing as you can. Exchange your paper with a classmate who has done the same assignment. Pinpoint the fallacies in each other's papers.
4. Write a one-page essay criticizing the view that Canada should stop extracting oil from northern Alberta's oil sands. Make use of at least the genetic fallacy and the slippery slope fallacy. Then write a one-page critique of your own paper, making sure to point out the fallacies and explaining why they are problematic.

PART THREE

ARGUMENTS

6 DEDUCTIVE REASONING
CATEGORICAL LOGIC

CHAPTER OBJECTIVES

Statements and Classes

You will be able to

- define subject term, predicate term, copula, quantifier, quantity, and quality.
- memorize the four standard-form categorical statements.

Translations and Standard Form

You will be able to

- translate ordinary statements into standard categorical form.
- translate singular statements into standard form.

Diagramming Categorical Statements

You will be able to

- construct a Venn diagram for any categorical statement.
- memorize the Venn diagrams for the four standard-form categorical statements.
- use Venn diagrams to tell if two statements are, or are not, equivalent.

Sizing Up Categorical Syllogisms

You will be able to

- understand the structure of categorical syllogisms.
- check the validity of a categorical argument by drawing Venn diagrams.

For centuries, philosophers, monks, scientists, linguists, and students have been enthralled by logic. Yes, *logic*. For many people—including some great thinkers such as Aristotle, Gottfried Leibniz, and Bertrand Russell—logic has been, ironically, a passion, something deemed worthy of deep study and long devotion. For hundreds of years, logic (along with philosophy) was a required course in universities and was regarded as one of the grand pillars upon which a liberal arts education was based (the others were grammar, rhetoric, arithmetic, music, astronomy, and geometry). Even today scholars continue to be drawn into the depths of logic, never seeming to tire of exploration and application.

> "The study of logic appeals to no criterion not already present in the learner's mind."
>
> —*C.I. Lewis*

But why do they bother? Why do they seem to think that logic is anything other than the dry and dusty preoccupation of dry and dusty philosophers? Well, maybe they bother because the study and use of logic, like the study and use of mathematics, is an exercise in exactitude, precision, clarity, and—above all—definite answers. All of which can be very satisfying. Or perhaps they bother because logic is the study of good reasoning or thinking and therefore should be part of every decision and every judgment we make.

> "Bad reasoning as well as good reasoning is possible; and this fact is the foundation of the practical side of logic."
>
> —*Charles Sanders Peirce*

Logic also produces real results for us. Out of the study of logic have come discoveries now used in electronic engineering, set theory, linguistics, mathematics, and, of course, philosophy. Investigations in logic have yielded insights that made the invention of computers possible. (See the box "Logic and Computers" in Chapter 7.)

We begin our study of formal logic by looking at **categorical logic.** The basic unit of concern in categorical logic is the *statement component*. We study the relationships, not between entire statements, but between components known as the subject and predicate of a statement. In Chapter 7 we will look at formal methods for assessing the relationships between entire statements, or propositions, when we study propositional logic.

categorical logic A form of logic whose focus is categorical statements, which make assertions about categories, or classes, of things.

Both types of reasoning—categorical and propositional—are deductive, and in both our ultimate goal is the evaluation of arguments. In propositional logic this task is made easier with "truth tables." In categorical logic the primary tools are diagrams and calculation rules.

In categorical reasoning the statements or claims of interest are **categorical statements**—those that make simple assertions about categories, or classes, of things. They say how certain classes of things are, or are not, included in other classes of things. For example: "All cows are vegetarians," "No gardeners are plumbers," or "Some businesspeople are cheats." Categorical statements like these play their part without the complexities that arise from conjunctive, disjunctive, or conditional statements.

categorical statement A statement or claim that makes a simple assertion about categories, or classes, of things.

Categorical logic is inescapable in daily life. Without thinking much about the process, we often use arguments composed of categorical statements.

CREDIT: S. Harris/Cartoon Stock

We may reason, for example, that no pocket knives are things permitted on a commercial airplane because no sharp instruments are things allowed on a commercial airplane, and all pocket knives are sharp instruments. In a real-life situation, we wouldn't state the argument so formally (and awkwardly), and we would probably make one of these premises implicit because it's too obvious to mention. Also, this whole process of reasoning would likely happen in seconds, with the argument zipping through our heads at top speed.

There are several good reasons why categorical logic—first formulated by Aristotle over 2000 years ago—is still around. Chief among these are that (1) it is part of everyday reasoning and (2) understanding its rules leaders to better, clearer thinking. If that is so, then learning how to use it well can only help us.

STATEMENTS AND CLASSES

The words in categorical statements that name classes, or categories, of things are called *terms*. Each categorical statement has both a **subject term** and a **predicate term**. Look, for example, at this claim:

subject term The first class, or group, named in a standard-form categorical statement.

predicate term The second class, or group, named in a standard-form categorical statement.

All cats are carnivores.

The subject term here is *cats*, and the predicate term is *carnivores*. The statement says that the class of *cats* is included within the class of *carnivores*. We can express the *form* of the statement like this:

All *S* are *P*.

standard-form categorical statement In categorical logic, a categorical statement that takes one of these four forms:

1. All S are P. (All cats are carnivores.)
2. No S are P. (No cats are carnivores.)
3. Some S are P. (Some cats are carnivores.)
4. Some S are not P. (Some cats are not carnivores.)

By convention, *S* stands for the subject term in a categorical statement; *P* stands for the predicate term.

This kind of statement—All *S* are *P*—is one of four **standard forms of categorical statements**. Here are all four of them together:

1. All *S* are *P*. (For example: All cats are carnivores.)
2. No *S* are *P*. (For example: No cats are carnivores.)
3. Some *S* are *P*. (For example: Some cats are carnivores.)
4. Some *S* are not *P*. (For example: Some cats are not carnivores.)

Standard-form statement 2, "No *S* are *P*," asserts that no member of the *S* class is included in the *P* class (no members of the class of cats are part of the class of carnivores). Statement 3, "Some *S* are *P*," asserts that some members of the *S* class are also members of the *P* class (some members of the class of cats are also members of the class of carnivores). Statement 4, "Some *S* are not *P*," asserts that some members of the *S* class are not members of the *P* class (some members of the class of cats are not members of the class of carnivores).

For the sake of simplicity, the terms in these statements about cats are single words, just nouns naming a class. But subject and predicate terms can also consist of noun phrases and pronouns. Noun phrases are used because several words may be needed to specify a class. Sometimes a noun like *cats* won't do, but a noun phrase like "cats that live outdoors and hunt mice" will.

In standard-form categorical statements, subject and predicate terms can't be *anything but* nouns, pronouns, and noun phrases. Only nouns, pronouns, and noun phrases can properly designate classes. So the statement "All cats are carnivores" is in standard form, but "All cats are carnivorous" is not, because "carnivorous" is an adjective, not a category of things.

As you might guess, many categorical statements you'll run into don't strictly fit any of these four patterns. But they should—if you want to easily evaluate the validity of arguments containing these statements. So part of the job of assessing such arguments is to translate the categorical statements found "in the wild" into the tamer and clearer configurations of the standard forms. The challenge is to do these translations while being faithful to the meaning of the original.

To translate categorical statements accurately, you need to know more about how they're put together. Categorical statements have four parts and several characteristics expressed in these parts. You already know about two of these parts, the subject term and the predicate term. They are joined together by a third part called the **copula**, a linking verb—either *are* or *are not*.

The fourth part is the **quantifier**, a word that expresses the **quantity**, or number, of a categorical statement. The acceptable quantifiers are *all*, *no*, or *some*. The quantifiers *all* and *no* in front of a categorical statement tell us that it's *universal*—it applies to every member of a class. The quantifier *some* at the beginning of a categorical statement says that the statement is *particular*—it applies to at least one member of a class.

Categorical statements can vary not only in quantity, but also in the characteristic of **quality**, being either *affirmative* or *negative*. A categorical statement that *affirms* that a class is entirely or partly included in another class is said to be affirmative in quality. A categorical statement that *denies* that a class is entirely or partly included in another class is said to be negative in quality.

copula One of four components of a standard-form categorical statement; a linking verb—either *are* or *are not*—that joins the subject term and the predicate term.

quantifier In categorical statements, a word used to indicate the number of things with specified characteristics. The acceptable quantifiers are *all*, *no*, or *some*. The quantifiers *all* or *no* in front of a categorical statement tell us that it's *universal*—it applies to every member of a class. The quantifier *some* at the beginning of a categorical statement says that the statement is *particular*—it applies to some but not necessarily all members of a class.

quantity In categorical statements, the attribute of number, specified by the words *all*, *no*, or *some*.

quality A characteristic of a categorical statement, determined by whether the statement affirms or denies that a class is entirely or partly included in another class. A categorical statement that affirms is said to be affirmative in quality; one that denies is said to be negative in quality.

With this technical vocabulary we can describe each of the standard forms of statements noted earlier.

1. All *S* are *P*. (All cats are carnivores.)
   This standard-form statement has a universal quantity and an affirmative quality. It *affirms* that *all* cats are included in the class of carnivores. So we characterize it as a *universal affirmative* statement, or claim.
2. No *S* are *P*. (No cats are carnivores.)
   This one *denies* that *all* cats are included in the class of carnivores. Put another way, the whole class of cats is *excluded* from the class of carnivores. It's a *universal negative* statement.
3. Some *S* are *P*. (Some cats are carnivores.)
   This one *affirms* that only *some* cats are included in the class of carnivores. It's a *particular affirmative* statement.
4. Some *S* are not *P*. (Some cats are not carnivores.)
   This one *denies* that only *some* cats are included in the class of carnivores. It doesn't refer to the whole class of cats, just as statement 3 doesn't refer to the whole class. But it denies, instead of affirms, that the partial class of cats is included in the class of carnivores. It's a *particular negative* statement.

Here are the four standard forms of categorical statements again with their quality and quantity listed:

A: All *S* are *P*. (universal affirmative)
E: No *S* are *P*. (universal negative)
I: Some *S* are *P*. (particular affirmative)
O: Some *S* are not *P*. (particular negative)

Notice that this time the statements are preceded not by numbers, but by the letters A, E, I, and O. These letters are the traditional designations for the four standard forms of categorical statements. We can say then, for example, that this or that statement is an A-statement or an O-statement, indicating the pattern of the arguments with an easy shorthand.

Something important to remember, even if it's obvious, is that all categorical statements should fit into one of these four standard forms, and all statements that do fit into one of these have the *same* form.

EXERCISE 6.1

Answers to exercises marked with an asterisk (*) may be found in Appendix B, Answers to Exercises.

For each of the following statements, identify the subject and predicate terms and the name of the form (universal affirmative, universal negative, particular affirmative, or particular negative). Also, state the traditional letter designation for each form (A, E, I, O).

*1. No scientists are Christians.
2. Some homes are condos.
3. No cats that have lived over 15 years in a domestic setting are pets free of health problems.
4. Most people do not like accounting.
*5. All theologians who have studied arguments for the existence of God are scholars with serious misgivings about the traditional notion of omnipotence.
6. No politicians are trustworthy.
7. All students who smoke marijuana are hipsters.
*8. Some people who play the stock market are not millionaires.
9. No taxpayers from the 2016 tax year are embezzlers.
10. No Canadian banks that had dealings with Enron are institutions that deserve our business!
11. All who sell homeopathic treatments are either delusional or fraudsters.
*12. Some terrorists are Saudi citizens.
13. No one who goes to university will be unemployed when they graduate.
14. Conservative backbenchers are pro-lifers.
15. Some of the protestors at the Occupy Wall Street protest are not poor.
*16. No "new Canadians" are supporters of changes in the immigration rules.
17. All child-abuse caseworkers are overburdened civil servants.

TRANSLATIONS AND STANDARD FORM

This is worth repeating: we translate ordinary statements into standard form categorical statements so that we can handle them more efficiently. We want to handle them efficiently so that we can more easily evaluate the validity of arguments composed of categorical statements. Translation is necessary to bring out the underlying structure of statements. It is also important because ordinary language is too imprecise and ambiguous to use in the analysis of statements and arguments. You will appreciate this fact more as you work with categorical statements.

Translating statements into standard form is a straightforward process consisting of a few simple steps and some rules of thumb. Knowing the steps and

FOOD FOR THOUGHT

Categorical Inspiration

Categorical statements don't have to sound like dry logical assertions. Artists, authors, poets, and songwriters have often used categorical statements to inspire. Here are a few examples:

"Every child is an artist." (Pablo Picasso)

"Some men see things as they are and ask why. Others dream things that never were and ask why not." (George Bernard Shaw)

"Any woman who understands the problems of running a home will be nearer to understanding the problems of running a country." (Margaret Thatcher)

"Let every man be respected as an individual and no man idolized." (Albert Einstein)

"No woman can call herself free who does not own and control her body. No woman can call herself free until she can choose consciously whether she will or will not be a mother." (Margaret Sanger)

"Love is the only gold." (Lord Alfred Tennyson)

"All you need is love." (John Lennon)

the rules is important, but getting some *practice* translating statements is vital if you want to know how to translate fast and accurately. If you don't understand a particular point, you'll have an easier time if you go over it until you do rather than skipping it and looking at it later.

Just as a reminder, here's the pattern of all standard-form categorical statements:

Quantifier . . . Subject Term . . . Copula . . . Predicate Term

You need to know how to handle each of these parts. Since the copula must always be either *are* or *are not*, you don't have to spend a lot time trying to determine the correct verb. But pinning down the terms and quantifiers is a little more challenging.

Terms

In translating statements, your first order of business is usually to identify the terms and ensure that they designate classes. Once you identify the terms and distinguish the subject term from the predicate term, you'll know in what order the terms must appear in the statement because the subject term must always precede the predicate term. Identifying the terms, though, often involves rewording them so they actually name classes. Consider these translations:

[Original] All dogs are loyal.
[Translation] All dogs *are* loyal animals.

[Original] Some guys have all the luck.
[Translation] Some guys *are* people who have all the luck.

[Original] No nations can survive without secure borders.
[Translation] No nations *are* things that can survive without secure borders.

Sometimes it's easy to locate statement terms but not as easy to tell which is the subject term and which is the predicate term. This can happen when the order of the subject and predicate is reversed:

Beyond the mountains stood the redwood trees.

Here the subject is "the redwood trees." The sentence has a normal variation of subject–predicate order, common in English. If you understand the structure of such grammatical reversals, you should be able to identify the true subject and predicate terms. To see this, ask yourself: what is the sentence *about?* Notice that the key verb is *stood*. Who or what is doing the standing? It's the redwood trees, and so they are the subject of the sentence.

Difficulty distinguishing subject and predicate terms can also arise when the word *only* is in a statement. For example, which is the subject term and which is the predicate in these A-statements?

1. Only palm readers are wise advisers.
2. Only if something is a music file is it a WAV file.
3. Hamburgers are the only real junk food.
4. The only crimes prosecuted are murders.

We can figure out statements 1 and 2 by using this formula: *The words "only" and "only if" precede the predicate term in an A-statement.* So the correct translations are:

1. All wise counsellors are palm readers.
2. All WAV files are music files.

The translations of statements 3 and 4 follow this formula: *The words "the only" precede the subject term in an A-statement.* Therefore the correct translations are:

3. All real junk food is hamburgers.
4. All prosecuted crimes are murders.

REVIEW NOTES

The Four Standard-Form Categorical Statements

A: All *S* are *P*. (universal affirmative)	"All cats are felines."
E: No *S* are *P*. (universal negative)	"No cats are felines."
I: Some *S* are *P*. (particular affirmative)	"Some cats are felines."
O: Some *S* are not *P*. (particular negative)	"Some cats are not felines."

> "Men are apt to mistake the strength of their feeling for the strength of their argument. The heated mind resents the chill touch and relentless scrutiny of logic."
>
> *–William E. Gladstone*

Now, what are the terms in these statements?

5. Chris Rock is a comedian.
6. Calgary is Canada's finest city.
7. Sunday is the first day of the week.
8. *The Matrix* is an amazing movie.
9. Alicia is not a good student.

FOOD FOR THOUGHT

Standard Form versus Fuzziness

We take the trouble to translate categorical statements into standard form for several reasons—one of them being that language is fuzzy, fuzzy, fuzzy. The famed logician Bertrand Russell agreed: "Because language is misleading, as well as because it is diffuse and inexact when applied to logic (for which it was never intended), logical symbolism is absolutely necessary to any exact or thorough treatment of our subject" (*Introduction to Mathematical Philosophy*).

We can see a good example of language fuzziness in this type of categorical statement: "All *S* are not *P*." Take the statement "All Bigfoot monsters are not apes." Does this mean that (1) no Bigfoot monsters are apes or (2) that some Bigfoot monsters are not apes? Statement 1 is an E-statement; statement 2 is an O-statement. To defeat fuzziness, we have to apply some categorical logic and translate the original sentence into either an E- or O-statement.

CREDIT: Mark Heath/Cartoon Stock

These are known as **singular statements**. Each one asserts something about a single person or thing, including objects, places, and times. Each subject term is a noun (including names), pronoun, or noun phrase referring to an individual, particular item. In a way, the predicate terms specify classes but, alas, the subject terms don't. We can transform such statements, though, into universal statements (A-statements or E-statements). The trick is to think of each subject term as naming a class in which there's just one member. We can, for example, treat the subject term in statement 5 ("Chris Rock") as designating a class with Chris Rock as one member of that class, like this:

singular statements In categorical logic, statements that assert something about a single person or thing, including objects, places, and times.

5. All persons identical to Chris Rock are comedians.

We can translate our other singular statements in similar fashion:

6. All places identical to Toronto are places that are Canada's finest city.
7. All days identical to Sunday are the first days of the week.
8. All things identical to the film *The Matrix* are amazing movies.
9. No persons identical to Alicia are good students.

Now we can see more clearly that statements 5–8 are A-statements and that statement 9 is an E-statement.

Granted, translations of ordinary statements into standard-form categorical statements can sometimes sound awkward, as the preceding translations surely do. But when we translate statements, we put them into a form that makes their logical connections transparent—an agreeable state of affairs when we're trying to check the validity of complex arguments.

Quantifiers

Some quantifiers may be in non-standard form, and some may be unexpressed. Consider these statements:

1. Every hockey player is an athlete.
2. Whoever is an artist is a genius.
3. Sharks are good swimmers.
4. Nothing for sale is truly valuable.
5. Comets are ice balls.

Each is a universal statement with a non-standard or unexpressed quantifier. Here are the translations with the proper quantifiers:

1. All hockey players are athletes.

2. All artists are geniuses.
3. All sharks are good swimmers.
4. No items for sale are truly valuable.
5. All comets are ice balls.

Statements 1, 2, and 4 have non-standard quantifiers; statements 3 and 5 have unexpressed quantifiers. Fortunately, most non-standard quantifiers are fairly easy to decipher. "Every professor," for example, obviously means all the professors. "Nothing" and "none" mean not any, which refers to all of them, whatever they are. Usually, unexpressed quantifiers are readily understood because of the nature of the terms. The statement "Sharks are good swimmers" clearly refers to all sharks, not just some of them. In some statements, though, the unexpressed quantifier is not obvious, as, for example, in "Trent University students are radicals." Is it "*All* Trent students" or "*Some* Trent students"? When in doubt, be charitable: assume the quantifier that you think would make the statement most likely to be true. In this case, "All Trent students . . ." is a sweeping generalization that's unlikely to apply to every single Trent student. The claim more likely to be true is "Some Trent students . . ."

Now consider these statements:

6. There are government workers who are spies.
7. Most movie stars are snobs.
8. Several politicians are space aliens.

These are all particular categorical statements. Their translations are:

6. Some government workers are spies.
7. Some movie stars are snobs.
8. Some politicians are space aliens.

The quantifier *some* is appropriate in all these statements because, in logic, it means "at least one." We therefore have only two options for expressing quantity in categorical statements: *all* and *fewer than all.* "Most," "a few," "several," "almost all," and similar terms are all translated as "some." Part of the reason for logic's restrictive definition of "some" is that, in everyday language, "some" is extremely vague. The word could mean "most," "two or three," "10 or more," or "many." Who knows? Logic, though, needs precision—more precision than is found in ordinary discourse.

FOOD FOR THOUGHT

Let Us Count the Ways . . .

Plenty of non-standard statements are equivalents of categorical statements in standard form.

A-Statement: "All S Are *P*"

Only scientists are experts.
Mathematicians are good acrobats.
Every general is a leader.
Only if something is a plant is it a flower.
Anything is a potential weapon.
Something is a true breakfast only if it includes eggs.
Whatever is a beaver is a rodent.
Every pediatrician is a doctor.
If something is not a vegetable, then it is not a potato.
All dictators are thugs.

E-Statement: "No S Are *P*"

If anyone is an artist, then she is not a banker.
All humans are non-reptiles.
Territories are not provinces.
Nothing that is a mind is a body.
Nothing red is a banana.
None of the vegetables are fruits.
It is false that some vegetables are fruits.

I-Statement: "Some S Are *P*"

There are engineers who are painters.
Most criminals are morons.
Several countries are islands.
At least one survivor is a hero.
A few lotteries are scams.
Many Europeans are Germans.

O-Statement: "Some S Are Not *P*"

Some philosophers are non-Christians.
Some non-Christians are philosophers.
Not all comedians are Canadian.
Many tents are not teepees.
Many maple trees are not sugar maples.
Most Quebecers are not separatists.
There are non-Christian philosophers.
Canadians are not always peacekeepers.
A few rock stars are not maniacs.

EXERCISE 6.2

Answers to exercises marked with an asterisk (*) may be found in Appendix B, Answers to Exercises.

Translate each of the following statements into standard categorical form and say whether the form is A, E, I, or O.

*1. All Habs fans are fanatical.
2. Most bears will try to eat you if they get the chance.
3. “Brave are the hearts that beat beneath Scottish skies.” (“Scotland the Brave”)
4. “He who laughs last, laughs best.”
*5. Only cellphone companies that keep up with the latest technology are good investments.
6. If it’s not alive, then it can’t be human.
7. “People with pinched faces often have poisonous hearts.” (Chinese proverb)
8. It’s impossible for any bachelor to also be married.
*9. “All intelligent thoughts have already been thought.” (Johann Wolfgang von Goethe)
10. “If it’s worth doing, it’s worth doing right.”
11. All bankers should be in jail.
12. Players who were injured in training didn’t suit up for the opening game.
*13. Some things are meant to be forgotten.
14. “There is no excellence without difficulty.” (Ovid)
15. Rap music is not very popular among senior citizens.
16. “All’s well that ends well.” (Shakespeare)

EXERCISE 6.3

Follow the instructions given for Exercise 6.2.

*1. Only a fool tests the depth of the water with both feet. (African proverb)
2. Work hard and you’ll get the marks.
3. “People who wish to salute the free and independent side of their evolutionary character acquire cats.” (Anna Quindlen)
*4. All androids like Commander Data are non-human.
*5. Nothing that satisfies the heart is a material thing.
6. It’s not often that you see CEO’s who aren’t overpaid.
7. Every political party that gets at least 20 per cent of the vote in a general election is a major player in Canadian politics.
*8. Most treatments said to be part of “alternative medicine” are unproven.

9. There are people among us here today who will one day rise to greatness.
10. "People who love only once in their lives are . . . shallow people." (Oscar Wilde)
11. Some Acadians settled on what is called the "French Shore" of Nova Scotia.
*12. Friday is the only day that gives her any joy.
13. Many critical thinking textbooks make good bedtime reading.
14. "All children are artists." (Pablo Picasso)
*15. The picture hanging on the wall is crooked.
16. Every time I try to go to the gym, I tire myself out just walking there.
17. "He that is born to be hanged will never be drowned." (French proverb)
18. Only you can stop forest fires!
19. It is not the case that all birds are non-flightless birds.
*20. "A nation without a conscience is a nation without a soul." (Winston Churchill)

DIAGRAMMING CATEGORICAL STATEMENTS

If you want more help in understanding the relationships between subject and predicate terms, you're in luck. You can represent such relationships graphically with the use of **Venn diagrams** (named after the nineteenth-century British logician and mathematician, John Venn). The diagrams consist of overlapping circles, each one representing a class specified by a term in a categorical statement. Here's an example:

Venn diagrams Diagrams consisting of overlapping circles that represent graphically the relationships between subject and predicate terms in categorical statements.

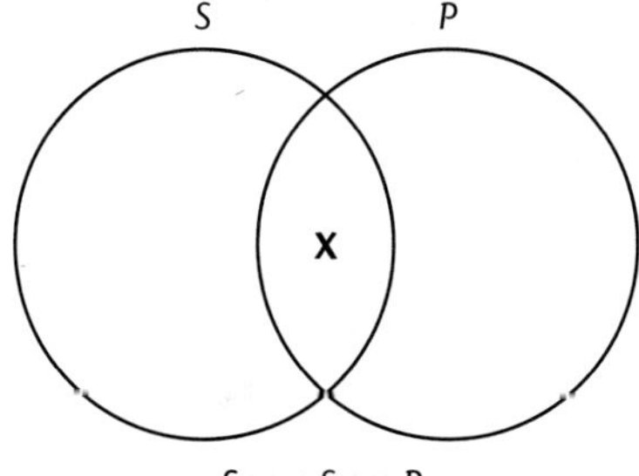

Some *S* are *P*.

This is the diagram for an I-statement: "Some *S* are *P*." The circle on the left represents the class of *S*; the circle on the right, the class of *P*. The area on the left contains only members of the *S* class; the area on the right contains only members of the *P* class. The area where the circles overlap means that both *S* members and *P* members are present. The X in the overlapped area, however, gives more specific information. It shows that *at least one* *S* member is a *P* member. That is, there is at least one *S* that also is a *P*. This diagram, of course, represents *any* statement of the form "Some *S* are *P*"—like, for instance, "Some cars are Fords." The X on the diagram where the circles overlap, then, would mean that *at least one* car is a Ford.

Now here's the diagram for an O-statement—"Some *S* are not *P*":

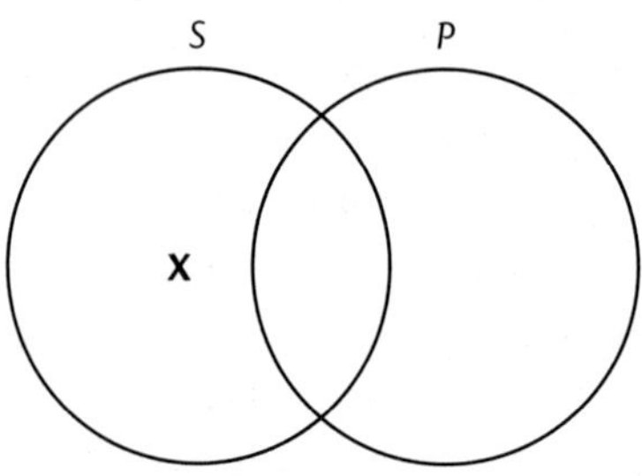

Some *S* are not *P*.

Here the X is in the *S* circle but outside the *P* circle, indicating that at least one *S* is not a *P*. In our car example (in which the *S* circle represents the class of cars and the *P* circle represents the class of Fords), this diagram would show that at least one car is not a Ford.

Here's the diagram for an A-statement—"All *S* are *P*":

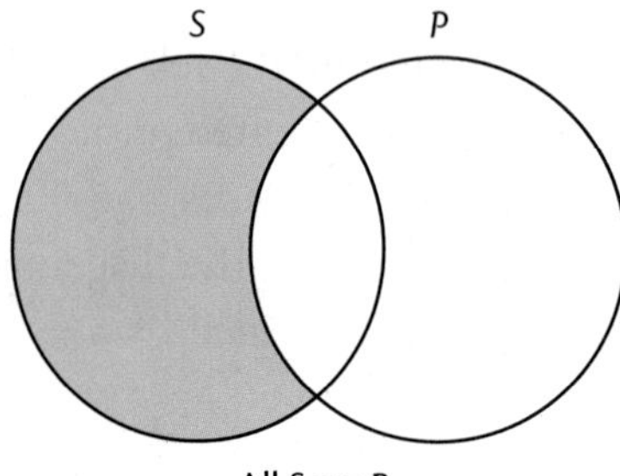

All *S* are *P*.

This diagram asserts that all members of the *S* class are also members of the *P* class ("All cars are Fords"). Notice that the part of the diagram where the *S* circle does not overlap the *P* circle is shaded, or "blacked out," showing that that area is "empty," or without any members. (If you want, think of it this way: in the shaded area, the lights are out because no one is home!) And this means

REVIEW NOTES

Three Steps to Diagramming a Categorical Statement

1. Draw two overlapping circles, each one representing a term in the statement.
2. Label the circles with the terms.
3. Shade an area of a circle to show that an area is empty; insert an X to show that at least one member of a class is also a member of another class.

that there are no members of *S* that are not also members of *P*. The remaining part of the *S* circle overlaps with the *P* circle, showing that *S* members—all of them—are also *P* members.

Finally, here is the diagram for an E-statement—"No *S* are *P*":

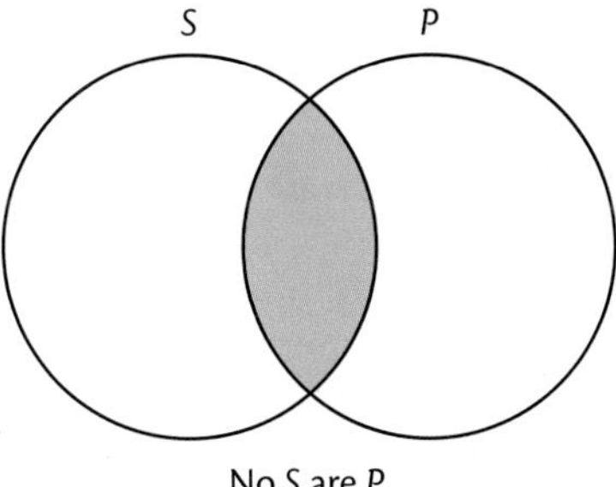

No S are P.

Here the area where the *S* circle and the *P* circle overlap is shaded (empty), meaning that there is no situation in which *S* overlaps with *P* (in which members of *S* are also members of *P*). So no members of *S* are also members of *P* ("No cats are vegetarians").

Venn diagrams can come in handy when you want to know whether two categorical statements are equivalent—that is, whether they say the same thing. Because sometimes we can say the same thing—make the identical logical claim—in two different ways. If the diagrams for the statements are identical, then the statements are equivalent.

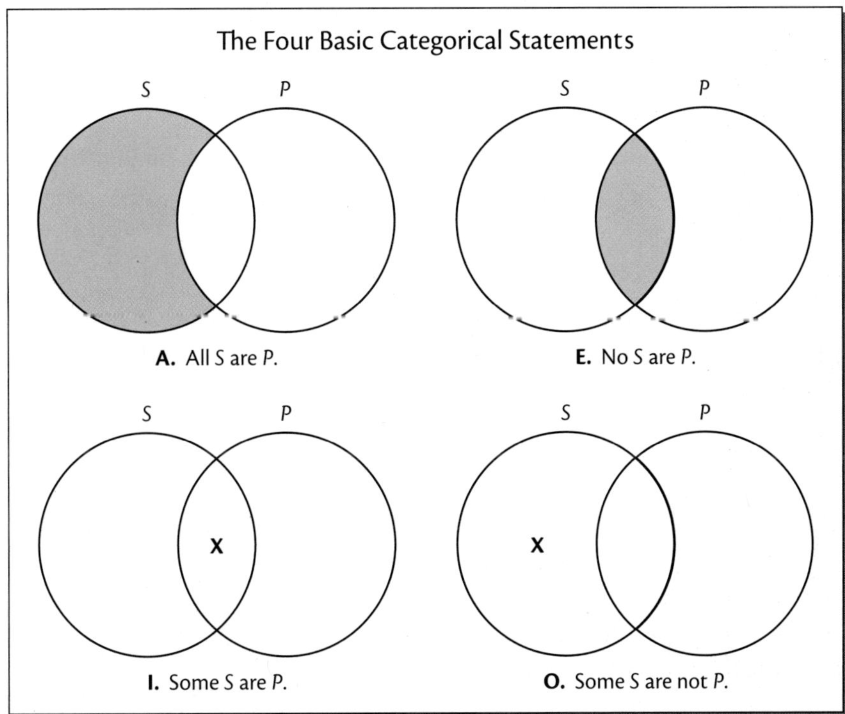

Let's say that you want to know whether the following two statements say the same thing:

No *S* are *P*.
No *P* are *S*.

If you diagram them both, you get your answer:

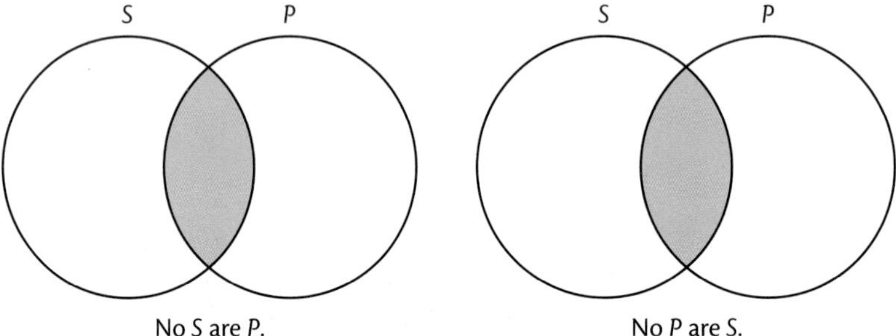

No S are P. No P are S.

You can see that the diagrams are identical—they both show the area of overlap between the two circles as shaded, signifying that there are no members of *S* that are also members of *P*, and vice versa. So the first statement ("No *S* are *P*," an E-statement) says the same thing as the second statement ("No *P* are *S*").

Likewise, if we compare the diagrams for "Some *S* are *P*" (I-statement) and "Some *P* are *S*," we can see that these statements are also equivalent:

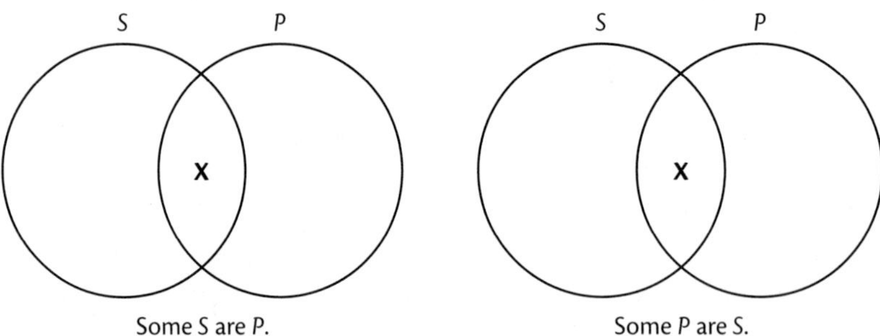

Some S are P. Some P are S.

On the other hand, by comparing diagrams we can see that A-statements and E-statements are *not* equivalent (something you knew already, of course):

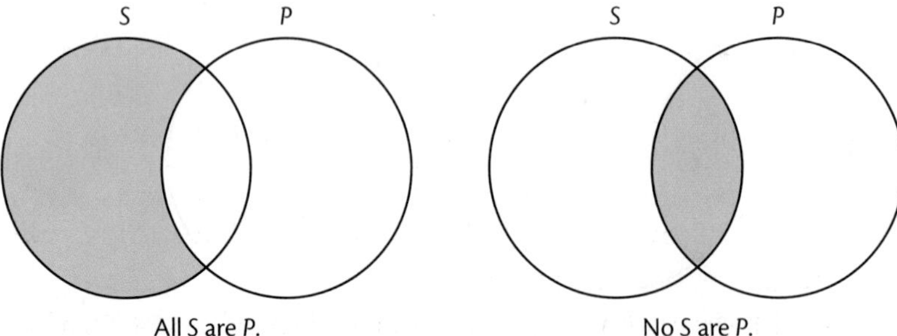

All S are P. No S are P.

Let's examine one final pair of statements:

All *S* are *P*.
No *S* are non-*P*.

The diagrams clearly show that these are equivalent:

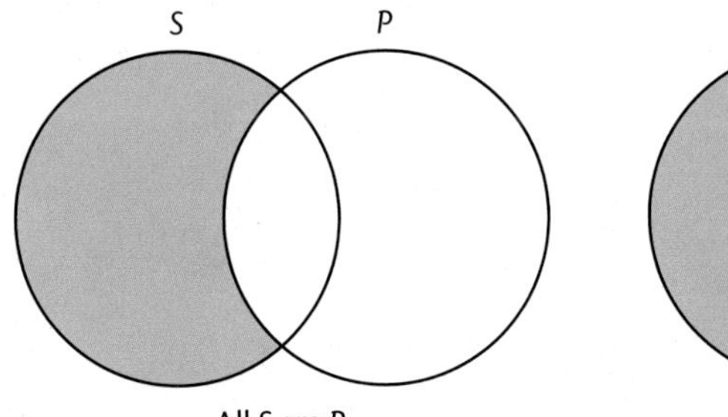

All S are *P*.

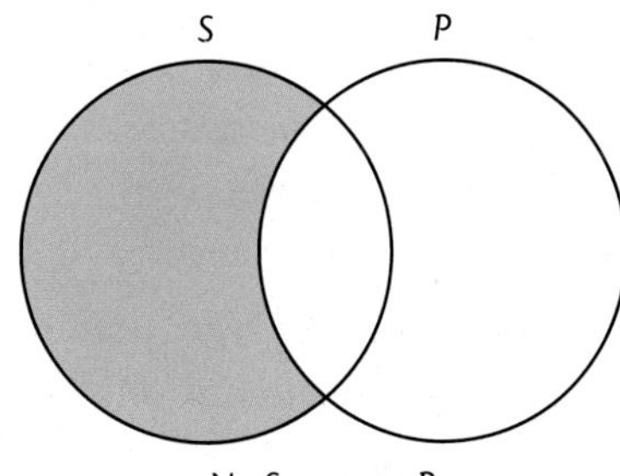

No S are non-*P*.

EXERCISE 6.4

Answers to exercises marked with an asterisk (*) may be found in Appendix B, Answers to Exercises.

Construct Venn diagrams for each of the following statements. Specify both the subject and predicate terms. If necessary, translate the statement into standard form before diagramming (A, E, I, or O).

*1. No one is exempt from federal income tax.
2. "No man is an island." (John Donne)
3. No one can legally drink at a bar or restaurant in Ontario unless they are 19.
4. Some animals are polar bears.
*5. "Nothing is more useless in a developing nation's economy than a gun." (King Hussein I of Jordan)
6. John Locke is one of the few philosophers whose ideas have truly shaped the modern world.
7. Some books are not written by either J.K. Rowling or Stephen King.
*8. Some good talkers are good listeners.
9. It is false that some sharks can breathe air.
10. Some people with excellent reputations are not persons of excellent character.
11. The man who invented matches didn't get rich from his invention.
*12. Every corporation has social obligations.
13. You can always rely on Acme knives because they never break and never get dull.
14. There are bad apples in every barrel.
15. "Few friendships could survive the moodiness of love affairs." (Mason Cooley)

EXERCISE 6.5

Construct Venn diagrams for each statement in the following pairs, and then say whether the statements are equivalent.

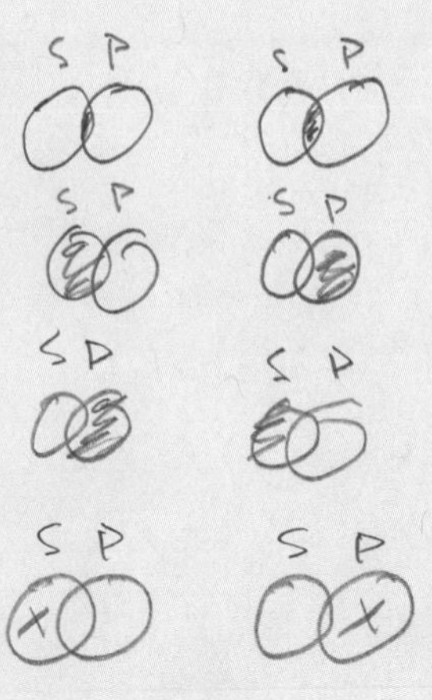

*1. No *P* are *S*; No *S* are *P*.
2. All *S* are *P*; Some *P* are non-*S*.
*3. All *S* are *P*; All *P* are *S*.
4. No *S* are *P*; All *P* are non-*S*.
5. Some *S* are *P*; Some *P* are *S*.
*6. All *P* are non-*S*; All *S* are non-*P*.
7. No non-*S* are *P*; No non-*P* are *S*.
8. No *S* are *P*; No *P* are *S*.
*9. Some *S* are not *P*; Some *P* are not *S*.
10. All *S* are non-*P*; No *P* are *S*.

SIZING UP CATEGORICAL SYLLOGISMS

> "Logical consequences are the scarecrows of fools and the beacons of wise men."
>
> —*Thomas Henry Huxley*

Once you understand the workings of categorical statements, you're ready to explore the dynamics of categorical arguments, or—more precisely—categorical syllogisms. As we saw in Chapter 3, a syllogism is a deductive argument made up of three statements: two premises and a conclusion. A categorical syllogism is one consisting of three categorical statements (A, E, I, or O) interlinked in a specific way. You can see the interlinking structure in this categorical syllogism:

1. All elected officials are civil servants.
2. All politicians are elected officials.
3. Therefore, all politicians are civil servants.

If we diagram this argument as we did in Chapter 3, we come up with this structure:

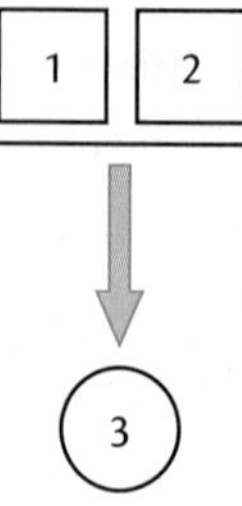

EVERYDAY PROBLEMS AND DECISIONS

Logic and Racism

Being bad at categorical logic is at the heart of an awful lot of racism and general prejudice against various ethnic, national, and religious groups. For example, in late 2014 an act of terrorism—a shooting—took place in Paris, at the offices of the satirical newspaper *Charlie Hebdo*. The killers were Muslims. Five people died and eleven more were injured. Such incidents are terrible tragedies. And the tragedy of such events is only amplified by the unthinking racism that often follows. Many people, unfortunately, leapt hastily from the fact that the *Charlie Hebdo* killers were Muslims to a general hatred or mistrust of Muslims. Consider what the relevant categorical syllogism would look like.

(1) Some killers (namely, the *Charlie Hebdo* killers) are Muslims.
(2) All killers are terrorists.
(3) Therefore, all Muslims are terrorists.

You can easily construct a Venn diagram to prove that this is a flawed syllogism. That is, the premises, even if they are true, are incapable of providing support for the conclusion. This is particularly important to see, given that the conclusion of this argument has led so many people to act badly toward their fellow human beings.

A good command of categorical logic can save you from being wrong about—and acting unethically toward—entire groups of people.

But this kind of diagram, though handy for understanding the overall structure of the argument, isn't much help here because it doesn't reveal the internal components and interlinking structure of the statements. Notice that each categorical statement has, as usual, two terms. But there are a total of only three terms in a categorical syllogism, each term being mentioned twice but in different statements. So in the preceding argument, *Politicians* appears in statements 2 and 3; *elected officials* in 1 and 2; and *civil servants* in 1 and 3.

In a categorical syllogism, we refer to the predicate term in the conclusion (*civil servants*, in this case) as the *predicate term* for the whole argument. The predicate term always also appears in one of the premises (premise 1, in the example above). The subject term in the conclusion is treated as the *subject term* for the whole argument. The subject term always also occurs in one of the premises (premise 2, in the argument above). The other term, the one that appears once in each premise but not in the conclusion, is referred to as the *middle term*. If we map out the argument with the terms labelled in this way, here's what we get:

Premise (1) [Middle term] [Predicate term].
Premise (2) [Subject term] [Middle term].
Conclusion (3) Therefore, [Subject term] [Predicate term].

We can symbolize this argument form with letters:

(1) All *M* are *P*.
(2) All *S* are *M*.
(3) Therefore, all *S* are *P*.

Here, *M* stands for the middle term, *P* for the predicate term, and *S* for the subject term.

So, summarizing, a categorical syllogism is one that has:

1. Three categorical statements—two premises and a conclusion.

FOOD FOR THOUGHT

Living by the Rules

Drawing Venn diagrams is a good way to both visualize what a syllogism is saying and test it for validity. But you can also check validity without diagrams. One technique is to assess the validity of a syllogism by determining if the argument follows certain rules. Some of these rules involve the fine points of syllogistic structure. But others are drawn from simple facts about syllogisms that you probably already know—or have suspected. Here are three such rules:

1. A valid categorical syllogism must possess precisely three terms.
2. A valid categorical syllogism cannot have two negative premises.
3. A valid categorical syllogism with at least one negative premise must have a negative conclusion.

Any standard-form categorical syllogism that breaks even one of these rules is invalid. (On the other hand, a categorical syllogism that does not violate any of these rules is not necessarily valid. It may be defective for other reasons.)

Here are some syllogisms that violate at least one rule:

All snakes are reptiles.
All reptiles are cold-blooded creatures.
Therefore, all lizards are cold-blooded creatures.
(Violates rule 1)

No criminals are law-enforcement officers.
Some law-enforcement officers are not bank robbers.
Therefore, some bank robbers are not criminals.
(Violates rule 2)

No Italians are Germans.
Some Inuit are Italians.
Therefore, some Inuit are Germans.
(Violates rule 3)

2. Exactly three terms, with each term appearing twice in the argument.
3. One of the terms (the middle term) appearing in each premise but not the conclusion.
4. Another term (the predicate term) appearing as the predicate term in the conclusion and also in one of the premises.
5. Another term (the subject term) appearing as the subject term in the conclusion and also in one of the premises.

A valid categorical syllogism, like a valid deductive argument of any other sort, is such that if its premises are true, its conclusion *must* be true. (That is, if the premises are true, the conclusion cannot possibly be false.) This fact, of course, you already know. Of more interest now is how we can *check the validity* of categorical syllogisms. Fortunately, there are several ways to do this, the simplest of which is the Venn diagramming method. This technique involves drawing a circle for each term (the subject, predicate, and middle term) in the argument (giving us three overlapping circles), then diagramming the premises on these circles (using shading and X's, as discussed in the previous section). If the resulting diagram reflects the assertion in the conclusion, the argument is valid.

If you know how to diagram categorical statements, you can diagram an entire categorical argument. Remember that since a categorical statement has two terms, we need two circles to diagram it—one circle for each term.

And since a categorical syllogism has three terms, we need three circles, overlapping like this:

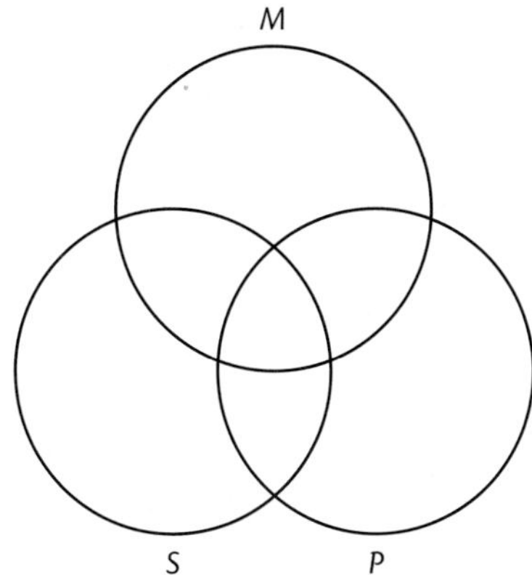

The top circle represents the class designated by the middle term (*M*); the bottom left circle, the subject term (*S*); and the bottom right circle, the predicate term (*P*). The two lower circles together represent the conclusion, since they stand for the relationship between the subject and predicate terms (*S* and *P*).

Let's diagram our syllogism about politicians and civil servants, diagramming one statement, or premise, at a time. We can start by labelling the diagram like this, with three empty, overlapping circles:

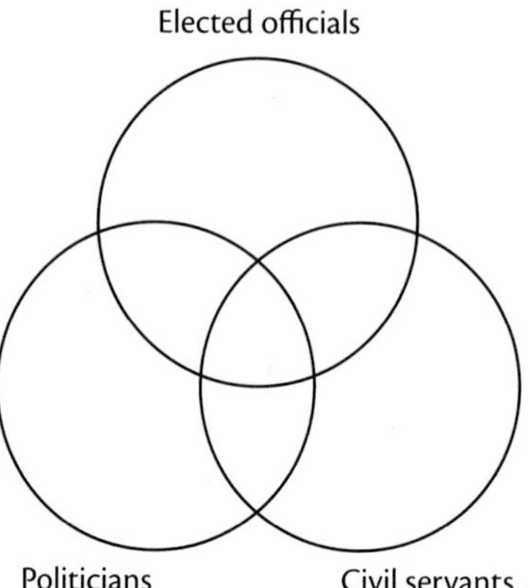

Now, we diagram the first premise ("All elected officials are civil servants"). To do this, we look *only* at the two circles involved in Premise 1—namely the "elected officials" circle and the "civil servants" circle. For now, *ignore the other circle entirely*. Premise 1 is an A-statement. So, to represent premise 1, we shade the part of the elected officials circle that does *not* overlap with the civil servants circle. This signifies that all the existing elected officials are also civil servants:

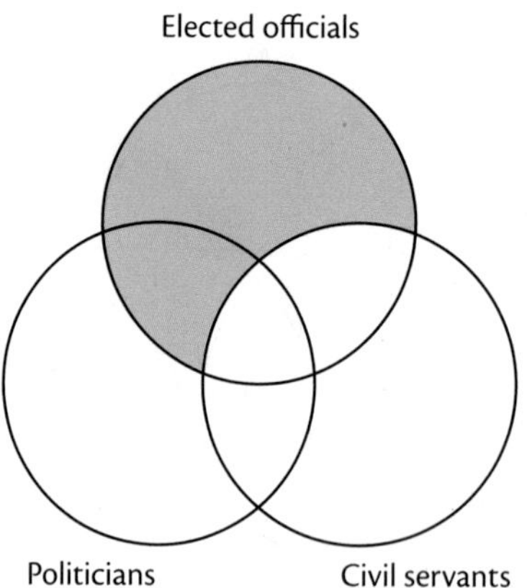

Notice that, if you just look at the two circles we're working with here, the diagram looks exactly like our original A-statement diagram on page 224. Diagrams of A-statements *always* look like that!

Next, we diagram premise 2 ("All politicians are elected officials"). Premise 2 is another A-statement, so we diagram it by shading the part of the politicians circle that does not overlap with the elected officials circle:

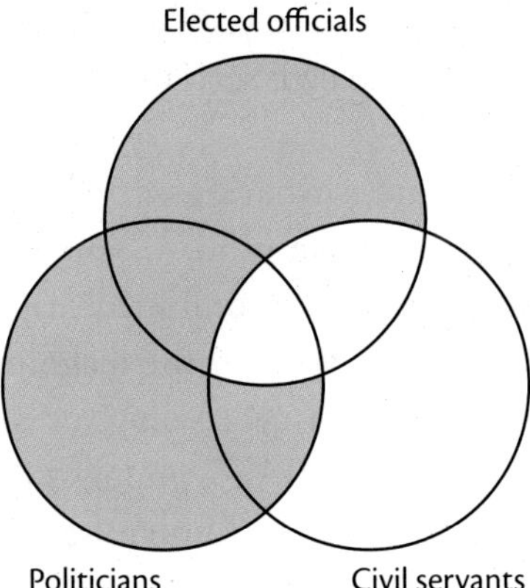

Now, we *stop drawing*. We diagram *only* the premises. We never, ever diagram the conclusion.

Why is that? Why not diagram the conclusion too? Recall that in a valid deductive argument, the premises imply the conclusion. So, once we diagram the premises, the resulting combined diagram is already supposed to represent the information in the conclusion ("Therefore, all politicians are civil servants").

REVIEW NOTES

Five Steps to Checking Validity with Venn Diagrams

1. Draw three overlapping circles, each circle representing a term in the syllogism, with the two circles representing the subject and predicate terms placed on the bottom.
2. Label the circles with the terms.
3. Diagram the first premise. (Diagram universal premises first. When diagramming a particular premise, if it's unclear where to place an X in a circle section, place it on the dividing line between subsections.)
4. Diagram the second premise.

NOW STOP. PUT DOWN YOUR PEN OR PENCIL. OK, now finally . . .

5. Check to see if the diagram represents what is asserted in the conclusion. If it does, the argument is valid; if not, it's invalid.

We can see that the politicians circle is shaded everywhere—except in the area that overlaps the civil servant circle. And this is how the diagram of the syllogism *should* be shaded to depict the statement "All politicians are civil servants." (Look at the diagram and ask yourself: where are the politicians? Most of the politician circle is shaded—empty. The only place you can find any politicians is in an area that overlaps with the civil servant circle. Hence, all politicians are civil servants.)

So the diagram does express what's asserted in the conclusion of our argument. The argument is therefore valid. If you diagram the premises of a categorical syllogism and the resulting combined diagram says the same thing as the conclusion, the syllogism is valid. If the diagram does not "contain" the conclusion (if information is missing), the syllogism is invalid.

This syllogism has two universal ("All") premises (both A-statements). Let's diagram one that has a particular ("Some") premise:

All robots are machines.
Some professors are robots.
Therefore, some professors are machines.

Here's the diagram properly labelled:

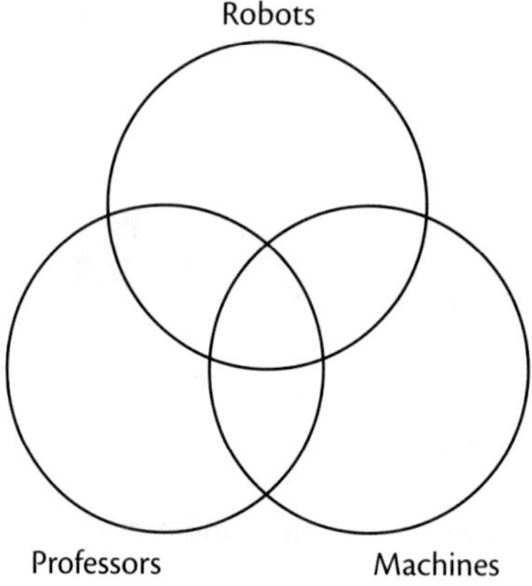

We'll diagram the first premise first ("All robots are machines")—but not just because it happens to be the first premise. In categorical syllogisms with both a universal and a particular premise, we should always diagram the universal premise first. The reason is that diagramming the particular premise first can lead to confusion. For example, in the argument in question, if we were to diagram the particular premise first ("Some professors are robots"), we would end up with an X in the area where the robots and professors circles overlap. That section, however, is split into two subsections by the machines circle:

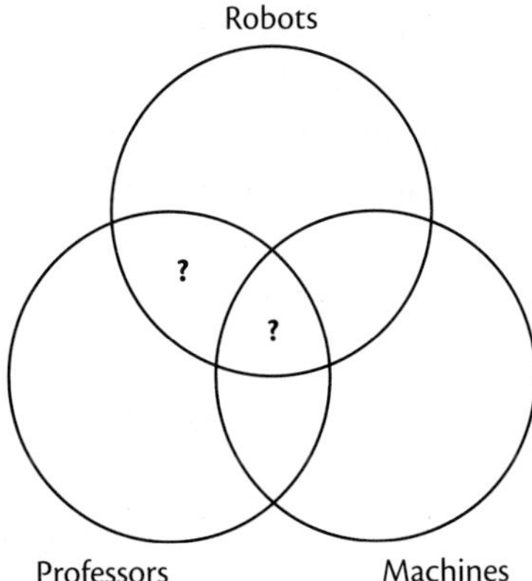

So then the question arises in which subsection we should place the X. (That's why there are question marks in the diagram above—to point out, just for now, the uncertainty). Should we put the X in the area overlapping with the machines circle—or in the part not overlapping with the machines circle? Our choice *does* affect what the diagram says about the validity of the argument. But if we diagram the universal premise first, the decision of where to insert the X is made for us because there would be only one relevant subsection left (and we can't place an X in a shaded area, because shaded means *empty*):

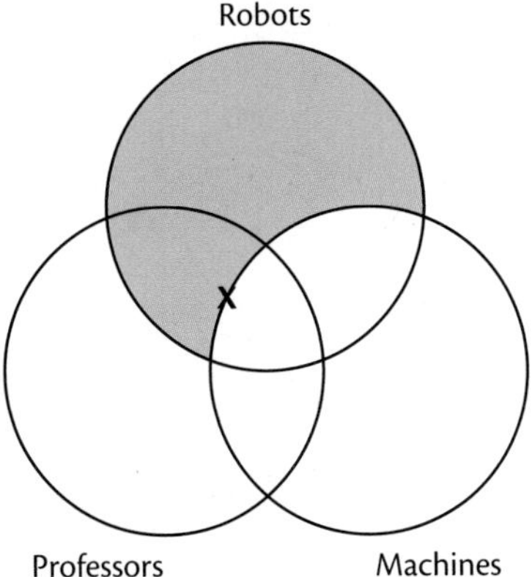

The resulting diagram represents the statement that some professors are machines, which is what the conclusion asserts. The syllogism, then, is valid.

But sometimes, diagramming the universal premise first still leaves us with a question about where the X should go. Consider this syllogism:

All barbers are singers.
Some Italians are singers.
Therefore, some Italians are barbers.

When we diagram the universal premise first, we see that the section where the Italians and singers circles overlap is divided between a subsection including barbers and a subsection excluding barbers. So the X could go in either subsection, and we have no way of knowing which:

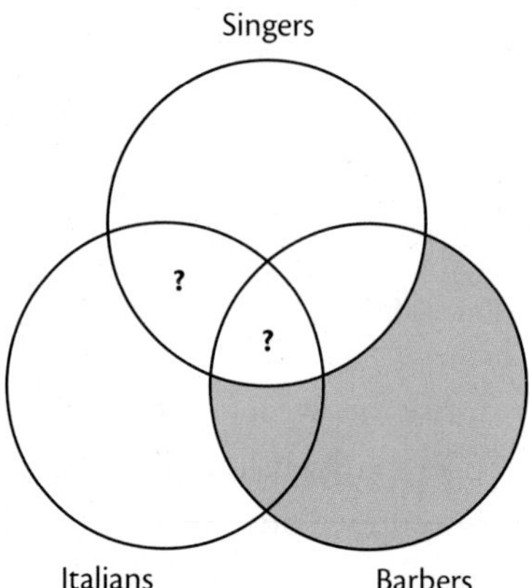

The question marks in the diagram above again suggest uncertainty. But question marks aren't really part of our diagramming method. So we need to decide where to put the X! In situations like this, the best approach is to indicate our uncertainty about where the X should go by placing it on the border between the two subsections, like this:

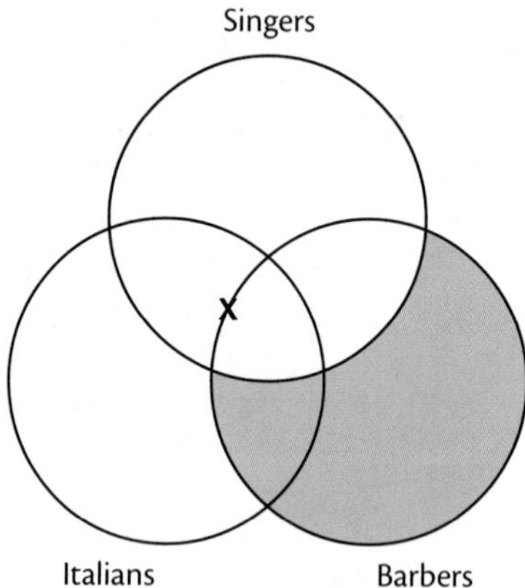

An X placed in this position means that among things that are both Italians and singers, something is either a barber or not a barber. Now, the conclusion says that some Italians are barbers. This conclusion is represented in the diagram only if there is an X *unquestionably* in the area where the barbers and Italians circles overlap. But we don't have an X unquestionably in that region; we have only an X that *may or may not be there*. That is, there's a question of just where the X is. Therefore, the diagram does not assert what the conclusion does, and the argument is invalid.

FOOD FOR THOUGHT

The Limits of the Venn Diagram Method

A hard problem in the study of logic is the question of whether a universal statement (like "All S are M" or "No S are M") has what is called "existential import." That is, does such a statement actually imply that something exists?

Consider this example. If you say that "None of the cars in the parking lot are Hondas," are you necessarily implying that there *are some* cars in the parking lot? You probably are; otherwise, it would be an odd thing to say in the first place. On the other hand, if you say that "No unicorns are dragons," are you necessarily implying that there *are some* unicorns in the world? Hopefully not! So the "existential import" of a universal statement—that is, whether or not it implies that some members of the predicate term actually exist—depends on the context. But formal logic is, well, formal, and so the systems we use to test logical statements look at the formal structure of an argument, independent of context.

But because of this problem, the Venn diagram method used in this textbook is not entirely foolproof. Consider the following syllogism:

All S are *M*
All *M* are *P*
Therefore some S are *P*.

Here's the Venn diagram for it:

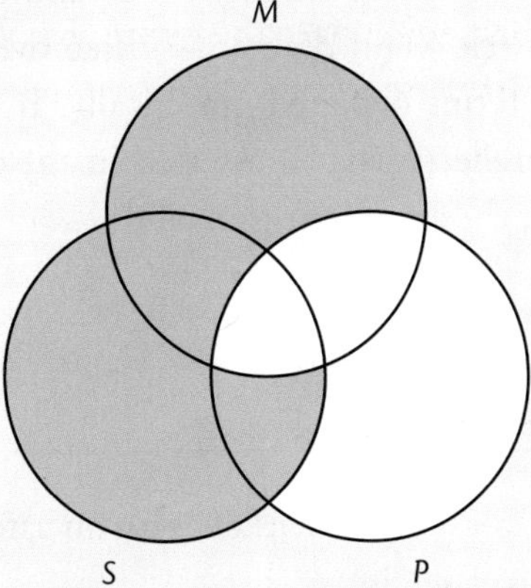

According to our method, the syllogism is invalid, because you can't look at the above diagram and *see* that "Some S are P." But is it *really* invalid? Unfortunately, that depends on what we're talking about.

What if the argument represented above is the following: "All cats are mammals. And all mammals are fur-bearing animals. So, some cats are mammals." That certainly seems valid. If the premises are true, how could it be false that at some cats are fur-bearing? After all, *some* in logic means "at least one."

The problem lies in the fact that *both* of this syllogism's premises are universal statements, and the conclusion is a particular statement.

The result is that the Venn diagram method used in this book will work for *nearly all* syllogisms you run across, and it will work for all the examples given in this book and in the Exercises throughout this chapter. But it won't work reliably for syllogisms that have two universal premises and a particular conclusion. Those are relatively rare, but keep your eyes open, and when you spot them, ask yourself, "Does the person putting this argument forward actually believe those exist?"

SUMMARY

Every categorical statement has a subject term and a predicate term. There are four standard forms of categorical statements: (1) universal affirmative ("All dogs are mammals"), (2) universal negative ("No dogs are mammals"), (3) particular affirmative ("Some dogs are mammals"), and (4) particular negative ("Some dogs are not mammals").

Categorical statements must be translated into standard form before you can work with them. Translating involves identifying terms, ensuring that they designate classes, and determining the quantifiers. Drawing Venn diagrams is a good way to visualize categorical statements and to tell whether one statement is equivalent to another.

A categorical syllogism is an argument consisting of three categorical statements (two categorical premises and a categorical conclusion) that are interlinked in a structured way. The syllogism consists of a subject term, predicate term, and middle term. The middle term appears once in each premise. The subject term appears in one premise and the conclusion, and the predicate term appears in the other premise and the conclusion. You can use Venn diagrams to represent categorical statements, showing how the terms are related.

The easiest way to check the validity of a categorical syllogism is to draw a three-circle Venn diagram—three overlapping circles with the relationship between terms depicted graphically. If, after diagramming each premise, the diagram reflects what is asserted in the conclusion, the argument is valid. If it does not, the argument is invalid.

EXERCISE 6.6

Answers to exercises marked with an asterisk (*) may be found in Appendix B, Answers to Exercises.

For each of the following arguments, label the subject term, predicate term, and middle term. Then translate each syllogism into symbolic form using *S*, *P*, and *M* to represent the terms.

1. All chickens are animals. All birds are animals. Therefore, all chickens are birds.

*2. All horses are mammals, and no mammals are lizards. Therefore, no lizards are horses.

3. No essays are poems. Some books are poems. So some books are not essays.

4. All corporations have limited liability, but some businesses don't have limited liability. That's why some businesses are not corporations.
5. All roads are highways to Rome, but no mere paths are roads. So no mere paths are highways to Rome.
*6. Some DVDs are not film classics, but all black-and-white movies are film classics. Therefore, some black-and-white movies are not DVDs.
7. Some cities are located in Canada. All cities located in Canada are great places to live. So some cities are great places to live.
8. All politicians are campaigners. All campaigners are money-grubbers. Therefore, all politicians are money-grubbers.
*9. No elm trees are cacti. Some tall plants are elm trees. So some tall plants are not cacti.
10. All thieves are criminals. All thieves are dangers to society. Therefore, all dangers to society are criminals.

EXERCISE 6.7

Draw Venn diagrams to test the validity of each of the arguments in Exercise 6.6. Answers are given for 2, 6, and 9.

EXERCISE 6.8

Translate each of the following arguments into categorical syllogistic form (premise, premise, conclusion), symbolize the argument (by using the conventional *S*, *P*, *M* variables), and draw a Venn diagram to test its validity.

*1. Some "alternative" medicines are cancer treatments, for all herbal medicines are "alternative" medicines and some herbal medicines are cancer treatments.
2. Bacon burgers are heart attack–inducing foods because all bacon burgers are high-fat foods, and some heart attack–inducing foods are not high-fat foods.
*3. All SUVs are evil vehicles because all SUVs are gas guzzlers and all gas guzzlers are evil vehicles.
4. Some buildings are unstable, so some skyscrapers must be unstable since all skyscrapers are buildings.
5. Cancer patients are not allowed to donate their organs because the organs could contain cancer. And no doctor would allow the donation of organs that could contain cancer.

6. Some children with autism are not children with developmental delays since all children with developmental delays are children with low IQs, and some children with autism are not children with low IQs.
7. Anyone who listens to his or her superiors without question might as well be a mindless robot. Since all of our soldiers are taught to obey their superiors without question, they might as well be an army of mindless robots.
*8. No wimps are social activists because no wimps are people of honest and strong convictions. And all social activists are people of honest and strong convictions.
9. Most people who drive SUVs are instant-gratification freaks who don't care about the environment or environmental issues. Instant-gratification freaks who don't care about the environment or environmental issues are the true enemies of the planet. Therefore, people who drive SUVs are the true enemies of the planet.
10. Vitamin pills are useless gimmicks promoted as sure cures for a variety of illnesses. Some useless gimmicks promoted as sure cures, though, are placebos that can make people feel good. So some vitamin pills are placebos that can make people feel good even if they don't cure anything.

Field Problems

1. Go online and check the opinion or editorial section of your local newspaper or one of the national newspapers (the *Globe and Mail* or *National Post*). Within one of the editorials or letters to the editor, find a categorical syllogism that you suspect is invalid. Assess its validity using the Venn diagram method. If it is indeed invalid, write a 150–200 word explanation of how you would explain, to someone who doesn't know about categorical logic, what's wrong with the argument.
2. Check recent news reports to find one categorical statement made by the prime minister of Canada, a federal cabinet minister, the mayor of your city, or one of the premiers. Translate the statement into standard form. (1) Construct a *valid* categorical syllogism using the statement as the conclusion and supplying whatever premises you deem appropriate. Assume that your premises are true. (2) Then construct an *invalid* syllogism using the same statement as the conclusion and supplying premises, also assumed to be true. In both arguments, try to keep the statements as realistic as possible (e.g., close to what you may actually read in a newsmagazine).

3. Think of a piece of *advice* you have been given that was presented in syllogistic form. (Hint: this often happens when a speaker's first premise is a general rule of thumb, and his or her second premise relates that rule to your current situation. The conclusion will be advice aimed specifically at you.) Is the argument a good one? Did you take the advice?

Self-Assessment Quiz

1. What is a quantifier? What are the two quantities that can be used in categorical statements?
2. What are the two qualities that can be expressed in categorical statements?
3. What are the four standard-form categorical statements? (Specify them by quality and quantity and by letter designation.)

For each of the following statements, identify the subject and predicate terms, the quality, the quantity, and the name of the form (universal affirmative, universal negative, particular affirmative, or particular negative).

4. Some inventions are not beneficial to humanity.
5. No matter how many reasons you give me, there just are no good reasons for supporting the death penalty.
6. Every employee who works under Francoise quits within a month.
7. Some ghost stories are not fabrications devised by true believers.

Translate each of the following statements into standard categorical form and indicate whether the form is A, E, I, or O.

8. A man without purpose cannot truly be called a man.
9. Hockey is the best sport.
10. Sheila is the finest scholar in the department.
11. Nobody who wants an A in this class would wait until the night before the exam to study.
12. "Slow and steady wins the race." (Aesop)
13. A politician is someone who firmly believes that getting elected makes one smart.
14. "A fanatic is someone who can't change his mind and won't change the subject." (Winston Churchill)

Construct Venn diagrams to test the validity of each of the following syllogisms.

15. All *M* are *P*. Some *S* are not *M*. Therefore, some *S* are not *P*.
16. No *M* are *P*. No *S* are *M*. Therefore, all *S* are *P*.
17. All *P* are *M*. No *S* are *M*. Therefore, no *S* are *P*.
18. Some *P* are not *M*. All *S* are *M*. Therefore, some *S* are not *P*.
19. All *M* are *P*. All *M* are *S*. Therefore, all *S* are *P*.
20. Some *S* are *M*. Some *M* are *P*. Therefore, some *S* are *P*.

Integrative Exercises

These exercises pertain to material in Chapters 1–6.

1. What is critical thinking?
2. What is an argument?
3. True or false: every argument must include at least two assertions or claims.
4. Can an inductive argument guarantee the truth of its conclusion?

For each of the following arguments, specify the conclusion and premises and indicate any argument indicator words.

5. Tanvir either forgot about our date or is just running very late. He definitely wouldn't forget, so he must just be running late.
6. I've worked for our boss for many years, and the only reasons he'd reprimand you like that are if she's in a bad mood or it's for the good of the company. Since I saw her looking really happy this morning, it must have been for the good for the company.
7. Either the crippled economy or the sex scandals will drive the British prime minister from office. If inflation rises, then there will be a crippled economy. Inflation will not rise. Therefore, the sex scandals will drive the British prime minister from office.
8. If you don't file your taxes on time, you'll get into trouble with the Canada Revenue Agency. However, since I know you filed your tax returns a month before the deadline, you'll be fine.
9. I will go to market unless the farmer objects, and I will stay home if the cows are sick. The cows aren't sick; therefore, I will go to market.

For each of the following arguments, determine whether it is deductive or inductive, valid or invalid, and strong or weak.

10. Either Ellen is shy or she is not. If her cheeks turn red, she's shy. If they don't turn red, she's not shy. Her cheeks are red. Ellen is shy.
11. Assad currently works for Microsoft and was hired six months ago. Anyone who isn't fired within three months of being hired by Microsoft will probably stay at the company for the rest of his or her career. That's why Assad will most likely spend the rest of his career at Microsoft.
12. "And certainly if its essence and power are infinite, its goodness must be infinite, since a thing whose essence is finite has finite goodness." (Roger Bacon, *The Opus Majus*)
13. The comet has appeared in the sky every 60 years for the past four centuries. It will appear in the sky again, right on schedule.

For each of the following arguments, identify the implicit premise that will make the argument valid.

14. Canadians dominate the National Hockey League. So Canada will likely win gold in Olympic Men's Hockey.
15. My friend Edward just called me and said that he's going to go pick up a package in a dark alley in the middle of the night in a sketchy part of town. I'll go wait for him at the hospital.
16. Either you ate the last piece of cake in the fridge or I did. So it must have been you!
17. The prime minister interfered in the decision making of a Crown corporation to benefit a friend of his. The prime minister should therefore resign.

Writing Assignments

1. Write a 600-word essay arguing either for or against solar energy. Structure your argument as a categorical syllogism.
2. Write a 300-word criticism of your own argument from Question 1 above. Focus your criticism on whichever of your categorical premises you think an opponent is most likely to focus on.
3. Write a 600-word rebuttal to Essay 5 ("How Ontario Ended Up with 'Cap and Trade'") in Appendix A. Make sure to note Essay 5's premises and conclusion.

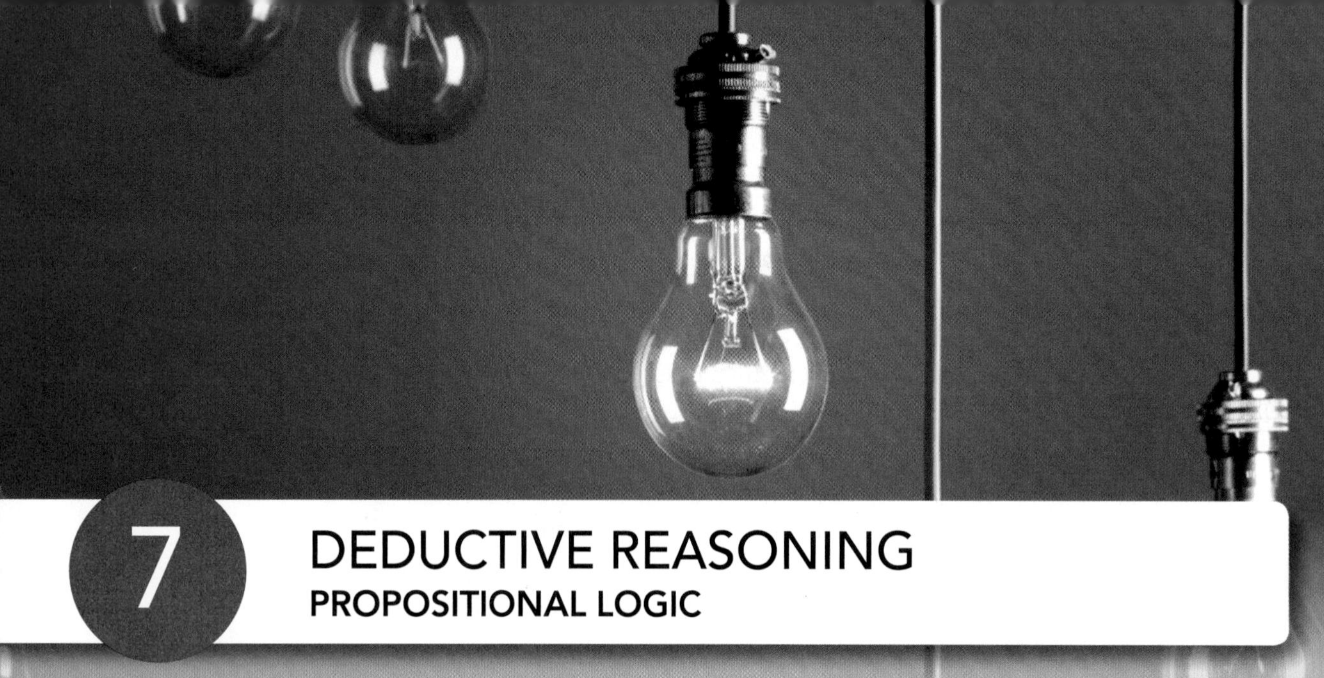

7 DEDUCTIVE REASONING
PROPOSITIONAL LOGIC

CHAPTER OBJECTIVES

Connectives and Truth Values

You will be able to

- understand the purpose and uses of propositional logic.
- understand the meaning, symbols, and uses of the four logical connectives—conjunction, disjunction, negation, and conditional.
- define *statement* and explain the distinction between simple and compound statements.
- translate simple statements into symbolic form.
- construct a truth table and use it to test the validity of arguments.
- identify the situations in which conjunctions, disjunctions, negations, and conditionals are true or false.
- understand the structure of conditional statements and the various ways in which they can be expressed.

Checking for Validity

You will be able to

- determine the validity of the very simple arguments using truth tables.
- use parentheses to express statements in symbolic form.
- use the short method to evaluate complex arguments.

We began our exploration of formal logic by exploring categorical logic. In categorical logic the basic unit of our concern was the *statement component*; that is, we were interested in the logical relationships between the subject and predicate of various statements.

propositional logic The branch of deductive reasoning that deals with the logical relationships among statements.

Here we take up an exploration of **propositional logic** (or truth-functional logic)—the branch of deductive reasoning that deals with the logical relationships among entire statements. In propositional logic, we use symbols to represent and clarify these relationships. If you master this material, you should reap at least two rewards right off. The first is a more thorough understanding of the power, precision, and dynamics of deductive reasoning. The second is the ability to evaluate the validity of very complex arguments.

How complex? Take a look at this deductive argument. Can you tell if it's valid?

(1) Canada will be a just society only if it improves the situation of its Aboriginal peoples.

FOOD FOR THOUGHT

What Hath Critical Thinking Wrought?

Every year the science humour magazine *Annals of Improbable Research* awards its infamous "Ig Nobel Prizes," which honour people whose achievements "cannot or should not be reproduced." We're talking here about actual research of dubious or curious value. We could argue that many Ig Nobel winners are living examples of what can happen when there are serious lapses in critical thinking. On the other hand, some of the wacky Ig Nobel accomplishments have the intended (or unintended) effect of making people laugh and then really think. You can judge the merits for yourself. Here's a partial list of the Ig Nobel Prizes for 2014:

- Physics: Kiyoshi Mabuchi, Kensei Tanaka, Daichi Uchijima, and Rina Sakai, for measuring the amount of friction between a shoe and a banana skin, and between a banana skin and the floor, when a person steps on a banana skin that's on the floor.
- Neuroscience: Jiangang Liu, Jun Li, Lu Feng, Ling Li, Jie Tian, and Kang Lee, for trying to understand what happens in the brains of people who see the face of Jesus in a piece of toast.
- Vlastimil Hart, Petra Nováková, Erich Pascal Malkemper, Sabine Begall, Vladimír Hanzal, Miloš Ježek, Tomáš Kušta, Veronika Němcová, Jana Adámková, Kateřina Benediktová, Jaroslav Červený, and Hynek Burda, for carefully documenting that when dogs defecate and urinate, they prefer to align their body axis with Earth's north–south geomagnetic field lines.
- Arctic Science: Eigil Reimers and Sindre Eftestøl, for testing how reindeer react to seeing humans who are disguised as polar bears.[1]

(2) Canada will improve the situation of its Aboriginal peoples only if doing so will not significantly reduce the standard of living of middle-class Canadians.
(3) If the standard of living of middle-class Canadians is reduced, then either Canada will not be a just society or it will not improve the situation of its Aboriginal peoples.
(4) Canada will not improve the situation of its Aboriginal peoples.
(5) Therefore, Canada will not be a just society.

If you don't know anything about propositional logic, the only way you can check this argument for validity is to rely on intuition, which is not a very reliable method. You just have to think it through, and the thinking it through will not be easy. But with a grounding in propositional logic, you can figure this one out in straightforward fashion with a high degree of certainty

CONNECTIVES AND TRUTH VALUES

As we've seen, arguments are composed of statements. In Chapter 3 we used symbols to represent the statements. Each symbol stood, not for a logical relationship between statements, but for a single statement. Propositional logic takes this symbolization to another level by using symbols to stand not just for statements but also for the *relationships between statements*—relationships that we specify with logical connective words, or connectives, such as "if . . . then" and "or." Propositional logic gets this work done by using the symbol language of **symbolic logic**, a branch of logic in its own right.

symbolic logic Modern deductive logic that uses symbolic language to do its work.

Because these logical connectives specify the relationships between statements, they shape the *form* of the argument. Recall that the validity of an argument is a matter of the argument's form; that's why we can judge the validity of an argument apart from any consideration of the truth of its premises. So propositional logic helps us assess the validity of an argument without being distracted by non-formal elements, such as the particular words used to express content.

variables In modern logic, the symbols, or letters, used to express a statement.

So the symbols used to express an argument are of two types. The first you're already familiar with; they're the lower-case letters, or **variables**, you use to represent propositions. For example, if *p*, then *q*. (There's no particular distinction in the letters *p* and *q*; any letters will do, as long as you use them consistently. That is, once you've chosen *p* to represent, say, "Alice rode her bike," *p* must consistently represent this same statement throughout the argument.) The second kind are the symbols for the logical connectives that indicate relationships between statements.

The following table presents the symbols for, and the meaning of, four logical connectives:

Symbol	Meaning	Example
&	Conjunction (and)	$p \& q$ Alice rode her bike, and John walked.
$\vee$	Disjunction (or)	$p \vee q$ Either Alice rode her bike, or John walked.
~	Negation (not)	$\sim p$ Alice did not ride her bike. It is not the case that Alice rode her bike.
$\rightarrow$	Conditional (if–then)	$p \rightarrow q$ If Alice rode her bike, then John walked.

These connectives are used in compound statements such as "The air is clean, and the sky is blue" or "If you stay up late, you will sleep in tomorrow." Remember that a **statement** (or **claim**) is an assertion that something is or is not the case. In other words, it is the kind of thing that can be either true or false. A **simple statement** is one that does not contain any other statements as constituents; a **compound statement** is composed of at least two simple statements.

statement (claim) An assertion that something is or is not the case.

simple statement A statement that doesn't contain any other statements as constituents.

compound statement A statement composed of at least two constituent, or simple, statements.

Every statement has a truth value. That is, a statement is either true or false. Or to be more precise, a true statement has a truth value of *true*, and a false statement has a truth value of *false*. In contrast, questions and exclamations don't have truth values: they are neither true nor false.

Now let's say that we have converted an argument into its symbolic form, and we list all the *possible* truth values of the argument's variables (statements). In other words, we list under what circumstances a statement is true or false because of the influence of the logical connectives. How would this information help us?

It could help us quickly uncover the validity or invalidity of the whole argument. Given the possible truth values of some statements in the argument, and given the relationships of the statements with one another as governed by the logical connectives, we could infer the possible truth values of all the other statements. Then we would have to answer just one question: *Is there a combination of truth values in the argument such that the premises could be true and the conclusion false?* If the answer is yes, then the argument is invalid. If there is no such circumstance, the argument is valid.

If you're a little fuzzy on all this, don't worry. It will become clearer as you digest the following examples and learn more about the dance between connectives and truth values. Let's look next at each of the four logical connectives introduced above.

Conjunction

conjunct One of two simple statements joined by a connective to form a compound statement.

conjunction Two simple statements joined by a connective to form a compound statement.

Two simple statements joined by a connective to form a compound statement are known as a **conjunction**. Each of the component statements is called a **conjunct**. For example:

Julio is here, and Juan is here.

Which we symbolize like this:

$p \,\&\, q$

The grammatical conjunction *and* is one of several terms that can express logical conjunction. Some others are *but*, *yet*, *nevertheless*, *while*, *also*, and *moreover*. In propositional logic, all these are logically equivalent; they are therefore properly symbolized by the ampersand (&). *Caution:* Make sure the connective really is conjoining two distinct statements and not a set of compound nouns as in "We went to Jack's bar *and* grill" or "Céline *and* Marie were a team."

The truth value of a conjunction is determined by the truth value of its parts, that is, by the truth value of its conjuncts. For example, look at this conjunction:

Last night I had a Coke, and I also had an order of poutine.

That conjunction is true if, and only if, it's true *both* that you had a Coke last night and that you had poutine last night. Maybe you did have Coke last night, and maybe you didn't. Maybe you had poutine last night, and maybe you didn't.

truth table A table that specifies the truth values for claim variables and combinations of claim variables in symbolized statements or arguments.

To identify and keep track of all the possible truth values of a conjunction, we can create a **truth table**, which is just a graphic way of displaying all the possibilities. Here's the truth table for the conjunction $p \,\&\, q$:

p	q	$p \,\&\, q$
T	T	T
T	F	F
F	T	F
F	F	F

At the top of the table, you see a column heading for each of the component statements (in this case, one for p and one for q) and one for the conjunction ($p \,\&\, q$) itself. The Ts and Fs below the line are abbreviations for *true* and *false*. The first two columns of Ts and Fs represent the four possible sets of truth values for the variables. Either *p* is true and *q* is true, or *p* is true and *q* is false, or *p* is false and *q* is true, or *p* is false and *q* is also false. Those are the only four combinations that are possible. The table shows, in other words, that there are only four combinations of truth values for the pair of variables *p* and *q*: T T, T F, F T, and F F. These are the only combinations possible for *any* conjunction (or any other two-variable compound).

The last column of Ts and Fs (under *p* & *q*) shows the possible truth values for the conjunction as a whole, given the four possible combinations of truth values of the pair of variables. This means that if you plug into the conjunction every possible pair of truth values, the conjunction will yield only these four truth values: T, F, F, and F.

In ordinary language, this is what each of the rows is saying:

Row 1: When *p* is true and *q* is true, *p* & *q* is true.
Row 2: When *p* is true and *q* is false, *p* & *q* is false.
Row 3: When *p* is false and *q* is true, *p* & *q* is false.
Row 4: When *p* is false and *q* is false, *p* & *q* is false.

(Think this through for yourself, using the example given above. If it's true that I had Coke last night, and also true that I had poutine last night, then the statement "I had Coke and also had poutine last night" is clearly true. But if it's true that I had Coke last night but false that I had poutine last night, then "I had Coke and also had poutine last night" is, as a whole, false. And so on.)

Maybe you've already guessed (by studying the truth table) an important fact about the truth value of a conjunction: If just one statement in the conjunction is false, the whole conjunction is false; only if both conjuncts are true is the whole conjunction true. The previous truth table reflects this state of affairs. In the table, we see that *p* & *q* is true only when *p* is true and *q* is true (in the first row)—and that *p* & *q* is false whenever at least one of the component statements is false (in the other three rows). This should make perfect sense to you, because in everyday speech, if one-half of a conjunction is false, we would normally regard the whole conjunction as false.

Alan Turing (1912–1954) was a mathematician and logician, and is considered the father of modern computer science. His work and life were recently portrayed in the historical thriller film *The Imitation Game*.

It's a good idea to remember the exact sequence of Ts and Fs in the first two columns of the previous truth table. That way you won't have to guess to make sure you include every possible combination

FOOD FOR THOUGHT

Logic and Computers

It is no exaggeration to say that without logic, there would be no computers of any kind—no laptops, no iPads, no Xbox. In fact, without logic we would have to do without all devices that run on microchips (or "integrated circuits"), including cellphones and calculators and even microwave ovens.

The ability to formalize statements in the way that propositional logic does is what allows computers to do their work. In fact, the basic operations of all computers are based on roughly the same set of logical operators that you are learning about in this chapter. In computers, "logic gates" are the basis for all circuitry. A logic gate is a physical device that implements a logical function such as negation (a "NOT gate") or conjunction (an "AND gate") or disjunction (an "OR gate").

As you may already know, the fundamental language of all computers is called "binary," a language that translates everything into 1s and 0s. In logical terms, the 1s and 0s of binary code work exactly like the Ts and Fs in our truth tables. In fact, look at how similar a computer scientist's "AND gate" (on the left, below) is to the truth table for conjunction!

A	B	Y
0	0	0
0	1	0
1	0	0
1	1	1

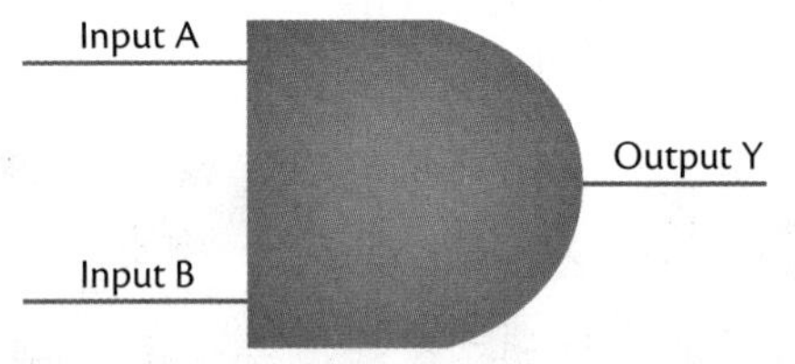

CREDIT: Pamela Moore/iStockphoto

Without logic, there would be no laptops, tablets, or cellphones. (There might not even be coffee.)

of truth values. The first few columns in any truth table are usually entered automatically as guides.

disjunct A simple statement that is a component of a disjunction.

disjunction A compound statement of the form "Either *p* or *q*." A disjunction is true even if only one disjunct is true, and false only if both disjuncts are false.

Disjunction

In a conjunction we assert that *p* and *q* are both true and that if just one conjunct is false, the whole conjunction is false. But in a **disjunction**, we assert that either *p* or *q* is true (though both might be) and that even if one of the statements is false, the whole disjunction is still true. Each statement in a disjunction is called a **disjunct**. For example:

Either Joan is angry or Ann is serene.

which we symbolize as

$p \vee q$

or

Either Joan or Ann will row the boat.

which we also symbolize as

$p \vee q$

The symbol for disjunction ($\vee$) is called a wedge, which is roughly equivalent to the word *or*. The word *unless* is also sometimes used in place of *or* to form a disjunction, as in "I will go to the movies unless I stay home." The words *either* and *neither* usually signal the beginning of a disjunction.

The truth table for a disjunction looks like this:

p	q	$p \vee q$
T	T	T
T	F	T
F	T	T
F	F	F

The table shows us that $p \vee q$ is true in every possible combination of Ts and Fs *except one*, where both p and q are false (in the last row). This situation just reflects the fact that for a disjunction to be true, only one of the disjuncts must be true. The disjunction here, for example, is true if (1) Joan is angry or (2) Ann is serene or (3) Joan is angry and Ann is serene.

An important point to keep in mind is that in English the word *or* has two meanings. It can mean "one or the other, or both," which is called the *inclusive* sense. In this sense, $p \vee q$ means "p or q or both" ("If he's sick or tired, he won't go jogging"). But *or* can also mean "either but not both," which is called the *exclusive* sense. In the exclusive sense, $p \vee q$ means "p or q but not both" ("You can have either the chicken or the fish as your in-flight meal"). Standard practice in logic is to assume the inclusive sense when dealing with disjunctions. This approach is reflected in the truth table for a disjunction, and it simplifies the evaluation of disjunctive arguments. It has no effect on our evaluation of disjunctive syllogisms (discussed in Chapter 3); they would be valid forms regardless of whether the disjunction was construed as inclusive or exclusive. Look:

"Logic is not a body of doctrine, but a mirror-image of the world. Logic is transcendental."

—*Ludwig Wittgenstein*

Either p or q.
Not p.
Therefore, q.

FOOD FOR THOUGHT

Arguments We Have Known and Loved

Virtually every field has its share of well-worn arguments that are used to establish this theory or that proposition. But the discipline of philosophy—because it is, well, philosophy—is studded from end to end with influential arguments, including some especially famous ones.

If all that exists is matter in motion, then there are no disembodied spirits.
All that exists is matter in motion.
Therefore, there are no disembodied spirits.

Whatever begins to exist has a cause.
The universe began to exist.
Therefore, the universe had a cause, namely God.

There is unnecessary evil in the world.
If there were an all-powerful, all-knowing, all-good being, there would be no unnecessary evil in the world.
Therefore, there is no all-powerful, all-knowing, all-good being.

If it's true that all our actions are determined by an indefinitely long chain of prior events, then people cannot perform free actions.
It's true that all our actions are determined by an indefinitely long chain of prior events.
Therefore, people cannot perform free actions.

We can't be certain that we are not dreaming.
If we can't be certain that we are not dreaming, we cannot be certain that what we sense is real.
If we cannot be certain that what we sense is real, we cannot acquire knowledge through sense experience.
Therefore, we cannot acquire knowledge through sense experience.

In the disjunctive syllogism one of the disjuncts is denied, so the argument is valid in any case. But if one of the disjuncts is affirmed, the argument is invalid when the disjunction is inclusive:

Either *p* or *q*.
p.
Therefore, not *q*.

Obviously, if the disjunction means "*p* or *q* or both," then by affirming *p* we cannot conclude not *q*.

If we know that the disjuncts in a disjunctive premise really are exclusive options ("either a boy or a girl"), then we can safely assume the exclusive meaning of *or* and examine the argument accordingly. Otherwise it's safest to stick to the inclusive sense.

Negation

A negation is the denial of a statement, which we indicate with the word *not* or some other term that means the same thing. For example, the negation of the statement "The price of eggs in China is very high" is as follows:

> The price of eggs in China is not very high.
>
> or
>
> It is not the case that the price of eggs in China is very high.
>
> or
>
> It is false that the price of eggs in China is very high.

Assuming we use p to represent the foregoing statement, here's how we would symbolize its negation:

> $\sim p$

The symbol ~ is called a "tilde," and when we state $\sim p$ aloud, we say "not p." When it appears in front of a statement, it indicates the reversal of the statement's truth value. A true statement becomes false; a false statement becomes true. One interesting consequence of this reversal is that a *double negation* is the same thing as *no* negation. For example, take the foregoing negation ("The price of eggs in China is not very high"). If you negate this negation ("It is not the case that the price of eggs in China is not very high") you end up with the positive statement, "The price of eggs in China is very high." The truth table for a negation explains why such reversals can happen:

p	$\sim p$
T	F
F	T

Conditional

Remember conditional statements? We looked at them when we discussed valid and invalid argument forms (*modus ponens*, denying the antecedent, etc.). The basic form of a conditional is "if . . . then . . ." For example: "If the cat is on the mat, then the rat will stay home." Symbolized, a conditional looks like this: $p \rightarrow q$, where an arrow represents the connective. Recall also that in a conditional, the first part (*p*) is the antecedent, and the second part (*q*) is the consequent.

Notice that a conditional asserts only that if the antecedent is true, then the consequent must be true. It does not assert that the antecedent is actually true or that the consequent is actually true—but only that under specified conditions a certain state of affairs will be actual.

At first, you may find that the truth table for conditionals seems a little odd. But it makes good sense when you think about it:

p	q	$p \rightarrow q$
T	T	T
T	F	F
F	T	T
F	F	T

The table shows that a conditional is false in only one situation—when the antecedent is true and the consequent is false. Put more precisely, a conditional statement is false if and only if its antecedent is true and its consequent is false. In all other possible combinations of truth values, a conditional is true—and this is the part that may strike you as odd.

Let's take each of the four combinations in turn and see how they work in this conditional statement: "If George is paid a dollar, then he'll jump out the window." The question we can ask is this: "Under what circumstances is the conditional statement (the whole statement, antecedent and consequent together) true?" Well, it should be clear that if George is indeed paid a dollar, and if he does jump out the window, then the whole conditional would be true. This is the situation in the first row of the truth table.

"The art of reasoning becomes of first importance. In this line antiquity has left us the finest models for imitation."

—*Thomas Jefferson*

What about the last row—what if the antecedent is false and the consequent is false? If it is false that George is paid a dollar, and it's false that he jumps out the window, there is no reason to think that the conditional itself is false. George could reasonably assert that the conditional statement isn't false if he isn't paid a dollar and doesn't jump out the window.

George could also reasonably assert that the conditional isn't false even when the antecedent is false and the consequent is true (the situation in the third row). If George isn't paid a dollar, and he still jumps out the window, that doesn't prove that the conditional is false.

This path brings us back to the fact that a conditional statement is false *only* when the antecedent is true and the consequent is false.

Conditional statements can be expressed in ways other than the if–then configuration, the standard form. Here are some conditionals in various patterns, with each one paired with the standard-form version:

EVERYDAY PROBLEMS AND DECISIONS

Propositional Logic and Bad Choices

A poor command of propositional logic can lead to bad choices in life! Consider the following argument about a very important life decision:

> If finishing a university degree were generally as useless as I think it is, then surely a genius like Bill Gates would know that and would not bother finishing university. And guess what? Bill Gates didn't bother to finish university. So, university is generally a bad idea. I might as well drop out now.

Hopefully you recognize this as an example of *affirming the consequent*, a fallacy first discussed in Chapter 3.

In symbolic form, a simplified version of this argument would look like this:

$p \rightarrow \sim q$

$\sim q$

$\therefore p$

You don't have to use symbolic logic every time you need to make a major life decision. But hopefully developing the relevant skills will help train your brain to recognize errors like this when you see them. The result is almost certain to be better decisions, including ones that matter a lot!

1. You will fall off that ladder if you're not careful.
   If you're not careful, you will fall off that ladder.
2. Gregory will excel in school provided that he studies hard.
   If Gregory studies hard, then he will excel in school.
3. Jenna would not have wrecked the car if she had not tried to beat that light.
   If Jenna had not tried to beat that light, she would not have wrecked the car.
4. I'll ride the bus only if I'm late.
   If I ride the bus, then I'm late.
5. Whenever I think, I get a headache.
   If I think, I get a headache.
6. I will walk the dog unless it's raining.
   If it's not raining, I will walk the dog.

Among these patterns, pair 4 and pair 6 are likely to cause you the most trouble. In pair 4, *only if* is the troublesome term. Just remember that *only if* introduces the *consequent* of a conditional. So in "I'll ride the bus only if I'm late," "only if" indicates that the consequent is "I'm late." So the antecedent is "If I ride the bus." You have to move *if* to the front of the antecedent to put the

REVIEW NOTES

Statements and Connectives

- A simple statement, or claim, is one that does not contain any other statements as constituents. A compound statement is one composed of at least two simple statements.
- Logical connectives:

  Conjunction (and): & If just one statement in a conjunction is false, the whole conjunction is false.
  Disjunction (or): ∨ A disjunction is true even if one of the disjuncts is false.
  Negation (not): ~ A negation "reverses" the truth value of any statement.
  Conditional (if–then): → A conditional is false if and only if its antecedent is true and its consequent is false.

- Words used in conditionals:

  if—introduces the antecedent; If *p*, then *q* = $p \rightarrow q$
  only if—introduces the consequent; *p* only if *q* = $p \rightarrow q$
  provided—introduces the antecedent; *p* provided *q* = $q \rightarrow p$
  unless—introduces the antecedent; *p* unless *q* = $\sim q \rightarrow p$
  whenever—introduces the antecedent; whenever *p*, *q* = $p \rightarrow q$

statement in standard form. In pair 6, *unless* is the sticking point. You need to understand that *unless* introduces the antecedent and means "if not." So here "unless it's raining" becomes "if it's not raining" in the antecedent position.

Because of such variations in conditional statements, it's important to translate conditionals into standard form before you try to assess their validity. To do that, you must identify the antecedent and consequent and put them in proper order (antecedent before consequent).

EXERCISE 7.1

Answers to exercises marked with an asterisk (*) may be found in Appendix B, Answers to Exercises.

Identify each of the following statements as a conjunction, disjunction, or conditional; identify its component statements; and indicate the symbol used to represent the connective.

*1. The Liberals raised taxes, and the Conservatives cut programs.

2. I'll have to vacation in Paris if I can't get a discount on those plane tickets to Japan.
3. If the Maple Leafs win this game, they'll be in the playoffs.
4. The chief financial officer of the company recently resigned; there had been rumours of "financial irregularities."
*5. If Taslima can read your mind, then you're in trouble.
6. Either the newspaper ad was misleading or it was meant as a joke.
*7. If God is all-powerful, then he can prevent evil in the world.
8. There's no way I'm going to get anything less than an A in this course!

EXERCISE 7.2

Translate each of the following statements into symbolic form. Use the letters in parentheses to represent each component statement. (Assume that the letters stand for positive statements so that a negated statement is indicated by putting a tilde [~] in front of a letter.)

*1. Either Herman does his homework, or he goofs off. (*p*, *q*)
2. If we don't start preserving the rain forests, many of the species that live there will end up going extinct. (*p*, *q*)
3. Many species will go extinct unless we start preserving the rainforests soon. (*x*, *y*)
*4. People die, but books live forever. (*e*, *f*)
5. Teasing a vicious dog is not a good idea. (*r*)
6. Provided Alex returns the money, he will not be prosecuted. (*x*, *y*)
7. "To fight this Lord Sidious, strong enough, you are not." (Yoda, in *Star Wars Episode III: Revenge of the Sith*) (*p*)
*8. He will not benefit from instruction, and he will not learn on his own. (*g*, *h*)
9. The Ebola outbreak in Africa will soon to spread to Canada unless we start extensive quarantine measures for people entering the country from Africa. (*j*, *k*)
10. That new Adam Sandler movie isn't all that bad. (*z*)
11. You will eventually discover the correct formula if you work systematically. (*x*, *y*)
12. Our opponents either cheated or got incredibly lucky. (*p*, *q*)
13. If Socrates is a man, he is mortal. (*d*, *e*)
*14. It is not the case that the zoo won't accept any more mammals. (*p*)
15. I wanted to go skiing this weekend, but it's just too cold. (*a*, *b*)
16. Either terrorists are hiding in every shadow, or someone is trying to convince us that they are! (*p*, *q*)

EXERCISE 7.3

Say which of the following compound statements are true and which are false on the basis of what you know about the truth value of their components.

1. It is currently winter in Australia ∨ It is currently winter in Canada.
*2. Alligators are reptiles & Dogs are reptiles
3. The Earth revolves around the sun & ~The moon revolves around the Earth
4. The volume of a cube increases → The surface area increases.
5. Cats have wings → Cats can fly
*6. ~ Dogs are mammals ∨ Snakes are reptiles
7. ~ Alligators are reptiles → Alligators are mammals
*8. Alligators can bark & ~ Dogs are reptiles
9. ~ ~ Dogs are mammals ∨ Snakes are reptiles
10. ~ ~ Dogs are mammals → ~ ~ Snakes are reptiles

EXERCISE 7.4

Indicate which of the following symbolized statements are true and which are false. Assume that the statements represented by the variables *a*, *b*, and *c* are true, and that the statements represented by *p*, *q*, and *r* are false.

1. $a \& p$
*2. $\sim a \lor \sim b$
3. $c \rightarrow p$
4. $\sim b \lor \sim c$
*5. $\mathrm{q} \rightarrow \mathrm{b}$
6. $a \& \sim q$
7. $b \lor \sim p$
8. $\sim b \& \sim q$
9. $b \rightarrow \sim c$
*10. $p \rightarrow \sim r$

EXERCISE 7.5

Translate each of the symbolic statements in Exercise 7.4 into a logically equivalent statement in English. Assume that the letters stand for positive statements. Possible answers are provided in Appendix B for 2, 5, and 9.

EXERCISE 7.6

Translate each of the following statements into symbolic form. Make sure that the letters you use stand for positive statements.

1. If you visited northern Manitoba in December, then you must have seen polar bears.

*2. Either Canada will become more European, or Canada will become more American.

3. "You either die a hero, or you live long enough to see yourself become the villain." (Harvey Dent, *The Dark Knight*)

4. Sure, I'm happy to stop at the grocery store on the way home, but I'm not going to buy you any of that awful instant coffee.

*5. Science will never triumph over religion unless science can offer a spiritual experience.

6. If you believed in animal rights, then you wouldn't eat meat.

7. Canada's oil sands are a very "dirty" source of oil, but most Canadians don't seem too concerned about that.

8. It is not the case that philosophy is dead, and it is not true that science has replaced it.

*9. Provided I pass my logic course, I will finally be able to understand political arguments.

10. Canadians say they support human rights, but they certainly aren't above buying cheap products produced by foreign companies with inhumane working environments.

CHECKING FOR VALIDITY

Now you're ready to put what you've learned about truth tables to use in determining the validity of arguments. The truth table test of validity is based on an elementary fact about validity that you've already encountered: *It's impossible for a valid argument to have true premises and a false conclusion.* So any procedure that allows us to easily check if the premises are true and the conclusion is false will help us test an argument for validity. Truth tables can do this. Devising truth tables for arguments, then, can reveal the underlying structure—the form—of the arguments, even those that are fairly complex.

Simple Arguments

Let's start by analyzing a very simple, silly argument involving a conjunction:

Ducks have webbed feet.
Ducks have feathers.
Therefore, ducks have webbed feet and ducks have feathers.

We symbolize the argument like this:

p
q
$\therefore p \,\&\, q$

Here we have each premise and the conclusion represented by variables, giving us a good look at the logical form of the argument. The symbol ∴ indicates that a conclusion follows (it's often translated as "therefore"). The argument is, of course, valid—a fact that you can quickly see without the aid of a truth table. But it makes for a simple illustration:

p	*q*	*p* & *q*
T	T	T
T	F	F
F	T	F
F	F	F

This truth table is a repeat of the one we looked at in the section on conjunctions. The top line of the table shows the two premises of the argument and its conclusion with their truth values listed below. Like all truth tables, this one shows every possible combination of truth values for the premises and conclusion.

When dealing with simple arguments, the first two columns of a truth table are guide columns in which the variables, or letters, of the argument are listed, followed by a column for each premise and then a column for the conclusion. In this case, though, the guide columns happen to be identical to the premise columns, so we won't repeat them.

> "Logic takes care of itself; all we have to do is to look and see how it does it."
>
> —*Ludwig Wittgenstein*

Now we can ask the big question: "Does the truth table show (in any row) a state of affairs in which the premises of the argument are true and the conclusion false?" If we can find even *one* instance of this arrangement, we will have shown that the argument is invalid. Remember that we are trying to judge the *validity* of an argument, which is a matter of argument *form*. So if we can discover that it's *possible* for a particular argument form to have true premises and a false conclusion, we will know without further investigation that the argument is invalid. Not only that, but we will know that *any* argument of the same pattern is invalid. The truth table can tell us definitively whether an argument is invalid because the table includes every possible combination of truth

REVIEW NOTES

Common Argument Forms Symbolized

***MODUS PONENS*, AFFIRMING THE ANTECEDENT (VALID)**

$p \rightarrow q$
p
$\therefore q$

HYPOTHETICAL SYLLOGISM (VALID)

$p \rightarrow q$
$q \rightarrow r$
$\therefore p \rightarrow r$

DENYING THE ANTECEDENT (INVALID)

$p \rightarrow q$
$\sim p$
$\therefore \sim q$

***MODUS TOLLENS*, DENYING THE CONSEQUENT (VALID)**

$p \rightarrow q$
$\sim q$
$\therefore \sim p$

DISJUNCTIVE SYLLOGISM (VALID)

$p \vee q$
$\sim p$
$\therefore q$

AFFIRMING THE CONSEQUENT (INVALID)

$p \rightarrow q$
q
$\therefore p$

values. If the truth table doesn't reveal a situation in which the argument has true premises and a false conclusion, then the argument is valid.

As you can see in the previous table, there is no row in which the premises are true (T T) and the conclusion false (F). Therefore, the argument is valid.

Here's a slightly more complex argument:

If the icebergs melt, the lowlands will flood.
The icebergs will not melt.
Therefore, the lowlands will not flood.

You should recognize this argument as an instance of denying the antecedent. Here it is symbolized, with negation and conditional connectives:

$p \rightarrow q$
$\sim p$
$\therefore \sim q$

And here's the truth table for the argument, with the premises and conclusion indicated for clarity:

p	q	$p \rightarrow q$ Premise	$\sim p$ Premise	$\sim q$ Conclusion
T	T	T	F	F
T	F	F	F	T
F	T	T	T	F
F	F	T	T	T

(Adding the labels "premise" and "conclusion" is totally optional. We won't always do that here in the text. But it may prove helpful in your own work.)

You can begin checking for validity in two different ways. You can first inspect all rows that have a false conclusion and then see if the premises in that row are true, indicating an invalid argument. Or you can zero in on rows showing all true premises and then check to see if they have false conclusions. In this case, the third row tells the tale: both premises are true and the conclusion is false. So the argument is invalid, and we need not check any other rows.

As we saw earlier, the truth value of a compound statement depends on the truth value of its components. That's why it's a good idea to start out with guide columns in a truth table. The truth value of these variables (letters) determines the truth value of statements that are composed of the variables. The truth value of these compound units in turn determines the truth value of any larger compound units.

In the truth table just given, the truth value of $\sim p$ is the contradictory of p, and the truth value of $\sim q$ is the contradictory of q. So whatever the truth value of a statement, the tilde (~) reverses it, from true to false or false to true.

Now let's try this one:

Either we fight for freedom or we give in to tyranny.
We won't give in to tyranny.
Therefore, we will fight for freedom.

Symbolized, it looks like this:

$p \vee q$
$\sim p$
$\therefore q$

And here is its truth table:

p	q	$p \vee q$ Premise	$\sim p$ Premise	q Conclusion
T	T	T	F	T
T	F	T	F	F
F	T	T	T	T
F	F	F	T	F

(Again, we've labelled the premises and conclusion in this truth table just to help you out, though it's not strictly part of the method.)

Is this argument valid? To find out, we need to check the table for any row that shows true premises and a false conclusion. The third row is the only one in which both premises are true—but the conclusion is also true. So this argument is valid.

Tricky Arguments

Arguments can get more complicated when variables and connectives are intricately combined into larger compounds and when the number of variables increases. In both these situations, truth tables can help you unravel the complexities. Let's examine an argument that has both these wrinkles. We'll go right to the symbolized form:

$p \rightarrow \sim(q \,\&\, r)$
p
$\therefore \sim(q \,\&\, r)$

Notice in these premises the use of parentheses to join variables. The parentheses enable us to symbolize arguments more precisely and to avoid confusion. In math, there is an obvious difference between 2 × (3 + 4), which equals 14, and (2 × 3) + 4, which equals 10. Likewise, there is a crucial difference between $p \rightarrow \sim(q \,\&\, r)$ and $(p \rightarrow \sim q) \,\&\, r$. The former symbolization would express a conditional such as "If it rains tomorrow, then Alice and Eric will not go to the movies." But the latter symbolization would represent a very different conditional, such as "If it rains tomorrow, then Alice will not go to the movies, and Eric will go to the movies." Such differences, of course, can affect the truth values of a statement and require a different truth table.

Here's a distinction involving parentheses that's worth committing to memory. Consider these two statements:

$\sim(q \,\&\, r)$
It is not the case that Leo sings the blues and Fats sings the blues.

$\sim q \ \& \sim r$
Leo does not sing the blues, and Fats does not sing the blues.

The first statement asserts that it is not the case that *both* Leo and Fats sing the blues. That is, it's not true that Leo and Fats are concurrently in the habit of singing the blues. Maybe Leo sings the blues, and Fats doesn't, or vice versa. On the other hand, the second statement says that Leo doesn't sing the blues and neither does Fats. If we hope that at least one of these guys sings the blues, we're out of luck.

Here's another distinction worth knowing. Look at these two statements:

$\sim(q \vee r)$
It is not the case that either Leo sings the blues or Fats sings the blues.

$\sim q \vee \sim r$
Either Leo does not sing the blues or Fats does not sing the blues.

The first statement says that neither Leo nor Fats sings the blues; it could also be symbolized as $\sim q \ \& \sim r$. The second statement says that it is not the case that *both* Leo *and* Fats sing the blues, which could also be expressed $\sim(q \ \& \ r)$.

Correctly symbolizing statements with parentheses is a straightforward business, but it requires close attention to what's being said. Your best clues to where to insert parentheses come from the words *either* and *neither*, conjunction and disjunction words such as *and* and *or*, and the punctuation in the sentences. Notice how the sentence clues in the following statements inform how the statements are symbolized:

If the next prime minister is from Ontario, then neither the West nor Atlantic Canada will be happy.

We can symbolize the statements with the following variables:

p—The next prime minister is from Ontario.
q—The West will be happy.
r—Atlantic Canada will be happy.
$p \rightarrow \sim(q \vee r)$

And:

Either John Oliver is funny or the show is rigged, or the network has made a bad investment.

p—John Oliver is funny.
q—The show is rigged.

r—The network has made a bad investment.
$(p \vee q) \vee r$

Arguments like these that have three variables instead of two may look scary, but they're not. The steps you use to check the validity of a three-variable argument are the same ones you apply in two-variable arguments. You devise a truth table, calculate truth values, and check for true premises with a false conclusion. The truth table, of course, has an additional guide column for the third variable, and there are more rows to accommodate the larger number of possible true–false combinations. In a two-variable table there are four rows; in a three-variable table there are eight rows, and thus eight combinations of truth values. Notice how the guide columns are laid out:

p	*q*	*r*
T	T	T
T	T	F
T	F	T
T	F	F
F	T	T
F	T	F
F	F	T
F	F	F

"Reason in man is rather like God in the world."

—*Thomas Aquinas*

To remember the truth values in each guide column, think of it this way: the first column is four Ts, then four Fs; the second column is alternating pairs of truth values beginning with T T; and the third column is alternating Ts and Fs starting with T.

Now let's test this argument for validity:

> If the Flames won game one, but didn't win game two, then they've only won one game. But it's not true that they won game one but didn't win game two. Therefore, it's not the case that they've only won one game.

p—The Flames won game one.
q—The Flames won game two.
r—The Flames have only won one game.

$(p \,\&\, {\sim}q) \rightarrow r$
${\sim}(p \,\&\, {\sim}q)$
$\therefore {\sim}r$

And here's the truth table for the argument:

	1 p	2 q	3 r	4 $p \& {\sim}q$	5 $(p \& {\sim}q) \rightarrow r$	6 ${\sim}(p \& {\sim}q)$	7 ${\sim}r$
1	T	T	T	F	T	T	F
2	T	T	F	F	T	T	T
3	T	F	T	T	T	F	F
4	T	F	F	T	F	F	T
5	F	T	T	F	T	T	F
6	F	T	F	F	T	T	T
7	F	F	T	F	T	T	F
8	F	F	F	F	T	T	T

This truth table has seven columns, and you can guess why six of them are there. The first three are the guide columns, and the last three are for the two premises and the conclusion. Column 4 is there because it simplifies the assigning of truth values to columns 5, 6, and 7—it is a component of the two premises. If we wanted, we could add more columns for other components such as ${\sim}r$ if the additions would make it easier to create the truth table.

The truth values for $(p \& {\sim}q)$ are, of course, determined by the truth values of its conjuncts. If just one conjunct is false, the conjunction is false (as it is in rows 1, 2, and 5 through 8). Only in rows 3 and 4 is the conjunction true. The truth value of the conditional $(p \& {\sim}q) \rightarrow r$ is based on the truth values of $(p \& {\sim}q)$ and r, with the conditional being false only when $(p \& {\sim}q)$ is true and r is false (row 4). In all other rows the conditional is true. The truth value of the premise ${\sim}(p \& {\sim}q)$ is the contradictory of the truth value for $(p \& {\sim}q)$. Likewise, the truth value of ${\sim}r$ is the contradictory of r.

Is there any row in which the premises are true and the conclusion false? Yes, that's the situation in rows 1, 5, and 7, so the argument is invalid.

Streamlined Evaluation

With truth tables, you can accurately assess the validity of any propositional argument, even some fairly complicated ones. But as the arguments get more complicated (when they have more than two or three variables, for example), you may want a more efficient technique for calculating validity. Here's a good alternative method—one that just happens to be easier to master if you already know the ins and outs of truth tables.

In this approach—which we'll call the *short method*—we don't bother to produce a whole truth table, but we do try to construct some truth table rows (maybe only one if we're lucky). The basic strategy is based on the same fact we relied on in the truth table test: it's impossible for a valid argument to have true premises and a false conclusion. So we try to discover if there's a way to make the conclusion false and the premises true by assigning various truth values to the argument's components. That is, we try to prove that the argument is invalid. If we can do this, then we'll have the proof we need.

Let's try the short method on this argument:

$\sim q$
$p \rightarrow (q \vee r)$
r
$\therefore p$

First we write out the argument so that the premises and conclusion are in a single row:

$\sim q \qquad p \rightarrow (q \vee r) \quad r \qquad p$

Now we examine the conclusion. What truth value must we assign to it to ensure that it's false? Obviously the answer is *false*—because there is only one variable in the conclusion, and the conclusion must be false. So we label p with an F in the conclusion and everywhere else in the argument. Then our row looks like this:

$\sim q$	$p \rightarrow (q \vee r)$	r	p
	F		F

Just one caution: as you work through the short method, you must remember that the truth values you mark under the argument row *apply to the variables (letters) only, not the premises*. To avoid any confusion, if you want you can write the truth values for the premises *above* the argument row. In this way you can indicate either (1) the premise truth values that you're trying for or (2) the premise truth values that result from your truth value assignments.

REVIEW NOTES

The Short Method: Step by Step

1. Write out the symbolized argument in a single row.
2. Assign truth values to the variables in the conclusion to make the conclusion false. (Write the appropriate Ts or Fs below the row.) Assign these truth values to the same variables elsewhere.
3. Consistently assign truth values to variables in the premises. Assign truth values first to premises where specific truth values are "locked in."
4. Try to make assignments that yield a false conclusion and true premises. If you can, the argument is invalid. If not, the argument is valid.

In this argument we can also tell right away that r *must* be true because it is a premise in the argument, and we're trying to see if we can make all the premises true (and the conclusion false). Then we have:

$\sim q$	$p \rightarrow (q \vee r)$	r	p
	F T	T	F

Now we look at the first column because it will be easy to determine its truth value. Since the first premise must be true and it's a negation, q, must be false. This fills out the whole argument with truth values:

$\sim q$	$p \rightarrow (q \vee r)$	r	p
F	F F T	T	F

We've shown then that the first and third premises are true. And we can now see that the second premise must also be true: the disjunction $(q \vee r)$ is true because one of the disjuncts is true (r). And the conditional (made up of p and the disjunction) is true because a false antecedent (p) and a true consequent $(q \vee r)$ yields a true conditional.

We have thus shown that this argument can have a false conclusion and true premises—the sign of an invalid argument.

Now let's try the short method on this argument:

$p \rightarrow q$
$q \rightarrow r$
$\sim r$
$\therefore \sim p$

Again, we write out the argument so that the premises and conclusion are in a single row:

$p \rightarrow q \quad q \rightarrow r \quad \sim r \quad \sim p$

Again, we start with the conclusion. Since the conclusion is a negation ($\sim p$), we know that there is only one way that the conclusion could be false—if p is true. We then must make p true everywhere else in the argument:

$p \rightarrow q$	$q \rightarrow r$	$\sim r$	$\sim p$
T			T

We now turn to the first premise, a simple conditional. The antecedent (p) is true, which means that if the conditional is to be true, its consequent (q) cannot be false (a true antecedent and a false consequent yields a false conditional). So we're forced to assign these truth values:

$p \rightarrow q$	$q \rightarrow r$	$\sim r$	$\sim p$
T T	T		T

FOOD FOR THOUGHT

Propositional Logic and Essay-Writing

Clarity of structure is an important element of any essay. This is especially true for argumentative essays, essays that are designed to convince the reader of some point of view. And believe it or not, a command of the basics of propositional logic can be a big help in this regard. In many cases, argumentative essays have an underlying structure that can be expressed in terms of propositional logic. Recognizing the structure of your own essay and writing it out using the methods explained in this chapter can help you organize your thoughts and can help ensure that the argument you are putting forward is a valid (and hopefully sound) one.

For example, imagine an essay that basically argues this: "Canada either has to increase expenditures on international aid, or admit to being a second-rate player on the international scene. But we cannot accept such a low status. Therefore we must increase spending on international aid." You probably recognize that as a simple disjunctive argument, which when translated into symbols would look like this:

$p \lor q$
$\sim q$
$\therefore p$

It would be easy to demonstrate using a simple truth table that this is a valid argument. And eventually your command of logic may get to the point where you will recognize instinctively that this argument is valid.

A short essay putting forward such a disjunctive argument would likely focus on the second premise, and explain in some detail why being a second-rate player on the international scene is such a bad thing. It would also have to explain why *those* are the two key options facing Canada, in order to avoid being accused of having put forward a false dilemma! If the dilemma is a false one, then this argument is valid but not sound.

An essay might instead have a simple *conditional* structure. Imagine an argument that says, "If Napoleon Bonaparte was a great leader, then he would have won the battle of Waterloo. But he did not win that battle. Therefore he was not a great leader."

$\mathrm{p} \rightarrow \mathrm{q}$
$\sim \mathrm{q}$
$\therefore \sim \mathrm{p}$

You may well recognize this argument structure as denying the consequent (*modus tollens*), a valid conditional argument structure. A full essay putting forward this argument about Napoleon would have to justify in detail the initial conditional claim about the significance of success at Waterloo. Is success in one particular battle really essential to establish a leader as a great one? If that conditional could be well supported, the argument would be a strong one, since the second premise (which states that Napoleon didn't *win* the battle) is a simple matter of historical fact upon which historians widely agree.

An essay of any substance is likely to have an underlying logical structure that is somewhat more complex than the two examples above. For example, an essay might have this slightly more complex version of a conditional structure:

$p \rightarrow (q \vee r \vee s)$
$\sim q$
$\sim r$
$\sim s$
$\therefore \sim p$

An example of an essay with that type of structure might read like this: "If government intervention in that industry is warranted, then it must be either because its product is dangerous, or its ads are dishonest, or its financial reports are incomplete. But its product is not dangerous. And its ads are not dishonest. And its financial reports are not incomplete. Therefore government intervention is not warranted." In an essay of any length, there would of course be a sub-argument establishing the truth of each of the premises. What is it, for example, that leads us to believe that the industry's products are not dangerous? If the argument for that is a propositional one, we could write it, too, in symbolic form.

What is the advantage of writing out the underlying logical structure of your essay's argument? There are at least three advantages. First, if you can write the structure of your argument using the tools of propositional logic, then you thereby reassure yourself that your essay does, in fact, have a logical structure. That is, you reassure yourself that you are putting forward a structured argument, rather than just subjecting your reader to a string of loosely connected ideas. Second, once you see the logical structure of your own argument, you can use the tools presented in this chapter to verify that your argument is valid. Finally, if you are able to represent your argument in terms of propositional logic, it is all the more likely that your readers, too, will be able to see that there is an underlying logic to your essay.

That leaves just *r* to deal with. Again we are forced to assign a truth value to it. Because the premise is a negation and it must be true, *r* has to be false. But if *r* is false, the second premise (another simple conditional) must be false (truth values for the premises are shown *above* the argument row):

```
  T        F       T     F
p → q    q → r    ~r    ~p
T   T    T   F     F     T
```

So we see that since there is only one way for the conclusion to be false, we are locked into truth values that prevented us from having all true premises. We simply cannot consistently assign truth values to this argument that will give us a false conclusion and true premises. Therefore, this argument is valid.

In using the short method like this, your overall goal is to see if you can prove invalidity in the most efficient way possible. You want to get the job done without a lot of unnecessary steps. The best strategy for doing this is to look for truth value assignments *that cannot be any other way* given the truth value assignments in the conclusion. That is, focus on premises with assignments that are "locked into" the argument by the truth values you've given the conclusion. Make assignments in those premises first, regardless of which premise you start with.

In the foregoing arguments, the conclusions could be made false in only one way, and that made the rest of the work easier. But sometimes a conclusion can be made false in more than one way. In such cases, your strategy should be to try each possibility—each way that the conclusion can be false—until you get what you're after: an argument with true premises and a false conclusion. As soon as you get it, stop. You've proven that the argument form is invalid, and there's no reason to continue making assignments. If you try all the possibilities and still can't prove invalidity, the argument is valid.

Let's take a look at one of these multiple-possibility arguments:

$p \rightarrow q$
$q \vee r$
$\sim q$
$\therefore p \,\&\, r$

$p \rightarrow q \qquad q \vee r \qquad \sim q \qquad p \,\&\, r$

In this argument the conclusion is a conjunction, and that means it can be made false by any one of these combinations of truth values: F–T, T–F, and F–F. If we make separate rows for each of these possibilities, they look like this:

	$p \rightarrow q$	$q \vee r$	$\sim q$	$p \,\&\, r$
1	F	T		F T
2	T	F		T F
3	F	F		F F

So can we consistently assign truth values to make the premises true and the conclusion false in any of these rows? We can forget about row 2 because in the first premise, q must be true (to avoid making the conditional false). And if q is true, the third premise would be false. Likewise, we must throw out row 3 because q again must be true (to ensure that the disjunction is true). And if q is true, we run into the same problem we have in row 2—the third premise must be false. Row 1, though, works. To make the third premise true, we must make q false. And when we assign a truth value of false to q in the rest of the argument, we make the premises true and the conclusion false. Therefore, the argument is invalid.

SUMMARY

In propositional logic we use symbols to stand for the relationships between statements—that is, to indicate the form of an argument. These relationships are made possible by logical connectives such as conjunction (and), disjunction (or), negation (not), and conditional (If . . . then . . .). Connectives are used in compound statements, each of which is composed of at least two simple statements. A statement is a sentence that can be either true or false.

To indicate the possible truth values of statements and arguments, we can construct truth tables, a graphic way of displaying all the truth value possibilities. A conjunction is false if at least one of its statement components (conjuncts) is false. A disjunction is still true even if one of its component statements (disjuncts) is false. A negation is the denial of a statement. The negation of any statement changes the statement's truth value to its contradictory (false to true and true to false). A conditional statement is false in only one situation—when the antecedent is true and the consequent is false.

The use of truth tables to determine the validity of an argument is based on the fact that it's impossible for a valid argument to have true premises and a false conclusion. A basic truth table consists of two or more guide columns listing all the truth value possibilities, followed by a column for each premise and the conclusion. We can add other columns to help us determine the truth values of components of the argument.

Some arguments are complex when variables and connectives are combined into larger compounds and when the number of variables increases. To prevent confusion, we can use parentheses in symbolized arguments to show how statement or premise components go together.

You can check the validity of arguments not only with truth tables but also with the short method. In this procedure we try to discover if there is a way to make the conclusion false and the premises true by assigning various truth values to the argument's components.

EXERCISE 7.7

Answers to exercises marked with an asterisk (*) may be found in Appendix B, Answers to Exercises.

Construct a truth table for each of the statements in Exercise 7.3. Answers are given at the back of the book for 2, 6, and 8.

EXERCISE 7.8

Construct a truth table for each of the following arguments and show whether the argument is valid or invalid.

1. $a \,\&\, b$
   $\therefore b$

*2. $p \to q$
   p
   $\therefore q$

*3. $p \vee q$
   q
   $\therefore \sim p$

4. $p \to q$
   $\sim p$
   $\therefore q$

5. $a \,\&\, b$
   $\sim a$
   $\therefore b$

6. $p \to q$
   $q \to r$
   $\therefore q$

*7. $p \to q$
   $\sim q \,\&\, r$
   $\therefore r$

8. $a \vee (b \,\&\, c)$
   $\sim (b \,\&\, c)$
   $\therefore a$

9. $x \to y$
   $y \to z$
   $\therefore x \to z$

10. $p \to q$
   $\therefore p \to (p \,\&\, q)$

11. $(a \,\&\, b) \to (b \to c)$
   $(a \,\&\, b)$
   $\therefore a \,\&\, b \,\&\, c$

12. $(a \to \sim b) \vee \sim c$
   c
   $\therefore \sim b$

13. $(p \vee q) \to (p \,\&\, q)$
   $p \,\&\, q$
   $\therefore p \vee q$

*14. $p \to q$
   $\sim (q \vee r)$
   $\therefore \sim p$

*15. $(d \vee e) \to (d \,\&\, e)$
   $\sim (d \vee e)$
   $\therefore \sim (e \,\&\, d)$

16. $(p \to q) \to (p \to r)$
   $\sim (p \to q)$
   $\sim r$
   $\therefore p$

17. $(d \vee e) \to f$
   $f \to (d \,\&\, e)$
   $\therefore (d \,\&\, e) \to (d \sim e)$

18. $\sim (d \,\&\, e)$
   $e \vee f$
   $\therefore \sim d \,\&\, e$

19. $a \,\&\, \sim b$
   $c \vee (a \to b)$
   $\therefore a \,\&\, c$

20. $d \vee \sim e$
   $f \to e$
   $\therefore d \to \sim f$

EXERCISE 7.9

For each of the following arguments, translate it into symbols, construct a truth table, and determine its validity.

1. If we give kidnappers the money that they demand, then further kidnappings will be encouraged. If we do not give kidnappers the money

that they demand, the kidnappers will kill the hostages. We will not give kidnappers the money that they demand. Therefore, the kidnappers will kill the hostages.

2. If the United States goes to war with Russia, then Canada will have to go to war with Russia as well. Canada also has a mutual protection pact with the United Kingdom and France. Since Russia has sworn not to go to war with France, they will not go to war with the United States either.
*3. This is either olive oil or canola oil. And it's not olive oil, so it must be canola oil.
4. "Men, it is assumed, act in economic matters only in response to pecuniary compensation or to force. Force in the modern society is largely, although by no means completely, obsolete. So only pecuniary compensation remains of importance." (John Kenneth Galbraith, *The New Industrial State*)
5. If the lake freezes, then the lake-effect snow will stop. If the lake-effect snow stops, the streets will be easier to plow. Therefore, the streets will be easier to plow.
6. Emilio will go to the concert with Joanne, only if Heather goes too. But Heather will only go to the concert if it's just she and Emilio. Joanne has stated that she'll only go if neither Emilio nor Heather do, since they're both being so annoying. Therefore, Joanne will go to the concert alone.
7. UN peacekeepers will not attack the local militants, provided that the militants behave themselves. The militants will not make trouble if the UN peacekeepers don't attack. Therefore, UN peacekeepers will not attack the local militants, and the militants will not make trouble.
8. "If then, it is agreed that things are either the result of coincidence or for an end, and these cannot be the result of coincidence or spontaneity, it follows that they must be for an end." (Aristotle, *Physics*)
9. Either there is evidence that women of supernatural powers (i.e., witches) exist, or there is no such evidence. If there is no such evidence, then we have no reason to believe in witches. If there is evidence, we do have reason to believe in witches. There is no such evidence. Therefore, we have no reason to believe in witches.
10. With great power comes great responsibility. Until you are ready for both, you can have neither. I have seen that you are irresponsible, so you will receive no powers from me.
*11. Either the herbal remedy alleviated the symptoms, or the placebo effect alleviated the symptoms. If the placebo effect is responsible for easing the symptoms, then the herbal remedy is worthless. The herbal remedy alleviated the symptoms. So the herbal remedy is not worthless.

EXERCISE 7.10

Use the short method to check the validity of the following arguments in Exercise 7.8: 1, 3, 5, 9, 10, 15, 16, and 18. Write the symbolized argument in one row and assign truth values to each variable. Then, above the argument row, assign truth values to the premises and conclusion. Answers are provided for 3, 10, and 15.

Field Problems

1. Find two deductive arguments on the Web or in a university newspaper. Go for variety: make sure one is a conditional argument and the other makes use of disjunction. Symbolize the arguments and determine the validity of each one by using the truth-table method.
2. Find a deductive argument in one of your textbooks (not this one!) Translate it into symbolic form and create a truth table to test its validity. Then devise a different argument that uses the same argument form as the one you found.
3. Think of a competitive activity that you enjoy participating in or watching – for example, football or online Scrabble or an Olympic sport. Can you think of a "standard" bit of wisdom related to that activity that takes the form of a conditional statement? (For example, "If you're in situation X, you should always do Y.) Write out both valid and invalid arguments that use that conditional statement as their first premise.

Self-Assessment Quiz

1. What are the four logical connectives used in this chapter? How is each one symbolized?
2. Construct the truth table for each logical connective.
3. Under what circumstances is a negation false?
4. Under what circumstances is a disjunction true?
5. Which of the following symbolized statements are true and which are false? Assume that *a*, *b*, and *c* are true, and *p*, *q*, and *r* are false.

   $c \rightarrow q$

   $q \rightarrow c$

   $a \ \& \sim q$

   $a \vee \sim q$

6. Put the following statement into symbolic form: "Either I'm seeing things or I just saw Professor MacDonald being interviewed on TV!"
7. Put the following into symbolic form: "You're sure to hit a home run. I mean, if you keep your eye on the ball."
8. Construct a truth table for each of the following arguments and indicate whether the argument is valid or invalid.

   $p \rightarrow q$ $p \vee (q \,\&\, r)$
   $r \rightarrow q$ $\sim(q \,\&\, r)$
   $\therefore q$ $\therefore p$

9. Translate this argument into symbols, construct its truth table, and indicate whether the argument is valid.

   If the office building is built too high, it will have a high probability of collapsing. If the construction company wants to make more money, it will build the office building too high. Either the construction company wants to make more money, or it wants to go bankrupt. Since no company wants to go bankrupt, the office building will have a high probability of collapsing.

10. Translate this argument into symbols, construct its truth table, and indicate whether the argument is valid.

    Either Joe goes to the movie, or Julia goes to the movie. If the movie is *The Imitation Game*, then Julia goes to the movie. So if Joe goes to the movie, the movie is not *The Imitation Game*.

Construct arguments in English for each of the following symbolized arguments.

11. $x \vee y$
    $y \vee z$
    $\therefore x \rightarrow z$
12. $a \rightarrow b$
    $\therefore a \rightarrow (a \,\&\, b)$
13. $a \,\&\, b$
    $\sim b$
    $\therefore a$
14. $(p \vee q) \rightarrow (p \,\&\, q)$
    $p \,\&\, q$
    $\therefore p \vee q$
15. $p \rightarrow q$
    $\sim p$
    $\therefore q$

Use the short method to check the validity of the following arguments. Write out the argument in a single row and assign truth values to each variable.

16. $p \rightarrow q$
    $\sim q$
    $\therefore \sim p$
17. $p \;\&\; q$
    $q \rightarrow r$
    $\sim q$
    $\therefore \sim r$
18. $p \rightarrow q$
    $q \rightarrow r$
    $\therefore p \rightarrow r$
19. $p \vee (q \;\&\; r)$
    $\sim p$
    $\sim q$
    $\therefore r$
20. $a \vee b$
    $b \vee c$
    $\therefore (b \;\&\; c) \vee (a \;\&\; b)$

Integrative Exercises

These exercises pertain to material in Chapters 3–7.

For each of the following arguments, determine whether it is deductive or inductive, valid or invalid, strong or weak. Then diagram it using the shapes-and-arrows method we learned in Chapter 3. Also state whether the argument contains any appeals to popularity or common practice.

1. "Proposals to reduce the criminal offence of euthanasia have been advanced, especially in light of the Latimer case. Some wish to create a new category of 'compassionate homicide.' For three reasons, it would be unwise public policy to enact this type of provision. (a) Killing someone is not an act of compassion. Compassionate homicide is an ethically flawed concept. (b) A separate crime for euthanasia would be discriminatory by (i) depriving the lives of sick and disabled persons of equal protection from murder; (ii) signifying that the lives of sick and disabled persons

have less value than others. (c) Public safety would be endangered." (Euthanasia Prevention Coalition of BC)

2. "Encouragement of contempt for laws is more dangerous to society than occasional use of marijuana. Severe laws against marijuana do not discourage use of marijuana, but rather breed this contempt not only for drug laws, but for laws in general. Therefore severe laws against marijuana are more dangerous to society than the activity which they are designed to prevent." (A. Blakeslee)
3. Homeopathy—the alternative "medicine" that uses infinitesimally small quantities of a substance diluted in water—is entirely bogus. If homeopathy worked, it would violate everything we know about how the human body works. In most cases, the effects people believe they experience can be chalked up to the placebo effect. And finally, scientists who have evaluated the clinical evidence agree that no one has ever proven any homeopathic remedy effective, despite many attempts to do so.
4. It is ridiculous for city council to pass a bylaw that bans smoking in all public places, including bars and private clubs. Many people enjoy smoking cigarettes and cigars, and in many cultures smoking has cultural and religious significance. A bylaw outlawing all forms of smoking is morally and legally unjustifiable.

For each of the following arguments, name the argument pattern—*modus ponens*, *modus tollens*, affirming the consequent, denying the antecedent, or none of these.

5. Installing an intrusion alarm in your home is very inconsiderate toward your neighbours. It is common knowledge that most alarms are set off by the careless actions of their own homeowners, so they are not useful. Moreover, the noise caused by these frequent mistakes, such as opening a window while the alarm is set, is very loud and disconcerting to everyone around the house. That's why nobody should install any sort of alarm in his or her house.
6. When there's an earthquake, houses shake. And we did feel our house shake, so there must have been an earthquake.
7. If there were structures in nature that were so complex that they could not possibly have evolved through natural selection, the theory of evolution must be false. There are such structures, however—like the human eye. Consequently evolution cannot be the right explanation for the existence of the peculiar life forms found on Earth.

Say which of the following symbolized statements are true and which are false. Assume that the statements represented by the variables *a*, *b*, and *c* are true, and *p*, *q*, and *r* are false.

8. $\sim b \vee b$
9. $\sim a \ \& \sim p$
10. $p \rightarrow a$
11. $b \rightarrow \sim r$

For each of the following arguments, specify the conclusion and premises (including any implied premises). Symbolize the argument and construct a truth table to determine the validity of the argument.

12. If the nuclear power industry improves its safety record and solves the nuclear waste problem, it will become the number one source of energy in the world. But it will never be able to change its safety record or solve the waste problem. Consequently, the industry will not become the primary source of the world's energy.
13. The *Mona Lisa* at the Louvre is either the original painted by Leonardo da Vinci or an extremely good fake. But if experts say it's real, then it's real. The painting's authenticity has been analyzed and verified by countless experts over the years. So it is highly unlikely that the *Mona Lisa* at the Louvre is a fake.
14. The surgery will be a success if blood loss can be controlled. The surgery is a success and the patient has spoken to the press. So blood loss must have been controlled.
15. If the other nine provinces want to keep Canada strong and united, then they will continue to recognize Quebec's special place in Confederation. If they continue to recognize Quebec's special place in Confederation, then Quebec's distinct culture will survive. Quebec's distinct culture will survive, so the other nine provinces will continue to recognize Quebec's special place in Confederation.

Translate each of the following arguments into categorical syllogistic form (premise, premise, conclusion), symbolize the argument (using the conventional *S*, *P*, *M* variables), and draw a Venn diagram to test its validity.

16. Some Muslims are not Sunni Muslims, for some Muslims are Shiite Muslims and no Shiite Muslims are Sunni Muslims.

17. Some computers are not laptops, but all netbooks are laptops. It follows that some computers are not netbooks.
18. Some shoes are inexpensive, and all shoes that are expensive are fancy. Therefore, not all shoes are fancy.
19. Mayor McTaggart will not support any proposal to soften the anti-smoking bylaw. He's a physician, and physicians never support proposals to soften anti-smoking bylaws.
20. Some contagious diseases are diseases caused by the influenza virus, and diseases caused by the influenza virus are always dangerous diseases. So some contagious diseases are dangerous diseases.

Writing Assignments

1. Write a 300-word essay that gives a deductive argument for why corporations should take their social responsibilities more seriously.
2. Select an issue from the following list and write a 500-word paper defending a claim pertaining to the issue. Use one or more deductive arguments to make your case.
   - Should people simply stop caring so much about privacy, in light of all the ways that modern technology makes it easier for our privacy to be invaded?
   - Should private clubs be permitted to ban members of the opposite sex from membership?
   - Should Canada expand the powers of law-enforcement agencies to combat terrorism?
   - Should there be an international court capable of charging entire countries with crimes?
3. Outline the argument in Essay 4 ("What's Wrong with Body Mass Index") in Appendix A, indicating the premises and the conclusion. Determine whether the argument is deductive or inductive.

8 INDUCTIVE REASONING

CHAPTER OBJECTIVES

Enumerative Induction

You will be able to

- define *enumerative induction* and explain how it's used.
- define *target population*, *sample*, and *relevant property*.
- understand the two ways in which an enumerative induction can fail to be strong.
- understand the error known as hasty generalization and know how to avoid it.
- understand the basics of opinion polls and know the definitions of *random sampling*, *self-selecting sample*, *margin of error*, and *confidence level*.

Statistical Syllogisms

You will be able to

- explain what a statistical syllogism is.
- define *individual*, *group*, *characteristic*, and *proportion*.
- understand three ways in which statistical syllogisms can fail to be strong.

Analogical Induction

You will be able to

- formulate and evaluate an argument by analogy.
- use the following criteria to evaluate arguments by analogy: relevant similarities, relevant dissimilarities, the number of instances compared, and diversity among cases.

Causal Arguments

You will be able to

- define *causal claims* and *arguments*.

- apply Mill's methods to the evaluation of causal arguments.
- recognize the ways in which people can make errors in causal reasoning.
- recognize and know how to avoid the post hoc fallacy.
- define necessary and sufficient conditions.
- distinguish between necessary and sufficient conditions in everyday contexts.

Mixed Arguments

You will be able to

- explain what a "mixed argument" is and what its key components are.
- evaluate a mixed argument.

We now pass from an exploration of deductive arguments to a close examination of inductive ones—a very small step since both these argument types are common features of our everyday lives. Recall that a deductive argument is intended to provide logically conclusive support for its conclusion; such an argument is either valid or invalid, sound or unsound. An inductive argument, on the other hand, is intended to supply only probable support for its conclusion, earning the label of "strong" if it succeeds in providing such support and "weak" if it fails. The conclusion of an inductively strong argument is simply more likely to be true than not. If the argument's premises are true, it is said to be cogent. Unlike valid deductive arguments, an inductively strong argument can never guarantee that the conclusion is true—but it can render the conclusion probably true, even highly likely to be true. Inductive arguments, then, cannot give us certainty, but they can give us high levels of probability—high enough at least to help us acquire knowledge in everything from physics to birdwatching.

"The rules of probable inference are the most difficult part of logic, but also the most useful."

—*Bertrand Russell*

Deductive logic is the invisible framework on which much of our reasoning hangs and the solid bond that holds together the logical frameworks of mathematics, computer science, and other theoretical or abstract disciplines. Inductive reasoning, though, gives us most of what we know about the empirical workings of the world, allowing us in science and in ordinary experience to soar reliably from what we know to what we don't. It allows us to reason "beyond the evidence"—from bits of what is already known to conclusions about what those bits suggest is probably true.

Inductive arguments come in several forms. In this chapter we will examine four of them and, as in previous chapters, we will focus on how to evaluate their merits in real-life contexts.

ENUMERATIVE INDUCTION

As you may have noticed in Chapter 3, sometimes an inductive argument reasons from premises about a group, or class, of things to a conclusion about a single member of the group (that is, from general to particular). For example:

> Almost all of the students attending this university want to be entrepreneurs.
> Wei-en attends this university.
> Therefore, Wei-en probably wants to be an entrepreneur.

> Eighty-two per cent of residents in this neighbourhood buy Girl Guide cookies.
> Sam is a resident of this neighbourhood.
> Therefore, Sam will probably buy Girl Guide cookies.

Far more inductive arguments, however, reason from premises about individual members of a group to conclusions about the group as a whole (from particular to general). In such cases we begin with observations about some members of the group and end with a generalization about all of them. This argument pattern is called **enumerative induction**, and it's a way of reasoning that we all find both natural and useful.

enumerative induction An inductive argument pattern in which we reason from premises about individual members of a group to conclusions about the group as a whole.

> Most peace activists I know are kind-hearted. So probably all peace activists are kind-hearted.

> Every Xphon computer I've bought in the last five years has had a faulty monitor. Therefore all Xphon computers probably have faulty monitors.

> Forty per cent of the pickles that you've sampled from the barrel are rotten. So 40 per cent of all the pickles in the barrel are probably rotten.

More formally, enumerative induction has this form:

> X per cent of the observed members of group A have property P. Therefore, X per cent of all members of group A probably have property P.

Translated into this format, our pickle argument looks like this:

> Forty per cent of the observed pickles from the barrel are rotten. Therefore, 40 per cent of all the pickles in the barrel are probably rotten.

Enumerative induction comes with some useful terminology. The group as a whole—the whole collection of individuals in question—is called the **target population** or **target group**. The observed members of the target group

target group (target population) In enumerative induction, the whole collection of individuals under study.

sample (sample member) In enumerative induction, the observed members of the target group.

relevant property (property in question) In enumerative induction, a property, or characteristic, that is of interest in the target group.

are called the **sample members** or **sample**. And the property we're interested in is called the **relevant property** or **property in question**. In the foregoing example, the target group is the pickles in the barrel, the sample is the observed pickles, and the property is the quality of being exceptionally good.

Now, using this terminology we can study arguments by enumeration a little closer. Remember that an inductive argument cannot only be strong or weak, but it can also *vary* in its strength—in the degree of support that the premises give to the conclusion. So the strength of the argument depends on the premises as well as on how much is claimed in the conclusion. Let's look at some examples.

Argument 1

All the corporate executives Jacques has worked for have been crooks. Therefore, all corporate executives are probably crooks.

The target group is corporate executives: that's what the conclusion is about. The sample is the corporate executives Jacques has worked for (those are the examples he looked at). And the relevant property—the characteristic he's interested in—is being a crook. We don't know how many corporate executives Jacques has worked for, but we must assume from what we know about employment patterns in corporate Canada that the number is small, probably no more than a dozen. Neither do we know exactly how many corporate executives there are, but we can safely guess that there are thousands or tens of thousands. It should be obvious, then, that this enumerative inductive falls short on at least one score: the sample is just too small. We simply cannot draw reliable conclusions about all corporate executives on the basis of a mere handful of them. The argument is therefore pretty weak.

"They're looking for someone who's well rounded and knows how to keep a cool head."

With such a small sample of the target group, we can't even conclude that *most* corporate executives are crooks. But we can make argument 1 strong by revising the conclusion to read, "*Some* corporate executives are probably crooks." This is a much more limited generalization that requires a more limited supporting premise.

We can fault this argument on another count: the sample is not representative of the target group. With thousands of corporate executives working for thousands of corporations, we must assume that corporate executives—in temperament, morality, demographics, and many other factors—are a diverse lot. It is therefore highly unlikely that Jacques's former bosses are representative of all corporate executives in their crookedness (the relevant property). Consider also that it is highly likely that most of Jacques's work experience has been within just one or two industries; and even if there are a lot of crooked executives in those industries, those industries might not be representative of the Canadian business world more generally. And if the sample is not representative of the whole, we cannot use it to draw accurate conclusions about the whole. Argument 1 is weak for that additional reason.

Consider this one:

Argument 2
Almost all of the blue herons that we've examined at many different sites in the nature preserve (about 200 birds) have had birth defects. Therefore, most of the blue herons in the nature preserve probably have birth defects.

In this argument the target group is the blue herons in the nature preserve, the sample is the 200 blue herons examined, and the relevant property is having birth defects. We would normally consider this a very strong enumerative induction. Assuming that the premise is true—that almost all 200 birds really did have birth defects—we would probably be surprised to discover that only a tiny minority of the target group as a whole had birth defects. Since the sample was drawn from many parts of the preserve, we would deem it representative of the target group. And because of the general uniformity of characteristics among birds in the wild, we would assume that a sample of 200 birds would be large enough to strongly support the conclusion. As it stands, argument 2 is strong.

On the other hand, a conclusion asserting that *all* of the target group had birth defects would normally go beyond what the evidence in the premise would support. There could easily be at least some blue herons in the preserve (assuming it to be large enough) that don't have birth defects, even if most do.

> "The deductive method is the mode of using knowledge, and the inductive method the mode of acquiring it."
>
> —*Henry Mayhew*

So you can see that an enumerative inductive argument can fail to be strong in two major ways: its sample can be (1) too small or (2) not representative. Of course, it's possible for an enumerative induction to be perfectly strong but to have false premises, in which case the argument isn't cogent. That is, the data (or evidence) stated in the premises could have been misinterpreted, misstated, or simply mistaken.

Sample Size

Let's say that you decide to conduct a survey of university students to determine their attitude toward premarital sex. So you stand around in the student centre and query the first five students that pass by. Four out of the five say that premarital sex is immoral. You conclude that 80 per cent (four-fifths) of the student body are against premarital sex. Should you send your findings to the school newspaper—or maybe even to the CBC?

No way. This survey is a joke—the sample is much too small to yield any reliable information about the attitudes of the students as a whole. That verdict may seem obvious, but just about everyone at one time or another probably makes this kind of mistake, which is known as **hasty generalization**. We're guilty of hasty generalization whenever we draw a conclusion about a target group on the basis of a too small sample. People regularly make this mistake when dealing with all sorts of enumerative inductive evidence—political polls, consumer opinion surveys, scientific studies (especially medical research), quality-control checks, anecdotal reports, and many others.

hasty generalization The fallacy of drawing a conclusion about a target group on the basis of too small a sample.

In our everyday experience, we may casually make, hear, or read hasty generalizations like these:

> You should buy a Dell computer. They're great. I bought one last year, and it has been really awesome.
>
> The only male professor I've had this year was a sexist pig. All the male professors at this school must be sexist pigs.
>
> Psychology majors are incredibly ignorant about human psychology. Believe me, I know what I'm talking about. My best friend is a psych major. What an ignorant goof!
>
> Americans are snobby and rude. Remember those two arrogant guys with really bad manners at the party? They're American. I rest my case.
>
> The food at Pappie's Restaurant is awful. I had a sandwich there once, and the bread was stale.

In general, the larger the sample, the more likely it is to reliably reflect the nature of the larger group. In many cases our common sense tells us when a sample is or is not large enough to draw reliable conclusions about a particular target group. A good rule of thumb is this: *the more homogeneous a target group is in traits relevant to the property in question, the smaller the sample can be; the less homogeneous, the larger the sample should be.*

For example, if we want to determine whether cottontail rabbits have teeth, we need to survey only a tiny handful of cottontail rabbits (maybe even just one) because cottontail rabbits are fairly uniform in their physical characteristics. In this sense, if you've seen one cottontail rabbit, you've seen them all: generally, all members of an animal species are very similar with regard to significant bits of anatomy. On the other hand, if we want to know the sexual preferences of South Asian Canadians who live in suburbs, surveying just a few won't do. Questioning a sample of 2 or 20 or even 200 suburban Asian

Canadians will not give us a reliable read on the sexual preferences of the target group. In social, psychological, and cultural properties, people are too diverse to judge a large target group by just a few of its members. In biological properties, however, *homo sapiens* is relatively uniform. We need to survey only one normal member of the species to find out if humans have ears.

Representativeness

In addition to being the proper size, a sample must be a **representative sample**—it must resemble the target group in all the ways that matter. If it does not properly represent the target group, it's a **biased sample**. An enumerative inductive argument is strong only if the sample is representative of the whole.

representative sample In enumerative induction, a sample that resembles the target group in all relevant ways.

biased sample A sample that does not properly represent the target group.

Many arguments using unrepresentative samples are ludicrous; others are more subtle:

> University students are glad that the Conservative Party is in power in Ottawa. Surveys of the members of the Campus Conservatives club on several university campuses prove this.

> Most nurses in this hospital are burned out, stressed out, and overworked. Just ask the ones who work in the emergency department. They'll tell you they're absolutely miserable.

> No one is happy. Almost everyone is complaining about something. Just look at the letters to the editor in any big-city newspaper. Complaints, complaints, complaints!

To be truly representative, the sample must be like the target group by (1) having all the same relevant characteristics and (2) having them in the same proportions that the target group does. The "relevant characteristics" are features that could influence the property in question. For example, let's say that you want to survey adult residents of Winnipeg to determine whether they favour distributing condoms in high schools. Features of the residents that could influence whether they favour condom distribution include political party affiliation, ethnic background, and being Catholic. So the sample of residents should have all of these features and have them in the same proportions as the target group (residents of Winnipeg). If half the adult residents of Winnipeg are Catholic, for example, then half the sample should consist of residents who are Catholic.

Say that we want to determine how the 10,000 eligible voters in a small town intend to vote in an upcoming federal election. We survey 1000 of them, which should be more than enough for our purposes. But the voters we poll are almost all over 70 years old and live in nursing homes. Our sample is biased because it does not reflect the makeup of the target group, most of whom are people under 45 who live in their own homes, work in factories or offices, and have school-age children. Any enumerative argument based on this survey would be weak.

> "You have to remember one thing about the will of the people: it wasn't that long ago that we were swept away by the Macarena."
>
> —*Jon Stewart*

We are often guilty of biased sampling in everyday situations. One way this happens is through a phenomenon called *selective attention* (see Chapters 2 and 4)—that is, the tendency to observe and remember things that reinforce our beliefs and to gloss over and dismiss things that undercut those beliefs. We may tell our friends that *The Walking Dead* is a lousy TV series because we remember that three episodes were boring—but we conveniently forget the four other episodes that we thought were amazing. Or we may be convinced that Dr Jones is one of the legendary "absent-minded professors." But this generalization seems plausible to us only because we're on the lookout for instances in which the professor's behaviour seems to fit the stereotype, and we don't notice instances that contradict the stereotype.

Opinion Polls

Enumerative inductions reach a high level of sophistication in the form of opinion polls conducted by professional polling organizations. Opinion polls are used to arrive at generalizations about everything from the outcome of federal elections to public sentiments about cloning babies to the consumer's appetite for tacos. But as complex as they are, opinion polls are still essentially inductive arguments (or the basis of inductive arguments) and must be judged accordingly.

So as inductive arguments, opinion polls should (1) be strong and (2) have true premises. More precisely, any opinion poll worth believing must (1) use a sample that is large enough to represent the target population accurately in all the relevant population features and (2) generate accurate data (that is, the results must correctly reflect what they purport to be about). A poll can fail to meet this latter requirement through data-processing errors, botched polling interviews, poorly phrased questions, and the like. (See the box "How Survey Questions Go Wrong" on page 311.)

In national polling, samples need not be enormous to be accurate reflections of the larger target population. Modern sampling procedures used in national polls can produce representative samples that are surprisingly small. Polling organizations such as Environics and Ipsos Reid regularly conduct polls in which the target group is Canadian adults (more than 25 million), and the representative sample consists of only 1000 to 1500 individuals.

random sample A sample that is selected randomly from a target group in such a way as to ensure that the sample is representative. In a simple random selection, every member of the target group has an equal chance of being selected for the sample.

How can a sample of 1000 be representative of more than 25 million people? By using **random sampling**. To ensure that a sample is truly representative of the target group, the sample must be selected *randomly* from the target group. In a simple random selection, every member of the target group has an

FOOD FOR THOUGHT

How Survey Questions Go Wrong

Many opinion polls are untrustworthy because of flaws in the way the questions are asked. The sample may be large enough and representative in all the right ways, but the poll is still dubious. Here are a few of the most common problems.

Phrasing of Questions

Poll results can be dramatically skewed simply by the way the questions are worded. A poll might ask, for example, "Are you in favour of Quebec tearing Canada in half by separating?" The question is apparently about Quebec's sovereignty. But the wording of the question practically guarantees that a very large percentage of respondents will answer "no." The politically and emotionally charged characterization of separation as "tearing Canada in half" would likely persuade many respondents to avoid answering "yes." More neutral wording of the question would probably elicit a very different set of responses.

Here's another example. Imagine a poll of people in your town that discovers that 95 per cent of the sample group approved of efforts by the municipal government to eliminate smoking in public places. Next, imagine that to get this huge approval rating, the survey question was worded like this: "Do you think that the government should work diligently to protect children, including by taking certain measures that would put some restrictions on when and where people can smoke?" Who would say "no" to protecting children? We shouldn't be surprised if such a question elicited an overwhelming number of "shoulds."

Such biased wording is often the result of sloppiness on the part of pollsters. Many other times it's a deliberate attempt to manipulate the poll results. The crucial test of polling questions is whether they're likely to bias responses in one direction or another. Fair questions aren't skewed this way—or are skewed as little as possible.

Order of Questions

The order in which questions are asked in a poll can also affect the poll results. Pollsters know that if the economy is in bad shape and they ask people about the economic mess first and then ask them how they like the prime minister, the respondents are likely to give the prime minister lower marks than if the order of the questions were reversed. Likewise, if you're asked specific questions about crimes that have been committed in your hometown, then you're asked if you feel safe from crime, you're more likely to say no than if you're asked the questions in reverse order.

Restricted Choices

Opinion polls frequently condense broad spectrums of opinions on issues into a few convenient choices. Some of this condensation is necessary to make the polling process manageable. But some of it is both unnecessary and manipulative and therefore seriously distorts the opinions of those polled. Daniel Goleman of the *New York Times* offers this example: "In one survey . . . people were asked if they felt 'the courts deal too harshly or not harshly enough with criminals.' When offered just the two options, 6 per cent said 'too harshly' and 78 per cent answered 'not harshly enough.' But when a third alternative was added—'don't have enough information about the courts to say'—29 per cent took that option, and 60 per cent answered 'not harshly enough.'"

equal chance of being selected for the sample. Imagine that you want to select a representative sample from, say, 1000 people at a football game, and you know very little about the characteristics of this target population. Your best bet for getting a representative sample of this group is to choose the sample members at random. Any non-random selection based on preconceived notions about what characteristics are representative will likely result in a biased sample.

Selecting a sample in truly random fashion is easier said than done (humans have a difficult time selecting anything in a genuinely random way). Even a simple process such as trying to pick names arbitrarily off a list of registered voters is not likely to be truly random. Your choices may be skewed, for example, by unconscious preferences for certain names or by boredom and fatigue. Researchers and pollsters use various techniques to help them get close to true randomization. They may, for instance, assign a number to each member of a population then use a random-number generator to make the selections.

One approach that definitely does *not* yield a random sample is allowing survey subjects to choose themselves. The result of this process is called a *self-selecting sample*—a type of sample that usually tells you very little about the target population. We would get a self-selecting sample if we published a questionnaire in a magazine and asked readers to fill it out and mail it in or if during

FOOD FOR **THOUGHT**

Mean, Median, and Mode

If you read enough opinion polls, you will surely encounter one of these terms: mean, median, or mode. These concepts are invaluable in expressing statistical facts, but they can be confusing. Mean is simply an average. The mean of these four numbers—6, 7, 4, and 3—is 5 (6 + 7 + 4 + 3 = 20 divided by 4 = 5). The median is the middle point of a series of values, meaning that half the values are above the point, and half the values are below the point. The median of these 11 values—3, 5, 7, 13, 14, 17, 21, 23, 24, 27, 30—is 17 (the number in the middle). The mode is the most common value. The mode in this series of values—7, 13, 13, 13, 14, 17, 21, 21, 27, 30, 30—is 13 (the most frequently appearing value).

The notions of mean, median, and mode are often manipulated to mislead people. For example, let's say that the dictator of Little Island Nation (population 1000) proposes a big tax cut for everyone, declaring that the mean tax savings will be $5000 (the total tax cut divided by 1000 taxpayers). The Islanders begin to gleefully envision how they will spend their $5000. But then they learn that the mean figure has been skewed higher because of a few millionaires whose tax savings will be $100,000 or more. The tax savings for the vast majority of taxpayers is actually less than $500. The $5000 figure that the dictator tossed out is the true mean, but it is painfully misleading. To the Islanders, what is much more revealing is the median tax savings, which is $400. The mode, the most common figure, is $300. When they get all the facts, the islanders stage a revolt—the first one in history caused by a better understanding of statistics.

a TV or radio news broadcast, we asked people to cast their vote on a particular issue by clicking options on a website or emailing their responses. In such cases, the sample is likely to be biased in favour of subjects who, for example, just happen to be especially opinionated or passionate; who may have strong views about the topic of the survey and are eager to spout off; or who may simply like to fill out questionnaires. Magazines, newspapers, talk shows, and news programs sometimes acknowledge the use of self-selecting samples by labelling the survey in question as "unscientific." But whether or not that term is used, the media frequently tout the results of such distorted surveys as though the numbers actually proved something.

"It is the mark of a truly intelligent person to be moved by statistics."

—*George Bernard Shaw*

So a well-conducted poll using a random sample of 1000 to 1500 people can reliably reflect the opinions of the whole adult population. Even so, if a second well-conducted poll is done in exactly the same way, the results will not be identical to that of the first poll. The reason is that every instance of sampling is only an approximation of the results that you would get if you polled every single individual in a target group. And, by chance, each attempt at sampling will yield slightly different results. If you dipped a bucket into a pond to get a one litre sample of water, each bucketful would be slightly different in its biological and chemical content—even if the pond's content was very uniform.

margin of error The variation between the values derived from a sample and the true values of the whole target group.

confidence level In statistical theory, the probability that the sample will accurately represent the target group within the margin of error.

Such differences are referred to as the **margin of error** for a particular sampling or poll. Competently executed opinion polls will state their results along with a margin of error. A poll, for example, might say that Candidate X will receive 62 per cent of the popular vote, plus or minus 3 percentage points (a common margin of error for polls). The usual way of expressing this number is 62 per cent ±3. This means that the percentage of people in the target population who will likely vote for Candidate X is between 59 and 65 per cent.

Connected to the concept of margin of error is the notion of **confidence level**. In statistical theory, the confidence level is the probability that the sample will accurately represent the target group within the margin of error. A confidence level of 95 per cent (the usual value) means that there is a 95 per cent chance that the results from polling the sample (taking into account the margin of error) will accurately reflect the results that we would get if we polled the entire target population. So if our aforementioned poll has a 95 per cent confidence level, we know that

CREDIT: Graham Harrop/Cartoon Stock

FOOD FOR THOUGHT

Polling the Clueless

Sometimes polls end up surveying, not the views of people with genuine opinions, but what has been called "non-attitudes." This happens when respondents answer polling questions even though they have no real opinion on the subject or no idea what the questions are really about. Presumably, people (being people) would rather give a bogus answer than admit that they are clueless.

In one landmark poll conducted in the United States many years ago, respondents were asked, "Some people say that the 1975 Public Affairs Act should be repealed. Do you agree or disagree with this idea?" One-third of those polled offered their opinion on the issue. Trouble was, the Public Affairs Act did not exist. The pollsters made it up.

there's a 95 per cent chance that the sampling results of 62 per cent ±3 points will accurately reflect the situation in the whole target group. Of course, this confidence level also means that there's a 5 per cent chance that the poll results will *not* be accurate.

Note that "confidence level" refers only to sampling error—that is, the probability that the sample does not accurately reflect the true values in the target population. It doesn't tell you anything about any other kinds of polling errors, such as bias, that can occur because of poorly worded questions or researchers who may consciously or unconsciously influence the kind of answers received.

Sample size, margin of error, and confidence level are all related in interesting ways.

- Up to a point, the larger the sample, the smaller the margin of error because the larger the sample, the more representative it is likely to be. Generally, for national polls, a sample size of 600 yields a margin of error of 4 per cent; a sample of 1000, 3 per cent; and a sample of 1500, 2.5 per cent. But enlarging the sample substantially, to well beyond 1000, does not substantially decrease the margin of error. Enlarging the sample from 1500 to 10,000, for example, pushes the margin of error down to only 1 per cent.
- The lower the confidence level, the smaller the sample size can be. If you're willing to have less confidence in your polling results, a smaller sample will do. If you can accept a confidence level of only 90 per cent (meaning there is a 10 per cent chance of getting inaccurate results), you don't need a sample size of 1500 to poll the adult population.
- The larger the margin of error, the higher the confidence level can be. With a large margin of error (20 per cent, for example), you will naturally

have more confidence that your survey results will fall within this wide range. This idea is the statistical equivalent of a point made earlier: you can have more confidence in your enumerative inductive argument if you qualify, or decrease the precision of, the conclusion.
- Here's a table showing roughly the relationship between sample size and margin of error for large populations (assuming a 95 per cent confidence level):

Survey Sample Size	Margin of Error
10,000	1.0%
2000	2.0%
1500	2.5%
1000	3.0%
500	4.5%
100	10.0%

To sum up, an enumerative induction, like any other inductive argument, must be strong and have true premises for us to be justified in accepting the conclusion. A strong enumerative induction must be based on a sample that is both large enough and representative. An opinion poll, as a sophisticated enumerative induction, must use a sufficiently large and representative sample and ensure that the data gathered reflect accurately what's being measured.

REVIEW NOTES

Enumerative Induction

- *Target group:* The class of individuals about which an inductive generalization is made.
- *Sample:* The observed members of a target group.
- *Relevant property:* The property under study in a target group.
- *Hasty generalization:* The drawing of a conclusion about a target group on the basis of a sample that's too small.
- *Biased sample:* A sample that is not representative of its target group.
- *Simple random sampling:* The selecting of a sample to ensure that each member of the target group has an equal chance of being chosen.
- *Margin of error:* The variation between the values derived from a sample and the true values of the whole target group.
- *Confidence level:* The probability that the sample will accurately represent the target group within the margin of error.

EXERCISE 8.1

Answers to exercises marked with an asterisk (*) may be found in Appendix B, Answers to Exercises.

For each of the following enumerative inductions, (1) identify the target group, sample, and relevant property; (2) indicate whether the argument is strong or weak; and (3) if it's weak, say whether the problem is a sample that's too small, not representative, or both. Assume that the information provided in the premises of each argument is true.

*1. A random, nationwide poll of several thousand readers of *Horse & Harness* magazine shows that 80 per cent of readers are against raising horses for their meat. Thus, most Canadian adults think Canada should ban the consumption of horse meat.
2. Most people agree that injecting hormones into livestock to make them bigger is a bad idea. A national newspaper recently went to PETA Canada's office and interviewed many of its members. They all stated that injecting hormones into livestock is painful for the animal and potentially a health hazard for the people that consume them.
3. Doctors used to think that anti-arrhythmic drugs were the cure for irregular heartbeats. They overprescribed these drugs and 50,000 patients died. Doctors used to believe that the cure for ulcers was a bland diet, but that turned out to be wrong too. Every new treatment we see these days sounds great. But history tells us that they will all turn out to be worthless or even deadly.
*4. For as long as records have been kept, Vancouver has received over 150 millimetres of rain in the month of December alone. Therefore, Vancouver is likely to get at least that much this December too.
5. Two-thirds of the adults in Toronto say they are in favour of permitting gay marriage. And almost 70 per cent of Montrealers are, too. This makes it perfectly clear that a large majority of people in this country are in favour of gay marriage.
6. I asked several of my university professors about the mayor's new transit plan and none of them approved of it. Clearly anyone with a decent intellect will agree that building subways is a bad idea.
7. Most newspaper reports of deaths involve either homicide or car crashes. Therefore, homicide and car crashes must be the leading causes of death.
*8. Eighty-five per cent of dentists who suggest that their patients chew gum recommend Brand X gum. Therefore, 85 per cent of dentists recommend Brand X gum.

9. Two hundred samples of water taken from many sites all along Lake Ontario show unsafe concentrations of toxic chemicals. Obviously the water in Lake Ontario is unsafe.
10. Clearly there is an epidemic of child abductions in this country. In the past year, major network news organizations have reported five cases of children who were abducted by strangers.
11. The cloud is definitely not a secure way to store your data. Case in point: the iCloud was recently hacked and many private photos of famous celebrities were leaked to the public. A few other cloud servers have also occasionally reported security issues that allowed unauthorized access to their stored data.

*12. Most Canadians are happy with their jobs and derive a great deal of satisfaction from them. A survey of 1500 adults with an annual income of $48,000 to $60,000, employed in various occupations, supports this assertion. When these subjects were asked if they were happy and satisfied with their jobs, 82 per cent said yes.

EXERCISE 8.2

For each of the enumerative inductions in Exercise 8.1, indicate whether the argument is strong or weak. If it's strong, explain how the sample could be modified to make the argument weak. If it's weak, explain how the sample could be modified to make the argument strong. Keep the modifications as realistic as possible. Answers are supplied for 1, 4, 8, and 12.

EXERCISE 8.3

For each of the following opinion polls, (1) determine whether the poll results offer strong support for the pollster's conclusion, and if they don't, (2) specify the source of the problem (sample too small, unrepresentative sample, or non-random sampling). Assume that the conducting of each survey is free of technical errors, such as mistakes in data processing or improper polling interviews.

*1. Lisa carried out a survey to determine if Canadians are willing to support the arts by contributing money directly to local theatre groups. One night she and her assistants interview 200 people who are attending an exhibition of sculpture at the city's biggest art gallery. To help ensure random selection, they purposely select every third patron they encounter for interviewing. There is only one interview question: "Are you willing to support the arts by giving money to local theatre groups?" Seventy-six per cent of the interviewees answer yes. Anita later reports that a majority of Canadians are willing to support the arts by giving money to local theatre groups.

2. A national polling organization surveys 1500 nurses chosen randomly from a national registry of this profession. The survey question is whether nurses are paid well enough for the difficult work they do. Ninety-four per cent of those surveyed say no. The pollsters conclude that there is a serious problem with how health care is funded in this country because most nurses are underpaid.
3. The local police department wants to find out how prevalent bullying is within the schools in their district. They distributed questionnaires to all of the students at the schools that asked them how often they were bullied or saw other students being bullied. About half of the questionnaires were returned to the police department, and most of them indicated that little to no bullying occurred at any of the schools. Using this information, the police department concluded that bullying is not a big problem in the community.
4. The *Winnipeg Free Press* website invites visitors to "speak out" by participating in "Today's Poll." One day, the question is "Should Canada be willing to negotiate with terrorists, as one Liberal MP has suggested?" That day, 3201 people visit the website and give their answers. Of those, 2204 answer "no." I therefore conclude that 69 per cent of Winnipeggers oppose the idea of Canada negotiating with terrorists.
5. A national women's magazine publishes a questionnaire on sexual harassment in the workplace. Respondents are asked to complete the questionnaire and mail it in to the magazine. The magazine receives over 20,000 completed questionnaires in the mail. Sixty-two per cent of the respondents say that they've been sexually harassed at work. The magazine reports that most women have been sexually harassed at work.

EXERCISE 8.4

For each of the following arguments, state which conclusions from the accompanying list would be strongly supported by the premise given. Assume that all premises are true.

*1. Five out of six vegetarians admit that they don't really like tofu.
   a. Eighty-three percent of vegetarians don't really like tofu.
   b. Most vegetarians don't like tofu.

   c. Most vegetarians and vegans don't like tofu.
   d. Vegetarians actually hate tofu.
2. By listening to music, 43 per cent of arthritis patients at the Drexell Clinic experience a decrease in pain in their knee and finger joints.
   a. By listening to music, 43 per cent of arthritis patients can experience a decrease in pain in their knee and finger joints.
   b. By listening to music, some arthritis patients can experience a decrease in pain in their knee and finger joints.
   c. By listening to music, some arthritis patients at the Drexell Clinic can experience a decrease in pain in their knee and finger joints.
   d. Music is good for your health.
3. Approximately 66 per cent of the 124 university students who responded to a questionnaire published in the campus newspaper are opposed to the federal government's vocal support for the Alberta oil sands.
   a. Sixty-six per cent of the readers of the campus newspaper are opposed to the federal government's vocal support for the Alberta oil sands.
   b. Sixty-six per cent of the students attending this school are opposed to the federal government's energy policies.
   c. Some students attending this school are opposed to the federal government's vocal support for the Alberta oil sands.
   d. Most readers of the campus newspaper are opposed to the federal government's vocal support for the Alberta oil sands.
   e. Some students don't understand why the oil sands are environmentally disastrous.
4. Alonzo told me that a number of his friends in the RCMP conduct illegal surveillance on people that they don't like.
   a. The RCMP approves of its officers conducting illegal activities.
   b. Most RCMP officers conduct illegal surveillance.
   c. Many RCMP officers conduct illegal surveillance.
   d. All RCMP officers conduct illegal surveillance.
   e. Some RCMP officers conduct illegal surveillance.
5. Seventy-seven per cent of adults interviewed in three Edmonton shopping malls (650 people) say they will vote Conservative in the next federal election.
   a. Most people will vote Conservative in the next federal election.
   b. Seventy-seven per cent of adult residents of Edmonton will vote Conservative in the next federal election.
   c. Many people in Edmonton will vote Conservative in the next federal election.
   d. A substantial percentage of people who shop at malls in Edmonton will vote Conservative in the next federal election.

EXERCISE 8.5

The following statements suggest modifications to each of the opinion polls in Exercise 8.3. In each case, determine whether the modification (and any associated change in poll results) would make the pollster's conclusion more likely to be true or not more likely to be true.

*1. Lisa supplements her research by conducting phone interviews of a random sample of 700 adult residents of her city (population 2 million), asking a slightly modified question: "Are you willing to support the arts by giving money to local theatre groups?" She conducts a similar poll in another large Canadian city. In both polls, at least 65 per cent of respondents say yes.
2. The national polling organization surveys 1500 health professionals (physicians, nurses, pharmacists, and others) randomly from various national registries. Ninety-five per cent of the respondents say that nurses are underpaid.
3. About 90 per cent of the questionnaires were returned (instead of 50 per cent) and about 10 per cent of them indicated that bullying was a frequent occurrence at school. However, most of the questionnaires that indicated frequent bullying originated from a single school.
4. Seven thousand people visit the website on the day that the poll is taken (instead of 3201), and of those, 6000 answer "no" to the question (instead of 2204).
5. The magazine receives over 30,000 completed questionnaires in the mail (instead of 20,000). Fifty-five per cent of the respondents say that they've been sexually harassed at work.

STATISTICAL SYLLOGISMS

Very often we have incomplete, but reasonably reliable, information about a group or category of things, and on the basis of that knowledge we can reach conclusions about particular members of that group or category. Will it be cold in Winnipeg on 12 January of next year? We don't know for sure, but we know that *most* January days in Winnipeg are cold, so we can reason inductively to a pretty firm conclusion. Will my flight from Halifax to Vancouver get there safely? Well, *virtually all* commercial air flights in Canada—hundreds every day—land perfectly safely. So we can assert pretty confidently that, yes, your flight will get to Vancouver just fine. Is that conclusion a *deductive certainty*? No, but it's still very, very reliable.

In Chapter 6 we dealt with categorical syllogisms, which were deductive arguments consisting of three elements: two categorical premises and a categorical conclusion. But there are also *statistical syllogisms*, which are *inductive* arguments that apply a statistical generalization—a claim about what is true of *most* members of a group or category—to a specific member of that group or category. Here are a few examples:

Argument 1
Premise 1: Over 80 per cent of Canadians live in cities.
Premise 2: You're a Canadian.
Conclusion: So you live in a city.

Argument 2
Premise 1: Most professional basketball players are well over six feet tall.
Premise 2: Paul plays for the Raptors.
Conclusion: Paul is over six feet tall.

Argument 3
Premise 1: Almost all countries in Africa are very poor.
Premise 2: Zimbabwe is in Africa
Conclusion: Zimbabwe is very poor.

Here is the pattern that all statistical syllogisms follow, when spelled out fully:

Premise 1: A proportion X of the group M have characteristic P.
Premise 2: Individual S is member of group M.
Conclusion: Individual S has characteristic P.

It is important, in analyzing a statistical syllogism, to be able to identify:

- The *individual* being examined.
- The *group* to which that individual is said to belong.
- The *characteristic* being attributed.
- The *proportion* of the group said to have that characteristic.

Sometimes the proportion will take the form of an actual statistic—that's where the term *statistical* syllogism comes from. It might be stated as a percentage (as in argument 1, above) or it could also be a fraction (such as 9/10). Sometimes specific numbers aren't available and an arguer will use a word like "most" or "almost all" or "most of the time." The point is that the first premise is a *generalization*—a statement (usually rooted in some evidence) about the members of a group or class. (In fact, very often the first premise of a statistical syllogism will be arrived at by—that is, it will be the *conclusion* of—an argument using enumerative induction. We'll return to this point shortly.)

Because they are a type of inductive argument, statistical syllogisms—even good ones, with acceptable premises—cannot guarantee their conclusions. So sometimes they can lead us astray. For example, imagine you're in southern Ontario and a friend points out a scary-looking spider in a woodpile. "It's OK," you say. "Spiders in Canada are generally harmless. So I'm sure it can't hurt you." That's a statistical syllogism. But is the conclusion true?

Here's that same argument, with its premises and conclusion spelled out:

Premise 1: In general, the spiders that live in Canada are harmless.
Premise 2 (unstated): That spider there is in Canada.
Conclusion: That spider is harmless.

If the spider in question is a black widow spider (a spider whose natural habitat includes parts of southern Ontario), your conclusion would be false—reasonable, but false!

Evaluating Statistical Syllogisms

Since statistical syllogisms, though very useful, are never airtight, we need a method for evaluating them.

Acceptable Premises

The first thing to consider, of course, is whether we have good reason to believe the premises. How is it that the generalization expressed in the first premise was arrived at? Is it common knowledge (such as "Most birds can fly" or "Most water on Earth is salt water")? Is it based on a careful survey, one with a large enough, randomly selected sample? Here we can apply all the tools learned in the previous section on enumerative induction. If the grounding of the generalization is weak, then the argument is weak.

Statistical Strength

Second, and perhaps most obviously, we should ask ourselves: just how strong is the generalization being offered? Clearly if our argument (about some member of the class M) is based on the claim that, say, "65 per cent of M are P," that's not nearly as strong as if that same argument were based on the claim that "99 per cent of M are P." We should clearly ask questions, then, when vague words such as *most* or *lots of* are used in statistical syllogisms. *Most* might just mean "51 per cent of," and that's a pretty weak basis for a conclusion about any particular member of that group.

Typical or Randomly Selected

Statistical syllogisms take a generalization about a group or class and apply that generalization to a specific, individual member of that group or class. This will make most sense for members that we have reason to believe are typical of that group or class. It is most reasonable to assume that the individual is typical when he, she, or it is selected randomly from the population. If you know, for example, that "85 per cent of Canadians don't know CPR," then it's reasonable to suspect, of any randomly selected Canadian, that he or she doesn't know CPR. But if you're talking to someone wearing a white coat at a hospital or working at a fire station, it's much less reasonable to assume that *that* person is part of the 85 per cent of Canadians who don't know CPR. That person, in fact, is highly likely to be part of the other 15 per cent. Or how about this: if I ask you, "How much do you think this stamp is worth?," you might well respond, "Well, most stamps are worth the value printed on them, and that one says '42 cents,' so it's worth 42 cents." In most circumstances, that might be a strong argument. But what if you have reason to believe that this particular stamp isn't a typical stamp? What if you happen to know that I'm a collector of rare and valuable stamps? In that situation, it's much more likely that the stamp I'm showing you is *not* a random or typical stamp, and so it would be unwise to jump too quickly to the conclusion that it's not worth much. Thus we should always consider whether the individual person or item under consideration is likely to be a typical member of the group, or whether you have reason to believe that he, she, or it is an exception to the rule.

EXERCISE 8.6

Answers to exercises marked with an asterisk (*) may be found in Appendix B, Answers to Exercises.

For each of the following statistical syllogisms, identify (1) the individual being examined; (2) the group to which that individual is said to belong; (3) the characteristic being attributed to that group and individual; and (4) the proportion of the group that is said to have that characteristic. You may need to supply missing parts.

*1. Barb rides recklessly. She rides her bike to work, and almost all people who ride their bikes to work ride recklessly.
2. There is only a 1 in 10 chance that anyone standing outside in the snow without a scarf will catch a cold. So even though Ben is standing outside in the snow without a scarf right now, he probably won't catch a cold.
3. Jerry has recently read a financial report that stated that only 0.01per cent of the world's population makes an annual net income of more than

$85,000. For this reason, he doubts his friend Jessica's claim that she makes more than $85,000.

*4. Almost every meal I've eaten at the Poolhouse Café has been wonderful. I'm sure the next one will be, too.

*5. That car of yours will never make it to Saskatoon. Most Fords are pieces of junk!

EXERCISE 8.7

Determine the most likely source of weakness for the following statistical syllogisms. (State whether the most likely problem is unacceptable premise, statistical weakness, or non-typical individual. Give a few words of explanation for why you think the argument is weak in that particular way.)

*1. I've met plenty of professional hockey players, and they all have inflated egos. Your boyfriend is a hockey player, eh? He must have a huge ego, too!

*2. Professor Norman grew up in a small mining town. Most people who grow up in small mining towns have never read Plato. So Professor Norman has never read Plato.

3. Most new businesses go out of business within the first two years. So I'm sure Barack Obama's plan to go into the consulting business after he's done being president is going to fail.

*4. Most people in this town who voted—53 per cent of voters—voted for Mayor Doran. You voted. So you supported Mayor Doran.

5. Only 1 per cent of women are colour-blind. You're a woman. So, you're likely not colour-blind.

ANALOGICAL INDUCTION

analogy A comparison of two or more things alike in specific respects.

An **analogy** is a comparison of two or more things alike in specific respects. In literature, science, and everyday life, analogies are used to explain or describe something. Analogies (often in the form of similes) can be powerful literary devices, both unforgettable and moving:

> . . . the evening is spread out against the sky.
> Like a patient etherized upon a table . . .
> (T.S. Eliot)

Just as the planets are connected to the sun and to each other,
so are people connected to kings and to each other.
(Epistles of the Brethren of Sincerity)

. . . Out, out brief candle!
Life's but a walking shadow, a poor player
That struts and frets his hour upon the stage
And then is heard no more. It is a tale
Told by an idiot, full of sound and fury,
Signifying nothing.
(*Macbeth*, Act V)

But an analogy can also be used to *argue inductively for a conclusion*. Such an argument is known as an **analogical induction**, or simply an **argument by analogy**. An analogical induction reasons this way: because two or more things are similar in several respects, they must be similar in some further respect. For example:

argument by analogy (analogical induction) An argument making use of analogy, reasoning that because two or more things are similar in several respects, they must be similar in some further respect.

Humans can move about, solve mathematical equations, win chess games, and feel pain.
Robots are like humans in that they can move about, solve mathematical equations, and win chess games.
Therefore, it's probable that robots can also feel pain.

This argument says that because robots are like humans in several ways (ways that are already known or agreed on), they must be like humans in yet another way (a way that the argument is meant to establish). So analogical induction has this pattern:

"All perception of truth is the detection of an analogy."
—*Henry David Thoreau*

Thing A has properties P_1, P_2, and P_3 plus the property P_4.
Thing B has properties P_1, P_2, and P_3.
Therefore, thing B probably has property P_4.

Argument by analogy, like all inductive reasoning, can establish conclusions only with a degree of probability. The greater the degree of similarity between the two things being compared, the more probable the conclusion is.

Recall that enumerative inductive has this form:

X per cent of the observed members of group A have property P.
Therefore, X per cent of all members of group A probably have property P.

Thus, the most blatant difference between these two forms of induction is that enumerative induction argues from some members of a group to the group as a whole, but analogical induction reasons from some (one or more) individuals to one further individual. Looked at another way, enumerative induction argues from the properties of a sample to the properties of the whole group; analogical induction reasons from the properties of one or more individuals to the properties of another individual.

Arguments by analogy are probably used (and misused) in every area of human endeavour—but especially in law, science, medicine, ethics, archaeology, and forensics. Here are a few examples:

Argument 4: Medical Science
Mice are mammals, have a mammalian circulatory system, have typical mammalian biochemical reactions, respond readily to high-blood-pressure drugs, and experience a reduction in blood cholesterol when given the new Drug Z. Humans are mammals, have a mammalian circulatory system, have typical mammalian biochemical reactions, and respond readily to high-blood-pressure drugs. Therefore, humans will also experience a reduction in blood cholesterol when given the new Drug Z.

Argument 5: Religion
A watch is a mechanism of exquisite complexity with numerous parts precisely arranged and accurately adjusted to achieve a purpose—a purpose imposed by the watch's designer. Likewise the universe has exquisite complexity with countless parts—from atoms to asteroids—that fit together precisely and accurately to produce certain effects as though arranged by plan. Therefore, the universe must also have a designer.

Argument 6: Law
The case before the court involves a search by the city police of a homeless man's cardboard shelter. At issue is whether it was improper for the police to enter the man's shelter without either permission or a warrant to search for evidence of a crime. A similar case—a relevant precedent—involved a search by the RCMP of an equipment trailer in which a man was living. In that case, the court ruled that the RCMP had violated section 8 of the Canadian Charter of Rights and Freedoms (the section that says, "Everyone has the right to be secure against unreasonable search or seizure.") Therefore, the court should also rule that the search by the city police of the homeless man's shelter violated section 8 of the Charter.

Argument 7: Forensics
Whenever we have observed this pattern in the spatter of blood, we have subsequently learned that the gunshot victim was about four feet from the gun when it was fired and was facing away from the assailant. In this crime scene, we have exactly the same pattern of blood spatter.

Therefore, the victim was about four feet from the gun when it was fired and was facing away from the assailant.

Arguments by analogy are easy to formulate—perhaps too easy. To use an analogy to support a particular conclusion, all you have to do is find two things with some similarities and then reason that the two things are similar in yet another way. You could easily reach some very silly conclusions. You could argue this, for instance: birds have two legs, two eyes, breathe air, and fly; and humans have two legs, two eyes, and breathe air; therefore, humans can also fly. So the question is, how do we sort out the good analogical inductions from the bad (or really wacky)? How do we judge which ones have conclusions worth accepting and which ones don't?

Fortunately, there are some criteria we can use to judge the strength of arguments by analogy:

1. Relevant similarities
2. Relevant dissimilarities
3. The number of instances compared
4. Diversity among cases

If you find yourself thinking that they make perfect sense, that's probably because you already use these criteria in your own arguments by analogy.

FOOD FOR THOUGHT

Analogical Induction in Ethical Reasoning

In Chapter 11 you will study in detail the uses of argument and critical thinking in ethical reasoning. For now, it's sufficient to know this: when we try to show that a particular action is right or wrong, we often rely on argument by analogy. We argue that since an action is relevantly similar to another action, and the former action is clearly right (or wrong), then we should regard the latter action in the same way. For example, we might propose an argument like this:

Premise 1: Caring more for the members of one's own family than outsiders is ethically permissible.

Premise 2: Canada's policy of giving more aid to its own citizens than to those of other countries is relevantly similar to caring more for the members of one's own family than outsiders.

Conclusion: Therefore, Canada's policy of giving more aid to its own citizens than to those of other countries is probably ethically permissible.

Here, as in any argument by analogy, the conclusion can be established only with a degree of probability. And we would evaluate its strength in the same way we would any other analogical argument.

Relevant Similarities

The more relevant similarities there are between the things being compared, the more probable the conclusion. Consider this argument:

> In the Vietnam War, the United States had not articulated a clear rationale for fighting there, and the United States lost. Likewise, in the present war the United States has not articulated a clear rationale for fighting. Therefore, the United States will lose this war too.

There is just one relevant similarity noted here (the lack of rationale). As it stands, this argument is weak; the two wars are only dimly analogous. A single similarity between two wars in different eras is not enough to strongly support the conclusion. But watch what happens if we add more similarities:

> In the Vietnam War, the United States had not articulated a clear rationale for fighting, there was no plan for ending the involvement of US forces (no exit strategy), US military tactics were inconsistent, and the military's view of enemy strength was unrealistic. The United States lost the Vietnam War. Likewise, in the present war, the United States has not articulated a clear rationale for fighting, there is no exit strategy, US tactics are inconsistent, and the military's view of enemy strength is naive. Therefore, the United States will also lose this war.

With these additional similarities between the Vietnam War and the current conflict, the argument is considerably stronger. (The premises, of course, may be false, rendering the argument not cogent, even if the inference were strong.) Arguments 4–7 (medical science, religion, law, and forensics) can also be strengthened by citing additional relevant similarities between the things compared.

Notice that this first criterion involves *relevant* similarities. The similarities cited in an analogical induction can't strengthen the argument at all if they have nothing to do with the conclusion. A similarity (or dissimilarity) is relevant to an argument by analogy if it has an effect on whether the conclusion is probably true. The argument on war that was just given mentions four different similarities between the Vietnam War and the present war, and each similarity is relevant because it has some bearing on the probability of the conclusion. But what if we added these similarities?

1. In both wars, some combatants have green eyes.
2. In both wars, some soldiers were left-handed.
3. During both wars, ticket sales to movies in the United States increased.

These factors would make no difference to the probability of the conclusion. They're irrelevant and can neither strengthen nor weaken the argument.

Of course, it's not always obvious what counts as a *relevant* similarity. To be relevant, a similarity cited as part of an analogical argument clearly has to be connected in some significant way to the conclusion being argued for. There's no plausible connection, for example, between the colour of soldiers' eyes and their success in war. So that factor isn't relevant. In some cases, an explanation may be required to show *why* a particular similarity is actually relevant. In this regard, the burden of proof (as discussed in Chapter 5) is on the person putting forward the argument.

Relevant Dissimilarities

Generally, the more relevant dissimilarities—or disanalogies—there are between the things being compared, the less probable the conclusion is. Dissimilarities weaken arguments by analogy. Consider argument 4 (regarding Drug Z). What if we discover that blood-pressure-lowering drugs that work in mice almost never work in humans? This one dissimilarity would severely weaken the argument and make the conclusion much less probable.

Pointing out dissimilarities in an analogical induction is a common way to undermine the argument. Sometimes finding one relevant dissimilarity is enough to show that the argument should be rejected. A familiar response to argument 5 (the watch argument) is to point out a crucial dissimilarity between a watch and the universe: the universe may resemble a watch (or mechanism) in some ways, but it also resembles a living thing, which a watch does not.

The Number of Instances Compared

The greater the number of instances, or cases, that show the relevant similarities, the stronger the argument. In the war argument, for example, there is only one instance that has all the relevant similarities: the Vietnam War. But what if there were five additional instances—five different wars that have the relevant similarities to the present war? The argument would be strengthened. The Vietnam War, though it is relevantly similar to the present war, may be an anomaly, a war with a unique set of properties. But citing other cases that are relevantly similar to the present war shows that the relevant set of similarities is no fluke.

Argument 7 (the forensics induction) is an especially strong argument in part because it cites numerous cases. It implies the existence of such instances when it says "Whenever we have observed this pattern . . . ."

Diversity among Cases

As we've seen, dissimilarities between the things being compared weaken an argument by analogy. Such dissimilarities suggest that the things being compared are not strongly analogous. And we've noted that several cases (instead of just one) that exhibit the similarities can strengthen the argument. In applying this criterion, however, we focus on a very different point: the greater the diversity among the cases that exhibit the relevant similarities, the stronger the argument.

Take a look at the following argument:

(1) In my first year of university, one of my courses was taught by a young philosophy professor who handed out a very clear syllabus, explained his expectations, and demonstrated early on that he was always willing to answer any question, and the course ended up being a very good course.
(2) In my second year of university, one of my courses was taught by a middle-aged sociology professor who handed out a very clear syllabus, explained his expectations, and demonstrated early on that he was always willing to answer any question, and the course ended up being a very good course.
(3) In my third year of university, one of my courses was taught by a very old English professor who handed out a very clear syllabus, explained his expectations, and demonstrated early on that he was always willing to answer any question, and the course ended up being a very good course.
(4) Now I'm in my fourth year, and I've got a middle-aged philosophy professor who has handed out a very clear syllabus, has explained his expectations, and has demonstrated early on that he is willing to answer any question.
(5) Therefore, this new course will be a good course, too.

Here we have several similarities in question, and they exist between the new professor situation (described in premise 4) and three other professors

REVIEW NOTES

Analogical Induction

ANALOGICAL ARGUMENT PATTERN

Thing A has properties P_1, P_2, and P_3, plus the property P_4.
Thing B has properties P_1, P_2, and P_3.
Therefore, thing B probably has property P_4.

CRITERIA FOR JUDGING ARGUMENTS BY ANALOGY

1. The number of relevant similarities.
2. The number of relevant dissimilarities.
3. The number of instances compared.
4. The diversity among cases.

(detailed in premises 1–3). But what makes this argument especially strong is that the cases are diverse despite the handful of similarities—one case involves a young philosophy professor; another a middle-aged sociology professor; and finally a very old English professor. This state of affairs suggests that the similarities are not coincidental or made up but are strongly linked even in a variety of situations.

As you know, an inductive argument cannot guarantee the truth of the conclusion, and analogical inductions are no exception. But by carefully applying the foregoing criteria, we can increase our chances of arriving at well-supported conclusions (or of identifying those conclusions that are not). This is a good thing—even though there is no magic formula for using the criteria in real-life situations.

EXERCISE 8.8

Answers to exercises marked with an asterisk (*) may be found in Appendix B, Answers to Exercises.

Evaluate each of the following passages and indicate whether it contains (1) an argument by analogy, (2) a literary analogy, or (3) an enumerative induction. If the passage contains an argument by analogy, indicate the total number of things (instances) being compared, the relevant similarities mentioned or implied, the conclusion, and whether the argument is strong or weak.

1. "People are like stained-glass windows. They sparkle and shine when the sun is out, but when the darkness sets in, their true beauty is revealed only if there is a light from within." (Elisabeth Kübler-Ross)

*2. "Duct tape is like the force. It has a light side, a dark side, and it holds the universe together." (Carl Zwanzig)

3. Interracial marriage is a bad idea. If a bird and a fish got married, where would they live?

4. "Look around the world: contemplate the whole and every part of it: you will find it to be nothing but one great machine, subdivided into an infinite number of lesser machines, which again admit of subdivisions, to a degree beyond what human senses and faculties can trace and explain. All these various machines, and even their most minute parts, are adjusted to each other with an accuracy, which ravishes into admiration all men, who have ever contemplated them. The curious adapting of means to ends, throughout all nature, resembles exactly, though it much exceeds, the production of human contrivance; of human design, thought,

wisdom, and intelligence. Since therefore the effects resemble each other, we are led to infer, by all the rules of analogy, that the causes also resemble; and that the Author of Nature is somewhat similar to the mind of men; though possessed of much larger faculties, proportioned to the grandeur of the work, which he has executed. By this argument *a posteriori*, and by this argument alone, do we prove at once the existence of a Deity, and his similarity to human mind and intelligence." (Cleanthes, in David Hume's *Dialogues Concerning Natural Religion*)

*5. My brother was always good at arithmetic, so he'll be a whiz at algebra.

6. Tolerating a vicious dictator is like tolerating a bully on the block. If you let the bully push you around, sooner or later he will beat you up and take everything you have. If you let a dictator have his way, he will abuse his people and rob them of life and liberty. If you stand up to the bully just once or—better yet—knock him senseless with a stick, he will never bother you again. Likewise, if you refuse to be coerced by a dictator or if you attack him, his reign will be over. Therefore, the best course of action for people oppressed by a dictator is to resist and attack.

*7. I like hamburger, and I like steak, and I like roast beef. So I will like tongue.

8. The brightness of our brief but beautiful lives is like that of a flash of lightning.

9. John S. Chen, the new CEO of BlackBerry, has been in the tech business for over 30 years. Referred to by some as "a doctor for businesses," he has a proven track record of helping failing tech companies get back on track. He'll be able to drag BlackBerry back to the top of the industry in no time.

10. Conducting an opinion survey is like shooting arrows at a target. The more arrows you shoot (the bigger your sample size) the more likely you are to hit your target.

*11. "Character is the foundation stone upon which one must build to win respect. Just as no worthy building can be erected on a weak foundation, so no lasting reputation worthy of respect can be built on a weak character." (R.C. Samsel)

EXERCISE 8.9

Evaluate each of the following arguments by analogy, indicating (1) the things (instances) being compared, (2) the relevant similarities mentioned or implied, (3) whether diversity among multiple cases is a significant factor, (4) the conclusion, and (5) whether the argument is strong or weak.

*1. Like two newlyweds, the countries of Europe have linked their economies together. Like newlyweds, they started out starry-eyed and optimistic about it all. And like newlyweds, the countries of Europe see clearly the benefits of this linking. But also like newlyweds, they are almost guaranteed to go through some tough times together. And eventually, like so many newlyweds, they may well end up regretting the whole idea.

2. Last year, our university expelled a student from our class for cheating on an exam. Just a couple months ago, another student was caught plagiarizing an essay. He got a zero on the paper, was suspended, and had it noted on his official transcript. One of my friends just got caught for posting test answers on Facebook, so the university will be punishing her very severely.

3. "If a single cell, under appropriate conditions, becomes a person in the space of a few years, there can surely be no difficulty in understanding how, under appropriate conditions, a cell may, in the course of untold millions of years, give origin to the human race." (Herbert Spencer)

4. Several new, modern manufacturing plants in the Toronto area have brought jobs to that area as well as improving the city's tax base, without causing significant amounts of pollution or noise or disrupting traffic. The same can be said for two new plants that have opened up on the outskirts of Montreal, as well as plants in Edmonton and Calgary. A plant built in Halifax will provide all the same benefits, also without disadvantages.

*5. Some people think suicide is immoral. But a well-established moral principle is that one is morally justified in using deadly force in self-defence when one is threatened with death or great pain from an assailant. A disease such as terminal cancer can also threaten one with death or great pain. So suicide—a use of deadly force—must sometimes be morally justified when it is an act of self-defence against an assailant (terminal disease) that threatens death or great pain. We are justified in using deadly force to avoid great pain, even when that deadly force is used against ourselves.

6. "If we survey the universe, so far as it falls under our knowledge, it bears a great resemblance to an animal or organized body, and seems actuated with a like principle of life and motion. A continual circulation of matter in it produces no disorder: a continual waste in every part is incessantly repaired: The closest sympathy is perceived throughout the whole system. And each part or member, in performing its proper offices, operates both to its own preservation and to that of the whole. The world, therefore, I infer, is an animal, and the Deity is the soul of the world, activating it and activated by it." (Philo, in Hume's *Dialogues Concerning Natural Religion*)

7. In her moral philosophy paper "A Defense of Abortion," Judith Jarvis Thomson writes, "[Imagine] you wake up in the morning and find yourself back to back in bed with an unconscious violinist. A famous

unconscious violinist. He has been found to have a fatal kidney ailment, and the Society of Music Lovers has canvassed all the available medical records and found that you alone have the right blood type to help. They have therefore kidnapped you, and last night the violinist's circulatory system was plugged into yours, so that your kidneys can be used to extract poisons from his blood as well as your own. [If he is unplugged from you now, he will die; but] in nine months he will have recovered from his ailment, and can safely be unplugged from you." Since most people would agree that you would be morally justified in unplugging yourself from the violinist, it also follows that it would be morally justified for a woman to abort (i.e., unplug herself from) her baby.

CAUSAL ARGUMENTS

Our world is a shifting, multi-stranded, complicated web of causes and effects—and that's an oversimplification. Incredibly, the normal human response to the apparent causal chaos is to jump in and ask what causes what. What causes breast cancer? What made Malcolm steal the car? What produced that rash on Norah's arm? What brought the universe into existence? Why have the New Democrats never won a federal election? When we answer such questions (or try to), we make a **causal claim**—a statement about the causes of things. And when we try to prove or support a causal claim, we make a **causal argument**—an inductive argument whose conclusion contains a causal claim.

causal claim A statement about the causes of things.

causal argument An inductive argument whose conclusion contains a causal claim.

Causal arguments, being inductive, can give us only probable conclusions. If the premises of a strong causal argument are true, then the conclusion is only probably true, with the probability varying from merely likely to highly probable. The probabilistic nature of causal arguments, however, should not be thought of as a failing or weakness. Causal reasoning is simply different from deductive reasoning, and it is our primary method of acquiring knowledge about the workings of the world. The great human enterprise known as science is concerned mainly with causal processes and causal arguments, and few people would consider this work inferior or unreliable because it was not deductively unshakeable. We now have very strong inductive arguments, for example, in favour of the claim that cigarettes cause cancer, that the HIV virus causes AIDS, and that chlorofluorocarbons cause depletion of Earth's ozone layer. Each of these causal conclusions is very reliable and constitutes a firm basis for guiding individual and collective behaviour.

Causal arguments can come in several inductive forms, some of which you already know about. For example, we sometimes reason about cause and effect by using enumerative induction:

> One time, when I made the aluminum rod come in contact with the rotating circular-saw blade, sparks flew.
> Another time, when I made the aluminum rod come in contact with the rotating circular-saw blade, sparks flew.
> Many other times, when I made the aluminum rod come in contact with the rotating circular-saw blade, sparks flew.
> Therefore, making the aluminum rod come in contact with the rotating circular-saw blade always causes sparks to fly.

"I would rather discover a single causal connection than win the throne of Persia."

—*Democritus*

Occasionally, we may argue to a causal conclusion by using analogical induction:

> Ten years ago a massive surge in worldwide oil prices caused a recession.
> Five years ago a massive surge in worldwide oil prices caused a recession.
> Therefore, the current massive surge in worldwide oil prices will cause a recession.

inference to the best explanation A form of inductive reasoning in which we reason from premises about a state of affairs to an explanation for that state of affairs:

> Phenomenon Q.
> E provides the best explanation for Q.
> Therefore, it is probable that E is true.

Most often, though, we use another type of induction in which we reason to a causal conclusion by pinpointing the best explanation for a particular effect. Let's say that after a hail storm you discover that the roof of your car, which you had left parked outside in the driveway, has a hundred tiny dents in it. You might reason like this: the dents could have been caused by the mischievous kids next door, by a flock of lunatic woodpeckers, or by the hail storm. After considering these options (and a few others), you decide that the best explanation (or hypothesis) for the dents is the hail storm. So you conclude that the hail storm caused the dents in your car's roof.

This is a very powerful and versatile form of inductive reasoning called **inference to the best explanation**. It's the essence of scientific thinking and a key part of our everyday problem solving and knowledge acquisition (whether causal or non-causal). Because of the importance and usefulness of such reasoning, this book devotes three chapters to it in Part 4. So we won't try to cover the same ground here. Instead, we'll concentrate on some other inductive patterns of reasoning that have traditionally been used to assess causal connections.

"I understand *how* I was born; I want to know *why*."

CREDIT: Jason Love/Cartoon Stock

FOOD FOR THOUGHT

Semmelweis, Clean Hands, and Childbed Fever

One of the most famous cases of successful causal reasoning in the history of science is the case of nineteenth-century Hungarian physician Ignaz Semmelweis. Semmelweis worked in the maternity section of the Vienna General Hospital, in Austria. During that time period, childbirth was quite dangerous; in fact, many women died in the process. Semmelweis noticed, however, a pattern. He noticed that women in one of the hospital's two maternity wards were several times more likely to die of a disease now known as "puerperal fever" (also known as "childbed fever") than were women in the other. He also noticed that women in the safer ward were cared for by midwives; women in the more dangerous ward were cared for by physicians, who often examined their patients directly after performing autopsies. Could there be a connection? Could the physicians be transferring something from the cadavers to their pregnant patients? Semmelweis believed so (even though scientists had not yet discovered the role of germs in producing disease). He instituted a policy under which all medical personnel were required to wash their hands with a chlorine solution after performing autopsies. In the months that followed, the death rate among women in the previously more dangerous ward dropped from 10 per cent to about 3 per cent. Semmelweis's careful causal reasoning saved lives.

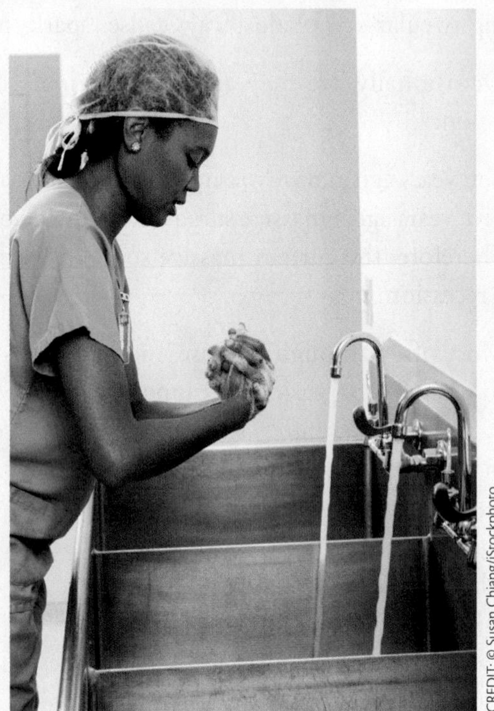

Causal reasoning saves lives every day.

CREDIT: © Susan Chiang/iStockphoto

Testing for Causes

The English philosopher John Stuart Mill (1806–73) noted several ways of evaluating causal arguments and formulated them into what are now known as "Mill's methods" of inductive inference. Despite their fancy name, however, the methods are basically commonsense and are used by just about everyone. They also happen to be the basis of a great deal of scientific testing. Let's look at a few of the more important ones.

Agreement or Difference

A modified version of Mill's Method of Agreement says that if two or more occurrences of a phenomenon have only one relevant factor in common, that factor must be the cause.

Imagine that dozens of people stop into Elmo's corner bar after work as they usually do and that 10 of them come down with an intestinal illness one hour after leaving the premises. What caused them to become ill? There are a lot of possibilities. Maybe a waiter who had a flu-like illness sneezed into their drinks, or the free tacos had gone bad, or another patron had a viral infection and passed it along via a handshake. But let's say that there is only one relevant factor that's common to all 10 people who got sick: they all had a drink from the same beer tap. We could then plausibly conclude that something in the beer probably caused the illness.

Public health officials often use the Method of Agreement, especially when they're trying to determine the cause of an unusual illness in a population of several thousand people. They might be puzzled, say, by an unusually large number of cases of rare liver disease in a city. If they discover that all the people affected have the same toxin in their bloodstreams—and this is the only common relevant factor—they have reason to believe that the toxin is the cause of the liver disease. In such situations, the poison may turn out to have an industrial or agricultural source.

Here's a schematic of an argument based on the Method of Agreement:

Instance 1: Factors *a*, *b*, and *c* are followed by *E*.
Instance 2: Factors *a*, *c*, and *d* are followed by *E*.
Instance 3: Factors *b* and *c* are followed by *E*.
Instance 4: Factors *c* and *d* are followed by *E*.
Therefore, factor *c* is probably the cause of *E*.

There's only one factor—factor *c*—that consistently accompanies effect *E*. The other factors are sometimes present and sometimes not. We conclude, then, that factor *c* brings about *E*.

Mill's (modified) Method of Difference says that the relevant factor that is present when a phenomenon occurs and that is absent when the phenomenon does not occur must be the cause. Here we look not for factors that the instances of the phenomenon have in common, but for factors that are points of difference among the instances.

Suppose that the performance of football players on a CFL team has been consistently excellent except for six players who have recently been playing the worst games of their careers. The only relevant difference between the high- and low-performing players is that the latter have been taking daily doses of Brand X herbal supplements. If the supplement dosing is really the *only* relevant difference, we could plausibly conclude that the supplements are causing the lousy performance. (Finding out if the supplements are indeed the only relevant difference, of course, is easier said than done.)

So arguments based on the Method of Difference have this form:

Instance 1: Factors *a*, *b*, and *c* are followed by *E*.
Instance 2: Factors *a* and *b* are not followed by *E*.
Therefore, factor *c* is probably the cause of *E*.

Both Agreement and Difference

If we combine these two reasoning patterns, we get a modified version of what Mill called the "Joint Method of Agreement and Difference." Using this joint method is, obviously, just a matter of applying both methods simultaneously —a procedure that generally increases the probability that the conclusion is true. This combined method, then, says that the likely cause is the one isolated when you (1) identify the relevant factors common to occurrences of the phenomenon (the Method of Agreement) and (2) discard any of these that are present even when there are no occurrences (the Method of Difference).

Let's apply this combined method to the mystery illness at Elmo's bar. Say that among the 10 patrons who become ill, the common factors are that they all drank from the same beer tap and they all had the free tacos. So we reason that the likely cause is either the beer or the tacos. After further investigation, though, we find that other patrons who ate the tacos did not become ill. We conclude that the beer is the culprit.

The schematic for arguments based on the Joint Method of Agreement and Difference is:

Instance 1: Factors *a*, *b*, and *c* are followed by *E*.
Instance 2: Factors *a*, *b*, and *d* are followed by *E*.
Instance 3: Factors *b* and *c* are not followed by *E*.
Instance 4: Factors *b* and *d* are not followed by *E*.
Therefore, factor *a* is probably the cause of *E*.

Factors *a* and *b* are the only relevant factors that are accompanied by *E*. But we can eliminate *b* as a possibility because when it's present, *E* doesn't occur. So *b* can't be the cause of *E*; *a* is most likely the cause.

You can see the Joint Method of Agreement and Difference at work in modern "controlled trials" used to test the effectiveness of medical treatments. In these experiments, there are two groups of subjects—one known as the experimental group; the other, the control group. The experimental group receives the treatment being tested, usually a new drug. The control group receives a bogus, or inactive, treatment (referred to as a placebo). This setup helps ensure that the two groups are as similar as possible and that they differ in only one respect—the use of the genuine treatment. A controlled trial, then, reveals the relevant factor *common* to the occurrence of the effect, which is the subjects' response to the treatment (Method of Agreement). And it shows the only important difference between the occurrence and non-occurrence of the effect: the use of the treatment being tested.

Correlation

In many cases, relevant factors aren't merely entirely present or entirely absent during occurrences of the phenomenon—they are closely *correlated* with the occurrences. The cause of an occurrence varies as the occurrence (effect) does. For such situations Mill formulated the Method of Concomitant Variation. This method says that when two events are correlated—when one varies in close connection with the other—they are probably causally related. For instance, if you observe that the longer you boil eggs, the harder they get (and no other relevant factors complicate this relationship), you can safely conclude that this correlation between boiling and hardening is a causal connection. You have good evidence that the boiling causes the hardening.

In medical science, such correlations are highly prized because direct evidence of cause and effect is so hard to come by. We don't *see* causation directly. Correlations are often indirect evidence of one thing causing another. In exploring the link between cigarette smoking and lung cancer, for example, researchers discovered first that people who smoke cigarettes are more likely to get lung cancer than those who don't smoke. But later research also showed that the more cigarettes people smoke, the higher their risk of lung cancer. Medical scientists call such a correlation a *dose–response relationship*. The higher the dose of the element in question (smoking), the higher the response (the more cases of lung cancer). This dose–response relationship between cigarette smoking and lung cancer is, when combined with other data, strong evidence that smoking causes lung cancer.

CREDIT: xkcd.com

FOOD FOR THOUGHT

Is It Causal Confusion or ESP?

For over two decades, scientist-writer Susan Blackmore (with degrees in psychology, physiology, and parapsychology) has been investigating the psychology of "psychic," or paranormal, experience. Her central hypothesis has been that people's supposed experience of extrasensory perception, or ESP (telepathy, clairvoyance, and precognition), is the result of errors in causal thinking. Specifically, people tend to mistake coincidence for causal connection. She writes:

> My hypothesis is that psychic experiences are comparable to visual illusions. The experience is real enough, but its origin lies in internal processes, not peculiarities in the observable world. Like visual illusions they arise from cognitive processes that are usually appropriate but under certain circumstances give rise to the wrong answer. In other words, they are a price we pay for using efficient heuristics.
>
> In the case of vision, illusions arise when, for example, depth is seen in two-dimensional figures and constancy mechanisms give the answer that would be correct for real depth. The equivalent in the case of psychic experiences may be the illusion that a cause is operating and an explanation is required when in fact none is. In other words, psychic experiences are illusions of causality. . . .
>
> Experiences of telepathy, clairvoyance, and precognition imply a coincidence that is "too good to be just chance." This is so whether the experience involves dreaming about a person's death and that person dies within a few hours, feeling the urge to pick up one's partner from the station and in fact he was stranded and needed help, or betting on a horse that later wins a race.
>
> Some people's response to such events is to say, "That was just a chance coincidence"; while others' is to say, "That cannot be chance." In the latter case the person will then look for a causal explanation for the coincidence. If none can be found, a "cause," such as ESP, may be invoked. Alternatively, some kind of noncausal but meaningful connection may be sought, such as Jung's "acausal connecting principle."
>
> There are two possible types of error that may be made here. First, people may treat connected events as chance coincidences, thereby missing real connections between events and failing to look for explanations. Second, they may treat chance events as connected and seek for explanations where none is required. In the real world of inadequate information and complex interactions one would expect errors of both types to occur. It is the latter type that, I suggest, gives rise to experiences of ESP. . . .
>
> One prediction of this approach is that those people who more frequently look for explanations of chance coincidences are more likely to have psychic experiences.
>
> Therefore, sheep [believers in ESP] should be those who underestimate the probability of chance coincidences.
>
> It has long been known that probability judgments can be extremely inaccurate. Kahneman and Tversky (1973) have explored some of the heuristics, such as "representativeness" and "availability," that people [are subject to]. [Other researchers (Fall 1982; Falk & MacGregor, 1983) found that adding] specific but superfluous detail can make coincidences

> seem more surprising, and things that happen to subjects themselves seem more surprising to them than the same things happening to other people. . . .
>
> There is, however, little research relating these misjudgments to belief in the paranormal or to having psychic experiences. Blackmore and Troscianko (1985) found that sheep performed worse than goats [skeptics about ESP] on a variety of probability tasks. For example, in questions testing for responsiveness to sample size, sheep did significantly worse than goats. The well-known birthday question was asked: How many people would you need to have at a party to have a 50:50 chance that two have the same birthday? . . . As predicted, goats got the answer right significantly more often than sheep.
>
> Subjects also played a coin-tossing computer game and were asked to guess how many hits they would be likely to get by chance. The correct answer, 10 hits in 20 trials, seems to be rather obvious. However, the sheep gave a significantly lower mean estimate of only 7.9, while goats gave a more accurate estimate of 9.6.[1]

We can represent arguments based on the Method of Concomitant Variation like this:

Instance 1: Factors *a*, *b*, and *c* are correlated with *E* being present.
Instance 2: Factors *a*, *b*, and increased-*c* are correlated with increased *E*.
Instance 3: Factors *a*, *b*, and decreased-*c* are correlated with decreased *E*.
Therefore, factor *c* is causally connected with *E*.

An important cautionary note must accompany this discussion of correlation: correlation, of course, does not always mean that a causal relationship is present. A correlation could just be a coincidence (as we will discuss in the next section of this chapter). An increase in home computer sales was correlated with a rise in the incidence of AIDS in Africa during the 1990s, but this doesn't mean that one was in any way causally linked with the other.

Causal Confusions

Mill's methods and other forms of causal reasoning may be common sense, and useful, but they're not foolproof. No inductive procedure can guarantee the truth of the conclusion. More to the point, it's easy to commit errors in cause-and-effect reasoning—regardless of the method used—by failing to take into account pertinent aspects of the situation. This section describes some of the more common causal blunders to which we're all prey.

Misidentifying Relevant Factors

A key issue in any type of causal reasoning is whether the factors preceding an effect are truly relevant to that effect. In using the Method of Agreement, for example, it's easy to find a preceding factor common to all occurrences of a phenomenon. But that factor may actually be irrelevant. In the case of Elmo's bar, what if all those who became ill had black hair? So what? We know that hair colour is very unlikely to be related to intestinal illness. *Relevant* factors include only those things that could possibly be causally connected to the occurrence of the phenomenon being studied. We could reasonably judge that factors relevant to the intestinal illness would include all the conditions that might help transmit bacteria or viruses.

Your ability to identify relevant factors depends mostly on your background knowledge—what you know about the kinds of conditions that could produce the occurrences in which you're interested. Lack of background knowledge might lead you to dismiss or ignore relevant factors or to assume that irrelevant factors must play a role. The only cure for this inadequacy is deeper study of the causal possibilities in question.

Mishandling Multiple Factors

Most of the time, the biggest difficulty in evaluating causal connections is not that there are so few relevant factors to consider—but that there are so many. Too often the Method of Agreement and the Method of Difference are rendered useless because they cannot, by themselves, narrow the possibilities to just one.

At the same time, ordinary causal reasoning is often flawed because of the failure to consider *all* the relevant antecedent factors. (Later chapters will refer to this problem as the failure to consider alternative explanations.) Sometimes this kind of oversight happens because we simply don't look hard enough for possible causes. At other times, we miss relevant factors because we don't know enough about the causal processes involved. This again is a function of skimpy background knowledge. Either way, there is no countermeasure better than your own determination to dig out the whole truth.

Being Misled by Coincidence

Sometimes ordinary events are paired in unusual or interesting ways. You think of Quebec, then suddenly a TV ad announces low-cost fares to Montreal; you receive some email just as your doorbell and the phone both ring; or you stand in the lobby of a hotel thinking of an old friend and then see her walk in. Plenty of interesting pairings can also show up in scientific research. Scientists might find, for example, that men with the highest rates of heart disease may also have a higher daily intake of water. Or women with the lowest risk of breast cancer may own Toyotas. Such pairings are very probably just coincidence, merely surprising correlations of events. A problem arises, though, when we think that there nevertheless *must be* a causal connection involved.

FOOD FOR THOUGHT

Coincidence, Birth Dates, and American Presidents

When we're tempted to say that the conjunction of two events "couldn't be just coincidence," we should think twice. People are often very bad at determining the true likelihood of events. Recall the birth date problem mentioned in Chapter 4. It's the classic example of misjudged probabilities: in a random selection of 23 people, what is the probability that at least 2 of them will have the same birthday? The answer: 50 per cent, or 50:50. People are usually shocked when they hear the answer. Part of the reason is that they usually underestimate how often oddball coincidences occur and fail to see that such strange conjunctions must occur from time to time. Here's a succinct explanation of the problem from social psychologist David G. Myers:

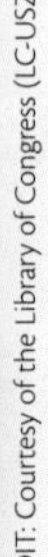

CREDIT: Courtesy of the Library of Congress (LC-USZ6212950)

> We've all marveled at such coincidences in our own lives. Checking out a photocopy counter from the Hope University library desk, I confused the clerk when giving my six-digit department charge number—which just happened at that moment to be identical to the counter's six-digit number on which the last user had finished. Shortly after my daughter, Laura Myers, bought two pairs of shoes, we were astounded to discover that the two brand names on the boxes were "Laura" and "Myers." And then there are those remarkable coincidences that, with added digging, have been embellished into really fun stories, such as the familiar Lincoln-Kennedy coincidences (both with seven letters in their last names, elected 100 years apart, assassinated on a Friday while beside their wives, one in Ford's theater, the other in a Ford Motor Co. car, and so forth). We also have enjoyed newspaper accounts of astonishing happenings, such as when twins Lorraine and Levinia Christmas, driving to deliver Christmas presents to each other near Flitcham, England, collided.

CREDIT: Arthur Rothstein

> My favorite is this little known fact: In Psalm 46 of the King James Bible, published in the year that Shakespeare turned 46, the 46th word is "shake" and the 46th word from the end is "spear." (More remarkable than this coincidence is that someone should have noted this!) . . .
>
> "In reality," says mathematician John Allen Paulos, "the most astonishingly incredible coincidence imaginable would be the complete absence of all coincidences." When Evelyn Marie Adams won the New Jersey lottery twice, newspapers reported the odds of her feat as 1 in 17 trillion—the odds that a given person buying a single

Continued

ticket for two New Jersey lotteries would win both. But statisticians Stephen Samuels and George McCabe report that, given the millions of people who buy US state lottery tickets, it was "practically a sure thing" that someday, somewhere, someone would hit a state jackpot twice. Consider: An event that happens to but one in a billion people in a day happens 2000 times a year. A day when nothing weird happened would actually be the weirdest day of all.[2]

For several reasons, we may very much *want* a coincidence to be the result of a cause-and-effect relationship, so we come to believe that the pairing *is* causal. Just as often we may mistake causes for coincidences because we're impressed or excited about the conjunction of events. Since the pairing of events may seem "too much of a coincidence" to be coincidence, we conclude that one event must have caused the other. You may be thinking about how nice it would be for your sister to call you from her home in the Yukon—then the phone rings, and it's her! You're tempted to conclude that your wishing *caused* her to call. But such an event, though intriguing and seemingly improbable, is not really so extraordinary. Given the ordinary laws of statistics, incredible coincidences are common and must occur. Any event, even one that seems shockingly improbable, is actually very probable over the long haul. Given enough opportunities to occur, events like this surprising phone call are virtually certain to happen to *someone*.

People are especially prone to think "it can't be just coincidence" because, for several psychological reasons, they misjudge the probabilities involved. They may think, for example, that a phone call from someone at the moment they're thinking of that person is incredible—but only because they've forgotten about all the times they've thought of that person and the phone *didn't* ring. Such probability misjudgments are a major source of beliefs about the paranormal or supernatural, topics that we address in Chapter 10. (See also the box "Is It Causal Confusion or ESP?" earlier in this chapter.)

Unfortunately, there is no foolproof way to distinguish coincidence from cause and effect. But this rule of thumb can help:

Don't assume that a causal connection exists unless you have good reason for doing so.

Generally, you have a good reason for suspecting that a causal connection exists if the connection passes one or more standard causal tests (such as the ones we've been discussing)—and if you can rule out any relevant factors that might undermine the verdict of those tests. Usually, when a cause-and-effect connection is uncertain, only further evaluation or research can clear things up.

Confusing Cause with Temporal Order

A particularly common type of misjudgment about coincidences is the logical fallacy known as ***post hoc, ergo propter hoc*** ("after that, therefore because of that"). It is true that a cause must precede its effect. But just because one event precedes another, that doesn't mean that the earlier one *caused* the later. To think so is to be taken in by this fallacy. Outrageous examples of post hoc arguments include "The rooster crowed, then the sun came up, so the rooster's crowing caused the sunrise!" and "Jasmine left her umbrella at home on Monday, and that caused it to rain." You can clearly see the error in such cases, but consider these arguments:

post hoc, ergo propter hoc ("after that, therefore because of that") The fallacy of reasoning that just because B followed A, A must have caused B.

Argument 8
After the training for police officers was enhanced, violent crime in the city decreased by 10 per cent. So enhanced training caused the decline in violent crime.

Argument 9
An hour after Julio drank the cola, his headache went away. The cola cured his headache.

Argument 10
As soon as Smith took office and implemented policies that reflected his conservative theory of economics, the economy went into a downward slide characterized by slow growth and high unemployment. Therefore, the Smith policies caused the current economic doldrums.

Argument 11
I wore my black shirt on Tuesday and got an F on a math quiz. I wore the same shirt the next day and flunked my psych exam. That shirt's bad luck.

The conclusion of argument 8 is based on nothing more than the fact that the enhanced training preceded the reduction in violent crime. But crime rates can decrease for many reasons, and the enhanced training may have had nothing to do with the decline in crime. For the argument to be strong, other considerations besides temporal order would have to apply—for example, that other possible causes or antecedent factors had been ruled out; that there was a close correlation between amount of training and decline in crime rates; or that in previous years (or in comparable cities) enhanced training was always followed by a decline in violent crime (or no change in training was always followed by steady crime rates).

Argument 9 is also purely post hoc. Such reasoning is extremely common and underlies almost all folk remedies and a great deal of quackery and bogus self-cures. You take a vitamin E capsule, and four hours later your headache is gone.

But was it really the vitamin E that did the trick? Or was it some other overlooked factor, such as something you ate, the medication you took (or didn't take), the nap you had, the change in environment (from, say, indoors to outdoors), or the stress reduction you felt when you had pleasant thoughts? Would your headache have gone away on its own anyway? Was it the *placebo effect*—the tendency for people to feel better when treated even when the treatment is fake or inactive? A chief function of controlled medical testing is to evaluate cause-and-effect relationships by systematically ruling out post hoc thinking and irrelevant factors.

Argument 10 is typical post hoc reasoning from the political sphere. Unless there are other good reasons for thinking that the economic policy is causally connected to specific economic events, the argument is weak and the conclusion unreliable.

Argument 11 is 100 per cent post hoc and undiluted superstition. There is no difference in kind between this argument and much of the notorious post hoc reasoning of centuries ago: "That woman gave me the evil eye. The next day I broke my leg. That proves she's a witch, and the Elders of Salem should have her put to death!"

Ignoring the Common Causal Factor

Sometimes A and B are correlated with each other, and genuinely causally connected, but A doesn't cause B and B doesn't cause A. Rather, both A and B are caused by some third factor, C, that they share in common. One often-cited

EVERYDAY PROBLEMS AND DECISIONS

Health Care Decisions

Some of the most critical decisions we make in life are about health care. Sometimes those decisions must be made on behalf of someone else, such as a child. In late 2014 and early 2015 the CBC reported on two different cases involving parents of girls with cancer. In both cases, the girls suffered from dangerous but treatable forms of cancer. In both cases, the parents opted to reject having their daughters treated at a hospital—treatment that would have included things like chemotherapy and perhaps radiation therapy—and instead opted for "natural" treatment options, including a vegan diet of raw, sugar-free foods.

It is interesting and instructive to ask about the thinking process that might have gone into such a decision. Clearly it had to be based on these parents' understanding of what would be best for their daughters. And that would surely be based on their understanding of the sum total of the available evidence about what would be most likely to help their daughters—that is, what would be most likely to cause them to get better. The physicians advising them told them that the existing scientific and medical evidence suggested that chemotherapy would be both necessary, and likely sufficient, to save the girls' lives. For whatever reason, both sets of parents rejected that advice.

One of the girls—Makayla Saulk—died in January of 2015. At the time of writing, the fate of the other girl, known as J.J., was still unclear.

example is this: there is a correlation between sales in ice cream and deaths due to drowning, across the months of the year. Does ice cream cause people to drown? No. Does drowning somehow cause a rise in ice cream sales? Highly unlikely! The truth is that both of those things are more common during a particular season, namely summer. In the heat of summer, more people go swimming and therefore the rate of drownings goes up. And sales of ice cream likewise go up in summer. So, summertime is the *common causal factor* shared by those two variables. (Note: *common* here means "shared," not "frequent.") Another example: imagine reading about a survey that suggests that Canadians with access to high-speed Internet tend to go out to see bands play live more than people with poor Internet access. Is there a causal connection between the two? Well, there might be: maybe people use the Internet to find out when good bands are playing, and Canadians without good Internet access are left out. But it's more likely that there's a common causal factor connecting the two: people who live in the city are much more likely to have high-speed Internet than people who live in rural areas. People who live in the city also tend to live near lots of clubs and bars where they can see live music. More evidence would be needed before we could be certain what the real causal story is.

How many women did the post hoc fallacy doom in Salem during the witch trials of the 1690s?

Confusing Cause and Effect

Sometimes we may realize that there's a causal relationship between two factors, but we may not know which factor is the cause and which is the effect. We may be confused, in other words, about the answers to questions like these:

> Does your coffee drinking cause you to feel stressed out—or do your feelings of being stressed out cause you to drink coffee?
>
> Does participation in high school sports produce desirable virtues such as courage and self-reliance—or do the virtues of courage and self-reliance lead students to participate in high school sports?
>
> Does regular exercise make people healthy—or are healthy people naturally prone to regular exercise?

As you can see, it's not always a simple matter to discern what the nature of a causal link is. Again, we must rely on our rule of thumb: *don't assume that a causal connection exists unless you have good reason for doing so*. This tenet applies not only to our ordinary experience, but also to all states of affairs involving cause and effect, including scientific investigations.

In everyday life, sorting cause from effect is often easy because the situations we confront are frequently simple and familiar—as when we're trying to discover what caused the kettle to boil over. Here, we naturally rely on Mill's methods or other types of causal reasoning. But as we've seen, in many other common circumstances, things aren't so simple. We often cannot be sure that we've identified all the relevant factors or ruled out the influence of coincidence or correctly distinguished cause and effect. Our rule of thumb, then, should be our guide in all the doubtful cases.

"Shallow men believe in luck. Strong men believe in cause and effect."

—*Ralph Waldo Emerson*

Science faces all the same kinds of challenges in its pursuit of causal explanations. And despite its sophisticated methods and investigative tools, it must expend a great deal of effort to pin down causal connections. Identifying the cause of a disease, for example, usually requires not one study or experiment, but many. The main reason is that it's always tough to uncover relevant factors and exclude irrelevant or misleading factors. That's why we should apply our rule of thumb even to scientific research that purports to identify a causal link. In Chapters 9 and 10, we'll explore procedures for evaluating scientific research and for applying our rule of thumb with more precision.

sufficient condition A condition for the occurrence of an event that guarantees that the event occurs.

necessary condition A condition for the occurrence of an event without which the event cannot occur.

Necessary and Sufficient Conditions

To fully appreciate the dynamics of cause and effect and to be able to skilfully assess causal arguments, you must understand two other important concepts: **necessary condition** and **sufficient condition**. Causal processes always occur under specific conditions. So we often speak of cause and effect in terms of *the conditions for the occurrence of an event*. Scientists, philosophers, and others go

REVIEW NOTES

Causal Confusions

- Misidentifying relevant factors
- Overlooking relevant factors
- Confusing coincidence with cause
- Confusing cause with temporal order (post hoc fallacy)
- Confusing cause and effect

a step further and emphasize a distinction between necessary and sufficient conditions for the occurrence of an event:

> *A necessary condition for the occurrence of an event is one without which the event cannot occur.*
>
> *A sufficient condition for the occurrence of an event is one that guarantees that the event occurs.*

Suppose you drop a water-filled balloon from the top of a building (aiming it at your least favourite professor, of course), and it breaks on the pavement. What are the *necessary* conditions for the breaking of the balloon (the effect)? There are several, including (1) your releasing the balloon, (2) the force of gravity acting on the water, (3) the weakness of the material that the balloon is made of (its breakability), and (4) the hardness of the pavement. If any one of these conditions is not present, the water balloon will not break. To state the obvious, if you don't release the balloon, it won't drop. If gravity is not in force, the balloon won't fall. If the balloon material isn't breakable, it won't break. If the pavement isn't hard enough, even a breakable balloon won't rupture. (For the sake of illustration, this list of necessary conditions is incomplete. Many, if not most, events in nature have large numbers of necessary conditions.)

What are the *sufficient* conditions for the balloon's breaking? Not one of the four conditions by itself is sufficient to cause the balloon to break. None *guarantees* the occurrence of the effect; none suffices to produce the event. But all the necessary conditions combined (these four and others) are sufficient to guarantee the balloon's breaking.

Failing to feed a healthy goldfish for a few weeks is a sure way to kill it. So this deprivation is a sufficient condition for its death, as is removing the water from its fishbowl. But neither taking away the fish's food nor draining its bowl is a *necessary* condition for a goldfish's death, because its death can be caused without resorting to either of these methods. On the other hand, necessary conditions for *sustaining* the fish's life include feeding it, providing it with water to live in, ensuring that the water is properly oxygenated, and so on. Again, in this instance, the whole set of the necessary conditions would constitute a sufficient condition for sustaining the fish's life.

In cases in which a complete set of necessary conditions constitutes a sufficient condition for an event, we say that the conditions are *individually necessary and jointly sufficient* for an event to occur. As the previous examples suggest, however, it's possible to have a set of conditions that are individually necessary but *not* jointly sufficient. Say some of the conditions necessary for sustaining the goldfish's life are present, but not all of them are. Because some necessary conditions are missing, the sufficient condition for keeping the fish alive would not exist. On the other hand, it is also possible to have a set of conditions that are jointly sufficient but not individually necessary. By not feeding a goldfish for weeks we would create a set of conditions sufficient for the death of the fish. But these conditions are not necessary for the death of a goldfish because we could ensure its death in other ways.

So there are conditions that are necessary but not sufficient for the occurrence of an event, and conditions that are sufficient but not necessary. There are also conditions that are *both* necessary and sufficient for an event. The Earth's being more massive than the moon is both a necessary and sufficient condition for the moon's being less massive than the Earth. A piece of paper's being heated to a sufficiently high temperature in the presence of oxygen is both a necessary and sufficient condition for the combustion of the paper.

In some situations, depending on our interests or practical concerns, we may focus on necessary causal conditions, and in other situations on sufficient causal conditions. When we're interested in *preventing or eliminating* a state of affairs, we often zero in on necessary causal conditions. If you were a scientist trying to discover how to prevent mosquito infestations, you would try to determine the necessary conditions for the occurrence of mosquito infestations. Uncovering and understanding just one necessary condition could give you everything you need to control the problem. If you found out, for example, that a necessary condition for mosquito breeding is standing water, you would need to look no further for an answer. Eliminating the standing water would prevent infestations.

When we're interested in *bringing about* a state of affairs, we're likely to focus on sufficient causal conditions. If you were a doctor devoted to treating clogged arteries in your patients, you would seek out treatments scientifically proven to be sufficient for alleviating the condition. The treatments might include surgery to remove the blockage or a procedure called balloon angioplasty to widen artery passageways.

Your success in appraising causal arguments often depends heavily on your ability to distinguish between statements expressing causes as necessary conditions and statements expressing causes as sufficient conditions. Consider:

> In the current situation, the prime minister will call an election if Parliament doesn't vote in favour of his proposal to cut taxes.

This statement says that the condition required for the prime minister to call an election is Parliament not supporting his proposal to cut taxes. But is this a necessary or sufficient condition? The use of the word *if* by itself signals a sufficient condition. If sufficient condition is what's meant, then the statement says that Parliament's refusal to support the tax cuts will automatically trigger an election call. This outcome is assured if Parliament doesn't co-operate.

But if the statement is meant to express the idea that Parliament's refusal to support the tax cut is a necessary condition, then we're talking about a very different situation. If Parliament's refusal is a necessary condition, then it *will not* unavoidably trigger an election call because the refusal may not be the *only* necessary condition. The idea of a necessary condition is expressed by the phrase "only if" before the stipulated condition. To express necessary condition, the statement should read:

> In the current situation, the prime minister will call an election only if Parliament doesn't vote in favour of his proposal to cut taxes.

So, depending on the kind of causal condition meant, the statement could describe an election that's sure to happen if the condition obtains—or an election that may not occur even if the condition obtains.

As you might expect, conditions that are *both* necessary and sufficient are indicated by the phrase "if and only if." For example:

> The paper will combust if and only if it's heated to a sufficiently high temperature in the presence of oxygen.

None of this discussion, however, should lead you to think that a causal condition must be *either* necessary or sufficient. It could be neither:

> Late delivery of the package caused John to miss his deadline.
> Ricardo's stubbornness caused the negotiations to break down.

EXERCISE 8.10

Answers to exercises marked with an asterisk (*) may be found in Appendix B, Answers to Exercises.

Analyze each of the following causal arguments. Identify the conclusion and say whether the argument appeals to the Method of Agreement, the Method of Difference, the Joint Method of Agreement and Difference, or correlation. In some cases the conclusion may be implied but not stated. State whether the argument is strong or weak.

1. Four people in this class failed the mid-term exam. The only common factors are that they have poor attendance records and they all ignored the instructions on Question 10.

*2. Research suggests that eating lots of fruits and vegetables may provide some protection against several types of cancer. Studies have revealed that the risk of getting cancer associated with the lowest intakes of fruits and vegetables is twice as high as that associated with the highest intakes. This association holds for several types of cancer, including cancers of the breast, colon, pancreas, and bladder.

3. Whenever a deadly virus hits the developed world, vaccines are developed quickly to combat it. However, when a deadly virus only affects the developing world, vaccines are usually nowhere to be found. It's clear that medical companies don't care about saving people in developing countries, probably because they don't have as much money.
4. We tested 20 samples of ground beef from six different processing plants across Canada. All samples were subjected to the standard test for *E. coli* O157:H7. Test results showed that 17 of them were free of *E. coli* and hence, in this regard, safe for human consumption. The other 3, however, showed significant levels of *E. coli.* The only relevant factor common to these 3 samples is that they all came from processing plants owned by a single company, JBR Meats, Inc. (and none of the 17 uncontaminated samples came from from a plant owned by JBR). We conclude that there are significant deficiencies in JBR's food-safety procedures.
5. A voluntary relationship survey conducted at my workplace showed that 30 per cent *more* people were now in a committed relationship compared to last year. Every single one of the people who reported having started a new relationship since last year's survey also stated that they had started using the new dating app called Tinder.
6. In Instance 1, when factors X, Y, and Z were present, E happened. In Instance 2, when factors X, Y, and P were present, E happened. In Instance 3, when factors X and Z were present, E did not happen. In Instance 4, when Z and P were present, E did not happen. And in Instance 5, when X, Z, and P were present, E did not happen. Therefore, Y caused E.

*7. Educators have frequently noted the connection between education level and salary. The higher a person's education level is, the higher his or her annual salary is likely to be. Education increases people's earning power.

8. "On 20 May 1747, I took twelve patients [with] scurvy on board the *Salisbury* at sea. Their cases were as similar as I could have them. They all in general had putrid gums, the spots and lassitude, with weakness of their knees. They lay together in one place, being a proper apartment for the sick in the fore-hold; and had one diet in common to all. . . . Two of these were ordered each a quart of cider a day. Two others took [25 drops of] vitriol three times a day. . . . Two others took two spoonfuls of vinegar three times a day. . . . Two of the worst patients [were given a half pint of sea water daily]. . . . Two others had each two oranges and one lemon given them everyday. . . . The two remaining patients took [small doses of nutmeg, garlic, mustard

seed, and a few other ingredients]. The consequence was that the most sudden and visible good effects were perceived from the use of the oranges and lemons; one of those who had taken them being at the end of six days fit for duty. . . . The other was the best recovered of any in his condition, and being now deemed pretty well was appointed nurse to the rest of the sick. As I shall have occasion elsewhere to take notice of the effects of other medicines in this disease, I shall here only observe that the result of all my experiments was that oranges and lemons were the most effectual remedies for this distemper at sea." (James Lind, *Of the Prevention of the Scurvy*, 1753)

9. Johnny owns a successful mid-sized telemarketing company. Three months ago, one of his best sales managers, Jeff, left to work elsewhere and Johnny hired Fred to replace him. Last week, while analyzing his employees' performance reports, he noticed many unfamiliar names. After a little digging, he discovered that the employee turnover rate at the store had increased substantially since Jeff left. Moreover, Fred had managed the vast majority of the employees that the store had lost. Therefore, Johnny concludes that Fred is an incompetent sales manager.
10. Scientists wanted to see whether giving pre-puberty children dietary supplements of calcium could significantly increase the density of the children's bones. (Bone density is a key part of bone strength.) So they selected 71 pairs of identical twins and gave one twin of each pair a daily supplement of extra calcium and the other twin a sugar pill (placebo). All the twins had diets that contained adequate amounts of all nutrients. The investigators monitored the twins and their diets for three years. The only relevant difference between the twins was the extra calcium that half of them received. At the end of the three years, the scientists found that the twins who had received the extra calcium had significantly greater bone density. They concluded that the extra calcium caused the increased density.
11. Baseballs and baseball gloves are complementary goods. That is, people who buy one often also buy the other. That's why a good way to sell more baseballs is to sell more baseball gloves.
12. The risk of atherosclerosis (hardening of the arteries) is linked to the amount of "bad" cholesterol (low-density lipoproteins) in the bloodstream. The higher those cholesterol levels, the greater the risk of atherosclerosis. There's a causal connection between levels of "bad" cholesterol and risk of atherosclerosis.

*13. Investigators tested the performance of four gasoline-powered lawnmowers before and after a tune-up. The machines differed in age, manufacturer, engine type, and controls. The performance of every mower was better after the tune-up, leading the testers to conclude that tune-ups can improve the performance of lawnmowers.

14. Minhiriath, Enedwaith, and Rohan are geographical regions that have similar climates year round. They are renowned for a unique flower that only grows within their borders, the Lissuin. Last year, Minhiriath experienced an unusual amount of rainfall, much more than Enedwaith and Rohan. Their Lissuin didn't grow properly, whereas those in the other two locations grew like they did every year. Therefore, growth of the Lissuin depends very heavily on the amount of rain the flowers receive.
15. Charlie was pretty happy all week, but then he started moping around as if he'd lost his dog or something. I think he's upset because he got word that his grades weren't good enough to get into medical school.
*16. The price of a barrel of oil on the world market has hit $40 only 12 times in the last 30 years. Sometimes major world economies were in recession, and sometimes they weren't. Sometimes there was an increase in the average fuel consumption of cars; sometimes not. War has been the only constant.
17. Sometimes my television reception is excellent, and sometimes it's terrible. There's only one important factor that seems to make a difference. When the reception is excellent, no other major appliances are running in the house. When it's terrible, at least one major appliance—like the dishwasher—is running. For some reason, running a major appliance interferes with my TV reception.
18. In our test, after people washed their hands with Lather-Up germicidal soap, no germs whatsoever could be detected on their hands. But under exactly the same conditions, after they washed their hands with Brand X germicidal soap, plenty of germs were found on their hands. Lather-Up is better.
*19. For years now, violent crimes in the downtown core of this city have consistently averaged three to four per month. After the police doubled foot patrols there, the rate has been one or two violent crimes every three months. That police presence has made a huge difference.
20. The cause of Barry's criminal behaviour—his involvement in pickpocketing and purse-snatching—is no mystery. Barry commits most of his criminal acts when the outdoor temperatures are highest. When it's very cold out, he behaves himself. In fact, the incidence of his criminal behaviour rises as the temperature rises. Barry's problem is that he has a heat-sensitive personality.

EXERCISE 8.11

For each argument in Exercise 8.10, identify errors in causal reasoning that are most likely to occur in the circumstances indicated. The possibilities include (a) misidentifying or overlooking relevant factors, (b) being misled by coincidence, (c) falling for the post hoc fallacy, and (d) confusing cause and effect. Answers are provided for 2, 7, 13, 16, and 19.

EXERCISE 8.12

For each of the following causal statements, say whether the specified cause is (a) a necessary condition, (b) a sufficient condition, (c) a necessary and sufficient condition, or (d) neither a necessary nor a sufficient condition.

*1. Sylvia's exposure to the influenza virus caused her to get the flu.
2. You've lied one too many times. I'm out of here!
3. The trees were cut down and then we sprayed pesticides on the remaining vegetation; next thing you know, all the animals that had lived there were just gone.
*4. Chopping off the head of the king put an end to him.
5. The mighty Casey hit the ball out of the park, winning the game by one run.
6. Dorothy's eagerness to get to class on time caused her to ride her bike right through a red light.
7. Taz yelled at the customer just because it was his last day at work so he knew couldn't be fired for it.
8. The dog bit Johann because he pulled its tail.
*9. A single spark started the internal combustion engine.
10. When carbon atoms are arranged in the proper crystalline arrangement, they make a diamond.

MIXED ARGUMENTS

We noted in Chapter 3 the distinction between deductive and inductive arguments. We said that a deductive argument is intended to provide logically *conclusive* support for its conclusion, and that an inductive argument is intended to provide *probable*—not conclusive—support for its conclusion. In Chapters 6 and 7 we discussed deductive reasoning in more detail and ways of evaluating deductive arguments. And here in Chapter 8 we've discussed several forms of inductive reasoning and ways of evaluating them. Since the processes for evaluating deductive and inductive arguments are so different, it makes sense to learn about them separately. But in real life, arguers will very

mixed argument An argument that includes both inductive and deductive elements.

often combine inductive and deductive elements within a single, compound argument. Let's look briefly at the notion of **mixed arguments** and how to evaluate them.

There are no limits to the ways in which arguers may try to combine deductive and inductive elements within a single, mixed argument. One of the simplest ways in which deductive and inductive elements may be combined is seen when one of the *premises* of a categorical syllogism is actually the *conclusion* of an inductive argument—say, an argument that uses enumerative induction. Here's an example:

> In our study, we gave 100 average Canadian consumers a simple quiz about basic science. None of them passed it. It seems average Canadian consumers just don't have an understanding of basic science. Only people who understand science should get to have a say on scientific issues like the safety of genetically modified wheat. So, average Canadians consumers should not have a say on genetically modified wheat.

The first part of that argument is an example of enumerative induction: it's a kind of survey, one that reaches a dramatic conclusion based on a rather small sample:

- *Target population:* Canadian consumer
- *Sample:* 100 Canadian consumers
- *Relevant property:* understanding of basic science
- *Conclusion:* 0 per cent of Canadian consumers understand basic science.

The second part of the argument is a categorical syllogism:

> Premise 1: No Canadian consumers understand basic science.
> Premise 2: All people who should get a say on the safety of genetically modified wheat are people who understand basic science.
> Conclusion: No Canadian consumers are people who should get a say on the safety of genetically modified wheat.

Let's look at those two components of the argument, beginning with the inductive part. How strong is the argument that "no Canadian consumers understand basic science?" The first thing to note, of course, is that the sample is very small: a sample of just 100 people leaves a very large margin of error. We also need more information about whether the sample was random or representative. We would also, ideally, want to ask questions about just what kind of quiz was administered and what the quiz givers count as "basic" science. But even with the minimal information available here, and especially given the small sample, it looks as if this inductive part of the argument is pretty weak.

But let's accept it for now, for the sake of argument, and move on to assess the deductive component of the argument.

Since the conclusion is about Canadian consumers and whether they're the sort who should have a say, we'll assign *S* and *P* (subject and predicate) this way:

S = Canadian consumers
P = people who should get a say on the safety of genetically modified wheat

We'll assign *M* (for middle term) to the term that's left, namely the bit about understanding basic science:

M = people who understand basic science

Next, let's take the categorical syllogism expressed above and put it into standard form, using the letters we just assigned:

No *S* are *M*.
All *P* are *M*.
Therefore, no *S* are *P*.

Now we can ask, is this a valid argument? Let's do a Venn diagram to figure it out. Diagramming the two premises produces a diagram like this:

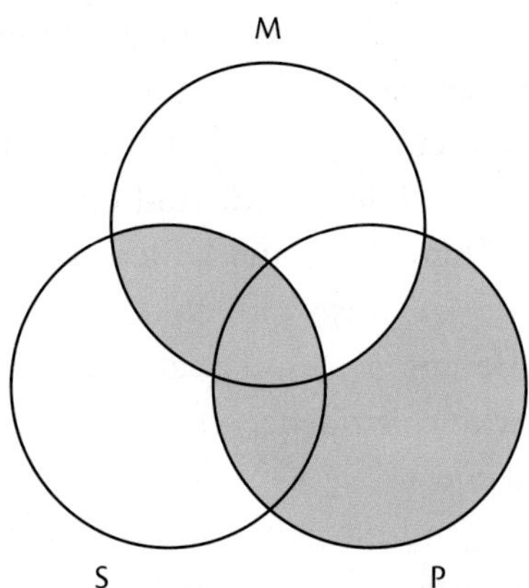

Does this diagram—with the premises drawn in—show the thing that is stated in the conclusion, namely that "No S are P"? Yes, you can clearly see that the area of overlap between the S circle and the P circle is entirely shaded out. It's empty, just as it should be to show that "no S are P." The deductive part of our overall argument, then, is valid.

So, what about our mixed argument as a whole? Well, the deductive part is fine. But since the inductive argument offered in support of one of the premises for the deductive part is quite weak, we should consider this mixed argument, as a whole, to be weak.

SUMMARY

An inductive argument is intended to provide only probable support for its conclusion, being considered strong if it succeeds in providing such support and weak if it does not.

Inductive arguments come in several forms, including enumerative, analogical, and causal. In enumerative induction, we argue from premises about some members of a group to a generalization about the entire group. The entire group is called the *target group*; the observed members of the group, the sample; and the group characteristics we're interested in, the relevant property. An enumerative induction can fail to be strong by having a sample that's too small or not representative. When we draw a conclusion about a target group on the basis of too small a sample, we are said to commit the error of hasty generalization. Opinion polls are enumerative inductive arguments, or the basis of enumerative inductive arguments, and must be judged by the same general criteria used to judge any other enumerative induction.

In analogical induction, or argument by analogy, we reason that since two or more things are similar in several respects, they must be similar in some further respect. We evaluate arguments by analogy according to several criteria: (1) the number of relevant similarities between things being compared, (2) the number of relevant dissimilarities, (3) the number of instances (or cases) of similarities or dissimilarities, and (4) the diversity among the cases.

A causal argument is an inductive argument whose conclusion contains a causal claim. There are several inductive patterns of reasoning used to assess causal connections. These include the Method of Agreement, the Method of Difference, the Method of Agreement and Difference, and the Method of Concomitant Variation. Errors in cause-and-effect reasoning are common. They include misidentifying relevant factors in a causal process, overlooking relevant factors, confusing cause with coincidence, confusing cause with temporal order, and mixing up cause and effect.

Crucial to an understanding of cause-and-effect relationships are the notions of necessary and sufficient conditions. A necessary condition for the occurrence of an event is one without which the event cannot occur. A sufficient condition for the occurrence of an event is one that guarantees that the event occurs.

Mixed arguments are ones that include both deductive and inductive elements within a single argument. These are quite common, as when the conclusion of an inductive argument is used as a premise for a deductive argument, such as a syllogism. In such cases, you will need to use the tools for evaluating both inductive and deductive arguments to determine the quality of the argument as a whole.

Field Problems

1. Devise an extended argument by analogy (250–300 words) to support the idea that giving a nice bottle of wine to your professor halfway through the term, as a token of your appreciation for help during his or her office hours, is just like giving a waiter or waitress a tip. Use several relevant similarities in your argument. Then write a *critique* of your argument (150–200 words), focusing especially on relevant dissimilarities and the number of relevant similarities.
2. Design an opinion poll to determine the percentage of people in the community where you live who believe that university tuition should be frozen at current levels. Specify all of the following parameters: (1) the target group, (2) the makeup and size of the sample, (3) the methods for ensuring a random sample, (4) the methods for ensuring a representative sample, (5) the exact phrasing of the polling question(s), (6) the method for gathering the responses (telephone survey, "man on the street" poll, email questionnaire, etc.), and (7) the acceptable margin of error. Explain the reasons for your choices.
3. Select a causal argument on a political issue from recent op-ed pages (in newspapers or on websites). Then critique it, explaining why it's strong or weak, specifically noting whether it misidentifies or overlooks relevant factors, confuses cause with coincidence, commits the post hoc fallacy, confuses cause and effect, or mishandles or misunderstands necessary and sufficient conditions.
4. Think of a causal claim that you recall being put forward by someone you know—perhaps a claim about what caused their cold, or an accident they saw happen, or their bad grade on a particular test at school. Did they put forward a causal argument, or merely a causal claim? Do you see any evidence of any of the "usual" errors that affect causal reasoning?

Self-Assessment Quiz

1. In enumerative induction, what do we mean by the terms "target group," "sample," and "relevant property"?
2. What is the logical form of enumerative induction, described schematically?
3. What are the two major ways in which an enumerative induction can fail to be strong?

4. In statistical syllogism, what do we mean by the terms *individual*, *group*, *characteristic*, and *proportion*?

For each of the following enumerative inductions, state whether the argument is strong or weak. If it's weak, indicate whether the problem is a sample that's too small, not representative, or both.

5. Look at the evidence! David Milgaard was wrongly convicted of murder in Saskatchewan in 1970. Donald Marshall Jr. was wrongfully convicted of murder in Nova Scotia in 1971. And Guy Paul Morin was wrongfully convicted, in 1994, of the 1984 murder of Christine Jessop in Ontario. People whose last names begin with an *M* get a raw deal from the Canadian justice system!
6. Over 90 per cent of the members of a national women's amateur hockey league (2500 members) are in favour of additional funding for amateur sports. Everyone in my running club is in favour of such funding. And all my pals from the gym are in favour of more funding for amateur sports. The fact is, almost all Canadians who are concerned with their fitness are in favour of additional funding for amateur sport.
7. My neighbour's chihuahua is a hateful little dog. No matter how hard I try to befriend it, it still barks menacingly at me whenever I walk by. It even tried to bite me once! I think all little dogs are just evil.
8. American football fans are a religious bunch. An online poll conducted by *Fox News* got over 1000 responses—and 43 per cent of them said that God directly helps particular quarterbacks win games.
9. I taught Nancy to play tennis last summer, and before long she was kicking my butt at it. And even though she just took up squash this year, she is already talking about joining a competitive league. That girl is good at just about any sport!
10. Media coverage of police brutality in New York has taught me that the cops are not to be trusted under any circumstances. They're just power-hungry bullies who will try to abuse their power whenever they can.

Evaluate each of the following arguments by analogy, indicating (1) the two things being compared, (2) the conclusion, and (3) whether the argument is strong or weak.

11. "Suppose that someone tells me that he has had a tooth extracted without an anaesthetic, and I express my sympathy, and suppose that I am then asked, How do you know that it hurt him? I might reasonably reply, 'Well, I know that it would hurt me. I have been to the dentist and know

how painful it is to have a tooth stopped without an anaesthetic, let alone taken out. And he has the same sort of nervous system as I have. I infer, therefore, that in these conditions he felt considerable pain, just as I should myself.'" (Alfred J. Ayer)

12. "As for one who is choosy about what he learns . . . we shall not call him a lover of learning or a philosopher, just as we shall not say that a man who is difficult about his food is hungry or has an appetite for food. We shall not call him a lover of food but a poor eater. . . . But we shall call a philosopher the man who is easily willing to learn every kind of knowledge, gladly turns to learning things, and is insatiable in this respect." (Socrates)
13. "In crossing a heath, suppose I pitched my foot against a stone, and were asked how the stone came to be there; I might possibly answer, that, for anything I knew to the contrary, it had lain there forever: nor would it perhaps be very easy to show the absurdity of this answer. But suppose I had found a watch upon the ground, and it should be inquired how the watch happened to be in that place; I should hardly think of the answer I had before given, that for anything I knew, the watch might have always been there. . . . There must have existed, at some time, and at some place or other, an artificer or artificers, who formed [the watch] for the purpose which we find it actually to answer; who comprehended its construction, and designed its use. . . . Every indication of contrivance, every manifestation of design, which existed in the watch, exists in the works of nature; with the difference, on the side of nature, of being greater or more, and that in a degree which exceeds all computation." (William Paley, *Natural Theology or Evidences of the Existence and Attributes of the Deity*) *Hint: Paley's conclusion is unstated.

Analyze each of the following causal arguments. Identify the conclusion and whether the argument is weak or strong. If it's weak, explain why with reference to the material in this chapter.

14. Cancer is mainly caused by technology. Cancer rates have risen through the twentieth century, as has our use of technology. Also, the main place people die of cancer is in hospitals, places that are just full of technology these days! Also, there are suspicions that cellphone use can cause brain cancer.
15. Smoking and exposure to second-hand smoke among pregnant women pose a significant risk to both infants and the unborn. According to numerous studies, each year the use of tobacco causes thousands of spontaneous births, infant deaths, and deaths from SIDS. Death rates for fetuses are 35 per cent higher among pregnant women who smoke than among pregnant women who don't smoke.

16. Why are crime rates so high, the economy so bad, and our children so prone to violence, promiscuity, and vulgarity? These social ills have arisen—as they always have—from the "moral vacuum" created when Canadians turn away from religion. Our current slide into chaos started when kids stopped saying "The Lord's Prayer" before class, and families stopped saying grace before dinner. And as God has slowly faded from public life, we have got deeper in the hole.
17. Ken's electronics store wanted to find out how to build the best computer so they conducted a multitude of tests on 20 different hardware configurations of computers. Of the 20 configurations, all of them scored highly on the energy efficiency test except the 1 computer with the newest NVidia graphics card. Thinking there might be a problem with the overall configuration of the computer, Ken decided to put the NVidia graphics card into the other 19 computers, while keeping all their other parts the same. He found that the energy efficiency test scores for all the other computers dropped dramatically after the graphics card was installed. Ken concludes that the newest NVidia graphics card makes computers less energy efficient and that he shouldn't use them.
18. I know for a fact that magnetic bracelets work. I've seen it first-hand! My mom started wearing one last year and she hasn't had a cold since!
19. Yesterday my astrological chart—prepared by a top astrologer—said that I would meet an attractive person today, and I did. Last week, it said I'd come into some money, and I did. (Jack paid me that $100 he owed me.) Now I'm a believer. The stars really do rule.
20. Most of the terminal cancer patients in this ward who had positive attitudes about their disease lived longer than expected. Most of the negative-attitude patients didn't live as long as expected. A positive attitude can increase the life expectancy of people with terminal cancer.

Integrative Exercises

These exercises pertain to material in Chapters 3 and 6–8.

For each of the following arguments, specify the conclusion and premises and say whether it is deductive or inductive. If it's deductive, use Venn diagrams or truth tables to determine its validity. If it's inductive, say whether it's an enumerative, analogical, or causal induction and whether it's strong or weak. If necessary, add implicit premises and conclusions.

1. Whenever George eats peanuts, he gets an allergic reaction. He just got an allergic reaction, so the chocolate bar he just ate must have peanuts in them.
2. Neighbours heard the dog barking just after 7 p.m.—and Mr Levin was found dead just after 8 p.m. This doesn't prove that the barking of the dog killed him, but it does show that the two events—the dog's barking and the death of Mr Levin—were somehow causally linked.
3. If society truly cared about the safety of our children, they would outlaw the civilian use and ownership of guns completely. Since our citizens can still own and use guns for hunting and recreation, our society must not care about the safety of our children.
4. "If we take in hand any volume; of divinity or school metaphysics, for instance; let us ask, Does it contain any abstract reasoning concerning quantity or number? No. Does it contain any experimental reasoning concerning matter of fact and existence? No. Commit it then to the flames; for it can contain nothing but sophistry and illusion." (David Hume)
5. Pharmacists aren't lacking in scientific knowledge. Anyone who has scientific knowledge knows that homeopathic remedies contain no active ingredients. So any pharmacist who sells or recommends a homeopathic remedy is selling or recommending something he or she knows has no active ingredient.
6. The new rules for student loans say that anyone who has missed two or more payments on any of their debts can be denied a loan. But anyone can miss a payment or two; in some cases, it happens because people just can't afford the payments. These new rules are punishing people for being poor.
7. All politicians are corrupt, so some corrupt people are effective leaders. Because, after all, some effective leaders are politicians.
8. If we increase security in the country because of terrorist attacks, our personal freedoms will be reduced. If we do not increase security in the country, terrorist attacks will increase. So either our personal freedoms will be curtailed or terrorist attacks will increase.
9. Because the core values of the Canada Health Act are universality and accessibility, we believe it is crucial that health care in Canada remain a public good, and we reject two-tier health care of any kind.
10. As former prime minister Pierre Elliott Trudeau argued when he was justice minister, "The state has no place in the bedrooms of the nation." This implies that governments should take no notice of people's gender or sexual orientation. When it comes to issuing marriage licences, then, all people must be equal under the law.
11. [Be careful: This one has an unstated conclusion.] The standard of living in Canada ranks among the very highest in the world. Yet that fact

glosses over the terrible living conditions endured by many of Canada's Aboriginal peoples. Despite its promises and obligations, the Canadian government has done little to improve the lot of its Aboriginal citizens, many of whom continue to struggle with poverty, poor health care, and substandard educational opportunities. And many Aboriginal communities continue to be plagued by crime and addiction.

12. Almost all of the owners of restaurants, bars, and clubs in Halifax are opposed to the city's total ban on smoking in indoor public places. The vast majority of Haligonians simply do not like this law.
13. Every student Maria knows who wears glasses also has a high grade-point average. So most students who wear glasses probably have high grade-point averages.
14. "The evils of the world are due to moral defects quite as much as to lack of intelligence. But the human race has not hitherto discovered any method of eradicating moral defects. . . . Intelligence, on the contrary, is easily improved by methods known to every competent educator. Therefore, until some method of teaching virtue has been discovered, progress will have to be sought by improvement of intelligence rather than of morals." (Bertrand Russell)
15. Television is destroying morality in this country. As TV violence, sex, and vulgarity have increased, so have violent crimes, sexual assaults, and violations of obscenity laws.
16. When dolphins are rewarded with food that they like, they are more likely to perform tricks. When provided with food that they didn't like, they often refused to perform any tricks altogether. So, researchers concluded that good food makes dolphins perform tricks.
17. "Some people would have us believe that the Supreme Court of Canada, emboldened by the Charter of Rights and Freedoms, has adopted an increasingly 'activist' stance and is now usurping powers that should legitimately be exercised by the legislature. . . . [But] it is highly misleading to speak as though the Supreme Court is taking power away from the legislature when it rules on charter cases. The role of the Supreme Court is to decide whether the legislature has satisfied the conditions required for the creation of legitimate law. Thus the only power that the Supreme Court takes away, when it rules against the legislature is the power to engage in an illegitimate use of force. And this is not a power that anyone should want the legislature to have." (Joseph Heath, "Why Have a Constitution at All?" *Policy Options*, October 2003)
18. When asked whether or not they recreationally smoked marijuana, 90 per cent of the students at QWE Community College said "yes." A recent scientific study shows that students who smoke marijuana recreationally end

up trying harder drugs. Since George will be attending QWE Community College, he will end up trying hard drugs.

19. The expansion of the new airport, on an island near downtown, has created serious traffic congestion. There's always a huge lineup of taxis near the ferry terminal waiting to pick up arriving passengers, and the excess traffic often backs up into neighbouring streets. I've lived here for years and have never seen such serious traffic delays downtown. Now, almost every weekday, traffic is a nightmare.
20. Look, you're either going to come out with us tonight or you're going to stay home. If you come out with us, you won't be able to study for tomorrow's quiz and so you'll probably fail it. If you stay home, you'll be able to study. But even if you study, the professor is totally unfair so you'll probably fail anyway. Either way, you're probably going to fail.

Writing Assignments

1. In a 250-word essay, use an enumerative inductive argument to argue that your campus is (or is not) relatively free of crime. Feel free to invent some plausible data to flesh out your argument.
2. Using either enumerative induction or argument by analogy, write a 500-word rebuttal to Essay 6 ("Raspberry Ketone, Pure Green Coffee Extract, Garcinia Cambogia, Weight Loss, and the Fallacy of Appealing to Authority") in Appendix A.
3. In a short essay (400–500 words), argue for or against one of the following claims. At the end of your essay, indicate in point form what type of argument you have produced (inductive or deductive, analogical, causal, etc.) and what the key strength of your argument is.
   - Canada is the best place in the world to live.
   - Everyone does what is in his or her own best interests.
   - Deadbeat dads (fathers who don't or won't pay child support that they are legally obligated to pay) should be put in jail.
   - Racial discrimination is not a problem at your school.
   - Competition is always a good thing.
   - Pornography should be banned on university campuses.

PART FOUR

EXPLANATIONS

9 INFERENCE TO THE BEST EXPLANATION

CHAPTER OBJECTIVES

Explanations and Inference

You will be able to

- define *inference to the best explanation* and understand how it differs from other kinds of induction.
- clarify what an explanation (including theoretical explanation) is and how it differs from an argument.
- appreciate how inference to the best explanation is used in all disciplines and in everyday life.
- demonstrate how to use inference to the best explanation in many different situations.

Theories and Consistency

You will be able to

- check an explanation for internal and external consistency.

Theories and Criteria

You will be able to

- understand the importance of using criteria to judge the adequacy of theories.
- list and explain the five criteria of adequacy.
- apply the criteria of adequacy to simple causal theories.
- define and explain an *ad hoc hypothesis*.

Telling Good Theories from Bad

You will be able to

- memorize and explain the four steps in the TEST formula.
- recognize the importance of considering alternative explanations.
- use the TEST formula to evaluate theories.

Let's take stock of the inductive terrain travelled thus far. In Chapter 8 we closely examined the nature and uses of inductive reasoning. We were reminded that a deductive argument, unlike an inductive one, is intended to provide logically conclusive support for its conclusion. If it succeeds in providing such support, it is said to be valid; if it does not, it is invalid. If a valid argument has true premises, it is said to be sound. But an inductive argument is intended to supply only probable support for its conclusion. If it manages to provide such support, it is said to be strong; if it does not, it is weak. The conclusion of an inductively strong argument is simply more likely to be true than not. If a strong argument has true premises, it's said to be cogent.

We also saw that inductive arguments come in several forms. One of them is enumerative induction, in which we reason from premises about *some* members of a group to a conclusion, or generalization, about the group *as a whole*. All the swans you have ever seen are white, so you conclude that *all* swans are white. Forty per cent of the students at your university have a driver's licence, so you conclude that 40 per cent of all students everywhere must have a driver's licence. (Whether these enumerative inductive arguments are strong or cogent is another matter.)

Another kind of inductive argument is argument by analogy (or analogical induction), in which we reason that since two or more things are similar in several respects, they must be similar in some additional respect. In an analogical induction you might argue that (1) since humans can move about, solve mathematical equations, win chess games, and feel pain, *and* (2) since computers (or robots) are like humans in that they can move about, solve mathematical equations, and win chess games, it is therefore probable that computers can also feel pain. Analogical induction, like all inductive reasoning, can establish conclusions only with a degree of probability.

REVIEW NOTES

A Look Back at the Basics

- *Statement (claim):* An assertion that something is or is not the case.
- *Premise:* A statement given in support of another statement.
- *Conclusion:* A statement that premises are intended to support.
- *Argument:* A group of statements in which some of them (the premises) are intended to support another of them (the conclusion).
- *Indicator words:* Words that frequently accompany arguments and signal that a premise or conclusion is present.
- *Deductive argument:* An argument intended to provide conclusive support for its conclusion.
- *Inductive argument:* An argument intended to provide probable support for its conclusion.

Finally, we saw that causal arguments—inductive arguments whose conclusions contain causal claims—can be enumerative inductions, analogical inductions, or arguments that rely on Mill's methods and similar kinds of inferences. Reasoning well about causal connections means avoiding numerous common errors, including misidentifying or overlooking relevant factors, confusing coincidence with cause, and committing the post hoc fallacy.

inference to the best explanation A form of inductive reasoning in which we reason from premises about a state of affairs to an explanation for that state of affairs:

Phenomenon Q.
E provides the best explanation for Q.
Therefore, it is probable that E is true.

We noted only in passing that there is another kind of inductive reasoning that is so important that all of Part 4 of this book is devoted to it: **inference to the best explanation**. Well, here we are in Part 4, and it's time to delve deep into this kind of inductive reasoning, perhaps the most commonly used form of inference and arguably the most empowering in daily life.

EXPLANATIONS AND INFERENCE

Recall from Chapter 1 that an explanation is a statement (or statements) asserting why or how something is the case. For example: the bucket leaks because there's a hole in it. He was sad because his dog had died. She broke the pipe by hitting it with a wrench. These explanations and all others are intended to clarify and elucidate, and thus to increase our understanding. Remember too our discussion of the important distinction between an explanation and an argument. Whereas an explanation tells us *why or how something is the case*, an argument gives us reasons for believing *that something is the case*.

As you've probably already guessed, there are also different kinds of explanations (see the box "The Lore of Explanations" on page 351). For instance, some explanations are what we might call procedural—they try to explain how something is done or how an action is carried out. ("She opened up the engine, then examined the valves, and then checked the carburetor.") Some are interpretive—they try to explain the meaning of terms or states of affairs. ("This word means 'fancy' or 'showy.'") And some are functional—they try to explain how something functions. ("The heart circulates and oxygenates the blood.")

theoretical explanation A theory, or hypothesis, that tries to explain why something is the way it is, why something is the case, or why something happened.

But the kind of explanation we're concerned with here—and the kind we bump into most often—is what we'll call, for lack of something snappier, a **theoretical explanation**. Such explanations are theories, or hypotheses, that try to explain why something is the way it is, why something is the case, or why something happened. In this category we must include all explanations intended to explain the cause of events—the causal explanations that are so important to both science and daily life. Theoretical explanations, of course, are claims. They assert that something is or is not the case.

Now, even though an explanation is not an argument, an explanation can be *part* of an argument. It can be the heart of the kind of inductive argument known as *inference to the best explanation*. And in this kind of inference, the explanations we use are theoretical explanations.

In inference to the best explanation, *we reason from premises about a state of affairs to an explanation for that state of affairs.* The premises are statements about observations or other evidence to be explained. The explanation is a claim about why the state of affairs is the way it is. The key question that this type of inference tries to answer is "What is the best explanation for the existence or nature of this state of affairs?" The best explanation is the one most likely to be true, even though there is no guarantee of its truth as there is in deductive inference.

> "There is nothing more practical than a good theory."
>
> —*Leonid Ilyich Brezhnev*

Recall that enumerative induction has this pattern:

> X per cent of the observed members of group A have property P.
> Therefore, X per cent of all members of group A probably have property P.

And recall that analogical induction has this pattern:

> Thing A has properties P_1, P_2, and P_3, plus the property P_4.
> Thing B has properties P_1, P_2, and P_3.
> Therefore, thing B probably has property P_4.

Inference to the best explanation, however, has this pattern:

> I've noticed phenomenon Q.
> E provides the best explanation for Q.
> Therefore, it is probable that E is true.

For example:

> The new quarterback dropped the ball again. The best explanation for that screw-up would be if he's nervous. So I think he's definitely nervous.

> The best explanation for Maria's absence today is that she's angry at the boss. Yeah, she's mad at the boss alright.

> The defendant's fingerprints were all over the crime scene, the police found the victim's blood on his shirt, and he was in possession of the murder weapon. The only explanation for all this that makes any sense is that the defendant actually committed the crime. So, he's guilty.

If the explanations in these arguments really are the best, then the arguments are inductively strong. And if the premises are also true, then the arguments are cogent. If they are cogent, we are justified in believing that the explanations for the phenomena are in fact correct.

Notice that an inference to the best explanation always goes "beyond the evidence"—it tries to explain facts but does so by positing a theory that is not derived entirely from those facts. It tries to understand the known by putting

forth—through inference and imagination—a theoretical pattern that encompasses both the known and unknown. It proposes a plausible pattern that expands our understanding.

The fact that there are *best* explanations, of course, implies that not all explanations for a state of affairs are created equal; some are better than others. Just because you've devised an explanation for something doesn't mean that you're justified in believing that the explanation is the right one. If other explanations are just as good, your explanation is in doubt. If other explanations are better than yours, you are not justified in believing yours. But much of the time, after further study or thought, you can reasonably conclude that a particular explanation really is the best explanation. (We'll see later how to evaluate the relative worth of explanations.) In this way you can come to understand the state of affairs better than you did before.

Inference to the best explanation probably seems very familiar to you. That's because you use it all the time—and need it all the time. Often when we try to understand something in the world, we construct explanations for why this something is the way it is, and we try to determine which of these explanations is the best. Devising explanations helps increase our understanding by fitting our experiences and background knowledge into a coherent pattern. At every turn we are confronted with phenomena that we can only fully understand by explaining them.

Sometimes we're barely aware that we're using inference to the best explanation. If we awaken and see that the streets outside are wet, we may immediately posit this explanation: it's been raining. Without thinking much about it, we may also quickly consider whether a better explanation is that a street-sweeper machine has wet the street. Just as quickly we may dismiss this explanation because we see that the houses and cars are also wet. After reasoning in this fashion, we may decide to carry an umbrella that day.

REVIEW NOTES

The Lore of Explanations

An explanation is a statement (or statements) asserting why or how something is the case. In traditional terminology, that which is to be explained in an explanation is called the *explanandum*, and that which does the explaining is called the *explanans*. Take this explanation: "The dog barked because a prowler was nearby." The explanandum is "the dog barked," and the explanans is "a prowler was nearby."

You can categorize explanations in many ways, depending on the kind of explanandum you're interested in. Here are a few of the more common categories:

- Teleological explanations try to explain the purpose of something, how it functions, or how it fits into a plan. (*Telos* is a Greek word meaning "end" or "purpose.")

  Example: The wall switch is there so you can turn off the lamp from across the room.
  Example: These wildflowers are here as a blessing from God.

- Interpretive explanations concern the meaning of terms or states of affairs. These explanations seek to understand not the purpose or cause of something, but rather its sense or semantic meaning.

  Example: When Mary smiled, she was indicating her agreement.
  Example: *Effect* means to accomplish, but *affect* means to influence.

- Procedural explanations try to explain how something is done or how an action is carried out.

  Example: To stop the chemical reaction, Ariana added sulphur.
  Example: He paid his taxes online by downloading the forms and then using his credit card number.

In all cases, remember that an example of an explanation is not always an example of a *good* explanation!

Let's consider a more elaborate example. Say you discover that your car won't start in the morning; that's the phenomenon to be explained. You would like to know why it won't start (the explanation for the failure) because you can't repair the car unless you know what the problem is. You know that there are several possible explanations or theories:

> "A superstition is a premature explanation that overstays its time."
>
> —*George Iles*

1. The battery is dead.
2. The fuel tank is empty.
3. The starter has malfunctioned.
4. A vandal has sabotaged the car.
5. All or several of the above.

So you try to figure out which theory is the most plausible, that is, most likely to be true. Let's say you see right away that there is snow around the car

FOOD FOR THOUGHT

Darwin and the Best Explanation

Charles Darwin (1809–82) offered the theory of evolution by natural selection as the best explanation for a wide variety of natural phenomena. He catalogued an extensive list of facts about nature and showed that his theory explained them well. He argued, however, that the alternative theory of the day—the view that God independently created various species—did not explain them. Darwin declared:

> It can hardly be supposed that a false theory would explain, in so satisfactory a manner as does the theory of natural selection, the several large classes of facts above specified. It has recently been objected that this is an unsafe method of arguing; but it is a method used in judging of the common events of life, and has often been used by the greatest natural philosophers.[1]

The blue-footed booby was one of the many species collected by Charles Darwin in the Galapagos Islands.

from yesterday's snowstorm—but there are no footprints (except yours) and no signs of tampering anywhere. So you dismiss theory 4. You remember that you filled up the gas tank yesterday, the fuel gauge says that the tank is full, and you don't see any signs of leakage. So you can safely ignore theory 2. You notice that the lights, heater, and radio work fine, and the battery gauge indicates a fully charged battery. So you discard theory 1. When you try to start the car, you hear a clicking sound like the one you heard when the starter had failed previously. Among the theories you started with, then, theory 3 now seems the most plausible. This means that theory 5 also cannot be correct since it entails two or more of the theories and you've already ruled out all but one.

If you wanted to, you could state your argument like this:

(1) Your car won't start in the morning.
(2) The theory that the starter has malfunctioned is the best explanation for the car's not starting in the morning.
(3) Therefore, it's probable that the malfunctioning starter caused the car not to start in the morning.

Note what you've done here: you've started with a description of a situation, evaluated possible explanations, and reasoned your way to a causal conclusion.

In science, where inference to the best explanation is an essential tool, usually the theories of interest are causal theories, in which events are the things to be explained and the proposed causes of the events are the explanations. Just

FOOD FOR THOUGHT

Sherlock Holmes and Inference to the Best Explanation

CREDIT: Jack Ziegler/The New Yorker Collection/The Cartoon Bank

The fictional character Sherlock Holmes owed his great success as a detective primarily to inference to the best explanation. He was so good at this kind of inference that people (especially his sidekick, Dr Watson) were frequently astonished at his skill. Holmes, however, was guilty of spreading some confusion about his ability. He called his method deduction, though it was clearly inductive. Here is Holmes in action:

> I knew you came from Afghanistan. From long habit the train of thoughts ran so swiftly through my mind that I arrived at the conclusion without being conscious of intermediate steps. There were such steps, however. The train of reasoning ran, "Here is a gentleman of medical type, but with the air of a military man. Clearly an army doctor, then. He has just come from the tropics, for his face is dark, and that is not the natural tint of his skin, for his wrists are fair. He has undergone hardship and sickness, as his haggard face says clearly. His left arm has been injured. He holds it in a stiff and unnatural manner. Where in the tropics would an English army doctor have seen much hardship and got his arm wounded? Clearly in Afghanistan."[2]

Here Holmes explains how he knew that a man had "gone about in fear of some personal attack within the last twelve-month":

> "You have a very handsome stick," I answered. "By the inscription I observed that you had not had it more than a year. But you have taken some pains to bore the head of it and pour melted lead into the hole so as to make it a formidable weapon. I argued that you would not take such precautions unless you had some danger to fear."[3]

as we do in everyday life, scientists often consider several competing theories for the same event or phenomenon. Then—through scientific testing and careful thinking—they systematically eliminate inadequate theories and eventually arrive at the one that's rightly regarded as the best of the bunch. Using this form of inference, scientists discover planets, viruses, cures, subatomic particles, black holes—and many things that can't even be directly observed.

And then there are all those other occupations and professions that rely on inference to the best explanation. Physicians use it to pinpoint the cause of multiple symptoms in patients. Police detectives use it to track down lawbreakers. Judges and juries use it to determine the guilt or innocence of accused persons. And mechanics use it to determine why a car is failing to function properly.

With so many people in so many areas of inquiry using inference to the best explanation, you would expect the world to be filled with countless theories proposed by innumerable people looking to explain all sorts of things.

And so there are. Here's a brief table of notable or interesting proposed theories and the phenomena they are meant to explain:

Theory	To Explain . . .
Atomic	Behaviour of subatomic particles
Germ	Spread of disease
HIV	Cause of AIDS
Oedipus complex	Behaviour of men and boys
Placebo effect	Apparent cure of disease
Bleak winters	Why Canadians are funny
Violent video games	Violence in children
El Niño	Bad weather
El Niño	Good weather
Incumbent politicians	A bad economy
Political sex scandals	Immoral behaviour of young people

Of course, it's often easy to make up theories to explain things we don't understand. The harder job is sorting out good theories from bad, a topic we'll explore more fully later in this chapter.

EXERCISE 9.1

Answers to exercises marked with an asterisk (*) may be found in Appendix B, Answers to Exercises.

1. What is an explanation?
2. What is inference to the best explanation?
3. Is inference to the best explanation inductive or deductive?
*4. What is it that theoretical explanations attempt to explain?
5. What is the basic logical pattern of inference to the best explanation? For enumerative induction? For analogical induction?
6. Under what circumstances can an inference to the best explanation be deemed strong? Cogent?

7. What is a teleological explanation? Interpretive explanation? Procedural explanation?
*8. What is a causal explanation? Are causal explanations used in inference to the best explanation?
9. How does the kind of explanation used in inference to the best explanation differ from a procedural explanation?
10. Have you used inference to the best explanation today? If so, how did you use it? (Give an example from the events of your day.)
11. Give an example of an occupation or profession, members of which make regular use of inference to the best explanation in their work.

EXERCISE 9.2

For each of the following explanations, say what state of affairs is being explained and what the explanation is.

1. Criminal behaviour is down these days because Canada's robust social "safety net" means that fewer people are driven by poverty to a life of crime.
*2. We all know that the polar bear is endangered, and the only explanation for that is the thinning of arctic ice, caused by global warming.
3. Why is Georgia wearing orange goggles? Because she's a bit eccentric, and she likes how they look.
4. Students love Professor Walton's class because she takes dull material and makes it interesting.
*5. Yes, I can tell you why the "hot" water from your faucet isn't very hot: your hot-water heater is over 20 years old and just can't keep up with modern water usage patterns.
6. Many consider crows to be one of the smartest animals in the world. They have been shown to be able to make and use rudimentary tools, and can even recognize human faces.
7. Americans are fond of the death penalty, but Europeans and Canadians are not. Americans just never got over the old Wild West eye-for-an-eye mentality. Europeans never had a Wild West, and Canada's West was kept orderly by the North West Mounted Police, the police force that eventually became the RCMP.
*8. Boy, are my hands shaking! I think I've been drinking too much coffee.
9. Corporate CEOs make so much money because the skills they have are highly in demand.
10. You don't understand . . . Jimmy *had* to sell the restaurant! "The Don" made him an offer he couldn't refuse!

EXERCISE 9.3

For each of the following, determine whether the type of explanation offered is theoretical (the kind used in inference to the best explanation) or non-theoretical (e.g., teleological, interpretive, procedural). Be careful to note any borderline cases (explanations that could be either theoretical or non-theoretical).

1. Dean moved to New York so that he could be closer to his son.
2. Homeopathic treatments are controversial because, while such treatments have many fans, scientists say they are entirely without scientific merit.
3. Ethics is the critical study of morality.

*4. Horatio caught a cold because he stood outside in the cold rain.

5. There is no peace in the Middle East—and there never will be—because of the stubbornness of both sides in the conflict.
6. A cat that has dilated pupils, an arched back, and ears folded all the way back is one that is ready to pounce.

*7. When you experience memory loss that can only mean one thing: Alzheimer's disease.

8. He broke the lock and pushed open the door—that's how he got in.
9. He did well on his essay by starting it early, writing a clear outline, researching the topic, and paying attention to how he expressed his ideas.
10. He keeps the music box on his desk because it reminds him of the love of his long lost love.
11. The towel is wet! Someone must have used the shower while we were gone.

*12. That painting is without vibrancy or cohesion. Just look at the dull colours and mishmash of forms.

13. Barry is single because he doesn't treat women well.
14. Sam has been weight training, so she's pretty buff.
15. Blech! I got food poisoning after eating a bad burger at the campus pub.
16. No one noticed the comet before because of cloud cover.
17. I always wear these socks when I play hockey—for good luck!

EXERCISE 9.4

In each of the following examples, a state of affairs is described. Devise two theories to explain each one. Include one theory that you consider plausible and one theory that you think is not plausible.

1. One of Harry Houdini's most famous acts was to free himself from a straightjacket while hanging from a rope in the middle of the street. Audiences were astounded by the feat and left wondering how such a thing was possible.

*2. When Jack came home, he noticed the window in the kitchen was broken, there were muddy footprints on the kitchen floor, and some valuable silverware was missing.
3. Mutilated cows have been found on the outskirts of several towns in western Canada. In each case organs are missing from the carcasses. There are never any signs of vehicle tracks or footprints. The cause of death is unknown. The method used to remove the organs is also unknown, although the wounds show indications that precise surgical tools were used.
4. Many Canadians are now avoiding travel to African countries. .
5. During the 1980s, the demand for food assistance rose dramatically and a massive charitable food-assistance system emerged.
*6. Alice has been taking vitamin C every day for a year, and during that time she has not had a cold or a sore throat.
7. I drank six glasses of red wine and ate a bag of chips last night. And this morning I woke up with a headache.
8. Scientists have discovered that there is a direct correlation between fat in people's diets and heart disease. The more fat, the greater the risk of heart disease.
9. Small, local restaurants in my area have all been closing down one by one over the past six months. None of the owners have given any explanation as to why. They've just gone without even saying goodbye. Some of my neighbours have noted that a lawyer who is notorious for having connections with the Mafia is buying up all the now-vacant locations.

EXERCISE 9.5

Read each of the following passages and answer these questions:

1. What is the phenomenon being explained?
2. What theory is suggested as a possible explanation for the phenomenon?
3. Is the theory plausible? If not, why not?
4. Is there a plausible theory that the writer has overlooked? If so, what is it?

Passage 1
Students who major in philosophy tend to do very well on the Law School Admissions Test (LSAT) and Medical College Admissions Test (MCAT). This is because studying philosophy gives students a chance to practise the abstract reasoning skills that are the key to success on such tests.

Passage 2
"Shark attacks around the world declined in 2003 for a third straight year, partly because swimmers and surfers grew more accustomed to thinking of the ocean as a wild and dangerous place. . . .

"The University of Florida, which houses the International Shark Attack File, said there were 55 unprovoked attacks worldwide, down from 63 reported in 2002 and lower than the previous year's 68 attacks.

"Four people were killed, compared to three in 2002, four in 2001 and 11 in the year 2000.

"Normally, scientists do not put much stock in year-to-year fluctuations in the number of attacks because they can be affected by such things as the weather and oceanographic conditions that drive bait fish closer to shore.

"But the third consecutive year of decline could indicate a longer term trend, the university said.

"'I think people are beginning to get a little more intelligent about when and where they enter the water,' George Burgess, director of the International Shark Attack File, said in a statement.

"'There seems to be more of an understanding that when we enter the sea, it's a wilderness experience and we're intruders in that environment.'"[4]

Passage 3

"Women who have been coloring their hair for 24 years or more have a higher risk of developing a cancer called non-Hodgkin lymphoma, researchers reported.

"They said their study of 1,300 women could help explain a mysterious rise in the number of cases of the cancer that affects the lymphatic system.

"Writing in the *American Journal of Epidemiology*, they said women who dyed their hair starting before 1980 were one-third more likely to develop non-Hodgkin lymphoma, or NHL, and those who used the darkest dyes for more than 25 years were twice as likely to develop the cancer.

"'Women who used darker permanent hair coloring products for more than 25 years showed the highest increased risk,' Tongzhang Zheng, associate professor of epidemiology and environmental health at Yale School of Medicine, said in a statement.

"Cancer experts note that a person's absolute risk of developing lymphoma is very low, so doubling that risk still means a woman who dyes her hair is very unlikely to develop lymphoma."[5]

Passage 4

In Canada, women are wildly under-represented on corporate boards of directors. Despite making up more than half the population, and a growing proportion of business-school graduates, women make up only about 20 per cent of the boards of publicly traded companies. But the reason is clear: women simply don't have business instincts required to be involved in the crucial task of guiding a big company. Besides, women generally don't want to be on boards—it seems like that's just not the kind of role women want. If they did want to play that kind of role, there would be more of them actively seeking board positions.

Abductive Reasoning

The process involved in making an inference to the best explanation is sometimes referred to by philosophers as **abduction**, or **abductive reasoning**. Abductive reasoning involves looking at a phenomenon, or a set of circumstances, and putting forward a hypothesis as to what would be a good explanation for that phenomenon or those circumstances.

abduction (abductive reasoning) The form of reasoning used when putting forward a hypothesis as to what would explain a particular phenomenon or set of circumstances.

For example, imagine you're at home and you hear a loud bang outside. Your mind immediately generates some possible explanations—some potential sources of such a noise. Maybe it occurs to you that the noise might have been produced by a car backfiring. You then have the option of looking outside to verify your hypothesis, or looking for other evidence that might tend to confirm or disconfirm it. Are there any cars on the street?

Abduction is sometimes half-seriously referred to as a process that involves making a guess. And it's true that abduction involves something like guesswork: if the facts of the case pointed to one, and only one, possible explanation, then we would be dealing with deduction rather than abduction. But although abduction involves taking a leap, it is not a leap into thin air. Our "guesswork" in such cases should be guided by our background knowledge and, where possible, by experience. If we have an upset stomach, our abductive reasoning about its cause will be guided by our knowledge of what sorts of things can and cannot cause an upset stomach. Of course, our background knowledge can sometimes be misleading, and our experience may be insufficient.

We can formalize the process of abduction as follows:

O = an observation (the phenomenon that needs to be explained)
T = a background theory (about how some part of the world works)
E = an explanation (of the observation)

In terms of the example cited above:

O = a bang outside
T = cars sometimes backfire, making a bang
E = a car backfired outside your house

The process of abduction involves first asking, "Is E consistent with T?" In other words, does E fit with your background knowledge of what sorts of things make loud bangs? Second, abduction involves asking, "Would O follow from E and T together?" In other words, if in fact cars backfiring sometimes make a bang, and if a car backfired outside your house, is it true that you would then hear a bang? That seems quite likely, so E is a pretty good explanation of O in this case.

But of course, that's just a start. Several possible Es may satisfy these conditions; lots may be consistent with both the initial observation and with your background knowledge. You must therefore use some commonsense to weed out all sorts of highly improbable possibilities (e.g., a meteor just landed outside your house). Once you've narrowed it down a bit—and your brain may well do that automatically—you can apply more formal rules, like our criteria of adequacy.

THEORIES AND CONSISTENCY

Very often we may propose a theory as an explanation for a phenomenon, or we may have a theory presented to us for consideration. In either case, we will likely be dealing with an argument in the form of inference to the best explanation. The conclusion of the argument will always say, in effect, *this* theory is the best explanation of the facts. And we will be on the hot seat trying to decide if it really is. How do we do that?

> "In making theories, keep a window open so that you can throw one out if necessary."
>
> —*Bela Schick*

The work is not always easy, but there are special criteria we can use to get the job done. Before we apply these criteria, though, we have to make sure that the theory in question meets the minimum requirement of *consistency*. A theory that does not meet this minimum requirement is worthless, so there is no need to use the special criteria to evaluate the theory or to compare it to other available theories. A theory that meets the requirement is at least eligible for further consideration. Here we are concerned with both *internal* and *external* consistency. A theory that is internally consistent is consistent with itself—it's free of contradictions. A theory that is externally consistent is consistent with the data it's supposed to explain—it fully accounts for the observable data.

If we show that a theory contains an internal contradiction, we have refuted it. A theory that implies that something both is and is not the case cannot possibly be true. By exposing an internal contradiction, Galileo once refuted Aristotle's famous theory of motion, a long-respected hypothesis that had stood tall for centuries. He showed that the theory implied two contradictory things, namely that a large, light object falls both faster and slower than a small, heavy one. Those things can't both be true, so there's a fatal internal contradiction in Aristotle's theory.

If a theory is externally inconsistent, we have reason to believe that it's false. Suppose you leave your car parked on the street overnight and the next morning discover that (1) the windshield has a large round hole in it, (2) there's blood

REVIEW NOTES

Minimum Requirement: Consistency

- *Internal consistency:* A theory that is internally consistent is free of contradictions.
- *External consistency:* A theory that is externally consistent is consistent with the data it's supposed to explain.

on the steering wheel, and (3) there's a brick on the front seat. And let's say that your friend Charlie offers this theory to explain these facts: someone threw a brick through your windshield. What would you think about this theory?

You would probably think that Charlie had not been paying attention. His theory is consistent with the fact that the windshield is broken, and it would explain why there's a brick on the seat. And it's not inconsistent with the observation of blood, though it doesn't explain it, either. But most important, Charlie's theory (that someone threw a brick—a sharp-edged, rectangular object—through your windshield) is inconsistent with the fact that the hole in the windshield is round. Charlie's theory is a good try, but it doesn't work. It's externally inconsistent—inconsistent with the data. Keep looking for a better answer!

THEORIES AND CRITERIA

For a moment let's return to our example, discussed earlier in this chapter, of the car that won't start. Recall that we examined five possible explanations for the non-start phenomenon:

1. The battery is dead.
2. The fuel tank is empty.
3. The starter has malfunctioned.
4. A vandal has sabotaged the car.
5. All or several of the above.

But what if someone suggested that our analysis of this problem was incomplete because we failed to consider several other possible theories that are at least as plausible as these five? Consider these, for example:

6. Each night, you are sabotaging your own car while you sleepwalk.
7. Your 90-year-old uncle, who lives 1000 kilometres away from you, has secretly been visiting at night and going for joyrides in your car, thus damaging the engine.

8. A poltergeist (a noisy, mischievous ghost) has damaged the car's carburetor.
9. Yesterday, you scrambled the electrical system by accidentally driving the car through an alternative space–time dimension.

What do you think of these theories? More specifically, are the last four theories *really* at least as plausible as the first five? If you think so, *why*? If you think not, *why not*?

A critical perspective is a good start. But next we want to give you some specific tools that you can use to evaluate theories. Remember that the strangeness of a theory is no good reason to discount it. It will not do simply to say that theories 6 to 9 are too weird to be true. In the history of science plenty of bizarre theories have turned out to be correct. (Quantum theory in physics, for example, is about as weird as you can get.) Earlier we concluded that theory 3 was better (more likely to be true) than theories 1, 2, 4, and 5. But what criteria did we use to arrive at this judgment? And on the basis of what criteria can we say that theory 3 is any better than theories 6 to 9? There must be *some* criteria because it is implausible that every theory is equally correct. Surely there is a difference in quality between a theory that explains rainfall by positing some natural meteorological forces and one that alleges that Donald Duck causes weather phenomena.

A simplistic answer to the problem of theory choice is this: just weigh the evidence for each theory, and the theory with the most evidence wins. As we will soon see, the amount or degree of evidence that a theory has is indeed a crucial factor—but it cannot be the sole criterion by which we assess explanations. Throughout the history of science, major theories—from the heliocentric theory of the solar system to Einstein's general theory of relativity—have never been established by empirical evidence alone.

criteria of adequacy The standards used to judge the worth of explanatory theories. They include *testability*, *fruitfulness*, *scope*, *simplicity*, and *conservatism*.

CREDIT: © AF Archive/Alamy

Some think that the technology may someday exist to enter the human mind through dream invasion, as depicted in the film *Inception*.

Fortunately, there are reasonable criteria and reliable procedures for judging the merits of eligible theories and for arriving at a defensible judgment of which theory is best. The **criteria of adequacy** are the essential tools of science and have been used (sometimes implicitly) by scientists throughout history to uncover the best explanations for all sorts of events and states of affairs. Science, though, doesn't own these criteria. They are as useful—and as used—among non-scientists as they are among men and women of science.

Applying the criteria of adequacy to a set of theories constitutes the ultimate test of a theory's value, for *the best theory is the eligible theory that meets the criteria of adequacy better than any of its competitors*. Here, *eligible* means that the theory has already met the minimum requirement for consistency.

All of this implies that the evaluation of a particular theory is not complete until alternative, or competing, theories are considered. As we've seen, there is seemingly no limit to the number of theories that could be offered to explain a given set of data. The main challenge is to give a fair assessment of the relevant theories in relation to each other. To fail to somehow address the alternatives is to overlook or deny relevant evidence, to risk biased conclusions, and to court error. Such failure is probably the most common error in the appraisal of theories.

A theory judged by these criteria to be the best explanation for certain facts is worthy of our belief, and we may legitimately claim to know that such a theory is true. But the theory is not then necessarily or certainly true in the way that the conclusion of a sound deductive argument is necessarily or certainly true. Inference to the best explanation, like other forms of induction, cannot guarantee the truth of the best explanation. That is, it is not truth-preserving. The best theory we have may actually be false. Nevertheless, we would have excellent reasons for supposing our best theory to be a true theory.

The criteria of adequacy are *testability*, *fruitfulness*, *scope*, *simplicity*, and *conservatism*. Let's examine each one in detail.

FOOD FOR THOUGHT

Inference to the Best Explanation and the External World

In Chapters 10 and 11 we will explore in detail how inference to the best explanation can be used to tackle some big issues. Here we just want to mention one of the "big questions" to which philosophers and other thinkers have applied inference to the best explanation.

A problem that has historically occupied thinkers in the history of philosophy is whether we have any good reasons to believe that there is a world outside our own thoughts. That is, is there an *external world* independent of the way we represent it to ourselves? Some people have denied that we have any such good reasons because we can never get "outside our skins" to objectively compare our subjective experiences with reality. All we know is the nature of our perceptions—which may or may not be linked to the "real world" in any way.

To this puzzle many philosophers have applied inference to the best explanation. They argue that we can indeed know that there is an external reality because that belief is the best explanation of the peculiar pattern of our perceptions. In other words, the best explanation—though admittedly not the only *possible* explanation—of why we seem to see a tree in front of us is that there *really is a real tree in front of us.*

Testability

testability A criterion of adequacy for judging the worth of theories. A testable theory is one in which there is some way to determine whether the theory is true or false—that is, it predicts something other than what it was introduced to explain.

Most of the theories that we encounter every day and all the theories that scientists take seriously are **testable**—*there is some way to determine whether the theories are true or false.* If a theory is untestable—if there is no possible procedure for checking its truth—then it is worthless as an explanatory theory. Suppose someone says that an invisible, undetectable spirit is causing your headaches. What possible test could we perform to tell if the spirit actually exists? None. So the spirit theory is entirely empty; we can assign no weight to such a claim.

Here's another way to look at it. Theories are explanations, and explanations are designed to increase our understanding of the world. But an untestable theory does not—and cannot—explain anything. It is equivalent to saying that an unknown thing with unknown properties acts in an unknown way to cause a phenomenon—which is the same thing as offering no explanation at all.

We often run into untestable theories in daily life, just as scientists sometimes encounter them in their work. Many practitioners of alternative medicine claim that health problems are caused by an imbalance in people's *chi*, an unmeasurable form of mystical energy that is said to flow through everyone. Some people say that their misfortunes are caused by God or the Devil. Others believe that certain events in their lives happen (and are inevitable) because of fate. And parents may hear their young daughter say that she did not break the lamp, but her invisible friend did.

Many theories throughout history have been untestable. Some of the more influential untestable theories are the theory of witches (some people called witches are controlled by the Devil), the moral fault theory of disease (immoral behaviour causes illness), and the divine-placement theory of fossils (God created geological fossils to give the false impression of an ancient Earth).

But what does it mean to say that a theory is testable or untestable? A theory is testable *if it predicts something other than what it was introduced to explain*. Suppose your electric clock stops each time you touch it. One theory to explain this event is that there is an electrical short in the clock's wiring. Another theory is that an invisible, undetectable demon causes the clock to stop. The wiring theory predicts that if the wiring is repaired, the clock will no longer shut off when touched. So it is testable—there is something that the theory predicts other than the obvious fact that the clock will stop when you touch it. But the demon theory makes no predictions about anything *except* the obvious, the very fact that the theory was introduced to explain. It predicts that the clock will stop if you touch it, but we already know this. So our understanding is not increased, and the demon theory is untestable.

Now, if the demon theory says that the demon can be detected with X-rays, then there is something the theory predicts other than the clock's stopping

REVIEW NOTES

Criteria of Adequacy

- *Testability:* Whether there is some way to determine if a theory is true.
- *Fruitfulness:* The number of novel predictions made.
- *Scope:* The amount of diverse phenomena explained.
- *Simplicity:* The number of assumptions made.
- *Conservatism:* How well a theory fits with existing knowledge.

when touched. You can X-ray the clock and examine the film for demon silhouettes. If the theory says the demon can't be seen but can be heard with sensitive sound equipment, then you have a prediction, something to look for other than clock stoppage.

So other things being equal, testable theories are superior to untestable ones; they may be able to increase our understanding of a phenomenon. But an untestable theory is just an oddity.

> "The weakness of the man who, when his theory works out into a flagrant contradiction of the facts, concludes 'So much the worse for the facts: let them be altered,' instead of 'So much the worse for my theory.'"
>
> —*George Bernard Shaw*

Fruitfulness

Imagine that we have two testable theories, theory 1 and theory 2, that attempt to explain the same phenomenon. Theory 1 and theory 2 seem comparable in most respects when measured against other criteria of adequacy. Theory 1, however, successfully predicts the existence of a previously unknown entity, say, a star in an uncharted part of the sky. What would you conclude about the relative worth of these two theories?

If you thought carefully about the issue, you would probably conclude that theory 1 is the better theory—and you would be right. Other things being equal, theories that perform this way—that successfully predict previously unknown phenomena—are more credible than those that don't. They are said to be **fruitful**—to yield new insights that can open up whole new areas of research and discovery. This fruitfulness suggests that the theories are more likely to be true.

fruitfulness A criterion of adequacy for judging the worth of theories. A fruitful theory is one that makes novel predictions.

If a friend of yours is walking through a forest where she has never been before, yet she seems to be able to predict exactly what's up ahead, you would probably conclude that she possessed some kind of accurate information about the forest, such as a map. Likewise, if a theory successfully predicts some surprising state of affairs, you are likely to think that the predictions are not just lucky guesses.

All empirical theories are testable (they predict something beyond the thing to be explained). But fruitful theories are testable and then some—they not

FOOD FOR THOUGHT

The Importance (and Fun) of Crazy Theories

Many theories proposed throughout the history of science have been, well, crazy. That is, they have been unorthodox or heretical, with a shockingly different take on the world. The heliocentric (or sun-centred) theory of our solar system is a prime example. Some of these crazy theories have turned out to be good theories—they measured up to the criteria of adequacy very well. So a crazy theory is not necessarily a bad theory. Science as a whole has always been open to offbeat explanations, but they had to be judged to have merit. Most crazy theories in science or on the fringes of science, though, usually fail the criteria of adequacy miserably. The challenge for scientists and other critical thinkers is to remain open to unorthodox theories but not be afraid to test them through critical reasoning. Besides, offbeat theories are fun. The following theories have been found on the Internet:

> "It is my belief that Mars was once a beautiful, fertile planet capable of sustaining life, much like our own, until some cataclysmic, global event changed everything. I believe that the survivors went searching for another planet, on which to live, and that they chose the Earth. We are their descendants. They were an advanced civilization who brought their technology with them. Upon reaching Earth, they proceeded to build the same type of structures that were familiar to them on Mars. That way, if there were more survivors they'd recognize the structures and know where the others were."

> "Trepanation is the practice of making a hole in the skull. It is sometimes spelled trephination. . . . Trepanation was practised on every continent through every time period and by every race of mankind until the advent of brain surgery in this century. Doctors today have been taught that trepanation was done in past centuries for superstitious, magical, or religious reasons. They generally look on trepanation as a practice akin to blood letting. They scoff at it. . . . The risk-to-benefit ratio would have to have been very favourable for the practice to have been so widely practised, but official investigators haven't been able to see that there is both a rationale and a benefit to this procedure."

> "Have you ever dreamed of travelling in time? Now you can experience what you have only dreamed of. With the Hyper Dimensional Resonator you can travel into the past or explore the future. The world will be at your beck and call and you will have all the time in the world to explore it. . . . I sell an instrument which can be used for both out of the body time travel and can also be used to help heal the sick."

only predict something, but they also predict something that no one expected. The element of surprise is hard to ignore.

Decades ago Einstein's theory of relativity gained a great deal of credibility by successfully predicting a phenomenon that was extraordinary and entirely novel. The theory predicts that light travelling close to massive objects (such as stars) will appear to be bent because the space around such objects is curved. The curve in space causes a curve in nearby light rays. At the time, however, the prevailing opinion was that light always travels in straight lines—no bends, no curves, no breaks. In 1919 the physicist Sir Arthur Eddington devised a way to test this prediction. He managed to take two sets of photographs of exactly the same portion of the sky—when the sun was overhead (in daylight) and when it was not (at night). He was able to get a good photo of the sky during daylight because there was a total eclipse of the sun at the time. If light rays really were bent when they passed near massive objects, then stars whose light passes near the sun should appear to be shifted slightly from their true position (as seen at night). Eddington discovered that stars near the sun did appear to have moved and that the amount of their apparent movement was just what the theory predicted. This novel prediction then demonstrated the fruitfulness of Einstein's theory, provided a degree of confirmation for the theory, and opened up new areas of research.

CREDIT: Betsy Streeter/Cartoon Stock

So the moral is that, other things being equal, fruitful theories are superior to those that aren't fruitful. Certainly many good theories make no novel predictions but are accepted nonetheless. The reason is usually that they excel in other criteria of adequacy.

Scope

Suppose theory 1 and theory 2 are two equally plausible theories to explain phenomenon X. Theory 1 can explain X well, and so can theory 2. But theory 1 can explain or predict *only* X, whereas theory 2 can explain or predict X—as well as phenomena Y and Z. Which is the better theory?

We must conclude that theory 2 is better because it explains more diverse phenomena. That is, it has more **scope** than the other theory. The more a theory explains or predicts, the more it extends our understanding. And the more a theory explains or predicts, the less likely it is to be false because it has more evidence in its favour.

scope A criterion of adequacy for judging the worth of theories. A theory with scope is one that explains or predicts phenomena other than that which it was introduced to explain.

A major strength of Newton's theory of gravity and motion, for example, was that it explained more than any previous theory. Then came Einstein's theory of relativity: it could explain everything that Newton's theory could explain *plus* many phenomena that Newton's theory could not explain. This increased scope of Einstein's theory helped convince scientists that it was the better theory.

Here's a more down-to-earth example. For decades psychologists have known about a phenomenon called *constructive perception* (discussed in Chapter 4). In constructive perception, what we perceive (see, hear, feel, etc.) is determined in part by what we expect, know, or believe. Studies have shown that when people expect to perceive a certain stimulus (say, a flashing light, a certain colour or shape, or a shadow), they often *do* perceive it, even if there is no stimulus present. The phenomenon of constructive perception then can be used to explain many instances in which people seem to perceive something when it is not really there or when it is actually very different from the way people think it is.

One kind of case that investigators sometimes explain as an instance of constructive perception is the UFO sighting. Many times people report seeing lights in the night sky that look to them like alien spacecraft, and they explain their perception by saying that the lights were caused by alien spacecraft. So we have two theories to explain the experience: constructive perception and UFOs from space. If these two theories differ only in the degree of scope provided by each one, however, then we must conclude that the constructive perception theory is better. (In reality, theories about incredible events usually differ on several criteria.) The constructive perception theory can explain not only UFO sightings but also all kinds of ordinary and extraordinary experiences—hallucinations, feelings of an unknown "presence," misidentification of crime suspects, contradictory reports in car accidents, and more. The UFO theory, however, is (usually) designed to explain just one thing: an experience of seeing strange lights in the sky.

Scope is often a crucial factor in a jury's evaluation of theories put forth by both the prosecution and the defence. The prosecution will have a very powerful case against the defendant if the prosecutor's theory (that the defendant did it) explains all the evidence and many other things while the defence theory (innocence) does not. The defendant will be in big trouble if the prosecutor's theory explains the blood on the defendant's shirt, the eyewitness accounts, the defendant's fingerprints on the wall, and the sudden change in his usual routine—*and* if the innocence theory renders these facts downright mysterious.

Other things being equal, then, the best theory is the one with the greatest scope. And if other things aren't equal, a theory with superior scope doesn't necessarily win the day because it may do poorly on the other criteria or another theory might do better.

Simplicity

Let's return one last time to the scenario about the non-starting car. Recall that the last four theories are as follows:

6. Each night, you are sabotaging your own car while you sleepwalk.
7. Your 90-year-old uncle, who lives 1000 kilometres away from you, has been damaging the engine by secretly visiting and going for joyrides in your car.

8. A poltergeist (a noisy, mischievous ghost) has damaged the car's carburetor.
9. Yesterday, you accidentally drove the car through an alternative space–time dimension, scrambling the electrical system.

By now you probably suspect that these explanations are somehow unacceptable, and you are right. One important characteristic that they each lack is **simplicity**. Other things being equal, the best theory is the one that is the simplest—that is, the one that makes the fewest assumptions. The theory making the fewest assumptions is less likely to be false because there are fewer ways for it to go wrong. Another way to look at it is that since a simpler theory is based on fewer assumptions, less evidence is required to support it.

simplicity A criterion of adequacy for judging how simple a theory is. A simple theory is one that makes as few assumptions as possible.

Explanations 8 and 9 lack simplicity because they each must assume the existence of an unknown and unproven entity (poltergeists and another dimension that scrambles electrical circuits). Such assumptions about the existence of unknown objects, forces, and dimensions are common in occult or paranormal theories. Explanations 6 and 7 assume no new entities, but they do assume complex and unlikely chains of events. This alone makes them less plausible than the simple explanation of 3, the starter malfunction.

The criterion of simplicity has often been a major factor in the acceptance or rejection of important theories. For example, simplicity is an important advantage that the theory of evolution has over creationism, the theory that the world was created all at once by a divine being (see Chapter 10). Creationism must assume the existence of a creator and the existence of unknown forces (supernatural forces used by the creator). But evolution does not make either of these assumptions.

Scientists eventually accepted Copernicus's theory of planetary motion (heliocentric orbits) over Ptolemy's theory (Earth-centred orbits) because the former was simpler (see Chapter 10). In order to account for apparent irregularities in the movement of certain planets, Ptolemy's theory had to assume that planets have extremely complex orbits (orbits within orbits). Copernicus's theory, however, had no need for so much extra baggage. His theory could account for the observational data without so many orbits within orbits.

Sometimes a theory's lack of simplicity is the result of constructing ad hoc hypotheses. An **ad hoc hypothesis** is one that cannot be verified independently of the phenomenon it's supposed to explain. If a theory is in trouble because it is not matching up with the observational data of the phenomenon, you might be able to rescue it by altering it—by positing additional entities or properties that can account for the data. Such tinkering is legitimate (scientists do it all the time) if there is an independent way of confirming the existence of these proposed entities and properties. But if there is no way to verify their existence,

ad hoc hypothesis A hypothesis, or theory, that cannot be verified independently of the phenomenon it is supposed to explain. Ad hoc hypotheses always make a theory less simple—and therefore less credible.

FOOD FOR THOUGHT

There's No Theory Like a Conspiracy Theory

Conspiracy theories try to explain events by positing the secret participation of numerous conspirators. The assassination of President John F. Kennedy, the terrorist attacks of 9/11, the Watergate scandal, the AIDS crisis—all these and more have been the subject of countless conspiracy theories, both elaborate and provocative. Some conspiracy theories, of course, have been found to be true after all. But most of them are implausible. The main problem with them is that they usually fail to meet the criterion of simplicity. They would have us make numerous assumptions that raise more questions than they answer. How do the conspirators manage to keep their activities secret? How do they control all the players? Where is the evidence that all the parts of the conspiracy have come together just so?

Nonetheless, many conspiracy theories remain quite popular, perhaps because they engage our imaginations. Here's a short list of things that, we are told, are the centre of a massive conspiracy:

- The terrorist attacks of 9/11
- The death of Elvis Presley
- The assassination of Martin Luther King Jr.
- The Oklahoma City bombing
- The death of Princess Diana
- The death of former Enron CEO Kenneth Lay

And here are a few of the alleged cabals that are doing all the dirty deeds:

- The US government
- The Vatican
- The CIA
- The Illuminati, a secret society controlling the government
- Doctors
- The Freemasons
- The pharmaceutical industry

the modifications are ad hoc hypotheses. Ad hoc hypotheses always make a theory less simple—and therefore less credible.

Conservatism

What if a trusted friend told you that—believe it or not—some dogs lay eggs just as chickens do? Let's assume that your friend is being perfectly serious and believes what she is saying. Would you accept this claim about egg-laying dogs? Not likely. But why not?

conservatism A criterion of adequacy for judging the worth of theories. A conservative theory is one that fits with our established beliefs.

Probably your main reason for rejecting such an extraordinary claim would be that it fails the criterion of **conservatism**, though you probably wouldn't state it that way. (Note: "conservatism" in this sense of has nothing to do with politics!) This criterion says that, other things being equal, *the best theory is the one that fits best with our established beliefs*. In other words, we want a theory that allows us to *conserve* or keep what we already know. We would reject the canine-egg theory because, among other things, it conflicts with our well-founded beliefs about mammals, evolution, canine anatomy, and much more. Humans have an enormous amount of experience (scientific and otherwise) with dogs, and none of it suggests that dogs can lay eggs. In fact, a great deal of what we know about dogs suggests that they *cannot* lay eggs. To accept the canine-egg theory despite its conflict with a mountain of solid evidence would be irrational—and destructive of whatever understanding we had on the subject.

Perhaps one day we may be shocked to learn that, contrary to all expectations, dogs do lay eggs. But given that this belief is contrary to a massive amount of credible experience, we must assign a very low probability to it.

We are naturally reluctant to accept explanations that conflict with what we already know, and we should be. Accepting beliefs that fly in the face of our knowledge has several risks:

1. The chances of the new belief being true are not good (because it has no evidence in its favour, while our well-established beliefs have plenty of evidence on their side).
2. The conflict of beliefs undermines our knowledge (because we cannot know something that is in doubt, and the conflict would be cause for doubt).
3. The conflict of beliefs lessens our understanding (because the new beliefs cannot be plausibly integrated into our other beliefs).

So everything considered, the more conservative a theory is, the more plausible it is.[6]

Here's another example. Let's say that someone claims to have built a perpetual motion machine. A perpetual motion machine is supposed to function without ever stopping and without requiring any energy input from outside the machine; it is designed to continuously supply its own energy.

Now, this is an intriguing idea—but one that we shouldn't take too seriously. The problem is that the notion of a perpetual motion machine is not conservative at all. It conflicts with a very well-established belief, namely, one of the scientific laws of thermodynamics. The law of conservation of mass-energy states that mass-energy cannot be created or destroyed. A perpetual motion machine, though, would have to create energy out of nothing. Like any law of nature, however, the law of conservation of mass-energy is supported by a vast amount of empirical evidence. We must conclude, then,

FOOD FOR THOUGHT

Was the Moon Landing a Hoax?

A stunning conspiracy theory says yes—NASA faked the whole thing. Here's NASA's side of the story:

> All the buzz about the Moon began on February 15th when Fox television aired a program called Conspiracy Theory: Did We Land on the Moon? Guests on the show argued that NASA technology in the 1960s wasn't up to the task of a real Moon landing. Instead, anxious to win the Space Race any way it could, NASA acted out the Apollo program in movie studios. Neil Armstrong's historic first steps on another world, the rollicking Moon Buggy rides, even Al Shepard's arcing golf shot over Fra Mauro—it was all a fake! . . .
>
> According to the show NASA was a blundering movie producer thirty years ago. For example, Conspiracy Theory pundits pointed out a seeming discrepancy in Apollo imagery: Pictures of astronauts transmitted from the Moon don't include stars in the dark lunar sky—an obvious production error! What happened? Did NASA film-makers forget to turn on the constellations?
>
> Most photographers already know the answer: It's difficult to capture something very bright and something else very dim on the same piece of film—typical emulsions don't have enough "dynamic range." Astronauts striding across the bright lunar soil in their sunlit space-suits were literally dazzling. Setting a camera with the proper exposure for a glaring spacesuit would naturally render background stars too faint to see.
>
> Here's another one: Pictures of Apollo astronauts erecting a US flag on the Moon show the flag bending and rippling. How can that be? After all, there's no breeze on the Moon. . . .
>
> Not every waving flag needs a breeze—at least not in space. When astronauts were planting the flagpole they rotated it back and forth to better penetrate the lunar soil (anyone who's set a blunt tent-post will know how this works). So of course the flag waved! Unfurling a piece of rolled-up cloth with stored angular momentum will naturally result in waves and ripples—no breeze required! . . .
>
> The best rebuttal to allegations of a "Moon Hoax," however, is common sense. Evidence that the Apollo program really happened is compelling: A dozen astronauts (laden with cameras) walked on the Moon between 1969 and 1972. Nine of them are still alive and can testify to their experience. They didn't return from the Moon empty-handed, either. Just as Columbus carried a few hundred natives back to Spain as evidence of his trip to the New World, Apollo astronauts brought 841 pounds of Moon rock home to Earth.
>
> "Moon rocks are absolutely unique," says Dr David McKay, Chief Scientist for Planetary Science and Exploration at NASA's Johnson Space Center (JSC). McKay is a member of the group that

CREDIT: NASA

oversees the Lunar Sample Laboratory Facility at JSC where most of the Moon rocks are stored. "They differ from Earth rocks in many respects," he added.

"For example," explains Dr Marc Norman, a lunar geologist at the University of Tasmania, "lunar samples have almost no water trapped in their crystal structure, and common substances such as clay minerals that are ubiquitous on Earth are totally absent in Moon rocks."

"We've found particles of fresh glass in Moon rocks that were produced by explosive volcanic activity and by meteorite impacts over 3 billion years ago," added Norman. "The presence of water on Earth rapidly breaks down such volcanic glass in only a few million years. These rocks must have come from the Moon!"[7]

that it is extremely unlikely that anyone could escape the law of conservation of mass-energy through the use of any machine. (This fact, however, has not stopped countless optimistic inventors from claiming that they've invented such devices. When the devices are put to the test, they invariably fail to perform as advertised.)

It's possible, of course, that a new theory that conflicts with what we know could turn out to be right and a more conservative theory could turn out to be wrong. But we would need good reasons to show that the new theory was correct before we would be justified in tossing out the old theory and bringing in the new.

Science looks for conservative theories, but it still sometimes embraces theories that are departures (sometimes *radical* departures) from the well-worn, accepted explanations. When this dramatic change happens, it's frequently because other criteria of adequacy outweigh conservatism. We'll explore the creation and evaluation of scientific theories in the next chapter.

Occult or paranormal theories often run afoul of the criterion of conservatism. Take *dowsing*, for instance. Dowsing is the practice of detecting underground water by using a hand-held Y-shaped stick (known as a divining rod or dowsing rod), a pendulum, or another device. It's a folk tradition that's hundreds of years old. Dowsers claim to be able to detect the presence of underground water by walking over a given terrain and holding the two branches of the dowsing rod (one in each hand) with its point facing skyward away from the body. (This claim, as it turns out, is unsupported.) When the point of the rod dips toward the ground, that's supposed to indicate that water is beneath the dowser. It seems to the dowser (and sometimes to observers) that the rod moves on its own, as though under the influence of some hidden force.

One theory to account for the rod's movements is that an unknown form of radiation emanating from the underground water pulls on the divining rod, causing it to move. (A well-supported alternative theory is that the movement of the divining rod in the dowser's hands is caused by suggestion and unconscious muscular activity in the dowser.) As it stands, the radiation theory is not testable, fruitful, or simple. But its major failing is its lack of conservatism. The claim about the strange, occult radiation conflicts with what scientists know about energy, radiation, and human sensory systems. It is possible that the dowser's radiation exists, but there is no reason to believe that it does and good reason to doubt it.

We will look at many more examples shortly, but before we go any further, you need to fully understand two crucial points about the nature of theory appraisal.

First, there is no strict formula or protocol for applying the criteria of adequacy. In deductive arguments there are rules of inference that are precise and invariable. But inference to the best explanation is a different thing altogether. There are no precise rules for applying the criteria, no way to quantify how a theory measures up according to each criterion, and no way to rank each criterion according to its importance. Sometimes we may assign more weight to the criterion of scope if the theory in question seems similar to other theories on the basis of all the remaining criteria. Other times we may weight simplicity more when considering theories that seem equally conservative or fruitful. The process of theory evaluation is not like solving a math problem—but more like diagnosing an illness or making a judicial decision. It is rational but not formulaic, and it depends on the dynamics of human judgment. The best we can do is follow some guidelines for evaluating theories generally and for applying the criteria of adequacy. Fortunately, this kind of help is usually all we need. (You'll get this kind of guidance in the following pages.)

Second, despite the lack of formula in theory assessment, the process is far from subjective or arbitrary. There are many judgments that we successfully make every day that are not quantifiable or formulaic—but they are still objective. We can agree, for example, on many key features that go into making a car a good one: various safety features, fuel efficiency, cargo space, and so on. We cannot say exactly how to rank those features, but that doesn't stop us from arriving at sound judgments; leaving aside questions of price, a BMW 520i is a better car than a Ford Fiesta. Of course, there are cases that are not so clear-cut that give rise to reasonable disagreement among reasonable people—various luxury sedans may be very similar in quality, with only minor differences. But there are also many instances that are manifestly unambiguous. Pretending that these questions of quality are unclear would be irrational. It would simply be incorrect to believe that a Toyota Yaris is "just as good" a car as an S-Class Mercedes. The same goes for evaluating theories. The criteria that apply are well understood. The fact that there's no formula for applying those criteria does nothing to prevent us from applying them in a sensible manner to tell good theories from bad ones.

EXERCISE 9.6

Answers to exercises marked with an asterisk (*) may be found in Appendix B, Answers to Exercises.

1. Is the quantity of evidence available for various theories a sufficient indication of which theory you should accept? Why or why not?
*2. In theory evaluation, what is the minimum requirement of consistency?
3. According to the text, what is a "best theory"? What does this imply about what it takes to completely evaluate a particular theory?
4. According to the text, what are the criteria of adequacy?
5. What does it mean for a theory to be testable? Fruitful? Conservative?
*6. What does it mean to say that a theory does not have much scope?
7. What does it mean when we say that a best explanation is not "truth-preserving"? Why is this important?
8. What role does the concept of simplicity important in determining the best theory? What are the risks involved in accepting a theory that is not simple?

EXERCISE 9.7

Following are several pairs of theories used to explain various phenomena. For each pair, determine (1) which theory is simpler and (2) which one is more conservative.

1. Phenomenon: Natural disasters have become more destructive and frequent all over the world. Theories: God has finally tired of humanity; global warming is affecting the Earth's complex weather systems.
*2. Phenomenon: Your cold symptoms end. Theories: Part of the natural cycle of the cold; the result of taking a homeopathic remedy with no measurable active ingredients.
3. Phenomenon: The winning of an election by a relatively unknown candidate. Theories: A last-minute blitz of TV ads; the candidate's endorsement by a famous convicted murderer.
*4. Phenomenon: A huge drop in the incidence of measles over the last 100 years. Theories: Mandatory immunization; lower levels of air pollution.
5. Phenomenon: The sudden friendliness of the Canadian government toward the conservative American government. Theories: The election of a Conservative government in Canada; change in attitude among Canadians regarding their neighbours to the south.

6. Phenomenon: Panic has spread among the people of your town. Theories: A serial killer has started a killing spree nearby and nobody knows who it is or who will be next victim; a new species of highly aggressive wasps has infested the town.
*7. Phenomenon: A hurricane hitting Nova Scotia. Theories: A pre-existing tropical storm was amplified by unusually warm ocean currents; radiation from outer space.
8. Phenomenon: A dream about bumping into an old friend comes true the next day. Theories: Coincidence; psychic connection between you and your old friend.

TELLING GOOD THEORIES FROM BAD

"For any scientific theory is born into a life of fierce competition, a jungle red in tooth and claw. Only the successful theories survive—the ones which in fact latched onto the actual regularities in nature."

—Bas Van Fraassen

Many (perhaps most) explanatory theories that you run into every day are easy to assess. They are clearly the best (or not the best) explanations for the facts at hand. The dog barked because someone was approaching the house. Your friend blushed because he was embarrassed. The mayor resigned because of a scandal. In such cases, you may make inferences to the best explanation (using some or all of the criteria of adequacy) without any deep reflection. But at other times, you may need and want to be more deliberate, to think more carefully about which explanation is really best. In either case, it helps to have a set of guidelines that tells you how your inquiry *should* proceed if you're to make cogent inferences. Here, then, is the **TEST formula**, four steps to finding the best explanation:

TEST formula A four-step procedure for evaluating the worth of a theory:

Step 1. State the **T**heory and check for consistency.
Step 2. Assess the **E**vidence for the theory.
Step 3. **S**crutinize alternative theories.
Step 4. **T**est the theories with the criteria of adequacy.

Step 1. State the **T**heory and check for consistency.
Step 2. Assess the **E**vidence for the theory.
Step 3. **S**crutinize alternative theories.
Step 4. **T**est the theories with the criteria of adequacy.

(In the next chapter, you will see that this formula is also one way of describing the general approach used in science to evaluate sets of theories.)

Step 1. State the theory and check for consistency. Before you can evaluate an explanatory theory, you must express it in a statement that's as clear and specific as possible. Once you do this, you can check to see if the theory meets the minimum requirement for consistency. If it fails the consistency test, you can have no good grounds for believing that it's correct. And, obviously, if the theory fails step 1, there's no reason to go to step 2.

Step 2. Assess the evidence for the theory. To evaluate any theory critically, you must understand any reasons in its favour—the empirical evidence or logical arguments that may support or undermine it. Essentially, this step involves an honest assessment of the empirical evidence relevant to the truth (or falsity) of the theory. To make this assessment, you must put to use what you already know about the credibility of sources, causal reasoning, and evidence from personal and scientific observations (topics covered in Chapters 4 and 8).

In this step, you may discover that the evidence in favour of a theory is strong, weak, or non-existent. You may find that there is good evidence that seems to count against the theory. Or you may learn that the phenomenon under investigation did not occur at all. Whatever the case, you must have the courage to face up to reality. You must be ready to admit that your favourite theory has little to recommend it.

Step 3. Scrutinize alternative theories. Inference to the *best* explanation will not help us very much if we aren't willing to consider *alternative* explanations. Simply examining the evidence relevant to an eligible theory is not enough.

Theories can often appear stronger than they really are if we don't bother to compare them with others. To take an outrageous example, consider this theory designed to explain the popularity and seeming omnipresence of an American icon. Mickey Mouse is not an animated character but a living, breathing creature that lives in Hollywood. The evidence for this explanation is the following: (1) millions of people (mostly children) worldwide believe that Mickey is real; (2) Walt Disney (Mickey's alleged creator) always talked about Mickey as if the mouse were real; (3) millions of ads, books, movies, and TV shows portray Mickey as real; (4) it's possible that through millions of years of Earth history a biological creature with Mickey's physical characteristics could have evolved; and (5) some say that if enough people believe that Mickey is real,

EVERYDAY PROBLEMS AND DECISIONS

Grades, Studying, and the Criteria of Adequacy

Explanations are important of everyday life, and inference to the best explanation is at the heart of many important decisions. Consider, for example, the question of what to do in the wake of poor performance on a test or quiz. Let's say you're a B+ student who gets a D on a particular quiz. Of course, you're disappointed, and maybe a little upset. But what should you do about it? What's your plan, as a student? Deciding what to do requires that you first figure out why the bad grade happened. What's the best explanation? So you start listing the possibilities. Maybe you didn't study enough. Maybe the test was unfair. Maybe the material was much harder than usual. Maybe the professor made a grading error. The Criteria of Adequacy can help you sort through what the most likely explanation is. And knowing what the most likely explanation is helps you know what to do next—both regarding this quiz and regarding how to prepare for the next one.

then—through psychic wish fulfillment or some other paranormal process—he will become real.

Now, you don't believe that Mickey is real (do you?), even in the face of reasons 1–5. But you might admit that the Mickey theory is starting to sound more plausible. And if you never hear any alternative explanations, you might eventually become a true believer. (Anthropologists can plausibly argue that various cultures have come to believe in many very unlikely phenomena and exotic deities in large part because of *a lack of alternative explanations.*)

When you do consider an alternative explanation—for example, that Mickey is an imaginary character of brilliant animation marketed relentlessly to the world—the Mickey-is-real theory looks a little silly. And once you consider the evidence for this alternative theory (e.g., documentation that Walt Disney created Mickey with pen and ink and that countless marketing campaigns have been launched to promote his creation), the other explanation looks even sillier.

Step 3 requires us to have an open mind, to think outside the box, to ask if there are other ways to explain the phenomenon in question, and to consider the evidence for those theories. Specifically, in this step we must conscientiously look for competing theories, *then apply both step 1 and step 2 to each one of them.* This process may leave us with many or few eligible theories to examine. In any case, it's sure to tell us something important about the strength or weakness of competing theories.

Many times the criteria of adequacy can help us do a preliminary assessment of a theory's plausibility without our surveying alternative theories. For example, a theory may do so poorly regarding a particular criterion that we can conclude that, whatever the merits of alternative explanations, the theory at hand is not very credible. Such a clear lack of credibility is often apparent when a theory is obviously neither simple nor conservative.

Skipping step 3 is an extremely common error in the evaluation of explanations of all kinds. It is a supreme example of many types of errors discussed in earlier chapters—overlooking evidence, preferring available evidence, looking only for confirming evidence, and denying the evidence.

Step 3 goes against our grain. The human tendency is to grab hold of a favourite theory—and to halt any further critical thinking right there.

Our built-in bias is to seize on a theory immediately—because we find it comforting or because we just "know" it's the right one—then ignore or resist all other possibilities. The result is a greatly increased likelihood of error and delusion and a significantly decreased opportunity to achieve true understanding.

Failure to consider alternative theories is the archetypal mistake in inquiries into the paranormal or supernatural (a topic we touch upon in Chapter 10). The usual pattern is this: (1) you come across an extraordinary or impressive phenomenon, (2) you can't think of a natural explanation of the facts, and

REVIEW NOTES

Evaluating Theories: The TEST Formula

Step 1: State the **T**heory and check for consistency.
Step 2: Assess the **E**vidence for the theory.
Step 3: **S**crutinize alternative theories.
Step 4: **T**est the theories with the criteria of adequacy.

(3) you conclude that the phenomenon must not be natural but paranormal or supernatural. This conclusion, however, would be unwarranted. Just because you can't think of a natural explanation doesn't mean that there isn't one. You may simply be unaware of the correct natural explanation. In the past, scientists have often been confronted with extraordinary phenomena that they couldn't explain—phenomena that were later found to have a natural explanation.

Step 4. Test the theories with the criteria of adequacy. As we've seen, simply adding up the evidence for each of the competing theories and checking to see which one gets the highest score will not do. We need to measure the plausibility of the theories by using the criteria of adequacy. The criteria can help us put any applicable evidence in perspective and allow us to make a judgment about theory plausibility even when there's little or no evidence to consider.

By applying the criteria to all the competing theories, we can often accomplish several important feats. We may be able to eliminate some theories immediately, assign more weight to some than others, and distinguish between theories that at first glance seem equally strong.

The best way to learn how to do step 4, as well as steps 1–3, is by example. Watch what happens when we assess the plausibility of theories for the following set of events.

A Doomed Flight

On 2 September 1998, Swissair Flight 111 crashed into the Atlantic Ocean not far from Peggy's Cove, Nova Scotia, killing all 229 people on board. The incident, like most airline disasters, prompted a search for explanations for the crash. The ensuing investigation was led by the Canadian Transportation Safety Board (TSB), with the co-operation of the US Federal Aviation Administration (FAA) and the aircraft manufacturers Pratt & Whitney. The investigation relied heavily on criteria of adequacy to sort through competing theories. After an investigation lasting five years, the TSB concluded that faulty wiring in the aircraft's entertainment system had started a fire that eventually brought the plane down.

Using this incident as inspiration and guide, let's devise another story of a mysterious jetliner crash and examine the main theories to explain it. We will assume that all the facts in the case are known, that all relevant reports are honest (no intent to deceive), and that no other information is forthcoming. In other words, this is a very contrived case. But it suits our purposes here just fine. Here goes.

The (made-up) facts of the case are these: at 8:30 p.m., Flight 222, a McDonnell Douglas MD-11, left JFK airport in New York on its way to Oslo, Norway. At 9:38 p.m. the crew issued a "Mayday" call, and at 9:42 the plane crashed into the ocean 50 kilometres off the coast of Newfoundland. The crash happened during a time of heightened awareness of possible terrorist attacks on aircraft.

Now let's try steps 1–4 on a supposedly popular theory and some of its leading alternatives. Here's the pop theory in question. Theory 1: *A missile fired by a terrorist brought down the plane.* This one meets the requirement for consistency, so our first concern is to assess the evidence for the theory. Those who favour this theory point to several pieces of evidence. Eyewitnesses said that they had seen a bright streak of light or flame speeding toward the plane. A few people said that they thought they were watching a missile intercept the plane. And a journalist reported on the Internet that the plane had been shot down by a missile fired from a boat.

There are, however, some problems with this evidence. Eyewitness reports of the movements of bright lights in a dark sky are notoriously unreliable, even when the eyewitnesses are experts. Under such viewing conditions, the actual size of a bright object, its distance from the observer, its speed, and even whether it's moving are extremely difficult to determine accurately by sight. Also, another phenomenon could have easily been mistaken for a speeding missile. It's known that an explosion rupturing a fuel tank on an aircraft's wing can ignite long streams of fuel, which from the ground may look like a missile heading toward the plane. In addition, the Canadian Coast Guard monitors boats and ships in the area in which Flight 222 crashed, and it says that there were none in the immediate area when the crash occurred. Because of the distances involved and other factors, firing a missile from the ground at Flight 222 and hitting it was virtually impossible. Finally, an unsupported allegation—whether from a journalist or anyone else—is not good evidence for anything.

Then we have this explanation. Theory 2: *An alien spacecraft shot the plane down.* For the sake of illustration, we will assume that this explanation meets the consistency requirement. The evidence is this: several people say that they saw a UFO fly near the plane just before the plane exploded. And tapes of radar images show an unknown object flying close to the MD-11.

These eyewitness accounts suffer from the same weakness as those mentioned in theory 1. Observations under the conditions described are not reliable. Thus many alleged alien craft have turned out to be airplanes, helicopters, blimps, meteors, and even the planet Venus, an extremely bright object in the sky. Radar tapes may show many objects that are "unknown" to untrained observers but are identified precisely by experts. The radar evidence would be more impressive if the flight controllers had not been able to account for an object flying close to Flight 222.

Theory 3: *A bomb on board the plane exploded, bringing the aircraft down.* This explanation is internally and externally consistent. The main evidence for it is the existence of trace amounts of explosive residue on a few of the recovered aircraft parts. Also, the story of the crash of Flight 222 resembles the media account of the crash of another jetliner that's known to have been brought down by an onboard bomb.

This resemblance, though, is only that—it's not evidence that counts in favour of the bomb theory. And the explosive residue is not so telltale after all. Investigators determined that the residues are most likely left over from a security training exercise conducted on the plane a week earlier. Moreover, examination of the wreckage and patterns of damage to it suggests that a bomb was not detonated inside the aircraft.

Theory 4: *A mechanical failure involving the fuel tanks caused the explosion that brought the plane down.* This is an eligible theory. It's backed by evidence showing that an explosion occurred in one of the plane's fuel tanks. Experts know that a short circuit in wiring outside a fuel tank can cause excess voltage in wiring that's inside the tank and thus ignite the fuel. Investigators found that there was indeed a short circuit in some of the fuel-tank wiring. In addition, explosions in several other large jets, some smaller planes, and various machine engines have been linked to faulty wiring in fuel tanks.

Theory 5: *A solar flare disrupted electrical circuits in the plane, releasing a spark that made the fuel tanks explode.* This too is an eligible theory. Solar flares are massive electromagnetic explosions on the surface of the sun. They can sometimes disrupt radio communications and even cause radio blackouts. Theory 5 says that a solar flare so dramatically affected electrical circuits in the plane that a spark was emitted that ignited the fuel. The rationale behind this theory is that flying planes, being closer to the sun, are more susceptible to the powerful effects of solar flares. The evidence for this theory, however, is nil. There is no good reason to believe that a solar flare could ever cause a spark in an electrical circuit.

Now let's apply the criteria of adequacy to these explanations. We can see right away that all the theories do equally well in terms of testability and fruitfulness. They're all testable, and none has yielded any surprising predictions. Except for theory 4, they also have equal scope because they explain only the phenomenon they were introduced to explain, the crash of Flight 222 (and perhaps similar airline crashes). Theory 4, however, has a slight edge because it can explain certain airline crashes as well as explosions in other systems that have wired fuel tanks. So if we are to distinguish between the theories, we must rely on the other criteria.

This is bad news for theories 2 and 5 because they fail the criteria of simplicity and conservatism. The evidence in favour of the alien spacecraft theory is extremely weak. Even worse, it conflicts with a great deal of human experience regarding visitors from outer space. We simply have no good evidence that anyone has ever detected any beings or technology from outer space. Moreover, the probability of the Earth being visited by beings from outer space must be considered low (but not zero) in light of what we know about the size of the universe and the physical requirements of space travel. Likewise, the solar flare theory has no evidence to support it, and it too conflicts with what we know. There are no documented cases of solar flares causing sparks in electrical wiring. And neither theory is simple. Theory 2 assumes an unknown entity (aliens), and theory 5 assumes unknown processes (solar flares causing sparks in wiring). These are excellent grounds for eliminating theories 2 and 5 from the running.

> "Science is organized common sense where many a beautiful theory was killed by an ugly fact."
>
> —*Thomas H. Huxley*

That leaves theories 1, 3, and 4, which we must also sort out by using the criteria of simplicity and conservatism. They fare equally well in terms of simplicity, because none assumes any unknown or mysterious entities or processes. Conservatism, though, is a different story. Neither theory 1 nor 3 accords with the evidence. In each case, existing evidence counts *against* the theory. Theory 4, though, accords well with the evidence. It not only doesn't conflict with what we know, but the evidence also supports the theory in important ways. Theory 4, then, is the best explanation for the crash of Flight 222 and the theory most likely to be true. And the explanation we started with, theory 1, is implausible.

Without a detailed formula, without a weighting system, and without quantifying any criteria, we have arrived at a verdict regarding competing theories. Deciding among theories is not always so straightforward, of course. But this lack of clear-cut answers is what gives rise to more research and more critical thinking.

EXERCISE 9.8

Answers to exercises marked with an asterisk (*) may be found in Appendix B, Answers to Exercises.

On the basis of what you already know and the criteria of adequacy, determine which theory in each group is most plausible.

1. Phenomenon: A man shows up at a local walk-in clinic, complaining of sinus congestion, a cough, and a sore throat.
   Theories: (1) lung cancer, (2) the common cold, (3) he has been poisoned by his wife.
2. Phenomenon: A sudden and dramatic drop in the price of many corporate stocks.
   Theories: (1) rumours of a recession, (2) manipulation of the stock market by one powerful shareholder, (3) particularly nasty weather on the east coast.

*3. Phenomenon: Extraordinarily large humanlike footprints in the snow on a mountainside.
   Theories: (1) the legendary man-beast known as the Yeti, (2) falling rocks from the sky, (3) a very big human mountain climber.

4. Phenomenon: A decrease in the number of subscribers for cable TV.
   Theories: (1) A decrease in the overall population, (2) The increasing popularity of on-demand Internet media streaming services such as Netflix, (3) The younger generation's preference for reading over watching television.
5. Phenomenon: A large increase in the incidence of heart disease among middle-aged women.
   Theories: (1) the result of an increase in violence against women, (2) an increase in the amount of fat consumed by women over age 45, (3) an increase in the number of women who marry late in life.

EXERCISE 9.9

Evaluate the following theories by using the TEST formula. As part of your evaluation:

a. State the claim to be evaluated.
b. Indicate what phenomenon is being explained.
c. Specify at least one alternative theory.
d. Use the criteria of adequacy to assess the two theories and determine which one is more plausible.
e. Write a paragraph detailing the reasons for your choice. Use your background knowledge to fill in any information about the theories and how well they do regarding each criteria.

1. A religious sect based in Montreal predicts that the end of the world will occur on 1 January 2017. The world, of course, does not end then. The leader of the sect explains that the prophecy failed to come true because members of the sect did not have enough faith in it.

2. A small, secret society of corporate CEOs and international bankers runs the economies of Canada, the United States, and Europe. For its own benefit and for its own reasons, the society decides when these nations go into and come out of recession, what levels of production will be achieved by the oil industry, and what each country's gross national product will be. Members of the society are so rich and powerful that they are able to hide the society's activities from public view and operate without the knowledge of governments and ordinary citizen.
3. I'm pretty sure I'm dying. I feel terrible. I threw up several times this morning. Last night, after getting home from the sushi restaurant, I had awful stomach cramps and so I went straight to bed, but I slept badly. I looked up stomach cancer online, and the article I read listed symptoms just like these. I'm pretty sure I have cancer.
4. Officer, it's not what it looks like! I know there's a dead body in the house, and the body belongs to the guy I found sleeping with my wife, and my fingerprints are on the knife that's in his chest, but I swear I didn't kill him!
5. What difference does footwear make? Well, your feet are connected to your legs, which are connected to your back, and your back includes your spine. And your spinal cord is the conduit for electrical impulses that either control or affect every major organ of your body. So we looked at the shoes people wear. We went out in public and found people wearing soft-soled sneakers, and asked them about their health. We also found people wearing hard-soled leather shoes, and asked them about their health. We also took both groups' blood pressure. We found that people wearing sneakers tended to be less overweight, and had lower blood pressure, and had fewer complaints about depression and anxiety. These results demonstrate that the right shoes can have a huge impact on your health.
6. Anaïs said farewell to her favourite uncle as he boarded a plane for Paris. That night she dreamed that he was flying in a jetliner that suddenly ran into a powerful thunderstorm and extreme turbulence. The plane rocked from side to side, then descended rapidly into the night. The jetliner crashed into a mountain, killing all onboard. When she awoke the next day, she learned that her uncle's plane had encountered violent turbulence on the way to Paris and that several passengers, including her uncle, had been injured during the flight. She had just had one of those rare experiences known as a prophetic dream.

EXERCISE 9.10

Read the following passages and answer these questions for each one:

1. What is the phenomenon being explained?
2. What theories are given to explain the phenomenon? (Some theories may be unstated.)
3. Which theory seems the most plausible and why? (Use the criteria of adequacy.)
4. Which theory is the least plausible and why?
5. Regarding the most credible theory, what factors would convince you to regard it as even more plausible?
6. What factors could persuade you to regard the least credible theory as at least somewhat more plausible?

Passage 1

Wrongdoing is apparently remarkably common in the world of politics. Some people think this is because the people who go into politics are already corrupt. Others think it is because the power that comes with political office automatically corrupts the holders of such offices. But politicians are in reality are no different from the rest of us, and probably no less ethical in office than they were in private life. The world of politics is full of regular, honest folks like you and me. They may even be more ethical, on average, given that many of them dedicate their lives to public service when they could easily make more money as private citizens with regular jobs. All the apparently unethical behaviour is just a reflection of the fact that politicians have very special jobs. Those jobs involve making very difficult decisions, decisions that often mean that some interested party is not going to get what they want. This means that political decisions inevitably make someone angry, and that angry individual is likely to feel injured and to think of the decision-maker is unethical.

Passage 2

"Parapsychologists claim man's ability to know when he is being stared at has existed since the time of primitive man and served, in those days, to warn him of impending danger and attack from savage beasts. They also believe this ability still exists in modern men and women today. Skeptics deny this claim and believe it is nothing more than superstition and/or a response to subtle signals from the environment that are not strong enough to let us know exactly what caused them. For example, if we are in a very dark room and we suddenly sense the presence of another person—even though we do not see or hear him—we may know he is there because of the person's shaving lotion, movement of air currents in the room, body heat, etc. In other words if we are warned of another's presence, it is likely due to subtle physical cues in the environment that we normally do not attend to—not to any so-called 'psychic' or paranormal ability!

"To determine if people can tell when they are being stared at, two demonstrations were completed. In the first, forty individuals were stared at for an average time of 8.6 minutes while they were eating, reading, or watching a computer screen or television. When they finished they were asked if they were aware they were being stared at. Of the forty a total of thirty-five reported they were 'totally unaware that anyone was looking at them.' For the other five there is good reason to believe they also were not aware they were being viewed. In the second demonstration fifty students sat at a table in front of a one-way mirror and were observed by two experimenters, one minute at a time, five times during a twenty-minute observation period. The students' task was to try to guess when they were being stared at and report their degree of certainty. None of the fifty were able to correctly guess when they were being stared at. The mean accuracy score for the group was 1.24; the chance score for guessing was 1.25 out of a total of five guesses."[8]

SUMMARY

Even though an explanation is not an argument, an explanation can be part of an argument—a powerful inductive argument known as inference to the best explanation. In inference to the best explanation, we reason from premises about a state of affairs to an explanation for that state of affairs. Such explanations are called *theoretical explanations*, or theories.

To be worthy of consideration, a theory must meet the minimum requirement for consistency. We use the criteria of adequacy to judge the plausibility of a theory in relation to competing theories. The best theory is the one that meets the criteria of adequacy better than any of its competitors. The criteria of adequacy are testability (whether there is some way to determine if a theory is true), fruitfulness (the number of novel predictions made), scope (the amount of diverse phenomena explained), simplicity (the number of assumptions made), and conservatism (how well a theory fits with existing knowledge).

Judging the worth of a theory involves using a four-step process called the *test formula*: (1) Stating the theory and checking for consistency, (2) assessing the evidence for the theory, (3) scrutinizing alternative theories, and (4) testing the theories with the criteria of adequacy.

Field Problems

1. Many companies have recently marketed products that are supposed to relieve various ailments (arthritis, low back pain, migraine headaches, tennis elbow, etc.) through the use of simple magnets. This "magnetic therapy" is said to work because magnetic fields generated by the magnets act on the body's processes or structures. Look at ads in magazines, on TV, or on the Internet to find a health claim made for one of these products. Then, in a 150-word paragraph, evaluate the claim in light of the criteria of simplicity and conservatism. Check for any relevant scientific research and information at www.quackwatch.com or www.sram.org (The Scientific Review of Alternative Medicine).
2. Using the TEST formula, evaluate the theory that if, on 2 February (Groundhog Day), a groundhog emerges from his burrow and sees his shadow, winter will end shortly after. Do some research to uncover any evidence pertaining to this theory. Write a 200-word essay summarizing your findings.
3. Go to the website of a major newspaper (or your own town's main newspaper). Find a story or editorial that presents an explanation for some public figure's decision or behaviour. Does the explanation presented pass the tests suggested in this chapter?

Self-Assessment Quiz

1. What is the basic pattern of inference to the best explanation? How does this pattern differ from that of enumerative induction? From analogical induction?
2. What is external consistency?
3. What are the criteria of adequacy?
4. According to the text, what does it mean for a theory to be testable or untestable?
5. What are the elements of the TEST formula?
6. According to the text, in theory evaluation, when is a theory properly considered the best?

Each of the following theories is offered to explain how it is that Arthur was aware that the mysterious stranger he met on the train was his long-lost brother,

Arnold, before they had even exchanged names or talked about their childhood. Indicate which theory (a) lacks simplicity, (b) is not conservative, (c) is untestable, and (d) has the most scope. (Some theories may deserve more than one of these designations.)

7. The fact that Arthur correctly guessed that the stranger was his brother was coincidence. We all feel from time to time that someone else is familiar, and perhaps connected to us somehow, and sometimes that feeling is bound to come true.
8. Arthur is a psychic.
9. This is an example of the strong "electric" bond between siblings and other blood relatives: their brains respond to each other's presence, even if they are not fully aware of the effect.
10. Arthur arrived at the conclusion mathematically: he met the "stranger" on the train on 13 January 2015, and his long-lost brother's birthdate was 13 January 1985. And of course 1985, subtracted from 2015, is 30. And they were on train number 30!

Indicate which theory in each of the following groups is most plausible.

11. Phenomenon: The rise in popularity of a newly elected prime minister.
    Theories: (1) the so-called honeymoon effect in which a new prime minister enjoys popularity until he or she is involved in serious or controversial decisions, (2) the systematic manipulation of all polling organizations by the prime minister's staff, (3) the influence of a powerful secret society controlling the media.
12. Phenomenon: You have noticed a large number of birds flying in a southerly direction.
    Theories: (1) The birds have sensed an impending natural disaster and are flying south to escape the worst of it, (2) air pollution in the local ecosystem has reached an all time high and is no longer suitable for birds to live in, (3) the birds are migrating south for the winter.
13. Phenomenon: Ships, boats, and planes have been disappearing off the coast of Prince Edward Island for years.
    Theories: (1) considering the meteorological and atmospheric conditions of the area, it's normal for some craft to be lost from time to time; (2) the craft have been hijacked; (3) the ships, boats, and planes are simply off course.
14. Phenomenon: An unusual number of cases of serious gastrointestinal illness among otherwise healthy people around Ontario.

Theories: (1) terrorists have been sneaking into people's homes and poisoning them, (2) they all ate contaminated meat products from the same meat-processing plant, (3) radiation from cellphones is making people sick.

Evaluate the following theories using the TEST formula. As part of your evaluation, (1) state the claim to be evaluated, (2) indicate what phenomenon is being explained, (3) specify at least one alternative theory, and (4) use the criteria of adequacy to assess the two theories and determine which one is more plausible.

15. Peter's credit card was declined at the supermarket today. Someone must have stolen his card and used up all the available credit.
16. Skeptical scientists have never been able to find evidence for cold fusion, try as they may. That's because their skepticism skews their observations.
17. People buy expensive products because of subliminal advertising—their minds are being influenced by imperceptible stimuli designed by advertising agencies.
18. Mark hired his sister, Jane, for the sales position because she had the most relevant working experience out of all the interviewees.
19. Schoolchildren who do poorly in school are not dumb and they do not have learning disabilities. They perform poorly for one reason only: low or negative expectations of their teachers.
20. The mayor has always been against the idea of having dedicated bike lanes. But suddenly, this year, he says he supports the idea. He also introduced a new plan to keep more of the city's athletic facilities open late. And have you noticed that he's lost a lot of weight, and looks more fit? I think it all has to do with the way he changed after that heart attack he had last fall.

Integrative Exercises

These exercises refer to lessons in Chapters 3 and 6–9.

1. What is a deductive argument?
2. What is an invalid argument?
3. What is an inductive argument?
4. What is the logical pattern of *modus tollens*?

For each of the following arguments, specify the conclusion and premises and state whether it is deductive or inductive. If it's deductive, use Venn diagrams or truth tables to determine its validity. If it's inductive, say whether it's an enumerative, analogical, or causal induction and whether it's strong or weak. If necessary, add implicit premises and conclusions.

5. Either you're here to collect the money I owe you, or you're here for a friendly visit. And that gun in your hand suggests you're not here for a friendly visit, so I'm guessing you're here to collect the money.
6. I've read a lot about relations between Canadian soldiers and the people of Afghanistan. Almost everything I've read has been positive. The Afghanis realize that our soldiers are there to help and have welcomed them with open arms. I even read about one woman whose house was damaged in a firefight between Canadian soldiers and Taliban fighters, and she said she was glad the Canadians were there.
7. It's vital for a businesses to attract and retain customers. Businesses that don't believe in this principle will never earn a profit and inevitably go bankrupt. That's why all businesses strive to treat their customers with respect.
8. The problem is that if people realized just how much their own health is within their control, they wouldn't go to doctors any more. But people don't realize that yet. So people will continue to go to doctors.
9. "Hence a young man is not a proper hearer of lectures on political science; for he is inexperienced in the actions that occur in life, but its discussions start from these and are about these; and, further, since he tends to follow his passions, his study will be vain and unprofitable, because the end aimed at is not knowledge but action." (Aristotle, *Nicomachean Ethics*)
10. Why should Canada be sending aid to foreign countries when there are people right here in Canada who need help? Every dollar spent on foreign aid could be better spent on problems right here at home!
11. He's in love with her. He giggles whenever she enters the room, and he won't look her in the eye.
12. I can tell he's the one who stole the new stapler off your desk. I noticed him shifting uneasily in his seat and avoiding eye contact whenever you walk by. He also has a nice shiny stapler on his desk, despite complaining recently that he didn't have one.
13. Every woman I know has a warped relationship with her mother. What is it with women? They're all a bunch of emotional wrecks.
14. Plenty of my friends' friends smoke weed and get really drunk. This leads me to believe that marijuana use results in a desire to drink excessive amounts of alcohol.

Evaluate each of the following theories and indicate whether it is plausible or implausible.

15. People are more likely to behave strangely, even violently, during a full moon.
16. David Milgaard was sent to prison for raping and murdering a nursing assistant, Gail Miller, and he spent 21 years behind bars. Three of Milgaard's friends testified against him in court. Milgaard was released in 1997 after DNA evidence supposedly proved he didn't commit the crime. But I'll trust the word of three witnesses over some fancy scientific test any day!
17. In Area 51, the famous portion of a military base near Groom Dry Lake in Nevada, the US government is concealing real alien visitors or an actual space vehicle used by the visitors to reach Earth.
18. People who complain about not being able to find a job are really saying that they can't find a job that they are willing to do. There are plenty of menial positions that need to be filled. People are just too lazy and entitled to actually work hard for their money.
19. The large network news organizations have ignored most of the anti-war protests staged since 9/11. Coverage of any anti-war sentiment seems to be against media policy. This can only mean that top network execs have decided together that such coverage is not in their best interests.
20. Multiple studies have shown that, despite having no plausible causal relationship to each other, there is a significant positive correlation between the amount of ice cream consumed and the number of violent crimes committed on the same day.

Writing Assignments

1. Think of the last few winters, and the way your overall level of health has varied from winter to winter. Perhaps some winters you've been perfectly healthy, and other winters you've had several bouts of cold and flu. Think back to a winter when you recall being sick a lot. Write a 250-word paper evaluating at least two theories that explain why you were sick so much. Use the TEST formula.
2. In a 300-word essay, evaluate the theory that all major decisions made by the president of your university are motivated by money and have very little to do with the merits of ideas or programs. Use the TEST formula.

3. Write a 500-word paper in which you use the TEST formula to assess two theories for the apparent huge popularity of Justin Bieber in Canada. One theory is the "subliminal advertising" theory (call that Hypothesis 1). On this theory, Bieber's record company is paying hundreds of millions of dollars to have persuasive pro-Bieber messages inserted into movies and TV shows in a way that makes them invisible to the conscious mind but effective at a subconscious level. The other theory (call it Hypothesis 2) is that Bieber is not really so popular after all: but the government of the Canada has issued secret legal orders, requiring radio and television networks to play Bieber's music and videos, and requiring newspapers to print bogus stories about how hordes of fans follow Bieber wherever he goes.

10 JUDGING SCIENTIFIC THEORIES

CHAPTER OBJECTIVES

Science and Not Science

You will be able to

- understand why science is not the same thing as technology, ideology, or scientism.

The Scientific Method

You will be able to

- list the five steps of the scientific method.
- understand the logic of scientific testing.
- understand why no scientific hypothesis can be conclusively confirmed or conclusively confuted.

Testing Scientific Theories

You will be able to

- use the steps of the scientific method, and be able to explain how a scientist would go about testing a simple hypothesis in medical science.
- understand why scientists use control groups, make studies double-blind, include placebos in testing, and seek replication of their work.

Judging Scientific Theories

You will be able to

- list the five criteria of adequacy and explain what they mean.
- understand how to apply the criteria of adequacy to the theories of evolution and creationism and why the text says that evolution is the better theory.

Science and Weird Theories

You will be able to

- explain why evaluating weird claims might be worthwhile.

Making Weird Mistakes

You will be able to

- understand why it can be so easy to err when trying to evaluate weird theories.
- explain three major errors that people often make when they are trying to assess extraordinary experiences and theories.
- explain the distinction between logical and physical possibility.

Judging Weird Theories

You will be able to

- use the TEST formula to evaluate extraordinary theories.
- understand why eyewitness testimony is often unreliable.

So the world is abuzz with claims in the form of explanations—*theoretical explanations*, to be more precise—about why something is the case or why something happens. An overwhelming number of such theories are offered to explain the cause of events, such as why the window broke, why the moon looks so pale, why Ralph stole the bike, why the stock market crashed. As critical thinkers, we do the best we can in evaluating these theories that come our way, testing them if possible, looking for alternative theories, and applying the criteria of adequacy. As it turns out, science is in the same line of work.

Science seeks to acquire knowledge and an understanding of reality, and it does so through the formulation, testing, and evaluation of theories. When this kind of search for answers is both systematic and careful, science is being done. And when we ourselves search for answers by scrutinizing possible theories—and we do so systematically and carefully—we are searching scientifically.

Let's examine the scientific process more closely.

SCIENCE AND NOT SCIENCE

First, let's explore what science is *not*.

Science is not technology. Science is a way of searching for truth—a way that uses what is often referred to as *the scientific method*. Technology, on the other hand, is not a search for truth; technology is the use of knowledge to do things in the world, and it is often embodied in products—DVDs, cellphones, laptop computers, robots that vacuum the carpet, better mousetraps. Technology applies knowledge acquired through science to practical problems that science generally doesn't care about, such as the creation of electronic gadgets. Technology seeks facts to use in producing stuff. Science tries to understand how the world works, not by merely cataloguing specific facts, but by discovering general principles that both explain and predict phenomena.

This nice distinction sometimes gets blurry when technologists do scientific research to build a better product or scientists create gadgets to do better scientific research. But, in general, science pursues knowledge; technology makes things.

Science is not ideology. Some people say that science is not a way of finding out how the world works, but a world view affirming how the world is, just as Catholicism or socialism affirms a view of things. To some, science is not only an ideology, but a most objectionable one—one that posits a universe that is entirely material, mechanistic, and deterministic. On this "scientific view," the world—including us—is nothing more than bits of matter forming a big machine that turns and whirs in predetermined ways. This mechanistic notion is thought to demean humans and human endeavours by reducing us to the role of cogs and sprockets.

But we can't identify science with a specific world view. At any given time, a particular world view may predominate in the scientific community, but this fact doesn't mean that the world view is what science is all about. Predominant world views among scientists have changed over the centuries, but the general nature of science as a way of searching for truth has not. For example, the mechanistic view of the universe, so common among scientists in the seventeenth century, has now given way to other views. Discoveries in quantum mechanics (the study of subatomic particles) have shown that the old mechanistic perspective is incorrect.

Science is not scientism. One definition of *scientism* is the view that science is the only reliable way to acquire knowledge. Put another way, science is the only reliable road to truth. But in light of the reliability of our sense experience under standard, unhindered conditions (see Chapter 4), this claim is dubious. We obviously do know many things without the aid of scientific methodology.

"Science is not gadgetry. The desirable adjuncts of modern living, although in many instances made possible by science, certainly do not constitute science."

—*Warren Weaver*

But there is a related point that is not so dubious. Science may not be the only road to truth, but it is an extremely reliable way of acquiring knowledge about the empirical world. (Many philosophers of science would go a step further and say that science is our *most reliable* source of knowledge about the world.) Why is science so reliable? Science embodies, to a high degree, what is essential to a reliable knowledge of empirical facts: systematic consideration of alternative solutions or theories, rigorous testing of them, and careful checking and rechecking of the conclusions.

Some would say that science is reliable because it is self-correcting. Science, when done properly, does not grab hold of an explanation and never let go. Instead, it looks at alternative ways to explain a phenomenon, tests these alternatives, and opens up the conclusions to criticism from scientists everywhere. Eventually, the conclusions may turn out to be false and scientists will have to abandon the answers they thought were solid. But usually, after much testing and thinking, scientists hit upon a theory that does hold up under scrutiny. They are then justified in believing that the theory is true, even though there is some chance that it is flawed.

THE SCIENTIFIC METHOD

The scientific method cannot be identified with any particular set of experimental or observational procedures because there are many different methods for evaluating the worth of a hypothesis. In some sciences, such as physics and biology, hypotheses can be assessed through controlled experimental tests. In other sciences, such as astronomy and geology, hypotheses must usually be tested through observations. For example, an astronomical hypothesis may predict the existence of certain gases in a part of the Milky Way, and astronomers can use their telescopes to check whether those gases exist as predicted.

The scientific method, however, does involve several standard steps, regardless of the specific procedures involved:

1. Identify the problem or pose a question.
2. Devise a hypothesis to explain the event or phenomenon.
3. Derive a test implication or prediction.
4. Perform the test.
5. Accept or reject the hypothesis.

Scientific inquiry begins with a problem to solve or a question to answer. So in step 1 scientists may ask: What causes X? Why did Y happen? Does hormone therapy cause breast cancer? Does Aspirin lower the risk of stroke? How is it possible for whales to navigate over long distances? How did early hominids communicate with one another? Was the Big Bang an uncaused event?

In step 2 scientists formulate a hypothesis that will constitute an answer to their question. In every case there are facts to explain, and the hypothesis is an explanation for them. The hypothesis guides the research, suggesting what kinds of observations or data would be relevant to the problem at hand. Without a hypothesis, scientists couldn't tell which data are important and which are worthless.

Where do hypotheses come from? One notion is that hypotheses are generated through induction—by collecting the data and drawing a generalization from them to get a hypothesis. But this can't be the way that most hypotheses are formulated because they often contain concepts that aren't in the data. (Remember, theories generally reach beyond the known data to posit the existence of things unknown.) The construction of hypotheses is not usually based on any such mechanical procedure. In many ways, they are created just as works of art are created: scientists dream them up. They, however, are guided in hypothesis creation by certain criteria—namely, the criteria of adequacy we examined in the last chapter. With testability, fruitfulness, scope, simplicity, and conservatism as their guide, they devise hypotheses from the raw material of the imagination.

Remember, though, that scientists must consider not just their favourite hypothesis, but alternative hypotheses as well. The scientific method calls for consideration of competing explanations and for their examination or testing at some point in the process. Sometimes applying the criteria of adequacy can immediately eliminate some theories from the running, and sometimes theories must be tested along with the original hypothesis.

In step 3 scientists derive implications, or consequences, of the hypothesis to test. As we've seen, sometimes we can test a theory directly, as when we simply check the gas tank of the lawnmower to confirm the theory that it won't run because it's out of gas. But often theories cannot be tested directly. How would we directly test, for example, the hypothesis that chemical X is causing leukemia in menopausal women? We can't.

> "The whole of science is nothing more than a refinement of everyday thinking."
>
> —*Albert Einstein*

So scientists test indirectly by first deriving a test implication from a hypothesis and then putting that implication to the test. Deriving such an observational consequence involves figuring out what a hypothesis implies or predicts. Scientists ask, "If this hypothesis were true, what consequences would follow? What phenomena or events would have to obtain?"

Recall that we derived test implications in the problem of the car that wouldn't start in Chapter 9. One hypothesis was that the car wouldn't start because a vandal had sabotaged it. We reasoned that if a vandal had indeed sabotaged the car, there would be tracks in the snow around it. But there were no tracks, disconfirming the sabotage hypothesis.

The logic of hypothesis testing, then, works like this: when we derive a test implication, we know that if the hypothesis to be tested (*H*) is true, then there is a specific predicted consequence (*C*). If the consequence turns out to be false (that is, if it does not obtain as predicted), then the hypothesis is probably false, and we can reject it. The hypothesis, in other words, is disconfirmed. We can represent this outcome in a conditional, or hypothetical, argument:

If *H*, then *C*.
Not *C*.
Therefore, not *H*.

FOOD FOR THOUGHT

Are You Scientifically Literate?

According to poll results reported in a July 2006 issue of *Maclean's*, 57 per cent of Canadians believe in ESP (extrasensory perception). This is despite these facts:

- No credible scientific evidence of ESP has *ever* been produced.
- The existence of ESP would contradict much of what is known about physics and human neurophysiology.

A little scientific literacy can help you avoid unreasonable beliefs!

Test *Your* Scientific Literacy!

True or False?

1. Lasers work by focusing sound waves.
2. Electrons are smaller than atoms.
3. The universe began with a huge explosion, the "Big Bang."
4. The earliest humans lived at the same time as the dinosaurs.
5. The hole in the ozone layer is responsible for global warming.
6. Artificial cloning usually involves transplanting the nucleus from one cell into another cell.

Answers: 1. False, 2. True, 3. True, 4. False, 5. False, 6. True.

This is, remember, an instance of *modus tollens*, a valid argument form. In this case, *H* would be false even if only one of several of its consequences (test implications) turned out to be false.

On the other hand, we would find ourselves in a very different situation if *C* turned out to be true:

If *H*, then *C*.
C.
Therefore, *H*.

Notice that this is an instance of affirming the consequent, an invalid argument form. So just because *C* is true, that doesn't necessarily mean that *H* is true. If a consequence turns out to be true, that doesn't *prove* that the hypothesis is correct. In such a result, the hypothesis is confirmed, and the test provides at least some evidence that the hypothesis is true. But the hypothesis isn't then established. If other consequences for the hypothesis are tested, and all the results are again positive, then there is more evidence that the hypothesis is correct. As more and more consequences are tested, and they are shown to be true, we can have increasing confidence that the hypothesis is in fact true.

As this evidence accumulates, the likelihood that the hypothesis is actually false decreases—and the probability that it's true increases.

In step 4 scientists carry out the testing. Usually this experimentation is not as simple as testing one implication and calling it quits. Scientists may test many consequences of several competing hypotheses. As the testing proceeds, some hypotheses are found wanting, and they're dropped. If all goes well, eventually one hypothesis remains, with considerable evidence in its favour. Then step 5 can happen, as the hypothesis or hypotheses are accepted or rejected.

Because scientists want to quickly eliminate unworthy hypotheses and zero in on the best one, they try to devise the most telling tests. This means that they are on the lookout for situations in which competing hypotheses have different test consequences. If hypothesis 1 says that *C* is true, and hypothesis 2 says that *C* is false, a test of *C* can then help eliminate one of the hypotheses from further consideration.

As we've seen, implicit in all this is the fact that no hypothesis can ever be *conclusively* confirmed. It's always possible that we will someday find evidence that undermines or conflicts with the evidence we have now.

Likewise, no hypothesis can ever be *conclusively* proven wrong. When scientists test hypotheses, they never really test a single hypothesis—they test a hypothesis together with a variety of background assumptions and theories. So a hypothesis can always be saved from refutation by making changes in the background claims. (As we detailed in the previous chapter, sometimes these changes are made by constructing ad hoc hypotheses—by postulating unverifiable entities or properties.) In such situations, no amount of evidence logically compels us to conclusively reject a hypothesis.

But our inability to confirm or confute a hypothesis conclusively does not mean that all hypotheses are equally acceptable. Maintaining a hypothesis in the face of mounting negative evidence is unreasonable, and so is refusing to accept a hypothesis despite accumulating confirming evidence. Through the

REVIEW NOTES

Steps in the Scientific Method

1. Identify the problem or pose a question.
2. Devise a hypothesis to explain the event or phenomenon.
3. Derive a test implication or prediction.
4. Perform the test.
5. Accept or reject the hypothesis.

use of carefully controlled experiments, scientists can often affirm or deny a hypothesis with a high degree of confidence.

TESTING SCIENTIFIC THEORIES

Let's see how we might use the five-step procedure to test a fairly simple hypothesis. Suppose you hear reports that some terminal cancer patients have lived longer than expected because they received high doses of vitamin C. And say that the favoured hypothesis among many observers is that the best explanation for the patients surviving longer is that vitamin C is an effective treatment against cancer. So you decide to test the hypothesis that high doses of vitamin C can increase the survival time of people with terminal cancer. (Years ago, this hypothesis was actually proposed and tested in three well-controlled clinical trials.[1]) An obvious alternative hypothesis is that vitamin C actually has no effect on the survival of terminal cancer patients and that any apparent benefits are due mainly to the placebo effect (the tendency for people to feel better temporarily after they're treated, even if the treatment is a fake). The placebo effect could be leading observers to believe that people taking vitamin C are being cured of cancer and are thus living longer. Or the placebo effect could be making patients feel better, thereby enabling them to take better care of themselves (by eating right or complying with standard medical treatment, for example) and increasing survival time.

Now, if your hypothesis is true, what would you expect to happen? That is, what test implication could you derive? If your hypothesis is true, you would expect that terminal cancer patients given high doses of vitamin C would live longer than terminal cancer patients who didn't receive the vitamin (or anything else).

> "The grand aim of all science is to cover the greatest number of empirical facts by logical deduction from the smallest number of hypotheses or axioms."
>
> *—Albert Einstein*

How would you conduct such a test? To begin with, you could prescribe vitamin C to a group of terminal cancer patients (called the *experimental group*) but not to another group of similar cancer patients (called the control group) and keep track of their survival times. Then you could compare the survival rates of the two groups. But many people who knowingly receive a treatment will report feeling better—even if the treatment is an inactive placebo. So any positive results you see in the treated group might be due not to vitamin C but to the placebo effect.

To get around this problem, you would need to treat both groups, one with vitamin C and the other with a placebo. That way, if most of the people getting the vitamin C live longer than expected and fewer of those in the placebo group do, you can have slightly better reason for believing that vitamin C works as advertised.

But even this study design is not good enough. It's possible for the people conducting the experiment, the experimenters, to bias the results unknowingly.

Through subtle behavioural cues, they can unconsciously inform the test subjects which treatments are real and which ones are placebos—and this, of course, would allow the placebo effect to have full reign. Also, if the experimenters know which treatment is the real one, they can unintentionally misinterpret or skew the study results in line with their own expectations.

This problem can be solved by making the study *double-blind*. In double-blind experiments, neither the subjects nor the experimenters know who receives the real treatment and who the inactive one. A double-blind protocol for your vitamin study would ensure that none of the subjects would know who's getting vitamin C, and neither would the experimenters.

What if you have a double-blind set up but most of the subjects in the vitamin C group were sicker to begin with than those in the placebo control group? Obviously, this would bias the results, making the vitamin C treatment look less effective—even if it *is* effective. To avoid this skewing, you would need to ensure that both groups are as much alike as possible to start—with all subjects being around the same age, having the same physical condition, being at the same stage of cancer, and so on.

Finally, you would need to run some statistical tests to ensure that your results are not a fluke. Even in the most tightly controlled studies, it's possible that the outcome is the result of random factors that cannot be controlled. Statisticians have standard methods for determining when experiment results are likely, or not likely, to be due to chance.

Suppose you design your study well and you conduct it. The results are that the patients receiving the high doses of vitamin C did not live longer than the placebo group. In fact, all the subjects lived about the same length of time. Therefore, your hypothesis is disconfirmed. On the other hand, the alternative hypothesis—that vitamin C has no measurable effect on the survival of terminal cancer patients—is confirmed.

Should you now reject the vitamin C theory? Not yet. Even apparently well-conducted studies can have hidden mistakes in them, or there can be factors that the experimenters failed to take into account. This is why scientists insist on study *replication*—the repeating of an experiment by different groups of scientists. If other scientists replicate the study and the study results hold up, then you can be more confident that the results are solid. In such a case, you could safely reject the vitamin C hypothesis. (This is, in fact, what scientists did in the real-life studies of vitamin C and cancer survival.)

At this point, when evidence has been gathered that can bear on the truth of the hypothesis in question, good scientific judgment is crucial. It's here that consideration of other competing hypotheses and the criteria of adequacy again come into play. At this stage, scientists need to decide whether to reject or accept a hypothesis—or modify it to improve it.

FOOD FOR THOUGHT

The Philosophy of Science

Many of the issues discussed in this and the previous chapter would be considered by philosophers to be part of the study of the philosophy of science. The philosophy of science is concerned with understanding the foundations, methods, and limits of science as a whole.

One of the key questions asked by philosophers of science is "What distinguishes science from non-science?" Certainly we can give *examples* of disciplines that we think of as branches of science, such as physics and biology and chemistry. But what, other than tradition, justifies designating them as sciences but not using that word to describe, for instance, astrology or engineering or needlepoint or the study of law? In this regard, some philosophers of science have focused on the scientific importance of generating knowledge through observation. Others (such as Karl Popper) have focused on the significance of *falsifiability*. In order for a claim or hypothesis to be scientifically meaningful, they argue, it must be possible, at least in principle, for there to be some empirical observation that would prove it false. As we pointed out in Chapter 9, if a theory makes no testable claims, it is of little use to us.

Another important set of debates within the philosophy of science has to do with what the proper goals of science are. Some—adherents of **scientific realism**—argue that the goal of science is to bring our understanding of the natural world closer and closer to the truth. Philosophers who hold this view would say, for example, that from Aristotle to Ptolemy to Copernicus and beyond, science has moved ever closer to a true understanding of planetary motion. Others, however, believe that this way of thinking about science is misguided. Those who hold the position known as **scientific instrumentalism** argue that it makes more sense to think in terms of the usefulness of scientific theories rather than their truth. On this view, a good theory is one that we find makes useful predictions, ones that help us predict and control the world around us.

It is also worth noting—after all the time we spent discussing inductive logic in Chapters 8 and 9—that philosophers of science have given considerable thought to what is known as the **problem of induction**. Science is fundamentally about devising theoretical explanations for how the world works and testing those theories through observation. As evidence builds up, scientists reason inductively to an eventual conclusion about which theory is best. However, as David Hume (1711–76) pointed out, no amount of evidence can ever allow us to generalize with certainty—we could still be missing crucial evidence. And besides, Hume pointed out, how do we even know that inductive reasoning is a good way to learn things? The answer, it seems, is that we figured that out inductively, by trial and error. But saying that we've learned inductively that induction works amounts to begging the question! This may not pose much of a problem for working scientists, but it poses a serious intellectual problem for philosophers of science, who are deeply concerned about understanding how, and why, science works.

Sir Karl Popper (1902–94) was one of the twentieth century's most important philosophers of science.

JUDGING SCIENTIFIC THEORIES

As you can see, theory testing is part of the broader effort to assess the merits of one theory against a field of alternatives. And as you know by now, this broader effort will always involve, explicitly or implicitly, the application of the criteria of adequacy to the theories in question:

- Testability: Whether there's some way to determine if a theory is true.
- Fruitfulness: The number of novel predictions made.
- Scope: The amount of diverse phenomena explained.
- Simplicity: The number of assumptions made.
- Conservatism: How well a theory fits with existing knowledge.

Let's study two important examples to see how scientists manage this task. The first is a classic case from the history of science; the second, a contemporary tale of what many perceive as a battle between science and religion. Notice that the steps itemized by the TEST formula are implicit in the evaluation process.

scientific realism The school of thought that says the goal of science is to bring our understanding of the natural world closer and closer to the truth.

scientific instrumentalism The school of thought that says the goal of science is to put forward theories that are useful in helping us predict and control the world around us.

problem of induction The philosophical question as to whether the process of induction can ever lead to real knowledge.

Copernicus versus Ptolemy

Consider the historic clash between the geocentric (Earth-centred) and the heliocentric (sun-centred) theories of planetary motion. It's difficult to imagine two rival theories that have more profoundly influenced how humanity views itself and its place in the universe.

In the beginning was the geocentric view. Aristotle got things going by putting forth the theory that a spherical Earth was at the centre of a spherical universe consisting of a series of concentric, transparent spheres. On one celestial sphere we see the sun, the moon, and the known planets. On the outermost sphere we behold the stars. All the heavenly bodies rotate in perfect circles around the stationary Earth. The heavenly bodies are pure, incorruptible, and unchanging; the Earth, impure, corruptible, and transient.

Then came the great astronomer and mathematician Ptolemy, who flourished in Alexandria between the years 127 and 148 CE (nearly 1900 years ago). He discovered inconsistencies in the traditional geocentric system between the predicted and observed motions of the planets. He found, in other words, that Aristotle's theory was not conservative, a crucial failing. So he fine-tuned the old view, adding little circular motions (called epicycles) along the planet orbits and many other minor adjustments. He also allowed for an odd asymmetry in which the centre of planet orbits was not exactly the centre of Earth—all this so the theory would match up with astronomical observations. By the time Ptolemy finished tinkering he had posited 80 circles and epicycles—80 different planetary motions—to explain the movements of the sun, moon, and five known planets.

FOOD FOR THOUGHT

Copernicus on Ptolemy's System

Copernicus was shocked at how complex and seemingly arbitrary Ptolemy's revered system was. He thought that Ptolemy, through countless revisions and additions, had created not a beautiful model—but a kind of monster. As Copernicus put it:

> It is as though an artist were to gather the hands, feet, head and other members for his images from diverse models, each part excellently drawn, but not related to a single body, and since they in no way match each other, the result would be a monster rather than a man.

The result was a system far more complex than Aristotle's. But the revised theory worked well enough for the times, and it agreed better than the earlier theory did with observational data. Despite the complications, learned people could use Ptolemy's system to calculate the positions of the planets with enough accuracy to manage calendars and astrological charts. So for 15 centuries astronomers used Ptolemy's unwieldy, complex theory to predict celestial events and locations. In the West, at least, Earth stood still in the centre of everything as the rest of the universe circled around it.

The chief virtue of the Ptolemaic system, then, was conservatism. It fitted, mostly, with what astronomers knew about celestial goings-on. It was also testable, as any scientific theory should be. Its biggest failing was simplicity—or the lack thereof. The theory was propped up by numerous assumptions for the purpose of making the theory fit the data.

Enter Nicolaus Copernicus (1473–1543). He was disturbed by the complexity of Ptolemy's system. It was a far cry from the simple theory that Aristotle had bequeathed to the West. Copernicus proposed a heliocentric theory in which Earth and the other planets orbit the sun, which is the true centre of the universe. In doing so, he greatly simplified both the picture of the heavens and the calculations required to predict the positions of planets.

"IT'S BLACK, AND IT LOOKS LIKE A HOLE. I'D SAY IT'S A BLACK HOLE."

Copernicus's theory was simpler than Ptolemy's on many counts, but one of the most impressive was retrograde motion, a phenomenon that had stumped astronomers for centuries. From time to time, certain planets seem to reverse their customary direction of travel across the skies—to move backward! Ptolemy had explained this retrograde motion by positing yet more epicycles, asserting that planets orbiting Earth will often orbit around a point on the larger orbital path. Seeing these orbits within orbits from Earth, an observer would naturally see the planets sometimes backing up.

But the Copernican theory could easily explain retrograde motion without all those complicated epicycles. As the outer planets (Mars, Jupiter, and Saturn) orbit the sun, so does Earth, one of the inner planets. The outer planets, though, move much more slowly than Earth does. On its own orbital track, Earth sometimes passes the outer planets as they lumber along on their orbital track, just as a train passes a slower train on a parallel track. When this happens, the planets appear to move backward, just as the slower train seems to reverse course when the faster train overtakes it.

Copernicus's theory, however, was not superior on every count. It explained a great many astronomical observations, but Ptolemy's theory did too, so they were about even in scope. It had no big advantage in fruitfulness over the Ptolemaic system. It made no impressive predictions of unknown phenomena. Much more troubling, it seemed to conflict with some observational data.

One test implication of the Copernican theory is the phenomenon known as *parallax*. Critics of the heliocentric view claimed that if the theory were true, then as Earth moved through its orbit, stars closest to it should seem to shift their position relative to stars farther away. There should, in other words, be parallax. But no one had observed parallax.

Copernicus and his followers responded to this criticism by saying that stars were too far away for parallax to occur. As it turned out, they were right about this, but confirmation didn't come until 1832, when parallax was observed with more powerful telescopes.

Another test implication seemed to conflict with the heliocentric model. Copernicus reasoned that if the planets rotate around the sun, then they should show phases just as the moon shows phases because of the light of the sun falling on it at different times. But in Copernicus's day, no one could see any such planetary phases. Fifty years later, though, Galileo used his new telescope to confirm that Venus had phases.

Ultimately, scientists accepted the Copernican model over Ptolemy's because of its simplicity—despite what seemed at the time like evidence against the theory. As Copernicus said, "I think it is easier to believe this [sun-centred view] than to confuse the issue by assuming a vast number of Spheres, which those who keep the Earth at the center must do."[2]

Evolution versus Creationism

Few scientific theories have been more hotly debated among non-scientists than evolution and its rival, creationism (or creation science). Both theories claim to explain the origin and existence of biological life on Earth, and each claims to be a better explanation than the other. Can science decide this contest? Yes. Despite the complexity of the issues involved and the mixing of religious themes with the non-religious, good science can figure out which theory is best. Remember that the best theory is the one that explains the phenomenon and measures up to the criteria of adequacy better than any of its competitors. There is no reason that the scientific approach cannot provide an answer here—even in this thorniest of thorny issues.

Neither the term *evolution* nor the concept began with Charles Darwin (1809–82), who is none the less regarded as the father of evolutionary theory. The word showed up in English as early as 1647. The ancient Greek philosopher Anaximander (c. 611–547 BCE) was actually the first evolutionary theorist, who inferred from some simple observations that humans must have evolved from an animal and that this evolution must have begun in the sea. But in his famous book *The Origin of Species* (1859), Darwin distilled the theory of evolution into its most influential statement.

> "It is a good morning exercise for a research scientist to discard a pet hypothesis every day before breakfast. It keeps him young."
>
> —*Konrad Lorenz*

Scientists have been fine-tuning the theory ever since as new evidence and new insights pour in from many different fields, such as biochemistry and genetics. But the basic idea has not changed: living organisms adapt to their environments through inherited characteristics, which results in changes to successive generations. Specifically, the offspring of organisms differ physically from their parents in various small but occasionally important ways, and these differences can be passed on genetically to their offspring. If an offspring has an inherited trait (such as sharper vision or a larger brain) that increases its chances of surviving long enough to reproduce, that individual is more likely to survive and pass the trait on to the next generation. After several generations, this useful trait, or adaptation, spreads throughout a whole population of individuals and differentiates the population from its ancestors. The name that Darwin gave to this process is *natural selection*.

Creation science, on the other hand, maintains that (1) the universe and all life was created suddenly, out of nothing, only a few thousand years ago (6000–10,000 is the usual range); (2) natural selection could not have produced living things from a single organism; (3) species change very little over time; (4) man and apes have a separate ancestry; and (5) the Earth's geology can be explained by catastrophism, including a worldwide flood.[3]

The first thing we should ask about these two theories is whether they're testable. The answer is yes. Recall that a theory is testable if it predicts or explains something other than what it was introduced to explain. On this

FOOD FOR THOUGHT

Can You See Evolution?

Critics of the theory of evolution often ask, "If evolution occurs, why can't we see it?" Here's how the US National Academy of Sciences responds to this objection:

> Special creationists argue that "no one has ever seen evolution occur." This misses the point about how science tests hypotheses. We don't see Earth going around the sun or the atoms that make up matter. We "see" their consequences. Scientists infer that atoms exist and Earth revolves because they have tested predictions derived from these concepts by extensive observation and experimentation.
>
> Furthermore, on a minor scale, we "experience" evolution occurring every day. The annual changes in influenza viruses and the emergence of antibiotic-resistant bacteria are both products of evolutionary forces. . . . On a larger scale, the evolution of mosquitoes resistant to insecticides is another example of the tenacity and adaptability of organisms under environmental stress. Similarly, malaria parasites have become resistant to the drugs that were used extensively to combat them for many years. As a consequence, malaria is on the increase, with more than 300 million clinical cases of malaria occurring every year.[4]

criterion, evolution is surely testable. It explains, among other things, why bacteria develop resistance to antibiotics, why there are so many similarities between humans and other primates, why new infectious diseases emerge, why the chromosomes of closely related species are so similar, why the fossil record shows the peculiar progression of fossils that it does, and why the embryos of related species have such similar structure and appearance.

Creationism is also testable. It too explains something other than what it was introduced to explain. It claims that Earth's geology was changed in a worldwide flood, that the universe is only a few thousand years old, that all species were created at the same time, and that species change very little over time.

Innumerable test implications have been derived from evolutionary theory, and innumerable experiments have been conducted confirming the theory. For example, if evolution is true, then we would expect to see a systematic change in the fossil record from simple creatures at the earlier levels to more complex individuals at the more recent levels. We would expect not to see a reversal of this configuration. And this sequence is exactly what scientists see time and time again.

Creationism, however, has not fared as well. Its claims have not been borne out by evidence. In fact, they have consistently conflicted with well-established scientific findings.

This latter point means that creationism fails the criterion of conservatism—it conflicts with what we already know. For example, the scientific evidence shows that Earth is not 6000–10,000 years old—but billions of years old. According to the US National Academy of Sciences:

> There are no valid scientific data or calculations to substantiate the belief that Earth was created just a few thousand years ago. [There is a] vast amount of evidence for the great age of the universe, our galaxy, the Solar system, and Earth from astronomy, astrophysics, nuclear physics, geology, geochemistry, and geophysics. Independent scientific methods consistently give an age for Earth and the Solar system of about 5 billion years, and an age for our galaxy and the universe that is two to three times greater.[5]

Creationism also fails the criterion of conservatism on the issue of a geology-transforming universal flood. Again, the National Academy of Sciences has this to say:

> Nor is there any evidence that the entire geological record, with its orderly succession of fossils, is the product of a single universal flood that occurred a few thousand years ago, lasted a little longer than a year, and covered the highest mountains to a depth of several meters. On the contrary, intertidal and terrestrial deposits demonstrate that at no recorded time in the past has the entire planet been under water. . . . The belief that Earth's sediments, with their fossils, were deposited in an orderly sequence in a year's time defies all geological observations and physical principles concerning sedimentation rates and possible quantities of suspended solid matter.[6]

Has either theory yielded any novel predictions? Evolution has. It has predicted, for example, that new species should still be evolving today; that the fossil record should show a movement from older, simpler organisms to younger, more complex ones; that proteins and chromosomes of related species should be similar; and that organisms should adapt to changing environments. These and many other novel predictions have been confirmed. Creationism has made some novel claims, as we saw earlier, but none of these have been supported by good evidence. Creationism is not a fruitful theory.

> "If we are going to teach creation science as an alternative to evolution, then we should also teach the stork theory as an alternative to biological reproduction."
>
> —*Judith Hayes*

The criterion of simplicity also draws a sharp contrast between the two theories. Simplicity is a measure of the number of assumptions that a theory makes. Both theories make assumptions, but creationism assumes much more. Creationism assumes the existence of a creator and unknown forces. Proponents of creationism readily admit that we do not know how the creator created nor what creative processes were used.

In this contest of theories, the criterion of scope—the number of diverse phenomena explained—is probably more telling than any of the others. Biological

FOOD FOR THOUGHT

Gaps in the Fossil Record?

Creationists hold that if evolution were true, then there should be fossil remains of transitional organisms. But, they insist, there are gaps where transitional fossils should be, so evolution didn't happen. But this claim is incorrect. There are transitional fossils:

CREDIT: Ted Daeschler/Academy of Natural Sciences/VIREO

In 2006 scientists discovered this 375-million-year-old fossil of a species that spans the gap between fish and land animals.

> Gaps in the fossil record are not even a critical test of evolution vs. progressive creation, as evolution also predicts gaps. There are some 2 million described species of living animals, but only 200,000 described fossil species. Thus, it is impossible to provide a minutely detailed history for every living species. This is because, first, the fossil record has not been completely explored. It is pretty hard to overlook a dinosaur bone! Yet, though dinosaurs have been excavated for over 150 years, 40 per cent of the known species were found in the last 20 years or so (*Discover*, March 1987, p. 46). It is likely many more dinosaur species remain to be found. Second, sedimentary rocks were formed locally in lakes, oceans, and river deltas, so many upland species were never fossilized. Third, many deposits that were formed have been lost to erosion. Thus, a complete record is impossible.
>
> However, there is a critical test. Evolution predicts that some complete series should be found, while [creationists predict] that none should ever be found. In fact, many excellent series exist. The evolution of the horse is known in exquisite detail from *Hyracotherium (Eohippus)* to the modern horse (G.G. Simpson, *Horses*, 2nd ed. Oxford, 1961). Scientific creationists have been forced to claim that the series is but allowed variation within a created "kind." If so, then rhinoceroses, tapirs, and horses are all the same "kind," as they can be traced to ancestors nearly identical to *Hyracotherium*! All of these fossils lie in the correct order by both stratigraphic and radioisotope dating.
>
> Another critical test is Darwin's prediction that ". . . our early ancestors lived on the African continent. . . ." (*The Descent of Man*, p. 158). An excellent, detailed series of skulls and some nearly complete skeletons now connect modern man to African australopithecines. Some of the extinct australopithecines had brains about the size and shape of those of chimpanzees.[7]

evolution explains a vast array of phenomena in many fields of science. In fact, a great deal of the content of numerous scientific fields—genetics, physiology, biochemistry, neurobiology, and more—would be deeply perplexing without the theory of evolution. As the eminent geneticist Theodosius Dobzhansky put it, "Nothing in biology makes sense except in the light of evolution."[8]

Virtually all scientists would agree—and go much further:

> It [evolution] helps to explain the emergence of new infectious diseases, the development of antibiotic resistance in bacteria, the agricultural relationships among wild and domestic plants and animals, the composition of Earth's atmosphere, the molecular machinery of the cell, the similarities between human beings and other primates, and countless other features of the biological and physical world.[9]

Creationism, however, can explain none of this. And it provokes, not solves, innumerable mysteries. What caused the worldwide flood? Where did all that water come from? Where did it all go? Why does Earth seem so ancient (when it's said to be so young)? How did the creator create the entire universe suddenly—out of nothing? Why does the fossil record seem to suggest evolution and not creation? So many questions are an indication of diminished scope and decreased understanding.

Note that creationism tries to explain biological facts by appealing to something that's incomprehensible—a creator and his means of creating. The creationist view is that something incomprehensible using incomprehensible means created the universe. But appealing to the incomprehensible does not increase our understanding. Creationism, then, explains nothing. Creationism has zero scope.

Good scientists must be prepared to admit this much: if creationism meets the criteria of adequacy as well as evolution does, then creationism must be as good a theory as evolution. But creationism fails to measure up to the criteria of adequacy. On every count it shows itself to be inferior. Scientists then are justified in rejecting creationism in favour of evolution—and this is exactly what they do.

EXERCISE 10.1

Answers to exercises marked with an asterisk (*) may be found in Appendix B, Answers to Exercises.

1. What is the difference between science and technology?
2. What is the scientific method?
3. According to the text, why is science not an ideology?
4. According to the text, why is science such a reliable way of knowing?
5. What are the five steps of the scientific method? (State them in order, if you can!)
6. Can hypotheses be generated entirely through induction? Why or why not?

*7. What does it mean to derive a test implication from a theory?
*8. What is the conditional argument reflecting the fact that a theory is disconfirmed? Is that argument valid or invalid?
9. What is the conditional argument reflecting the fact that a theory is confirmed? Is that argument valid or invalid?
10. Can theories be conclusively confirmed? Why or why not?
*11. Can theories be conclusively disconfirmed? Why or why not?
12. What is the difference between scientific realism and scientific instrumentalism?
13. What is falsifiability? Why is it important in the consideration of claims and hypotheses?

EXERCISE 10.2

For each of the following phenomena, devise a hypothesis to explain it and derive a test implication to test the hypothesis.

1. The probability of getting hit by lightning is much higher for a person living in Florida than it is for someone living in Ontario.
*2. Jamal found giant footprints in his backyard and mysterious tufts of brown fur clinging to bushes in the area. Rumours persist that Bigfoot, the giant primate unknown to science, is frequenting the area. Two guys living nearby also claim to be perpetrating a hoax about the existence of the creature.
3. Students who tend to skip classes also tend to commit plagiarism more often.
4. In the months directly following the tragedy of 11 September 2001, there were no major terrorist attacks in the United States or Canada.
5. There is a positive correlation between the number of suicides in a community and the average number of hours a worker spends in the workplace per week.
*6. Weight trainers swear that the supplement creatine dramatically improves their performance.
7. Many people who take B vitamins for their headaches report a lower incidence of headaches.
8. "Whenever I think back to my childhood, all I remember are really great times and really bad times. I guess life was just never dull when I was a kid!"
9. When John got home, he found that the lock on his door had been broken and his high-definition, flat-panel TV was missing.

10. The economic gap between the very rich and the very poor widened considerably in 2011.

EXERCISE 10.3

Using your background knowledge and any other information you may have about the subject, devise an alternative theory to explain each of the following and then apply the criteria of adequacy to both of them—that is, ascertain how well each theory does in relation to its competitor on the criteria of testability, fruitfulness, scope, simplicity, and conservatism.

1. Phenomenon: A significant number of political science majors end up going to law school after they graduate.
   Theory: Job prospects in the political world are low for recent graduates because in general, society trusts experience over youth.
2. Phenomenon: Your mild-mannered friend suddenly goes into a violent rage.
   Theory: Your friend has schizophrenia.
*3. Phenomenon: The unexpected melting of massive chunks of the world's glaciers.
   Theory: Local climate changes are melting glaciers.
4. Phenomenon: Unethical behaviour seems unusually common in the banking industry, and in the finance industry more generally.
   Theory: Banking attracts unethical people to work in it.
5. Phenomenon: The average Fortune 500 CEO makes a salary that far exceeds that of even the highest paid doctors.
   Theory: Our society values making a profit over saving lives.
6. Phenomenon: Species of flightless birds on two adjacent islands are genetically closely related.
   Theory: Both are descended from the same flying ancestor.
*7. Phenomenon: A lot of crime is committed by people who are in financial need.
   Theory: Poverty fosters crime.
8. Phenomenon: After an embarrassing loss, the coach of the basketball team yelled at the team for 20 minutes. They did better during their next game.
   Theory: Yelling at basketball players motivates them to try harder.
9. Phenomenon: Over the past year, two terminally ill cancer patients in Broderick Hospital were found to be cancer-free.
   Theory: Treatment with a new type of chemotherapy put these patients into remission.

10. Phenomenon: Entrance marks required to get into most Canadian universities are at their highest level in years.
    Theory: Increased immigration is resulting in greater competition from new Canadians, which drives up the entrance requirements.

EXERCISE 10.4

For each of the following theories, derive a test implication and indicate whether you believe that such a test would likely confirm or disconfirm the theory.

1. Birds evolved from flying mammals, such as bats, rather than from reptiles as is generally believed by scientists.
*2. Ever since the city installed brighter streetlights, the crime rate has been declining steadily.
3. The J-Ray bracelet emits energy that improves athletic performance.
4. The Dodge Intrepid is more a reliable car than the BMW 325i.
5. Practitioners of transcendental meditation can levitate—actually ascend unaided off the ground without physical means of propulsion.
*6. Eating foods high in fat contributes more to being overweight than eating foods high in carbohydrates.
7. All corporations are driven primarily by the pursuit of profits.
8. Cats are exclusively carnivores.

EXERCISE 10.5

Read the passages below and answer the following questions for each one:

1. What is the phenomenon being explained?
2. What theories are advanced to explain the phenomenon? (Some theories may be unstated.)
3. Which theory seems the most plausible and why? (Use the criteria of adequacy.)
4. Regarding the most credible theory, is there a test implication mentioned? If so, what is it? If not, what would be a good test implication for the theory?
5. What test results would persuade you to change your mind about your preferred theory?

Passage 1

The Roswell UFO incident is considered by some conspiracy theorists to be one of the biggest cover-ups in history. In the summer of 1947, an unidentified flying object crash-landed onto a ranch near Roswell, New Mexico. Initially, the military reported that the object was just a normal weather balloon, but this ran contrary to eyewitness reports that stated that the debris contained pieces of metal and rubber. This led many to believe that the military was engaging in a cover-up, and that the wreckage was that of an alien spaceship. In the 1990s the military admitted that there really was a cover-up, but not for the discovery of extraterrestrials. They stated that the crash was actually that of a nuclear test monitor, which the military was using at the time to check if the Russians were conducting nuclear weapons tests. However, many conspiracy theorists still maintain that this is just another attempted cover-up to draw our attention away from the fact that aliens did indeed crash land on Earth and that the US government is now in possession of extraterrestrial life and technology.

Passage 2

"Michael Behe, a Lehigh University biochemist, claims that a light-sensitive cell, for example, couldn't have arisen through evolution because it is 'irreducibly complex.' Unlike the scientific creationists, however, he doesn't deny that the universe is billions of years old. Nor does he deny that evolution has occurred. He only denies that every biological system arose through natural selection.

"Behe's favorite example of an irreducibly complex mechanism is a mouse trap. A mouse trap consists of five parts: (1) a wooden platform, (2) a metal hammer, (3) a spring, (4) a catch, and (5) a metal bar that holds the hammer down when the trap is set. What makes this mechanism irreducibly complex is that if any one of the parts were removed, it would no longer work. Behe claims that many biological systems, such as cilium, vision, and blood clotting, are also irreducibly complex because each of these systems would cease to function if any of their parts were removed.

"Irreducibly complex biochemical systems pose a problem for evolutionary theory because it seems that they could not have arisen through natural selection. A trait such as vision can improve an organism's ability to survive only if it works. And it works only if all the parts of the visual system are present. So, Behe concludes, vision couldn't have arisen through slight modifications of a previous system. It must have been created all at once by some intelligent designer. . . .

"Most biologists do not believe that Behe's argument is sound, however, because they reject the notion that the parts of an irreducibly complex system could not have evolved independently of that system. As Nobel Prize–winning biologist H.J. Muller noted in 1939, a genetic sequence that is, at first, inessential to a system may later become essential to it. Biologist H. Allen Orr describes the processes as follows: 'Some part (A) initially does some job (and not very well, perhaps). Another part (B) later gets added because it helps A. This new part isn't essential, it merely improves things. But later on A (or something else) may change in such a way that B now becomes indispensable.' For example, air bladders—primitive lungs—made it possible for certain fish to acquire new sources of food. But the air bladders were not necessary to the survival of the fish. As the fish acquired additional features, however, such as legs and arms, lungs became essential. So, contrary to what Behe would have us believe, the parts of an irreducibly complex system need not have come into existence all at once."[10]

EXERCISE 10.6

Read the following passage about a study conducted on the use of vitamin C to treat cancer. Identify the hypothesis being tested, the consequences (test implication) used to test it, and whether the hypothesis was confirmed or disconfirmed.

Passage 1

"In 1978, the Mayo Clinic embarked on a prospective, controlled, double-blind study designed to test Pauling and Cameron's claims [for the effectiveness of vitamin C in treating cancer]. Each patient in this study had biopsy-proven cancer that was considered incurable and unsuitable for further chemotherapy, surgery, or radiation. The patients were randomized to receive 10 grams of vitamin C per day or a comparably flavored lactose placebo. All patients took a glycerin-coated capsule four times a day.

"The patients were carefully selected so that those [in the] vitamin C [and] placebo groups were equally matched. There were 60 patients in the vitamin C group and 63 in the placebo group. The age distributions were similar. There was a slight predominance of males, but the ratio of males to females was virtually identical. Performance status was measured using the Eastern Cooperative Oncology Group Scale, a clinical scale well recognized by cancer researchers. Most study patients had some disability from their disease, but only a small proportion were bedridden. Most patients had advanced gastrointestinal or lung cancer. Almost all had received chemotherapy, and a smaller proportion had undergone radiation therapy.

"The results were noteworthy. About 25 per cent of patients in both groups showed some improvement in appetite. Forty-two per cent of the patients on placebo alone experienced enhancement of their level of activity. About 40 per cent of the patients experienced mild nausea and vomiting, but the two groups had no statistically significant differences in the number of episodes. There were no survival differences between patients receiving vitamin C and those receiving the placebo. The median survival time was approximately seven weeks from the onset of therapy. The longest surviving patient in this trial had received the placebo. Overall, the study showed no benefit from vitamin C."[11]

SCIENCE AND WEIRD THEORIES

What good are science and inference to the best explanation in the realm that seems to lie *beyond* commonsense and scientific inquiry—the zone of the extraordinary, the paranormal, and the supernatural? In this land of the weird—the interesting and mysterious domain of UFOs, ESP, ghosts, psychic predictions, tarot card readings, and the like—exactly what work can science do?

> "I maintain there is much more wonder in science than in pseudoscience. And in addition, to whatever measure this term has any meaning, science has the additional virtue, and it is not an inconsiderable one, of being true."
>
> —*Carl Sagan*

From reading Chapter 9, you probably have already guessed that science and critical reasoning can be as useful in assessing weird claims as they are in sizing up mundane ones. Inference to the best explanation—whether used in science or everyday life—can be successfully applied to extraordinary theories of all kinds. Fortunately for critical thinkers, the TEST formula outlined in Chapter 9 for finding the best theoretical explanation is not afraid of ghosts, zombies, or space aliens. In the next few pages, we will get a good demonstration of these points by examining some extraordinary theories in much greater detail than we have previously.

Science has always been interested in the mysterious, and from time to time it has also ventured into the weird. In the past 150 years, scientists have tested spiritualism, clairvoyance, telepathy, telekinesis, astrology, dowsing, the Loch Ness monster, faith healing, firewalking, and more. Among these we should also count some bizarre phenomena that scientists never tire of studying—black holes, alternative dimensions of space, and the micro-world of subatomic particles, where the laws of physics are crazy enough to make Alice in Wonderland scream.

FOOD FOR THOUGHT

Critical Thinking and "Magic"

Some of the most well-respected stage magicians and escape artists of all time have dedicated themselves to demonstrating to the public that many weird beliefs—including belief in psychics, telekinesis, and "real" magic—are false.

Harry Houdini was a stage magician and the most famous escape artist of all time. Back in the 1920s, Houdini devoted himself—when he wasn't on stage—to debunking psychics who said they could tell the future and mediums who claimed to speak to the dead. He used his own knowledge of how stage magic works to show the tricks that allowed whose who claimed supernatural powers to fool the gullible.

The heir to Houdini's role as debunker of the paranormal was James Randi, who went by the stage name "The Amazing Randi" when he performed stage magic in the 1960s and '70s. Like Houdini, Randi was an expert stage magician who thought it unethical to use the tricks of that trade to fool people, especially for money. In 1996 he founded the James Randi Educational Foundation, an organization whose mission is to educate the public about the risks of accepting unproven paranormal claims, and to subject such claims to controlled scientific investigation. The foundation also administers a million dollar prize: they will give $1 million to anyone who can prove, under controlled circumstances, that they have any supernatural ability. To date, the prize has not yet been claimed.

Today, the illusionist duo Penn and Teller likewise use their skill at stage magic both to entertain and to educate. Some of their best illusions end with the pair demonstrating to the crowd precisely the tricks of the trade, revealing how their "magic" is accomplished.

But why should anyone bother to learn how to evaluate weird claims in the first place? Well, for one thing, some weird claims are widely believed and they are often difficult to ignore. They are, after all, heavily promoted in countless television programs, movies, books, magazines, and tabloids. And—like claims in politics, medicine, and many other fields—they can dramatically affect people's lives, for better or worse. It's important, then, for anyone confronted with such popular and influential claims to be able to assess them carefully.

In addition, if you really care whether an extraordinary claim is true or false, there is no substitute for the kind of critical evaluation discussed here. Accepting (or rejecting) a weird claim solely because it's weird will not do. A hearty laugh is not an argument, and neither is a sneer. Weird claims often turn out to be false, but as the history of science shows, they sometimes surprise everyone by being true.

MAKING WEIRD MISTAKES

So in science and in our own lives, the critical assessment of weird theories is possible, but that doesn't mean the process is without risks. It's easy for a scientist or anyone else to make mistakes when thinking about extraordinary claims. Weird claims and experiences have a way of provoking strong emotions, preconceived attitudes, and long-held biases. In the world of the weird, people (including scientists and other experts) are often prone to the kinds of errors in reasoning we discussed in Chapter 4, including resisting contrary evidence, looking for confirming evidence, and preferring available evidence. Those who contemplate extraordinary things also seem to be especially susceptible to the following errors.

Leaping to the Weirdest Theory

When people have an extraordinary experience, they usually try to make sense of it. They may have a seemingly prophetic dream, see a ghostly shape in the dark, watch their astrologer's prediction come true, think they've witnessed a miracle, or feel they have somehow lived another life centuries ago. Then they cast about for an explanation for such experiences. And when they cannot think of a natural explanation, they often conclude that the explanation must be paranormal or supernatural. This line of reasoning is common but fallacious. *Just because you can't think of a natural explanation doesn't mean that there isn't one.* You may just be ignorant of the correct explanation. Throughout history, scientists have often been confronted with astonishing phenomena that they could not explain in natural terms at the time. But they didn't assume that the phenomena must be paranormal or supernatural. They simply kept investigating—and they eventually found natural explanations. Comets, solar eclipses, meteors, mental illness, infectious diseases, and epilepsy were all once thought to be supernatural or paranormal but were later found through scientific investigation to have natural explanations. When confronted then with a phenomenon that you don't understand, the most reasonable response is to search for a natural explanation.

"They seem friendly enough so far."

The fallacious leap to a non-natural explanation is a version of the appeal to ignorance discussed in Chapter 5. People think that since a paranormal or supernatural explanation has not been shown to be false, it must be true. This line, though logically fallacious, can be very persuasive.

The failure to consider alternative explanations is probably the most common error in assessing paranormal claims. As we've seen, this failure can be willful. People can refuse to consider seriously a viable alternative. But honest and intelligent people can also simply be unaware of possible natural explanations. Looking for alternative explanations requires imagination and a deliberate attempt to "think outside the box."

Mixing What Seems with What Is

Sometimes people leap prematurely to an extraordinary theory by ignoring this elementary principle: *just because something seems real doesn't mean that it is.* Because of the nature of our perceptual equipment and processes, we humans are bound to have many experiences in which something appears to be real but is not. The corrective for mistaking the unreal for the real is to apply another important principle that we discussed in Chapter 4: it's reasonable to accept the evidence provided by personal experience only if there's no good reason to doubt it. We have reason to doubt if our perceptual abilities are impaired (we are under stress, drugged, afraid, excited, etc.), we have strong expectations about a particular experience (we strongly expect to see a UFO or hear spooky noises, for example), and observations are made under poor conditions (the stimuli are vague and ambiguous or the environment is too dark, too noisy, too hazy, etc.). Since scientists can falter here just as anyone else can, they try to use research methods that minimize reasons for doubt.

Misunderstanding the Possibilities

Debates about weird theories often turn on the ideas of possibility and impossibility. Skeptics may dismiss a weird theory by saying, "That's impossible!" Believers may insist that a state of affairs is indeed possible, or they may proclaim, "*Anything* is possible!" Such protestations, however, are often based on misunderstandings.

The experts on the subject of possibility (namely, philosophers) often talk about *logical possibility* and *logical impossibility*. Something is logically impossible if it violates a principle of logic (that is, if it involves a logical contradiction). Something is logically possible if it does not violate a principle of logic (does

REVIEW NOTES

Common Errors in Evaluating Extraordinary Theories

1. Believing that just because you can't think of a natural explanation, a phenomenon must be paranormal.
2. Thinking that just because something seems real, it is real. (A better principle is that it's reasonable to accept the evidence provided by personal experience only if there's no good reason to doubt it.)
3. Misunderstanding logical possibility and physical possibility. Also, believing that if something is logically possible, it must be actual.

not involve a logical contradiction). Anything that is logically impossible can't exist. We know, for example, that there are no married bachelors because these things involve logical contradictions (male humans who are both married and not married). Likewise we know that there are no square circles because they involve logical contradictions (things that are both circles and not circles). We must conclude from all this that, despite what some people sincerely believe, it is not the case that anything is possible. If a weird phenomenon is logically impossible, we needn't investigate it further because it can't exist. Most alleged paranormal phenomenon, however, are not logically impossible. For example, ESP, UFOs, reincarnation, dowsing, spontaneous human combustion, and out-of-body experiences do not generally involve any logical contradiction.

Philosophers also refer to *physical possibility* and *physical impossibility*. Something is physically impossible if it violates a law of science. Whatever violates a law of science cannot occur. We know that travelling faster than the speed of light is physically impossible because such an occurrence violates a law of science. Perpetual motion machines are physically impossible because they violate the law of science known as the conservation of mass energy. Thus, if an extraordinary phenomenon violates a law of science, we know that it cannot be.

EVERYDAY PROBLEMS AND DECISIONS

Conspiracy and Vaccines

Being a parent means making many critical decisions, including decisions about your child's health care. One of the most important steps in insuring a child's health is making sure that he or she gets properly vaccinated. Standard vaccinations for infants include vaccinations that protect against diphtheria, tetanus, influenza, measles, mumps, rubella, polio, and more. Some of the diseases that these vaccines help prevent are deadly. Many of them have been virtually eliminated in countries like Canada and the United States, due in large part to the fact that almost all children are now vaccinated against them. But many of them are still a frequent cause of illness and death in parts of the world where vaccination is unavailable or unaffordable.

Some parents in Canada and the United States, however, still opt not to have their children vaccinated. In some cases, they fear the side effects they believe the vaccines to have. It is true that all vaccines can have side effects, but most of them are very minor (like a sore arm or a mild fever) and more serious side effects are extremely rare. In other cases, parents may believe that the vaccines are simply unnecessary, and that their widespread use is the result of an evil scheme, a conspiracy funded by the major pharmaceutical companies that make the vaccines. Is that possible? Perhaps, but is it likely? Parents who choose not to have their children vaccinated are ignoring the guidance of the entire medical profession, the conclusions of epidemiologists (scientists who study the spread of disease), and the advice of every single public health agency. Which theory stands up best when subjected to the tests provided in this chapter and the previous one?

Some things that are logically possible, however, are physically impossible. It's logically possible for Vaughn's dog to fly to another galaxy in 60 seconds. Such an astounding performance would not violate a principle of logic. But it does violate laws of science pertaining to speed-of-light travel and gravitation; it is therefore physically impossible. The upshot of all this is that, contrary to what some people would have us believe, the fact that something is *logically* possible that doesn't mean it's *physically* possible. That is, if something is logically possible, that doesn't mean it happened or exists—many logically possible things may not be real.

JUDGING WEIRD THEORIES

Now let's do a detailed evaluation of an extraordinary theory using the TEST formula from Chapter 9. Recall the four steps of the procedure:

Step 1. State the theory and check for consistency.
Step 2. Assess the evidence for the theory.
Step 3. Scrutinize alternative theories.
Step 4. Test the theories with the criteria of adequacy.

Science uses such a procedure to assess all manner of extraordinary explanations, and—by proceeding carefully and systematically—so can you.

Talking with the Dead

Some people claim that they can communicate with the dead, providing impressive and seemingly accurate information about a person's dead loved ones. They are called psychics (a century ago they were called mediums), and they have gained the respect of many who have come to them in search of messages from the deceased. They appear on television programs, publish books, and offer seminars to thousands. The most famous among these modern-day mediums are psychics John Edward, Theresa Caputo ("Long Island Medium"), and Lisa Williams. Their performances assure many people that their loved ones who "have passed over" are fine and that any unsettled issues of guilt and forgiveness can be resolved.

> "The most beautiful thing we can experience is the mysterious. It is the source of all true art and science."
>
> —*Albert Einstein*

What is the best explanation for these otherworldly performances in which the psychics appear to be in contact with the dead? Several theories have been proposed. One is that the psychics are getting information about the dead and their loved ones ahead of time (before the performances begin). Another is that the psychics are using telepathy to read the minds of the living to discover facts about the dead. But for simplicity's sake let's narrow the list of theories down to the two leading ones.

"We [psychics] are here to heal people and to help people grow . . . skeptics . . . they're just here to destroy people. They're not here to encourage people, to enlighten people. They're just here to destroy people."

—*James Van Praagh*

"Death is a part of life, and pretending that the dead are gathering in a television studio in New York to talk twaddle with a former ballroom-dance instructor is an insult to the intelligence and humanity of the living."

—*Michael Shermer*

Step 1. Here's the psychics' theory.

Theory 1: The psychics are communicating information or messages to and from the disembodied spirits of people who have died. In other words, the psychics are doing exactly what they claim to be doing. They are somehow identifying the appropriate deceased spirit, receiving and decoding transmissions from that spirit, conveying the information to the living, and sending messages back to the dead.

Step 2. The main evidence in support of this theory is the psychics' performance. They usually perform before an audience and talk to audience members who have lost loved ones. The psychics appear to know facts about the dead that they could only know if they were actually communicating with the dead. They also seem to inexplicably know things about members of the audience. Often they also provide incorrect information (such as saying that a member of the audience has lost her mother when in fact the mother is very much alive). But their "hits" (times when they produce correct information) occur often enough and seem to be specific enough to impress.

Psychics have rarely been tested scientifically. The few experiments conducted to date have been severely criticized for sloppy methodology. And those tests that have been conducted properly have failed to find any evidence at all of psychic ability. So there is no good scientific evidence to support theory 1. Investigators who have seen the psychics' live performances (not just the edited versions of the TV programs) report that the hit rates (the percentage of hits out of the total number of statements or questions) are actually much lower than most people realize. They have found hit rates as low as 5 per cent, with the highest being well under 50 per cent. The low hit rate, though, may not be apparent on TV shows because misses are often edited out. Psychics tend to explain their misses with ad hoc hypotheses (explanations that cannot be verified).

CREDIT: Mike Flanagan/Cartoon Stock

Step 3. Here's the main alternative to the psychics' theory.

Theory 2: The psychics are doing "cold reading." Cold reading is a very old skill practised by fortune tellers, tarot-card readers, and mentalists (performers who pretend to read minds). When done well, cold reading can astonish and appear to be paranormal. In cold reading, the psychic reader surreptitiously acquires information from

FOOD FOR THOUGHT

Eyewitness Testimony and Extraordinary Things

A great deal of the evidence for paranormal phenomena is eyewitness testimony. Unfortunately, research suggests that eyewitness testimony generally can't be trusted—especially when the testimony concerns the paranormal. For example, in some studies people who had participated in a seance later gave wildly inaccurate descriptions of what had taken place. Researchers have found that people's beliefs and expectations seem to play a big role in the unreliability of testimony about the paranormal.

> Different people clearly have different beliefs and expectations prior to observing a supposed psychic—skeptics might expect to see some kind of trickery; believers may expect a display of genuine psi [parapsychological phenomena]. Some 70 years ago Eric Dingwall in Britain speculated that such expectations may distort eyewitness testimony: the frame of mind in which a person goes to see magic and to a medium cannot be compared. In one case he goes either purely for amusement or possibly with the idea of discovering "how it was done," whilst in the other he usually goes with the thought that it is possible that he will come into direct contact with the other world.
>
> Recent experimental evidence suggests that Dingwall's speculations are correct.
>
> Wiseman and Morris in Britain carried out two studies investigating the effect that belief in the paranormal has on the observation of conjuring tricks. Individuals taking part in the experiment were first asked several questions concerning their belief in the paranormal. On the basis of their answers they were classified as either believers (labelled "sheep") or skeptics (labelled "goats").
>
> In both experiments individuals were first shown a film containing fake psychic demonstrations. In the first demonstration the "psychic" apparently bent a key by concentrating on it; in the second demonstration he supposedly bent a spoon simply by rubbing it.
>
> After they watched the film, witnesses were asked to rate the "paranormal" content of the demonstrations and complete a set of recall questions. Wiseman and Morris wanted to discover if, as Hodgson and Dingwall had suggested, sheep really did tend to misremember those parts of the demonstrations that were central to solving the tricks. For this reason, half of the questions concerned the methods used to fake the phenomena. For example, the psychic faked the key-bending demonstration by secretly switching the straight key for a pre-bent duplicate by passing the straight key from one hand to the other. During the switch the straight key could not be seen. This was clearly central to the trick's method; and one of the "important" questions asked was whether the straight key had always remained in sight. A second set of "unimportant" questions asked about parts of the demonstration that were not related to the tricks' methods. Overall, the results suggested that sheep rated the demonstrations as more "paranormal" than goats did, and that goats did indeed recall significantly more "important" information than sheep. There was no such difference for the recall of the "unimportant" information.[12]

people (the subjects) by asking them questions, making statements, observing how people behave, and listening to what they say. Good cold readers always give the impression that the information actually comes from some mysterious source, such as the spirits of the departed. Anyone can learn to do cold reading. It doesn't require any exotic skills or special powers. All that's needed is the practised ability to deftly manipulate a conversation to elicit information from the subject.

Note that theory 2 does not say that the cold reading is necessarily done to deliberately deceive an audience. Cold reading can be done either consciously or unconsciously. It's possible for people to do cold reading while believing that they are getting information via their psychic powers.

To get the relevant information (or appear to have it), a psychic reader can use several cold-reading techniques, including the following:

1. The reader encourages the subject to fill in the blanks.

   READER: I'm sensing something about the face or head or brow.
   SUBJECT: You're right, my father used to have terrible headaches.
   READER: I'm feeling something about money or finances.
   SUBJECT: Yes, my mother always struggled to pay the bills.

2. The reader makes statements with multiple variables so that a hit is very likely.

   READER: I'm feeling that your father was dealing with a lot of frustration, anguish, or anger.
   SUBJECT: Yes, he was always arguing with my brother.

3. The reader makes accurate and obvious inferences from information given by the subject.

   READER: Why was your father in the hospital?
   SUBJECT: He had had a heart attack.
   READER: Yes, he struggled with heart disease for years and had to take heart medication for a long time. You were really worried that he would have another heart attack.

4. The reader asks many questions and treats answers as though they confirmed the reader's insight.

   READER: Who was the person who got a divorce?
   SUBJECT: That was my daughter. She divorced her husband in 1992.
   READER: Because I feel that the divorce was very painful for her, that she was sad and depressed for a while.

5. The reader makes statements that could apply to almost anyone.

   READER: I'm sensing something about a cat or a small animal.
   SUBJECT: Yes, my mother owned a poodle.

With such cold-reading techniques a reader can appear to read minds. Theory 2 is bolstered by the fact that the psychics' amazing performances can be duplicated by anyone skilled in the use of cold reading. In fact, magicians, mentalists, and other non-psychic entertainers have used cold-reading techniques to give performances that rival those of the top psychics. Regardless of their authenticity, the performances of Van Praagh, Edward, and other psychics seem to be indistinguishable from those based on cold reading. The psychics may indeed be communicating with the dead, but they look as if they're using cold-reading techniques.

Step 4. Now we can apply the criteria of adequacy to these two competing explanations. Both theories are testable, and neither has yielded any novel predictions. So we must judge the theories in terms of scope, simplicity, and conservatism. And on each of these criteria, theory 2 is clearly superior. Theory 1 explains only the psychics' performances as described earlier, but theory 2 explains these performances plus other kinds of seemingly psychic readings, including tarot-card reading, fortune telling, mentalist acts, and old-fashioned spiritualist seances. Theory 1, of course, fails the criterion of simplicity because it assumes the existence of unknown entities (disembodied spirits with certain abilities) and unknown processes (communication to and from the dead); theory 2 makes no such assumptions. Finally, theory 1 is not conservative. It conflicts with everything we know about death, the mind, and communication. Theory 2, though, fits with existing knowledge just fine.

Here are these judgments in table form:

Criterion	Theory 1	Theory 2
Testable	Yes	Yes
Fruitful	No	No
Scope	No	Yes
Simple	No	Yes
Conservative	No	Yes

We must conclude that theory 1 is a seriously defective theory. It is unlikely to be true. Theory 2, however, is strong. It is not only superior to theory 1, but it is also a better explanation than other competing theories we haven't discussed in that it can explain most or all of the psychics' hits. If the cold-reading

FOOD FOR THOUGHT

Why People Believe Psychic Readings

Ray Hyman is professor emeritus of psychology at the University of Oregon and an expert on the scientific investigation of paranormal claims, including psychic readings. Years of research have led him to be skeptical of the validity of psychic readings, but he used to be a true believer. He explains why he went from believer to skeptic:

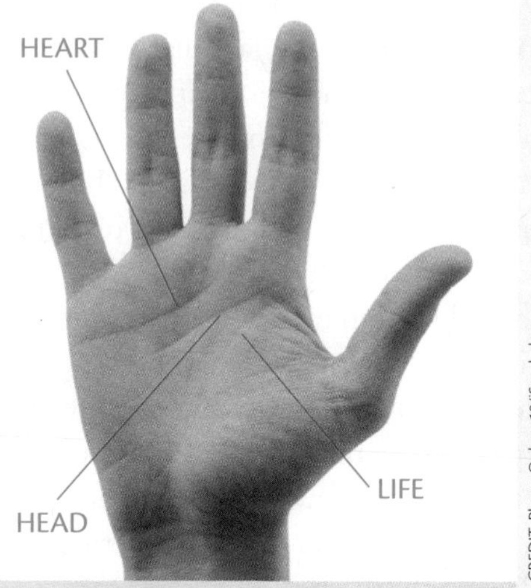

CREDIT: Photo © dem 10/iStockphoto

What is this palm saying? Psychologists think they know.

> Now it so happens that I have devoted more than half a century to the study of psychic and cold readings. I have been especially concerned with why such readings can seem so concrete and compelling, even to skeptics. As a way to earn extra income, I began reading palms when I was in my teens. At first, I was skeptical. I thought that people believed in palmistry and other divination procedures because they could easily fit very general statements to their particular situation. To establish credibility with my clients, I read books on palmistry and gave readings according to the accepted interpretations for the lines, shape of the fingers, mounds, and other indicators. I was astonished by the reactions of my clients. My clients consistently praised me for my accuracy even when I told them very specific things about problems with their health and other personal matters. I even would get phone calls from clients telling me that a prediction that I had made for them had come true. Within months of my entry into palm reading, I became a staunch believer in its validity. My conviction was so strong that I convinced my skeptical high school English teacher by giving him readings and arguing with him. I later also convinced the head of the psychology department where I was an undergraduate.
>
> When I was a sophomore, majoring in journalism, a well-known mentalist and trusted friend persuaded me to try an experiment in which I would deliberately read a client's hand opposite to what the signs in her hand indicated. I was shocked to discover that this client insisted that this was the most accurate reading she had ever experienced. As a result, I carried out more experiments with the same outcome. It dawned on me that something important was going on. Whatever it was, it had nothing to do with the lines in the hand. I changed my major from journalism to psychology so that I could learn why not only other people, but also I, could be so badly led astray. My subsequent career has focused on the reasons why cold readings can appear to be so compelling and seemingly specific.
>
> Psychologists have uncovered a number of factors that can make an ambiguous reading seem highly specific, unique, and uncannily accurate. And once the observer or client has been struck with the apparent accuracy of the reading, it becomes virtually impossible to dislodge

the belief in the uniqueness and specificity of the reading. Research from many areas demonstrates this finding. The principles go under such names as the fallacy of personal validation, subjective validation, confirmation bias, belief perseverance, the illusion of invulnerability, compliance, demand characteristics, false uniqueness effect, foot-in-the-door phenomenon, illusory correlation, integrative agreements, self-reference effect, the principle of individuation, and many, many others. Much of this is facilitated by the illusion of specificity that surrounds language. All language is inherently ambiguous and depends much more than we realize upon the context and non-linguistic cues to fix its meaning in a given situation.[13]

theory really is better than all these others, then we have good reasons to believe that Edward, Caputo, Williams, and other psychics perform their amazing feats through simple cold reading.

SUMMARY

Science seeks knowledge and understanding of reality, and it does so through the formulation, testing, and evaluation of theories. Science is a way of searching for truth. It is not the only way to acquire knowledge, but it is, however, a highly reliable way of acquiring knowledge of empirical facts.

The scientific method cannot be identified with any particular set of experimental or observational procedures. But it does involve several general steps: (1) identifying the problem, (2) devising a hypothesis, (3) deriving a test implication, (4) performing the test, and (5) accepting or rejecting the hypothesis.

This kind of theory testing is part of a broader effort to evaluate a theory against its competitors. This kind of evaluation always involves, implicitly or explicitly, the criteria of adequacy.

Inference to the best explanation can be used to assess weird theories as well as more commonplace explanations in science and everyday life. However, when people try to evaluate extraordinary theories, they often make certain typical mistakes. They may believe that because they can't think of a natural explanation, a paranormal explanation must be correct. They may mistake what seems for what is, forgetting that we shouldn't accept the evidence provided by personal experience if we have good reason to doubt it. And they may not fully understand the concepts of logical and physical possibility. In both science and everyday life, the test formula enables us to appraise fairly the worth of all sorts of weird theories, including those about communication with the dead, which we examined in this chapter.

EXERCISE 10.7

Answers to exercises marked with an asterisk (*) may be found in Appendix B, Answers to Exercises.

1. Why is it unreasonable to accept an extraordinary claim solely because of its weirdness?
2. Why is it unwise to reject an extraordinary claim solely because of its weirdness?
3. Why is it unreasonable to conclude that a phenomenon is paranormal just because you cannot think of a natural explanation?

*4. What logical fallacy is the fallacious leap to a non-natural explanation an example of?

5. What is the critical thinking principle that can help you avoid mistaking how something seems for how something is?

*6. What is logical possibility? What is logical impossibility?

7. What is physical possibility? What is physical impossibility? How would changes in our understanding of science affect our perception of these terms?
8. Is it true that "anything is possible?" If not, why not?
9. Are pigs (or pig-like things) that fly logically possible?
10. Can something be logically impossible but physically possible? How about logically possible but physically impossible?

EXERCISE 10.8

In each of the following examples, a state of affairs is described. Devise three theories to explain each one. Include two plausible theories that are natural explanations and one competing theory that is paranormal.

1. Madame Florence gazed into my eyes, and held my hand. "I see good things in your future," she said. "You will have very good luck this week!" The next day, I got a call offering me that great new job I applied for.

*2. Jacques lived in a house built back in the 1940s and that was now in disrepair. As he sat reading in the living room, he heard creaking sounds coming from upstairs.

3. Selena found herself thinking about the camping trip that she had gone on in British Columbia several months ago. She was remembering the morning she woke up to find her tent crawling with ladybugs. As she was

pondering the ladybugs, she suddenly noticed a ladybug on the windowsill near her chair.

4. Some people report that in the past when they needed help in a risky situation (e.g., when they were in a car accident or when they were lost in a crime-ridden neighbourhood), they were aided by a stranger who never gave his or her name and who left the scene quickly after rendering assistance. They claim that the stranger must have been their guardian angel.
5. "Want to hear something strange? One time when I was a kid we went camping and in the middle of the night we heard these eerie sounds and when we looked out of our tent we saw a bright light flash across the sky. It was definitely nothing we had ever seen before!"
6. For her seventeenth birthday, Lil really wants a car of her own. Her neighbour is selling a relatively nice one, but another neighbour warns her that the seller's father had died of a heart attack while driving the car, and that "everyone says" his spirit still lives in the car. Ignoring the warning, Lil buys the car and parks it in her garage. The next day, she wakes up to find the garage empty—the car is gone.

*7. Wayne dreamed that his uncle was killed by a bear in Algonquin Provincial Park. When Wayne woke up, he got a call from his mother saying that his uncle had been injured in a car accident near the park: his car had hit a bear!

8. Reginald had begun acting strangely. Soon after his seventieth birthday, he began speaking incoherently, as if in some bizarre foreign language, and he sometimes looked at his family as if he had no idea who they were.

EXERCISE 10.9

Using your background knowledge and any other information you may have about the subject, devise a competing, naturalistic theory for each paranormal theory that follows, and then apply the criteria of adequacy to both of them—that is, ascertain how well each theory does in relation to its competitor on the criteria of testability, fruitfulness, scope, simplicity, and conservatism.

1. Phenomenon: Yolanda awoke one morning and remembered having a strange dream. She dreamed that space aliens came into her bedroom while she was sleeping and abducted her. The dream seemed extremely vivid. Later in the day, she noticed some scratches on her ankle. She didn't know how they got there.
   Theory: Yolanda was abducted by aliens.

2. Phenomenon: Christopher and Andrew are twins. They often seem to know what each other is thinking and can finish each other's sentences. Many times they report knowing what the other is up to, even when miles apart.
   Theory: The twins share a special psychic connection.

*3. Phenomenon: In 1917 in Cottingley, England, three little girls claimed to have taken photos of fairies who played with them in the garden. The photos showed the girls in the garden with what appeared to be tiny fairies dancing around them. (The 1997 movie *Fairy Tale* was about the girls and their story.)
   Theory: Fairies really do exist, and the girls photographed them.

4. Phenomenon: Ogopogo is alleged to be a large water serpent inhabiting Okanagan Lake in British Columbia. The creature is unknown to science. The serpent was known as N'ha-a-itk by the Interior Salish First Nations tribe, and there have been many reported sightings over the years. There is no hard evidence proving that the monster exists.
   Theory: Ogopogo actually exists.

5. Phenomenon: The Bermuda Triangle is an infamous region of the North Atlantic Ocean that is notorious for the number of ships and planes that have mysteriously disappeared while travelling through it. Some believe that the mythical lost city of Atlantis is submerged somewhere within the Triangle, and that it is some unknown, long-lost technology emanating from the city that is causing the disappearances.
   Theory: The lost city of Atlantis is responsible for the unexplained disappearances of ships and planes in the Bermuda Triangle.

Field Problems

1. Find a controversial health or medical theory on the Internet and design a study to test it. Indicate the makeup and characteristics of any group in the study, whether a placebo group is used, whether the study is double-blind, and what study results would confirm and disconfirm the theory.
2. Find a controversial theory in the social sciences (e.g., anthropology, economics, psychology, political science) on the Internet and design a study to test it. Indicate the makeup and characteristics of any group in the study, whether a placebo group is used, whether the study is double-blind,

and what study results would confirm and disconfirm the theory. If the theory is one that you strongly believe, indicate the kind and level of evidence that could convince you to change your mind about it.

3. Think of someone you know, and engage in a bit of scientific reasoning about him or her. In particular, formulate a theory about *what it is that is this individual's main motivator.* Is it money? Grades? Vanity? What makes him or her do what he or she does? Then, devise a way of testing your theory. (Note: you don't need to carry out your test! Just design it.)

Self-Assessment Quiz

1. What is a test implication?
2. Are hypotheses generated purely through induction? Why or why not?
3. When a test implication is disconfirmed, what conditional argument is exemplified?
4. When a test implication is confirmed, what conditional argument is exemplified?
5. Why can't scientific hypotheses be conclusively confirmed?
6. Briefly explain three common errors that people make when evaluating extraordinary theories.

For each of the following phenomena, devise a hypothesis to explain it and derive a test implication to test the hypothesis.

7. There are multiple police cruisers parked outside of my neighbour's house and drug dogs are sniffing around his garage.
8. Cornelius has been brought to the hospital's emergency ward unconscious, with a small round hole in his blood-stained shirt.
9. Steffi, while walking through a wooded area near her Winnipeg home, spots a blue-and-yellow macaw—a kind of parrot that she knows is definitely not native to Canada.

For each of the following phenomena, suggest (1) a possible hypothesis to explain it, (2) a possible competing hypothesis, (3) a test implication for each hypothesis, and (4) what testing results would confirm and disconfirm the hypothesis.

10. Community members have noticed that the water in the lake near the automotive factory has taken on a strange green hue.

11. Students at St Ignatius Boys' School who were put into a class taught by a male teacher showed an improvement in their grades.
12. Public health officials report a significant increase in levels of stress in people who live or work in Toronto.
13. Since the newspapers ran stories about how poorly workers in factories in the developing world are treated, our company has made a huge effort to make sure workers at our suppliers' factories in China are treated well.

For each of the following hypotheses, specify a test implication and say what evidence would convince you to accept the hypothesis.

14. The risk of serious injury while riding a motorcycle is greater than the risk of serious injury while driving a car.
15. Most people—regardless of ethnicity—are economically better off now than their parents were 30 years ago.
16. Canada is closer to a two-tier health care system today than it was 10 years ago.

Each of the theories that follow is offered to explain why an astrological reading by a famous astrologer turned out to be wildly inaccurate. On the basis of a person's horoscope, he had predicted that the person was a nice man who could work well with other people. The person turned out to be Josef Mengele, the Nazi mass murderer. Say which theory (a) lacks simplicity, (b) is not conservative, (c) is untestable, and (d) has the most scope. (Some theories may merit more than one of these designations.)

17. Theory: Astrology—the notion that the position of the stars and planets at your birth controls your destiny—has no basis in fact.
18. Theory: Astrology works, but the astrologer read the horoscope wrong.
19. Theory: An unknown planetary force interfered with the astrological factors that normally determine a person's destiny.

Evaluate the following theory using the TEST formula. Say what phenomenon is being explained. Use your background knowledge to assess the evidence. Specify one alternative theory, use the criteria of adequacy to assess the two theories, and determine which one is more plausible.

20. Carlos has always been a little strange and a bit of a loner. Recently however, his behaviour has gone from strange to frightening. He has begun reading the ideologies of known terrorist leaders and radical thinkers. He's also been following the social media accounts of notable terrorist

organizations and has posted in the forums of websites that openly support terrorism against the Western world. Yesterday, he was spotted behaving suspiciously around the local public school. I think he's planning a terror attack on the school!

Integrative Exercises

These exercises pertain to material in Chapters 3–5 and 8–10.

1. What is an enumerative induction?
2. What is an analogical induction?
3. What is a necessary condition? What is a sufficient condition?
4. What is the appeal to ignorance?

For each of the following arguments, specify the conclusion and premises. If necessary, add implicit premises and conclusions.

5. "The proper thing for the state to do, faced with disagreement about the nature of marriage that goes to the very core of what marriage is, is to get out of marriage as the relevant factor for the determination of state benefits. There should be no marriages (civil or religious) that the state should care about. Leave 'marriage' to those who have some kind of theory about it. The non-religious marriages will be tiny in number in comparison with traditional marriages in any case." (Iain T. Benson, http://centre blog.blogspot.com)
6. "Privatization is neither an efficient nor an effective response to the shortage of long-term care facilities. Some Regional Health Authorities see [privatization] as an obstacle to the provision of well-coordinated and fiscally-responsible care. Centralized administration of public health care provides both lower administrative costs and economies of scale. Indeed, the fact that health care costs so much more in the US than in Canada—13.5 per cent of GDP in the US compared with 9.2 per cent in Canada—is largely the result of higher administrative costs in a system comprised of numerous competitive insurance firms, hospitals, clinics, and so on." (Editorial, *Canadian Centre for Policy Alternatives*, www.policyalternatives.ca)
7. "The current tax burden is massively distorted by land values (since buildings depreciate as they get older) and falls heavily on those in built-up areas where values reflect scarcity, not service costs or incomes.

> The perverse impact is to push residents and small businesses out of denser areas on the basis of high taxes. That's totally at odds with the city's development plan to encourage inner-city growth. And it is simply wrong and completely backwards for the city to dictate where you can live or where you do business just to maximize taxes on property.
>
> "Homeowners have some protection under an assessment cap, but this only puts more burden on small business. Instead, we need a new system based on actual service costs and real ability to pay, and that doesn't tax people out of homes and business locations they can otherwise afford and want to remain in." (Editorial, *Halifax Chronicle-Herald*, 25 January 2012)

For each of the following phenomena, suggest (1) a possible hypothesis to explain it, (2) a possible competing hypothesis, and (3) a test implication for each hypothesis.

8. The accident rate on Highway 401 was very high but was reduced considerably after the speed limit was lowered to 90 km/h and billboards urged drivers to obey the law.
9. The sales numbers of guitars in the country have risen ever since Justin Bieber became famous.
10. There are several new businesses on the east side of town despite the fact that the new Walmart there resulted in several small stores closing. Indeed, business near the new Walmart seems to be booming!

Evaluate each of the following theories by using the TEST formula. Use your background knowledge to assess the evidence. Specify one alternative theory, use the criteria of adequacy to assess the two theories, and determine which one is more plausible.

11. Canada's prominent role as an international peacekeeper has resulted from the respect our military has earned through aggressive use of its awesome firepower over the last 30 years.
12. The key to a long and healthy life is a simple diet consisting mostly of grains, fruits, and vegetables.
13. The NDP has never formed a federal government in Canada because influential Americans have worked hard to prevent Canada from becoming "too left-wing."
14. Controlling the supply of illegal firearms in Canada is so hard because the lax gun laws in the United States makes smuggling guns from the US into Canada much easier.

Writing Assignments

1. In a one-page essay, use the TEST formula to evaluate one of the following theories:
   a. Phenomenon: People with the flu report feeling better after drinking chamomile tea.
      Theory 1: Chamomile tea cures the flu.
      Theory 2: The placebo effect.
   b. Phenomenon: A temporary drop in the crime rate in Regina occurred just after a visit from US president Barack Obama.
      Theory 1: Obama had a calming effect on local criminal gangs.
      Theory 2: Extra police presence deterred crime.
   c. Phenomenon: We took six puppies to a nursing home for senior citizens one morning, and nurses reported that the patients generally reported fewer minor health problems during the rest of the day.
      Theory 1: Puppies prevent minor illnesses.
      Theory 2: Puppies improve patients' mood, which results in them complaining less about their health.
2. Read Essay 10 ("Unrepentant Homeopaths") in Appendix A and write a 500-word essay evaluating homeopathy, by comparing the following two theories: (1) Homeopathy is an elaborate system of placebos, without any real effect; (2) Homeopathy is effective in a way not fully understood today by science. Use the TEST formula.
3. Devise two theories to explain the prevalence of "binge drinking" among university students, and then write a 500-word paper evaluating the worth of the two theories.

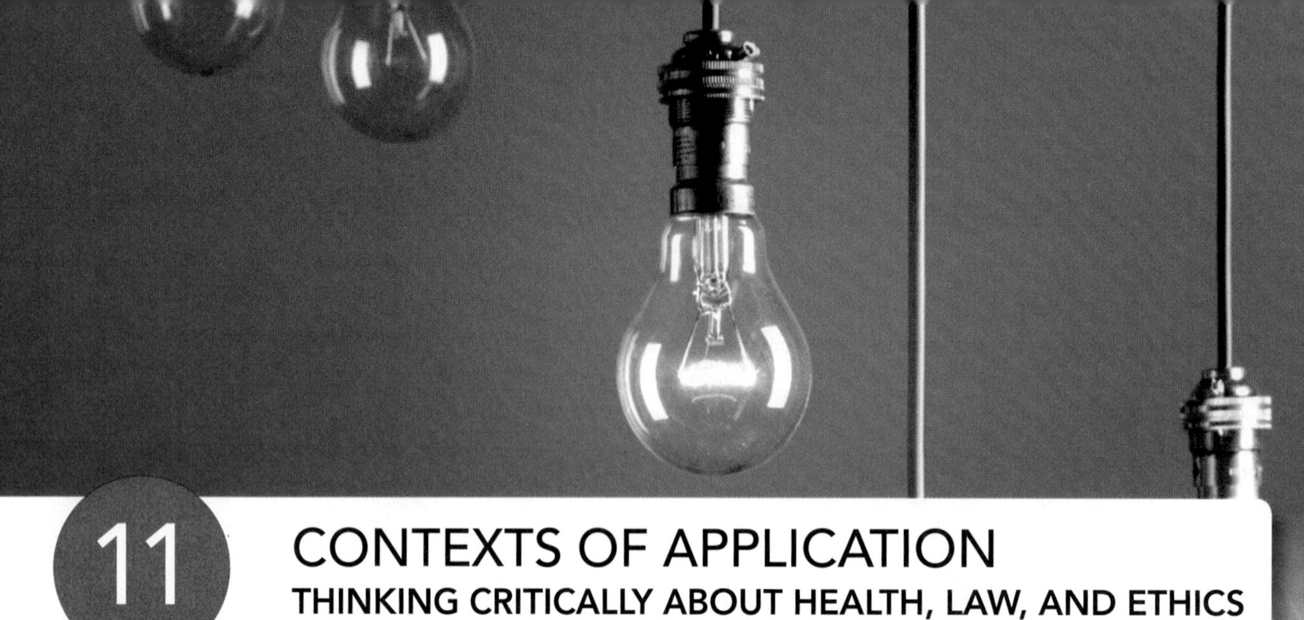

11 CONTEXTS OF APPLICATION
THINKING CRITICALLY ABOUT HEALTH, LAW, AND ETHICS

CHAPTER OBJECTIVES

Thinking Critically about Health and Health Care

You will be able to

- appreciate the risks posed by various causal confusions in reasoning about health.
- understand the importance of critically evaluating all news reports related to health.
- recognize the importance and limits of expert advice related to health.
- avoid the most common fallacies found in reasoning about health.

Thinking Critically about the Law

You will be able to

- appreciate the role of "inference to the best explanation" in legal reasoning.
- understand the way that legal reasoning involves application of categorical logic.
- recognize the significance of key fallacies as they appear in legal reasoning.

Thinking Critically about Ethics

You will be able to

- distinguish between ethical claims and descriptive claims.
- appreciate why critical thinking skills are as relevant to ethical claims as they are to other sorts of claims.
- distinguish among ethical premises that draw upon the three historically important traditions of ethics.

In this chapter, we turn to examining several contexts in which the application of critical thinking skills is especially important. In Chapter 10 we applied our critical thinking skills to the world of science. But there is a sense in which science, rather than being an area of application, is really just a specialized form of critical thinking itself. In the present chapter, we will look at four different areas of decision making in which the sorts of skills you have learned in the preceding chapters turn out to be especially important.

THINKING CRITICALLY ABOUT HEALTH AND HEALTH CARE

There are few decisions that we make in life that are more important than the decisions we make about our health. When it comes to our health, good decision making can literally be a matter of life and death. Making good decisions depends on figuring out what to believe, and that is precisely the business of critical thinking.

This textbook began with the observation that all of us are faced with the challenge of figuring out what to believe given the enormous number of possible beliefs vying for space in our brains. This is nowhere more obvious than in the world of health. Every day we are bombarded with news reports detailing medical breakthroughs, friendly advice on how to stay healthy, and half-remembered lessons taught to us by our parents. We are faced with claims about what kinds of foods we should eat, how much exercise we should get, what sorts of personal habits will keep us healthy, and what to do when we get sick. It can all be truly bewildering.

Key Skills

In order to make sense of this flood of information, we really do need to apply the full range of critical thinking skills and techniques. But a few skills stand out as being particularly useful in evaluating health information.

The most basic critical thinking skill when it comes to thinking critically about your health is the ability to engage in reasoning about causation. In essence, almost all significant health claims are answers to questions about causation. That is true whether we are interested in the cause of illness or what will reverse illness and maintain health. With regard to the causes of illness, we need to find good answers to questions like these:

- What sorts of foods lead most readily to obesity?
- Can a sexually transmitted infection like herpes or chlamydia *really* be transmitted by the seat of a public toilet?

- Will lack of sleep make me more likely to "get run down" and catch a cold or the flu? If I get extra sleep later, will that let me "catch up"?
- What are the most likely causes of a headache or a rash or aches and pains?
- Is it risky to shake hands with someone who has HIV/AIDS?

With regard to preserving or restoring health, we need to be able to evaluate causal claims to answer questions such as the following:

- Does drinking red wine reduce our risk of heart attacks?
- Will taking an antibiotic cure my cold?
- How important is exercise in maintaining a strong immune system?
- Does stretching before running make it less likely that I will pull a muscle?
- Are herbal remedies a safe and effective way to treat various illnesses?

As a starting point, evaluating such claims requires that you recall the lessons learned about causal reasoning in Chapter 8. But in many cases, evaluating causal claims related to health will require that you critically examine the arguments behind various causal claims. To begin with, you need to remember that causal reasoning is a branch of inductive logic. As such, causal reasoning can only ever give us conclusions that are probable, rather than certain—although in some cases, the weight of available evidence is sufficient to make particular conclusions *highly* probable. For example, the evidence marshalled over the last several decades makes it *highly probable* that smoking cigarettes has a strong tendency to cause cancer. This is not a deductive argument, so it can never guarantee its conclusion. But the evidence in this case is so strong that it would be foolish not to believe this causal claim.

But as in all situations requiring the evaluation of causal explanations or hypotheses, we must be on guard against various causal confusions. For example, we must be careful not to be misled by coincidence. Imagine you notice that every time you've caught a cold over the last year it has happened just before a major essay is due at school. Is it really likely that having an essay due is *causing* you to catch a cold? Is that consistent with what you know about the role of viruses in causing colds? Another common causal confusion involves confusing temporal order with causation. As we learned in Chapter 8, if we assume that simply because A is followed by B, then A must have caused B, we commit the fallacy known as *post hoc, ergo propter hoc* ("after that, therefore because of that"). If you take a homeopathic remedy on the third day of a bad cold, you may well find that the cold goes away two or three days later. Is that because the homeopathic remedy was effective, or because the average cold only lasts a total of seven days anyway? Likewise, we must be careful not to

"Something's just not right—our air is clean, our water is pure, we all get plenty of exercise, everything we eat is organic and free-range, and yet nobody lives past thirty."

CREDIT: Alex Gregory/The New Yorker Collection/Cartoon Bank

ignore common-causal factors. When A is found to be correlated with B, is that because one of them causes the other, or is it instead because both are caused by some third factor, C? For example, you might have heard that knee trouble is common among people who also have heart disease. But does knee trouble cause heart disease? Does heart disease cause knee trouble? We might be tempted by one of those causal hypotheses until we consider that both of those ailments are known very often to result from a common cause—namely, obesity.

Of course, in many cases we do not evaluate causal hypotheses ourselves, but instead rely—directly or indirectly—on expert opinion. Sometimes expert opinions come to us directly, from our physician or from other health professionals, and sometimes expert opinions are related to us by the news media.

Evaluating Health Claims in the News

Another important skill is the ability to critically evaluate claims in the news. To begin with, we need to adopt a critical attitude to the process by which news—including health news—is reported. As outlined in Chapter 4, not all news is created equal. The quality of reporting varies enormously, especially, perhaps, with regard to health. For example, a 2011 study published in the journal *Public Understanding of Science* examined claims made in news stories about the relationship between various foods and people's health. The authors of the study systematically looked at items reported in various UK newspapers and examined whether various health claims were justified based on available scientific evidence. They concluded that 72 per cent of health claims made in UK newspapers were supported by levels of evidence *lower* than what would be thought of as "convincing," and 68 per cent were supported by levels of evidence lower than what would be required even to make those claims "probable."[1] This suggests that we cannot take health claims found in the news at face value. In part, this may be a result of the very fact that health is so important to us. News outlets are motivated to feature stories that will get our attention, and they know that stories about food and health are likely to do just that. In some cases, that motivation is liable to outweigh their motivation to report carefully and critically. It is also worth pointing out that, in some cases, reporters themselves may lack the necessary skills to evaluate claims about health science. The result can be reporting that exaggerates the significance of new scientific findings, or that fails to ask hard questions about just how much evidence there is in favour of particular points of view.

In evaluating novel health claims made in news stories, you should ask yourself the following questions:

- Does the news story report a range of views, including the opinions of experts who are skeptical of those novel claims?
- Are the opinions cited in the story the opinions of people with genuine, relevant expertise?
- Does the reporter make an effort to explain the overall body of evidence with regard to the topic at hand, or does he or she merely report narrowly on what is newest and apparently most exciting?
- Is the reporter experienced at reporting on health and science?
- Finally, is the media outlet doing the reporting a credible source of information? Major news outlets like the *Globe and Mail* and the *New York Times* have reputations for high-quality reporting. That doesn't mean they don't make mistakes, but it does tend to make their reporting more reliable.

It is also important to read beyond the headlines. In many cases, sensationalistic headlines accompany news stories about scientific findings related to health that are actually much more bland and unexciting. A headline may trumpet a "PROMISING NEW TREATMENT FOR CANCER!" even though the story below it merely describes a relatively small advance in scientific understanding of one aspect of one type of cancer.

Finding and Evaluating Expert Advice

"Be careful of reading health books. You may die of a misprint."

—*Mark Twain*

There are many health issues that we are all perfectly capable of thinking through on our own. Most of us don't need outside advice to understand the health dangers of sharp objects, or to know that a diet consisting entirely of butter would be bad for us. But in some cases, understanding what will cause health problems or what will prevent or cure them requires the input of experts. As we learned in Chapter 4, an expert is someone who is more knowledgeable in a particular subject area or field than most others are. When experts tell us some claim (in their area of expertise) is true, they are more likely to be right than we are. Experts on health are more likely to be right because (1) they have access to more information on health than we do, and (2) they are better at judging health information than we are. They tend to have access to vast quantities of data and are specially trained at evaluating such data to arrive at useful conclusions.

As we also noted in Chapter 4, the special insight that experts have means that they can help us evaluate novel claims, and that includes claims about health.

If a health claim conflicts with the opinion of a health professional, we have good reason to doubt it.

But of course, there are plenty of occasions on which experts disagree with each other with regard to health. There is expert disagreement, for example, about the value of various health-screening tests—such as cholesterol testing, Pap smears, prostate cancer screening, and so on—at least for particular populations. In such situations, we should recall a further principle from Chapter 4, regarding expert disagreement:

When health experts disagree about a health claim, we have good reason to doubt it.

However, with regard to our health we often cannot afford simply to throw up our hands when faced with disagreement among experts. We can *doubt* whether a particular claim is true or not, but that doesn't necessarily help us make a decision. If a particular health issue is of specific significance for us, we can ask the following questions to help us navigate through expert disagreement:

1. Are the experts involved all true experts, with relevant expertise? (Make sure the apparent disagreement, in other words, is not a disagreement between health researchers on one hand and concerned celebrities on the other!)
2. Does the issue in question deeply divide the population of relevant experts, or are there just a few experts who disagree with the majority? In such situations, you still have *reason to doubt*, but if you need to make a decision about your health, you should take expert opinions as bits of evidence, and—as we have said previously—*proportion your belief to the evidence.*
3. You should consider whether expert disagreement is rooted in evidence about the particular segment of the population of which you are part. For example, there might be expert disagreement concerning the value of cholesterol testing for the general population, yet wide expert agreement concerning the importance of such testing for people of *your* age group.

We should also remember that disagreement among experts often pertains to small details, which can sometimes distract us from broad expert agreement on more important issues. They might disagree, for example, about the exact kind and quantity of exercise that is required to keep us healthy—and newspapers might make a big deal out of such disagreement—despite fundamental agreement on the importance for all of us to maintain an active lifestyle.

FOOD FOR THOUGHT

Critical Thinking and Health Professionals

How does critical thinking fit into the world of health professionals? Obviously, critical thinking plays an essential role in that world; we rely on health professionals precisely because they are able to critically evaluate health information, including the information relevant to diagnosing and treating our illnesses.

It may already have occurred to you that health professionals are *experts* in the sense discussed in Chapter 4. That is true, and it has implications for their ability to assess and understand claims about health and health care. As we noted in Chapter 4, experts have an advantage in that they have access to more information on the subject of health than the average consumer does, and they are better at judging that information than the average consumer is. A well-trained doctor, pharmacist, or nurse, for example, knows a good deal about how to evaluate the conclusions reached by particular scientific studies—the announcement of a breakthrough in cancer care, for example. They also know how to assess the cumulative weight of the various pieces of evidence that are relevant to a particular question, such as whether acupuncture is effective at treating back pain.

But health professionals themselves face challenges in deciding what to believe. After all, the amount of relevant information is enormous and growing rapidly; it is probably impossible for any health professional to keep up with all the latest findings in anything but a very narrow specialty. And expertise is always limited in scope. A nurse or pharmacist will generally not know as much about diagnosing illness as a physician does; a physician or nurse will generally not know as much about the interactions of different drugs as a pharmacist does; and a pharmacist or physician will generally not know as much about measuring and recording a patient's vital signs (pulse, blood pressure, etc.) as a nurse does. Outside of his or her own specialty, a health professional may be more knowledgeable than the average person, but not a true expert. When health professionals are faced with claims on topics that fall partly or entirely outside their field of practice, they must be cautious: they must not only proportion their belief to the evidence, but must also temper their degree of belief according to what they know to be the limits of their own ability to judge that evidence.

Stumbling Blocks

"He who has health, has hope; and he who has hope, has everything."

—*Thomas Carlyle*

Deciding what to believe with regard to staying healthy and responding to illness is an effort that is subject to many of the fallacies discussed in Chapter 5. Think, for example, of the prominence of *appeal to tradition* and *appeal to popularity* in the realm of health. For instance, you may have been told that "everyone knows" that you can catch a cold if you go outside in winter without a scarf. But of course, that's pure appeal to popularity—just because it is widely believed, that doesn't mean it's true. Such appeals are particularly worrisome with regard to health. Health is a complex matter, and there are many subtopics on which the general public simply is not well informed.

Similarly, your grandmother may tell you that the best cure for a cold is chicken soup, or a "mustard plaster" applied to your chest while you rest in bed. Why? Because that's what her mother told her, and what her mother's mother told her, and so on. But of course, that doesn't make it true. That's just an appeal to tradition. Appeal to tradition is particularly problematic in the realm of health, because advances in health science have resulted in enormous changes in what we know about how to stay healthy, how we get sick, and what we should do about it when we do. For centuries, people believed that a healthy diet had to include meat, and plenty of it. Today there is growing evidence that meat should play only a relatively small role in our diets, and many experts recommend a vegetarian or even vegan diet. Appealing to tradition, here, does not serve us well! The same goes for treating illness. The fact that a particular treatment—some mixture of herbs, for example—was used "for hundreds of years" within a particular culture doesn't prove that that treatment was effective; it merely proves that it was popular, and perhaps that those people had no alternatives that were superior.

It is also worth noting the sense in which evaluating health claims often amounts to a process very much like the one we described in Chapter 10 for judging scientific theories. Do WiFi signals (radiation given off by wireless Internet) cause health problems? In determining whether that theory is credible, we ought to ask whether that theory is testable and fruitful, whether it is broad in scope, whether it is simple, and whether it is conservative. It is worth noting that most so-called alternative medicines do very badly when evaluated

FOOD FOR THOUGHT

Hey, Doc! Don't Look for Zebras!

One particular critical thinking challenge faced by health professionals has to do with availability error, which we discussed in Chapter 4. Recall that the availability error has to do with the human mind's tendency, when evaluating various risks, to think first of the most exciting and exotic possibilities. We pointed out that most people think of shark attacks as a relatively common source of danger, despite the fact that shark attacks are actually incredibly rare, because when such attacks do happen they are so gruesome and frightening. As a result, it is easy for us to vividly imagine a shark attack when asked to close our eyes and imagine something dangerous.

When this tendency is observed in physicians, it often takes the form of what is known as the "zebra problem." It is summed up in the diagnostic rule of thumb often taught to medical students: "When you hear the beat of hooves, think 'horse' not 'zebra.'" In other words, when diagnosing a patient, don't think *first* of the most exotic possible explanation for the patient's symptoms—begin instead with the most common and likely possibilities. For instance, when a patient has a rash, don't think first of rare and exotic diseases like Legionnaires' disease or the bubonic plague! Work first to rule out simple, commonplace causes like chicken pox or poison ivy. That is very likely also to be good advice for the average individual: your headache at the end of a long and stressful day is probably not an indication that you've got a brain tumour.

in this way. Some of them fail the test of conservatism because they assume the existence of strange flows of "energy" through the human body, energy of a kind not known to modern physics. Others turn out not to be very broad in scope. Homeopathy, for example, is a form of alternative therapy that assumes that water has a "memory" of every molecule it ever came in contact with, and so medicines diluted beyond the point at which there is any active ingredient left can, supposedly, still have an effect on our bodies. Yet homeopaths assert that this effect only becomes relevant in the manufacture of homeopathic remedies: it supposedly has no implications whatsoever for the water we drink!

Weird theories of all kinds are especially common with regard to health. And so it is particularly important to avoid the temptation, noted in Chapter 10, to leap to weird theories in the absence of evidence. In the face of unusual experiences, our "background knowledge" may let us down and we may be tempted to jump to unwarranted conclusions. If you are not accustomed to getting headaches, the sudden onset of a headache may cause you to assume the worst: maybe it's a brain tumour! The fact that you can't happen to think of a more mundane explanation for your headache doesn't mean that no such explanation exists.

THINKING CRITICALLY ABOUT THE LAW

Nowhere is critical thinking more essential than in the application of law. The law represents the strongest rules of behaviour in any society, rules typically enforced by means of the full power and authority of government. When individuals are found to have violated the law, they may be subject to substantial fines or imprisonment. Taking away an individual's freedom is a very serious matter, and doing so should only be done in full light of the facts, evaluated according to the strictest possible standards of critical thinking.

Critical thinking is relevant to many aspects of the law. Members of Parliament and their staff must think critically about the need for, and wording of, new legislation if they are to make sure that new laws are both clearly needed and clearly worded. Police officers must use critical thinking skills in applying the law. For example, police officers must apply the law without bias resulting from *hasty generalization*. Citizens, too, must use their critical thinking skills with regard to the law. If the law forbids "vehicles" in the park, does that include *toy* vehicles or wheelchairs?

In this section, however, we will focus on the application of critical thinking skills to deliberations in the courtroom. That is, we will focus on the need for critical thinking skills on the part of judges, lawyers, and members of juries in criminal proceedings.

Critical thinking is particularly important in a court of law for a couple of reasons. The first reason has to do with the importance of such proceedings: as noted above, legal proceedings can result in individuals being thrown in jail, losing their freedom along with the ability to have regular contact with friends and family. The second reason has to do with the adversarial nature of our legal system. Under the current system, any time someone is charged with a crime the court is faced with the challenge of evaluating two competing points of view. On one side is the Crown attorney, representing the government. His or her job is to attempt to convince the court that the accused is guilty and ought to be punished. On the other side are the accused and his or her defence counsel. The defence counsel's job is to attempt to convince the court that the accused is innocent, has been wrongly charged, and ought to be set free. Neither side is responsible for presenting a balanced view of the evidence. It is the job of the Crown to argue vigorously for a guilty verdict, just as it is the defence counsel's job to argue zealously for a finding of innocence. And in most cases the truth of the matter will not be obvious. The court must hear the evidence, weigh it carefully, and reach a verdict. In some circumstances, that task falls to one or more judges, and in other circumstances it falls to a jury of 12 regular citizens. Either way, it is a task that requires the most serious attention to the demands of critical thinking.

EVERYDAY PROBLEMS AND DECISIONS

Jury Duty

One of the most important decisions any citizen can make, or help make, is the decision to send a fellow citizen to jail. As a member of a jury in a criminal trial, you are part of a group of 12 citizens making just such a decision.

If you serve on a jury in such a case, what factors should you take into consideration? Most generally, a juror's job is to take into consideration all information presented during the trial. And, importantly, that is *all* that should influence a juror. It is a juror's duty to do his or her best not to be influenced by other factors, such as prejudices or biases. A juror needs to use good judgment and common sense to evaluate the evidence presented. Of course, jurors are not experts in the law. (In fact, lawyers are not eligible to serve as jurors in Canada.)

The relevant legal expertise is provided by the two lawyers (the prosecutor and defence counsel) and by the judge. It is the task of the prosecutor and defence counsel to present evidence and to explain to the jury what they take to be the key aspects of the relevant laws. They will naturally do so in a way that is intended to persuade jurors. The prosecutor will try to convince the jury that the defendant is guilty, and the defendant's lawyer will try to convince the jury that the defendant is innocent—or, at least, that the prosecutor has not provided enough evidence to prove guilt. After all evidence is presented, the judge will instruct the jury, in an impartial way, on what the relevant laws say, and on what factors they must—and what factors they must not—take into consideration.

Key Skills

Of all of the critical thinking skills needed in a court of law, the most fundamental is a good command of what we referred to in Chapter 9 as "inference to the best explanation." Recall that inference to the best explanation is a form of inductive argument in which the arguer gives reason for believing one explanation for a set of facts rather than another. And that, of course, is precisely what goes on in a court of law. In a criminal trial, various kinds of evidence are presented to the court: a body was found; the accused, Mr Levin, was found near the scene with blood on his hands; an eyewitness testifies to having seen Mr Levin arguing with the victim just a few hours earlier; DNA evidence suggests the involvement of some third party; and so on. After such evidence is presented, each lawyer—the Crown attorney and the defence counsel—will provide a story, an account of the events of the day that they will argue constitutes a good explanation for that evidence, taken as a whole. And the court—the judge or the jury—must evaluate those competing explanations to determine which is best.

Recall from Chapter 9 that all instances of inference to the best explanation follow this pattern:

Phenomenon Q.
E provides the best explanation for Q.
Therefore, it is probable that E is true.

"He's big, all right, and he's definitely a wolf, but it'll be up to a jury to decide whether or not he's bad."

CREDIT: Michael Maslin/The New Yorker Collection/The Cartoon Bank

In a criminal trial, "Phenomenon Q" would be the crime in question—on the murder, the theft, etc. "E" would be one or another of the explanations offered by the competing lawyers—either that the defendant committed the crime or she did not. The middle premise, then, would be that E provides the best explanation for how the crime happened. And the conclusion of the argument—the verdict of the trial—would be either that the defendant did or did not commit the crime.

In most instances of inference to the best explanation, we say that the argument that presents the best explanation is inductively strong. But in a criminal trial, we are looking not just for a *strong* argument regarding whether the accused is guilty or innocent, but for a *compelling* argument. During criminal proceedings, the burden of proof (a notion discussed in Chapter 5) rests squarely upon the prosecution. The accused, in other words, is "innocent until proven guilty," and in order to be punished must be found "guilty beyond a reasonable doubt." The reason for this high standard is clear. First, as noted above, the stakes in criminal trials are very high. Second, our legal system is rooted in the principle that it is a heinous wrong to convict someone who is in fact innocent, and that if errors are to be made, it is much better that they be made in favour of the defendant. As the eighteenth-century English judge William Blackstone famously put it, it is "better that 10 guilty persons escape than that one innocent suffer." Finally, note that the individual accused generally faces significant disadvantages. He is, after all, just one person with one lawyer, being prosecuted by a Crown attorney who is backed, in principle, by the very considerable resources of the entire government. The government, it is believed, has so many obvious advantages that the least we can do is ask the Crown to bear the burden of proof.

Finally, it is worth noting that many aspects of legal reasoning involve categorical logic of the kind we studied in Chapter 6. In determining whether a person violated the law, we are essentially determining whether his or her actions fall into a particular category of prohibited behaviours. Look, for example, at the start of Section 221 of the Criminal Code of Canada, the section dealing with homicide:

> A person commits homicide when, directly or indirectly, by any means, he causes the death of a human being.

Though it may not look like it, this is a categorical statement—specifically, a universal affirmative statement. An argument rooted in that section might look like this:

> Mr Levin indirectly caused the death of a human being. According to the Criminal Code, anyone who causes the death of a human being, even indirectly, is guilty of homicide. So Levin must be found guilty of homicide.

Put into standard form, that argument might look like this:

P1. All persons who are Mr Levin are persons who directly or indirectly caused the death of a human being.

P2. All persons who directly or indirectly cause the death of a human being are persons who have committed homicide.

C. Therefore, all persons who are Mr Levin are persons who committed homicide.

Simplifying, this becomes:

All *S* are *M*.
All *M* are *P*.
Therefore, all *S* are *P*.

And we can easily demonstrate, using a Venn diagram, that this is a valid argument. The key problem for the court to decide, of course, is whether the key premise—premise 2—is in fact true!

The way convicted criminals are sentenced is also a matter of categorical logic. For example, according to Section 47 of the Criminal Code of Canada:

> *Every one who commits high treason is guilty of an indictable offence and shall be sentenced to imprisonment for life.*

This, too, is a categorical claim of the universal affirmative variety, one that would serve as the foundation for a categorical argument regarding the appropriate punishment for a particular individual.

Stumbling Blocks

Most fundamental among the critical thinking challenges faced in modern courts of law is the difficulty implied by the need to evaluate competing theories—that offered by the Crown and that offered by the defence—in light of what may be an absolutely overwhelming quantity of evidence. But we can also identify a number of other, more specific, challenges.

Judges and juries must be on guard against the effect of many of the argumentative fallacies discussed in Chapter 5. Prosecutors, for example, may offer juries a *false dilemma*: either convict the accused, or let a vicious killer go free. Prosecutors might be tempted to make *ad hominem* arguments. If they can make the accused seem like a bad person, it may make it easier for a jury to believe that he has committed the crime of which he is accused. But, strictly speaking, the character of the accused is not relevant. People with histories of wrongdoing are sometimes wrongly accused, and people of good character do, unfortunately, sometimes commit crimes. So character is beside the point; what matters is whether the facts support the conclusion that the accused actually committed the crime in question. Jurors may also be tempted to *beg the question* against the accused. If the accused weren't guilty, they might wonder, why would he be accused of this vicious crime? After all, only criminals get arrested, right? But that of course is a premise that assumes the very thing we are trying to determine, namely whether the accused should be considered a criminal or not. The accused, for his part, might attempt an *appeal to emotion*: please don't convict me, because I've got a family to support. The judge and jury must of course do their best to avoid being influenced by such considerations; their job is to judge the evidence, to believe one theory or the other in proportion to the evidence, and to return the verdict that fits best.

In legal contexts, we must also beware of the risks of faulty conditional reasoning. Look, for instance, at this imaginary (but not unlikely) bit of legal reasoning:

> Ladies and gentlemen of the jury, it is clear what has happened here. If Mr Alkoby committed this crime, we would surely find his fingerprints on the knife that killed Ms Swansburg. And his fingerprints were indeed found on that weapon! It is clear that Mr Alkoby committed this gruesome crime.

This sounds like a compelling argument! But notice the argument's logical structure: it is a piece of propositional logic—more specifically, a conditional argument of a particular kind, first discussed in Chapter 3. If you look carefully, you'll see that this is an example of *affirming the consequent*, which we know is always invalid. Of course, the fact that the defendant's fingerprints were found on the murder weapon is not irrelevant. At the very least, that is likely to be an important part of a strong inductive argument for the defendant's guilt. But here, even more essentially than in other instances, we must avoid being drawn in by the deductive style of the prosecutor's argument, which tends to suggest to our mind that the argument is much stronger than it actually is.

Finally, criminal courts must also be wary of the limits on the reliability of eyewitness testimony. An eyewitness is someone who reports, in court, things he or she claims to know from personal experience. In Chapter 4, we learned about the worrisome effect of things like impairment and expectation on the reliability of personal experience. And, according to Toronto defence lawyer Jaki Freeman, Canadian courts have long been aware of these problems:

> For years, Canadian courts have been aware that eyewitness evidence is remarkably frail and fraught with problems. Such evidence has been identified as a major source of wrongful convictions in Canada. A number of factors influence the accuracy of an identification of a suspect by a witness, such as whether the suspect is known or a stranger to the witness, the circumstances surrounding the contact between the suspect and the witness, the individual make-up of the witness, and the nature and methods used during any pre-trial identification of the suspect. There are multiple reasons for this frailty including that the initial contact between witness and suspect is often made under traumatic and unexpected circumstances and when the observation conditions are not ideal. In addition to the factors present at the time of the observations and the personal characteristics of the observing witness, postevent identification procedures can influence the identification of a

> particular person. Pre-trial identification procedures may be flawed and designed—intentionally or unintentionally—to influence the witness so that a particular suspect is identified.[2]

In other words, courts of law do and should worry—for many of the same reasons discussed in Chapter 4—about relying on personal experience in the form of eyewitness testimony.

THINKING CRITICALLY ABOUT ETHICS

> "In matters of conscience, the law of the majority has no place."
>
> —*Mahatma Gandhi*

Finally, we turn to the topic of ethics. Some will be surprised at the very idea of applying critical thinking skills to the realm of ethics. After all, ethics is about what is right and wrong from a moral point of view, and isn't that a personal matter? Don't we all have—and aren't we all entitled to—our own views on that? Shouldn't we respect each other's opinions on ethics rather than adopting a critical attitude?

There is, of course, something right in this: we ought to adopt a respectful attitude to other *people* and take their points of view seriously. But this doesn't imply an exception to the general need to think critically. We don't, after all, want to commit to the *subjectivist fallacy* discussed in Chapter 2. Recall that subjective *relativism* is the idea that truth depends on what someone happens to believe—that believing something is enough to make it true. But that view is no more credible with regard to ethics than it is with regard to other sorts of claims. It just doesn't make sense to think, as subjective relativism implies, that none of us is ever wrong about anything related to ethics. We are all fallible, capable of making mistakes, and that's as true with regard to ethics as it is with regard to anything else. Our claims about ethics deserve to be backed up by good arguments. And when confronted with new ethical claims, we need to be able to evaluate critically the arguments offered in support of those claims.

Key Skills

ethics The critical, structured examination of how we ought to behave when our behaviour affects others.

Ethics is the critical, structured examination of how we ought to behave when our behaviour affects others. The most fundamental critical thinking skill when it comes to ethics is perhaps the very basic ability, learned in Chapter 3 of this book, to identify the fundamental building blocks out of which an ethical argument is constructed. Ethical claims are often put forward with considerable passion, and so a systematic approach can help us move past emotion to look carefully at the structure of an ethical argument.

As with other sorts of arguments, the basic building blocks of ethical arguments are claims or statements. Ethical claims come in many forms. Claims about how we ought to behave may take the form of claims about particular behaviours, the outcomes of our choices, or the kinds of people we should be. Such claims answer questions regarding what kinds of behaviour are right and what kinds are wrong, and about what kinds of outcomes and what kinds of character traits are good or bad. Consider the following examples:

- Serena should keep her promise to you.
- It is wrong to treat James so harshly.
- Abortion is immoral.
- We ought to protect Liu from the angry mob.
- My father is a good man.

CREDIT: © Brigida_Soriano/iStockphoto

With regard to ethics, Socrates (469–399 BCE), in Plato's *Republic*, noted that "We are discussing no small matter, here, but how we ought to live."

Ethical claims can be differentiated from plain descriptive claims, such as the following:

- Serena did not keep her promise to you.
- James was fired.
- Some people think abortion is immoral.
- Liu was protected from the angry mob.
- My father tried to be a good man.

Most ethical arguments in fact feature some combination of ethical and descriptive claims. In one standard kind of ethical argument, the arguer puts forward a general ethical principle of some sort, then describes some action to which that principle applies, and then concludes that the action is either right or wrong. For example:

> Ethical Premise: It is unethical to take other people's belongings without their permission.
> Descriptive Premise: You borrowed my sweater without my permission.
> Ethical Conclusion: You did something unethical.

Note first that this argument has two premises. One is about ethics and one is merely descriptive—it describes the facts of the case in a general way. This is, in fact, an important thing to note about ethical arguments. Every ethical argument, once its premises are made explicit, *must* contain at least one ethical premise and one descriptive premise. Without a descriptive premise, we don't know the facts of the case under consideration; without an ethical premise, the argument has no ethical or moral foundation at all. As the eighteenth-century philosopher David Hume pointed out, mere facts alone cannot support an ethical conclusion. Or to put it another way, descriptive premises only tell you how the world is; an ethical conclusion tells you how the world *should* be. Logic won't take you from the former to the latter without an ethical premise to help.

What does spelling out the premises and conclusions of an ethical argument accomplish? For one thing, we achieve a certain amount of clarity just by putting it all there in black and white. Keep in mind that in real conversation, ethical arguments will often have pieces missing. In many instances, arguers simply leave out ethical premises that they think are too obvious to state. By making those pieces explicit, we are able to examine them carefully to see if they are plausible.

Making the parts of an ethical argument explicit can also help us see its structure, the way its premises work to attempt to support its conclusion. Notice, for example, that the two premises in the argument above need each other. They are, in other words, *dependent premises*, something we learned about in Chapter 3. That means that if either premise fails to be plausible, then the entire argument falls apart.

Notice also that the argument above is made up entirely of categorical claims—or, at least, claims that can be reworded slightly to make them into categorical claims. Put in categorical terms, that argument might look like this:

> All instances in which you took my sweater are instances of taking other people's belongings without their permission.
>
> All instances of taking other people's belongings without their permission are unethical actions.
>
> Therefore, all instances in which you took my sweater are unethical actions.

Putting it this way is somewhat awkward, but it accurately reflects the meaning of the original argument. Further, we can go ahead and put that argument into standard form, as follows:

> All *S* are *M*.
> All *M* are *P*.
> Therefore, all *S* are *P*.

And of course, once we see the argument in this form, we can evaluate it as we would any other categorical syllogism, for example, by constructing a Venn diagram.

Categorical arguments of this sort are very common. In such an argument, the arguer tries to fit a particular action into a category of actions generally acknowledged to be either ethical (e.g., keeping promises) or unethical (e.g., stealing). It also happens to be a kind of syllogism that is a valid argument. (Check for yourself and see!) This means that, presented with such an argument, you can proceed directly to evaluating the premises to determine if they are reasonable. Did the person in question really take the sweater without permission? Is it really true that taking things without the owner's permission is always unethical? Are there exceptions? Do the exceptions apply to this case?

Next, consider the following ethical argument:

> Ethical Premise: If Earl was a good man, he would take care of his family.
> Descriptive Premise: But Earl has not taken care of his family.
> Ethical Conclusion: Earl is not a good man.

Notice the structure of this argument. You might begin by noting that the first premise—the ethical premise—is a conditional statement, a statement with an "if–then" structure. This suggests that the argument here can be evaluated using the tools of propositional logic, as discussed in Chapter 7. So we could, in principle, construct a truth table to evaluate this argument. But there's no need for that in this particular case. If you look closely, you'll see that the argument above is an instance of denying the consequent, an argument structure that is always *valid*.

But compare that to this argument:

> Ethical Premise: If you're a good person, you keep your promises.
> Descriptive Premise: You keep your promises.
> Ethical Conclusion: So, you're a good person.

Notice that again, we have a conditional argument, an instance of affirming the consequent. And so again, there's no need for a truth table: arguments that affirm the consequent are always invalid.

So much for the logical structure of ethical arguments. How can we tell whether the premises of an ethical argument are acceptable? Well, to begin, we noted above that every ethical argument will have at least one descriptive premise, and we can evaluate that just as we would evaluate the claims made in any other kind of argument. (For more on that, see Chapter 4.) But what about ethical premises? The evaluation of ethical claims, and the standards to which ethical claims should be subjected, is a vast topic, one that is the subject of extensive philosophical debates. We cannot delve into those debates in any detail, but will provide here just a couple of hints at how an assessment of ethical premises might begin.

First, we can apply the ethical component of what we referred to in Chapter 4 as our background information—that huge collection of very well-supported beliefs that we all rely on to inform our actions and choices. That background information includes not just descriptions, but also ethical rules and standards. The fact that it is generally wrong to lie or to hurt people is so well-established that for most purposes it is unreasonable to doubt it.

Another tactic we can apply is to look for certain structural features that experts generally think ethical claims ought to have. One such feature is universality. An ethical starting point ought to be one that could apply to all persons in the relevant circumstances. For example, "It is wrong to lie" is universal in the relevant sense. It doesn't claim to apply to just one or a few people—by default, it applies to everyone. (In fact, we could reasonably, though awkwardly, reword that claim as a universal affirmative categorical statement: "All persons are persons who should not lie.") A claim that singles out a particular individual for special treatment is usually not acceptable as a foundation for an ethical argument. We can, of course, arrive at *conclusions* that are about specific

individuals, but those conclusions must be reached as the result of an argument rooted in an ethical premise that is universal in its scope.

Another key feature to look for in ethical claims is consistency. This means that our ethical judgments should be the same for situations that have the same features. If someone proposes an ethical rule for one situation, it ought to apply also in relevantly similar situations. For example, if someone says "taking office supplies home is morally justified," we are justified in asking whether that person thinks that stealing is justified in other situations, too. To think that a particular kind of behaviour is permissible in one situation but not in situations that share the relevant characteristics is inconsistent. An ethical premise that demonstrates inconsistency need not be taken very seriously.

Finally, we can gain some confidence in specific ethical premises if they are drawn from one or more of the great traditions of philosophical ethics. The Western philosophical tradition stretches back more than 2000 years, and during that time philosophers have proposed and debated an enormous number of ethical theories claiming to sum up everything that needs to be said about the topic. Today, no one theory stands out as having won that grand intellectual struggle. But a few contenders have stood the test of time, and continue to be defended by at least a respectable subset of philosophers. We cannot discuss these theories in any detail here, but for our purposes it will be enough to point out that each of these theories represents a tradition of moral thinking that has stood the test of time. Each of them proposes a respectable set of principles or ethical reasons that can serve as premises for ethical arguments.

These three grand traditions of ethics are as follows:

- **Argument from consequences**. Arguments rooted in this tradition take as a starting point the idea that our most fundamental ethical obligation is to produce certain kinds of outcomes. In other words, in making ethical choices, it is the expected consequences of our behaviour that matters. Arguments rooted in an appeal to consequences will generally point out that certain actions have a tendency to make people better off, to prevent harm, to make people happy, and so on. In philosophical terms, this tradition is known as *consequentialism*, and the most respected form of consequentialism is known as *utilitarianism*. This tradition is most famously represented by the English philosopher John Stuart Mill (1806–1873).

argument from consequences An ethical argument that takes as a starting point the idea that our most fundamental ethical obligation is to produce certain kinds of outcomes.

- **Argument from rights and duties**. Arguments grounded in this tradition focus not on outcomes, but on performing or avoiding certain kinds of actions. This tradition holds that there are certain actions that we must always avoid doing (like killing innocent persons) and certain actions that it is our duty always to do (such as, perhaps, keeping promises). It

argument from rights and duties An ethical argument that begins with the notion that there are certain kinds of actions that we must always do or always avoid doing.

is from this tradition that we get the notion of human rights—the idea that humans are to be respected, and therefore there are certain ways they must be treated. Philosophically, this tradition is referred to as *deontology* and is most famously associated with the work of the German philosopher Immanuel Kant (1724–1804).

argument from character An ethical argument that proceeds from the assumption that what really matters ethically is character, rather than the nature or outcome of particular actions.

- **Argument from character.** Arguments rooted in this tradition start from the assumption that what really matters, ethically, is character. That is, the key is not so much the individual choices we make on particular occasions, but the kinds of people we show ourselves to be through our actions. Arguments of this kind will tend to focus on whether specific behaviours—or more likely, patterns of behaviour—demonstrate one or another of various desirable traits of character, such as honesty and bravery and compassion. To philosophers, this tradition is known as *virtue theory*, and is associated historically with the highly influential work of the ancient Greek philosopher Aristotle (384–322 BCE).

In contrast, there are ethical points of view that have not stood the test of time. These include ethical egoism (the theory that the only relevant ethical reason is self-interest) and ethical relativism (the theory that all that matters is the moral beliefs of your own society).

Finally, it is worth pointing out that premises rooted in these different ethical traditions sometimes point to quite different conclusions. Argument from rights and duties, for example, is often seen as providing a counterweight to reasoning that is rooted entirely in argument from consequences. It is easy to imagine a situation in which a police officer, for example, believes she could do some good—achieve some good outcome—by framing an innocent man. When ethical premises from different ethical traditions conflict, there is no formula for settling the debate.

Stumbling Blocks

We have already noted that the subjectivist fallacy is perhaps the greatest barrier to clear thinking about ethics. If we are even to begin to apply the tools of critical thinking to various ethical claims, we must first get past the unhelpful notion that ethics is all just a matter of personal opinion.

But a number of other fallacies are likewise common in ethical arguments. Among the most common, perhaps, is the appeal to popularity. Appeal to popularity, as we learned in Chapter 5, occurs when we cite the popularity of some idea—the sheer number of people who believe it—as evidence that it must be true. Historically, a kind of appeal to popularity was likely responsible for the perpetuation of injustices against women, minority groups, and homosexuals. Prior to 1919, the year when Canadian women were granted the right to vote, it was sometimes argued that "everyone knows" that women have no ability to understand politics, and would just vote for whichever candidate was the most handsome! Of course, critical thinkers recognize that the fact that many people "know" (or rather *believe*) something doesn't make it true. It's also worth pointing out that sometimes appeal to popularity is combined with appeal to tradition: "everyone knows" that Group X isn't worthy of being treated equally, and "that's the way it has always been." A critical approach to ethics is dedicated to pointing out such fallacies and to questioning the factual basis for the claims they make use of.

Another common fallacy found in arguments concerning ethics is the straw man fallacy. Recall that in a straw man, the arguer presents a distorted, weakened, or oversimplified version of someone's position so that it can be more easily attacked or refuted. Occurrences of the straw man fallacy happen very easily when discussing ethics. It is relatively easy to produce cartoonish versions of someone else's subtle ethical claims or arguments. If Mark argues that companies in developing nations might be justified in failing to use expensive safety equipment, an opponent might express horror at Mark's belief that "workers' lives have no value." Similarly, if Josephine argues that, out of concern for the effects of climate change, Canada ought to consider reducing industrial greenhouse gas emissions, an opponent might be tempted to make her look foolish by accusing her of wanting to shut down Canada's industrial sector altogether, thereby wrecking our economy.

Finally, we must also be on guard for instances of the slippery slope fallacy when discussing ethics. Recall that a slippery slope involves arguing, without good reason, that taking some particular step will inevitably lead to some further, highly undesirable step. Such arguments are common in ethics precisely because discussions of ethics are so often focused on what we should or should not do. Note also that ethics is generally about rules of behaviour, about drawing lines between acceptable and unacceptable actions. So it is often tempting for us to worry that some action that is on *this* side of the line separating right from wrong is going to lead to some other action that is on *the other* side of that line, especially if we don't look carefully at what the relevant differences might be between the two things. Slippery slope arguments sometimes arise in discussions of physician-assisted suicide, for example. Advocates might argue that, under some circumstances, it might be reasonable for an individual with a serious, chronic illness to ask a physician for help in dying. Critics of such a view may suggest that if we allow physicians to help the seriously ill to commit suicide, what's to stop them from deciding on their own to start killing patients. "Next thing you know," the critic may conclude, "no one will be safe in a hospital." But of course, that doesn't obviously follow. Supporters of physician-assisted suicide typically only argue for the availability of a fully voluntary process. They also often recommend safeguards, such as the participation of an entire committee of physicians and a requirement that the patient's desire to die be documented as persisting over a number of weeks. The slope from physician-assisted suicide to rampant murder by doctors, in other words, is not necessarily so slippery!

As with other kinds of arguments, we must recall that the fact that someone has offered a fallacious argument for a particular ethical point of view doesn't mean that their view is incorrect. All it means is that the argument *as presented* does not work. As critical thinkers, we recognize that we can, and should, do better.

SUMMARY

Health care, law, and ethics are among the most important topics that any of us deals with in our daily lives. Clear thinking about health is among our greatest challenges. Health is universally agreed upon as fundamental to a good life, an essential precondition to the enjoyment of whatever particular projects and pastimes bring us joy. Clear thinking in courts of law is essential to making sure that justice is served—that the guilty are punished and the innocent are not. And clear thinking about ethics is the foundation of a morally good life. The very best—that is, the most reliable—thinking in health care, in law, and in ethics relies heavily on the tools of critical thinking.

EXERCISE 11.1

Review Questions

Answers to exercises marked with an asterisk (*) may be found in Appendix B, Answers to Exercises.

*1. According to the text, what is the most basic critical thinking skill when it comes to thinking about health?
2. Is causal reasoning part of inductive or deductive logic?
3. If an argument is fallacious, does that mean that the conclusion is false?
4. According to the study cited in this chapter, roughly what per cent of health claims reported in UK newspapers are supported by good evidence?
5. What is the most reasonable attitude to adopt toward health claims that conflict with expert opinion?
6. Name two key questions you should ask yourself when you see novel health claims being published in the news.

7. When engaging in "inference to the best explanation" in criminal trials, what constitutes the phenomenon to be explained?
*8. How does the concept of "burden of proof" apply to criminal trials?
9. What is one argumentative fallacy that is common in legal reasoning?
10. Why is subjectivism about ethics tempting?
11. Why is subjectivism about ethics a mistake?
12. What is the difference between an ethical claim and a descriptive claim?
13. What constitutes our background information with regard to ethics?
*14. Name the three "grand traditions" of ethics discussed in this chapter.

EXERCISE 11.2

On the basis of claims you already have good reason to believe, your background information, and your assessment of the credibility of any cited experts, indicate for each of the following statements whether you would accept it, reject it, or proportion your belief to the evidence. Give reasons for your answers. If you decide to proportion your belief to the evidence, state generally what degree of plausibility you would assign to the claim.

*1. An apple a day keeps the doctor away!
2. Everyone should get at least a couple of hours of exercise every week to promote long-term health.
*3. Dr Campagna, my physics teacher, says that WiFi radiation is pretty much harmless.
4. Dr Samuelson, famous author and young earth creationist, supports the idea that smoking increases a person's chance of contracting lung cancer.
5. Possession of marijuana is illegal in Canada.
6. Mr Abdolmalaki is a Crown attorney, and he says very few people in Canada go to jail for simple possession of marijuana.
7. Of course Bartkiw is guilty. It doesn't matter that his plane ticket shows he was in another country at the time an eyewitness described him almost perfectly as the one who stole the jewels!
8. I'm innocent. Just ask my lawyer, and she'll tell you.
*9. Killing innocent people is wrong.
10. Killing another person is never ethically justified.
11. Katy Perry says that celebrities have a moral obligation to support charities.
12. My ethics professor, Professor Li, says that he has studied the debate carefully and there simply are no philosophically sound arguments against allowing all people to marry regardless of sexual orientation.

EXERCISE 11.3

For each of the following claims, name the fallacy or fallacies involved, if any.

1. Wow, that herbal remedy grandma recommended was awesome. I had a cold for a week, and then I took that stuff and the cold was gone the next day!
*2. I don't believe that a diet with lots of meat in it is bad for you. My family is German, and we've always loved lots of meat products—bratwurst, schnitzel, liverwurst, you name it!
3. Please, Your Honour, you can't find me guilty! If I go to jail, who's going to feed my kids?
4. How can cheating on my taxes be wrong? Everyone does it!
*5. Shahram is obviously guilty of this crime. He's a notorious thug with a long history of criminal behaviour.
6. Fresh air from an open window is good for a sleeping baby. Every parent knows that!
*7. Who do you think you are, telling me I shouldn't hit my kids? I'm entitled to my own morals, and that includes how to raise my own children.
*8. I can't believe you think it's OK to download "pirated" music. I'm amazed that you think it's better for struggling artists to starve rather than being paid for their music!
9. If you commit first-degree murder, you should go to jail. But my client didn't commit first-degree murder, so he should not go to jail.

EXERCISE 11.4

For each of the following arguments, construct a Venn diagram to assess for validity. If the argument is valid, give a brief outline of whether the argument's premises are acceptable. (Hint: you may need to supply a missing premise or conclusion.)

*1. Anyone who smokes heavily is sure to get cancer. And you're a heavy smoker!
2. Skiing is dangerous. After all, people have died doing "backcountry" skiing, and any sport where people have died should be considered dangerous.
3. Some muggers are thieves and some thieves go to jail. So, some muggers go to jail.

4. Anyone who takes office supplies home for personal use is a thief. That's exactly what Alison did. So . . . !
5. Killing is wrong. So capital punishment is wrong.
6. You're a moral person. All moral persons must avoid lying. So you must avoid lying.
*7. Some people who lie have good reasons. Some people who have good reasons are actually saints. So some people who lie are saints.

Field Problems

1. Go online and find the Letters to the Editor section of the website for your local newspaper or a national (Canadian) newspaper (such as the *Globe and Mail* or *National Post*). Identify a letter to the editor that makes an ethical argument—an argument about some ethical issue. Does the writer commit any logical fallacies? Overall, is his or her argument a strong one?
2. Think of something you believe to be true with regard to staying healthy—some claim either about what helps you stay healthy or about what would make you get sick. What reasons do you have for believing that claim? Go online and find at least three reputable websites that offer support for that claim. Is the support for it strong, or weak?
3. Imagine that you've been charged—falsely!—with a serious crime. What critical thinking tools from this textbook would you most want your lawyer to understand? What critical thinking skills would be most important in order for your lawyer to help keep you out of jail?

Self-Assessment Quiz

1. How should a critical thinker regard unsupported health claims that conflict with a lot of his or her background information?
2. According to the text, what form of reasoning is most important in reasoning about health?
3. Give one of the five questions the text says you should ask yourself when evaluating novel health claims made in news stories.

4. Explain the risk that the availability error poses in medical diagnosis.
5. Give one reason why the burden of proof lies with the prosecution in criminal cases in Canada.
6. According to the text, which standard form categorical statement best represents the Criminal Code description of a crime?
7. What form might an ad hominem argument take in a court of law?
8. Define *ethics*.
9. Why must all ethical arguments have at least one ethical premise?
10. Name one of the key features of any ethical premise.

For each of the following claims, state whether it is (a) probably true, (b) probably false, (c) almost certainly true, (d) almost certainly false, or (e) quite uncertain.

11. Butter is better for you than margarine.
12. Too much salt is bad for you.
13. Pomegranate juice prevents cancer.
14. My baby has been crying and has little red bumps. I'm sure she's got skin cancer!
15. Joon was found near the murder scene with blood on his hands. He committed the murder!
16. Mr Veltmeyer was in another country when the crime took place. He cannot be directly responsible.
17. Saying you're sorry when you aren't actually sorry is the same as lying.
18. Treating two people differently without being able to cite a relevant difference between them is unjust.
19. It's unfair that the company refused to hire Sui because she's Chinese.
20. Killing an innocent person is always unethical.

Writing Assignments

1. Write a 250-word essay explaining which of the domains discussed in this chapter—health, law, or ethics—should be thought of as requiring the highest standard of evidence. Explain your point of view, and explain whether society in general behaves in a way that is consistent with your view.
2. Go online and find a website that supports one health-related myth. Write a 300-word essay explaining why it is a myth and providing one fallacious argument that tends to perpetuate that myth.

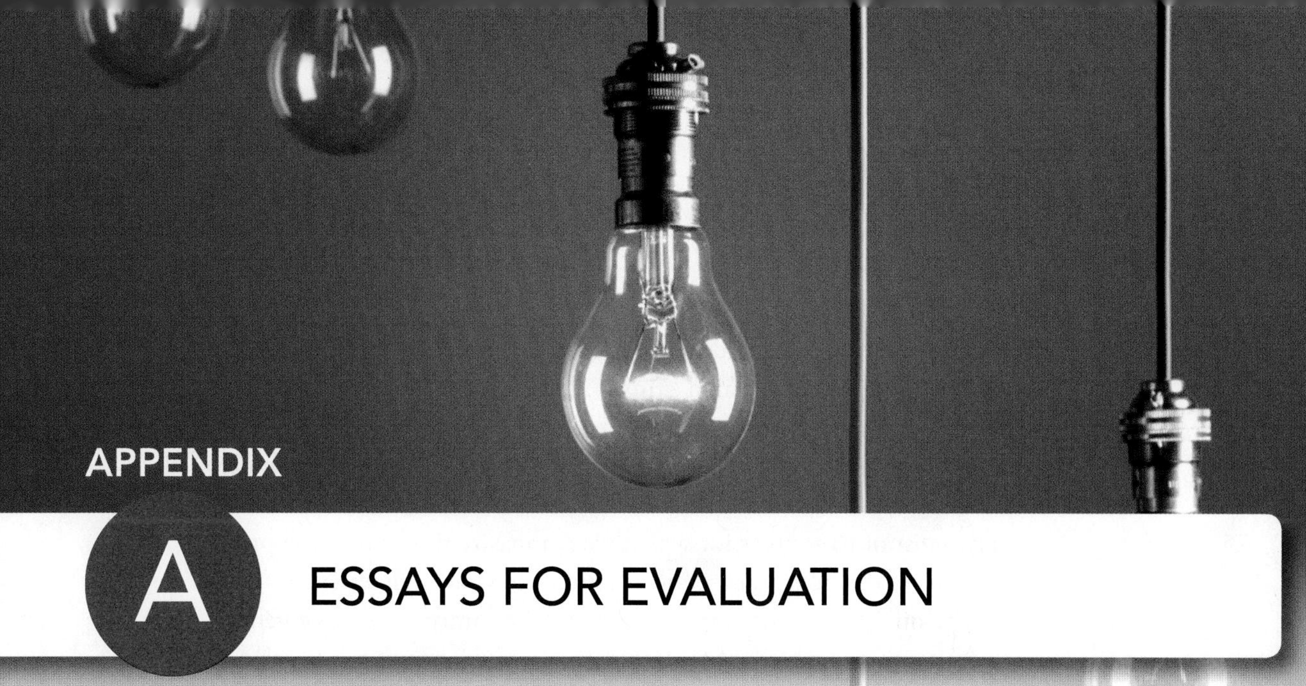

APPENDIX A ESSAYS FOR EVALUATION

ESSAY 1*

Deterrence

by David M. Paciocco

The theory of deterrence has two components. The first, known as "specific" or "individual" deterrence, is that punishment will discourage the offender from committing further offences in the future. The second, known as "general deterrence," is that punishing offenders will discourage other like-minded people from committing offences.

Based on its 1987 study, *Sentencing Reform*, the Canadian Sentencing Commission gave up on specific deterrence. It acknowledged that the claim that punishment is effective in reducing the tendency to reoffend is undermined by rates of recidivism (or repeat offending), the apparent "undeterrability" of certain groups of offenders, and the "acknowledged fact" that most prison inmates have been convicted on prior occasions.[1] Anyone who has the time should sit in provincial court and watch offenders being sentenced. As a prosecutor, I became so accustomed to finding a copy of the criminal record in the file that if there wasn't one, I would look around the floor to see if I had dropped it.

In spite of our failure to intimidate offenders from reoffending by punishing them, we continue to rely on specific deterrence as a justification for punishment. If we are going to send a first offender to jail, our preference is to give a "short, sharp" sentence that will "send a message" to him or her. This practice shares a philosophical kinship with giving a child a sharp smack to

---

* Source: David M. Paciocco, "Deterrence," in *Getting Away with Murder: The Canadian Criminal Justice System*, (Toronto, Irwin Law, 1999).

the back of the head, and is probably about as effective. It is, however, a lot more expensive.

General deterrence, the theory that punishing offenders will intimidate others into being law-abiding, is even more central to our theories of punishment. For the most hated crimes, those involving sexual assault, violence causing bodily harm, robbery, and drugs, the primary sentencing principle is general deterrence. Trial judges are overruled by appeal courts when they fail to give general deterrence sufficient weight in sentencing offenders. Yet, paradoxically, most of the crimes for which we emphasize this sentencing principle are the kinds of offences that are most resistant to general deterrence.

The official position appears to be that we must accept the general deterrence theory as a matter of faith, but that we cannot put too much faith in it. The Canadian Sentencing Commission asked Professor Cousineau of Simon Fraser University to review the latest literature. He concluded that "there is little or no evidence to sustain an empirically justified belief in the deterrent effect of legal sanctions."[2] In spite of this report, the commission could not bring itself to reject the intuitively appealing notion that if people know there is a heavy cost associated with their conduct, they may, as rational people, opt not to engage in that behaviour.[3] But even the Sentencing Commission was guarded in its assessment. It cautioned that there is no reason to believe that legal sanctions can be used to deter specific crimes, or to believe that making an example out of a particular offender will have any effect on other potential offenders. It therefore concluded its discussion of general deterrence by saying that "deterrence is a general and limited consequence of sentencing."[4]

A moment's reflection will demonstrate why general deterrence is so ineffective. Deterrence is based on theories of rational decision making. It presupposes that actors weigh to a nicety the pros and cons of their acts before action. The most dangerous criminals do not fit that model. They are not people renowned for their good judgment and considered action. At the same time, the most horrendous crimes do not lend themselves to this kind of judgment. Sexual offenders give in to vile urges. Assailants strike out in anger. Homicide, in particular, is primarily a crime of passion. It is only rarely a contract hit or a neatly planned exercise. It is more often the worst result of the free reign of jealousy, rage, vindictiveness, hatred, and anger, the most powerful of human emotions. Even when not spontaneous, it is still most commonly done in the throes of extreme emotion. In 1995, by no means an exceptional year, 9 per cent of killers committed suicide, almost invariably immediately after they had killed.[5] If these people are not afraid to inflict mortal violence on themselves as the price for their crime, what makes us think we can deter them by threatening them with a cell with a television?

Some Canadians believe that the television in the cell is part of the reason that general deterrence does not work; we are not hard enough on criminals. If we ratcheted up the sentences, they believe, and began to treat criminals as criminals, we might just reduce crime. In fact, there is "a great deal of empirical research in the United States and elsewhere [that] has shown that crime rates are not greatly affected by changes to the severity of penalties imposed."[6] The Canadian Sentencing Commission came to the same conclusion.[7] This result has been effectively demonstrated in Canada with respect to the offence of murder. Murder rates did not rise with the abolition of capital punishment in 1976. They went down and stayed down. One of the great American ironies is that those states with the highest murder rates are the same ones that invoke the death penalty most frequently.

The Ontario Court of Appeal was recently asked to increase the typical sentencing range for men who attempt to murder their female partners. Sentences for that offence range around ten years. The court was right to reject the submission that imposing higher sentences would discourage men from trying.[8] By definition, these men are attempting to succeed in killing their spouses. If they succeeded, they would get life imprisonment, subject to lengthy parole ineligibility. How can anyone think that a man who knows he might get life if he succeeds is going to sit down and say, "OK. If I fail they are going to give me 12 years instead of ten, so I had better not do it." This is simply silly. Even at 20 or 30 or 40 years, there would be no difference. The violent among us are destructive actors, not constructive thinkers.

Cesare Beccaria, sometimes called the father of criminology, was a proponent of general deterrence. He nonetheless sensed that employing brutal punishments would do nothing to reduce crime rates: "The countries and times most notorious for severity of penalties have always been those in which the bloodiest and most inhumane deeds were committed, for the same spirit of ferocity that guided the hand of the legislators also ruled that of the parricide and assassin."[9] Savage punishments reinforce savage attitudes in some people. For the just, savage punishments defeat themselves. They can cause a humane public to rebel against the values demonstrated by the administration of justice, thereby undermining the educational effect of criminal prosecutions. Experience has shown that they can even cause courts to rebel by finding technical ways to prevent imposing the punishment.[10] When felons were executed for minor felonies in England, judges became creative in finding ways not to convict.

Even if the theory of general deterrence is sound, its promise is easily defeated in practice. It is universally accepted that to be effective systematically, general deterrence depends more than anything else on the certainty of punishment. That is why high-profile RIDE programs and high police presence in crime areas can help produce a reduction in crime rates, but an abstract fear of being caught is tremendously less effective. Some commentators have added that the punishment must also be swift for general deterrence to work. For reasons we can do nothing about, punishment in our system is neither certain nor swift. In terms of the certainty of punishment, with the exception of homicide, where detection and conviction rates are high, only a very small percentage of offenders are even sentenced. This is partially because of the chronic underreporting of most offences, and partially because some crimes are simply not solved by the police. There are also incredibly high attrition rates for most offences. Complaints tend not to get to trial, either because there is insufficient evidence, the complainants recant, witnesses disappear, the accused disappears, the matter is judged not serious enough to proceed, or the case otherwise falls through the cracks. Some cases end up in acquittals. A leading English academic, Andrew Ashworth, estimates that, in Britain, only 3 per cent of actual offences end up at the sentencing stage.[11] The John Howard Society of Alberta estimated that the clearance rate by conviction in Canada in 1987 was unlikely to exceed 20 per cent.[12] Even if both these figures are gross underestimates, they demonstrate poignantly that we will never attain certainty of punishment, no matter how much money we throw at the system or how much we tinker with its rules.

All indications are that general deterrence, in the form of creating conditions through the punishment of offenders that will make others decide not to offend, is woefully ineffective for most crimes. It is particularly so for crimes of violence. If the marginal return of general deterrence was the only gain to be made by incarcerating violent offenders, it would not make economic sense to do so. Our continued reliance on it as a reason for the punitive sentencing of such people is therefore misleading and distorting. It creates a public expectation that cannot be satisfied.

Notes

1. Canadian Sentencing Commission, *Sentencing Reform: A Canadian Approach* (Ottawa: Ministry of Supply and Services, 1987), 135. Between 1975 and 1985, 60 per cent of those released on mandatory supervision were readmitted to federal penitentiary, while 49 per cent of those who had been released on parole were readmitted.
2. Ibid., 136.
3. Ibid., 136–7.
4. Ibid., 138.
5. Statistics Canada, Canadian Centre for Justices Statistics, *Homicide in Canada—1995* 16, no. 11 (1996): 5.
6. Julian V. Roberts, "New Data on Sentencing Trends in Provincial Courts" (1994), 34 CR (4th) 181: 194.
7. Canadian Sentencing Commission, *Sentencing Reform.* 137.
8. *R. v. Edwards* (1996), 28 OR (3d) 54 (CA).
9. Daniel J. Curran and Claire M. Renzetti, *Theories of Crime* (Boston: Allyn and Bacon, 1994), 13.

10. H.R.S. Ryan, *The Theory of Punishment* (1970), Study Note, reproduced in Don Stuart and R.J. Delisle, *Learning Canadian Criminal Law*, 5th ed. (Carswell: Toronto, 1995), 139.
11. Andrew Ashworth, *Sentencing and Criminal Justice* (London: Weidenfeld & Nicoloson, 1992), 23.
12. Canadian Sentencing Commission, *Sentencing Reform,* 148.

ESSAY 2*

Hurray! No One's Watching: The Olympics' Decline Signals Their Success, But Now What?

by Andrew Potter

Has the Olympic movement run its course? Television ratings in both Canada and the United States were way down for these Games, with both the CBC and NBC prime-time broadcasts losing out to new programming from their competitors. Over in Turin, many supposedly marquee events, notably figure skating, took place in half-empty arenas. Is this the beginning of the end for the largest sporting event in the world?

The *Wall Street Journal* thinks so. In an editorial published just days into the Turin Games, the paper argued that the chief appeal of the Olympics in the past was that, of all the proxy wars fought between the forces of freedom and the forces of totalitarianism, ice dancing and the luge were probably the most benignly entertaining. With the end of the Cold War and the rise of globalization, international events such as the Olympics are obsolete. But, if the *Journal* is right, then perhaps we shouldn't actually think of the declining interest in the Olympics as a sign of the movement's failure, but as its success.

The relationship between Olympism and nationalism has always been pretty confused. On the one hand, the fundamental principles of the Olympic movement sound like the lyrics to John Lennon's *Imagine* remixed in bureaucratese. The Olympic Charter explicitly states that the Games "are competitions between athletes in individual or team events and not between countries." The Olympic Truce, first declared in 1992, holds that athletic competition has the power to promote unity and peace by abolishing boundaries.

You could have fooled me. The charter may endorse sport as "a way of life based on the joy found in effort," but it promotes that way of life through flag-waving, anthem playing, and a rank ordering of nations by medal count. The fact is, for all its hippyish ideology, the Olympic movement has always found raw nationalism convenient. It is all well and fine for everyone to

* Source: Andrew Potter, "Hurray! No One's Watching. The Olympics' Decline Signals Their Success. But Now What?," *Maclean's*, 1 March 2006, 8.

routinely denounce Hitler for using the 1936 Berlin Games as a showpiece for Nazism, or to express horror at the 1972 Munich murder of 11 members of the Israeli team by Palestinian terrorists, but that's what happens when you allow sport to become the pursuit of politics by other means.

As countries stop mattering at the Games, we shouldn't be surprised to find that fewer people are tuning in to watch. Many of the traditional events don't really pull their weight as spectator sports, as evidenced by the absence of a serious luge league or Nordic combined circuit. More often than not, the athletes' skill or training or art is invisible to the untrained viewer, revealed through microsecond differences in split times or hinted at in the inscrutable decisions of an anonymous politburo of judges. What makes the Olympics worth watching is not what the athletes are doing, but the uniforms they are wearing. Those of us who cheered on Pierre Lueders in the bobsleigh event did so because he's Canadian, not because we have the foggiest appreciation for why the sport even exists.

There was always something rather ridiculous about the International Olympic Committee founder Pierre de Coubertin's idea that a quadrennial gathering of leisured aristocrats would lead the way to a borderless world of peace and harmony. Unsurprisingly, commercialization and professionalization appeared at the modern Games almost immediately, along with other complications such as drug use and the participation of women. In his excellent book *Olympics in Athens 1896*, the British diplomat Michael Llewellyn Smith suggests that, instead of lamenting the tawdry affair that the Olympics has become, we should embrace it "as a triumph of modernity, capitalism, commerce, sporting prowess and celebrity culture."

To really embrace the modern world, the IOC just needs to go an extra step and become truly cosmopolitan by doing away with countries at the Olympics altogether: get rid of the flags and make the Games a genuine competition between individuals under the Olympic banner. Or, if we must have teams, here's an idea. Many athletes already get the bulk of their funding from corporate sponsorships, so why not let corporations sponsor entire teams? I'd just as soon see Wal-Mart or Starbucks at the top of the medal standings as I would China or Sweden.

One likely consequence of all of this would be a serious overhaul of the schedule of events: out with the old and aristocratic, in with the extreme and populist. This is in fact what the IOC is already doing, to a certain extent. The sports that got most of the attention (and fans) at Turin were the ones with all of the fancy branding and the hyper marketing. Events such as snowboarding and freestyle skiing ruled the Winter Games, just as beach volleyball is far and away the most popular sport at the Summer Games. Not only might such a move help revive the Games' sagging fortunes, but it would be more faithful to the transnationalist spirit of the Olympic movement.

Meanwhile, nothing would prevent countries from continuing to invest in amateur sport. Indeed, if we truly value one of the fundamental principles of the Olympic movement—that "sport is at the service of the harmonious development of man, with a view to encouraging the establishment of a peaceful society"—then national pride is irrelevant, is it not? Governments should invest in amateur sport simply because it makes better citizens, and if it doesn't, then it isn't clear why governments should be involved. If the Games can't survive a move to true commercialized cosmopolitanism, then Olympism is a more obsolete ideal than it already seems.

ESSAY 3*

Marine Parks

by Bill Daly

The issue of whether we should allow marine parks to stay open has been widely debated in our community recently. It is an important issue because it concerns fundamental moral and economic questions about the way we use our native wildlife. A variety of different arguments have been put forward about this issue. This essay will consider arguments for having marine parks and point to some of the problems with these views. It will then put forward reasons for the introduction of laws that prohibit these unnecessary and cruel institutions.

It has been argued that dolphin parks provide the only opportunity for much of the public to see marine mammals (Smith, 1992). Most Australians, so this argument goes, live in cities and never get to see these animals. It is claimed that marine parks allow the average Australian to appreciate our marine wildlife. However, as Smith states, dolphins, whales, and seals can be viewed in the wild at a number of places on the Australian coast. In fact, there are more places where they can be seen in the wild than places where they can be seen in captivity. Moreover, most Australians would have to travel less to get to these locations than they would to get to the marine parks on the Gold Coast. In addition, places where there are wild marine mammals do not charge an exorbitant entry fee—they are free.

Dr Alison Lane, the director of the Cairns Marine Science Institute, contends that we need marine parks for scientific research (*The Age*, 19 February 1993). She argues that much of our knowledge of marine mammals comes from studies that were undertaken at marine parks. The knowledge obtained

* Source: Bill Daly, "Marine Parks." For further information about this resource, contact williamjdaly@gmail.com.

at marine parks, so this argument goes, can be useful for planning for the conservation of marine mammal species. However, as Jones (1991) explains, park research is only useful for understanding captive animals and is not useful for learning about animals in the wild. Dolphin and whale biology changes in marine park conditions. Their diets are different, they have significantly lower life spans and they are more prone to disease. In addition, marine mammals in dolphin parks are trained and this means that their patterns of social behaviour are changed. Therefore research undertaken at marine parks is generally not reliable.

It is the contention of the Marine Park Owners Association that marine parks attract a lot of foreign tourists (*The Sun-Herald*, 12 April 1993). This position goes on to assert that these tourists spend a lot of money, increasing our foreign exchange earnings and assisting our national balance of payments. However, foreign tourists would still come to Australia if the parks were closed down. Indeed, surveys of overseas tourists show that they come here for a variety of other reasons and not to visit places like Seaworld (*The Age, Good Weekend*, 16 August 1993). Tourists come here to see our native wildlife in its natural environment and not to see it in cages and cement pools. They can see animals in those conditions in their own countries. Furthermore, we should be promoting our beautiful natural environment to tourists and not the ugly concrete marine park venues.

Dolphin parks are unnecessary and cruel. The dolphins and whales in these parks are kept in very small, cramped ponds, whereas in the wild they are used to roaming long distances across the seas. Furthermore, the concrete walls of the pools interfere with the animals' sonar systems of communication. In addition, keeping them in pools is a terrible restriction of the freedom of fellow creatures who may have very high levels of intelligence and a sophisticated language ability. Moreover, there are many documented cases of marine mammals helping humans who are in danger at sea or helping fisherman with their work.

In conclusion, these parks should be closed, or at the very least, no new animals should be captured for marine parks in the future. Our society is no longer prepared to tolerate unnecessary cruelty to animals for science and entertainment. If we continue with our past crimes against these creatures we will be remembered as cruel and inhuman by the generations of the future.

References

Jones, G. 1991. "The Myths about Animal Research in Marine Parks," *Scientific Australian* 12, 3.
Smith, H. 1992. "Marine Parks: Good for Business, Good for Australia," *Leisure Business Review* 24, 4.
The Age. 19 February 1993.
The Age, Good Weekend. 16 August 1993.
The Sun-Herald. 12 April 1993.

ESSAY 4*

What's Wrong with "Body Mass Index"

by Samantha Brennan

I'd like us to ditch all talk of Body Mass Index (BMI) as a meaningful measure when it comes to individuals. And please don't say it's better than weight because it's just weight + height taken into account. Insofar as weight is a problematic measure and BMI relies on weight, so too is BMI problematic. I've long loved Kate Harding's project "BMI Illustrated" over at *Shapely Prose* (kateharding.net/bmi-illustrated). She describes it this way, "I put together a slideshow to demonstrate just how ridiculous the BMI standards are." This isn't to deny that BMI talk is useful about populations and big picture trends, it's just that I think it's misleading and harmful when it comes to individuals.

Lots of thin people are falsely reassured by their BMI, while lots of people with BMIs in the "overweight/obese" categories might be worrying with no good reason. Fit and fat are linked but not in the ways most people think. I worry that lots of fat people don't exercise because they worry what people will think especially if you exercise and don't get any smaller. Yet fat and fit people can be very healthy. "People can be obese yet physically healthy and fit and at no greater risk of heart disease or cancer than normal weight people, say researchers. The key is being "metabolically fit," meaning no high blood pressure, cholesterol, or raised blood sugar, and exercising, according to experts. Looking at data from over 43,000 US people they found that being overweight per se did not pose a big health risk," reports the BBC (www.bbc.co.uk/news/health-19474239).

I love my family doctor who cheered me up immensely when she looked at my chart and said, "This is the part of the visit when, given your weight, I should warn you about the health problems associated with overweight and obesity. However, given that you've got low to normal blood pressure, no sugar issues, and the best ratio of good to bad cholesterol we've ever seen at this clinic, I can't in good conscience do that. You're extremely healthy. Whatever you're doing, keep doing it."

A few years ago I tried Weight Watchers—for probably the sixth time in my life, will I never learn?—and I was shocked at their weight range for my height. Weights I haven't seen since Grade 6. And to give you some perspective they were also weights I never weighed even when at 5' 7" I wore size 8 clothing. The so-called "healthy" or "normal" weight range for me has never seemed plausible.

* Source: Samantha Brennen, "Fit, Fat, and What's Wrong with BMI," *Fit Is a Feminist Issue*, 9 September 2012 http://fitisafeministissue.com/2012/09/09/fit-fat-and-whats-wrong-with-bmi. Reproduced with permission of the author.

I had an interesting experience recently. This summer I was measured in the BodPod at the Fowler Kennedy Sports Medicine Clinic which tells you exactly how much of your body is fat and how much is muscle, bone etc. I was happy to see that to weigh what Weight Watchers thought of as my ideal, I'd be allowed a mere 20 lbs of body fat. I won't discuss exact weights today but I will tell you that I'm 122 lbs of not fat. It's my goal as part of my "fittest at fifty" plan to improve my ratio of lean body mass. I plan to both develop my muscles and lose some body fat. I'd also like to lose pounds in absolute numbers too, mostly though to make running easier on my joints and to make it easier to get up hills faster on the bike! Hill climbing on the bike is all about power to weight ratio and so I'll never be a climber but I hate to get dropped on hills on a regular basis. According to BMI, I'll likely always be overweight or obese and I've made my peace with that.

Marc Perry notes in *Get Lean* that according to BMI most American football players count as obese. So too do many Olympic athletes. You can find a list online of all of the gold medal athletes from the 2004 Olympics in Athens who count as overweight or obese according to BMI. We need to change our image of what athletes look like. Usually they don't look like fitness models.

ESSAY 5*

How Ontario Ended Up with "Cap and Trade"

by Joseph Heath

Like many people, I was encouraged to see the Government of Ontario finally stepping into the breach and taking action on the climate change issue, but I was very disappointed to see them choosing to go with a cap-and-trade system rather than a carbon tax. Prior to yesterday, there were two models out there: BC's carbon tax and Quebec's cap-and-trade system. Ontario joining Quebec probably represents a tipping point that will push the country as a whole in the direction of cap and trade, which is, as far as I'm concerned, a second-best outcome.

How did we wind up here? This is all a consequence of what I consider to be the most important political shift to have occurred in Canada in the past two decades, which is the near-total collapse of moderate conservatism. Indeed, it's not a surprise that the major spokespersons of the centre-right in Canada—Andrew Coyne, Tasha Kheiriddin, etc.—were lining up today to criticize the

* Source: Joseph Heath, "Ontario Chickens out, Chooses Cap-and-Trade," *In Due Course*, 14 April 2015. http://induecourse.ca/ontario-chickens-out-chooses-cap-and-trade. Reproduced with permission of the author.

Ontario plan. And yet the problem, ultimately, stems from the failure of the centre-right in Canada to control their own political parties. And if they're looking for someone to blame, they should be pointing the finger at Canadian prime minister Stephen Harper, not Ontario premier Kathleen Wynne.

Right now, the policy space on climate change can be organized in the following way (starting with positions that involve the least government involvement in the economy, moving down to those that involve the most):

1. *The Alberta fantasy.* Under this scenario, we just keep on digging up bitumen and selling synthetic oil, investing in new mines, processing and pipeline infrastructure, subject to absolutely no constraints and a carbon price of zero. And people don't have to pay taxes, because, yay! we're digging money out of the ground.
2. *Carbon tax.* The government puts a price on carbon emissions, which raises the price of fossil-fuel derived energy relative to other forms. The price is adjusted until the desired quantity of emissions is achieved.
3. *Cap and trade.* Firms are issued permits to produce emissions. If their emissions exceed the quantity permitted, they must purchase additional permits on the market. If they are under their emissions quota, they can sell their unused permits.
4. *The "planning and banning" fantasy.* Here the government gets involved in micro-managing the transition, mandating specific technology for emitters, and subsidizing what it considers to be promising technologies.

I think everyone can see why, for people who have a distrust of government, scenario 1 is the best and scenario 4 is by far the worst. But why is 2 (carbon tax) ahead of 3? It's because cap and trade is so much easier for governments to fiddle around with. In particular, it allows the government to play around with the permit allocations, giving specific firms or industries special exemptions, or extra permits. That's why the NDP supports it (keeping in mind that there is significant alignment of interest between the Canadian Auto Workers and the automobile industry—a major beneficiary of these fiddles). It also appeals to some of the worst political instincts of the Ontario Liberal Party, and of Kathleen Wynne specifically, who is constantly going on about how government needs to be a "partner" in all major economic activity in the province—which basically means subsidizing manufacturing in ways both subtle and gross.

The nice thing about a carbon tax is that it's really hard to fiddle. So while in practice cap and trade and carbon tax come to the same thing, in reality they don't. This is Andrew Coyne's major complaint. And yet he fails to note that if you survey the political landscape in Canada, you find that no major political party (with the exception of the BC Liberals), is willing to champion option 2. In other words, the centre-right in this country is missing in action. Both the Liberals and the NDP are now down into zones 3 and 4 (the Liberals having been pushed there by conservative rhetoric) while the federal Conservative party, not to mention the various provincial Progressive Conservative parties, including Ontario's, remain resolute champions of option 1—the Alberta fantasy.

There are two reasons for this. First, conservative political parties in Canada have largely been captured by ideological extremists. One can see this very clearly with the federal Conservative Party in Canada—up to and including the prime minister—which can best be described as "anti-environmental." There is simply no one there willing to champion market-based approaches to solving environmental problems. One can see the same thing in the Ontario Progressive Conservative Party, where the idea of "promoting a market solution" to a public problem seems to be confused with "doing nothing" or "pretending that there is no problem." The second reason is connected to the first, and it has to do with electoral strategy. Roughly speaking, the reason that ideological extremists have had such success in controlling conservative parties is that their particular brand of "common sense" conservatism produces a set of incredibly powerful electoral strategies (far better than anything the centre-right can come up with). For instance, the "job-killing carbon tax" sound bite is so powerful that it has taken on a life of its own, effectively tying the hands of the federal government on this issue. (One can see it as well in the current contest for the leadership of the Ontario PC party, where both candidates have locked themselves into supporting option 1, because of the power of the anti-tax sound bite.)

In other words, the reason that option 2 winds up being a political orphan is that the people who champion this sort of an approach can't win elections. Indeed, the Liberal Party of Canada started out supporting option 2, and got slaughtered by the Conservatives for it. (Indeed, there are striking similarities between the Conservative treatment of carbon taxes in Canada and the Republican approach to health care reform in the United States, where Mitt Romney wound up disavowing his own health care reform plan, because there was so much mileage to be had from demonizing "Obamacare." As a result, conservatives in both countries have wound up taking positions that put them completely outside the space of reasonable policy disagreement, largely for reasons of electoral strategy.)

The irony is that, by insisting on getting option 1—and by painting themselves into a corner with their rhetoric—what conservatives are winding up with is option 3. In fact, what they're winding up with is even worse: First, they are getting a provincial patchwork rather than a more efficient national system. And second, they are getting cap and trade, a system that is more open to government meddling in the economy. It's almost as though, what they need to learn to do is *compromise*, and speak out in favour of option 2. Unfortunately, in order to get option 2 onto the table, someone on the right in this country would need to figure out how to control—or even influence—Stephen Harper, and apparently no one is able to do that.

I understand that it's no fun being a moderate. But seriously, someone on the right in Canada needs to step up to the plate. Is there *any* politician in Ontario—not a journalist, a politician—willing to stand up to the government and say, "we should have a carbon tax instead"? Because so far all I've heard from the opposition has been the same old fantasy, that all taxes are evil, and that we should be doing nothing about climate change.

ESSAY 6*

Raspberry Ketone, Pure Green Coffee Extract, Garcinia Cambogia, Weight Loss, and the Fallacy of Appealing to Authority

by Tracy Isaacs

My usually skeptical husband forwarded me an email message late last week with the subject "weight loss." It contained a short video of Dr Oz endorsing pure green coffee bean extract as a miracle weight loss potion. My husband's question to me: "What do you think?"

The clip I watched showed an enthusiastic Dr Oz with the creator of the product. Oz declared it a weight loss miracle. When I went back to the link a few days later, the link led me to something different. This time, Dr Oz was interviewing someone about a different weight loss miracle: Garcinia Cambogia. Apparently it's also an amazing fat burner! Like pure green coffee bean extract, this product is supposed to result in weight loss without any changes to diet or activity.

Neither the green coffee bean extract page nor the garcinia cambogia page would let me leave them without not one but two pop-ups asking me if I was sure I wanted to leave that page.

Dr Oz has also spoken highly of "raspberry ketone." Available in pill form (because you'd have to eat NINETY pounds of raspberries to get the appropriate "dose"), raspberry ketone is no less than "a fat-burner in a bottle," according to Dr Oz.

---

* Source: Tracy Isaacs, "Raspberry Ketone, Pure Green Coffee Extract, Garcinia Cambogia, Weight Loss, and the Fallacy of Appealing to Authority," *Fit Is a Feminist Issue*, 24 January 2013 http://fit isafeministissue.com/2013/01/24/raspberry-ketone-pure-green-coffee-extract-garcinia-cambogia-weight-loss-and-the-fallacy-of-appealing-to-authority. Reproduced with permission of the author.

His website states that "research has shown that raspberry ketone can help in your weight-loss efforts, especially when paired with regular exercise and a well-balanced diet of healthy and whole foods." I love the addendum "especially when paired with regular exercise and a well-balanced diet . . . ."

I think I will stick to the regular exercise and healthy whole foods and save myself the $180 for a 90-day supply.

Most reviews of these products that I've read have questioned the research. A *Globe and Mail* article notes that the study on which the main claims about green coffee bean extract were based involved very few participants. Moreover, participants also lost weight during the placebo phase of the trial.

A *Canadian Living* article on raspberry ketone notes that so far mice have been the only research subjects. Both articles quoted credible MDs claiming that, surprise, surprise: There are no magic solutions!

From the Globe and Mail: *"Usually when studies break the physical laws of the universe, there's usually something wrong with the study itself," said Dr Yoni Freedhoff, medical director of Ottawa's Bariatric Medical Institute, who writes Weighty Matters, a popular blog on nutrition issues. (http://www.theglobeandmail.com/life/health-and-fitness/health/green-coffee-bean-extract-does-it-really-help-you-lose-weight/article 6116816)*

I haven't linked to Dr Oz's website and I am not going to say a lot more about these products. Both his site and the products are easy to find on the Internet.

What I do want to say is this: there is a well-known fallacy that we learn about in philosophy called "the appeal to authority." Appealing to authority is not a good strategy for those seeking truth claims. Just because some authority like Dr Oz said it's true doesn't mean it's true. Of course we do not need to dismiss the claims of experts. Good science is based on sound studies that have undergone peer review and are based on approved methodologies and ample evidence.

Unfortunately, Dr Oz is not an expert in most of what he goes on about. And yet he is accepted as an authority by countless people. His stamp of approval on some product or health claim is taken as gospel by many people. It boosts sales the way Oprah's endorsement of books used to (perhaps still does) have undue influence in the publishing industry.

This is not to say that everything he says is false. It is only to say that just because he said it doesn't make it true. We need more evidence than that.

But the medical community has long told us that there are no magic pills for weight loss. Dr Oz's claims about these miracle weight loss products are just plain irresponsible, given his level of influence.

I've heard all sorts of claims about this and that miracle food or product. When I was a teenager, people took caffeine pills to lose weight. As an undergraduate, smoking cigarettes was the thing. At one time or another, the special powers of cabbage, grapefruit, and bananas took centre stage in the weight loss culture. Now it's more likely to be raspberry ketone, pure green coffee bean extract, or garcinia cambogia.

And I haven't even touched on fad diets like eating for your blood type (based on totally ungrounded claims), the lemon–cayenne pepper–maple syrup–water detox, or any variant of a low carb/high protein plan (my first diet—circa 1980—was the Scarsdale diet, a high protein low carb plan that people loved because you got to eat "plenty of steak" for dinner).

If healthy and sustainable weight loss is what you are seeking, none of these supplements or plans will work. They are not sustainable ways of eating for the rest of your life. And like the claim about raspberry ketone, pair anything with regular exercise and healthy eating and you're good to go.

No magic and no surprises. As *Globe and Mail* reporter Carly Weeks says in her evaluation of raspberry ketone, the bottom line hasn't much changed: "While the promise of the synthetic compound sounds alluring, the best way of losing weight hasn't changed: It's still diet and exercise."

I would only add that "diet" shouldn't be taken to mean "diets," those restricted eating plans designed to lose weight. Diets don't work. In this context we should understand "diet" to mean simply the way we eat on a regular basis. We talk a lot on our blog about why weight loss alone is not a great measure of fitness and why we're not big fans of dieting. . . .

Just to reiterate: "Dr Oz said it" is not a reason on which you can base a strong conclusion. In philosophy we call that an appeal to authority, and it's a fallacy.

ESSAY 7*

Yes, Human Cloning Should Be Permitted

by Chris MacDonald

Patricia Baird's discussion of human cloning (*Annals* RCPSC, June 2000) challenges the prospect of nuclear-transfer cloning for the purposes of human reproduction. Baird reviews a long list of familiar worries about human cloning, but the most striking feature of her discussion is its frankness in placing the onus of justification on the shoulders of those who would permit human cloning. The reasons for permitting cloning, she argues, are "insufficiently compelling," so cloning should be prohibited. The implication is that any new

* Source: Chris MacDonald, "Yes, Human Cloning Should Be Permitted," *Annals of the Royal College of Physicians and Surgeons of Canada* 33, 7 (October 2000): 437–8. Reprinted by permission of the author.

technology should be forbidden unless and until enough justification can be found for allowing its use.

Baird is to be commended for her frankness. But the onus is misplaced, or at least too severe. One need not be a single-minded defender of liberty to think that, contrary to Baird's implication, we need good reasons to limit the actions of others, particularly when those actions do no clear and specific harm. The fact that a portion of society—even a majority—finds an activity distasteful is insufficient grounds for passing a law forbidding it. For example, it is presumably true that at one point, roughly 90 per cent of the public (the same proportion that Baird says is against human cloning) was opposed to homosexuality. Does (or did) this justify action on the part of government to ban homosexual lifestyles? Surely not.

There may be a flaw in my analogy. Human cloning, according to critics, has harmful effects (or at least risks). Indeed, Baird suggests that the arguments regarding potential physical and psychological harm to clones have been "well delineated." In fact, a convincing case has yet to be made for the claim that the physical and psychological risks to clones are more severe than, or different in kind from, those faced by children produced in more traditional ways. Identical twins live with the psychological "burden" of not being genetically unique. Children born to women over 35 are at an increased risk of genetic illness. Children resulting from in-vitro fertilization or other reproductive technologies live with the knowledge that their origins were unusual. They may even live with the knowledge that their genetic profile has been manipulated (for example, through pre-implantation selection of embryos). Human cloning for reproductive purposes is another novel—and as yet untested—medical technology. As such, it should be approached with caution. Thorough animal trials should be completed before attempts on humans are contemplated. But this is true of any new medical technology.

Baird worries about the shift that human cloning might provoke in the way that we view children. This in turn would change the type of community that we are. The central worry is that human cloning "commodifies" children (i.e., that cloning may make us think of children as a commodity or product to be bought and sold). Why would cloning have this effect? Is it simply because it is likely to be expensive, so that it costs money to have children? Surely this is insufficient to worry us. Raising children already costs money—the statistics show us how many hundreds of thousands of dollars it costs to raise a child through to adulthood. Yet no one has suggested that we see our children as products, or love them any less. (In the mid 1940s—before publicly funded health care—my grandparents sold their car to pay the hospital bill related to my father's birth, so "purchasing" the birth of a child is nothing new!)

Baird argues that an "important part of human identity is the sense of arising from a maternal and a paternal line while at the same time being a unique individual." Yet without supporting evidence, this sounds like pop psychology. And we can reply in kind: most people I know do not identify with both their maternal and paternal lineages. One of my friends, who was raised by a single mother, identifies with her maternal eastern European heritage, and not with the French paternal heritage implied by her surname. Another friend identifies with his father's black heritage, rather than with his maternal Chinese lineage, despite his Asian physical features. Such patterns are not unusual. Dual heritage may be normal, but it hardly seems central to our conception of ourselves as humans. And identical twins seem none the worse for the knowledge that they are not genetically unique individuals. Claims about challenges to what makes us "human" may be powerful rhetorical devices, but they must be substantiated if they are to be convincing.

Baird is correct to exhort us to look beyond harms to identifiable individuals, to the social implications that human cloning might have. As a comparison, think of fetal sex selection. Most of us think that sex selection is a bad thing—not because of any purported harm to the child, but because we worry about the social implications of valuing children of one sex over those of another. So Baird rightly reminds us that focusing on potential harms to individuals constitutes a "dangerously incomplete framing" of the problem. Furthermore, cloning (and genetic technology in general) is sufficiently new—and its implications sufficiently poorly understood—to warrant a healthy respect, and even the allowance of a margin of safety. But this does not suggest the need for the ban that Baird (with others) proposes. What these worries suggest is a need for caution, for discussion, and for regulation. For instance, laws limiting the number of clones that might be created from one individual, restricting the combination of cloning with genetic modification, and defining lines of parental obligation, would alleviate many of the concerns associated with human cloning. (Françoise Baylis argues that cloning is so likely to be used in combination with gene transfer that we should think of cloning as an enhancement technology rather than as a reproductive technology, in her article "Human Cloning: Three Mistakes and a Solution," which has been accepted for publication in the *Journal of Medicine and Philosophy*.)

What I have said here should not be taken as an absolute defence of human cloning in all circumstances. (Indeed, there may be only a few circumstances in which cloning is appropriate.) Nor have I suggested that public monies should be spent on cloning research. All I have suggested is that a ban on research leading toward human cloning is unwarranted by the arguments raised thus far. Caution and discretion are warranted; a ban is not.

Finally, I worry that Baird's point of view exemplifies the way in which human reproductive cloning is being singled out, among cloning-related techniques, as a bogeyman. Almost in chorus, scientists are pleading with regulators not to place restrictions on cloning experimentation per se. At the same time, most scientists seem to be more than willing to swear off reproductive cloning, and indeed to wring their hands over the moral implications of its use. Yet this has the air of a too-hasty concession. The scientific community seems to be too willing to condemn one unpopular application of cloning technology, on the basis of too little convincing argumentation, to appease those who oppose cloning technology in general. But human cloning for reproductive purposes has legitimate, morally acceptable applications—for example, for infertile couples, and for gay couples. And none of the criticisms have been convincingly made. We should not let reproductive human cloning be abandoned as the moral sacrificial lamb of the cloning debate.

ESSAY 8*

RIM Is Dead

by Henry Blodget (CEO/EIC, Business Insider*)*

By creating the BlackBerry, Research In Motion revolutionized mobile productivity. For nearly a decade, the company easily fended off the competition by providing the best personal-information gadget on the market. It silenced its critics. It reduced Palm, a previous leader in mobile gadgets, to a pile of rubble. And it made its shareholders rich.

But now, Research In Motion's amazing run appears to be over. The company has lost its lead in the smartphone market, and its market share is falling rapidly. And many long-time addicts like me have switched to iPhones or Android phones.

There are three main reasons RIM's fortunes have turned south.

First and foremost, RIM's products are no longer the best on the market. Although some diehard business users still cling to their BlackBerrys—and insist that the devices are better for email and calendar management than anything else out there—these folks are increasingly a minority. The rest of smartphone users prefer the broader capabilities of iPhones and Android phones, especially apps and Web browsing.

Second, the smartphone market has become a "platform" game. As Microsoft's Windows demonstrated in the PC era, technology markets in which

* Sources: Henry Blodget, "RIM Is Dead" and Nick Waddell, "Long Live RIM," *Canadian Business*, 19 May 2011 www.canadianbusiness.com/technology-news/rim-is-dead/ and www.canadianbusiness.com/technology-news/long-live-rim-2/.

third-party companies build programs or applications to run on top of a particular operating system or other product—"platform markets"—tend to standardize around one or two market leaders. Thanks to the explosion of "apps" available for iPhones and Android phones, the smartphone market is increasingly becoming a platform market. Research In Motion has fewer developers building apps for BlackBerry than Apple and Google do for their platforms, and this lack of apps makes the products less useful for consumers. RIM has tried to encourage developers in recent years, but it still lags badly as an app-development platform.

Third, one of the biggest selling points for BlackBerrys has always been their security and integration with corporate computing systems, most notably Microsoft's Exchange. Increasingly, however, companies are allowing employees to use whichever devices they prefer. And many employees are choosing iPhones and Android phones. In addition, many companies are officially equipping employees with iPhones and iPads, something that was nearly unheard of only a few years ago.

Is there anything that could turn RIM's fortunes around?

Yes. If RIM actually could deliver a product that was a "quantum leap" over the latest iPhone or Android phone, consumers would respond accordingly. The one benefit about competing in the smartphone market is that consumers tend to upgrade their phones every year or two, and they tend to be seduced by the latest, greatest phone on the market.

The most likely scenario for RIM is that it becomes Nokia, a company that once dominated the cellphone market but lost several steps and is now scrambling to stay relevant. A worse scenario would be that RIM becomes the next Palm, a one-time leader that falls on its face and is eventually sold for scrap to a larger technology player.

Long Live RIM

by Nick Waddell (Founding Editor, Cantech Letter*)*

To a certain class of pundit, Research In Motion is already a dinosaur. The Waterloo tech giant, which made its name by practically inventing the smartphone category, sells products that to some seemed antiquated compared to slicker iPhones, iPads, and Android devices. But all is not lost for RIM. Its obsession with making its devices secure now shows extended vision, given recent high-profile security gaffes from industry leaders Amazon, Apple, and Sony. And RIM is hardly floundering financially; the global mobile player is in outstanding fiscal shape. Marked for extinction by many, RIM itself is preparing for evolution instead.

It's hard to ignore that RIM's transformation into an also-ran occurred alongside Apple's stunning and sustained resurgence. Comparisons between

RIM and Apple are commonplace. Nervy analysts these days are just as likely to set RIM against beleaguered mobile pioneer Palm.

Palm's Palm Pilot popularized the personal digital assistant, or PDA. Released in 1996, the device effectively launched an industry that ultimately morphed into the devices we see today. But for numerous reasons, many related to a seemingly endless string of spinoffs and corporate restructurings, Palm lost its way and failed to jump on the lucrative opportunity of combining an electronic organizer with a cellular phone. Palm was ultimately acquired by HP for a fraction of the value it once commanded.

In a recent interview with *Forbes*, Rob Enderle of the Enderle Group said RIM "started out as a much-loved enterprise product, but that market has changed to one that is more consumer-driven in that the business line managers are more inclined to make IT decisions." His conclusion about RIM? "They are trending to be the next Palm." Others, however, say the RIM-Palm comparison doesn't really stand up to examination.

Casual observers might be surprised to learn of the company's astonishing growth over the past three years. Between fiscal 2008 and 2011, RIM's top-line revenue more than tripled, from just over $6 billion to nearly $20 billion. Of course, this number is less than a third of the $65 billion that Apple posted in fiscal 2010. But dig a little deeper into the books of both companies and a curious stat stands out. In the most recent fiscal year, Apple spent $1.78 billion on research and development, a number equal to 2.73 per cent of its top line. In contrast, RIM has been much more R&D intensive; the $1.35 billion it spent on R&D in the last fiscal year was 6.78 per cent of its total revenue.

So what is RIM up to with all this spending? Paradigm Capital analyst Barry Richards sees evidence of a sea change at RIM that is punctuated by 14 recent acquisitions, including last year's snagging of highly regarded QNX Software, which makes operating systems used in "mission critical" environments such as high-speed trains and nuclear power plants. QNX is now expected to become nothing less than the default operating system for all BlackBerry devices.

The acquisition of QNX was another in a series of RIM moves that had tech geeks buzzing. Navneet Alang, a writer for the Techi website, agrees, saying, "Blackberry have suddenly got a lot of talent for creating a successor to their clunky and old-fashioned—if eminently practical—Blackberry OS." Richards believes RIM's new PlayBook tablet, which also operates on the QNX architecture, "takes RIM back to its roots in secure data for enterprises."

Indeed, a growing amount of evidence suggests that mobile security could be the issue that slowly levels the playing field between RIM and the more tony Android and Apple devices. In April, security researchers discovered that the location-based services in Apple's iOS 4+ devices, including the iPhone, had been collecting comprehensive and detailed information on their users' location in an unencrypted file. Apple is now facing at least one class-action lawsuit. . . .

With a strong balance sheet, a robust and powerful new operating system, and a global smartphone market that is growing at a frenetic pace, rumours of RIM's demise may [. . .] be greatly exaggerated. In the meantime, tech investors looking to identify the next killer app might be surprised to find that apps in general are fast being overshadowed by more menacing security concerns. To the great favour of Research In Motion, 2011 will almost certainly be more about encryption, and less about Angry Birds.

ESSAY 9*

The Letter

by Nancy Walton

Trust me—this is the most difficult column I've ever written. It may surprise you and it may not be exactly what you want to hear.

Plenty of media attention, radio and television air time and space on social networking sites has been devoted to a hate-filled letter to a mother whose son has autism in Newcastle, Ontario. You've seen it, I'm sure. But if you've been living under a large heavy rock and wearing earplugs for the last few days, the short version is this: the family of a 13-year-old boy with autism received an anonymous letter suggesting that the boy either leave the neighbourhood, or be euthanized.

At first, I didn't want to write about this. In fact, I didn't talk about it much or post about it on Facebook. But when my lovely editor at *Bunch* asked me if I wanted to write some kind of response, I saw an opportunity. I'm not here to rant, or knee-jerk, to scream, vilify, or to blame, but simply to talk. To talk about what kinds of things this letter asks me to remember.

First, this letter asks me to remember sadness and compassion. For the woman who wrote it, for the family who received it, and for the world in general. I'm loath to post the letter—or the words therein—on my social network profiles, in a world where everything goes viral. Somehow providing more attention to the words—and reacting with anger and rage towards the woman who wrote it—seems to feel not as good as it should. It should feel justified to react to a letter like that with anger and, as some have, a wish for karma to *do*

* Source: Nancy Walton, "Life With Georgia Reflects on the Letter," *Life With Georgia*, 21 August 2013 http://lifewithgeorgia.com/2013/08/21/life-with-georgia-reflects-on-the-letter/. Reproduced with permission of the author.

its thing for the writer. Yet reflecting anger back with anger does not feel right. This may be, in part, due to my own career and experiences: first, training as a nurse and working in an acute-care hospital, doing graduate work in ethics and now working as a professor, teaching others how to be good nurses. Something we teach and learn is that you'll inevitably encounter angry, highly disagreeable people all the time—who are, at that moment, your patients—who you may not like at all, whose values are not aligned with yours, and whose views or words you may find repugnant.

But everyone has a story. And somewhere in that story is a hint about why they ended up the way they did. As a nurse, I provided care to patients who expressed views or practices that I would not tolerate in other contexts: racist, homophobic, misogynistic views that were inherently misaligned with my own values. I cared for patients who struck me, who told me to fuck off, who sexualized me, who insulted me. I nursed others who I didn't know well, whose values I never explored, and for all I know may have been murderers, abusers, or bullies. But I cared for them, talked to them, ensured that they were pain-free and comfortable as I would for any patient. I demonstrated compassion in the face of adversity and I challenge my students to do the same: to act with care and humanity to someone who you might think, really deep down, doesn't deserve it. In no way does that condone their views or suggest implicit agreement—it demonstrates a kind of compassion that we need to keep in the world. It is what a nurse must do, day after day. And that practice has, in some way, spilled into the rest of my life.

The letter asks me to remember that there are many battles to be fought. My job, as Georgia's mom, is to figure out which ones I need to fight. While I acknowledge that the content of this letter is extreme and terrible in terms of the reaction to a child with autism, I experience the range of reactions to the "difference" that is Georgia in the world every day: fear, discomfort, disgust, impatience, agitation. I'm okay with her differences. But trust me, a great many are not. Many more than you would think, hope, or predict. I'm sensitized to it and never miss it. You've seen a view of her in this column that is cute at times, compelling and loveable. Yet this is not what everyone sees. Yesterday the cashier at our local Metro backed up from her cash register as Georgia approached, too close for comfort. Half-frightened and half-disgusted, she glared at Georgia who was drooling just a little bit with messy hair and a grubby face and t-shirt. On a regular basis, I experience the ultra hip, trendy downtown moms in Trinity Bellwoods—they must be cool with everything, right?—who are highly uncomfortable with my kid who is happily barking at the swing, or just standing and watching the other kids play. The mothers stare. They let their children stare. They shoo their children away from her. They catch my eye and, embarrassed, they smile awkwardly. Occasionally, I have been known to inform them out loud that autism, as far as we know, is not yet contagious.

The world is a cruel and intolerant place. There are people who write horrible letters to mothers of children with autism. There are others who vilify those who love people of the same sex. Some believe that those who practise a different religion or love a different god do not deserve to live. Others are sure that the lives of men are worth more than the lives of women and that female children should not be educated, valued, or even fed. Some people abuse their elderly parents. Children are enslaved, victimized, mutilated, assaulted, and killed. There are still those who believe that the colour of your skin makes you either a far better or a less worthy person. There are people who will beat a dog, drown a kitten, or kill a random innocent young man because "they were bored." From the random utterings of "Hey retard!" or "Hey fatso!" to the gunning down of those who have differing values, we live in a world in which hate, abuse, bullying, misogyny, marginalization, bigotry, and discrimination happen.

Sadly.

I'm not saying that I simply accept these things. Not at all. Rather, I have to pick my own fights. If I got angry every time someone was uncomfortable with my child being around or wished desperately that Georgia was something else or somewhere else, I'd have no energy left for anything else. The fight would be monumental, constant, and would flavour my entire child-rearing experience.

I do get angry. All the time. I recently stood cutting vegetables at the kitchen counter, sobbing with anger. I was listening to a CBC radio documentary on Betty Anne Gagnon, a woman with a developmental disability who was horribly abused by her family caregivers. The story talked about how her caregivers would punish her by making her drink Clorox, how they failed to provide Betty Anne with a life, with adequate food, or with love and compassion. How the system failed her, ignored her, forgot about her. This makes me angry. It makes me angry that there aren't enough high quality, accessible services and safeguards for kids and youth with autism and the often-lost or neglected adults they will become. It makes me angry that our government can spend thousands of dollars on senator audits but fail to provide social services for the many individuals and families who just fall through the cracks. It angers me that so many people are raging about this terrible letter but so few understand just how badly our system consistently fails children, youth, and adults with autism, and their families who struggle and deal with hardship without respite on a level that is, for some, unsustainable. This letter reminds me about just how much there is to be angry about.

The last thing this letter does is ask me to remember the compassion that I see in all the good things and the good people I experience all the time. The woman in the dentist's office who didn't mind that Georgia bumped her arm at least once a minute in the waiting room and was cheering for the Raptors (yes, in the dental office) too loud and too often. The police officer who invited us into the horse trailer to pet the horses, out of the blue. The firefighter on the street who lifts Georgia into the truck for a look around. The shopkeeper on Queen West who takes great pleasure in offering Georgia a chair and a chat. My 86-year-old neighbour who tells Georgia that she is loved and presses a well-used Ziploc bag of too-old hard candy into her hand. The father with a baby, in a restaurant, who makes sure that he not only tells Georgia what the baby's name is, but chats with her about the baby. Fellow vacationers who know Georgia loves a good splash in the pool and go out of their way to execute a quick cannonball jump in the deep end as they walk by, purely for her amusement. Our good friends who let Georgia run about their farm, walk their dogs, and drive the tractor. Our babysitter who would lift up a car to free this kid. My family who embraces this wonderful girl and find great pleasure in her difference. All the surprisingly compelling and touching gestures from people who do not understand Georgia perfectly, but are willing to come a little closer. That is what that letter asks me to remember.

ESSAY 10*

Unrepentant Homeopaths

by Scott Gavura

Alternative medicine is ascendant in Canada. From the dubious remedies that are now stocked by nearly every pharmacy, to the questionable "integrative medicine" at universities, there's a serious move to embrace treatments and practices that are not backed by credible evidence. Canada's support for alternative medicine, and for its "integration" into conventional health care, is arguably worse than many other countries. Canada's drugs regulator, Health Canada, has approved hundreds of varieties of sugar pills and declared them to be "safe and effective" homeopathic remedies. Some provinces are even moving to regulate homeopaths as health professionals, just like physicians, nurses, and pharmacists. Given the regulatory and legislative "veneer of legitimacy" that homeopathy is being granted, you can see how consumers might be led to believe that homeopathic remedies are effective, or that homeopaths are capable of providing a form of health care. The reality is far uglier, and the consequences may be tragic. Canadian homeopaths are putting the most vulnerable in society at risk by selling sugar pills to consumers, while telling them that they're getting protection from communicable diseases.

---

* Source: Scott Gavura, "Unrepentant Homeopaths Still Selling Sugar Pills to Prevent Infectious Disease," *Science-Based Pharmacy*, 7 December 2014 https://sciencebasedpharmacy.wordpress.com/2014/12/07/unrepentant-homeopaths-still-selling-sugar-pills-to-prevent-infectious-disease. Reproduced with permission of the author.

CBC Marketplace, a consumer affairs show, recently used hidden cameras to record reporters asking homeopaths about vaccines. The show sent young mothers (with their babies) to speak with homeopaths about immunizations and vaccines in Toronto and Vancouver.

Of the five homeopaths filmed, four warned the mothers against vaccines, and advised them to avoid giving basic vaccinations like MMR (measles, mumps, and rubella). Only brief clips are shown in the episode, but the standard anti-vaccination tropes and misinformation are all there, such as saying that vaccines "overwhelm" the immune system, or blaming autism on vaccines. After the fear is created, then the sales pitch comes. Homeopaths just happen to have a substitute for real medicine and its toxic vaccines. The solution is sugar pills. The homeopaths pull out their homeopathic "nosodes" and offer them as "risk-free" substitutes, claiming that they have effectiveness rates of "93–95 per cent." It's appalling and frightening. As I watched the sales pitch, I wondered how many times homeopaths have counselled parents against vaccines—and how many parents actually knew that they'd been sold an expensive placebo, with zero ability to protect their children from infectious disease.

How did it ever come to this?

If you're new to the world of alternative medicine, you might think of homeopathy as a variation of herbalism. The marketing and labelling of homeopathic "remedies" encourages you to think this, describing it as a "gentle" and "natural" system of healing, and putting cryptic "30C" codes beside long Latin names. But with herbalism, at least you're getting some herb. Homeopathy's remedies contain no medicine at all—herbal, natural, or otherwise. They are inert. Homeopathy is the air guitar of alternative medicine, going through the motions of medicine, without actually providing medicine. How water and sugar pills are thought to heal is based on nonsensical, prescientific ideas about biology, biochemistry, and medicine itself. Homeopathy is based on the idea that "like cures like" (which is simply a form of magical thinking) and then performing successive dilutions of substances in water. Each dilution is believed to *increase*, not decrease, the "potency" of the final product. And these are serious dilutions. Think of putting one drop of a substance into a container of water. Only that container is 131 light-years in diameter. That's the "30C" dilution you'll see on packages. Homeopaths believe that the water molecules retain a "memory" of the original substance (while somehow forgetting all the other products it has come in contact with). The final remedy is diluted so completely that most "remedies" *don't contain a single molecule* of the original substance you started with. The CBC used a great image to illustrate the absurdity—a tablet *the size of the Earth* might contain a single molecule of the original substance. The rest is sugar.

You might wonder how homeopathy could ever be approved as "safe and effective" by a drug regulator. It comes down to how you define "effective." In the case of homeopathy, regulators diluted the standards just like homeopaths dilute their remedies. Health Canada was required to collect and evaluate some sort of evidence of effectiveness for each product it was responsible for regulating. But it realized that homeopathy could never meet conventional scientific standards of evidence. Consequently it allows citations about homeopathy from texts that date back to the 1800s as "evidence" that homeopathy is effective. To put this in perspective, this means that homeopaths can cite "evidence" that precedes germ theory. Forget about randomized controlled trials—this is anecdote-based medicine.

Through this process, Health Canada approved 82 homeopathic "nosodes" for sale over the years. A "nosode" is a remedy that starts with infectious material, like polio, measles, or smallpox, and then it's diluted sequentially until mathematically, there's nothing left but water. Those appear to be the remedies the CBC caught the homeopaths selling as vaccine substitutes. Last year the advocacy group Bad Science Watch (www.badsciencewatch.ca) launched a public campaign against nosodes, and succeeded in getting Health Canada's agreement to force commercial manufacturers to place a label on their products stating "This product is not intended to be an alternative to vaccination." This was the warning *CBC Marketplace* was looking for on the packages sold on camera. The warning wasn't there—because Health Canada apparently doesn't require the warning when the remedy is produced by the homeopaths themselves, only when the products are commercially prepared. Rather than reflecting on CBC's question and Health Canada's intent, homeopaths are instead gloating about their supposed "victory" over a requirement to give consumers a fair warning. No regulator is going to stop Canada's homeopaths from selling fake vaccines to Canadians, it seems.

This isn't the first time *CBC Marketplace* has scrutinized homeopathy. A 2011 episode asked if homeopathy was a "Cure or Con" and came to the expected conclusion. This episode had a similar reaction, with homeopaths outraged over the "bias" from CBC. (For LOLs, check out the Homeopathy and CBC Marketplace Facebook page, at www.facebook.com/Homeopathyand-CBC). CBC notes that not one of the five homeopaths filmed on camera was willing to go back on camera to defend their actions. Nor was any homeopathy spokesperson from the various homeopathy organizations that exist in Canada. But now that the show has been broadcast, several homeopaths are defending themselves in print. Their own words are further evidence that homeopaths do not appear to comprehend the risks they are taking with the health of children.

While these homeopaths may genuinely believe their homeopathic "remedies" are effective, their customers are not receiving full disclosure of the scientific facts. This is where homeopathy can harm. Choosing homeopathy over a vaccine is a *decision to forsake immunization*, something a homeopath's customers may not even realize—and seemingly something homeopaths have no intention of disclosing, even when they know the product should be labelled this way. Frustratingly, regulation has given homeopaths an opportunity, and now they're exploiting it, suggesting that homeopathy may offer something valuable. It does not. Regulating homeopathy and its providers makes as much sense as regulating magic carpets and their vendors.

Why is all this so important? Because vaccines work. And we need high vaccination rates to control or eradicate disease. Vaccines are one of the most remarkable health interventions ever developed. This fact has been written about countless times in this blog, so I won't rehash that evidence.

Millions of lives saved by an inexpensive and safe medical intervention. The potential that we'll be able to eradicate a disease from the earth, like we did with smallpox. That's what vaccines are doing. And that's why the actions of homeopaths are so frustrating. With vaccine rates dropping in some areas (some Toronto public schools have up to 40 per cent of students with "exemptions" from the vaccination schedule), health professionals and public health advocates need to be prepared to recognize and address the antagonism against vaccines that's fostered by homeopaths.

Another image that really hit home for me recently was a photo series from Anne Geddes, whom you probably associate with photos of cute children. She recently did a photo session with the victims of meningococcal disease, an illness that can steal limbs and even kill within 24 hours. The photos are beautiful but heartbreaking, and speak to the catastrophic harm that this infectious disease can cause. Amazingly, this infection is now vaccine preventable. But you need to be vaccinated with medicine—not sugar pills.

Anti-vaccine sentiment is ugly, and it's even uglier when there's a profit motive behind it. I commend *CBC Marketplace* for yet again taking a hard look at homeopathy from a consumer protection perspective, as it's something that regulators like Health Canada seem to show little interest in. The evidence is unequivocal—homeopathy has nothing to contribute to immunization or public health issues. One thing that you can do to counter-balance the harms of Canadian homeopaths is to contribute to vaccine programs directly, like those coordinated by Bill Gates or by other organizations. I've just contributed to UNICEF's program and bought vaccines (https://shop.unicef.ca/vaccine-pack) which should prevent measles, tetanus, and polio in 139 children. The costs are modest, the risks are low, and the vaccines will save lives. If only this type of health care was supported by homeopaths.

•

APPENDIX

B ANSWERS TO EXERCISES

CHAPTER 1

Exercise 1.1

1. Critical thinking is the systematic evaluation or formulation of beliefs, or statements, by rational standards.
4. Critical thinking operates according to rational standards in that beliefs are judged by how well they are supported by reasons.
6. The *critical* in critical thinking refers to the exercising of careful judgment and judicious evaluation.
8. A statement is an assertion that something is or is not the case.
11. An argument is a group of statements in which some of them (the premises) are intended to support another of them (the conclusion).
14. In an argument, a conclusion is a statement that premises are intended to support.
17. No.
19. Indicator words are words that frequently accompany arguments and signal that a premise or conclusion is present.
23. Look for the conclusion first.

Exercise 1.2

1. Not a statement
4. Not a statement
7. Statement
10. Not a statement

Exercise 1.3

1. Argument
   Conclusion: You should try coffee.

7. Not an argument
11. Argument
    Conclusion: Don't outlaw guns.
15. Argument
    Conclusion: Noisy car alarms should be banned.

Exercise 1.4

1. Argument
   Conclusion: Raising the price of our shoes is sure to dampen sales.
   Premise: It's a law of economics that if prices go up, demand will fall.
4. Argument
   Conclusion: The flu epidemic on the east coast is real.
   Premise: Government health officials say so.
   Premise: I personally have read at least a dozen news stories that characterize the situation as a "flu epidemic."
7. Not an argument
10. Not an argument

Exercise 1.5

3. Premise 1: Freedom to seek out food to sustain oneself and one's family is a basic moral right.
   Premise 2: Treaties signed by the Canadian government state that Aboriginal Canadians will always be able to hunt and fish.
6. Premise 1: MacDonald has admitted that he knows nothing about animals.
   Premise 2: The Society for the Prevention of Cruelty to Animals has declared MacDonald a dummy when it comes to animals.
9. Premise 1: The Internet has led to the capture of more terrorists than anything else.
   Premise 2: The attorney general of Canada has asserted that the Internet is the best friend that anti-terrorist teams have.
12. Premise 1: All the top TV critics agree that *The Walking Dead* is the greatest series in television history.
    Premise 2: I have compared *The Walking Dead* to all other TV series and found that the show outshines them all.

Exercise 1.6

2. Conclusion: Several Canadian cities can expect to see an overall decline in smoking.
4. Conclusion: As a married person, you are happier than people who aren't married.
8. Conclusion: Canadian society doesn't care about its children.

Exercise 1.7

1. Argument
   Conclusion: Advertising isn't manipulative.
   Premise: The main thing advertising does is provide information about products.
   Premise: Ads that don't seem to provide much information are really just trying to entertain us, not manipulate us.
3. Argument
   Conclusion: There is no archaeological evidence for the [biblical] Flood.
   Premise: If a universal Flood occurred between 5000 and 6000 years ago, killing all humans except the eight on board the Ark, it would be abundantly clear in the archaeological record.
   Premise: The destruction of all but eight of the world's people left no mark on the archaeology of human cultural evolution.

CHAPTER 2

Exercise 2.1

1. For critical thinking to be realized, the process must be systematic, it must be a true evaluation or formulation of claims, and it must be based on rational standards.
5. We take things too far when we accept claims for no reason.
7. You are most likely to let your self-interest get in the way of clear thinking when you have a significant personal stake in the conclusions you reach.
11. Group pressure can affect your attempts to think critically by allowing your need to be part of a group or your identification with a group to undermine critical thinking.
14. A world view is a set of fundamental ideas that helps us make sense of a wide range of issues in life.
17. Critical thinking is concerned with objective truth claims.
21. Reasonable doubt, not certainty, is central to the acquisition of knowledge.

Exercise 2.2

1. Self-interest
4. Face-saving
7. Group pressure
10. Self-interest

Exercise 2.3

1. a. The charges are false.

   c. Important evidence that would exonerate Father Miller was not mentioned in the newspaper account.
3. a. A study from McGill shows that women are less violent and less emotional than men.
6. No good reasons listed.

Exercise 2.4

1. Better-than-others group pressure. Possible negative consequence: Failure to consider other points of view; discrimination against people who disagree with Marie-Eve.
3. It's not entirely clear what the group's motivations are. This passage could easily be an example of better-than-others group pressure.
7. Appeal to popularity. Possible negative consequence: Overlooking other factors that might be a lot more important than popularity.

Exercise 2.5

1. Face-saving. Possible negative consequences: Continued poor performance due to misidentifying problems; alienation of workers.
2. Self-interest. Possible negative consequences: Wasting taxpayers' money; being thrown out of office for misconduct.

CHAPTER 3

Exercise 3.1

4. Deductive
8. Sound
12. No

Exercise 3.2

1. Step 1: Conclusion: She has a superior intellect.
   Premises: Ethel graduated from Queen's University. If she graduated from Queen's, she probably has a superior intellect.
   Step 2: Not deductively valid.
   Step 3: Inductively strong.
   Step 4: Does not apply.
6. Step 1: Conclusion: Thus, every musician has a university degree.
   Premises: Every musician has had special training, and everyone with special training has a university degree.
   Step 2: Deductively valid.
   Step 3: Does not apply.
   Step 4: Does not apply.

9. Step 1: Conclusion: So some actors who sing also play a musical instrument.
   Premises: Some actors sing, and some play a musical instrument.
   Step 2: Not deductively valid.
   Step 3: Not inductively strong.
   Step 4: Intended to be deductive.
15. Step 1: Conclusion: So it's impossible for androids to have minds.
   Premises: If minds are identical to brains—that is, if one's mind is nothing but a brain—androids could never have minds because they wouldn't have brains. Clearly, a mind is nothing but a brain.
   Step 2: Deductively valid.
   Step 3: Does not apply.
   Step 4: Does not apply.

Exercise 3.3

3. Valid
8. Valid
14. Valid
18. Valid
23. Invalid

Exercise 3.4

I.

1. The honourable member from Algoma-Manitoulin-Kapuskasing was caught misusing campaign funds.
5. She's not incompetent.
10. Only someone who is pro-American would fail to criticize US military action in the Gulf War or in the war in Afghanistan.

II.

3. Sixty per cent of the teenagers in several scientific surveys love rap music.
6. Assad's fingerprints are on the vase.
9. Add a premise to the effect that the murder rates in almost all cities in central Canada are very low, too.

Exercise 3.5

1. Valid; *modus tollens*
6. Valid; *modus tollens*
9. Valid; *modus ponens*

Exercise 3.6

2. If Lino is telling the truth, he will admit to all charges.

Lino is telling the truth.
So he will admit to all charges.
If Lino is telling the truth, he will admit to all charges.
He will not admit to all charges.
So he is not telling the truth.

5. If religious conflict in Nigeria continues, thousands more will die.
   The religious conflict in Nigeria will continue.
   Therefore, thousands more will die.
   If religious conflict in Nigeria continues, thousands more will die.
   Thousands more will not die.
   Therefore, the religious conflict in Nigeria will not continue.
9. If solar power can supply six megawatts of power in Vancouver (which is certainly not the sunniest place in the world), then solar power can transform the energy systems in sunnier places like Edmonton and Calgary.
   Solar power can supply six megawatts of power in Vancouver.
   So solar power can transform the energy systems in sunnier places like Edmonton and Calgary.
   If solar power can supply six megawatts of power in Vancouver (which is certainly not the sunniest place in the world), then solar power can transform the energy systems in sunnier places like Edmonton and Calgary.
   But solar power cannot transform the energy systems in sunnier places like Edmonton and Calgary.
   So solar power cannot supply six megawatts of power in Vancouver.

Exercise 3.7

The sample answers below are some possible solutions. Remember, you've been asked to use the counterexample method, which means there are lots of possible answers that are correct (but also lots that are incorrect).

4. Not possible to construct a counterexample. This is a valid argument (denying the consequent).
   If ~*a*, then *b*.
   ~*b*.
   Therefore, *a*.
5. One possible counterexample: If Stephen Harper was the prime minister of Canada in 1970, then he would be a Canadian.
   Stephen Harper was not prime minister of Canada in 1970. Therefore, he is not a Canadian.
   If *a*, then *b*.
   Not *a*.
   Therefore, not *b*. (That's denying the antecedent, an invalid argument form.)

7. One possible counterexample: If Vaughn is a dog, he is a mammal.
   He is a mammal.
   Therefore, he is a dog.
   If *a*, then *b*.
   b.
   Therefore, *a*. (That's affirming the consequent, an invalid argument form.)
8. One possible counterexample: If ducks are sea turtles, then they are at home in the water.
   Ducks are not sea turtles.
   Therefore, ducks are not at home in the water.
   If *a*, then *b*.
   Not *a*.
   Therefore, not *b*. (That's denying the antecedent, an invalid argument form.)
11. One possible counterexample: If Victoria is the capital of British Columbia, then Victoria is in British Columbia.
   Victoria is in British Columbia.
   Therefore, Victoria is the capital of British Columbia.
   If *a*, then *b*.
   b.
   Therefore, *a*. (That's affirming the consequent, an invalid argument form.)

Exercise 3.8

1. Any argument that provides three separate, stand-alone reasons supporting a single conclusion will do. For example:

   (1) The stores are closed. (2) We have no money. (3) And we have no way of travelling to any place of business. (4) Therefore, we are just not going to be able to go shopping right now.

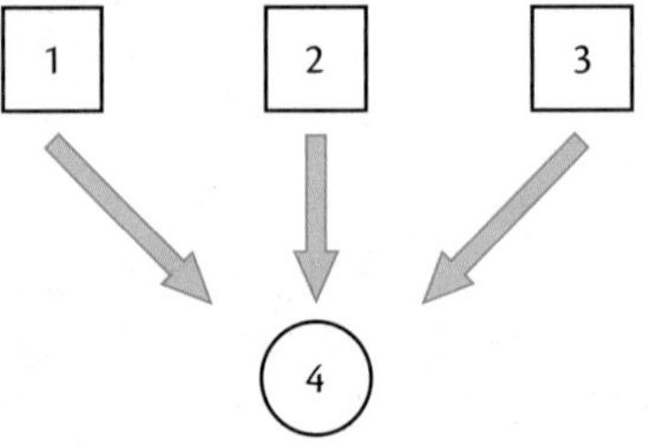

The queen is not alive.
Therefore, Charles is king.

4. (1) If the pipes have burst, there will be no running water. (2) The pipes have burst. (3) And if all the water is rusty, we won't be able to use it anyway, (4) and all the water is rusty. (5) So we have no usable water at this point.

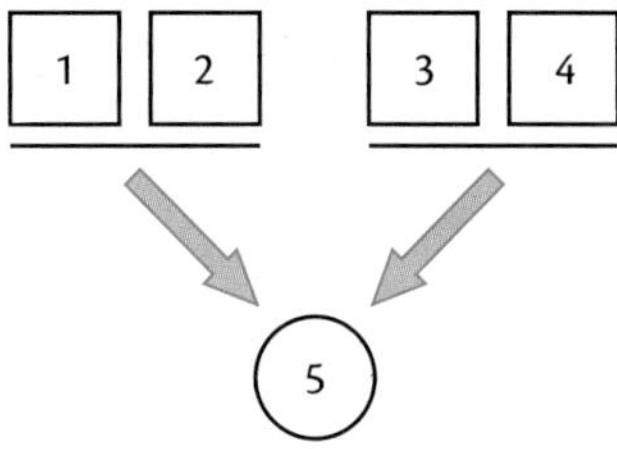

Exercise 3.9

6. (1) If Marla buys the house in the suburbs, she will be happier and healthier. (2) She is buying the house in the suburbs. (3) So she will be happier and healthier.

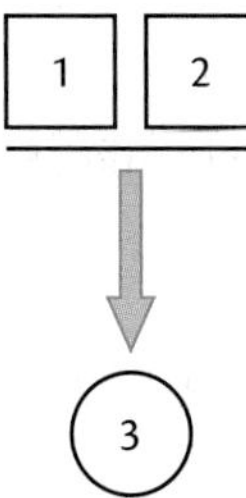

10. (1) The existence of planets outside our solar system is a myth. (2) There is no reliable empirical evidence at all showing that planets exist outside our solar system.

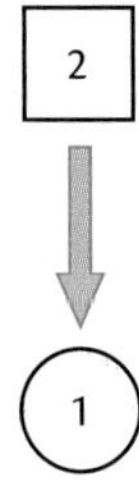

17. ~~(1) There are at least two main views regarding the morality of war. (2) Pacifism is the view that no war is ever justified because it involves the taking of human life. (3) Just-war theory is the view that some wars are justified for various reasons—mostly because they help prevent great evils (such as massacres, "ethnic cleansing," or world domination by a madman like Hitler) or because they are a means of self defence.~~ (4) I think that

our own moral sense tells us that sometimes (in the case of the World War II, for example) violence is occasionally morally justified. (5) It would be hard for anyone to deny that a war to prevent something like the Holocaust is morally right. [Implied conclusion] (6) Just-war theory is correct.

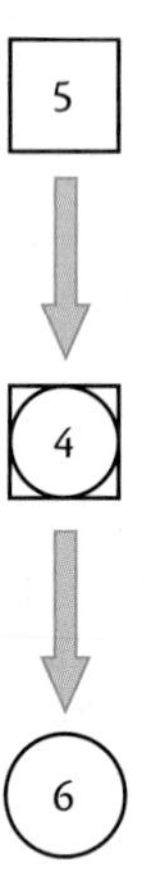

20. (1) The picnic will probably be spoiled because (2) there is a 90 per cent probability of rain.

Exercise 3.10

1. Conclusion: (9) You should skip the supplements.
   Premises: (2) There's no persuasive evidence yet to suggest that collagen supplements help with joint pain. (3) Collagen is a specific thing (something unstated). (4) Collagen is absorbed in a certain (unstated) way. (5) Collagen is synthesized in the body in a certain (unstated) way. (6) It's implausible that a small supplement of amino acids consumed daily will have any meaningful therapeutic effects. (8) Genacol, like other collagen supplements, appears to be little more than an expensive protein supplement.

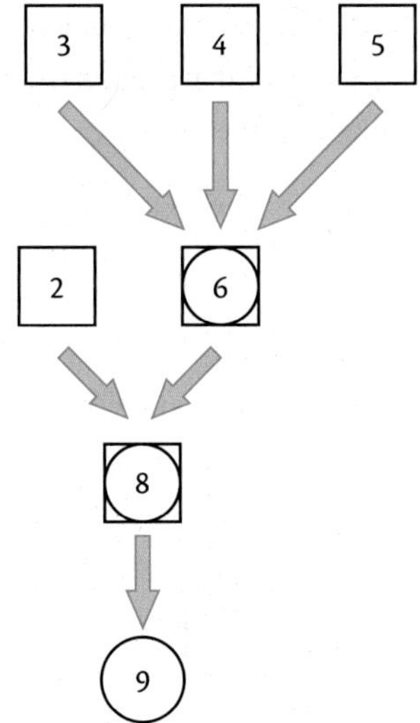

CHAPTER 4

Exercise 4.1

4. We should proportion our belief to the evidence.
10. Two additional indicators are reputation among peers and professional accomplishments.
17. By making a conscious effort to consider not only information that supports what we believe, but also the information that conflicts with it.

Exercise 4.2

4. Proportion belief to the evidence; the claim is not dubious enough to dismiss out of hand, and not worthy of complete acceptance. Low plausibility.
6. Reject it; it conflicts with a great deal of background information.
10. Proportion belief to the evidence; the claim is not dubious enough to dismiss out of hand, and not worthy of complete acceptance. Moderate plausibility.
14. Reject it; it conflicts with a great deal of background information.
17. Reject it; it conflicts with a great deal of background information.

Exercise 4.3

3. Do not agree. Persuasive evidence would include the body of an alien or the alien craft itself, both scientifically documented as being of extra-terrestrial origin.

8. Do not agree. Persuasive evidence would include several double-blind, controlled trials demonstrating that meditation and controlled breathing shrink tumours.

CHAPTER 5

Exercise 5.1

4. The fallacy of composition involves arguing that what is true of the parts must be true of the whole. The fallacy of division does the opposite: it involves arguing that what is true of the whole must also be true of the parts.
10. They are fallacious because they assume that a proposition is true merely because a great number of people believe it, but as far as the truth of a claim is concerned, what many people believe is irrelevant.
15. Yes.
19. A false dilemma may assert that there are only two alternatives to consider when there are actually more than two, or assert that there are two distinct alternatives that may in fact not be mutually exclusive. People are often taken in by false dilemmas because they don't think beyond the alternatives laid before them.

Exercise 5.2

1. Composition
5. Genetic fallacy
10. Appeal to the person
14. Equivocation (the word *desirable* is used as if it means "capable of being desired" and also as if it means "worthy of being desired"). Alternatively: faulty analogy
20. Appeal to the person

Exercise 5.3

4. False dilemma
6. Hasty generalization
10. False dilemma

Exercise 5.4

3. Jones says that Mrs Anan deserves the Nobel Prize. But he's a real jerk. Clearly, then, Mrs Anan does not deserve the Nobel Prize.
6. In light of ethical considerations, Scouts Canada should allow gay kids to be members. The reason is that banning gay kids from the organization would be in conflict with basic moral principles.

11. Newfoundland's fisheries are a mess because the Department of Fisheries and Oceans—a federal department—has too much power over them. Nobody likes intrusive governments!

CHAPTER 6

Exercise 6.1

1. *S* = scientists, *P* = Christians; universal negative; E.
5. *S* = theologians who have studied arguments for the existence of God, *P* = scholars with serious misgivings about the traditional notion of omnipotence; universal affirmative; A.
8. *S* = people who play the stock market, *P* = millionaires; particular negative; O.
12. *S* = terrorists, *P* = Saudi citizens; particular affirmative; I.
16. *S* = new Canadians, *P* = immigration reform supporters; universal negative; E.

Exercise 6.2

1. All Habs fans are fanatical fans (or, are people who are fanatical). A.
5. All good investments in cellphone companies are investments in cellphone companies that keep up with the latest technology. A.
9. All intelligent thoughts are thoughts that have already happened. A.
13. Some things are things meant to be forgotten. I.

Exercise 6.3

1. All people who test the depth of the water with both feet are fools. A.
4. All androids like Commander Data are non-humans. A.
5. No things that satisfy the heart are material things. E.
8. Some treatments said to be part of "alternative medicine" are unproven treatments. I.
12. All days that give her any joy are Fridays. A.
15. All pictures identical with the one hanging on the wall are things that are crooked. A.
20. All nations without a conscience are nations without souls. A.

Exercise 6.4

1. No persons are persons exempt from federal income tax.
   S = persons; *P* = persons exempt federal income tax.

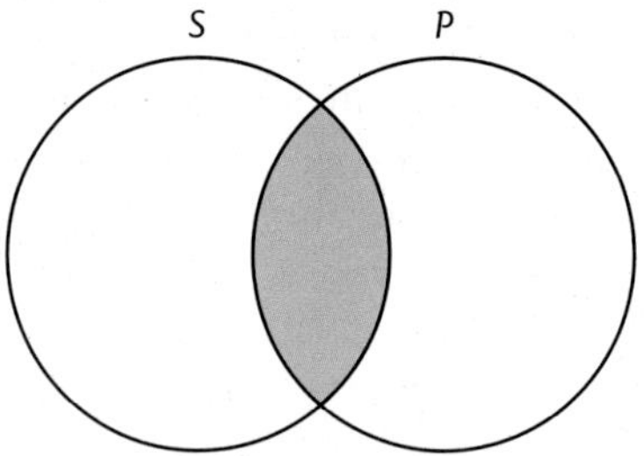

5. No things are things more useless in a developing nation's economy than a gun.
   S = things; *P* = things more useless in a developing nation's economy than a gun.

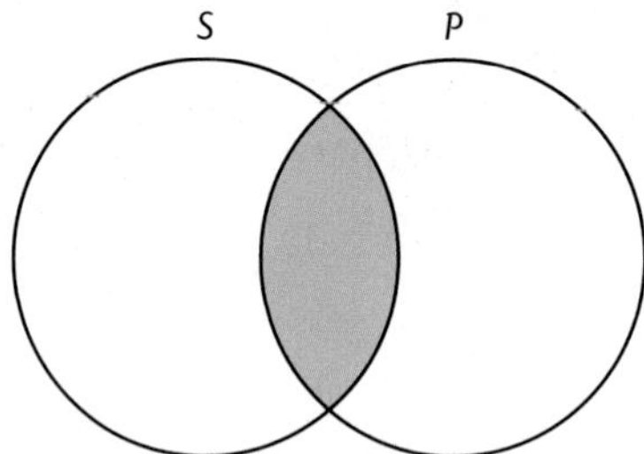

8. Some good talkers are good listeners.
   S = good talkers; *P* = good listeners.

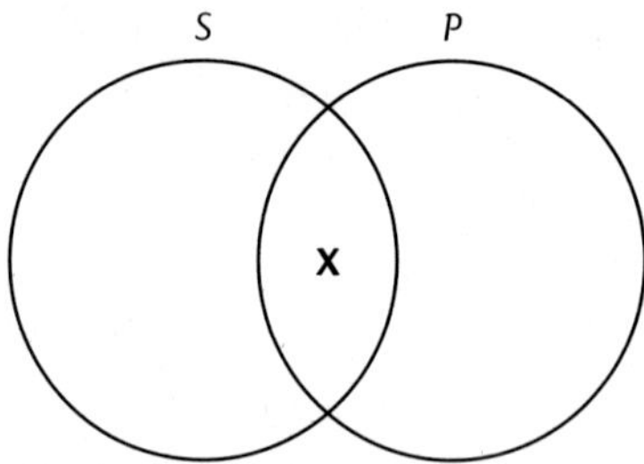

12. All corporations are corporations with social obligations.
    S = corporations; *P* = corporations with social obligations.

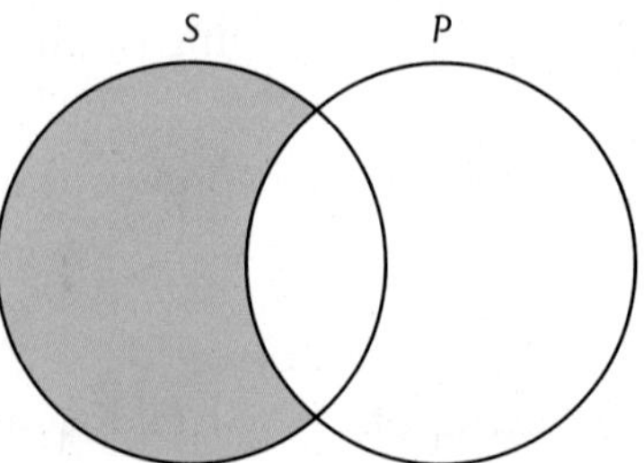

Exercise 6.5

1. No *P* are *S*; No *S* are *P*.

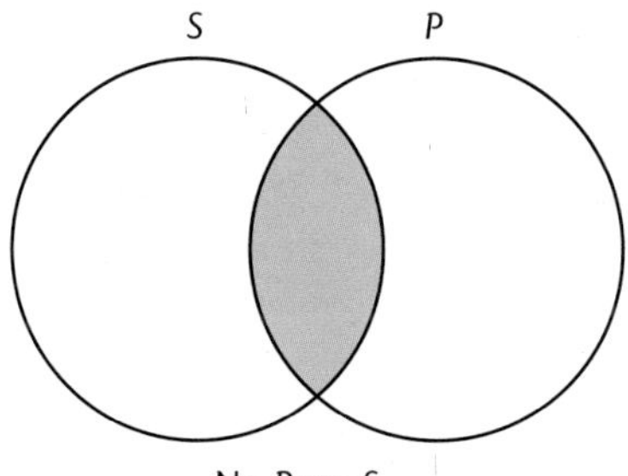

No *P* are *S*.

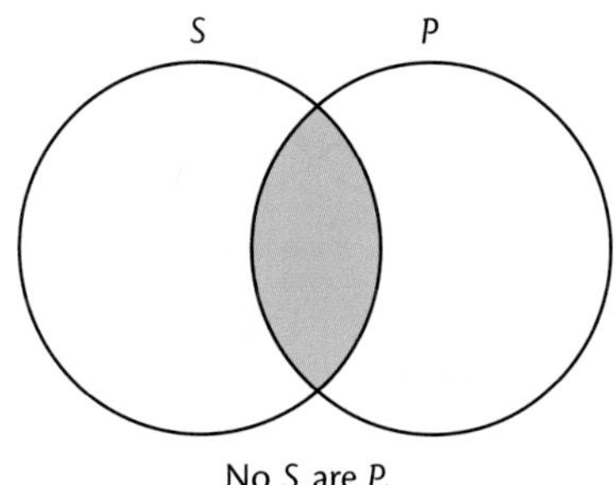

No *S* are *P*.

   Equivalent.

3. All *S* are *P*; All *P* are *S*.

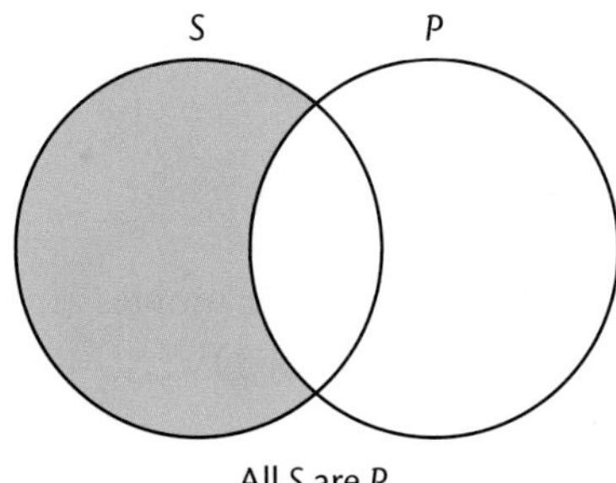

All *S* are *P*.

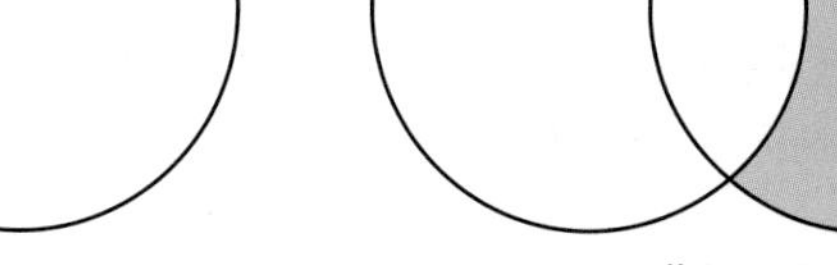

All *P* are *S*.

   Not equivalent.

6. All *P* are non-*S*; All *S* are non-*P*.

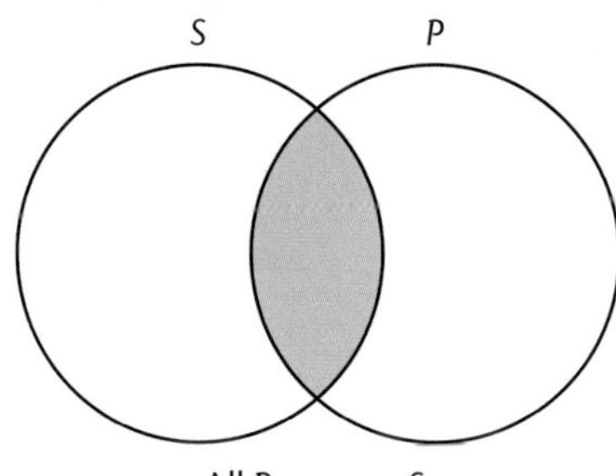

All *P* are non-*S*.

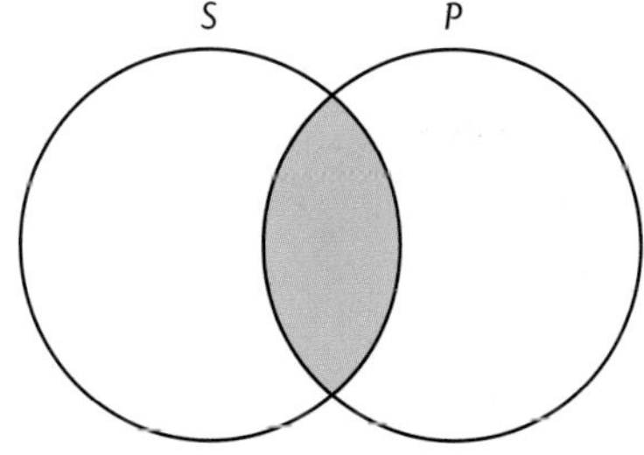

All *S* are non-*P*.

   Equivalent.

9. Some *S* are not *P*; Some *P* are not *S*.

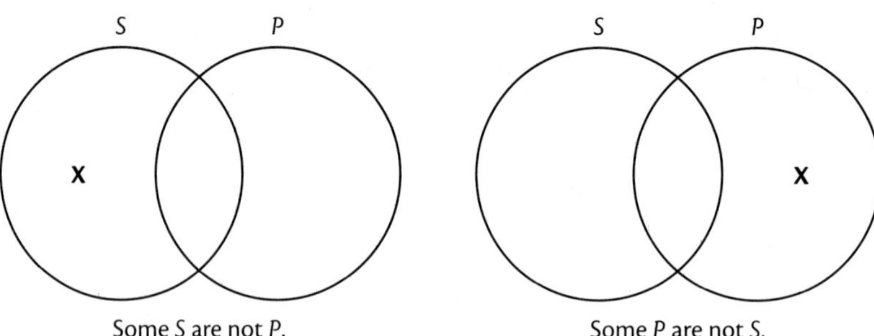

Some *S* are not *P*.   Some *P* are not *S*.

Not equivalent.

Exercise 6.6

2. All horses are mammals, and no mammals are lizards. Therefore, no lizards are horses.
   S = lizards
   P = horses
   M = mammals
   All *P* are *M*.
   No *M* are *S*.
   Therefore, no *S* are *P*.
6. Some DVDs are not film classics, but all black-and-white movies are film classics. Therefore, some black-and-white movies are not DVDs.
   S = black-and-white movies
   P = DVDs
   M = film classics
   Some *P* are not *M*.
   All *S* are *M*.
   Therefore, some *S* are not *P*.
9. No elm trees are cacti. Some tall plants are elm trees. So some tall plants are not cacti.
   S = tall plants
   P = cacti
   M = elm trees
   No *M* are *P*.
   Some *S* are *M*.
   Therefore, some *S* are not *P*.

Exercise 6.7

2. All *P* are *M*.
   No *M* are *S*.
   Therefore, no *S* are *P*.

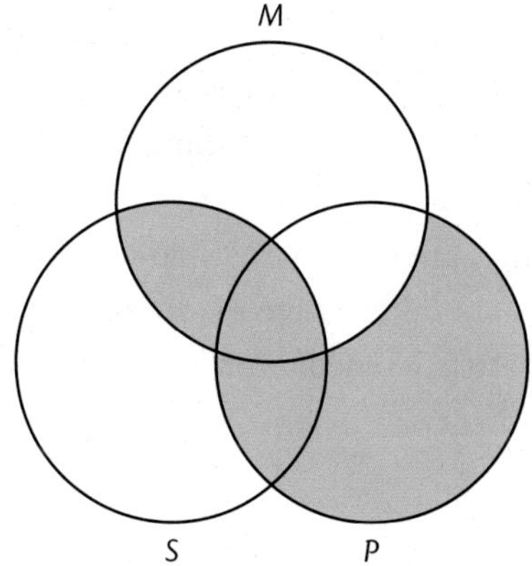

Valid.

6. Some *P* are not *M*.
   All *S* are *M*.
   Therefore, some *S* are not *P*.

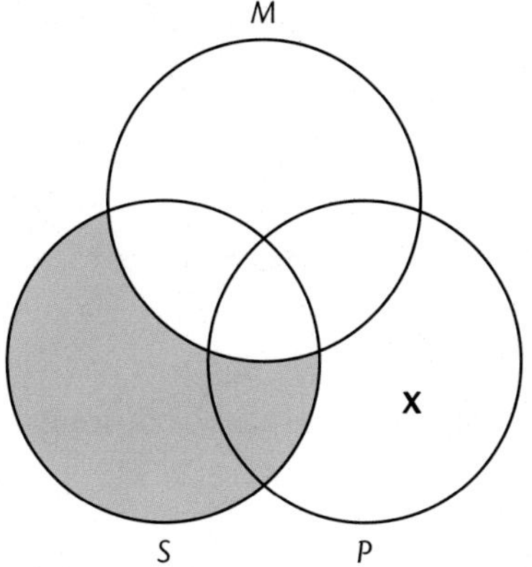

Invalid.

9. No *M* are *P*.
   Some *S* are *M*.
   Therefore, some *S* are not *P*.

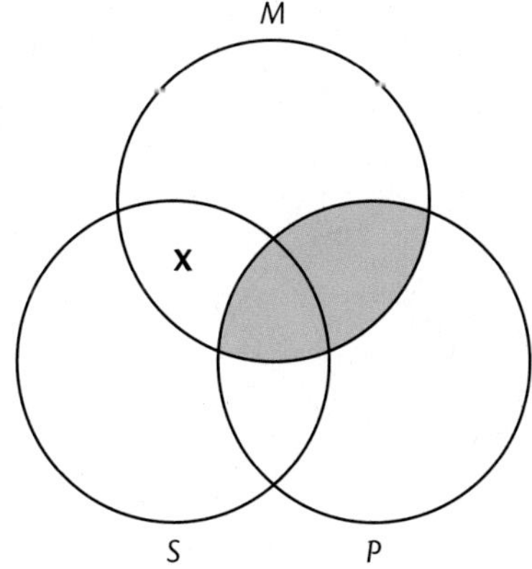

Valid.

Exercise 6.8

1. Some "alternative medicines" are cancer treatments, for all herbal medicines are "alternative medicines," and some herbal medicines are cancer treatments.
   Some herbal medicines are cancer treatments.
   All herbal medicines are "alternative medicines."
   Therefore, some "alternative medicines" are cancer treatments.
   Some *M* are *P*.
   All *M* are *S*.
   Therefore, some *S* are *P*.

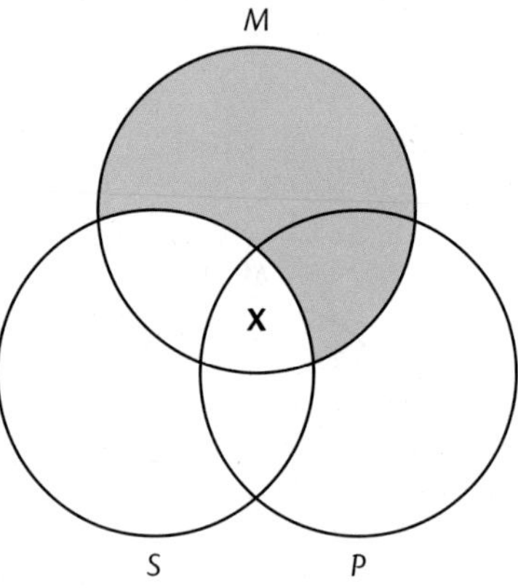

   Valid.

3. All SUVs are evil vehicles because all SUVs are gas guzzlers, and all gas guzzlers are evil vehicles.
   All gas guzzlers are evil.
   All SUVs are gas guzzlers.
   Therefore, all SUVs are evil vehicles.
   All *M* are *P*.
   All *S* are *M*.
   Therefore, all *S* are *P*.

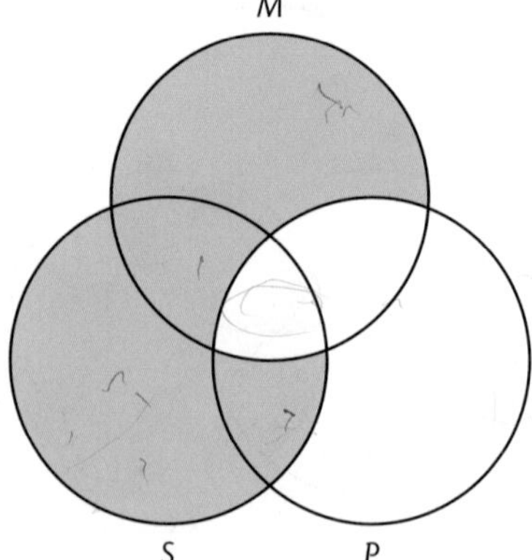

   Valid.

8. No wimps are social activists because no wimps are people of honest and strong conviction. And all social activists are people of honest and strong conviction.
   All social activists are people of honest and strong convictions.
   No wimps are people of honest and strong convictions.
   Therefore, no wimps are social activists.
   All *P* are *M*.
   No *S* are *M*.
   Therefore, no *S* are *P*.

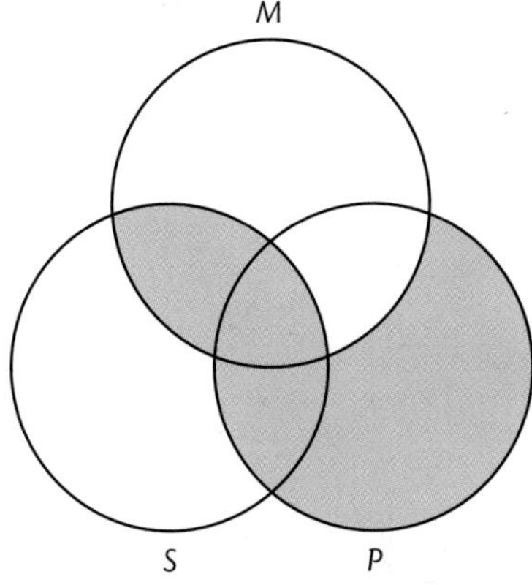

   Valid.

CHAPTER 7

Exercise 7.1

1. Conjunction. Components: The Liberals raised taxes, The Conservatives cut programs; &
5. Conditional. Components: Taslima can read your mind, You're in trouble; →
7. Conditional; Components: God is all-powerful, He can prevent evil in the world; →

Exercise 7.2

1. $p \vee q$
4. $e \& f$
8. $\sim g \& \sim h$
14. $\sim\sim p$

Exercise 7.3

2. False
6. True
8. False

Exercise 7.4

2. False
5. True
10. True

Exercise 7.5

2. Either John is not home or Mary is not home.
5. If the sun is shining, then we will go outside.
10. If the day goes well, then we will not regret our efforts.

Exercise 7.6

2. $p \lor q$
5. $\sim a \rightarrow \sim b$
9. $p \rightarrow q$

Exercise 7.7

2. Alligators are reptiles and dogs are reptiles.

a	*d*	*a* & *d*
T	T	T
T	F	F
F	T	F
F	F	F

6. Either dogs are not mammals, or snakes are reptiles. [Hint: To avoid confusion, you can *add* columns after the guide columns, such as the one for *~d* in this truth table. This extra column reminds you that the truth values for *~d* are the flip side of those for *d*.]

d	*s*	*~d*	*~d* ∨ *s*
T	T	F	T
T	F	F	F
F	T	T	T
F	F	T	T

8. Alligators can bark, and dogs are not reptiles.

a	*d*	*~d*	*a & ~d*
T	T	F	F
T	F	T	T
F	T	F	F
F	F	T	F

Exercise 7.8

2. Valid

$p \rightarrow q$
p
$\therefore q$

p	*q*	*p → q*	*p*	*q*
T	T	T	T	T
T	F	F	T	F
F	T	T	F	T
F	F	T	F	F

7. Valid

$p \rightarrow q$
$\sim q \;\&\; r$
$\therefore r$

p	*q*	*r*	*~q*	*p → q*	*~q & r*	*r*
T	T	T	F	T	F	T
T	T	F	F	T	F	F
T	F	T	T	F	T	T
T	F	F	T	F	F	F
F	T	T	F	T	F	T
F	T	F	F	T	F	F
F	F	T	T	T	T	T
F	F	F	T	T	F	F

14. Valid

$p \rightarrow q$

$\sim(q \vee r)$

$\therefore \sim p$

p	q	r	$\sim p$	$p \rightarrow q$	$\sim(q \vee r)$	$\sim p$
T	T	T	F	T	F	F
T	T	F	F	T	F	F
T	F	T	F	F	F	F
T	F	F	F	F	T	F
F	T	T	T	T	F	T
F	T	F	T	T	F	T
F	F	T	T	T	F	T
F	F	F	T	T	T	T

Exercise 7.9

3. This is either olive oil or canola oil. And it's not olive oil, so it must be canola oil.

$o \vee c$

$\sim o$

$\therefore c$

o	c	$o \vee c$	$\sim o$	c
T	T	T	F	T
T	F	T	F	F
F	T	T	T	T
F	F	F	T	F

Valid

11. Either the herbal remedy alleviated the symptoms, or the placebo effect alleviated the symptoms. If the placebo effect is responsible for easing the symptoms, then the herbal remedy is worthless. The herbal remedy alleviated the symptoms. So the herbal remedy is not worthless.

$h \vee p$

$p \rightarrow w$

h

$\therefore \sim w$

h	p	w	$h \vee p$	$p \rightarrow w$	h	$\sim w$
T	T	T	T	T	T	F
T	T	F	T	F	T	T
T	F	T	T	T	T	F
T	F	F	T	T	T	T
F	T	T	T	T	F	F
F	T	F	T	F	F	T
F	F	T	F	T	F	F
F	F	F	F	T	F	T

Invalid

Exercise 7.10

3. $p \vee q$
   p
   $\therefore \sim q$
   T T F
   $p \vee q$ p $\sim q$
   T T T T
   Invalid

10. $p \rightarrow q$
    $\therefore p \rightarrow (p \,\&\, q)$
    F F
    $p \rightarrow q$ $p \rightarrow (p \,\&\, q)$
    T F T T F
    Valid

15. $(d \vee e) \rightarrow (d \,\&\, e)$
    $\sim(d \vee e)$
    $\therefore \sim(d \,\&\, e)$
    T F F
    $(d \vee e) \rightarrow (d \,\&\, e)$ $(d \vee e)$ $\sim(d \,\&\, e)$
    T T T T T T T T
    Valid

CHAPTER 8

Exercise 8.1

1. Target group: Canadian adults; sample: several thousand horse owners; relevant property: being in favour of banning horse meat. The argument is weak because the sample is not representative.

4. Target group: Decembers in Vancouver; sample: many years of Decembers in Vancouver; relevant property: receiving over 150 millimetres of rain. The argument is strong.
8. Target group: dentists; sample: dentists who suggest that their patients chew gum; relevant property: recommending Brand X gum. The argument is weak because the sample is not representative.
12. Target group: Canadians; sample: adults with an annual income of $48,000–$60,000; relevant property: being happy and satisfied with one's job. The argument is weak because the sample is not representative. (Middle-income workers are likely to have attitudes toward job satisfaction that are different from those of workers in other income brackets, especially lower ones.)

Exercise 8.2

1. Weak. To ensure a strong argument, draw the sample randomly from the entire Canadian population, not just from horse owners.
4. Strong. To make this into a weak argument, rely on a much smaller sample, such as "the last few Decembers."
8. Weak. To ensure a strong argument, draw the sample randomly from the set of all dentists, not just the dentists who recommend gum.
12. Weak. To ensure a strong argument, draw the sample randomly from the set of all Canadian workers, including respondents representative of all income groups.

Exercise 8.3

1. Does not offer strong support for the conclusion. The problem is non-random—and therefore non-representative—sampling.

Exercise 8.4

1. a, b

Exercise 8.5

1. More likely to be true.

Exercise 8.6

1. Individual: Barb; group: people who ride their bikes to work; characteristic: riding recklessly; proportion: almost all.
4. Individual: next meal eaten at the Poolhouse Café; group: meals eaten at the Poolhouse Café; characteristic: being wonderful; proportion: almost every.

5. Individual: your car; group: Fords; characteristic: work poorly; proportion: most.

Exercise 8.7

1. Statistical weakness (given weak anecdotal evidence)
2. Non-typical individual (being a professor makes Professor Norman unusual; professors are more likely than most people to have read Plato)
4. Statistically weak (53 per cent might technically be "most," but just barely)

Exercise 8.8

2. Literary analogy.
5. Argument by analogy. Two things being compared; relevant similarity: working with numbers; conclusion: "he'll be a whiz at algebra;" weak argument.
7. Argument by analogy; four things being compared; relevant similarity: being beef; conclusion: "I will like tongue;" weak argument.
11. Argument by analogy; two things being compared; relevant similarity: being foundations; conclusions: "no lasting reputation worthy of respect can be built on a weak character;" weak argument.

Exercise 8.9

1. Instances being compared: the economic joining of newlyweds, on one hand, and the countries of Europe on the other; relevant similarities: linked economic fate; optimism; seeing benefits; likelihood of tough times together; diversity among cases not a significant factor; conclusion: The countries of Europe may regret linking their economies; weak argument (because of several unmentioned dissimilarities—including very different reasons for joining together and different degrees of linkage)
5. Instances being compared: having terminal cancer and being threatened by an assailant; relevant similarities: being threatened with death or great pain; diversity among cases not a significant factor; conclusion: "suicide must sometimes be morally justified when it is an act of self-defence against a terminal disease that threatens death or great pain." This is a strong argument—*if* all the relevant similarities and dissimilarities have indeed been taken into account. A critic could argue, though, that killing oneself in self-defence is just not relevantly similar to killing another human in self-defence. The critic, then, would have to specify what the significant difference is.

Exercise 8.10

2. Conclusion: "Research suggests that eating lots of fruits and vegetables may provide some protection against several types of cancer." Correlation. The argument is strong. The conclusion is a limited claim ("*may* provide some protection . . ."), which the stated correlation could easily support.
7. Conclusion: "Education increases people's earning power." Correlation. The argument is strong.
13. Conclusion: "Tune-ups can improve the performance of lawnmowers." Correlation. The argument is strong.
16. Conclusion: [Implied] "Having a major war somewhere in the world causes the price of oil to hit $40 a barrel." Method of agreement. The argument is strong if all relevant factors have been taken into account, which may not be the case.
19. Conclusion: Police presence has caused the reduction in crime. Method of difference. The argument is relatively strong. More information is needed in order to rule out other possible causes.

Exercise 8.11

2. a, d (It may be that a diagnosis of cancer leads people to start eating healthier!)
7. a
13. a
16. a, b, d
19. a, b, d

Exercise 8.12

1. a
4. b
9. a

CHAPTER 9

Exercise 9.1

4. A theoretical explanation is an explanation that serves as a theory, or hypothesis, used to explain why something is the way it is, why something is the case, or why something happened.
8. A causal explanation is a kind of theoretical explanation. Like all theoretical explanations, causal explanations are used in inference to the best explanation.

Exercise 9.2

2. The state of affairs being explained is the endangered status of the polar bear. The explanation is the thinning of arctic ice, caused by global warming.
5. The state of affairs being explained is the "hot" water from your faucet not being very hot. The explanation is that your hot-water heater is old and can't keep up.
8. The state of affairs being explained is the fact that your hands are shaking. The explanation is that you've had too much coffee.

Exercise 9.3

4. Theoretical
7. Theoretical
12. Interpretive

Exercise 9.4

2. Theory 1: Jack's house was burglarized.
   Theory 2: Jack's dog went on a rampage.
6. Theory 1: Alice was not exposed to any germs.
   Theory 2: Vitamin C supercharged Alice's immune system.

Exercise 9.6

2. The minimum requirement of consistency is the criterion that any theory worth considering must have both internal and external consistency—that is, be free of contradictions and be consistent with the data the theory is supposed to explain.
6. A theory that does not have much scope is one that explains very little—perhaps only the phenomenon it was introduced to explain and not much else.

Exercise 9.7

2. The first theory is both simpler and more conservative.
4. The first theory is both simpler and more conservative.
7. The first theory is both simpler and more conservative.

Exercise 9.8

3. Theory 3

CHAPTER 10

Exercise 10.1

7. It means to ask yourself, "If this theory were true, what testable consequences would follow from it?"
8. Denying the consequent. Valid.
11. No. Hypotheses are tested together with other hypotheses. A hypothesis can always be saved from refutation by making changes in one of the accompanying hypotheses.

Exercise 10.2

2. Hypothesis: Two guys are perpetrating a Bigfoot hoax. Test implication: If the two guys are perpetrating a hoax, then monitoring their behaviour day and night should yield evidence of hoaxing activity.
6. Hypothesis: Creatine dramatically increases the performance of weight trainers. Test implication: If creatine increases performance, then giving creatine to weight trainers in a controlled way (in a double-blind controlled trial) should increase various measures of performance in the trainers compared to weight trainers who get a placebo (inactive substance).

Exercise 10.3

3. Theory: Local climate changes are melting glaciers.
   Competing theory: Heat from volcanic activity around the planet is melting the glaciers.
   Both theories are about equal in terms of testability, fruitfulness, and scope. The volcanic theory, however, is neither simple nor conservative. It's not simple because it assumes an unknown process. It's not conservative because it is not consistent with what is known about the effects of heat from volcanoes.
7. Theory: Poverty fosters crime.
   Competing theory: People commit crimes because they lack basic human values.
   Both theories are about equal in terms of testability, fruitfulness, scope, and simplicity. The values theory, though, is not conservative. It conflicts with what we know about those who commit crimes. Some crimes are indeed committed by people who lack basic human values (for example, sociopaths) but that is not true for *most* crime.

Exercise 10.4

2. Test implication: If brighter street lights decrease the crime rate, then reducing the brightness of the lights (while keeping constant all other factors, such as police patrols) should increase the crime rate. The test would likely confirm the theory.
6. Test implication: If eating foods high in fat contributes more to being overweight than eating foods high in carbohydrates, then over time people should gain more weight when they are eating X number of grams of fat per day than when they are eating the same number of grams of carbohydrates per day.

Exercise 10.7

4. The appeal to ignorance.
6. Something is logically impossible if it violates a principle of logic; something is logically possible if it does not violate a principle of logic.

Exercise 10.8

2. Theory 1: The aging of the building materials in the house caused creaking.
   Theory 2: The wind blowing against the house caused the creaking.
   Theory 3: A ghost caused the creaking.
7. Theory 1: A coincidental matching between the dream and real events made the dream seem prophetic.
   Theory 2: Wayne had the same dream every night because he was concerned about his uncle, so there was a good chance that the dream would match something in reality.
   Theory 3: The dream was a genuine prophetic dream.

Exercise 10.9

3. Alternative theory: As a prank, the little girls cut drawings of fairies out of a book, posed them in the garden, and took photos of themselves with the cutouts. Then they claimed that the photos showed actual fairies. Both theories seem to be about equal in testability and fruitfulness. The prank theory has more scope because faked photos can explain many other phenomena, including many different kinds of paranormal hoaxes. The fairy theory is neither simple nor conservative. Fairies are unknown to science, and claims about their existence conflict with many things that we know.

CHAPTER 11

Exercise 11.1

1. The ability to carefully reason about causation.
8. The burden of proof is always on the prosecution, which means that the defendant is considered innocent until proven guilty.
14. Argument from consequences, argument from rights and duties, argument from character.

Exercise 11.2

1. If taken literally, reject it. The idea that eating apples literally prevents the need to see a doctor conflicts with a great deal of background knowledge.
3. Proportion belief to the evidence. The expert cited likely has relevant expertise. But the study of the effects of WiFi radiation is relatively new, and new technologies may change existing estimates of risk. High plausibility.
9. Accept it. Although we might be able to think of exceptions, the idea that killing innocent people is unethical is widely agreed upon and is an essential rule for a stable society.

Exercise 11.3

2. Appeal to tradition
5. Ad hominem
7. Subjectivist fallacy
8. False dilemma; appeal to emotion

Exercise 11.4

1. Anyone who smokes heavily is sure to get cancer. And you're a heavy smoker!
   All smokers are people who will get cancer.
   All people who are identical with you are smokers.
   Therefore, all people who are identical with you will get cancer. [hidden conclusion]
   All *M* are *P*.
   All *S* are *M*.
   Therefore, all *S* are *P*.

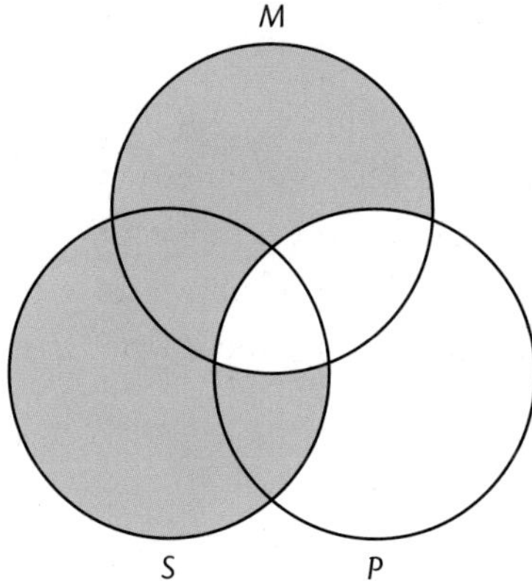

The argument is valid.
The first premise is not acceptable. Many people who smoke get cancer, but not all of them do.

7. Some people who lie have good reasons. Some people who have good reasons are actually saints. So some people who lie are saints.
   Some people who lie are people who have good reasons (to lie).
   Some people who have good reasons (to lie) are saints.
   Some people who lie are saints.
   Some *S* are *M*.
   Some *M* are *P*.
   Some *S* are *P*.

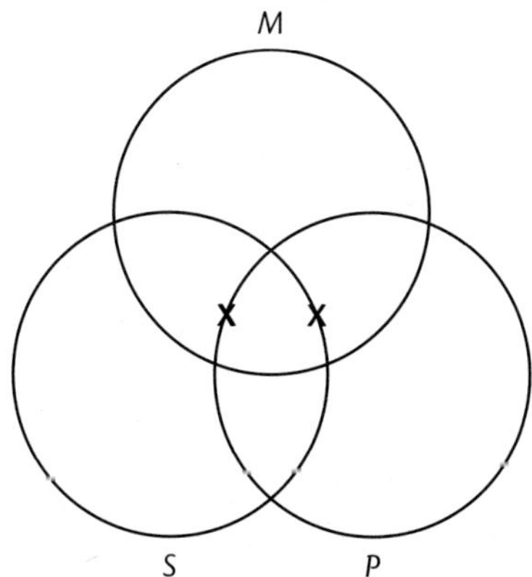

Not Valid

GLOSSARY

abduction (abductive reasoning) The form of reasoning used when putting forward a hypothesis as to what would explain a particular phenomenon or set of circumstances.

ad hoc hypothesis A hypothesis, or theory, that cannot be verified independently of the phenomenon it is supposed to explain. Ad hoc hypotheses always make a theory less simple—and therefore less credible.

ad hominem *See* appeal to the person.

affirming the antecedent *See modus ponens.*

affirming the consequent An invalid argument form:

> If *p*, then *q*.
> *q*.
> Therefore, *p*.

analogical induction *See* argument by analogy.

analogy A comparison of two or more things alike in specific respects.

antecedent The first part of a conditional statement (If *p*, then *q*), the component that begins with the word *if. See* conditional statement.

appeal to authority The fallacy of relying on the opinion of someone deemed to be an expert who in fact is *not* an expert.

appeal to common practice The fallacy of accepting or rejecting a claim solely on the basis of what groups of people generally do or how they behave (when the action or behaviour is irrelevant to the truth of the claim).

appeal to emotion The fallacy of using emotions in place of relevant reasons as premises in an argument.

appeal to ignorance The fallacy of arguing that a lack of evidence proves something. In one type of this fallacy, the problem arises by thinking that a claim must be true because it hasn't been shown to be false. In another type, the breakdown in logic comes when you argue that a claim must be false because it hasn't been proven to be true.

appeal to popularity (or **to the masses)** The fallacy of arguing that a claim must be true merely because a substantial number of people believe it.

appeal to the person (or ad hominem) The fallacy of rejecting a claim by criticizing the person who makes it rather than the claim itself. *Ad hominem* means "to the man."

appeal to tradition The fallacy of arguing that a claim must be true just because it's part of a tradition.

argument A group of statements in which some of them (the premises) are intended to support another of them (the conclusion).

argument by analogy (analogical induction) An argument that makes use of analogy by reasoning that because two or more things are similar in several respects, they must be similar in some further respect.

argument from character An ethical argument that proceeds from the assumption that what really matters ethically is character, rather than the nature or outcome of particular actions.

argument from consequences An ethical argument that takes as a starting point the idea that our most fundamental ethical obligation is to produce certain kinds of outcomes.

arguments from rights and duties An ethical argument that begins with the notion that there are certain kinds of actions that we must always do or always avoid doing.

background information The large collection of very well-supported beliefs that we all rely on to inform our actions and choices. It consists of basic facts about everyday things, beliefs based on very good evidence (including our own personal observations and excellent authority), and justified claims that we would regard as "common sense" or "common knowledge."

begging the question The fallacy of attempting to establish the conclusion of an argument by using that conclusion as a premise. Also called arguing in a circle.

biased sample A sample that does not properly represent the target group. *See* representative sample.

burden of proof The weight of evidence or argument required by one side in a debate or disagreement.

categorical logic A form of logic whose focus is categorical statements, which make assertions about categories, or classes, of things.

categorical statement A statement or claim that makes a simple assertion about categories, or classes, of things.

causal argument An inductive argument whose conclusion contains a causal claim.

causal claim A statement about the causes of things.

claim A statement; an assertion that something is or is not the case.

cogent argument A strong inductive argument with all true premises.

composition The fallacy of arguing that what is true of the parts must be true of the whole. The error is to think that the characteristics of the parts are somehow transferred to the whole, something that is not always the case.

compound statement A statement composed of at least two constituent, or simple, statements.

conclusion In an argument, the statement that the premises are intended to support.

conditional statement An "if–then" statement; it consists of the antecedent (the part introduced by the word *if*) and the consequent (the part introduced by the word *then*).

confidence level In statistical theory, the probability that the sample will accurately represent the target group within the margin of error.

conjunct One of two simple statements joined by a connective to form a compound statement.

conjunction Two simple statements joined by a connective to form a compound statement.

consequent The part of a conditional statement (If *p*, then *q*) introduced by the word *then*.

conservatism A criterion of adequacy for judging the worth of theories. A conservative theory is one that fits with our established beliefs.

copula One of four components of a standard-form categorical statement; a linking verb—either *are* or *are not*—that joins the subject term and the predicate term.

criteria of adequacy The standards used to judge the worth of explanatory theories. They include *testability*, *fruitfulness*, *scope*, *simplicity*, and *conservatism*.

critical thinking The systematic evaluation or formulation of beliefs or statements by rational standards.

deductive argument An argument intended to provide logically conclusive support for its conclusion.

denying the antecedent An invalid argument form:

> If *p*, then *q*.
> Not *p*.
> Therefore, not *q*.

denying the consequent *See modus tollens.*

dependent premise A premise that depends on at least one other premise to provide joint support to a conclusion. If a dependent premise is removed, the support that its linked dependent premises supply to the conclusion is undermined or completely cancelled out.

disjunct A simple statement that is a component of a disjunction.

disjunction A compound statement of the form "Either *p* or *q*." A disjunction is true even if only one disjunct is true, and false only if both disjuncts are false.

disjunctive syllogism A valid argument form:

> Either *p* or *q*.
> Not *p*.
> Therefore, *q*.

In the second premise of a syllogism, either disjunct can be denied.

division The fallacy of arguing that what is true of the whole must be true of the parts. The error is thinking that characteristics of the whole must transfer to the parts or that traits of the group must be the same as traits of individuals in the group.

enumerative induction An inductive argument pattern in which we reason from premises about individual members of a group to conclusions about the group as a whole.

equivocation The fallacy of using a word in two different senses in an argument.

ethics The critical, structured examination of how we ought to behave when our behaviour affects others.

expert Someone who is more knowledgeable in a particular subject area or field than most others are.

explanation A statement or statements intended to tell why or how something is the case.

fallacy An argument form that is both common and defective; a recurring mistake in reasoning.

false dilemma The fallacy of asserting that there are only two alternatives to consider when there are actually more than two.

faulty analogy A defective argument by analogy.

fruitfulness A criterion of adequacy for judging the worth of theories. A fruitful theory is one that makes novel predictions.

gambler's fallacy The error of thinking that previous events can affect the probabilities in the random event at hand.

genetic fallacy The fallacy of arguing that a claim is true or false solely because of its origin.

hasty generalization The fallacy of drawing a conclusion about a target group on the basis of too small a sample.

hypothetical syllogism A valid argument made up of three hypothetical, or conditional, statements:

> If *p*, then *q*.
> If *q*, then *r*.
> Therefore, if *p*, then *r*.

independent premise A premise that does not depend on other premises to provide support to a conclusion. If an independent premise is removed, the support that other premises supply to the conclusion is not affected.

indicator words Words that frequently accompany arguments and signal that a premise or conclusion is present.

inductive argument An argument in which the premises are intended to provide probable, not conclusive, support for its conclusion.

inference The process of reasoning from a premise or premises to a conclusion based on those premises.

inference to the best explanation A form of inductive reasoning in which we reason from premises about a state of affairs to an explanation for that state of affairs:

> Phenomenon Q.
> E provides the best explanation for Q.
> Therefore, it is probable that E is true.

invalid argument A deductive argument that fails to provide conclusive support for its conclusion.

logic The study of good reasoning, or inference, and the rules that govern it.

margin of error The variation between the values derived from a sample and the true values of the whole target group.

mixed argument An argument that includes both inductive and deductive elements.

modus ponens **(affirming the antecedent)** A valid argument form:

> If *p*, then *q*.
> *p*.
> Therefore, *q*.

modus tollens **(denying the consequent)** A valid argument form:

> If *p*, then *q*.
> Not *q*.
> Therefore, not *p*.

necessary condition A condition for the occurrence of an event without which the event cannot occur.

peer pressure Group pressure to accept or reject a claim solely on the basis of what one's peers think or do.

philosophical skepticism The view that we know much less than we think we do or that we know nothing at all.

philosophical skeptics Those who embrace philosophical skepticism.

post hoc, ergo propter hoc **("after that, therefore because of that")** The fallacy of reasoning that just because B followed A, A must have caused B.

predicate term The second class, or group, named in a standard-form categorical statement.

premise In an argument, a statement, or reason, given in support of the conclusion.

problem of induction The philosophical question as to whether the process of induction can ever lead to real knowledge.

property in question *See* relevant property.

propositional logic The branch of deductive reasoning that deals with the logical relationships among statements.

quality A characteristic of a categorical statement, based on whether the statement affirms or denies that a class is entirely or partly included in another class. A categorical statement that affirms is said to be affirmative in quality; one that denies is said to be negative in quality.

quantifier In categorical statements, a word used to indicate the number of things with specified characteristics. The acceptable quantifiers are *all*, *no*, or *some*. The quantifiers *all* and *no* in front of a categorical statement tell us that it's *universal*—that is, that it applies to every member of a class. The quantifier *some* at the beginning of a categorical statement says that the statement is *particular*—it applies to some but not all members of a class.

quantity In categorical statements, the attribute of number, specified by the words *all*, *no*, or *some*.

random sample A sample that is selected randomly from a target group in such a way as to ensure that the sample is representative. In a simple random selection, every member of the target group has an equal chance of being selected for the sample.

red herring The fallacy of deliberately raising an irrelevant issue during an argument. The basic pattern is to put forth a claim and then couple it with additional claims that may seem to support it but that, in fact, are mere distractions.

relevant property (property in question) In enumerative induction, a property, or characteristic, that is of interest in the target group.

representative sample In enumerative induction, a sample that resembles the target group in all relevant ways. *See* biased sample.

sample (sample member) In enumerative induction, the observed members of the target group.

scientific instrumentalism The school of thought that says the goal of science is to put forward theories that are useful in helping us predict and control the world around us.

scientific realism The school of thought that says the goal of science is to bring our understanding of the natural world closer and closer to the truth.

scope A criterion of adequacy for judging the worth of theories. A theory with scope is one that explains or predicts phenomena other than that which it was introduced to explain.

simple statement A statement that doesn't contain any other statements as constituents.

simplicity A criterion of adequacy for judging the worth of theories. A simple theory is one that makes as few assumptions as possible.

singular statements In categorical logic, statements that assert something about a single person or thing, including objects, places, and times.

slippery slope The fallacy of arguing, without good reasons, that taking a particular step will inevitably lead to further, undesirable steps.

social relativism The view that truth is relative to societies.

sound argument A deductively valid argument that has true premises.

standard-form categorical statement In categorical logic, a categorical statement that takes one of these four forms:

1. All *S* are *P*. (All cats are carnivores.)
2. No *S* are *P*. (No cats are carnivores.)
3. Some *S* are *P*. (Some cats are carnivores.)
4. Some *S* are not *P*. (Some cats are not carnivores.)

statement (claim) An assertion that something is or is not the case.

stereotyping Drawing conclusions about people without sufficient reasons.

straw man The fallacy of distorting, weakening, or oversimplifying someone's position so it can be more easily attacked or refuted.

strong argument An inductive argument that succeeds in providing probable—but not conclusive—support for its conclusion.

subjective relativism The idea that truth depends on what someone believes.

subjectivist fallacy Accepting the notion of subjective relativism or using it to try to support a claim.

subject term The first class, or group, named in a standard-form categorical statement.

sufficient condition A condition for the occurrence of an event that guarantees that the event occurs.

syllogism A deductive argument made up of three statements—two premises and a conclusion. *See modus ponens* and *modus tollens*.

symbolic logic Modern deductive logic that uses symbolic language to do its work.

target group (target population) In enumerative induction, the whole collection of individuals under study.

testability A criterion of adequacy for judging the worth of theories. A testable theory is one in which there is some way to determine whether the theory is true or false—that is, it predicts something other than what it was introduced to explain.

TEST formula A four-step procedure for evaluating the worth of a theory:

Step 1. State the **T**heory and check for consistency.
Step 2. Assess the **E**vidence for the theory.
Step 3. **S**crutinize alternative theories.
Step 4. **T**est the theories with the criteria of adequacy.

theoretical explanation A theory, or hypothesis, that tries to explain why something is the way it is, why something is the case, or why something happened.

truth-preserving A characteristic of a valid deductive argument in which the logical structure guarantees the truth of the conclusion if the premises are true.

truth table A table that specifies the truth values for claim variables and combinations of claim variables in symbolized statements or arguments.

tu quoque **("you're another")** A type of ad hominem fallacy that argues that a claim must be true (or false) just because the claimant is hypocritical.

valid argument A deductive argument that succeeds in providing conclusive support for its conclusion.

variables In modern logic, the symbols, or letters, used to express a statement.

Venn diagrams Diagrams consisting of overlapping circles that graphically represent the relationships between subject and predicate terms in categorical statements.

weak argument An inductive argument that fails to provide strong support for its conclusion.

world view A philosophy of life; a set of fundamental ideas that helps us make sense of a wide range of important issues in life. A world view defines for us what exists, what should be, and what we can know.

NOTES

Chapter 2

1. Bertrand Russell, *Let the People Think* (London: William Clowes, 1941), 2.
2. W.K. Clifford, "The Ethics of Belief," in *The Rationality of Belief in God*, ed. George I. Mavrodes (Englewood Cliffs, NJ: Prentice-Hall, 1970), 159–60.
3. Shirley MacLaine, *It's All in the Playing* (New York: Bantam Books, 1987), 171–2.
4. For a thorough review of various forms of relativism, see Theodore Schick and Lewis Vaughn, *How to Think about Weird Things*, 3rd ed. (Mountain View, CA: Mayfield, 1999), 68–92.

Chapter 3

1. This step-by-step procedure is inspired, in part, by Greg Bassham et al., *Critical Thinking: A Student's Introduction* (San Francisco: McGraw-Hill, 2002), 56–62.
2. This procedure is inspired, in part, by Brooke Noel Moore and Richard Parker, *Critical Thinking*, 6th ed. (Mountain View, CA: Mayfield, 2001), 274–5.

Chapter 4

1. Russell, *Let the People Think*, 1.
2. Adapted from Duke University Libraries, "Evaluating Web Pages," http://library.duke.edu/services/instruction/library guide/evalwebpages.html (accessed 8 September 2009).
3. Elizabeth Loftus and Hunter G. Hoffman, "Misinformation and Memory: The Creation of New Memories." *Journal of Experimental Psychology: General* 118, no. 1 (March 1989): 100–4.
4. Terence Hines, *Pseudoscience and the Paranormal* (Buffalo, NY: Prometheus Books, 1988), 170.
5. This example was inspired by L.W. Alvarez, letter to the editors, *Science* (18 June 1965): 1541.
6. Hines, *Pseudoscience and the Paranormal*, 4–5.
7. Thomas Gilovich, *How We Know What Isn't So* (New York: Free Press, 1991), 54.
8. J. Cocker, "Biased Questions in Judgment of Covariation Studies," *Personality and Social Psychology Bulletin* 8 (June 1982): 214–20.
9. Michael Sivak and Michael Flannagan, "Flying and Driving after the September 11 Attacks," *American Scientist* (January–February 2003): 6–8.
10. John Ruscio, "Risky Business," *Skeptical Inquirer* (March 2000), 22–6.
11. Peter Kan, Sara E. Simonsen, Joseph L. Lyon, and John R. W. Kestle, "Cellular Phone Use and Brain Tumor: A Meta-analysis," *Journal of Neurooncology* 86 (2008): 71–8; Institute of Medicine, *Immunization Safety Review: Vaccines and Autism* (National Academies Press, 2004).
12. Leonard Downie Jr. and Robert G. Kaiser, *The News About the News* (New York: Vintage Books, 2003), 9–10.
13. Carl Campanile, "Work Farce," *New York Post*, 26 June 2003, http://nypost.com/2003/07/03/work-farce-probers-nab-repair-loaf/.
14. Niles Lathem, "Soldiers Sweep Up Saddam's Hit Goons," *New York Post*, 1 July 2003, http://nypost.com/2003/07/01/soldiers-sweep-up-saddams-hit-goons/.

Chapter 5

1. The inspiration for this unconventional categorization comes primarily from Ludwig F. Schlecht, "Classifying Fallacies Logically." *Teaching Philosophy* 14, no. 1 (1991): 53–64; and Bassham et al., *Critical Thinking: A Student's Introduction* (San Francisco: McGraw-Hill, 2002).
2. W. Ross Winterowd and Geoffrey R. Winterowd, *The Critical Reader, Thinker, and Writer* (Mountain View, CA: Mayfield, 1992), 447–8.
3. Reported in Richard Whately, *Elements of Logic* (London: Longmans, Green, and Co., 1826).
4. Schick and Vaughn, *How to Think About Weird Things*, 192.
5. Student paper reproduced by permission of Mitchell S. McKinney, University of Missouri, www.missouri.edu/_commpjb/comm104/Sample_Papers/Free_Speech/free_speech.html.

Chapter 7

1. *Annals of Improbable Research*, http://www.improbable.com/ig/2014/

Chapter 8

1. Susan Blackmore, "Psychic Experiences: Psychic Illusions," *Skeptical Inquirer* 16: 367–76.
2. David G. Myers, "The Power of Coincidence," *Skeptic Magazine* 9, no. 4 (September 2002).

Chapter 9

1. Charles Darwin, *The Origin of Species* (New York: Collier, 1962), 476.

2. Arthur Conan Doyle, *A Study in Scarlet* (New York: P.F. Collier and Son, 1906), 29–30.
3. Arthur Conan Doyle, "The 'Gloria Scott,'" *Memoirs of Sherlock Holmes* (London: George Newnes, 1894).
4. "Shark Attacks Are Down for Third Year in a Row," CNN.com (29 January 2004), http://www.cnn.com/2004/TECH/science/01/29/shark.attacks.down.reut/.
5. "Study Examines Cancer Risk from Hair Dye," CNN.com (28 January 2004).
6. W.V. Quine and J.S. Ullman, *The Web of Belief* (New York: Random House, 1970), 43–4.
7. NASA, "The Great Moon Hoax," NASA Science, http://science.nasa.gov/science-news/science-at-nasa/2001/ast23feb_2/
8. Robert A. Baker, "Can We Tell When Someone Is Staring at Us?," *Skeptical Inquirer* (March/April 2000), 34.

Chapter 10

1. See Stephen Barrett et al., *Consumer Health*, 6th ed. (New York: McGraw-Hill, 1993), 239–40.
2. Thomas S. Kuhn, *The Copernican Revolution: Planetary Astronomy in the Development of Western Thought* (Cambridge, MA: Harvard University Press, 1957), 179.
3. Section 4a of Act 590 of the Acts of Arkansas of 1981, "Balanced Treatment for Creation-Science and Evolution-Science Act."
4. National Academy of Sciences, *Science and Creationism,* 2nd ed. (Washington: National Academies Press, 1999). http://books.nap.edu/html/creationism/evidence.html.
5. National Academy of Sciences, *Science and Creationism* (Washington, DC: National Academy Press, 1998).
6. Ibid.
7. George S. Bakken, "Creation or Evolution?" *Skeptic Report*, September 10, 2004, www.skepticreport.com/sr/?p=216.
8. Theodosius Dobzhansky, quoted in National Academy of Sciences, *Science and Creationism*, ix.
9. National Academy of Sciences, "Preface," in *Science and Creationism*, xi.
10. Schick and Vaughn, *How to Think about Weird Things*, 190–1.
11. Stephen Barrett, "High Doses of Vitamin C Are Not Effective as a Cancer Treatment," Quackwatch.com, revised 3 October 2011, www.quackwatch.org/01QuackeryRelatedTopics/Cancer/c.html.
12. Richard Wiseman, Matthew Smith, and Jeff Wiseman, "Eyewitness Testimony and the Paranormal," *Skeptical Inquirer* (November/December 1995) www.csicop.org/SI/show/eyewitness_testimony_and_the_paranormal/.
13. Ray Hyman, "How *Not* to Test Mediums," *Skeptical Inquirer* (January/February 2003) www.csicop.org/si/show/how_not_to_test_mediums_critiquing_the_afterlife_experiments.

Chapter 11

1. Ben Cooper et al. "The Quality of the Evidence for Dietary Advice Given in UK National Newspapers," *Public Understanding of Science* (April 2011), 664–73.
2. Jaki Freeman, "The Supreme Court of Canada and Eyewitness Identification—*R. v. Bruce*, 2011 S.C.C. 4." *Briefly Speaking* 20, no. 2 (May 2011).

INDEX

abduction, 359–60
adequacy: *see* criteria of adequacy
ad hoc hypothesis, 369–70
ad hominem fallacy, 173–5, 186, 448
advertising, 151–6; cost of, 151–2; news media and, 147; purpose of, 153; techniques of, 153–5
affirming the antecedent, 85, 261
affirming the consequent, 87–8, 261, 449
agreement: causal arguments and, 314–17
aircraft crash example, 379–82
ambiguity: semantic, 119; syntactic, 119; writing and, 118–20
ampersand, 248
analogical induction, 302–12; causal arguments and, 313; uses of, 304–5
analogy, 302–3; arguments by, 192, 302–12; faulty, 153, 192–3
Anaximander, 406
antecedent, 85, 86–7, 254; affirming, 85, 261; denying, 86–7, 261
appeal to authority, 129–30, 153
appeal to common practice, 179, 186
appeal to emotion, 153, 182–3, 186; law and, 448–9
appeal to ignorance, 134, 180–2, 418
appeal to popularity, 153, 178–9, 186; group pressure and, 42–3; health decisions and, 442–3; law and, 456–7
appeal to the masses, 42–3, 178–9, 186
appeal to the person, 173–5, 186, 448
appeal to tradition, 179–80, 186; health decisions and, 442–3
applications: critical thinking and, 436–62
Aquinas, Thomas, 86, 265
architecture: critical thinking and, 8
argumentative essays, 29–32, 61–2, 117–20; thesis and, 61–2
argument from character, 456
argument from consequences, 455
argument from rights and duties, 455–6
arguments: argumentative essays and, 29, 30–1; assessment of, 64–116; causal, 312–33, 437–9; cogent, 69, 70, 282, 349; compelling, 447; conditional, 84–90, 188–9, 449; deductive, 65–73, 84–90, 333–5; definition of, 11; diagramming, 92–105, 231–8; disjunctive, 188–9; emotion and, 62; essay writing and, 166–7; good/bad, 65; inductive, 65–73, 333–5; influential, 252; invalid, 66–70, 86–90; long, 105–11; missing parts of, 78–82; mixed, 333–5; opposing, 61; patterns of, 83–92; reasons and, 11–16; simple, 259–63; sound, 69–70; strong, 67–70, 282, 349; structure of, 65–70; three-variable, 265; tricky, 263–6; valid, 66–70, 84–6, 246; weak, 67–70, 282
Aristotle, 18, 360, 403, 456
assessment: of arguments, 64–116; of objections, 29, 31
assumptions (implicit premises), 78–82
A statements (universal affirmative), 214, 217–19, 221
attention, selective, 40–1, 288
authority: appeal to, 129–30, 153; Internet and, 132–3; *see also* experts
availability error, 143, 144–6, 191; health decisions and, 443; paranormal and, 318–19

background information, 124–6, 127; ethics and, 454; abduction and, 359
begging the question, 186–7, 193, 448
beliefs: conflict of, 371, 373
Bergamin, José, 126
bias: cognitive, 4; confirmation, 142–3; definition of, 44; double-blind studies and, 400–1; experts and, 131–2; Internet and, 133
Blackmore, Susan, 318
Blackstone, William, 447
Blodget, Henry, 480–1
Bohr, Niels, 132
Borg, 41
Brennan, Samantha, 471–2
Brezhnev, Leonid Ilyich, 349
Buddha, 42
burden of proof, 181–2; law and, 447

Caputo, Theresa, 421
Carlyle, Thomas, 442
categorical logic, 210–43; ethics and, 452–3; law and, 447–8
categorical statements, 211, 212–15, 228; affirmative, 213–14; negative, 213–14; particular, 213–14; standard forms of, 212–15; universal, 213–14
categorical syllogisms, 228–38; diagramming, 231–8; rules of, 230–1, 233; validity of, 230–3
causal arguments, 312–33; common factor and, 324–5, 439; health decisions and, 437–9; temporal order and, 323–6; testing, 314–19
causal confusions, 319–26; health decisions and, 438–9
cause: effect and, 325–6
character: argument from, 456
claims, 9–11; causal, 312; conflicting, 124–7, 134–5; evaluating, 122–65; positive, 181–2; unsupported, 123; *see also* statements (claims)
classes: terms and, 216–17
Clifford, W.K., 40
cognitive biases, 4

coincidence: causal connection and, 318, 319, 320–2; health decisions and, 438; misjudging of, 139
"cold reading": psychics and, 422, 424–7
common causal factors, 324–5, 439
common practice: appeal to 179, 186
"common sense/knowledge," 125
comparisons, misleading, 154
composition: fallacy of, 175–6, 186
computers: logic and, 250
conclusions, 11–12; deductive arguments and, 65–70; diagramming, 223; disguised, 15–16; essay, 29, 31, 167–8; identifying, 16–18; indicator words and, 15; inductive arguments and, 65–70; long arguments and, 106; true, 69–70
conditional arguments, 84–90, 188–9; faulty, 449
conditional statements, 247, 253–6; translation of, 254–6
conditions, necessary/sufficient, 326–9
confidence level, 291–3
confirmation bias, 142–3
conflict of interest, 132
conjunct, 248
conjunction, 247, 248–50, 256
connectives, 246–59; symbols for, 247
connotation, 169–70
consequences: argument from, 455; hypotheses and, 397–400
consequent, 85, 254; affirming, 87–8, 261, 449; denying, 85
consequentialism, 455
conservatism, 363, 370–4, 382, 403
consistency: ethics and, 455; external, 360–1; internal, 360; theories and, 360–1
conspiracy theories, 370, 410
control group, 316–17, 400–1
controlled trials, 316–17, 400–1
Copernicus, Nicolaus, 369, 403–5
copula, 213, 216
correlation, 317–19
counterexample method, 89–90
courts: critical thinking and, 444–50
creationism: evolution and, 189, 369, 406–10
creativity: critical thinking and, 7–8
Criminal Code of Canada, 437
criteria of adequacy, 361–76; science and, 393, 397, 403–10, 425; TEST formula and, 378, 379; weird theories and, 425
critical thinking: applications of, 436–62; barriers to, 33–60; criticisms of, 6–7; definition of, 3; importance of, 4–9; introduction to, 2–32; lack of, 8–9
Cronkite, Walter, 147

Daly, Bill, 469–70
Darwin, Charles, 352, 406, 409
dead: communication with, 421–7
deductive arguments, 65–73, 84–90, 333–5; conditional, 84–90; identifying, 71–3
deductive reasoning, 210–43; propositional logic and, 244–80
definitions: essay writing and, 120, 168–70; lexical, 168; persuasive, 168; precising, 168; stipulative, 168
Democritus, 313
Dennett, Daniel, 127
denying the antecedent, 86–7, 261
denying the consequent, 85
deontology, 456
"Deterrence," 463–7
diagramming: arguments, 92–105; categorical statements, 223–8; categorical syllogisms, 231–8; premises, 223
difference: causal arguments and, 314–17
dilemma, false, 187–90, 193, 448
Dingwall, Eric, 423
Diogenes, 184
disjunct, 88–9, 250
disjunction, 188–9, 247, 250–3, 256, 261
disjunctive syllogism, 88–9, 261
Disraeli, Benjamin, 37
dissimilarities, relevant, 305, 307
diversity: analogic induction and, 305, 307–9
division: fallacy of, 176–7, 186
Dobzhansky, Theodosius, 409
domain name, 133
domino theory, 190
double-blind studies, 401
doubt, possible/reasonable, 49
dowsing, 373–4
drafts: essay, 31–2; first, 165–70
Dunning-Kruger effect, 5
dysphemisms, 169

Eddington, Arthur, 367
editing, essay, 32
Edward, John, 421
effect: cause and, 325–6
Einstein, Albert, 216, 366–7, 397, 421; aim of science and, 400
Emerson, Ralph Waldo, 326
emotions: appeal to, 153, 182–3, 186, 448–9; arguments and, 62; critical thinking and, 38
emphasis, false, 151
enumerative induction, 283–98; causal arguments and, 312–13
equivocation: fallacy of, 177–8, 186
errors: availability, 143, 144–6, 191, 318–19, 443; causal arguments and, 319–26; margin of, 291, 292–3; reasoning and, 3–4, 417–21; sampling, 292
essays: annotated sample, 203–8; argumentative, 29–32, 61–2, 117–20; elements of, 166; first draft of, 165–6; guidelines for, 31–2; propositional logic and, 269–70; sample, 203–8, 463–89; structure of, 29–31; thesis and, 61–2; writing, 29–32, 61–2, 117–20
E statements (universal negative), 214, 218, 219, 221
ethical egoism, 456
ethical relativism, 456

ethics: analogic induction and, 305; critical thinking and, 450–8; philosophical traditions and, 455–6
ethnocentrism, 43
euphemisms, 169–70
evaluation: critical thinking and, 3
evidence: available, 144–6; confirming, 142–3, 145, 150; contrary, 40–1, 61, 140–2, 145; disconfirming, 142–3; expectation and, 135–7; experts and, 127–35; fooling ourselves and, 140–6; lack of, 180–2; news media and, 146–51; opposing, 40–1, 61, 140–2, 145; personal experience and, 135–40; strength of, 126; TEST formula and, 376–7; theories and, 362; *see also* support
evolution: creationism and, 189, 369, 406–10; theory of, 352
expectation: personal experience and, 135–7
experimental group, 400–1
experiments: controlled, 316–17, 400–1; science and, 396, 400–1
experts, 127–35; health decisions and, 440–2; prerequisites for, 130–1; relevant expertise and, 130
explanandum, 351
explanans, 351
explanations: alternative, 377–9, 397, 418–19; arguments and, 14; best, 346–92; causal, 348; functional, 348; inference and, 348–60; interpretive, 348, 351; procedural, 348, 351; teleological, 351; theoretical, 348–54, 394; types of, 348, 351; *see also* theories
external world: reality of, 363
extrasensory perception (ESP), 318, 398; *see also* paranormal
eyewitness testimony, 423, 449–50

facts: opinion and, 125
fallacies, 171–202; ad hominem, 173–5, 186, 448, advertising and, 153; appeal to authority, 129–30, 153; appeal to common practice, 179, 186; appeal to emotion, 153, 182–3, 186, 448–9; appeal to ignorance, 134, 180–2, 418; appeal to popularity, 42–3, 153, 178–9, 186, 442–3, 456–7; appeal to the masses, 42–3, 178–9, 186; appeal to the person, 173–5, 186, 448; appeal to tradition, 179–80, 186, 442–3; composition, 175–6, 186; division, 176–7, 186; equivocation, 177–8, 186; ethical thinking and, 450, 456–8; gambler's, 139; genetic, 172–3, 174, 186; health decisions and, 442–4; legal thinking and, 444, 448–50; *post hoc, propter hoc*, 323–6, 438; red herring, 183–4, 186; slippery slope, 190–1, 193, 457; straw man, 80, 184–5, 186, 457; subjective, 46–7, 450, 456; *see also* hasty generalization
false dilemma, 187–90, 193, 448
falsifiability, 402
faulty analogy, 153, 192–3
folk psychology, 127
formulation: critical thinking and, 3
fossil record: gaps in, 409
framing, 4
Freeman, Jaki, 449–50
"Free Speech on Campus" (annotated sample paper), 204–7
fruitfulness, 363, 365–7, 403

Galileo, 360, 405
gambler's fallacy, 139
Gandhi, Mahatma, 450
Gavura, Scott, 486–9
generalization: enumerative induction and, 283; *see also* hasty generalization
genetic fallacy, 172–3, 174, 186
Gilovich, Thomas, 142
Gladstone, William E., 218
Goleman, Daniel, 289
gravity: theory of, 367
group pressure: as barrier, 41–5
"guesswork," 359

hasty generalization, 145, 191–2, 193; advertising and, 153; inductive reasoning and, 286; law and, 444
Hayes, Judith, 408
health: advice on, 129, 131; critical thinking and, 324, 420, 437–44
health professionals: critical thinking by, 442
Heath, Joseph, 472–5
Hines, Terrence, 137
hit rate: psychics and, 421, 425
Holmes, Sherlock (fictional character), 353
homeopathy, 444
Houdini, Harry, 417
"How Ontario Ended Up with 'Cap and Trade'," 472–5
Hubbard, Elbert, 3
human rights, 455–6
Hume, David, 7, 12, 402, 452
"Hurray! No One's Watching: The Olympics' Decline Signals Their Success, But Now What?," 467–9
Huxley, Thomas Henry, 40, 228
Hyman, Ray, 426–7
hypnagogic imagery, 38
hypotheses: ad hoc, 369–70; alternative, 397; scientific, 396–400
hypothetical syllogism, 85–6, 261

identification: advertising and, 153
ideology: science and, 395
if and only if, 329
"Ig Nobel" prizes, 245
ignorance: appeal to, 134, 180–2, 418
Iles, George, 351
impairment: personal experience and, 135–7
implications: theory and, 397–400
independent premises, 96
indicator words, 14–15; deductive/inductive arguments and, 72–3; diagramming, 92–3
induction: problem of, 402, 403

inductive arguments, 65–73, 333–5; identifying, 71–3
inductive reasoning, 181, 281–343; analogic, 302–12, 313; enumerative, 283–98, 312–13; health decisions and, 438; inference to the best explanation and, 346–92
inference, 4, 12; explanations and, 348–60
inference to the best explanation, 313, 346–92; guidelines for, 376–9; law and, 446–7; pattern of, 349
innumeracy: evidence and, 139–40
instances: number of, 305, 307
instrumentalism, scientific, 402, 403
Internet: evaluating, 132–3
introduction, essay, 29, 30, 166
invalid arguments, 66–70; conditional, 86–90; *see also* validity
Isaacs, Terry, 475–7
I statements (particular affirmative), 214, 218, 221

James, William, 43
James Randi Educational Foundation, 417
Jefferson, Thomas, 254
"Joint Method of Agreement and Difference," 316–17
jury duty, 445

Kahneman, Daniel, and Amos Tversky, 318
Kant, Immanuel, 456
Kennedy–Lincoln coincidences, 321

La Bruyère, Jean de, 177
law: critical thinking and, 444–50
Lennon, John, 216
"Letter, The," 483–6
Lewis, C.I., 211
Lincoln–Kennedy coincidences, 321
logic, 4, 211; categorical, 210–43, 452–3, 447–8; computers and, 250; deductive, 210–80; essays and, 269–70; inductive, 283–98, 302–13, 346–92, 438; propositional, 211, 244–80; symbolic, 246; truth-functional, 245; *see also* reasoning
"Long Live RIM," 481–3

MacDonald, Chris, 477–80
MacLaine, Shirley, 47
magic: debunking, 417
Maimonides, Moses, 173
margin of error, 291, 292–3
"Marine Parks," 469–70
Mars, 137
masses: appeal to, 42–3, 178–9, 186
mathematics, 211
Maurois, André, 79
Mayhew, Henry, 285
mean, 290
meaning, word, 169–70, 177–8
media: advertising and, 151; news, 146–51
median, 290
memory: impairment of, 136–7; unreliability of, 38
"Method of Agreement," 314–16
"Method of Concomitant Variation," 317–19
middle term (M), 229–30
Mill, John Stuart, 314, 455
"Mill's methods," 314–19
Mitchell, Maria, 136
Mizner, Wilson, 17
mode, 290
modus ponens, 85, 261
modus tollens, 85, 261
moon: landing hoax and, 372–3; "lunacy" and, 143
Myers, David G., 321

NASA, 372–3
National Academy of Sciences (US), 407, 408
natural selection, 406; *see also* evolution
necessary conditions, 326–9
negation, 247, 253, 256; double, 253
news media, 146–51; alternative, 151; health claims and, 439–40; quality of, 147; reliability of, 150–1
newsworthiness, 148–9
Newton, Isaac, 367
Nietzsche, Friedrich, 66
"non-attitudes," 292
nouns/noun phrases: categorical statements and, 213

objections: assessment of 29, 31
observations: science and, 396
only, 217
only if, 217, 329
opinion polls, 288–93; unscientific, 290–1; untrustworthy, 289
opinions: facts and, 125; unsupported, 107
or, inclusive/exclusive, 251–3
O statements (particular negative), 214, 218, 221
outline, essay, 31, 117–18, 165–6

Paciocco, David M., 463–7
paragraphs, essay, 166
parallax, 405
paranormal, 318, 398, 418; criterion of conservatism and, 373–4; evidence and, 141; testing, 421–7
pareidolia, 38, 138
parentheses, 263–4
particular affirmative statement (I), 214, 214, 218, 221
particular negative statement (O), 214, 214, 218, 221
Paulos, John Allen, 321
peer pressure, 42–3
Penn and Teller, 417
perception: constructive, 367–8; expectations and, 138; impairment of, 135–7
person: appeal to, 173–5, 186, 448

personal attack, 174
personal experience: as evidence, 135–40; weird theories and, 419
personal stake: as barrier, 37–9
philosophical factors: as barriers, 34, 45–50
philosophical skepticism/skeptics, 49
philosophy, 211; of science, 402; traditions of, 455–6
physicians: as experts, 131
Picasso, Pablo, 216
Pierce, Charles Sanders, 211
placebo, 316, 324, 400–1
planetary motion, 369, 403–5
"poisoning the well," 175
Popper, Karl, 402
possibility, logical *v.* physical, 419–21
post hoc, propter hoc, 323–6, 438
Potter, Andrew, 467–9
predicate term (P), 212–15, 216; subject and, 211; translation of, 217–222
prejudice, 44, 229
premises, 11–12; deductive arguments and, 65–70; dependent, 96; diagramming, 223; identifying, 16–18; independent, 96; indicator words and, 14–15; inductive arguments and, 65–70; irrelevant, 172–86; long arguments and, 106; number of, 15; true, 68–70; unacceptable, 172, 186–94; unstated, 78–82
Principle of Charity, 80
probability, 139–40; causal arguments and, 312; inductive reasoning and, 282; misjudgments of, 322
pronouns: categorical statements and, 213
property, relevant, 284, 287, 319–20
propositional logic, 211, 244–80
psychics, 421–7
psychological factors: as barriers, 34–45
psychology, folk, 127
Ptolemy, Claudius, 369, 403–5
"puffery," 154

qualifiers: weasel words and, 155
quality, 213
quantifiers, 213, 216; non-standard/unexpressed, 219–21
quantity, 213
questions: opinion polls and, 289

racism, 44, 229
Randi, James, 417
random sampling, 288, 290–1
"Raspberry Ketone, Pure Green Coffee Extract. . .," 475–7
rational standards: critical thinking and, 3
realism, scientific, 402, 403
reasoning: abductive, 359–60; circular, 186–7; common errors in, 3–4; deductive, 210–80; faulty, 171–202; inductive, 181, 281–343, 346–92; passion and, 7; *see also* logic
reasons: arguments and, 11–16; claims and, 9–11
red herring, 183–4, 186
relativism: ethical, 456; social, 47; subjective, 46–7, 450
relativity: theory of, 366–7
relevant property, 284, 287; misidentifying, 319–20
replication, 401
representativeness, 287–8, 318–19
retrograde motion, 405
revising, essay, 32
rhetoric, 182–3
rights and duties: argument from, 455–6
"RIM Is Dead," 480–1
Ruscio, John, 144
Russell, Bertrand, 37, 39, 48, 124, 126; language and logic and, 218; probability and, 282

Sagan, C., 416; and P. Fox, 137
sample (sample members), 284–93; biased, 287–8; random, 288, 290–1; representative, 287–8, 318–19; self-selecting, 290–1; size of, 285–7, 288, 292–3
sampling error, 292
Samuels, Stephen, and George McCabe, 321
Sanger, Margaret, 216
Schick, Bela, 360
science: crazy theories and, 366; critical thinking and, 437; non-science and, 394–6, 402; philosophy of, 402; as self-correcting, 396; theories and, 393–435; weird theories and, 416–27
scientific instrumentalism, 402, 403
scientific method, 394, 396–400
scientific realism, 402, 403
scientism, 395
scope, 363, 367–8, 403
selective attention, 40–1, 288
self-image: as barrier, 36–7, 39
self-interest: as barrier, 35–41; overcoming, 37–41
semantic ambiguity, 119
Semmelweis, Ignaz, 314
Shaw, George Bernard, 216, 365
short method (propositional validity), 266–71
similarities, relevant, 305, 306–7
simplicity, 363, 368–70, 382, 403
singular statements, 219
skepticism, 48–9
slant: news and, 149–50
slippery slope fallacy, 190–1, 193, 457
slogans, advertising, 153–4
social relativism, 47
Socrates, 5, 9
some, 220
sound arguments, 69–70
sound bites, 151
source: news media and, 150–1
standard forms of categorical statements, 212–22
statement component, 211

statements (claims), 9–11; categorical, 211, 212–15, 228; compound, 247; conditional, 247, 253–6; simple, 247; singular, 219; *see also* thesis statement
statistical syllogisms, 298–302; evaluating, 300–1
stereotyping, 43
Stewart, Jon, 288
straw man fallacy, 80, 184–5, 186, 457
strong arguments, 67–70, 282, 349
subject term (S), 212–15, 216; predicate and, 211; translation of, 217–222
subjective fallacy, 46–7, 450, 456
subjective relativism, 46–7, 450
sufficient conditions, 326–9
suicide, physician-assisted, 457–8
support: conclusive/probable, 282, 333; degree of, 284; *see also* evidence
syllogisms, 85–6; categorical, 228–38; disjunctive, 88–9, 261; hypothetical, 85–6, 261; statistical, 298–302
symbolic logic, 246
syntactic ambiguity, 119

target population/group, 283–93; homogenous, 286–7
technology: science and, 394–5
Tennyson, Lord Alfred, 216
terms: translation of, 216–19
testability, 363, 364–5, 403
TEST formula, 376–9; weird theories and, 421–7
test implications: hypotheses and, 397–400
testing: hypotheses and, 397–9; TEST formula and, 379; theories and, 400–2
Thatcher, Margaret, 216
theoretical explanations, 348–54; science and, 394
theories, 348–54; assessing, 376–86, 393–435; consistency and, 360–1; conspiracy, 370, 410; crazy, 366; criteria of adequacy and, 361–76; eligible, 363; notable, 354; scientific, 393–435; TEST formula and, 376; testing, 400–2; uses of, 352–4; weird, 416–27, 444; *see also* explanations
thesis statement, 29, 30, 31, 61–2, 117, 166
"thinking outside the box," 7–8
Thoreau, Henry David, 302
tilde, 253; domain names and, 133
tradition(s): appeal to, 179–80, 186, 442–3; philosophical, 455–6
transitional words/phrases, 167
translation: categorical statements and, 213, 215–22; conditionals and, 254–6
"truth-preserving," 66
truth tables, 211; conditional and, 254; conjunction and, 248–50; disjunction and, 251; negation and, 253; simple arguments and, 260–1, 262, 263; three-variable arguments and, 265; tricky arguments and, 263–6
truth values, 246–59
tu quoque, 174
Twain, Mark, 440

universal affirmative statement (A), 214, 217–19, 221
universality: ethics and, 454–5
universal negative statement (E), 214, 218, 219, 221
universal statements, 213–14, 219
"Unrepentant Homeopaths," 486–9
utilitarianism, 455

vaccines, 420
vagueness: advertising and, 154
validity, 66–70, 84–6; categorical statements and, 215; categorical syllogisms and, 230–3; propositional logic and, 246, 247, 259–72; short method of assessing, 266–71; truth table test of, 259–66
Van Fraassen, Bas, 376
variables, 246
Venn diagrams, 335; categorical arguments and, 231–8; categorical statements and, 223–8; limits of, 237
virtue theory, 456

Waddell, Nick, 481–3
Walton, Nancy, 483–6
weak arguments, 67–70, 282
weasel words, 155
Weaver, Warren, 395
websites: evaluating, 132–3
weird theories, 416–17, 444; errors of reasoning and, 417–21; testing, 421–7
"What's Wrong with 'Body Mass Index'," 471–2
Williams, Lisa, 421
Wiseman, R., and R.L. Morris, 423
Wittgenstein, Ludwig, 251, 260
words: connotation and, 169–70; indicator, 14–15, 72–3, 92–3; meaning of, 169–70, 177–8; transitional, 167; weasel, 155
world view, 45–6
writing: argumentative essay and, 29–32, 61–2, 117–20; first draft and, 165–70; logic and, 269–70; sample paper and, 203–8

"Yes, Human Cloning Should be Permitted," 477–80

"zebra problem," 443

CREDITS

Literary credits

Page 107–8, block quote: © 2002 National Review, Inc. Reprinted by permission.

Page 109–10, block quote in Exercise 3.10 (2): Sarah Foster / InformedOpinions.org

Page 160: "Work Farce." From *New York Post*, 26 June 2003. © 2003 *New York Post*. All rights reserved. Used by permission and protected by the Copyright Laws of the United States. The printing, copying, redistribution, or retransmission of this Content without express written permission is prohibited.

Page 162: "Soldiers Sweep Up Saddam's Hit Goons." From *New York Post*, 1 July 2003 © 2003 *New York Post*. All rights reserved. Used by permission and protected by the Copyright Laws of the United States. The printing, copying, redistribution, or retransmission of this Content without express written permission is prohibited.

Page 318-19, block quote: Used by permission of the *Skeptical Inquirer* magazine. www.csicop.org

Page 321-2, block quote: From *Skeptic* magazine.

Page 357-8, Exercise 9.2, Passage 2: From reuters.com, 29 January 2004 © 2004 reuters.com. All rights reserved. Used by permission and protected by the Copyright Laws of the United States. The printing, copying, redistribution, or retransmission of this Content without express written permission is prohibited.

Page 358, Exercise 9.2, Passage 3: From reuters.com, 28 January 2004 © 2004 reuters.com. All rights reserved. Used by permission and protected by the Copyright Laws of the United States. The printing, copying, redistribution, or retransmission of this Content without express written permission is prohibited.

Page 372-3: NASA

Page 385-6, Exercise 9.10, Passage 2: Used by Permission of the *Skeptical Inquirer* magazine www.csicop.org

Page 409, block quote in box: George S. Bakken/National Centre for Science and Education

Page 415, Exercise 10.6, Passage 1: Quackwatch

Page 423, block quote: Used by Permission of the *Skeptical Inquirer* magazine www.csicop.org

Page 426, block quote: Used by Permission of the *Skeptical Inquirer* magazine www.csicop.org

Page 449-50, block quote: Briefly Speaking

Design credits

Map/magnifying glass: Pixel Embargo/Shutterstock
Clipboard: Pixel Embargo/Shutterstock
Chain links: d3 images/Shutterstock
Lightbulb: Pixel Embargo/Shutterstock
Pen and paper: Pixel Embargo/Shutterstock